The New Sociology of Modern Britain

Eric Butterworth is Reader in Social Policy at the University of
York where he has been on the staff since 1966. Since graduating in
history from the University of Cambridge he has had wide
experience both in teaching social sciences and history and in the
practice of community work, as well as in research in these fields, in
Britain and Australia. His publications include *A Muslim
Community in Britain*, *Immigrants in West Yorkshire* and (with Ray
Lees and Peter Arnold) *The Challenge of Community Work*.

David Weir is Professor of Organizational Behaviour at the
University of Glasgow. After graduating from Queen's College,
Oxford, he held the post of research sociologist at Aberdeen
University and subsequently taught sociology at the universities of
Leeds, Hull and Manchester before joining Glasgow. Among his
other books are *Men and Work in Modern Britain*, *Social Problems
of Modern Britain* (Fontana; co-edited with Eric Butterworth) and
Cities in Modern Britain (Fontana; co-edited with Camilla
Lambert).

Edited by
Eric Butterworth and David Weir

The New Sociology of Modern Britain

An Introductory Reader

Fontana Paperbacks

First published by Fontana Paperbacks
as *The Sociology of Modern Britain* 1970
Eighth impression 1974
Second edition first published 1975
Seventh impression 1982
Third edition first published as
The New Sociology of Modern Britain 1984

Set in 9 on 10½ Times
Reproduced, printed and bound in Great Britain
by Hazell, Watson and Viney Limited,
Member of the BPCC Group,
Aylesbury, Bucks.

Contents

3. Socialization

4. Work

5. Class

Preface

Over the fifteen years since the preparation of the reader we have had cause to be grateful to a wide range of friends, colleagues and critics, too numerous to mention by name, for the help, advice and criticism they have given us.

More specifically we should like to thank Maureen Christie, in particular, for the work she has done in preparing this edition for the press.

ERIC BUTTERWORTH
DAVID WEIR

General Introduction

Preamble

This reader was the first of its kind on modern Britain when it was published in 1970. Since then it has been widely used and read by people interested in learning more about their society, including many taking courses at various levels on modern Britain. We present the third edition of our book.

Our purposes now combine the original format and approach, with its focus on seven specific topics which form the chapters, with a view of themes which are of particular concern now and are likely to remain extremely important for the rest of this century: these include changes in the structure of the family and the nature of family life; the issues of social change and development in inner city areas; work, satisfaction and unemployment; concentrations of power and the legitimacy of politics; questions about socialization, gender and the media; the effect of traditional practices and attitudes on Britain as a society, its performance, and its place in the world, and the 'breaking of the mould' of the two-party system – if that is what it turns out to be.

We have never tried to relate our content specifically to particular examination courses. Our original idea for the book came from our experience with adults, in traditional liberal adult education classes, teaching postgraduates, and on courses for a wide range of occupational groups. What such students wanted was a focus around which thinking and discussion could take place, to which personal experience could be related. They were not into rote learning, the regurgitation of chunks of textbooks (without any first-hand contact with what they read about, in experience or in books) in order to pass examinations. Nor, in our view, should students taking examinations be. Our book is intended to be a starting point, limited in certain aspects, inadequate, too, because we have had to make choices given the scope of the work. Its objectives at least are clear, and we think that from an educational point of view they are of overwhelming importance.

Approach

We have aimed, in the first place, to provide material which can be used to answer crucial questions about the nature and state of British society. We start from the standpoint that sociology is a humanistic and humane study, whatever may be said about it as a 'science' of society, and we bear in mind what C. Wright Mills said about 'scientific' approaches: 'Much that has passed for "science" is now felt to be dubious philosophy; much that is held to be "real science" is often felt to provide only confused fragments of the realities among which men live.'

The reader needs a frame of reference within which to study the society. Part of this is provided by relevant theories, set in an appropriate context; part by documentation, and part by a perspective which includes some perception of important historical events and developments, of possibilities in the future, and of the place of the society among others in the modern world. Since people living in Britain have their main experience of life there, it is desirable to look first at how the perceptions of the world they develop provide them with a viable tool for the analysis of this and other societies. We believe that there is merit in focusing study on one's own society before extending this study outside familiar boundaries. It is not because living in a society necessarily provides an *objective* view: class bias (in the way considered by Spencer in the reading in Chapter 7) may prevent this. But the society can provide a continuing opportunity for analysis and judgement to correct initial impressions. There is no 'right' way to look at a society, no 'correct' conclusion to come to about it: the study of modern Britain should be about a society which is clearly recognizable in its main features, with evidence about it which sets it in its position in the world, and in a perspective which takes into account the sources from which it came and the directions in which it may go. Such an approach leads not to the simplification of the issues but to an awareness of their complexity. However, limits must be set to the number of substantive issues which are considered. We have made no attempt to go back to first principles in, for example, our consideration of the family. We are not concerned as such with the extent to which it is similar to families in other societies studied by social anthropologists. This is not because these are not relevant. Rather, we are interested in the family's particular nature in Britain, the forms it takes, alternatives to it and informal structures which relate to it. Our main aim is to make clear, within the limits of such a book, the origins of the modern family in Britain, its rationale, the logic of its structures and its links with the other institutions of society.

Our view about theory is not that it is irrelevant but that the study of the kind of grand theories which present a world view follows the detailed consideration of empirical evidence, subjective impressions and 'theories of the middle range'; that is, analytical perspectives that provide coherent explanations of the evidence. If some of these are not acceptable then they provide at least a standpoint against which other perspectives may be assessed.

The study of society requires an open mind and not one closed off by theories. As Dennis H. Wrong says in a famous article, 'If the initiating questions are forgotten, we readily misconstrue the task of theory, and the answers previous thinkers have given become narrowly confining conceptual prisons, degenerating into little more than a special, professional vocabulary applied to situations and events that can be described with equal or greater precision in ordinary language.' If platitude and jargon result from this kind of professionalization then undoubtedly sociology is too important to be left to the sociologists. We include writing by several authors who are not sociologists.

Our aim throughout is to maximize the advantages of a reader over a textbook. The reader allows the authors to speak with their own voices. There is less emphasis on covering all aspects of *every* subject and more on providing data, perspective, analysis or at times even polemic, which will lead on to more difficult questions about the society under discussion and to continuing systematic work. We wish to avoid the impression that what we present is a snapshot at a particular point in time, without reference to the historical experience that has preceded it; nor is it a compilation which attempts to cover everything on the subject. Up-to-date material for its own sake can soon become extremely dated, and the only way to cope with this is to choose subjects for study which are of continuing importance.

We hope our reader will be looked on more as a *source-book which offers a point of entry to study*. Despite the organization around the major themes, it can be viewed and used in different ways. For example, for the student of ethnic groups and minority relations there are readings in Chapters 2, 3 and 7 which are explicitly relevant, and other material related to these subjects can be found elsewhere in the book. A wide range of approaches to *research and information-gathering* are included: from the descriptive data in the Scarman report, through surveys and sophisticated interviewing techniques used by researchers in Chapters 4, 5 and 6, to the interpretative and analytical work by Bott and Werbner in Chapters 1 and 2 respectively.

Reading and Further Study

There are four sources of further reading which are suggested from this book. First, we recommend anyone wishing to study specific issues in greater depth to consult the full versions of the readings we present, since the majority are only part of the author's work; moreover, for reasons of space, we have had to omit most of the readings' references. Second, the Further Reading at the end of each chapter includes important studies and some books referred to in the readings. The third source is in the Textbook Reference at the end of the book, which mentions some of the main sources of factual data on Britain, and provides cross-referencing between our reader and the main textbooks which are currently in use.

Finally, it is worth pointing out that this is one of a series on modern Britain. A companion volume, on *Social Problems*, complements the approach and material presented here.

E. B.

D. W.

1. Family

The definition of the family by G. P. Murdock is a useful starting point for our study:

> The *family* is a social group characterized by common residence, economic cooperation, and reproduction. It includes adults of both sexes, at least two of whom maintain a socially approved sexual relationship, and one or more children, own or adopted, of the sexually cohabiting adults. The family is to be distinguished from marriage, which is a complex of customs centring upon the relationship between a sexually associating pair of adults within the family. Marriage defines the manner of establishing and terminating such a relationship, the normative behaviour and reciprocal obligations within it. . . .

Although our own society is generally monogamous, this definition of the family does not limit it to any particular form of marriage. Moreover, traditions within some ethnic minorities, particularly those from the Indian subcontinent, involve forms such as the joint family system where a three-generational family depending on the authority of the senior male is to be found, and, among Muslims in their own countries of origin, perhaps some polygamous arrangements. This may be modified over time, but there are significant differences in structure of authority, relationships within the family and the prominence of the arranged marriage which will continue. Some of these features are given more attention in Werbner's reading on Manchester Pakistanis in Chapter 2. Both in families and also within wider kinship structures and elsewhere the importance of the primary group is apparent.

A *primary group* is characterized by features such as face-to-face association, small numbers, the unspecialized character of the association, relative permanence and comparative intimacy. The most obvious examples are the family, face-to-face contact in the old-fashioned locality, and a group of friends. The primary group develops among its members insights into the mood and states of mind of others, leading among other consequences to shared sentiments and attitudes. Such a group is fundamental in forming the social nature and ideals of the person concerned, a sense of belonging to that group and the wider society, and for most of us the family is the first and most significant experience of this.

However, as Cooley wrote: 'It is not to be supposed that the unit of the primary group is one of mere harmony and love. It is always a differentiated and usually a competitive unit, admitting of self-assertion and various appropriative passions; but these passions are socialized by sympathy, and come or tend to come, under the discipline of a common spirit.'

Another relevant concept is that of *norms*. These are social rules or beliefs which tell us the behaviour that is appropriate in a given situation. W. G. Sumner distinguished between folkways and mores, the latter being stronger and involving, for instance, prohibitions against murder and actions which would set at risk the fabric of the society, whereas the former had to do with etiquette and other matters at the level of social convention. A hierarchy of shared rules, shared beliefs and shared expectations therefore develops. Where goals are widely shared in society – for example, the desire to enter high-status occupations – these are referred to as values. The definition of a social norm is set out clearly by Johnson: it 'would state (1) who is expected, (2) by whom, (3) to do what, or refrain from doing what, (4) in what circumstances. In addition, it would specify (5) what penalties will be forthcoming if the norm is violated, or what rewards if it is conformed to, (6) what circumstances surrounding a violation will be regarded as extenuating, and (7) who will administer the penalties or give the rewards. The laws of the state are easiest to describe in this way,' Johnson goes on. 'But social interaction is governed by many other norms as well, explicit and implicit.'

It is usual to think of the family as composed of husband, wife and their children. This is the *nuclear* family which is the normal household unit in Britain. Members of this family are usually biologically related, although this is not invariably the case: the institution of adoption provides the same legal basis as for any other family. There are differences in the way the term 'nuclear family' is used: in most cases it refers to parents and children living together, but sometimes it is used to describe members of a nuclear family wherever they might happen to be.

Most people are members of two families during their lives. The first is the family of *origin* (or orientation) in which our earliest experiences take place. The second is the family of *marriage* (or procreation) in which we play the roles of parents. The functions of the family involve on the one hand *internal processes*, the ways in which the family operates as a system of relationships, and on the other those which relate to the wider society.

In common with other advanced industrial societies of the West, the nuclear family is the primary unit, but the *extended* family can still remain important. This term refers to a grouping which is wider than the nuclear family but involves those related by marriage or kinship. The studies of Bethnal Green by Young and Willmott and by Townsend provide interesting evidence for the continuing vitality of one kind of extended family. Among some ethnic minorities in Britain, for example Pakistanis and Indians, the norm remains the joint family based on the authority, for certain defined purposes, of the head of this three-generation grouping, but in practice more and more begin to live in modified forms of the nuclear family, possibly with certain relatives present in the household unit. The definition of household used in the ten-yearly census is: 'one person living alone or a group of persons living together, partaking of meals prepared together and benefiting from a common housekeeping'.

The need to study the family from an historical perspective is the assumption behind the reading from **Young and Willmott** which starts our chapter. Three stages of family life, from the pre-industrial to the present day, are outlined. In the first, the pre-industrial stage, the family was usually the unit of production, working together in a number of complementary or similar roles. After industrialization the members of the family tended to become individual wage-earners, and this was a process likely, it is suggested, to tear apart the working-class family. In the present stage the unity of the family has been restored around the functions of consumption, as opposed to the functions of production in Stage 1.

Certain characteristics of the modern, or Stage 3, family are suggested, among them 'home-centredness', especially when the children are young; the greater importance of the nuclear family as opposed to the extended family (of relatives); and finally the diminishing segregation of the roles of the sexes. (These points may be linked with those made by Bott in another reading in this chapter.) There are class aspects of the extent to which families are to be formed with the characteristics of Stage 3, and it is suggested in the reading that examples of all three stages are still to be found. Two trends are discernible in Stage 3: one is the extent to which women work outside the home, and the other is the large amount of work now done in the home by men. These trends are so advanced that there is no kind of work in the home which is strictly reserved for the wives, and sharing of tasks is probably increasing. Information from the sample of families indicated that time, too, is shared much more – less so if only the weekdays are taken into account. If weekends are included, more time is spent with the family than at work.

Technology and greater living space for family members have led to more comfort and more inclination for adults to be in the home. Activities previously of a communal kind, which almost inevitably involved contact with neighbours, such as drawing water or using the wash-house, are now provided for in the home. Light and heat are much more efficiently supplied to houses, and higher living standards and smaller families have a bearing on these changes. What has been achieved, in the opinion of the authors, is a new sort of integration arising from the historical experience and from social changes such as the limitation of families and the extension of women's rights.

The reading by **Rimmer and Wicks** provides a basis of information on a range of issues to do with the family. It indicates clearly the extent to which only a minority of families falls into the group of 'married couple with children' around which the media and popular perceptions are focused. The information is worth examining in the light of the stages of the family cycle developed later in this chapter by Rosser and Harris, who set out findings from their research in Swansea about twenty years ago. The figures quoted from *Social Trends* by Rimmer and Wicks are not exactly comparable with those of the Swansea research, but both indicate the extent to which the family with dependent children is in a minority. Rimmer and Wicks also indicate a significant variation in the proportion of this group in different parts of the country for reasons associated with a number of factors including the age-structure of the population, its ethnic composition, and its religious affiliations.

The reading shows how popular marriage has become, maintaining in the twentieth century a far higher rate than any attained in the nineteenth. Furthermore there has been a remarkable change in the ratios between males and females of marriageable age, reversing the situation before 1939 when more girls than boys survived infancy and where the imbalance was made worse by the deaths of men in the First World War. Now there is a preponderance of males in age groups up to forty-four. The rate of divorce has increased proportionately more than the increase in the rate of marriage, though the inference from high rates of remarriage must be that marriage is an extremely popular institution.

The brief information contained in this reading is more up-to-date than that in the reading on divorce by Chester later in this chapter, but the analysis that Chester provides remains valid. It has been predicted that at least one in four marriages currently taking place will end in divorce, with a much higher rate among those who marry young. Partly as a consequence of this, the number of one-parent families has risen considerably: at the beginning of the 1980s one household in eight is headed by a single parent. Despite the limitations of such statistics, the economic and social consequences of being a member of a one-parent family, and for that matter of a larger-than-average family, are often serious.

A relatively large number of single parents are in the work force, but the effects of growing unemployment, which is likely to remain at a high level for at least the rest of this decade, may affect them disproportionately. The great enlargement of the work force from 1961 to 1975 was the result of an increasing number of women joining it, and women's work remains crucial for the standard of living of many families. (The reading later in this chapter by Oakley sets issues about the position of women in a more general context.)

From a more specifically social view, the increasing number of elderly people (those over retirement were 6 per cent of the total population in 1901 and 17 per cent in 1978) has consequences for family and social policy, particularly since the four-generational family – a result of the younger ages at which women have had children in the recent past, and of higher expectations of life – will become more common. Apart from the unmarried the majority of the population will increasingly be part of at least a three-generational family. However the proportion over retirement age is expected to fall slightly by the end of the century since the low birth rates in the interwar period, 1919–39, mean that there are fewer people in that age group to survive to old age.

The next reading arises from research undertaken by **Rosser and Harris** in the Swansea area and demonstrates that the period during which family life revolves around young children takes up less than half of the normal cycle of family life. In future this stage of procreation (phase II), taken to be the period from the birth of the first child to the marriage of the first child, will take up a smaller proportion of the family cycle because of changes which result from earlier ages of marriage, fewer children born within a shorter period during marriage, and greater expectation of life. The other phases which they identify are: phase I, home-making, from marriage to the birth of the first child; phase III, dispersion, from the marriage of the first child to the marriage of the last child; and phase IV, from the marriage of the last child to the death of the original partners. As Rosser and Harris point out, each phase of the cycle has its characteristic patterns of household composition, family behaviour and social participation in the life of the community.

The rise in the divorce rate is the subject of widespread and often uninformed speculation. That there has been a substantial growth is undeniable: **Chester** considers this in relation to the complex of factors which involve both personal relationships and expectations and social conditions. He concludes that contemporary marriages are more vulnerable to divorce than were wartime marriages and that the differentials are increasing (i.e., marriages of the late 1960s, for example, will be more prone to divorce). Two main questions are considered. First, are contemporary couples having more divorces or divorces earlier in marriage (since the British evidence contrasts with that from the United States in that a majority of those divorcing in the past thirty years have been married for over ten years)? Secondly, are couples experiencing more marriage breakdowns or merely resorting more readily to divorce in the event of breakdown? It is suggested that in the future there will be more divorce and earlier divorce.

Chester shows how divorce is not to be taken as an index of marriage breakdown. In the experience since 1900 separation often became an alternative to divorce whereas more recently those who separate may go on to divorce, thereby appearing twice in the figures (and leading the unwary to declarations of doom about the future of the family).

Finally, divorce is related to statistics of other forms of personal behaviour and experience which relate to moral norms: illegitimate births, venereal disease, crime and others. It is made abundantly clear that the statistics have to be interpreted with great care, and that changes in personal and social values are of great relevance.

Chester's examination of variant family forms complements the discussion on divorce. A pluralistic family system has, by its nature, consequences for child development, as well as wider implications. Divorce brings about two of the important variant family forms, the one-parent family (usually headed by a female) and what Chester defines as the reconstituted family.

The one-parent family has attracted more and more attention since the publication of the Finer report. Recent evidence indicates the groups into which such families fall, and emphasizes that they do not form a homogeneous category: while the majority are divorced or single women, one in nine is a lone father. The reading provides much-needed information about the characteristics of one-parent families, and the extent to which they receive support from members of their family – for example, living with relatives or others – or how far they are alone. Over recent years features have emerged which are disturbing from a policy point of view. It has been estimated that a child born in 1977 has a one in two chance of being in a one-parent family before the age of sixteen. Moreover, there are much greater concentrations in certain parts of the country: nearly one family in three is headed by a single parent in inner London.

Many diverse stereotypes of one-parent families exist. The usual structure of sociability geared to couples can lead to social isolation for the lone parent as well as severe problems arising from carrying sole responsibility for the family. One of the consequences is pressure to remarry, and this is the commonest outcome of divorce. There are certain vulnerable areas for these 'reconstituted' families, including trauma, unresolved guilt, and other psychic consequences. The formulation of appropriate policies for family and divorce requires an appreciation of the problems faced by these kinds of families. Chester's view is that progress has been made in redefining divorce and facilitating its increase but that this has not been accompanied by a general re-examination of the functions of the family. This is considered later in the chapter in the reading by Morgan.

The work of **Bott** is taken from her intensive study of twenty families in London reflecting different structures and forms of organization. As she points out, all three of the types of organization she discusses were found in all families but the relative amounts varied considerably. She relates the type of organization which predominates in a family to the external social relationships of its members. One implication from her work is that if the family moves from the area where husband and wife have connected social networks and segregated roles to perform, to another where they are on their own as a nuclear family, this is likely to have consequences for their roles and their way of life. This reading is relevant for the classification it provides of family organization. It has had a profound importance for many studies of family life. Among the more recent, set in a wider context, is that of Werbner on Manchester Pakistanis in Chapter 2.

The reading from work by **Macdonald and Mars** is chosen for two reasons. There has been a 'real increase in the numbers of people who enter some form of unmarried cohabitation'. Evidence from England and Wales has suggested that the number of couples who lived together before their first marriage more than tripled in less than a decade up to 1975. The figure of 10 per cent living together before marriage was suggested. This reflects a trend documented also in countries such as the United States and, most notably, Sweden. In the latter country cohabiting couples made up less than 1 per cent of the total of married and unmarried couples about twenty years ago, but by 1974 the figure appeared to have increased to about 12 per cent. Our purpose is to pose questions about the extent to which informal marriage is an alternative to, or anticipation of, formal marriage, and to indicate the significance of this development which a generation ago would have been regarded as being morally quite unacceptable to the great majority. Perhaps most striking are the indications of similarities between formal and informal marriage.

Studies of the family rarely give any prominence, except in most general terms, to the prevalence of that other informal arrangement, the extramarital affair. Despite the liberalization of the law on divorce, adultery is still cited in 30 per cent of divorces as causing the irretrievable breakdown which has become the precondition of divorce. The reading by **Lake** contains material which considers the affair as an alternative marriage in certain circumstances. Lake goes on to suggest that the justifications used for lying and cheating reflect attitudes formed in childhood. Finally he points up a 'functional homogeneity' between affair and marriage as extensions of the socialization process. Both Macdonald and Mars and Lake write interestingly and provocatively about 'informal' structures, often disregarded by sociologists, and these form the subject of a reading by Henry in Chapter 7.

The thesis put forward by **Dennis** is that in an increasingly specialized society the family is the only social institution in which people are perceived and valued as whole persons, and marriage the only place where the individual can expect esteem and love. The emphasis upon this and upon sociability helps to account for the increasing popularity of marriage even when the divorce rates are rising. Dennis suggests that romantic love becomes the only valid basis for marriage, unlike the situation which prevails among minorities from Asia living in Britain where marriage is viewed as an alliance between families of roughly equivalent social status.

The discussion of romantic love is taken further by **Little**. He shows how the link between love and marriage which is now taken for granted is the product of historical circumstances, and discusses how this delimits the individual's area of responsibility more successfully than is possible in societies whose kinship patterns reflect much more detailed and wide-ranging obligations to a wider range of kinsfolk.

Kinship and the wider bonds of family are seen in two contrasting settings in the next readings. **Loudon** deals with an area in the Vale of Glamorgan and the way in which shared kinship connections and gossip provide a social cement for the established residents, setting them off from newcomers who are unaware of kinship links. His reference to 'affines' (the spouse and other relatives-in-law) raises the question of the terminology of kinship. Although it has been assumed that kinship among the middle class is less important than among working-class groups, some evidence suggests that although kinship may involve different things for the middle classes it remains important. **Hubert** suggests that frequency of contact, for instance, cannot, among the middle class, be taken as the sole criterion of a close relationship. In her sample from Highgate in London it was not possible to assume that ties of affection were unimportant even where contact was infrequent. The interchange of daily services played little part in the lives of those interviewed.

Although restricted to certain middle-class groups, the so-called 'dual-career family' is now established. In a book recommended for further reading the Rapoports consider the extent to which this pursuit of individual careers by professional spouses while they maintain a family life together is becoming more pervasive. The satisfaction gained from the pursuit of careers is seen as extending to more and more people, in consequence of affluence, and in particular to women. The women graduates studied showed three major work and family patterns: the conventional, whereby the woman abandons her career on marriage and does not return to it; the interrupted, where she intends to resume when her children grow older; and the continuous, where the career is interrupted through childbirth either minimally or not at all. The women who work appear to gain from their opportunities for self-expression. In this sample, children, despite problems raised by mothers having careers, were reported as showing independence and resourcefulness and contributing to meeting overall family needs.

In the reading taken from her analysis of women's experience in society today **Oakley** considers the question, 'What are husbands for?' and points out that early anthropologists saw the Victorian patriarchal family as the last and most civilized form of human relations. Certainly, men claimed 'the family' as their property. She examines critically the all-pervasive conventional family ideal, and also the strangeness of the view that although divorce is much more common, marriage is really working very well. On the structural issue to do with the institutions of marriage and the family, she indicates the very different, and in some ways contradictory, socialization of boys and girls (a subject on which there is other material in Chapter 3) and questions the idea of complementarity between the sexes. The idea of the family as a haven from the outside world is challenged, and the author concludes: 'The family is not what it is held out to be – for men, women or children.'

In the final reading in this chapter **Morgan** considers three issues of great importance for the family. He begins by examining differing perspectives about the place of the family in modern society. At one extreme these range from views that the family is in decline or marginal, to others indicating it remains too much at the centre and retains too much power. There is a wide range of attitudes about the desirability or otherwise of these changes. This leads on to definitions about kinship structures, and the delineation of family boundaries which arise from on-going contacts within the family and the interchanges between the family and the wider society. In a final section from the reading Morgan discusses the family and ideology. Many of the ideas and views expressed bring together and extend what are continuing themes in the chapter.

The Symmetrical Family
M. Young and P. Willmott

Reprinted with permission from Michael Young and Peter Willmott, *The Symmetrical Family*, Routledge and Kegan Paul, 1973, pp. 27–32, 93–100

On our main subject there l .s been no full history. 'It is a sad comment on British historiography that while we have a great many studies of political parties, trade unions and religious bodies, there is not a single history of the basic social institution of British life, the family. Until some attempt has been made to fill this gap it is impossible to write with assurance about family life in the nineteenth century, or to do more than hazard a few guesses at the nature of the impact of industrialism upon the home.' After Harrison wrote that statement, Anderson went some way towards filling the gap by documenting kinship patterns in one town, Preston, as well as in rural Lancashire and Ireland. The fourfold scheme that we put forward in this book will obviously become more differentiated, the interpretations more sophisticated, when the whole job has been done by historians, rather than sociologists, and changes in family structure related in all their complexity to demography.

But we believe enough is already known to allow a partial reconstruction to be made. The process of change, as we are interpreting it, has so far proceeded through three stages. Even though there is so much in common between family life at each stage, and even though the boundaries between one stage and another are somewhat arbitrary, the rough-and-ready division seems to us useful, as does the generalization, even though it cannot any more than most generalizations do justice to all the evidence. In the first stage, the pre-industrial, the family was usually the unit of production. For the most part, men, women and children worked together in home and field. This type of economic partnership was, for working-class people, supplanted after a bitter struggle by the Stage 2 family, whose members were caught up in the new economy as individual wage-earners. The collective was undermined. Stage 2 was the stage of disruption. One historian has pointed the contrast in this way:

Women became more dependent upon the employer or the labour market, and they looked back to a 'golden' period in which home earnings from spinning, poultry and the like, could be gained around their own door. In good times the domestic economy, like the peasant economy, supported a way of life centred upon the home, in which inner whims and compulsions were more obvious than external discipline. Each stage in industrial differentiation and specialization struck also at the family economy, disturbing customary relations between man and wife, parents and children, and differentiating more sharply between 'work' and 'life'. It was to be a full hundred years before this differentiation was to bring returns, in the form of labour-saving devices, back into the working woman's home. Meanwhile, the family was roughly torn apart each morning by the factory bell.

The process affected most the families of manual workers (and not all of these by any means). The trends were different in the middle-class family, where the contrasts for both husbands and wives were somewhat less sharp than they had been in the past. But as working-class people were preponderant most families were probably 'torn apart' by the new economic system. In the third stage the unity of the family has been restored around its functions as the unit not of production but of consumption.

It is clearly not possible, since social history is unlike political or military history, to do more by way of dating than to indicate in a rough manner when the successive waves of change started moving through the social structure. The Stage 1 family lasted until the new industry overran it in a rolling advance which went on from the eighteenth well into the nineteenth century. The development of the new industry was uneven as between different parts of the country, coming much later to London than to the industrial north. It also outmoded the old techniques of production more slowly in some occupations than in others. But come it did, eventually, along with many other forms of employment which shared one vital feature, that the employees worked for wages. This led to the Stage 2 family. The third stage started earlier in the twentieth century and is still working its way downwards. At any one period there were, and still are, families representing all three stages. But as first one wave and then another has been set in motion, the proportions in Stage 2 increased in the nineteenth century and in Stage 3 in the twentieth.

The new kind of family has three main characteristics which differentiate it from the sort which prevailed in Stage 2. The first is that the couple, and their children, are very much centred on the home, especially when the children are young. They can be so much together, and share so much together, because they spend so much of their time together in the same space. Life has, to use another term, become more 'privatized'. . . .

The second characteristic is that the extended family (consisting of relatives of several different degrees to some extent sharing a common life) counts for less and the immediate, or nuclear, family for more. We have not been able to discover much documentary evidence about kinship patterns in nineteenth-century England. People certainly often lived with or near relatives, and we would expect that daughters more often maintained close links with their parents, and particularly with their mothers, than sons did with theirs. Extended families must have been used for mutual aid. But we doubt, along with Anderson, whether they became so pervasive and so much the arena of women's lives until this century. Our belief is that since the second war, in particular, there has been a further change and that the nuclear family has become relatively more isolated in the working as in other classes.

The third and most vital characteristic is that inside the family of marriage the roles of the sexes have become less segregated. The difference between two contemporary families of the 1950s, with and without segregated roles, has been well described by Bott.

There was considerable variation in the way husbands and wives performed their conjugal roles. At one extreme was a family in which the husband and wife carried out as many tasks as possible separately and independently of each other. There was a strict division of labour in the household, in which she had her tasks and he had his. He gave her a set amount of housekeeping money, and she had little idea of how much he earned or how he spent the money he kept for himself. In their leisure time, he went to cricket matches with his friends, whereas she visited her relatives or went to a cinema with a neighbour. With the exception of festivities with relatives, this husband and wife spent very little of their leisure time together. They did not consider that they were unusual in this respect. On the contrary, they felt their behaviour was typical of their social circle. At the other extreme was a family in which husband and wife shared as many activities and spent as much time together as possible. They stressed that husband and wife should be equals: all major decisions should be made together, and even in minor household matters they should help one another as much as possible. This norm was carried out in practice. In their division of labour, many tasks were shared or inter-changeable. The husband often did the cooking and sometimes the washing and ironing. The wife did the gardening and often the household repairs as well. Much of their leisure time was spent together, and they shared similar interests in politics, music, literature, and in entertainment. Like the first couple, this husband and wife felt their behaviour was typical of their social circle, except that they carried the inter-changeability of tasks a little further than most people.

Bott was writing fifteen years ago, and not many families have yet got as far as the second couple. Power has not been distributed equally in more than a few families. Division of labour is still the rule, with the husband doing the 'man's' work and the wife taking prime responsibility for the housekeeping and the children. We believe that this applies to the majority of families. But the direction of change has, we believe, been from Bott's first to her second type.

Many different terms have been used for the new kind of family that is emerging. Since it has so many facets to it, a single apt word is not easy to find. Burgess and Locke said, a quarter of a century ago, that the family had moved from 'institution to companionship', and their words 'companionship family' have sometimes found favour, although not with us. The members of a family are more (or less) than companions. For the same reason we do not like 'companionate', as employed by Goldthorpe and his colleagues. We have ourselves talked about 'partnership' and the 'home-centred' family, but these words too are open to objection, the former because it is so general as to be applicable to all forms of marriage, and the latter because, although it stresses one of the distinguishing characteristics we have just mentioned, it does not now seem to us to stress the most important of them, the de-segregation of roles. The new family could be labelled simply egalitarian. But that would not square with the marked differences that still remain in the human rights, in the work opportunities and generally in the way of life of the two sexes. The term which is best, in our view, is the one used by Gorer, the 'symmetrical family', although the emphasis we want to give is not the same as his. He said that, 'In a symmetrical relationship A responds to B as B responds to A; the differences of temperament, of function, of skills are all minimized.' We think it is closer to the facts of the situation as it is now to preserve the notion of difference but ally it to a measure of egalitarianism. In this context the essence of a symmetrical relationship is that it is opposite but similar. If all segregation of roles ever disappeared (apart from that minimum prescribed by the dictatorship of a biology from which there is for most people no escape) then one might properly talk about egalitarian marriage. But to be fair to what has happened in this century a term is needed which can describe the majority of families in which there is some role-segregation along with a greater degree of equality than at Stage 2.

We must make it clear, in case we have failed to do so up to now, that we do not think that the Principle of Stratified Diffusion applied until the second half of the nineteenth century to family structure or indeed to much else. It had to wait until the new ideas of democracy had freed people's aspirations and the new products of industry had satisfied some of them. So the middle classes did not lead the movement from the first to the second stage. Their families were not broken up in the way that Thompson described, nor were those of many skilled workers. But the middle classes were the first to enter the third stage, reducing the numbers of their children and adopting other features of the new family. They have been followed by successive strata of the population. The main question posed by the 1970 survey is whether a new, fourth phase is now being initiated in the same class to ripple its way with the same wave-motion through the structure of society in the next century.

Less segregation of roles

These various historical processes are still working their way through the social structure which means that, in many if not all respects, they have had a fuller effect on the families of richer than poorer people, and of younger rather than older. With poorer and with older people the vestiges of Stage 2 are still very much apparent. But the great majority of married people in our sample were members of the dominant type of new family.

In Stage 2 families there was segregation of roles in many more ways than those to do with money. If husbands did any 'work' at all at home the tasks that they, and their wives, thought proper to them were those to which male strength and male manual skill lent themselves. It was not a man's place to do woman's work any more than the other way round. All that has now changed. Wives are working outside the home in what is much less of a man's world than it used to be.

Husbands also do a lot of work in the home, including many jobs which are not at all traditional men's ones – which is one reason why the distinction between work and leisure is now a great deal less clear for men than it used to be. It never was very distinct for women. There is now no

Table 1. Occupational class and husband's help in the home (main sample: married men working full-time)

Reported help to wife at least once a week	Profes- sional and managerial	Clerical	Skilled	Semi- skilled and unskilled	All
None	14%	13%	14%	24%	15%
Washing up only	16%	7%	13%	12%	13%
Other tasks (cleaning, cooking, child care etc.), with or without washing up	70%	80%	73%	64%	72%
Total %	100%	100%	100%	100%	100%
Number	171	70	236	107	585

sort of work in the home strictly reserved for 'the wives'; even clothes-washing and bed-making, still ordinarily thought of as women's jobs, were frequently mentioned by husbands as things they did as well. The extent of the sharing is probably still increasing. The latest reading that we have is recorded in Table 1. What husbands did in detail varied according to occupational class. The people at the top helped rather less than others with house-cleaning, for instance. But taking all forms of help into account it was still true that fewer semi-skilled and unskilled workers contributed at all in this sort of way.

The relationship can also be looked at in another way. Table 2 shows that on weekdays men spent more time with colleagues than they did with family. But take account of the weekend and the picture changes. If the week is treated as a whole the immediate family wins out in the competition for time against its main rival, people at work.

Table 2. Average hours spent with immediate family compared to others (diary sample: married men aged 30 to 49)

	Weekday	Saturday	Sunday	Total for week
Family	5·7	8·7	9·5	46·7
Family together with friends or relatives	0·5	1·9	2·3	6·7
Total with family	6·2	10·6	11·8	53·4
Work colleagues without family	7·1	2·6	1·0	39·1
Friends or relatives without family	0·7	1·1	0·8	5·4
Alone	2·1	1·1	0·7	12·3
Total waking hours accounted for	16·1	15·4	14·3	110·2
Number of men	203	197	197	—

In this and later tables time is expressed not in hours and minutes but in hours and tenths of hours. The total for the week has been calculated by multiplying the sample weekday by five and adding the two weekend days. Time has been excluded for which there was no record about who was present with the diarist.

They shared their work; they shared their time. But if the trend was towards it, most married couples were obviously still a long way from the state of unisex that some young people had arrived at. There were many roles which were still primarily the prerogative of one sex or another, particularly in the classes which were not so far on in the process of change. In 1970 the general rule in working-class families with cars was still that the husbands were the drivers and the wives passengers, like the children. But this role, too, was well on the way to being shared. Mr Barwick, a carpenter in Sutton, described what he did at 7 p.m. one Saturday.

I took Beryl out for a driving lesson just to polish up on turns in the road etc. The kids enjoy Mum driving for a change. Beryl's driving is a bit of a thing in the family at the moment. There is a bit of a competition going on with Dot, one of our friends who is learning as well. There was the usual inquest on the phone tonight after the lessons they had both had.

Just as it was in some families still thought rather strange for women to be drivers, it was in virtually all not expected that men should do more than *help* their wives at the work of child-rearing and housekeeping. The primary responsibilities for home and work were still firmly with one sex or the other.

Miniaturization of machines

The symmetrical family would not have developed as it has without the aid of technology, which has been responsible for the last change we want to mention. If technology had made it impossible to operate within the small frame of the home – if it had turned out that consumption had to be, like production, organized in large groups such as Robert Owen thought could be the salvation of mankind in his mill at New Lanark and in his community at New Harmony in Hampshire, and the builders of the *kitbbutzim* in Israel likewise in this century – then the family would perhaps have bent to technical necessity. As it is, technology has played new tunes on the same old theme of the primacy of the primordial.

It was not like that in Stage 2 of our scheme. People were thrust into an industrial economy before the houses and consumer goods to put in them had properly arrived. Almost the only luxury was provided in the tavern, and this was largely reserved for men. Along with their work-mates they could find in the warmth and conviviality of the pub some comfort to compensate them for the harshness of their working conditions, as well as abatement for the thirst which the hardness of the work stimulated. The weekends could, as incomes grew, be so uproarious that absenteeism on 'St Monday', as it was known even in the nineteenth century, was much higher than on any other day. The homes could not compete. They were small. They were full of wailing infants, at any rate where the parents did not keep them quiet (and sometimes stunt them for life) by feeding them with the opium-derived 'Godfrey's Cordial'. The Temperance Reformers, whether religious or secular, sometimes had success with their fearful stories of nemesis for the drinker which were the nineteenth-century counterpart of the statistics about lung cancer which the doctors and their allies have been producing in this. But often not. The space that mattered most for the husband used to be the collective space of the alehouse. As the amount of private space has increased there has been more physical room for the husband at home, more comfort and more room for receiving friends.

The water, before it was piped into an individual supply, used to come from a collective well or stand-pipe in the street or on the landing of one of the tenements built by the Peabody, Guinness, Sutton and other philanthropic housing trusts. The washing was done in communal wash-places. If people took baths at all, they did so in the public slipper-baths. The entertainments were also collective long after a public hanging on Tyburn Hill, near where the Marble Arch now stands, ceased to be the greatest sight in London, drawing crowds of a hundred thousand. The street-markets were an entertainment, as they and football and horse-racing, almost alone of the collective spectacles of the past, still are. The city burst out on Bank Holidays as it had long before when archery practice had been compulsory. Transport was collective. The music hall was collective, as was its successor, the cinema. And for a time it looked as though the big would go on getting bigger, outside as well as at work. In the 1930s Llewellyn Smith drew from his survey the conclusion that:

the supply of some of the more important forms of amusement has become mechanized, with consequent results which, *mutatis mutandis*, bear some analogy to those which follow the mechanization of industrial processes. The most characteristic instrument of popular entertainment today is the cinema, of which the first beginnings under the name of the 'bioscope' were referred to by Charles Booth. Today the 258 cinemas within the County of London, with their 344,000 seats and their repeated performances, are capable of entertaining a quarter of the whole population on any one day.

The extent of the change is obvious. What kept people out of the home (and especially husbands with their superiority of command over the money) was the absence of attraction within it. A city of small workshops was also a city of mass life. In this century a city of large factories and offices is also a city of miniature life on the family scale. It is as though the giant of technology has laboured only with one end, to produce tiny reproductions of itself . . ., and so to make up for the damage it did to the family in the past. Gas light and electric light were inventions as crucial as piped water; at least husbands could see the faces of their wives after dark without too great an expense. The fractional horse-power motor was another key invention, powering home-laundries, home ice-makers, tiny cold stores, floor cleaners and cooking aids. The average housewife has been given 'about the same amount of mechanical assistance (about two horsepower) as was deployed by the average industrial worker around 1914'. These inventions have, perhaps, done more for the wife than for the husband. But he has been just as absorbed as she by the machines which have brought entertainment into the home, starting with the gramophone and ending (so far) with colour television, and more so than she by the new style of do-it-yourself handicraft production with its power tools and extension ladders and stick-on tiles and emulsion paints. All in all, the machine has by mimicking man, from his fingers to his brain, enabled modern man to mimic his forbears. A partnership in leisure has therefore succeeded a partnership in work.

We do not know how much time people used to spend in and out of the home. But we do know what people who completed the diaries said about their custom in 1970. The figures are in Table 3. We very much doubt whether, before homes became Home, men at any rate would have passed more than half their time there.

Table 3. Proportion of total time spent at home by husbands and wives (diary sample: married men and women aged 30 to 49: total number of people shown in brackets)

	Weekday	Saturday	Sunday
Men	55%	66%	76%
	(203)	(197)	(197)
Women working outside the home	71%	75%	83%
	(132)	(127)	(127)
Women not working outside the home	87%	82%	87%
	(76)	(73)	(74)

We have been sketching out the manner in which family patterns have changed in the last two centuries. The pre-industrial family in which husbands, wives and children were partners in production (if far from equal partners) was in the end unable to resist the force of a much wider division of labour than could be managed within its tiny compass. The new economy did not smoothly incorporate the old or produce a new moral or any other sort of order by which the family could be sustained. Only slowly, and after a great deal of suffering of which women and children were the victims even more than men, has a different sort of integration been achieved around the functions of the family as a unit of consumption rather than production. Various changes, starting first in the middle classes, have been both interacting causes and consequences of the general transformation. The struggle for women's rights has gradually changed the mental climate, as well as bringing material benefits like family allowances to the aid of wives and children; and each victory has set off a campaign for another. Just because their husbands have been willing to cooperate in the process, the limitation of families has emancipated women more than anything else, and as success has been achieved both wives and children have become more rewarding to cooperate with. The acquisition of better homes has (except for those left out of the general advance) made it more worthwhile for husbands to spend money on them, and their occupants. There is then less reason for a sharp segregation of incomes. And if contraception and more tolerant husbands enable wives to go out to work, they can win for themselves a measure of financial independence.

The Family Today
L. Rimmer and M. Wicks

Reprinted with permission from Lesley Rimmer and Malcolm Wicks and the Study Commission on the Family, 1983

What do we mean by 'the family' in Britain today? Most people probably think in terms of a married couple with children. This is certainly not the only popular conception, but it is the view presented in advertising and by the media. It is also the family type that is usually implicitly assumed by government in framing its policies.

There have, however, been and continue to be, important changes in family patterns. A model of the typical family as, 'a nuclear family unit comprising the two natural parents and their respective legitimate child or children living together in their own homes' is, in some senses, increasingly unrealistic. As Table 1 shows, married couple families, with dependent children living with them, make up only about one-third of *households* at any one time – and only about 40 per cent if independent children are included. If the stereotype is drawn even more tightly – with mother at home and father as 'breadwinner' – then this would apply to only about 15 per cent of households. If only 'natural' parents were included, it would be a smaller proportion still. Increasing divorce and remarriage, the rising numbers of one-parent families, more dual-worker families and the different patterns among ethnic minority groups are changing the meaning of 'family' for a substantial minority of parents and children.

Table 1. Households: by type   Great Britain

	% 1961	1966	1971	1976	1978	1979
NO FAMILY: One person – under retirement age	4	5	6	6	7	8
over retirement age	7	10	12	15	15	15
Two or more people – one or more over retirement age	3	3	2	2	2	2
All under retirement age	2	2	2	1	1	1
ONE FAMILY: Married couple only	26	26	27	27	27	27
Married couple with 1 or 2 dependent children	30	27	26	26	26	25
Married couple with 3 or more dependent children	8	9	9	8	7	6
Married couple with independent child(ren) only	10	10	8	7	7	7
Lone parent with at least one dependent child	2	2	3	4	4	4
Lone parent with independent child(ren) only	4	4	4	4	3	4
TWO OR MORE FAMILIES:	3	2	1	1	1	1
TOTAL HOUSEHOLDS	100	100	100	100	100	100

Source: *Social Trends 11*, Table 2.2

Let us consider the major trends in more detail.

MARRIAGE

During the twentieth century there has been a remarkable increase in the marriage rate – in this sense at least, marriage has become more popular. Today about 90 per cent of men and women will have been married by the age of forty.

Increasing marriage rates among women have been largely dependent on the ratio of bachelors to spinsters and there have been some important changes since the mid-nineteenth century. As the Finer Report observes: 'In mid-Victorian England, almost one-third of the women aged twenty to forty-four had to remain spinsters because differential mortality and large-scale emigration so depleted the reservoir of men that there were not enough to go round.' There is now a more even balance between males and females of marriageable age and indeed since 1951 there has been an excess of males in the younger age groups which by 1961 had extended to all age groups up to forty-four years of age.

While marriage has become more popular in this sense, divorce has increasingly to be seen as an integral part of marriage and family patterns.

DIVORCE

There has been a long upward trend in the number of civil divorces since these first became available in 1857. Prior to 1914, the annual number of divorces never exceeded 10,000 in England and Wales, and 1000 in Scotland.

There were substantial increases in the wake of both world wars, but the numbers fell back during the 1950s. However, from the early 1960s there has been an upward trend, with the 1970 figure being more than double that of 1960. The Divorce Reform Act of 1969, which took effect in 1971, gave a sharp upward shift to the total number of divorces. Over the last twenty years there has been a 400 per cent increase in the divorce rate and in 1978 there were 143,667 divorces – a rate of 11.6 divorces per 1000 married people. Divorce rates peak between the ages of twenty-five and twenty-nine, and since 1970, divorce rates have doubled for ages above twenty-five and tripled for those below twenty-five.

Overall on this basis it is probable that one in four of marriages currently taking place will end in divorce. For those marrying young the rate is much higher: one-third of women marrying below the age of twenty will probably be divorced in fifteen years.

REMARRIAGE

Increasing divorce has been paralleled by an increase in rates of re-marriage. This suggests that a bad experience of marriage the first time round does not always put people off the idea as a whole. Today about 34 per cent of all marriages involve a remarriage for one or both of the partners. And if these trends continue, it has been estimated that by the year 2001 some 20 per cent of men in England and Wales will have been married more than once. However, remarriages are not immune to divorce. And while we do not yet know whether remarriages are more prone to divorce than first marriages, the proportion of divorces involving couples where one partner has been married before has risen from 12 per cent in 1973 to 15 per cent in 1978.

ONE-PARENT FAMILIES
Perhaps one of the most often identified consequences of the increase in marriage breakdown is the rising proportion of one-parent families in the population. In 1971 it is estimated that there were some 570,000 one-parent families, and by 1979 this had risen to 920,000 – with the care of over 1½ million children.

Overall the number of one-parent families is rising at about 6 per cent a year, and currently one in eight families is headed by a lone parent. Reliable estimates of the number of parents and children living in one-parent families have been difficult to produce, partly because of the lack of administrative statistics covering some of the routes into and out of one-parent status – separation and cohabitation, for example. And a very serious limitation of many existing statistics on one-parent families is that they show a 'snap-shot' at one point in time – that is, they are cross-sectional. Such estimates may appreciably understate the cumulative number of parents and their children in the population who have ever lived, or will live, in a one-parent family at some time. But until more comprehensive information is available on the 'risk' of becoming a one-parent family, it seems certain that the issues surrounding lone parenthood will be underappreciated.

There is far less evidence available on the number of families which are reconstituted or 'blended' – with parents and children from more than one marriage. But with the high rate of remarriage for some groups of divorcees it seems certain that the issues surrounding step-parenting are likely to become increasingly important.

The other major change in family patterns is the emergence of smaller families. In 1900 one-quarter of the married women were in childbirth every year. Yet thirty years later that proportion was down by one-half to one in eight.

Indeed, during the first years of this century the proportion of families with only two children almost doubled. Today over 40 per cent of married couples will have only two children and only 7 per cent will have four or more.

FOUR-GENERATION FAMILIES
At the other end of the family cycle increased life expectancy and growing numbers of the old have dramatically changed our concept of family. The

number of people over retirement age has increased from 2.4 million in 1901 to 9.5 million in 1978. The retirement age groups represented 6 per cent of the total population in 1901 and 17 per cent in 1978.

This 'ageing of the population' has been particularly marked in recent times. Between 1966 and 1976, the number of people aged sixty-five and over increased by 20 per cent, and while the period of rapid increase in the total number of elderly people is now over, there are extremely important changes occurring *within* the elderly population. Most importantly, the numbers of the very aged are increasing at a rapid rate. Those aged seventy-five or over are estimated to increase by 760,000 between 1975 and the end of the century, and two-thirds of this increase will occur in the decade 1975–85. Most of the very aged are women and many are widows.

Compared with earlier periods, then, today's children are more likely to have grandparents alive during much of their childhood and some will have one or more great-grandparents, too. In the future we must begin to think of 'family' in terms of children and *dependent parents*, as well as parents and dependent children.

WOMEN

Many of the important changes that have affected the family as a unit have had a particularly dramatic effect on women.

Increasing life expectancy, lower fertility, less infant mortality and the trend towards smaller families have had profound effects. For example, by the time the typical mother of today has virtually completed the cycle of motherhood she still has practically half her total life expectancy to live.

More women now undertake paid work outside the home and it has been suggested that the pattern of women's employment is likely to be of full-time work with a short break for childbearing. Indeed more women now work between marriage and the birth of their first child, and return to work once the children are at school. Between 1961 and 1975 the working population grew from 23.8 to 25.6 million and the whole of this increase was accounted for by the increase in the number of women by 30 per cent, from 7.7 million to 9.8 million.

Although more women in Britain (and Denmark) work outside the home than in other EEC countries, a much higher percentage of women in Britain work part-time, and it is the increase in part-time employment which wholly accounts for the increased employment of women with dependent children in the 1970s. In 1977 49 per cent of women without dependent children were working full-time compared with only 33 per cent of those with dependent children. Today one in six of the working population is a woman engaged in part-time work.

Ability to work outside the home still reflects family responsibilities – only 12 per cent of women with three or more dependent children work

full-time and the proportion of women working (at all) increases with the age of the youngest child. It should be noted that most preschool children still have non-working mothers. In 1978 only 5 per cent of children under two had a mother who worked full-time (another 19 per cent had a mother who worked part-time). For children of three to four years the proportions rise to 6 per cent and 25 per cent respectively.

An important change in family patterns, then, is the dual-worker household, and it has been shown that women's wages may make a crucial contribution to a family's standard of living. Indeed between three and four times as many families would be in poverty were it not for the wife's earnings.

Family patterns and public policy

A vast range of public policies have a direct bearing on families and the nature of family life. Many of these issues have been dealt with elsewhere and here we focus on a few illustrations.

THE FINANCIAL SUPPORT OF FAMILIES

Bringing up children is an expensive business, as any parent knows, and an adequate income is one of the most important requirements for the family. Most families, of course, depend for their main source of income on wages or salaries. Some 96 per cent of two-parent families rely on wages as their main source of income, but the proportion is only 40 per cent for one-parent families, and over 40 per cent of one-parent families rely on supplementary benefit. Increasing rates of unemployment are also having a major effect and the evidence shows that large families are particularly likely to suffer from unemployment. The heads of large families also have lower hourly rates of pay and they work longer hours. But earned income does not always fully meet family needs and it is important to look at the adequacy of the financial support that is offered by the state to families with children.

There is no one coherent system of social security provision. For most families child benefits provide the main source of state support, but for poor families there is a very wide range of means tested benefits available. And, of course, the taxation system, with its own reliefs and allowances, crucially affects family finances.

To some it seems surprising that family poverty remains a major problem in Britain and it is one that is exacerbated by growing unemployment and increasing numbers of one-parent families. The most recent evidence, for 1977, shows that there were 420,000 children in families with incomes below the supplementary benefit level; 990,000 children in families receiving supplementary benefit; and altogether there are as many as 3,550,000 children in families with incomes up to 40 per cent above the benefit level.

Apart from the question of family poverty, there is also interest in the question of how *all* families with children fare financially compared with those without children. Some argue that the position of such families has deteriorated relative to others and it is felt that this has occurred in terms of both taxation and family allowance/child benefits. For example, over the period from 1964/65 to 1978/79 the tax burden of a single person on average earnings increased by 36 per cent points while for a married couple with two children the increase was in the order of 144 per cent points. Also in the years since 1948 pensions and other main benefits have been increased twenty-two times. In contrast, family allowances/child benefits have been increased only ten times.

A particularly urgent question is the fragmented system of income support for lone parents and their children. Public policy is failing to come to terms with the scale of marriage breakdown, and in consequence, state support for children in one-parent families is woefully inadequate. Some 55 per cent of one-parent families are in poverty and 60 per cent of all children in families in receipt of supplementary benefit come from such families. Some children indeed may spend much of their 'formative years' at the levels of living provided by the Supplementary Benefits System. And these levels of living have been described by the body which used to administer the scheme as 'barely adequate' to meet the needs of families with children at a level consistent with normal participation in the relatively wealthy society in which they live.

Family Structure
C. Rosser and C. C. Harris

Reprinted with permission from C. Rosser and C. C. Harris, *The Family and Social Change*, Routledge and Kegan Paul, 1965, pp. 164–7

So far we have been examining the composition of the households in which our subjects lived at the time of our survey. For purposes of analysis and exposition, we have classified these into a series of 'household types', following the categories used by Young and Willmott in their study of Bethnal Green. The result is an essentially static, 'snap-shot' view of Swansea at a particular point in time. We must now emphasize the somewhat obvious, but neglected, point that from the point of view of invidivual families these are not separate 'household types' but phases in a continuous cycle of development. Domestic groups are 'born' at marriage, expand with births, reach a sort of climax as the period of procreation is passed and as the children grow to maturity, and decline as the children

marry and 'leave the nest' to found elementary families (and separate domestic groups) of their own. The original domestic group finally disintegrates with the death of one or both of the original partners. This is the normal and universal familial process. With each phase of the cycle, the composition of the domestic group alters – as children are born, or as they leave home on marriage (or bring in their spouses to form composite households). This natural and continuous rhythm of the successive generations must obviously underlie any discussion either of household composition or of family relationships external to the individual household. Here in this endless process are the essential dynamics of family life. It is of course a continuous process within each individual family, though it can without great difficulty be divided into a series of arbitrary but recognizable phases, much as can the life-span of a particular individual. As there are 'seven ages of man', so there seem to be four ages of the family. In the table, we show the phases into which we have divided this continuous and repetitive cycle of growth and decline, together with the numbers and proportions of the persons in our Swansea sample who fell by our definitions into each phase (taking married persons only of course, since marriage is the starting point of the cycle):

Table 1. The family cycle

Family phase	Definition	Numbers in our sample	Percentage of total
Phase I: Home-making	From marriage to the birth of the first child	297	17
Phase II: Procreation	From the birth of first child to the marriage of the first child	808	47
Phase III: Dispersion	From the marriage of the first child to the marriage of the last child	262	16
Phase IV: Final	From marriage of last child to death of original partners	358	20
Total		1725	100

We have taken these particular beginning and ending points for the four phases because they can be easily identified for the persons in our sample, and because of course they do represent clear and distinct milestones in

the progress of an individual family through this typical cycle. In the average case, with marriage about the age of twenty-three, the first phase lasts about two years, the second about twenty-three years (since it is from the birth to marriage of the first child). The length of the final two phases depends on the number of children born and on the facts of longevity. There have been dramatic changes in this average and normal family cycle over the last half-century or so with the striking decline in family size and the marked improvement in life expectancies. And it is useful in order to clarify and emphasize these changes, particularly those in family size, to divide Phase II which we have called the Phase of Procreation, into two subphases – 'childbearing' during which births are actually occurring, and 'childrearing' in which the children born are growing to maturity. It is the very great shortening of the actual period of childbearing, comparing say the present generation of women with that of their grandmothers, which has produced the most marked change in this family cycle.

Each age or phase has its characteristic pattern of household composition, of family behaviour, and of social participation in the life of the community of which the family concerned is a component. The dominant social characteristic of the first phase is that it is a period of very considerable adjustments and rearrangements in relationships, particularly with the sudden arrival on the scene of a new set of relatives – the in-laws. Our survey revealed that the majority of marriages begin with the newly married couple living temporarily with relatives, more often than not in the home of the bride's parents. Hence characteristically this first phase of the family cycle is often spent wholly or partly in a composite household. In the second phase of the cycle, the characteristic domestic group for the larger part of this period consists of parents and dependent children, though towards the end of this phase it is not uncommon for a composite household covering three generations to be again formed with an elderly parent or parents from either the wife's or the husband's side (more usually the former) coming to live with the family.

The Phase of Dispersion begins with the marriage of the first child and continues until all the children are married. As the children marry and leave home, the domestic group goes through a period of declining size, though commonly the size of the group may expand temporarily as one or other of the married children starts off marriage by bringing the spouse into the parental household. The partial rupture of relationships characteristic of this phase may thus be softened by the formation of a temporary composite household. When all the children have in fact married, even if they have not all left home, the family concerned has entered the last phase of the cycle – and in most cases the original couple find themselves on their own once more.

This, briefly expressed, is of course a model of the life cycle covering the normal or typical case. There are, it scarcely needs to be emphasized, numerous variations in practice on this general model of the four ages of the family. Some persons never marry and thus never enter on this cycle. Others marry but never have any children and are thus permanently halted as it were in the first phase. In other cases the cycle is abnormal through the death of one or both partners early in the marriage, or through 'broken homes' produced by separations or divorces (though these latter accounted for only 1.5 per cent of the cases in our sample). In yet others, one or more of the children may never marry and remain permanently in the parental home – the case for example of the spinster daughter living with and caring for her elderly father and mother, or of the bachelor son maintaining the home for his widowed mother. In some cases the couple concerned may have well above the 'normal' number of children which will affect in their case the length of the two final phases. These many variations are, however, minority instances. In the vast majority of cases the process that we have outlined above does in fact represent the pattern of family development over the succeeding generations.

Divorce
R. Chester

Reprinted with permission from Robert Chester, 'Divorce in the Nineteen Sixties', *Marriage Guidance*, vol. 14, no. 2, 1972, pp. 35–9

Between 1959 and 1969 the annual number of petitions for divorce and annulment in England and Wales increased by 133 per cent. This represents an average growth of 9 per cent per annum compound, and the rise in numbers was from 26,000 to 61,000. The trend shows no sign of levelling off, and the growth rate is likely to be given at least a temporary acceleration by the new divorce law operating from January 1971. It is necessary, of course, to allow for the increase in the number of marriages during the period, and the *divorce rate* per 1000 married population shows an increase of 100 per cent (against the 133 per cent increase for petitions). During the 1960s, that is to say, the divorce rate doubled. At the 1969 rate, almost four million adults will have the experience of divorce during the remaining three decades of this century, and perhaps two million children under school-leaving age will be affected. Clearly divorce is now a mass experience, and it is possible that these estimates understate the future magnitude.

Divorce has not been very much studied by social scientists in England. When they have studied it, the tendency has been to explain the historical increase (from under 1000 per annum at the turn of the century) in terms of population growth, the disturbing effects of war, and the increased availability of divorce. Certainly availability has been increased by such measures as sex-equalization in 1923, extensions of grounds in 1937, and the provisions of the Legal Aid Act 1949. Factors of this kind, however, can hardly be responsible for the recent great increase in divorce, and it has become necessary to look elsewhere for an explanation. It begins to seem probable that changes in social conditions developing throughout the postwar years are now being reflected in the statistics of various kinds of personal behaviour, and that there have been changes in the norms of marriage. The study of contemporary divorce is in part a study of social change, and closer analysis of recent divorce trends reveals some suggestive patterns.

Analysis by cohort

Some light can be thrown on changing behaviour by the method which is technically known as cohort analysis. The idea underlying this procedure is basically very simple. In carrying it out, all the members of a particular 'generation' – say, all those who were born or married in a particular year – are followed through to see what their total experience has been at different points in time. It is possible, for instance, to take all the marriages in 1960, and to calculate the proportion which have ended in divorce by each successive anniversary of the marriage. We can then have a running account of their experience, and the people in this group can be compared with those who married earlier or later to see if there are any changes in behaviour between the cohorts or 'generations'. Calculations for each annual marriage cohort of the 1960s are shown in the table, together with the figures for those who married in 1942/43. The latter

Table 1. Percentage of successive marriage cohorts divorced at various durations of marriage. England and Wales

Those married in the year	Duration of marriage in years					
	4	5	6	7	8	9
1960	0·70	1·54	2·37	3·22	4·05	4·89
1961	0·76	1·62	2·52	3·38	4·35	—
1962	0·85	1·80	2·73	3·73	—	—
1963	0·95	2·00	3·10	—	—	—
1964	1·03	2·20	—	—	—	—
1965	1·19	—	—	—	—	—
1942/43	—	1·08	1·98	2·73	3·44	4·01

figures are included because these wartime marriages were supposed to be peculiarly vulnerable to breakdown and had accumulated historically record figures for divorce.

To compare the experience of cohorts, readings should be made *down* the columns, and it will immediately be seen that each successive marriage group shows a higher incidence of divorce than its predecessor at any given duration of marriage. For instance, those who married in 1960 show 1.54 per cent divorced at the end of five years of marriage, whereas by the time *they* had been married five years the couples of 1964 show 2.20 per cent, an increase of one-third. Similarly, after six years of marriage 2.37 per cent of the 1960 couples had divorced, but the figure for those marrying in 1963 is 3.10 per cent. Of the 1960 marriages almost 5 per cent had divorced before ten years of marriage, and those marrying later in the decade seem set to exceed this, probably quite considerably in the case of the most recent marriages. The universal tendency is for each marriage group to have higher divorce figures than the one before, and there is no evidence that the upward trend is diminishing.

A further point shown by the table is that even the lowest divorce figures for marriages of the sixties (those for 1960) are greater than those for the highest wartime figure. That is, as measured by this technique, contemporary marriages are more vulnerable to divorce than war marriages. At nine years' duration the 1960 marriages had accumulated 4.89 per cent divorced, against 4.01 per cent for the war marriages, an excess of more than one-fifth, and on the evidence of the table the marriages of the late 1960s will experience much wider differentials still.

There is another trend which can be shown by cohort analysis, and this relates to youthful marriages. It is possible for any given year to divide marriages into those where the bride is a teenager and those where she is twenty or more, and to follow each group separately. When this is done it can be seen both that the younger marriages are most prone to divorce and that this group shares the pattern of increasingly higher figures successively throughout the decade. Of the teenage girls marrying in 1960 (82,000), approximately 9 per cent had become divorced by the end of 1969, and later marriage groups seem certain to exceed this. The relationship between young age at marriage and marital instability is not well understood, but clearly such marriages are very hazardous.

In seeking to interpret the figures so far given, two questions in particular seem to need exploring, viz:

(1) Are contemporary couples having more divorces, or are they merely having divorce earlier in marriage?

(2) If having more divorces, are modern couples also experiencing more *marriage breakdown*, or merely resorting more readily to divorce in the event of breakdown?

More divorce or only earlier divorce?

Obviously contemporary cohorts are experiencing more early divorce, but there is no way of relating the percentage of a marriage group divorced by any particular anniversary to the percentage of that group which will divorce in the long run. It could be that the more recent couples are having most of their divorces in the early years of marriage, and that ultimately no greater proportion will be divorced. This seems unlikely, however. In the past, divorcing has continued up to advanced durations of marriage, with rather more than half occurring later than the tenth anniversary. After a twenty-year period in which petitions have first halved and then more than doubled it would be foolish to dogmatize on this point, and the new law will in any case create a 'bulge' which will temporarily obscure the trend. But whichever way it is measured divorce is increasing fast, and it seems unlikely that statistics in the next decade will show other than a modern propensity to have more divorce as well as earlier divorce. While only guesswork is possible, it may be that as many as one in eight, or even more, of contemporary marriages will end in divorce.

More breakdown or only more divorce?

Rising divorce figures are viewed with concern by many people because it is assumed that divorce provides an index of marriage breakdown. The relationship between divorce and the total volume of marriage breakdown, however, is a very uncertain one, both because of the difficulty of defining marriage breakdown and the impossibility of measuring all its components. Some would want to include in marriage breakdown those unions where the couple continue to cohabit, but only in deep disharmony and failure of emotional support. In practice we know nothing of the dimensions of this group of marriages, and we must measure breakdown only in terms of situations where there is deliberate absence of a spouse through divorce, annulment, separation or desertion. Marriages, that is, which have broken up as well as broken down.

Even here, however, accurate numbers of breakdowns cannot be given, because only some components are exactly known. Divorce and annulment figures are reliable, because marriages can be dissolved only by public processes. Figures for separated spouses, however, are currently a mystery. Some couples part purely informally, and the numbers and trends of these are completely unknown. Figures are available for breakdowns which are dealt with in the Magistrates' Courts, and these have remained roughly stable throughout the 1960s at approximately 32,000 per annum. These numbers, however, cannot simply be added to divorces to give an annual total of legally recorded breakdowns, because some who separate via lower courts go on to divorce later on, thus presenting a problem of double-counting. Probably about half of those obtaining magistrate's orders go on to divorce, although this is only a 'best estimate'. On the basis of a number of assumptions which are fully explained elsewhere, it seems possible that the annual numbers of *recorded* breakdowns increased during the 1960s by about 65 per cent, against 100 per cent for the divorce rate, and 133 per cent for the number of petitions. These figures indicate the unreliability of divorce figures alone in the estimation of marriage breakdown, and of course they leave out of account the category of informally broken marriages. It might be expected that modern couples would be more ready than others in the past to regularize unsatisfactory marital situations, and that the number of unrecorded breakdowns has been falling. If such is the case, this would reduce still further the total increase of marriage breakdown from the 65 per cent suggested above. In other words, if fewer couples part informally, then recorded breakdowns come to be a truer reflection of the total, and increases therein would not necessarily indicate a commensurate increase in marital instability. At the very minimum, however, current figures suggest a greater propensity than in the past to dissolve a failed union. Contemporary marriages certainly have higher *recorded* breakdown rates, and they very probably have higher total breakdown rates, although the latter conclusion should be regarded as tentative.

Estimating the future is a hazardous exercise, but it may be worthwhile to speculate what proportion of contemporary marriages may ultimately succumb to one form or another of marriage breakdown. It seems possible that 12–15 per cent of marriages may come to an end via application to the divorce court or to magistrates. This leaves unaccounted for both unrecorded separations, and empty but legally intact marriages if a fuller definition of marriage breakdown is employed. One estimate puts the figure at 5–10 per cent of marriages for both kinds of breakdown combined, and adding these to recorded breakdowns it seems possible that between one-sixth and one-quarter of contemporary marriages may experience failure through termination, separation, or internal collapse. We cannot be certain that such high rates are historically new, and in any case historical comparisons may be unwise or misleading when people in the periods concerned have very different conceptions and expectations of marriage. What we can be certain of is that marriage difficulties are very widespread in modern society.

Conclusion

Since the mid-1950s there have been increases in the recorded statistics of various forms of personal behaviour and experience which relate to moral norms. Apart from divorce, such increases are seen, for instance, in illegitimate births, legitimate births premaritally conceived, venereal disease, crimes known to the police and (possibly) attempted suicide. As with marriage breakdown, there are problems concerning the compilation and verification of all these statistics, and they must be treated with caution. Nevertheless, the coincidence of timing and trend might plausibly indicate a shift in personal and social values commencing with the second decade after the war. It is not intended here to explore the changes in social conditions which may cumulatively have led to changes in the values of individuals and social groups, and it is certainly not the intention to deplore the 'permissive' or 'affluent' society. Such stereotyped catch phrases have very doubtful usefulness for serious social analysis, and the issues involved are so new and complex that no one can yet pretend to fully understand them.

Nevertheless, many observers have commented that the 1960s saw a breakthrough into a new kind of society, based on a relative if uneven afluence, and possessing a more *laissez-faire* approach to matters of personal behaviour. Social change is always likely to make most impact on the young, and those born since the late 1930s have matured into a world in which many orthodoxies have been challenged or overthrown, and many previously tractable groups have become self-consciously assertive, not least young people themselves, and women. There has been a general revolution of rising expectations, and such a situation is unlikely to leave unchanged the previous norms of marriage behaviour and family relationships. Our information is incomplete and unsatisfactory in many ways, but it seems to indicate that high manifest levels of marital instability should be expected to become an integral feature of individual and social experience.

Variant Family Forms

R. Chester

Reprinted with permission from Robert Chester, *The Family*, Office of Population Censuses and Surveys, Occasional Paper 31, 1983, pp. 103–4. Presented at the British Society for Population Studies Conference, September 1983

It is a sociological commonplace that the family system is becoming pluralistic, and it is natural to ask whether all variant forms are equally competent in sustaining the assigned family functions. The nature of the consequences for child development is clearly a central issue here, but there are others, such as whether particular variant family forms are able to fulfil adult needs, whether they have access to the resources necessary for adequate functioning, and whether they are able to maintain their boundaries to create the privacy for family processes to operate. Such questions are wider than divorce, but divorce is the major cause of two important variant forms, the one-parent family (usually female-headed), and the reconstituted family, which is conventional in personnel structure but not in family career or internal relationships.

For a significant part of their lives large numbers of children now do not experience the constellation of family roles and their development which is postulated in the Parsonian model, and evidence suggests that the functionality of the one-parent family is threatened in various ways. Economic deprivation has already been mentioned, and the probability of a female head of household. The lesser social standing of women means that the gatekeeping function tends to be less powerfully exercised, so that such families may be less autonomous and more vulnerable to surveillance and intervention by neighbours or officials. There is evidence that at the community level one-parent families are stigmatized by adverse stereotypes, and incommoded by the ambiguity of status which follows from failure to institutionalize post-divorce relationships, so that members have difficulties in negotiating a legitimate social identity. The couple-oriented nature of the structure of sociability can lead to social isolation for the lone parent, and single-handed responsibility for the household creates severe problems of time and energy allocation. Fatigue and frustration can follow from the absence of relief and mediation which parents can conventionally offer each other in dealings with children, while children may experience parental behaviour which is indecisive or unduly rigid. Social welfare agencies have not been successful in creating supportive services for such families, and the absence of good social credentials may mean that community supports are also sometimes lacking.

Altogether it is clear that one-parent families are vulnerable to many difficulties, but it is also clear that some of these are not so much entailed in the condition as they are the product of institutional and cultural responses and omissions which enhance the possibility of inadequate functioning. Not all of the difficulties of such families would be policy-responsive, but some would be, and the current situation seems to reflect social reluctance to assimilate fully the consequences of divorce. Society is thus left worrying (as it does) about the functional adequacy of a unit which it permits to be created by its divorce policies but is prevented from endorsing by its other value-commitments.

The unfavourable circumstances of one-parent families could be construed as latent coercions which sustain the ethic of conjugality by pressing towards remarriage. It is true that certain difficulties stand in the way of remarriage, such as social isolation, the age-specific nature of courtship institutions, financial austerity, and surveillance by children (as well as sometimes by the community and by welfare officials). Nevertheless, remarriage is the commonest outcome of divorce, and where children are involved this creates step-relationships within the reconstituted family. Literature on such families in this country is scarce. However, there are reasons to believe that step-families too have problems of social credentials, and may be hampered in their functioning because they are liable to experience both unique problems and more acute versions of ordinary problems. The acquisition of family roles is usually gradual and sequenced, with opportunity to negotiate the marital relationship in advance of parenthood, achieve parental role-orientation by stages, and establish the generational distance upon which discipline and the incest barrier are based. In step-families developmental stages are collapsed, and solidarities which normally grow slowly have to be more quickly achieved. Step-parents may find themselves sharing role-modelling, maintenance and nurturing with the absent natural parent, and there are contradictory pressures concerning how they should regard themselves. There are incentives to become indistinguishable from ordinary families, but they are also pressed not to supplant the absent parent. Again such families often appear odd through an incongruous collection of children, or because of complications of surnames and kin networks. The identity of the family thus invites questions, and may be spoiled.

Reconstituted families also have certain vulnerabilities. Some members may have experienced trauma, there are possible issues of unresolved guilt, and there are the potential psychic consequences of having been a one-parent family. There are material and symbolic residues of the previous family, one aspect of which is that step-children are perennial reminders of a partner's previous sexual life. Norms of behaviour and relationship are not institutionalized, and legal relationships are not like those of ordinary families (the absence of an incest bar, for instance).

There are, therefore, issues concerning how far present arrangements and practices facilitate reconstitution. It is certain that the dynamics of reconstituted families are different, and likely that they are more problematical, than those of ordinary families.

It is not the intention here to denigrate one-parent or reconstituted families, or to imply that they are universally malfunctioning. For one thing, these situations may be superior for those concerned to any available alternative, and for individuals there are benefits as well as costs to both conditions. Nevertheless, research reports indicate that problems exist of the kind outlined, and some of these derive from current social arrangements and attitudes. Society's divorce policies foster the creation of family variants of uncertain functionality, while social irresolution concerning the family prevents adequate acknowledgement of what has been wrought, and adequate attention to policies which are conceivably needed to facilitate the achievement of functions which are still deemed to be vital and still assigned to the family. It is true, of course, that the family is not the only agency of maintenance, socialization and stabilization of adult personality, and that human resilience can overcome many difficulties. Problems associated with divorce-created family variants may be historically transient, a property of pioneer cohorts of the new divorce era. Even so, the importance of the functions concerned and the welfare needs of children, suggest that development of the family should not be left to omission, indirection, and piecemeal and uncoordinated response together with the unguided ingenuity of individuals.

The social agenda

The burden of the above discussion is that society has not fully accommodated to the consequences of mass divorce because it has not resolved its attitude towards the phenomenon itself. A leap has been made in redefining divorce and facilitating its increase, but this has not been accompanied by a general rethinking of the family and its functions. Even although divorce rates have risen to unprecedented levels there are historical and cultural factors which militate against any easy acceptance of divorce or of notions that divorce may have positive aspects. The increased frequency of divorce against an unfavourable cultural background makes for a situation of sociological interest because society is faced with large and persistent discrepancies between traditional moral attitudes and current behaviour. Current divorce levels are an index of social change, but they are an index also of strain in the social structure which presses for alleviation.

Where social behaviour diverges widely from traditional social codes, in a liberal democracy at least, the political dynamics tend towards the modification of the codes in a 'liberal' direction. Contemporary Western societies seldom contain the preconditions for programmes of 'moral regeneration', so that law reforms on social issues, while often delayed, are generally in the direction favoured by 'progressive' opinion. The recent evolution of divorce law is an example of this, although it should be noted that law-makers were slow to act, and the reform could be seen as only keeping up with changes which had already occurred in behaviour and normative climate. The reform occurred only after the upward trend in divorce numbers was already well established, and after court practice had already shorn the concept of the matrimonial offence of much of its influence. In such areas as sex, marriage and reproduction legislators are rarely *avant-garde*, and they commonly operate by piecemeal reform rather than major reconstruction. It is for such reasons that ambiguities and disjunctions now exist in the way in which the family is regarded within the institutional framework.

The recent evolution of divorce has to be understood in the context of the new kind of society which has emerged since 1945. New kinds of value-orientations have appeared, such as self-realization, autonomy, equality and spontaneity, in contrast to inherited values such as self-denial, conformity and obligation. Traditional moral authorities have been challenged, and moral orthodoxies have been subverted by the thrust of new or revivified social tendencies, not least of which is the new feminist impulse. Whatever valuation may be placed on these changes, they seem integral to new social and economic conditions, and are the moral component of the revolution of rising expectations. Within marriage there is a shift in emphasis from the institutional and dutiful to the romantic and compassionate elements. Jural rigidity, male authority and fixed roles give way to flexibility, equality and intimacy, and marriage is recast into primarily a personal relationship. From this angle divorce might be viewed sociologically as part of the process by which the family system generates novel modes of domicile, economic activity, parental styles and sexuality in response to contemporary conditions and their attendant values.

However, while divorce reform may enable adults to be more readily freed of their existing marital ties, it does not of itself facilitate the finding of a reputable and unproblematical alternative life, and it does not touch upon other aspects of family functions. Because it refers only to adult needs, divorce reform fragments the unity of hitherto family functions. From the adult viewpoint, although released from a particular relationship he or she is threatened (on the evidence) with life experiences which are unlikely to enhance the probability of a stabilization of personality and satisfaction of emotional needs. From the viewpoint of the child, the whole nurturing and socializing function is put in question, and this has social as well as individual implications. The stability and functional adequacy of the family *system* are compatible with high divorce rates, as cross-cultural evidence testifies, but for this to be so the social structure has to be adapted to the fragility of marriage. Such is not the case in Britain (or other Western countries), where other assumptions concerning marriage and the family are still enshrined in public rhetoric and embodied in the institutional framework and policy agencies of society. To remedy this situation, and to safeguard the functions hitherto entrusted to the nuclear family, more would be needed than *ad hoc* adjustments. Mass divorce creates the need for reassessment and potential change on a very broad front. Doubtless such changes would constitute a major social overhaul, and would be seen by some as the abandonment of concern for the family. However, failure to adapt to the consequences of divorce means that the functions of the family outlined at the beginning of this paper will be put in question, and there will remain confusions and ambiguities in concepts of the family which produce individual and social problems.

Family Activities
E. Bott

Reprinted with permission from Elizabeth Bott, *Family and Social Network*, Tavistock Publications, 1957, pp. 52–61

The organization of familial activities can be classified in many ways. I find it useful to speak of 'complementary', 'independent', and 'joint' organization. In complementary organization, the activities of husband and wife are different and separate but fitted together to form a whole. In independent organization, activities are carried out separately by husband and wife without reference to each other, in so far as this is possible. In joint organization, activities are carried out by husband and wife together, or the same activity is carried out by either partner at different times.

All three types of organization were found in all families. In fact, familial tasks could not be carried out if this were not so. But the relative amounts of each type of organization varied from one family to another. The phrase *segregated conjugal role-relationship* is here used for a relationship in which complementary and independent types of organization predominate. Husband and wife have a clear differentiation of tasks and a considerable number of separate interests and activities. They have a clearly defined division of labour into male tasks and female tasks. They expect to have different leisure pursuits, and the husband has his friends outside the home and the wife has hers. The phrase *joint conjugal role-relationship* is here used for a relationship in which joint organization is relatively predominant. Husband and wife expect to carry out many activities together with a minimum of task differentiation and separation of interests. They not only plan the affairs of the family together but also exchange many household tasks and spend much of their leisure time together.

Among the research couples, there were some general resemblances in the type of organization characteristically followed in a particular type of activity but, within these broad limits, there was a great deal of variation. Thus in all families there was a basic division of labour, by which the husband was primarily responsible for supporting the family financially and the wife was primarily responsible for housework and childcare; each partner made his own differentiated but complementary contribution to the welfare of the family as a whole. But within this general division of labour, there was considerable variation of detail. Some wives worked, others did not. Some families had a very flexible division of labour in housework and childcare by which many tasks were shared or inter-changeable, whereas other families had a much stricter division into the wife's tasks and the husband's tasks.

Similarly, there were some activities, such as making important decisions that would affect the whole family, that tended to be carried out jointly by husband and wife. But here too there was considerable variation. Some husbands and wives placed great emphasis on joint decision, whereas others hardly mentioned it. Couples who stressed the importance of joint decisions also had many shared and interchangeable tasks in housework and childcare.

In activities such as recreation, including here entertaining and visiting people as well as hobbies, reading, going to the cinema, concerts, and so forth, there was so much variation that it is impossible to say that one form of organization was consistently dominant in all families.

The research couples made it clear that there had been important changes in their degree of conjugal segregation during their married life. In the first phase, before they had children, all couples had had far more joint activities, especially in the form of shared recreation outside the home. After their children were born the activities of all couples had become more sharply differentiated and they had had to cut down on joint external recreation. Data from the group discussions with wives in the third phase, when the children were adolescent and leaving home, suggest that most husbands and wives do not return to the extensive joint organization of the first phase even when the necessity for differentiation produced by the presence of young children is no longer great.

But the differences in degree of segregation of conjugal roles among the research families cannot be attributed to differences in phase development, because all the families were in more or less the same phase. Early in the research, it seemed likely that these differences were related in some way or another to forces in the social environment of the families. In first attempts to explore these forces an effort was made to explain conjugal segregation in terms of social class. This attempt was not very successful. The husbands who had the most segregated role-relationships with their wives had manual occupations, and the husbands who had the most joint role-relationships with their wives were professional or semi-professional people; but there were several working-class families that had relatively little segregation, and there were professional families in which segregation was considerable. Having a working-class occupation is a necessary but not a sufficient cause of the most marked degree of conjugal segregation. An attempt was also made to relate degree of segregation to the type of local area in which the family lived, since the data suggested that the families with most segregation lived in homogeneous areas of low population turnover, whereas the families with predominantly joint role-relationships lived in heterogeneous areas of high population turnover. Once again, however, there were several exceptions.

Because I could not understand the relationship between conjugal segregation, social class, and neighbourhood composition, I put social class and neighbourhood composition to one side for the time being and turned to look more closely at the immediate environment of the families, that is, at their actual external relationships with friends, neighbours, relatives, clubs, shops, places of work, and so forth. This approach proved more fruitful.

First it appeared that the external social relationships of all families assumed the form of a network rather than the form of an organized group. In an organized group, the component individuals make up a larger social whole with common aims, interdependent roles, and a distinctive sub-culture. In network formation, on the other hand, only some, not all, of the component individuals have social relationships with one another. For example, supposing that a family, X, maintains relationships with friends, neighbours, and relatives who may be designated as A, B, C, D, E, F . . . N, one will find that some but not all of these external persons know one another. They do not form an organized group in the sense defined above. B might know A and C but none of the others; D might know F without knowing A, B, or E. Furthermore, all of these persons will have friends, neighbours, and relatives of their own who are not known by family X. In a network the component external units do not make up a larger social whole; they are not surrounded by a common boundary.

Second, although all the research families belonged to networks rather than to groups, there was considerable variation in the 'connectedness' of their networks. By connectedness, I mean the extent to which the people known by a family know and meet one another independently of the family. I use the word 'close-knit' to describe a network in which there are many relationships among the component units, and the word 'loose-knit' to describe a network in which there are few such relationships. Strictly speaking, 'close-knit' should read 'close-knit relative to the networks of the other research families', and 'loose-knit' should read 'loose-knit relative to the networks of the other research families'. The shorter terms are used to simplify the language, but it should be remembered that they are shorthand expressions of relative degrees of connectedness and that they are not intended to be conceived as polar opposites.

A qualitative examination of the research data suggests that the degree of segregation of conjugal roles is related to the degree of connectedness in the total network of the family. Those families that had a high degree of segregation in the role-relationship of husband and wife had a close-knit network; many of their friends, neighbours, and relatives knew one another. Families that had a relatively joint role-relationship between husband and wife had a loose-knit network; few of their relatives, neighbours, and friends knew one another. There were many degrees of variation between these two extremes. On the basis of our data, I should therefore like to put forward the following hypothesis: the degree of segregation in the role-relationship of husband and wife varies directly with the connectedness of the family's social network. The more connected the network, the greater the degree of segregation between the roles of husband and wife. The less connected the network, the smaller the degree of segregation between the roles of husband and wife.

At first sight this seems to be an odd relationship, for it is hard to see why the social relationship of other people with one another should affect the relationship of husband and wife. What seems to happen is this. When many of the people a person knows interact with one another – that is, when the person's network is close-knit – the members of his network tend to reach consensus on norms and they exert consistent informal pressure on one another to conform to the norms, to keep in touch with one another, and, if need be, to help one another. If both husband and wife come to marriage with such close-knit networks, and if conditions are such that the previous pattern of relationships is continued, the marriage will be superimposed on these pre-existing relationships, and both spouses will continue to be drawn into activities with people outside their own elementary family (family of procreation). Each will get some emotional satisfaction from these external relationships and will be likely to demand correspondingly less of the spouse. Rigid segregation of conjugal roles will be possible because each spouse can get help from people outside.

But when most of the people a person knows do not interact with one another, that is, when his network is loose-knit, more variation on norms is likely to develop in the network, and social control and mutual assistance will be more fragmented and less consistent. If husband and wife come to marriage with such loose-knit networks or if conditions are such that their networks become loose-knit after marriage, they must seek in each other some of the emotional satisfactions and help with familial tasks that couples in close-knit networks can get from outsiders. Joint organization becomes more necessary for the success of the family as an enterprise.

Informal Marriage
P. Macdonald and G. Mars

Reprinted with permission from Petrine Macdonald and Gerald Mars, 'Informal Marriage', in Stuart Henry (ed.), *Can I Have It in Cash? A Study of Informal Institutions and Unorthodox Ways of Doing Things*, Astragal Books, 1981, pp. 150-6

The question of why people live together without being married proves to be important when one examines and tries to understand the initial stages of informal marriage. Diana Barker in 'A Proper Wedding' notes that, whatever the pros and cons of marriage, the wedding ceremony itself is significant both to the couple concerned and to their relations and friends. Most weddings involve some organization and planning; the wedding is an event anticipated by the people concerned for several weeks, and in some cases for several months, before it actually takes place. This period is renowned for short tempers, arguments and last-minute second thoughts, as the many separate elements of the event are organized and arrangements made. However, it is an important period, for it gives the participants time to absorb and discuss the implications of the wedding and what marriage will involve. This element of a 'proper wedding' or the lack of it, is also important when one considers informal marriage.

At the beginning of our research we suspected that informal marriage might also be marked by tension in the parallel period between the decision to live together and actually moving in with a partner. Since this period can be seen as a 'safety gap', we suggested that informal marriages involving such a period would be likely to be more stable and longer lasting than informal marriages which were less well considered. This suspicion, however, has so far proved unfounded. In only a very few cases did we find couples with anything like a waiting period between their decision to live together and its implementation. The great majority of people interviewed revealed that their initial moving in together had been either somewhat casual: 'We didn't discuss it but it seemed silly to pay two rents'; or due to force of circumstances: 'I didn't have anywhere to live and she said that I could stay with her.' But this set of findings needs further examination. It may be said that our original suspicion has some foundation and that the couples we interviewed who are still together, are together in spite of the lack of forethought. To answer this question we need to interview couples who have lived together but who later separate and see whether their relationships began in a different way. This material will be obtained during the course of our study.

More importantly, assuming the significance of the initial planning and decision-making phase, we suggest that informal marriage can be seen as one alternative to marriage; that it is the same as formal marriage without the legal and religious sanctions. If the distinction between trial marriage and informal marriage is maintained, this does not ignore other interpretations of cohabitation. If the participants viewed their relationship at an early stage as trial marriage then our findings regarding the lack of formalization of the beginning of the arrangement are much less surprising in the same way that one would not expect a couple to plan and discuss their first date at great length or see it as a necessarily significant step. Alternatively, however, should we find evidence of such a prior waiting period before a couple decide to live together then this would support our notion of their cohabitation as informal marriage.

We do not mean to suggest by this that all cohabitation must be seen as an informal alternative to marriage. It is obvious that this is not the case. Some cohabiting relationships are clearly a reaction against rising divorce rates; some arise from legal wrangles between those separated from their spouses; while others have to do with changing notions of conjugal rights in a context of the growth of the women's movement. Yet others are the result of changing courtship patterns and will be ended by traditional marriage or by the couple separating because they feel that they are not suited.

Ambiguity in social relationships: the problems of informal marriage

When considering the effects that informal marriage has on the existing social structure, one major point seems to us of particular interest: informal marriage creates ambiguities in the relationships of the couple with the outside world. While both formal and informal marriages involve a rearrangement of the partners' immediate relationships with their families of origin, the lack of public ceremony in the case of an informal marriage adds to the ambiguity of their situation and further bedevils the relationships between the generations.

As we have said, legal marriage generally involves a number of prearranged steps which culminate in a ceremony. This ceremony marks, among other things, that control of the couple has passed from the senior to the junior generation; the sexuality of the couple is no longer under the nominal control of their parents and any services which the couple performed for their parents, such as contributing money to the household, helping around the house, are formally withdrawn in favour of the new household which the couple will set up. In the case of informal marriage, however, there are no socially marked demonstrations indicating that this has happened and, from the point of view of the parental generation, the change of control from one generation to the next appears to happen without their foreknowledge, consent or even involvement. The fact that all but one of those interviewed by us had already left the parental home before they cohabited, suggests that in these cases parental control had already been relaxed, surrendered or displaced before the start of the informal marriages. Despite this, ambiguities still remained, perhaps because there was no formal or conscious expression of what the new situation involved for the parties concerned.

This ambiguity is reflected in the fact that approximately half those interviewed admitted to never actually telling their parents of their informal marriage. This is not to say that the parents of these people were unaware of the situation but that they were left to glean the information for themselves: 'I never actually told them but they are not daft, they worked it out.' 'They knew we lived in the same flat and I was always talking about him so, eventually, they must have put two and two together.' When asked why they had not told their parents, some of those interviewed said that it was a private arrangement and, therefore, did not concern their parents. In the case of a number of women, the reason given was that they felt it would upset and disappoint their parents and so the situation was left deliberately vague or not admitted. In several cases the pretence was carried to the extent that parents visiting one partner caused the other to move out of the home temporarily so that the parents would be unaware of the nature of the relationship. Of those people who did tell their parents about the arrangement, we found that women tended to want to tell their parents in person while men were more unconcerned about the method of breaking the news. There is therefore a suggestion here that control over procreation by the senior generation is regarded as significant by their juniors.

We found the ambiguity further reflected in answers to questions about sleeping arrangements during overnight visits to parents and relations. In cases where couples did not sleep together at their parents' home, the reason given was that either their parents would not permit it or that the couple themselves were reluctant to raise the matter. In some cases, after a time parents changed the sleeping arrangements without prompting, which the couple took as a sign that their relationship had become more acceptable to their parents.

On the other hand, in all cases but one, where it was applicable, parents staying overnight at the couple's home assumed that the couple would sleep together there. In the one case where this did not apply, the mother, who was a regular churchgoer, refused to visit the couple. However, she did permit both her husband and her daughter to visit and stay overnight. It would seem from this that people respect and abide by the informal rules operating in the home that they are visiting and that, if they feel unable to do this, they avoid the situation altogether.

The ambiguous nature of informal marriage extends to the couple's relationship with the wider social structure and it does so in a variety of ways. For example, where both unmarried partners work they are typically taxed as two single people and, therefore, pay higher tax than a married couple. In the UK this aspect of informal marriage costs them £195 per annum. On the other hand, if one of the partners applies for social security, the earnings of the other will be taken into account when the case is being assessed, as is the case with a married couple. Legally, the status of an unmarried couple varies with the particular law invoked. In the UK, in the absence of a will, one unmarried partner cannot automatically inherit from the other because they are not legally next of kin. However, in several cases recently, the ownership of the home has been awarded to the surviving partner where they have been able to prove that this was the deceased's intention.

While the colloquial term for informal marriage is the same as that for cohabitation, namely 'living together', the ambiguity of the institution is perhaps most obviously represented by the fact that there is no commonly used, unambiguous word in the English language to describe the partners of an informal marriage. Most of the people interviewed by us said that they found referring to their partner when talking to stangers difficult because of the absence of a suitable word. The words 'boyfriend' and 'girlfriend' were used in the main, although all said that if a shopkeeper or tradesman referred to their partner as husband or wife, they rarely corrected the misunderstanding since it was not important to do so, and indeed it may be important not to do so. It is interesting that the English language has responded so quickly to the women's movement by the introduction, if not widespread acceptance of, the term 'Ms' for both married and unmarried women, and yet no word has so far emerged to describe the partners of an informal marriage. It may be argued, however, that the women's movement has existed in one form or another for many years and in comparison, the institutionalization of informal marriage is relatively new. Of course, people living together in a permanent arrangement without marriage is not a new phenomenon in itself. In the recent past, couples in such a relationship tended to live *as though* they were married; the women used their partner's name, wedding rings were worn and, generally, the impression given to outsiders was that the couple had actually married. The phenomenon of living together relatively permanently without the pretence of religious or legal sanctions as with informal marriage is of relatively recent origin and it is this that perhaps accounts for this linguistic gap.

The normality of informal marriage

When considering the effect social structure has on the form and duration of informal marriage, the point which stands out, perhaps surprisingly, is the similarity between informal marriage and its formal counterpart. We argue that this similarity can be accounted for by the influence of existing social pressures and the strength of existing formal institutions.

Although informal marriage may seem to many a radical and somewhat shocking departure from traditional legal marriage, we found the couples we interviewed remarkably conformist in their approach to their relationship and that the pattern of most of their informal marriages paralleled traditional ones in major ways. At its most basic, the influence of formal marriage can be seen in the fact that all those interviewed had chosen to live as part of a couple rather than as part of a threesome, foursome etc. (We realize, of course, that there is a relatively small number of people who have chosen to live in large sexual groups as in 'group marriage' or in certain communes.) Further, we found that the informal marriages we studied entailed the same kind of sexual obligation as in traditional marriage in that the ideal of sexual exclusivity was subscribed to. In several cases interviewees said that they felt this exclusivity was important and that it entailed rejecting other boyfriends/girlfriends at the beginning of the relationship. All those interviewed said they would marry if they had children and thus the duration of informal marriages seems to be greatly affected by the social pressures regarding illegitimacy. The legal position of illegitimate children does not, in itself, appear a major factor in determining the duration of informal marriages.

As far as domestic duties are concerned, while equal sharing tended to be seen as the ideal, in fact the women interviewed did more than the men and, more importantly, took more of the responsibility for such work. This finding echoes those of an American study by Stafford, Backman and Dibona which compared the division of labour among married and unmarried couples. The authors of this study conclude: 'The persistence of the traditional division of labour among both the cohabiting and married couples is neither the outcome of a power struggle nor the differential availability of time. Rather it is the nonconscious ideology developed from parental modeling that preserves traditional sex roles.'

Finally, the normality of informal marriage is underlined when the couples split up. Current research being conducted by Kitty Mika of the

University of Colorado suggests that couples who live together can find breaking up as traumatic as do married couples getting a divorce. Indeed, since commitment has been found to be as critical a variable in the adjustment of cohabiting couples as it is in formal marriages, it is perhaps not surprising that couples find opting out of the relationship less easy than they originally believed.

So far our tentative findings would confirm that, in spite of what people might think or fear, and not discounting the minor interactual difficulties faced by all kinds of cohabiting partners, informal marriage is rather less radical than it is often described. As Bowman and Spanier have said, 'It is sometimes assumed not only by the individuals involved but by outside observers, that every seeming innovation represents the point of a wedge of social change. If we learn anything from history we learn that many such apparent innovations either remain as the lifestyles of small minorities or are gradually phased out.' To this we might add that even if such innovations become established as an institution they take on a form not so dissimilar from existing comparable institutions. Thus informal marriage seems far less a reflection of major new directions in social organization and more a reminder of the strength of existing social forces.

Affairs
T. Lake

Reprinted with permission from Tony Lake, 'The Extramarital Affair', in Stuart Henry (ed.), *Can I Have It in Cash? A Study of Informal Institutions and Un-orthodox Ways of Doing Things*, Astragal Books, 1981, pp. 159–65

If the essence of formal marriage can be described – and there are those who would argue that it cannot – then it probably lies in the *exclusive mutuality* of the contract between man and wife, in the scope of this mutuality, and in the ideal nature of the aspirations upon which marriage is founded. In the ideal marriage nothing of importance happens to either partner which is not then shared as part of an overt process of mutual enrichment and growth. Individual need-fulfilment can be seen to encompass the meeting of many objectives in the social, economic, sexual, emotional, and intellectual life of the person. When a couple marry, they publicly declare their commitment to achieve all their individual objectives together, in the interests of the furtherance of their unity as man and wife.

It is arguable that this ideal task is a practical impossibility. Few people are sufficiently resourceful and well matched to become an unlimited source of growth for one another for the rest of their lives. Even where this happens, they are unlikely to be able to act as the exclusive source of growth for one another. People require stimulation from other company outside marriage. Most marriage is therefore based on a series of compromises which falls short of the ideal, but which maintains certain elements of exclusivity acceptable to both partners. For example, it is common for the husband to take the major share of economic and intellectual growth and to share the benefits of this growth vicariously with his wife. It appears to be normative, also, for the husband to have more social enrichment than the wife, although this norm is probably less rigid now than it was two decades ago. The view is still widely held, however, that sexual enrichment, and to some extent emotional enrichment should be a joint activity. In marriages which are seen as 'stable', it is generally assumed that the marital relationship is built upon interrelated compromises – give and take – of the homeostatic nature. When the balance is disturbed by a breach of mutuality, the couple discuss this and stabilize their feelings by affirming the nature of their homeostatic contract.

Such an analysis is incomplete, however, unless account is also taken of the part played by marriage in socialization. Traditionally marriage is the final stage in the socialization of the adolescent. Marriage is therefore a continuation of the aims and purposes of the parental marriages – an extension of the objectives of the family of origin of the husband and of the wife. These vary widely from class to class, and from family to family. Broadly, they are concerned with the achievement of *survival and physical growth* – a person is 'old enough' to get married; the achievement of *economic self-sufficiency*, and the attainment of *responsible fertility* – often expressed as 'time to settle down'. The status of 'being married' marks people out as socially adult. In the middle classes emotional and intellectual maturity are particularly stressed as an indication of a sufficient socialization for marriage. In all classes the continuity between family of origin and family of marriage is a major influence upon whom one marries, when, and where. People choose as spouse a person who seems most likely to be able to contribute to the meeting of the ideals of marriage with the minimum of effort, and this usually means someone who is like the parent so that continuity of socialization will proceed.

Extramarital affairs disrupt this continuity by contravening the mutuality of the marital contract. An extramarital affair is a sexual relationship between two people in which either partner or both is actively married to somebody else, and in which deceit is used to conceal the relationship from the spouse so as to produce or preserve the appearance of stability in the marriage. Seen from the point of view of the marriage, an affair is an act of individual enrichment which robs the spouse of what is rightfully his or her own. For example, time which could have been spent with the spouse is spent with the lover instead. Money which could have been spent on joint comforts is used privately on another person. Love, sexual pleasure, and enhanced self-esteem, which the legitimate partner has a right to expect exclusively, is shared with an illicit partner. Intellectual respect towards the spouse is seen as diminished because more is given to a lover. Indeed, the ideal mutuality of marriage is so all-encompassing that any private enrichment can be seen as an *ipso facto* deprivation of the official partner. An affair is also a breach of the continuity of socialization with the family of origin. People who have affairs therefore not only hide them from the spouse, but usually also from their own parents.

But it frequently happens that affairs take on many of the qualities of marriage, and that the mutuality of the illicit couple becomes more significant to them than the life experiences they continue to share with their partners in the extant marriages. It is in this sense that some affairs act as alternative marriages. The lover replaces the spouse to a significant degree in the individual growth and socialization of the person having the affair, but not necessarily to the extent that the affair replaces and destroys the marriage. It is not uncommon for an affair to be the ultimate stimulus for a divorce which is then followed by the marriage of the two people having the affair. But it may be far more usual than is commonly recognized for affairs to last for many years as undiscovered and unrevealed parallel or alternative marriages, skilfully concealed by each lover from their spouse. The individual having the affair sees it in terms of the continuity of his or her own private growth, and the conflict arises because he or she sees this growth, in terms of objectives which are not conceded by the 'official' partner (and often the family of origin), to be legitimate aims on his part. . . .

The affairs which become alternative marriages arise as alternative strategies of individual development within the continuity of growth from childhood to adolescence and beyond to the wider objectives of adult self-realization. This usually means that an affair enables the married person to tackle again those aspects of the adolescent agenda which were left uncompleted at the time of the marriage, and which were abandoned early in the marriage as incompatible with its total mutuality. People cheat in order to grow. In doing so they are often repeating behaviour required of them during childhood. For this reason, further insight into the nature of affairs can be gained from an analysis of why and how people justify their deceit.

Why people cheat

In producing justifications for lying and cheating the three or four principal actors in the drama of an affair frequently give away clues as to the attitudes they learned in childhood from their own parents. The following are six of the most commonly encountered groups of justifications.

Love justifies everything: deceit is justified on the grounds that love transforms the sordid business of cheating into something noble, or something beyond the control of the deceiver because a person who is in love lives on a higher plane than normal. Underlying this type of justification is a defence against guilt about sex. It is not only the sordid business of lying, but also the sordid business of sex which becomes sacred and pure by the addition of love. The myth of the one true love, often carefully fostered by adults during the deceiver's childhood and adolescence, can clearly be seen as a parental way of controlling both the child and the parent's own fears about sex. The same controlling myth can be seen in the argument that for two people to be truly right for one another the 'chemistry' must be right. Many affairs are justified as alternative marriages because they continue to meet the objectives of socialization laid down by the parents in controlling myths of this kind. For example, a woman who has an affair with a person who makes a better lover than potential husband will justify it on the grounds that it makes her 'happy' – thus meeting the criterion of marriage set her by her parents, but meeting it outside marriage. 'Happiness' and 'love' are transmuting processes which help her cope with a fear of sex transmitted to her by her parents during socialization.

It was nothing to do with my wife/husband: children are often made aware of the fact that if it was not for them their parents would separate. The child's role in holding the marriage together actively involves him in producing two sets of acceptable behaviour – one for each parent – which differ in several respects. This can lead to conflicting agendas in adolescence, typified by conspiracy with one parent against the other – for example, 'I shouldn't tell your father just yet' – and then the reverse conspiracy: 'Mummy said I shouldn't tell you, so please do not let her know I have.' When such a person marries it is often to suit one parent rather more than the other. The affairs which follow then meet the objectives on the list of the parent who least approved of the marriage. They are 'nothing to do with the spouse' in the same way that covert arrangements with one parent were nothing to do with the other parent.

He lies about his affairs – why shouldn't I about mine?: the competitive 'tit-for-tat' affair, in which a married person gives the impression of his marriage as a race to score the most extramarital scalps, is probably the cruellest of marital 'games'. The lover is used as a pawn in the power struggle between the married partners. In the same way the child is often used as a pawn in its parents' marriage, being given extremes of attention – neglected and spoiled by turns. The child's method of coping is to resort to tantrums, which are then rewarded with massive attention. Very often, however, the child is competing with a parent who also throws tantrums.

Two wrongs are seen to be an effective substitute for justice. When affairs start they are often justified on the grounds that the other spouse started it first.

I make it right in other ways: the idea that a marriage depends on the happiness of both partners individually, and that how this is achieved matters less than its effects lies behind this group of justifications for cheating. Similar justifications include: 'What he/she doesn't know can't hurt him/her' and 'As long as she knows I'll never leave her, she will trust me.' The affairs in question are often seen as props to the marriage, and the lies are 'white' lies. Provided that the lover accepts this role, affairs of this kind often have a rock-like quality, and last for years as alternative marriages. The guilt is assuaged by careful, and as far as possible, equal attention and love from the person having the affair to both lover and the spouse. Often in cases of this kind lover and spouse are socially connected and accept one another as friends, neighbours, or colleagues. The lover has the major disadvantage, in that he or she carries the burden of jealousy to save the spouse from feeling it, and to avoid upsetting the carefully constructed balance of power. The adulterous spouse is, however, usually very jealous if his or her quasi-wife takes a second lover. 'Making things right in other ways' usually applies from the person having the affair to both the official and unofficial spouse, and if the latter is unfaithful this often hurts more than if the former were so. The childhood equivalent behaviour is that of keeping both parents happy, by following a jointly agreed agenda of socialization.

He/she just could not take it: to tell about an affair which is serious, or to have one discovered is often the most difficult crisis a married person can face. The partner having an affair, therefore, often justifies deceit on the grounds that he is afraid to hurt the spouse in this way. Not only will all the trust and faith on which a marriage has been built be destroyed, but it seems also as though the spouse will be irreparably hurt. In many marriages there is a one-sided emotional development which leads to extremes of dependence. But the roots of this justification probably go deeper, to the parental control of the child through the stricture that some things are totally unforgivable. The child is led to believe that there is a special category of sin which would physically harm the parent, which would be 'the death of me', as some parents put it. Yet others are told they would 'never' be forgiven for some transgressions. To a young child, 'never' is difficult to grasp, but utterly terrifying. The fear of permanent rejection lies deep within many children who have been banished under indeterminate sentences before they were old enough to understand time. The fear that a spouse would never forgive, or be totally destroyed by revelations of infidelity seems to be a reliving of such punishments.

It doesn't mean anything: the reduction of the status of the affair from serious to casual – at least, as far as the spouse is concerned – is another form of deceit. In one or two cases the interviewee said that the spouse suspected an affair, and that suspicions had been allayed by saying it had been casual and was now over. More usually, this form of deceit was used for affairs which really were casual, but here the adultery took the form of a long series of relatively petty infidelities in the form of 'one-night stands', rather like some forms of teenage rebellion.

Conclusion: the function of the affair

The structure of marriage acquires its cohesion from the mutual behaviour of the partners. Mutual behaviour is made up of actions which cannot be separately apportioned to the individual participants without doing damage to the relationship – for example, joint ownership of property, joint status as man and wife, emotional interdependence, the conception and upbringing of children, parenthood itself, etc. In perhaps the majority of marriages, the partners love one another sufficiently for many such mutual activities to bind them together too far for divorce ever to appear likely. To the extent that divorce and separation are traumatic this is due to the necessity of apportionment of mutual behaviours and the products of mutuality. The structure of many serious affairs is also reinforced by mutuality.

The affair often resembles marriage for this reason. There is also, however, a functional homogeneity between affair and marriage in that both are extensions of the socialization process which is the primary task of the family of origin in the life of the individual. The affair seems to continue the objectives of marriage by other, alternative means. In part this shows in the way so many people having serious affairs return to the unfinished agenda of their adolescent growth. In part it also shows in the extent to which deceit is justified by arguments repeating the self-control mechanisms imposed by parents on the person during childhood. The affair often becomes a re-enacted drama in which the unknowing spouse stands in for the punitive parent.

Relationships
N. Dennis

Reprinted with permission from Norman Dennis, 'Relationships', *International Journal of Comparative Sociology*, vol. II, 1962, pp. 86–8

The need which can be satisfied *outside* the family with increasing difficulty only is the need to participate in a relationship where people are perceived and valued as whole persons.

In urban industrial society it is necessary to collaborate with one set of people in order to earn a living, with another to worship, with a third set to be educated, with a fourth for amusement, with a fifth in seeing to the affairs of the neighbourhood, and so on. Minute differentiation of function is the secret of productivity. But the one thing which this type of organization of roles cannot 'produce' are the values of what Toennies called 'mutual furtherance and affirmation'. In the elaboration of modern social institutions, marriage has become the only place in which the individual can demand and expect esteem and love. Adults have no one on whom they have a right to lean for this sort of support at all comparable to their right to lean on their spouse. The marriage relation, to a far greater extent than in systems where communal type solidarities exist between fellow-workmen, neighbours, and extended kin categories, is in a strategic position in this respect.

In contributing to one another love, dignity and emotional support in spite of failures in specific roles or particular tasks, the spouses are fundamentally alike. Yet this is a special case of cooperation where likeness of contribution nevertheless produces great interdependence. This is so for two reasons. Unlike, say, housework, where the task could be carried out by a single person, and more than one person does it for reasons of convenience, sociability essentially requires the interplay of feelings for its fruition. The man and woman give each other something they could not provide for themselves. Unlike, say, sexual intercourse, which is possible in casual liaisons, companionship needs time and conditions suited to the emergence of primary-type ties, and these conditions do not flourish outside the family. James Thurber's 'One is a Wanderer' well describes the futility in the big city of the search for companionship outside of the family setting. Not only is it practically difficult to find communal satisfactions in modern society. The norms do not allow men and women not married to one another to indulge in tender companionate relationships. Any friendship between males tends to be stigmatized by attributing to it a homosexual basis. These rules are functional. They prevent obligations arising in communal type relationships from contaminating complex and fractionalized utilitarian relationships in the economy and in society at large.

The changing grounds of recruitment to the role of spouse support this interpretation. Sentiments turn increasingly towards the notion of romantic love as not just preferable but as the inevitable and only valid basis for marriage. Values emphasize personal response to the exclusion of economic advancement or social standing. A second tendency has been the increased obscurity of standards of choice where these are not connected with the romantic motif. 'In all the conversation about courtship there appears to be a lack of any definite criteria for liking or disliking . . . expectations which are vague and diffuse are more easily met and adjustment between husband and wife . . . may therefore be less difficult than in cases where both partners know exactly what they want.'

The divorce figures themselves support this interpretation. Primary relations which are sought for themselves, as contrasted with those which emerge as the by-product of other cooperative activities, are difficult to sustain. The well documented and much discussed 'loss of functions' of the family has reduced the possible volume of by-product primary group satisfactions. It is not surprising therefore that the divorce figures should have reached their present level. When people marry under the influence of romantic love, as Bertrand Russell has said, 'each imagines the other to be possessed of more than mortal perfections and conceives that marriage is going to be one long dream of bliss . . . In America, where the romantic view of marriage has been taken more seriously than anywhere else, and where law and custom alike are based on the dreams of spinsters, the result has been an extreme prevalence of divorce and an extreme rarity of happy marriages.' In so far as companionship, a close, durable, intimate, and unique relationship with one member of the opposite sex becomes the prime necessity in marriage, a failure in this respect becomes sufficient to lead to its abandonment. But it is significant that divorced people nevertheless remarry at about the rate at which bachelors and spinsters marry. They are discontented with a particular spouse. They cannot do without marriage if their primary social needs are to be met.

The spouse relationship, as has been indicated, is reorganized around this new balance of functions. Getting a living and making a comfortable and beautiful home are subordinated to companionship. Raising a family is also assessed within this context.

The Basis of Marriage
K. Little

Reprinted with permission from Kenneth Little, 'The Strange Case of Romantic Love', the *Listener*, 7 April 1966

I call romantic love 'strange' because in some societies a strong love attraction is socially viewed as a laughable and tragic aberration. Individual love relationships seem to occur everywhere; but a romantic complex is entirely absent from many societies, and our own Western civilization is almost unique in this respect. I mean by this the idea that falling in love is a highly desirable basis of courtship and marriage.

This special feature of our culture can be traced back to feudalism during the eleventh century. Among the ruling class at that time marriage was a mere commercial enterprise, an assignment forced upon the two interested parties by their overlords and guardians. It was destitute of love. Indeed, the wife of the knight or baron has been described as a serf and a chattel whom he kept in order by such corporal chastisement as circumstances might require.

With the ending of the struggle between Christendom and the pagan or infidel invaders, the castle became the centre of social intercourse. The knight who was now free to remain at home instituted a court. This gave women a chance to express feminine interests and graces.

This change of attitude, which lifted the woman of noble birth from conditions of savagery, was associated with the troubadours. They effected her rescue not by encouraging wives to love their husbands or husbands to cherish their wives but by propounding a code of gallantry. This required knights and squires, as part of their chivalric duty, to gain the favour of a lady, and having won it to make it the lodestone of their lives. The relationship was supposed to be restrained on the physical side, rapturous, beautiful, and tender but entirely extramarital. Marriage was regarded as the most formidable obstacle and dangerous enemy of love.

The medieval concept had drawn a line between the spiritual and the sexual aspects of love. The court society of the baroque and the rococo periods rewarded the gallant's deeds and duels with carnal favours. This integrated love and sex, though only outside marriage.

The idea that love and sex could be combined then filtered down from the castle to the city. It appealed to the rising merchant classes, but illicit relationships did not square with puritanism and thrift. Consequently, the verbiage of courtly love was now addressed not to the married women but to the marriageable maiden. This meant that between engagement and marriage the man was expected to court the girl and display emotional fervour. Association with the opposite sex was not supposed to take place before the betrothal. Nevertheless, the aim at last was to integrate love and marriage. Young people were to make their own choice of partner on the basis of their feelings. Thus, for the first time, the spirituality of love and the marital sex relationship became the same. The conjugal union was to be sanctified by the former.

I have explained that romance first connoted love outside marriage. Marriage was arranged, hence it was assumed that only extramaritally could people make true love choices. The significant change is that romance has come to be the predominant factor. The connubial state as well as courtship should be rapturous. At first romance was monopolized by aristocratic ladies and by conveying the idea that amorous dalliance was a mark of noble birth, gave to love-making a high social status. It encouraged courtship among the bourgeois family, placing its woman members on a special pedestal. Their duty, by the middle of the nineteenth century, was to keep alive virtues and graces that the sterner sex had no chance of developing. The latter – the sons of manufacturers – had to be converted into gentlemen. So, protected from vice and from danger, protected even from serious work, the wife or daughter symbolized her menfolk's aspirations. She was their surrogate in the upper-class world of gentility.

How, then, did romance manage to survive the subsequent emancipation of women? George Bernard Shaw has given part of the answer. His plays show clearly how romance has adapted to feminine needs. Girls, he declares, are right to choose their own spouses; it enables them to deal with the opposite sex as equals. The ethic laid it down that love is profaned by marrying for money, but there is nothing wrong about marrying for love: on the contrary, it is everyone's simple duty. So popular proved this theme that with the development of mass media of communication it became the principal stock-in-trade of major industries. In other words, not only were the traditional barriers down, but the wheel had turned full circle. Who could question this when, as it appeared, thrones were abdicated and royal families did not deny commoners as suitors – all for the sake of romantic love?

I exaggerate, but only because some psychologists have dismissed this emotion as adolescent frenzy. Instead, perhaps romantic love is one of society's methods of rationalizing changes in the organization of marriage. Abstractions come easier in the context of a different culture and so, finally, an example from West Africa. Traditionally, among the people there the bride is chosen by the family, who expect her to produce children and help economically. There, unlike here, even in monogamy a man's closest relationship is not with his wife but with his kinsfolk.

Nowadays, however, educated young West Africans have discovered the alleged virtues of romantic love. They stress the idea of marriage being a true union of husband and wife as well as an economic partnership. Love will be the most important thing when they marry. These younger people have new opportunities in West Africa today. Particularly if educated, there are careers in which they can often rise quickly. But to advance individualistically may seriously offend respected older kinsfolk and relatives. Having partly paid for a man's education, they will expect a return and to share in his subsequent prosperity. It is difficult for him to refuse, because this wide family system has ingrained deep feelings of obligation. He has somehow to square personal interests – his ambition – with kinship sentiment.

Western marriage, therefore, may be an emotional solution. It emphasizes love for a single partner and so reduces the extent of moral obligation customarily felt. This is what I meant by romantic love having a rationalizing function. It helps in the dilemma described to ease an otherwise guilty conscience.

Kinship 1
J. B. Loudon

Reprinted with permission from J. B. Loudon, 'Kinship and Crisis in South Wales', *British Journal of Sociology*, vol. 12, no. 4, 1961, pp. 347–9

It is on ceremonial occasions that people reveal the extent to which they are aware not only of the details of their own kin ties but of those of members of other 'families'. One of the chief difficulties facing newcomers is their lack of knowledge of the key kinship connections between their long-settled neighbours. This is not only or chiefly because they are liable in their ignorance to ally themselves irrevocably with the wrong people when they arrive, or with members of one or other faction in a long-standing local feud. The real point is that without some knowledge of kin ties they can take little part in local gossip.

Gossip is undoubtedly the most important channel for constant reaffirmation of shared values about behaviour. Those who cannot join in gossip about their neighbours, friends and relatives, especially gossip which requires that kind of intricate map-reading of kinship connections which comes as second nature to those with lifelong familiarity with the local genealogical landscape, soon find themselves excluded from conversations at local gatherings. Nuances of expression escape them when discussion turns on the relevance to the speaker's long held opinion of a particular family of the latest example of the behaviour of one of its members. Even where the individual under discussion is referred to by more than his Christian name, more often than not it is by one of half a dozen common Welsh surnames or by the name of a house or farm; and his behaviour may well be related to that of members of earlier generations of his family now all dead.

Conversely, the newcomer tends to be treated by his neighbours with that reserve which is appropriate towards people who have no easy way of expressing, in relation to particular individuals and instances familiar to their audience, their general ideas about what is right and wrong, still less of showing that they share the expectations of their neighbours regarding customary behaviour in specific contexts. It should not be thought that kinship as a means of evaluating behaviour and placing people is primarily employed by women. It is true that, in general, women appear to have a more detailed and systematic knowledge of kin ties than men do, in the Vale as elsewhere in Britain. Men's knowledge of genealogical connections, while usually pragmatic, is often no less extensive than that of women. People who live in small rural neighbourhoods in the Vale and who cannot be identified in terms of local kin ties are often regarded with latent suspicion by their neighbours.

The importance of this process is obviously dependent on the proportion of the inhabitants who have local kinship connections. In one typical village in the Vale there are 112 people living in 31 households. Only 5 households, comprising 21 individuals, lack kin ties with people living less than 10 miles away. A further 5 households, comprising 19 individuals, are linked through kinship with people living in neighbouring parishes. Each of the remaining 21 households, comprising 72 individuals, have kin ties with other households in the village as well as with other people living elsewhere in the Vale. It is sometimes said by informants that people who have moved into the Vale never 'belong' until at least one of their children has married a member of a local family. In general, informants have no clear definition of what they mean by a local family, though those who consider themselves to be members of one often differentiate between what they call 'real Vale people' and others in discussing marriage preferences. Such preferences, colloquially expressed in a variety of ways, oblique, derisive or simply practical, are often best identified by reference to the informant's evaluation of exceptions rather than in looking for statements of rules. A woman is said by her husband's kin and neighbours to be a successful farmer's wife in spite of the fact that she is not a farmer's daughter and was born and brought up in a town. A rich member of a long-established gentry family marries, as his second wife, a woman who was originally a servant in his household and his relatives say: 'But she's really a decent little woman and Freddy has never been looked after so well in his life', or the envious say, with a sigh, of a marriage between people much better off than themselves, 'Well, money marries money, doesn't it?'

Impressions gained from such items of gossip may be confirmed by survey material. The vast majority of farmers' wives are, in fact, the daughters of farmers. Most members of the upper class, however defined, marry members of the upper class. Affinal ties tend to reinforce business connections between entrepreneurs.

The evaluative function of kinship is of particular importance in any study of the ways in which members of a local community identify and deal with unusual behaviour. The social roles, including kinship roles, filled by an individual actor are related to the readiness with which his family, friends and neighbours regard certain kinds of behaviour on his part as unusual. Furthermore, the readiness with which some kinds of unusual behaviour are recognized as evidence of mental disorder, by doctors as well as others, is related to the perceived social status of the individual. In relatively small communities, especially among what have been described as the highly homogeneous sections of the local population, kin ties are often more important than factors such as occupation, education and economic resources in the perception of social status in certain contexts. Where an individual has no extensive local network of kin ties, evaluation of unusual behaviour is often in terms of general or 'national' norms of expectation regarding the performance, for example, of occupational or 'social class' roles. Unusual behaviour on the part of those with 'close-knit' networks is more likely to be assessed in terms of flexible local norms which are adaptable to particular circumstances.

Kinship 2
J. Hubert

Reprinted with permission from *International Journal of Comparative Sociology*, 1966, pp. 61, 63–5, 79–80

This paper deals with a small sector of the results of research in progress among a set of middle-class families in London. The object of the study is to analyse the structure and estimate the magnitude and social significance of the kinship systems of British middle-class families.

It started with a pilot investigation of thirty families living on a private housing estate in North London, generally considered to be a 'good middle-class area', and having a high proportion of professional people living on it. Following the pilot survey, a random sample of sixty households was taken of the total population of electors' households on the estate (about 250 in all). This sample was heterogeneous in terms of marital status, family stage, age, religion and occupation, though the majority of individuals are married with children, Protestant, and the occupations of the heads of households fall within the broad band of 'middle-class' occupations . . .

The majority of the individuals in the Highgate sample are not born Londoners. Twenty-two out of sixty were born in London, the rest elsewhere. This is not surprising since one might expect a metropolitan population to be drawn from all over the country. But it contrasts with the origins of the working-class informants in Young and Willmott's survey of Bethnal Green, where 85 per cent of men and 85 per cent of women were born in London. Taking very crude geographical areas, a similar number of the Highgate individuals were born in the south (including the south-west) of England, and the north of England – eleven in each: six were born in Scotland, one in Ireland, and none in either Wales or East Anglia. A surprising number, nine out of thirty-eight non-Londoners, were born abroad, but only in rare cases were they born of foreign parents – in most cases their parents were living abroad, which in itself has some kinship relevance.

Most of the Highgate informants are thus migrants to London, and come from a wide range of different areas. By definition, all thirty married couples now live in London, and over two-thirds of them also first met their spouses in London; of the twenty-one pairs who met there, in only five cases were both born there; only two couples first met in any other 'home town' of either of them, the rest elsewhere in the country or abroad. Thus there was in nearly every case some degree of mobility before marriage, on the part of both men and women. Spouses were not, on the whole, drawn from a home environment and very few met either directly or indirectly through kin.

The two couples who met in their home town first met as children, which may or may not be considered to be meeting through kin. Of the others, only four couples met through relatives of some kind. Eleven couples met through their training, or in connection with their work, the other thirteen either socially or in some indeterminate way. The high proportion of couples who met through college and work is perhaps typical of a professional group of people.

The fact that most informants married spouses from different areas implies that either their parents moved from the place they were born, or that the informants themselves left home before marriage. In fact in most cases both men and women had been living away from home for some time before they were married. This is not unexpected in the case of the men, but is so with the high proportion of women. Exactly two-thirds of the wives were living away from home before they married, all of them for over a year, and the majority of them for five or more years.

What emerges from this is that the informants, and in particular the women, were independent of their parents before they married, at least in terms of residence. This contrasts with the working-class situation usually described, in which a girl lives at home until she marries and possibly for some time after she marries, until the couple can afford a place of their own. This early independence of girls from their parents, and especially from their mothers, is significant because it affects the type of relationship they have with their mothers, and attitude towards them, in adult life. Certainly we have not found situations at all like those described by Young and Willmott in Bethnal Green, where married daughters depend on their mothers not only for day-to-day services in the house, but also for emotional support in their daily life. The fact that this does not commonly occur in Highgate does not mean that the young wives do not have strong affective ties with their mothers, but residential independence long before marriage, combined with professional training and general independence of outlook, must lead to at least a different sort of relationship between married daughters and their mothers; one expressed not in terms of daily contact and moral support, but in perhaps maturer ways, with dependence only in times of crisis, e.g. in confinements and illness, not in the daily running of their lives.

Independence from parents is not merely an accidental concomitant of professional life. In most cases there is explicit agreement that children should be independent of their parents. This is manifested in earlier life by the willingness to send children to boarding schools. This attitude is apparent, when their children marry, in the strong preference on both sides for the young couple to set up house on their own, and in order that this should be possible parents will provide money towards a house rather than let them have to move in with them.

This stress on independence is significant as one of the main factors in the formation and development of kin relationships and attitudes. It means that young people can choose to live where they like, or where their work takes them, because the sort of relationship they grow up to have with their parents, and thus with their other kin, does not depend on frequent and intense contact of any kind. From childhood onwards there are different attitudes and expectations of parent-child behaviour, and different ways of expressing emotion.

This fact makes the assessment of relationships with kin somewhat more difficult. It means that frequency of contact cannot be taken in isolation as the criterion of a close relationship, and in fact it may sometimes be misleading as an indication of the strength of an affective tie between two kinsmen.

The relative freedom, in intellectual and emotional terms, of children from their parents, is important in various ways in their subsequent relationships with extra-familial kin in general. In one respect merely being residentially independent, especially in order to get professional training of some kind, enables persons to widen the scope of their contacts, and to meet people with whom they have things in common, e.g. similar training and intellectual disciplines. Young people will be freer to choose as friends people they like, and this may extend to members of the family as well. 'Community of interest' is often quoted as one of the most important things in the choice of friends from within the family. These people, by virtue of their background, education and occupation, have additional criteria to apply in their selection of kin. In fact one might have expected far fewer and less intense relationships with kin than is the case. What is surprising is not the paucity of kin relationships, but the number and richness of them considering the alternatives open to these individuals, and in many cases the lack of common interests between them.

To return to residential independence – it can be seen that it is not only our informants that have moved from their parental home or home area, but the majority of their kin have scattered too, in this and previous generations.

This does *not* mean that relationships are ineffective or necessarily distant between parents and children, or between other sorts of kin. The expected patterns of behaviour are based on strong affective ties which are not, however, expressed in frequent and intense interchange of contact and services or mutual dependence. Just because there is not frequent and intense contact does not mean that the affective tie does not exist. Nor that, in certain circumstances, kin are not called upon for assistance or advice. It is significant that certain services are given regardless of the geographical distance between kin. For example, one of the situations in which mothers are most frequently called in to help is at the birth of a baby. Nearly all the young wives had their mothers to stay in the house at least during one confinement, i.e. when she herself was in hospital. Many mothers travelled from great distances to do this, one or two even from abroad. Thus it can be seen that distance is no barrier to the sort of services these sort of people tend to need. Neither mothers nor daughters expect or want daily exchange of household services in normal circumstances, neither do they generally want constant contact with each other.

The type of relationship between parents and children obviously determines to a large extent the sort of relationships an individual will have with the rest of his or her kin. If a relationship with a parent is not manifested in constant interaction then two things result. Firstly, the ideology and attitudes with which a child is brought up will be of such a kind that he does not expect a close relationship with his extra-familial kin, and secondly, because of relatively infrequent contact with parents and siblings, genealogically more distant kin will enter into his life even less, and ties even with relatives who may be in constant contact with a parent may be dropped or maintained according to individual preferences. In this sense geographical distance may enable ties to be dropped without, generally, upsetting the relationships between other kin.

Considering a wide divergence of occupations and cultural interests and, in some cases, of class background, a great many ties are maintained with relatives. Generally, contact is not frequent, but this seems to bear little direct relation to geographical distance except insofar as the latter acts as an extreme limiting factor. Where people want to see their kin, wide distances are covered relatively often. Expectations of extra-familial kin behaviour do not usually demand frequent contact, even when proximity allows it. With closer kin, specifically parents and siblings, there is more evidence to support the hypothesis (often held for all kin) that as much interaction will take place as possible at all times. Even for parents and siblings this is not entirely so, but here behaviour approximates more to this hypothesis, and this is so in spite of the ideology of independence with which children grow up, and the complex set of circumstances arising out of a wide range of occupations and cultural interests.

Ties with kin outside the family of origin are maintained on a more selective basis, and they are often manifested only in contact of an intermittent nature. Partly, this is because these ties are not often of a very strong kind – it is fair to say that to a great extent these people function independently of the majority of their kin. But it is also partly because more overt behaviour patterns of any more intense nature are not expected between members of these families.

Happy Families
A. Oakley

Reprinted with permission from Ann Oakley, *Subject Women*, Martin Robertson, 1982, pp. 236–8, 239–46

What are husbands for?

Most girls in the last decades of the twentieth century are still brought up to envisage their destinies in the cloudless, confetti-bedecked land of Mr Right, the tall, dark, handsome stranger who will colonize their lives and make them happy ever after. Interviewing London schoolgirls in 1976, Sue Sharpe found that 82 per cent of fifteen-year-old girls wanted to marry, a third by the time they were twenty. Very few girls did not see their lives as centred on married bliss; few saw any conflict between their future as wives and mothers and their future as workers (or as divorcees or as mothers of adult and absent children).

When girls describe their future projected lives, men – as husbands and fathers – are important, but they have a strangely insubstantial existence. Joyce Joseph, analysing girls' written accounts of their projected lives, said:

> One of the interesting facts which emerged when the life stories were examined was that large numbers of girls reported the deaths of their husbands when their husbands had performed the limited function of providing them with children. In some the husband died and the woman went back to her job, or more commonly went to live with, or near, her children. Some married again, or lived alone as a romantic widow enlivened by visits of their grandchildren, or even replaced their husband by a dog.

A third of Joseph's 'husband killers' dispensed with their husbands when the children became self-supporting. Men, thus, have a symbolic significance. They are recognized to be economic providers, bestowers of status and marks of respectability. What, after all, are husbands for? This question, whose answer comes so easily to fifteen-year-old schoolgirls, has preoccupied anthropologists for decades. The quandary is usually put in these terms: the relation of women to children is biological – through gestation and lactation the tie is visible to everyone; but the relation of men to children and of men to the mothers of children is hidden or may (in the former case) be strictly unknowable. So what accounts for the personal and publicly legitimized connections between men, on the one hand, and women and children, on the other, in most, if not all human societies? What about this slippage between 'most' and 'all' – is it sensible or warranted to claim the universality of the family as the achievement that makes us different from ('better than') apes?

The early anthropologists saw the Victorian patriarchal family as the last and most civilized form of human relations. 'Primitive' societies, they thought, were just that: riddled with promiscuity and with such morally disreputable arrangements as group marriage and communal childrearing, which attached no value to the singular, lifelong, family-creating union of one man and one woman. (Of course such arrangements gave greater recognition to the sexuality and independence of women, but that was one reason why nineteenth- and early twentieth-century anthropologists disliked them.)

By the 1950s, this belief in 'primitive communism' had died out, and it was speedily becoming 'an article of faith with most students of society that one can find everywhere the individual or "nuclear" family of a man and woman with their children'. This article of faith persists. Most sociologists today find a way of interpreting other cultures' arrangements for licensing heterosexual unions and legitimizing and rearing children so that they are essentially no different from Mr and Mrs Jones in their suburban home in Birmingham (England or Alabama) with their wedding photographs in the drawer, their mortgage and their 2.4 children. . . .

The licensing of sexual relations, the legitimizing of children, their socialization, the inheritance of property between generations, the provision of food, clothes, shelter and other material resources – these are conditions of social life that every human culture must meet, but not necessarily in the same way.

However, it has to be said that men have a problem. As Mead has put it: 'The recurrent problem of civilization is to define the male role satisfactorily enough – for men, that is.' Women's achievements are listed by nature: childbearing is their authentic accomplishment *as women*. By comparison, the achievements of men have no ready-made definition, but have to be wrestled out of a strictly cultural mould. Husbands, cross-culturally,

> are important mainly as fathers; that is to say, as men who give their name, their status in so far as this is inherited, and the right to inherit their property, to the children of a woman with whom they have made a particular kind of contract. [L. Mair]

It is important for men to claim 'the family' as their property (*pace* the term 'a family man') for three reasons: first, it subjects the realm of the natural to the reign of the social; secondly, it gives them control over women and children; thirdly, where families are basic units of social organization, there are political advantages to be had in being their managing directors.

Happy families

If the satisfactoriness of marriage and family life is to be gauged from the extent to which people enter these institutions, then pledging oneself to *one* man (or one woman) must make people very happy indeed. 'Marriage', it is said, 'has never been more popular' (*The Times,* 17 August 1976). Since the mid-1940s in Europe and the USA marriage rates have increased enormously and the age of marriage has fallen.' In Britain, by the mid-1960s, 95 per cent of men and 96 per cent of women were, or had been, married by the age of forty-five compared with 88 per cent and

In Britain, the 1970 Family Law Reform Act lowered the age at which parental consent for marriage was not needed from 21 to 18, and helped to account for a drop in the average age of first marriage immediately after. Since the early 1970s the decline in the age of first marriage has halted somewhat.

83 per cent in 1921. Since the mid-1960s, there has also been a growth in the popularity of remarriage among both widowed and divorced persons; one index of this change is that chances of remarriage by the age of thirty-five doubled for British women born in 1940 as compared with those born in 1930. International trends in marriage and remarriage are very similar, though there are differences in detail from one country to another; for example, a post-1970s fall in first marriage rates has been particularly pronounced in Scandinavia, where larger numbers of couples cohabit than in the less sexually libertarian countries.

Twenty years ago Margaret Mead noted a paradox behind the growing popularity of marriage. Almost every human need, she said,

that has historically been met in the home can now be met outside it: restaurants serve food; comics, movies and radio provide amusement, news and gossip; there are laundries and dry-cleaners and places that mend one's socks and store one's winter coat, wash one's hair and manicure one's nails and shine one's shoes. For sex satisfaction it is no longer necessary to choose between marriage and prostitution; for most of those without religious scruples sex is available on a friendly and amateur basis and without responsibility. The automobile has made it even unnecessary for one of a pair of temporary sex partners to have an apartment. Entertaining can be done in a hotel or at a club. When one is sick, one goes to a hospital, and when one dies, one can be buried quite professionally from an undertaking establishment. A telephone service will answer one's telephone, and a shopping service do one's shopping. The old needs of food, shelter, sex, and recreation are all efficiently met outside the home – and yet more people are married today than ever before in the country's recorded history.

Why? Replacing some of the functions of the family with purchased services outside it obviously calls for money that some people do not have. Extracting labour from the unpaid duty of wives is cheaper than paying its market price. But, aside from this, it is not a general rule in other areas of life that as something becomes increasingly archaic and useless it becomes more popular. Horses are not purchased in large numbers as cars become assets within the reach of more and more people; pianos move out of people's front rooms and into junk shops as radios, television, records and cassettes spread music to places it never went before. A reservation has to be added to this general rule: the tendency for useless items of social life to drop out of fashion can be reversed by a well-mounted advertising campaign. Hence white sugar, cigarettes, instant puddings, unreliable cars, immediately breakable toys – things that are not only useless but positively dangerous to human health and happiness – can be kept in circulation if enough money is spent on telling people they cannot live without them. It is not too far-fetched to see marriage and the family in these terms. Thus, one answer to the question, 'why is marriage so popular?' is that people are constantly told it is good for them. The second answer is that statistics of marriage's popularity hide its failures, which are many. Rephrasing these answers from the point of view of women, we can say that women are encouraged to believe that they will find lifelong happiness in monogamous unions with men, but what they are in fact likely to find is that it is precisely marriage that oppresses, suppresses and depresses them.

THE CONVENTION OF CONVENTIONAL FAMILIES

The nuclear family is a state of mind rather than a particular kind of structure or set of household arrangements. It has little to do with whether the generations live together or whether Aunt Mary stays in the spare bedroom. Nor can it be understood with kinship diagrams and figures on family size. [E. Shorter]

It can, in fact, only be understood as ideology. 'The' family or 'the family' is the major paradigm of social relations in which the inhabitants of modern technologically complex societies are encouraged to believe. 'The family' in its attenuated, conventionalized form (two parents, 2.4 children, father breadwinning and mother housekeeping, each family in a home of its own) is held out to be both the normal way of living and the happiest place to be. But 'the family' is also 'mapped on' to the cartography of other social institutions. As the radical psychiatrists Laing and Cooper have observed, its gender and generation hierarchies provide a powerful model for the social relations of factories, schools, universities, business corporations, religious organizations, political parties, governments, armies and hospitals. It is because the character and function of women is so typed by the convention of their place in the family, and especially by their relation to men as husbands and fathers, that the politics of female-male relationships are echoed throughout society.

Some origins of the idealized image of the conventional family have been explored earlier in this book. So far as present-day society is concerned, this imagery is ubiquitous – informing the socialization of children, the educational system, employment opportunities, health and welfare provision, language, advertising, and the media generally. The paradigm of the conventional family is part of the ideological apparatus of the state. Thus, official morality has mushroomed to lay down the rules for non-marital heterosexual relationships:

> Where a husband and wife are members of the same household their
> requirements and resources shall be aggregated and shall be treated as
> the husband's, and similarly, unless there are exceptional circum-
> stances, as regards two persons cohabiting as man and wife. [Second
> Schedule to the Ministry of Social Security Act, 1966, para.3(1)]

This provision of the Ministry of Social Security Act, 1966 – the infamous
'cohabitation' rule – enabled the British exchequer to save £887,000 in
1971 by cutting supplementary benefits to unsupported women and
children. The women involved were those who could be construed by
social security officers to be having a relationship with a man upon whose
shoulders the financial burden of fatherhood and/or husbandhood could
be said (by the state) to fall. Since what (according to the Supplementary
Benefits handbook) has to be established is that a man and woman are
living together 'as man and wife', the strategies adopted are most revealing of official definitions of marriage. Sharing a home, sharing a bed and
swapping housekeeping and income-providing services, so that the
woman provides the first for the man and the man provides the second for
the woman, are the necessary criteria. Examination of actual cases, however, shows that social security officers attach 'undue attention . . . to the
question of sexual relations'.

> A typical case was that of Mrs Brown. Her boyfriend had been a friend
> of her husband's from whom she was separated. He had continued
> seeing her after the separation out of sympathy and had started staying
> the night. He usually slept at Mrs Brown's four or five times a week,
> but considered his home to be at his mother's. He kept all his clothes in
> his bedroom at his mother's house and contributed to her household
> expenses. He went home each morning to collect his sandwiches and
> ate his evening meal with his mother. He made no contribution to Mrs
> Brown's household other than to provide the Sunday lunch which he
> ate with them. He had no intention of supporting Mrs Brown and the
> question of marriage had never been discussed. Mrs Brown tried to
> make clear to the officer that it was purely a sexual relationship, that
> 'Mr X does not live here, he just shares my bed'. However, neither the
> Commission nor the appeal tribunal were able to grasp the distinction
> that she made between a man staying with her and his living with her.
> [R. Lister] ‑

Sexual services are something a man is supposed to pay for – inside and
outside marriage. Or, to put it another way, if women are allowed to draw
supplementary benefits regardless of the income of any man with whom
they happen to be associated, the Supplementary Benefits Commission
will be involved in paying women who are unable to take a job because

they are looking after children. The cohabitation rule is 'logic's last bulwark against the spectre of wages for housework', a distinctly anti-conventional-family demand.

In view of the all-pervasiveness of the conventional family ideal, it is hardly surprising that the two questions 'should I marry?' and 'should we have children?' apparently do not occur to most people.

> Parenthood, like marriage, was taken for granted [says Lyn Richards of Australian couples she interviewed]. 'Why not stay single?' and 'Why not stay childless?' had been equally non-questions. Virtually none of the men or women had asked either question of themselves or their partners . . . Almost everyone interviewed remembered people expecting them to have children. Having children . . . had been expected from childhood . . . marriage and children were part of the same unquestioned assumption about growing up.

Marriage establishes the credentials of maturity, of personal and sexual competence. For women the idea of a 'proper' marriage with all its romantic trimmings is also a cover for economic realism – the only way to improve on the economic standing of their family of origin and to combat their disadvantaged labour market position.

DOING RIGHT BUT FEELING BAD

Like white sugar and cars, marriage may be popular but it is definitely hazardous. Of British marriages made in the 1970s, more than a quarter will end in divorce at some point in the next thirty years; for American couples, the figure is nearer 40 per cent. Some guide to the accelerated growth in the divorce industry is provided by the British *Family Formation* survey. In this, information about marriage-related behaviour was obtained from 6589 women in England, Wales and Scotland in 1976. A tenth of women first married in 1966–70 were separated from their husbands within five years of marriage, a figure similar to the proportion separating after ten years of marriage among women married in 1961–5, and to the proportion separating after fifteen years of marriage among the cohort married in 1956–60.

It can be, and has been, argued that more divorce does not mean less happiness; men and women are simply freer to discard unsatisfactory marriages than they used to be. The reasoning is that romantic love and the emancipation of women have improved marriage but made it inherently unstable; however, this instability is no bad thing since it indicates 'an enlarged degree of opportunity and happiness'. Furthermore, 75 per cent of divorcees remarry, which hardly suggests that marriage is a decaying institution.

It seems a little strange to argue that the fact that something breaks down a lot proves that it is really working very well. A more convincing argument is that, for one reason or another, people want to retain their faith in marriage's successful functioning in the face of considerable evidence to the contrary. Problems with marriage are not new. Julia Spruill's commentary on *Women's Life and Work in the Southern Colonies* notes that

> Those who point to the colonial period as a golden age of family relationships can hardly be acquainted with the eighteenth century discussions lamenting the decadence of the domestic virtues, with the suspicion and distrust reflected in private papers, with the large number of public notices of absconding wives and voluntary separations, and with the many complaints by husbands and wives in court records.

'Reflections on unhappy marriages', a favourite journalistic subject then, paralleled the 'Is the family a dying institution?' articles today. In both cases the cause of the trouble is seen to lie in individuals (emancipated undomesticated wives, broken homes, adulterous husbands) or in particular social circumstances (changes in divorce laws, more contraception and choice in childbearing). Unsuccessful marriages are interpreted as problems, not solutions to problems; yet, as Wright Mills observed, the imaginative enterprise of connecting personal troubles and public issues must suggest that divorce statistics indicate, not a proliferation of unique personal difficulties, but 'a structural issue having to do with the institutions of marriage and the family'.

There are two sides to this structural issue. One is that the cultural expectation of great intimacy between men and women clashes with the very different and, in some ways, contradictory, socializations of the sexes. Men and women are reared primarily as masculine and feminine individuals, the one to notions of potency, public-mindedness and emotional invulnerability, the other to standards of fragility, domesticity and emotional hypersensitivity. While individuals with such dissimilar preparations for adulthood might be expected to find some way of cooperating with one another residentially and economically, it is hard to see how they can hope to be one another's greatest friends. And, as for the idea of complementarity – another fashionable idiom in which the marital relations of the sexes are discussed – surely this is just a euphemism for uncomfortable division and difference?

The second structural consideration is that discussed by Christopher Lasch in his suggestively named *Haven in a Heartless World*. Lasch's contention is that the family is conventionally regarded as a haven, but that the realities of present-day society have stripped it of even this mystification. Capitalist industry profits from the concentration of psychological welfare work in the family. Indeed, it promotes this work under the guise of the family being a free and sacred retreat from the exigencies of paid labour. Yet in fact

> the modern world intrudes at every point and obliterates its privacy. The sanctity of the home is a sham in a world dominated by giant corporations and by the apparatus of mass promotion. . . . The same historical developments that have made it necessary to set up private life – the family in particular – as a refuge from the cruel world of politics and work, an emotional sanctuary, have invaded this sanctuary and subjected it to outside control. A retreat into 'privatism' no longer serves to shore up values elsewhere threatened with extinction. [C. Lasch]

Thus, the family is not what it is held out to be – for men, women or children. It is not an easy answer to the drudgery of work or to the heartlessness of the outside world.

The Centrality of the Family
D. H. J. Morgan

Reprinted with permission from David Morgan, *Social Theory and the Family*, Routledge and Kegan Paul, 1975, pp. 204–13

Let us start with an apparently insurmountable problem: the fact that many different writers come to radically different conclusions about the place of the family in modern society. As will be shown, this is not simply a matter of a distinction between functionalist and anti-functionalist, between abolitionist or retentionist or between optimist and pessimist but more a matter of points of view that arise out of the intersection of these opposing positions. The following five positions – while certainly not exhausting the possibilities – reflect some of the main strands of argument:

1. The family is of decreasing importance in modern society. The first major blow the family suffered was industrialism and the overthrow of the traditional patriarchal structure. Since then the family has become smaller, weaker and less able to fulfil the few functions left to it. Many important functions have been taken over by outside agencies and the family has been eroded by the development of a 'mass society'. People cling to the form of the family and the ideology surrounding the family although the content has effectively withered away. To adopt Weber's memorable phrase on the secularization of the Protestant Ethic: 'The idea

of duty in one's calling prowls about in our lives like the ghost of dead religious beliefs.' We should not spend time in mourning the death of the family. Marcuse and Reich would argue that the central problems lie elsewhere and Barrington-Moore would suggest that we should give the family a decent burial. Horkheimer, while sharing this general analysis of the loss of family functions and centrality, is more worried by the apparent dangers of this and so would probably be classed with the pessimists.

2. The first group of pessimists would agree that the family has been declining in the way outlined by members of the first group but would also argue that the overall effect of this decline will be disastrous for social life generally. A modified version of this pessimistic perspective is presented by the contributors to the volume edited by Anshen, most of whom would appear to argue that the family has a vital role to play in social life generally, that it is under considerable strain in modern society and that the main solution is the strengthening of the democratic, open form of family structure. Less ambiguous and more pessimistic is Zimmerman; in a recent statement he argues, 'When the ideological structure of the family system loses its virility and strength the social system generally gets into trouble.'

3. Another, probably smaller, group would express pessimism not because the family is becoming increasingly marginal but because the family remains firmly at the centre. There are several overlapping arguments here, including the argument that the modern family is too well adjusted to a destructive culture and that the distinction between normal and pathological families would appear to be that in the latter the victims become too painfully obvious to the outside world. This group is pessimistic in that there appears to be little discussion of the way out in alternative family or non-family systems. Laing has presented little in the way of wide-ranging alternatives to the family so far and Henry adopted an even less ambiguously tragic stance in relation to the modern family.

4. If this second group of pessimists argue that the family is well – too well – adjusted to modern society, the optimists would support this argument but reject the tone. Their main argument, however, would be with those who argue that the family is in decline. Instead they would argue that the family has become more specialized but no less vital. Under this heading we would, of course, include Parsons together with Fletcher, Aron and McGregor. Also included here would be the supporters of the 'modified extended family' argument, whatever disputes they might have with Parsons over the structure of the family in modern society.

5. Finally we may note those who argue that the family is central but not essential and who would concentrate on the dysfunctions of the family rather than the eufunctions. Here we would include Reich with his analysis of the way in which authoritarianism is supported by the family structure and, more recently, the radical feminists who would argue that

the abolition of the family as we know it is essential for the development of a society not structured around sex roles. While members of this group would support the critiques of the family provided by Laing and Henry they would be more optimistic about the possibilities of developing alternatives.

How can we resolve these apparently different perspectives? Part of the answer must obviously be to examine more clearly what is being meant by such words as 'family', 'central', 'marginal' and so on. Yet it is clear that even greater specification of terms would not resolve the conflict between, say, a functionalist approach that leans heavily on the instrumental-expressive distinction and, on the other hand, the radical feminists who reject such a distinction and the analysis that follows from it. Moreover, it would seem likely that these differing perspectives and differing definitions are themselves *part* of the reality and that any attempt to freeze that reality by arbitrarily imposing one definition over another would be to impose one version of reality over others. These assessments and definitions are not merely the province of professional sociologists or family therapists but are also used and *lived* by 'laymen' in their everyday lives. (Including, of course, professional sociologists, etc., when they are 'living in the world'.)

It would follow also that such differences of opinion or interpretation are not likely to be resolved merely by an accumulation of more empirical material. What is important is the *kind* of material that we seek to gather; in particular we must ask does it seek to capture the multiplicity of lay meanings, definitions and understandings of the family in its approach rather than to impose certain externally derived definitions by fiat? Similarly, the mere imposition of lists of functions on to a frozen entity called the family will not resolve these differing perspectives. In what follows I shall attempt to give recognition to the fact that there are not only many 'types' of family in modern society ('types' usually referring to an externally derived set of typifications) but that there are also many ways of understanding families. My family may be an imperfect but deliberately willed attempt to conform to some ideal of 'the Christian home' or it may be a series of traps, a thing out of control, threatening and stifling. I may wear my family lightly, ready to put it aside should the opportunity or occasion arise, or it may be an ever present cross to bear. My family may resemble the Mafia or the brittle ease of a Noël Coward comedy. These definitions, these understandings, these evaluations (which may well cut across class and status differences) must be part of my definitions, understandings and evaluations of family life. Furthermore, the diversity of these definitions itself arises out of a situation where the 'family' as an institution possesses a degree of autonomy in relation to the wider society.

The delineation of familial boundaries

In our society there are no clear rules as to what we mean by 'relatives' or 'kindred'. By definition these are not bounded units since they are based on Ego's definition of the situation. Thus the picture of the kinship universe is one of increasing fuzziness at the edges and more definite, but still flexible, notions of duty, reciprocity, closeness (with the possibilities of conflict) nearer the centre. Moreover, this kinship universe is subject to change over time as a result of changes in one's own life cycle as an individual and as a member of two intersecting and changing nuclear families and changes in the individual and family life cycles of significant related others.

However vague and fluctuating this outer cloud of relationships might be, the inner nuclear core of parents and children would appear to be much more definite. At least that is the impression presented by, say, Laing on the one hand and Parsons on the other. Our dwellings, terms like 'family car' or 'family entertainment', and images presented through the media by advertisers, politicians and clergymen reinforce and maintain this definitive image of the family, one requiring the co-presence of parents and children and the relative absence of others. Yet, simply because this image is so widely disseminated does not necessarily mean that it always accords with subjectively understood reality. And, if indeed it is the case that many people understand and live their family this way for most of the time, we should perhaps regard this accomplishment as something worth investigating, a stimulus to our curiosity rather than something merely taken for granted as 'given'.

Some partial clues to understanding this aspect of family living are provided by Berger and Kellner in their interesting paper on 'Marriage and the Construction of Reality'. This paper, which is an application of Berger's general concern in widening the sociology of knowledge to include everything that generally passes for knowledge, starts with Durkheim's insight that marriage serves as a protection against anomie for the individual. This is, however, too negative, they argue; we must look at the positive side of marriage and they suggest that we may see it as a 'nomos-building instrumentality'. Reality is socially constructed. This everyday reality is not something fixed and 'out there' but something which is constantly being constructed and built up through conversation with significant others. Marriage, which in our society entails the coming together of two relative strangers who do not usually have a shared past, is a particularly crucial arena for the building of reality through conversation. A new reality is posited in the process of conversation and interpersonal relations within the marital relationship. In marriage the partners construct the present, reconstruct the past and develop a commonly projected future. In this phenomenological approach to marriage, possibilities become facticities. Clearly this kind of analysis can be extended to other relationships in the family and elsewhere. Berger and Luckmann present a similar account to the process of primary socialization. In this process, the outside world is presented to the child through the double filter of the immediate family and the position of that family in the social structure. Socialization may be viewed as a kind of 'confidence trick' where the outside world is presented as the reality to the child in a 'quasi-inevitable' way.

Part of this reality which is constructed through marriage and the socialization process is the reality of the family itself, the boundaries, its members and its differences from other families. Thus the delineation of familial boundaries is not to be seen merely in terms of the imposition of a structure or set of terms devised by the analyst but in terms of the members themselves. The meaning of the family, the solidarity or fuzziness of its boundaries, is something which is built up, modified and redefined over time through living, talking and interacting in the family context. This world building is often extended beyond the boundaries of the immediate nuclear family to include significant members of the wider kinship universe. The naming of children may symbolically define certain significant ties and continuities beyond and outside the immediate nuclear family. The use of kinship terminology in relation to non-related but significant adults may be part of the same process. Among other mechanisms or resources used in this process of reality construction we may note the following:

1. The major events and crises that go to make up 'family themes'. These family themes may provide a central strand of experience for the family members – the prolonged illness or physical incapacity of one member, the use of a mentally handicapped child as a scapegoat or the labelling of a child as being 'bad' or 'difficult' – or they may be a set of shared experiences and events which are interwoven and periodically recognized, called upon and used in the business of socially constructing the everyday world of the family. A holiday, a move, a period of unemployment and many other events and minor crises may be woven into the particular history of a family and may be used, heightened in recall, in the process of constantly reconstructing the family and its boundaries.

2. The use of 'ritual in family living'. Ritual may enter into family life in a variety of ways. There may be national or religious rituals that are celebrated and given particular meaning in a family context such as Christmas or Thanksgiving. There may be rituals associated with the individual or family life cycle – anniversaries, birthdays, weddings, etc. – which are again celebrated in terms of the family with the family as the main focus. There are rituals which are elaborations of daily routines, sometimes as a result of externally imposed timetables, such as going to work or school, mealtimes or bedtimes. And finally there are the more

idiosyncratic rituals which are developed in the context of a particular family and which become elaborated over the years. The father who brings home small gifts for the children on Friday night is an example of an elaboration of this kind. Whatever the ritual, it is possible to view it as playing an important part in the social construction of reality and the delineation of familial boundaries.

3. The dwelling and the use of space. The authors of *Crestwood Heights* have provided a detailed analysis of the social meaning of the home and space within the home. The house provides a solid representation of the family to its members and differentiates that family from non-family members. Family members have free access to the dwelling, while non-family members are admitted and selected on the basis of invitations, the use of door bells, etc. Certain rooms may be reserved for the entertainment of guests (when the family puts on a performance for non-family members) and to be treated fictitiously as 'one of the family' is often a matter of being allowed unmediated access through, say, the back door.

The use of family themes, ritual and domestic space are some of the mechanisms through which the family as a social reality is defined and redefined. Two further points must be noted. In the first place it would be wrong to see these mechanisms in simple functional (or eufunctional) terms. Bossard and Boll note that ritual may have its dysfunctional aspects and that mechanisms such as we have described may become desperate attempts to maintain a reality which is no longer appropriate. The clear dysfunctions of the scapegoating mechanism as part of the family theme have already been noted. Second, it would be wrong to assume that these mechanisms serve to create the family reality as an undifferentiated whole. Rituals, as anthropologists have long observed, serve as much to emphasize divisions and separations as well as unities. The family meal, for example, may dramatize sex and age status divisions as well as the unity of that family. Children may not be accorded the same unlimited use of domestic space as adults; thus parents may implicitly claim free access to their children's rooms, a privilege which may well not be reciprocated.

It will be recognized that while all families operate some boundary-maintaining mechanisms not all families are equally successful in this process and, more positively, not all families present the boundaries in such clear forms. Laing's schizophrenogenic families, where the mother may seek to define the outside world as uniquely dangerous and seek to enclose the members of the family within its constructed boundaries, often with the collusion of other family members, represents one extreme rather than a model for all family forms. The current debate about 'open families', while presented largely in terms of the equal participation of the husband and wife in home and work alike, may remind us of other possibilities. In order to analyse the degree and kinds of openness or closure of families we need, of course, not merely to look at the processes of creating family worlds within the families themselves, but also at the place of the families in the wider society. Berger and Kellner recognize that their particular approach to marriage receives particular strength in the context of a society where family living is relatively 'privatized' and Henry makes much the same point in his detailed case studies. In a fascinating historical study, Sennett contrasts the two kinds of family living in the same residential area of Chicago at different periods in the late nineteenth century. In the early period there were upper-class families based on relatively open, wide-ranging networks of primary relationships. These families were replaced by more privatized middle-class families, whose family worlds were, Sennett argues, formed in defence against the urban and occupational worlds that they encountered.

It is clear that future investigations into the family must recognize the variety of family experiences and the various ways in which families define themselves in relation to the outside world. One possibly fruitful classification has been developed by Ponsioen in a study of family change in the Netherlands. He distinguishes between (a) patriarchal families; (b) open families within a closed village or neighbourhood; (c) the closed family in an open society; (d) the counterfeit family (where the ideal is the closed family but the reality falls short of this goal); (e) the boarding house type; and (f) the open family in the open society. Network analysis may be elaborated to distinguish not merely between close-knit and loose-knit networks but also between networks based primarily on kin and those based primarily on non-kin. Work in these directions could fruitfully involve a two-way process between the concepts analysts use to construct reality and the concepts actually used by actors in their daily business of living in families.

Family and the family ideology

We have discussed the problem of the delineation of familial boundaries largely in terms of viewing this as an on-going accomplishment of the actors themselves and also as arising out of the interchanges between the family and the wider society. But we should note that these family boundaries are not merely neutral social facts but also that these boundaries have a normative dimension. Family boundaries and family relationships are shaped not merely by concepts or constructions as to what is but also by normative conceptions as to what ought to be. By using the label 'ideology' in this context (rather than 'norms', 'values', 'mores', etc.) we hope to convey the possibility that certain agencies are more specifically concerned with the generation of familial ideology, the relative (although admittedly long-term) contingency of this ideology and the possibility of there being 'deviant' or counter-ideologies. To label something as 'ideology' is to attempt to relativize the absolute, to bring out into the open what was previously thought not to exist. Ideology functions best when it does not bear the name 'ideology'; when the label ideology is successfully applied it has to begin to struggle for existence.

Nowhere is this more clearly seen than in the context of the family. For here, in the process known as primary socialization, the adult who says 'don't' is at the same time asserting his right to say 'don't'. The rituals, use of space and family themes outlined in the last section recreate the particular family and the 'idea' of the family at the same time. Socialization is, for the most part, indirect and unobtrusive, as much a matter of silences as of conversations, of examples rather than direct instruction. Even when the outside world (school, peer group, the mass media) makes its presence felt and may provide alternative definitions as to what is and what ought to be, these experiences may, to some extent at least, be filtered through and appraised by the family. And, if the analyses of Berger and the authors of *Crestwood Heights* are correct, the family is increasingly to be seen as the central arena for 'normal' behaviour, for being one's true self, for letting one's hair down and so on. The family provides the main legitimate arena for the expression of sexual passion, anger, exhilaration, coldness, frustration, happiness and despair. Large-scale bureaucratically organized and urbanized society, on the other hand, it is argued, can only take these emotions and passions in small doses, if at all.

There are a multiplicity of ways in which ideology and the family become interwoven. In some cases, the family and elements of family structure may be viewed as an ideal model for society as a whole. The 'patriarchalism' analysed by some of the radical feminists and by Reich refers directly to the process of mapping ideal sets of relationships from one domain on to another. Patriarchalism, then, involves two dominances, that of men over women and parents (particularly fathers) over children. These patterns of dominance are learned in the family, projected on to the wider society, encountered in the wider society and reflected back from that society on to the family. There is a strong reinforcing overlap between father and son, master and apprentice, head of the family firm or farm and heir to the estate. While today the patriarchal model of family and society is felt to be inappropriate, the relative power of familial symbols when applied to non-familial realtionships – father, brother, sister, mother – is still maintained and tells us something about the ideal qualities of family relationships as well as about the ideal expectations of the particular situations – trade unions, religious orders – to which they are applied.

More explicit ideological formulations may be made about the nature of the family and its importance in the wider society. It has been noted that the various theories that have been cited as to whether the family is in decline and whether or not this decline, if it is occurring, is likely to have a damaging effect on society as a whole are not merely theories developed by sociological analysts but are also theories which are widely held and used by various agencies. In modern society these ideologies may be made most explicitly when the family appears to be under threat. Some of the concern about women and children working in the early nineteenth-century factories was not just about the hours and the working conditions but about the fact that they were there at all and these concerns provided an occasion to dramatize the values of family life and sexual relationships which, it was felt, were being threatened by this particular feature of the factory system. Similarly the proposal of legislation about divorce or abortion provides another occasion to dramatize particular familial values. Ideological statements, therefore, concern themselves with the nature and central significance of family life and the ideally expected quality of relationships within the family.

The examination of the source and effects of ideology in society is a complex business and involves many difficult problems which are, in many respects, central to sociological analysis. What is involved here is the attribution of a specific set of normative ideas to a particular group in society, the argument that these ideas become, in some way, more widely diffused and, finally, that they become part of the objective reality for a significant proportion of the population. To state the problem in these terms is to demonstrate the large amount of work that needs to be done in the analysis of the interconnections between ideology and society; clearly simple references to the ideas of 'the ruling class' can only serve as a starting point in this analysis. Berger and Luckmann, in their imaginative fusion of themes from Durkheim, Mead, Weber, Parsons and Schutz, have provided some valuable insights into the latter stages of the process, that is how ideas are sustained, internalized and projected in order to shape the facticity of the social world. They perhaps pay less attention to the notion of ideology in the Marxist sense, to the idea that particular groups or interests may have greater weight and power in the defining of everyday reality. What may be said in the analysis of this process is that, in connection with the family, ideological prescriptions would appear to have less work to do in so far as the family already is an on-going reality in some form or other, that most people live or have lived in families and that alternatives may often seem remote or identified with groups readily accorded the label of 'deviant' (religious groups, hippies, etc.).

There is not the space to pursue this topic further, only to state that the ideological dimension is an important, and often absent, part of the analysis of family relationships. Yet we may leave this theme with a contradiction. To say that there is an ideological dimension to family living which is not solely a product of the on-going business of family living itself is to say that there are agencies outside the family – churches, political parties, experts of one kind or another – with a particular interest in the family and its functioning (this interest is, of course, especially an interest in the 'younger generation'). Yet paradoxically, the assertion of some kind of outside interest in the family is to deny the priority of the family, is to challenge the exclusive legitimacy of family authority. In many cases, it may be expected, this paradox is successfully obscured by projecting the ideal model of the family into the natural world, that is by attempting to place the family outside historical contingency. But in some cases this paradox may give rise to contradictory trends and definitions. Thus the English (and American) Puritan family stressed the concepts of order and unity but it was possible that these very ideas might be seen as having priority over potentially self-centred family relationships. Thus some of the more radical sects in the English Civil War discussed the possibilities of polygamy, marriage within forbidden degrees and feminism. That these views did not 'succeed' is less significant than the fact that they were expressed and that they had their origin in the same set of values that attempted to set up the ideal model of the family. We should not necessarily dismiss the popular polemics that mock the practice of a celibate priest giving advice on the quality of family living (a kind of double-bind situation), but see in it the paradox arising out of a tension between rational world religions and the institution of the family, a tension which is often successfully obscured or contained but which sometimes is resolved in the living out of radical alternatives to the family.

Further Reading: Family

M. ANDERSON, *Family Structure in 19th Century Lancashire*, Cambridge University Press, 1971.

C. R. BELL, *Middle Class Families*, Routledge and Kegan Paul, 1968.

N. W. BELL and B. F. VOGEL (eds.), *A Modern Introduction to the Family*, The Free Press, 1960.

J. BERNARD, *The Future of Marriage*, Penguin, 1976.

D. COOPER, *Death of the Family*, Penguin, 1972.

N. DENNIS, F. HENRIQUES and C. SLAUGHTER, *Coal is Our Life*, Eyre and Spottiswoode, 1956.

F. ENGELS, *The Origin of the Family, Private Property and the State*, Lawrence and Wishart, 1972 (first published 1884).

N. HART, *When Marriage Ends*, Tavistock, 1976.

R. D. LAING, *The Politics of the Family*, Penguin, 1976.

P. LASLETT, *Family Life and Illicit Love in Earlier Generations*, Cambridge University Press, 1977.

G. P. MURDOCK, *Social Structure*, The Free Press, 1965.

A. OAKLEY, *Housewife*, Allen Lane, 1974.

T. PARSONS, *Essays in Sociological Theory*, (Chapter IX), The Free Press, 1954.

M. PRINGLE, *The Needs of Children*, second edition, Hutchinson, 1980.

R. and R. RAPOPORT (eds.), *Working Couples*, Routledge and Kegan Paul, 1978.
E. SHORTER, *The Making of the Modern Family*, Fontana Paperbacks, 1977.
P. TOWNSEND, *The Family Life of Old People,* revised edition, Penguin, 1963.
J. TUNSTALL, *The Fisherman,* MacGibbon and Kee, 1962.
M. YOUNG and P. WILLMOTT, *Family and Kinship in East London,* Routledge and
Kegan Paul, 1957.

2. Community

Community is a difficult term to define acceptably because it is used in so many different ways: for example, to describe an area where all the inhabitants are able to have face-to-face contacts, or an area the size of a large town or city. The word has also been used to describe groups of people, physicians, lawyers, and others, who are in the same kind of occupation or profession. For some the boundaries of their area may reflect merely administrative convenience; for others they may represent strong feelings of common interest. Community tends to be a God word. In many circumstances, when it is mentioned, we are expected to abase ourselves before it rather than attempt to define it. For our purposes it contains some or all of the following: a territorial area, a complex of institutions within an area, and a sense of 'belonging'.

The notion of territorial area is present in most definitions of community, though even here qualifications have to be made. Locality is relevant for one reason or another in all the readings which follow. Within the distinct area which it covers, the boundaries of which may be blurred for all kinds of reasons, the community contains certain types of institutions which lead to the development of distinctive sets of social relationships.

Communities vary a good deal in the ways in which they are independent of, or dependent upon, close ties with other communities. Isolation in Britain tends to exist only in remote rural areas, and the character of the fifth of the population living in rural areas is influenced by the increasing presence of former town-dwellers who come to live in the country though often continuing to work in the towns. The sense of community, of belonging, is not confined to those living in close-knit villages: it has been documented in the studies of East London by Young, Willmott and others. In his consideration of the characteristics of the city, Wirth emphasized a set of social conditions, notably the size of the population, the density of settlement, and the heterogeneity of the inhabitants.

Certain factors help to determine the nature of the development of a community. They include: time and common residence, shared activities and the degree of involvement in them, the characteristics of members (especially where they come from), and the kinds of leadership which are present. Frankenberg provides a useful continuum of communities, from 'truly rural' to examples drawn from housing estates and central areas of cities. In some cases the feeling of community may be only a residue after the bonds which kept the community together begin to disintegrate.

A classification some time ago by Curle of villages in Devon into four types of social subsystem provides a useful frame of reference, distinguishing between two types which are 'closed' and two which are 'open'. Closed but integrated is the relatively static traditional type whereas closed but disintegrating represents its decay and loss of vitality (in part because of the age structure) in the interaction between the inhabitants. Open but not integrated reflects the 'atomized' pattern of new suburbs transported to a rural setting, whereas open and integrated suggests open and flexible but equipped with common standards and a strong sense of community.

The first two readings relate to the 'common bonds' which members of a community share. These are considered, by **Morris and Mogey** in the first, in relation to five basic roles – of new householder, tenant, neighbour, parent, together with a residential community role – which assume different degrees of importance with the passage of time or because of the changed family circumstances of the inhabitants. Berinsfield, where the survey was conducted, was an untypical example of a new housing development in that most of the inhabitants previously lived together in a hutted group of buildings where levels of amenity were low. Their previous acquaintance made for certain differences, as did the scheme for rehousing whereby no pair of neighbours was housed together, but the bonds can be considered, with others, in relation to any neighbourhood.

Since 1919 a larger and larger proportion of the population have been housed in public housing on 'estates'. The reading about Watling by **Durant** was one of the earliest studies of such a development. It has a continuing relevance because it raises questions about the community life which develops and the kinds of pressures which affect the forms it takes. In particular, brief reference here is made to the factors leading to differentiation, among them the growth of organizations and the economic standing of the families. One of the crucial points is the way in which the sense of community which originally arose from facing common problems dissipated itself when new and sectional loyalties began to develop.

Questions about the journey to work and the mobility of the population, and the effect of these on the level of commitment to any 'community', arise from the study since for the inhabitants Watling and their life there 'belonged to only part of their day, and merely to a passing period of their lives'.

Cohen focuses upon the East End of London as a 'reception centre' for newcomers, with each group bringing distinctive traditions and cultural values. Much current writing about minorities concentrates on the processes of assimilation or accommodation but, as Cohen points out, there was no question for these subcommunities of assimilation into a dominant indigenous culture. It was a pattern of integration which, until recently, meant newcomers starting as outsiders and becoming insiders later by dissociating themselves from more conspicuous outsiders. The process has gone on through conflict rather than harmony. The three social factors which underpinned the integration are seen as the extended kinship structures, regulating socialization in each subcommunity, the ecological structure of the working-class neighbourhood, and the structure of the local economy, all of which interacted with each other. With their elimination, Cohen suggests, the present state of tension has developed. He identifies three distinct strata within both the community as a whole and the subcommunities: the socially mobile elite, the respectables, and the lumpen.

The changes began to gather momentum from the 1950s, when new towns and estates were built and large-scale redevelopment took place, leading to the entry of new minorities such as West Indians and Pakistanis. Families leave, firms move out and property speculators enter, and the neighbourhood changes its nature. Trends in industry that developed affected the craft industries and small-scale production in the East End, and the situation is made worse by what is seen as a crisis of indigenous leadership. The East End is a large area to generalize about but the analysis indicates clearly the interrelationship of the different elements in the life of communities of this kind and their changing patterns of life.

The 'riots' that occurred in parts of London and other inner city areas in Britain in 1981 were not unique, nor were they particularly severe. Nevertheless they involved, in Brixton, South London, injury to many policemen and ordinary people, and considerable damage to property, including cars. They raise questions about many aspects of life in these places and about the apparent inability of the social system to deal successfully with areas where there is racial tension, unemployment and the cumulative effects of urban deprivation. The riots in Brixton were the subject of an inquiry headed by Lord Scarman, an eminent judge, whose report contained many recommendations both about the way the police should operate and be trained, and about the ways in which life within the local community could be organized so as to minimize the strains particularly felt by members of ethnic groups.

The reading from **Scarman** is about the social conditions in Brixton which contributed to the outbreaks of violence. Brixton itself had been damaged by 'planners' blight' – a series of indecisive attempts to tackle serious questions about urban renewal, physical decay and economic decline. The area contained many more than the average number of unfit houses. There was considerable overcrowding and a high incidence of housing stress, evidenced by large numbers of homeless families, and groups, including young single people, who were in vulnerable conditions.

What follows is part of a community profile which looks at the population and the black community, including provision of education, family situations, the effects of discrimination, and the growing problem of youth unemployment. In its approach, and its stress on 'facts', it contrasts with other readings in this chapter (for example those by Cohen and Werbner).

The findings of the Hytner report, summarized by **Venner**, about the disturbances in Moss Side, Manchester, in September 1981, show marked similarities with the Scarman report on the Brixton disorders. (In fact, they were published a little before Scarman.) The report examines important questions about inner city areas, pointing to the effects of a population structure heavily weighted towards younger age groups at a time when unemployment was running at 60 per cent for under-nineteen-year-olds, the rate being even higher among black teenagers. Since that time the rate is likely to have worsened, with even more devastating effects on young people. This links with the material on social conditions in Brixton in the reading by Scarman. The evidence about police-community relations emphasizes the inexperience of some young policemen, in contrast to the work of Community Contact Police who visit schools, organize activities for young people and so on. There were criticisms of police complaints procedure. The great hostility to the police was marked, as was the sense of disaffection among the young. However, the panel largely dismissed suggestions of outside involvement of political groups from the ultra-right or the ultra-left, though at least two on the left were thriving. The report argues that extremists are not such a threat as are the social conditions on which they feed, and that Rastafarians and other peaceful 'black consciousness' groups should not be treated as 'extremists' by the police. The events in Moss Side were a self-fulfilling prophecy, as it was there that trouble was expected in Manchester. This is even though recent redevelopment had changed its image of being a slum, with a large West Indian population, associated with prostitution and crime, especially drugs and illegal drinking, and expectations of racial tension had diminished. There were genuine grievances in the area, and many reasons for feeling alienated from society, but the outbreak appeared to be fortuitous even though it led to three nights of rioting. Moreover, differently motivated groups joined in, including those who looted, who were apparently mainly middle-aged and white. This brief account of the main findings of the Hytner report illustrates the range of issues and the varying motivations and actions of those involved. It complements the other readings in this chapter concerned with social conditions in multiracial areas, the position of ethnic groups in British society, and the origins of public violence.

A small but growing number of ethnic minorities from the New Commonwealth, and also Pakistan, live in Britain. The migration of these groups has taken place mainly in the past thirty years. An increasing number of the children and young people in these groups were born in Britain. Most of those who migrated to Britain were from the West Indies, India, Pakistan (including East Pakistan, which became Bangladesh), Hong Kong, and Asian minorities from Kenya and Uganda. Some information about the black, mainly West Indian, population of Brixton has been provided already in the reading from Scarman. From a different perspective **Werbner** considers the lifestyles of Pakistanis in Manchester, which will serve as an illustration of aspects of social living among ethnic minorities from the Indian subcontinent. The questions with which the reading is mainly concerned, which have a wealth of illustrative material accompanying them, have to do with the threefold model of lifestyle 'messages', geared to 'dominance', 'conformity' or 'independence', shown by Manchester Pakistanis. In a variety of ways the information about interpersonal relationships provides additional insights into urban social structures beyond what is available through studies of, for example, occupation or class. The reading offers a consideration of several, apparently disparate, social aspects of urban living, including the existence of distinctive 'exclusive' cultural beliefs and practices, the 'shape' of social networks and how they are recruited, and the division of labour in the home. The account that emerges is much subtler than those often presented, which contrast 'traditional' Asian villagers and 'middle-class' Asian townspeople. It contradicts many popular assumptions about such ethnic minorities and should lead us to reconsider them.

In some respects **Raban**, in the next reading, projects a view of the city and in particular of metropolitan life which echoes sociologists such as Durkheim, Wirth and others who stressed the anonymity, impersonality and segregation of the city. But he does identify the gathering together of a group, or 'a community of people' as he calls them, who share ideas: 'narrow, passionate *cognoscenti* bolstered by received ideas, given to clubs and cliques and intense sectarian debates'. He sees them as part of the essence of city life, drawn together by political or religious beliefs, common-interest groups, keeping the outside world at bay. Raban suggests it would be easy to see beliefs such as those of the Krishna people as merely grotesque, but that they are a response to the unreality and diversity of the city. In his view they are symptoms of serious urban conditions: clubs, cliques, cells and the like are 'foxholes for all those whom the city has isolated, for whom no larger reality is habitable'. For them the city is a place to live out the dream.

Mobility, and the confrontation of 'old' and 'new', may lead to changes in the structure of power. **Elias and Scotson**, in the reading on the theme of leadership, discuss what they call the quality of 'sociological oldness' whereby working-class families living for a long time in the same area may exercise power by monopolizing key positions in local institutions rather than by the inheritance of property. This arises, the authors suggest, from the greater cohesion and solidarity, and the greater uniformity of norms of the group. The study was undertaken in a rural area of Leicestershire where the old-established 'villagers' came into conflict with the inhabitants of the new estate grafted on to the old village. This is shown to be the result of becoming interdependent as neighbours. Finally, the stereotyped image of the Estate in the minds of the villagers was reinforced by a minority of Estate youngsters whose behaviour was bad.

The reading by **Newby** considers the transformation of some agricultural settlements in lowland England since the end of the war in 1945. During that time there has been a great decrease in employment opportunities and those workers who left for the towns were replaced in many areas by an overwhelmingly middle-class population drawn by cheap housing (until the late 1960s) and an idealized view of rural life. The arrival of the newcomers creates new class antagonisms that replace those of the old occupational community, as well as petty conflicts apparent in background and lifestyles. Although there is limited competition between the two groups, and their children, in the labour market, this is not so in the housing market. Newcomers compete with locals, contributing to higher demand and extensive changes in the market; they are scapegoated for the difficulties locals have in finding housing, although the situation is more complicated. In addition, newcomers tend to oppose new building of council housing to try and preserve the 'picturesque, ancient and unchanging' qualities of the English village as they see them. This leads to conflict on environmental issues, especially to do with conservation and modern farming methods, and often unintentional problems because of the desire of newcomers to treat surrounding farmland at times 'as though it were a vast municipal park'. For farm workers there may be a sense of loss because newcomers are unappreciative of their skills at work on which their status was once based. Instead, urban criteria of 'conspicuous consumption', in Veblen's phrase, are substituted, such as size of house, quality of car, possession of other consumer durables, and so on. Contacts between the two groups will be limited because of this 'reserve', or worse, shown by the locals in response to attempts by newcomers to allot the farm workers their places as, in Pahl's words, 'props on the rustic stage'. In face of these and other changes the local population, in Newby's view, has turned in on itself in such villages, and many newcomers may be unaware of the feelings they arouse.

It is appropriate to end this chapter with a reading about villages where new social divisions and conflicts have arisen to challenge once again the idealized view of community, deriving from such villages quite frequently, which many people still retain. Such a view would stress above all those qualities of hierarchy, order and harmony, leading to social integration, which the historical village was supposed to have. Some of the most interesting and stimulating work in sociological research in recent years has gone on in the area of rural sociology, by Newby, his colleagues and others, extending our perceptions of ways of life and the sources and nature of social change in the village. (A brief reading by Littlejohn is to be found in Chapter 4 about another, very different kind of village.) Together with the earlier readings in this chapter about a wide range of locations (inner city, housing estates, urban areas in places like London and Manchester); from a range of perspectives, and on issues as diverse as relationships between and within ethnic and other groups, policy on community and police relationships, what emerges is the continuing relevance of the focus upon local social systems. This, in Stacey's words, 'involves not only what institutions are present, but the processes of their operation. . . . Processes take *time* and the dimension of time is therefore . . . essential to the conceptualization of any social system.'

Common Bonds 1
R. N. Morris and J. Mogey

Reprinted with permission from Raymond Morris and John Mogey, *The Sociology of Housing*, Routledge and Kegan Paul, 1965, pp. 44–53

Informants perceived five common bonds which could be expressed in role terms. First, all were new-house dwellers. The 'householder role' covers all references to problems of gardening, and the maintenance and furnishing of the new house. Secondly, all were tenants of the same local authority. The 'tenant role' covers activities in this role-set: notably the payment of rent and complaints about the house and amenities, in so far as these were actually voiced corporately through the tenants' association. Thirdly, everyone had to adjust to new neighbours, as no pair of old neighbours was rehoused together. 'Neighbour roles' include adjustments to the neighbours, and the establishment of norms of neighbourly behaviour.

Fourthly, nearly all informants had young children. 'Parental roles' comprised those needs which were related to the children's behaviour, or suggested provisions for their welfare. Finally, many families felt the need to join with other residents in organizing social activities and entertainments, or in providing other services, designed to benefit all adults. 'Residential community roles' includes all references to the residential community as a whole. Most of these references were to the social centre, the need for more amenities, or to the provision of social events for the adults.

The common bonds of the householder role were mainly intangible. There was, first, widespread excitement and pride occasioned by living in a new house, after experience of a hut or of life with in-laws. This normally found expression through delight with the running hot water, the bathroom and the w.c. These correlated consistently and highly with house satisfaction. One respondent assured us that her ten-year-old son was so thrilled that he had insisted on taking a bath every day since they had moved into their new home. At the time of the interview, this remarkable performance had been maintained for three months. Similarly, many families took a new pride in themselves and their appearance.

The second common bond of the householder role concerned the process of adjustment to the new home – finding the appropriate furniture and cultivating the garden:

This is the first place where we could take an interest in the garden and surroundings and home.

For the first few months, this process was so universal that whenever a householder looked out of the window he could see others coping with the same problems. New furnishings and appliances were a constant source of interest:

The usual way – you start off with a pushbike and finish up with a car. Everyone's trying to be better, buying new furniture.

The interest was not simply part of the competition for status which occurs in any relatively new group; it was also an attempt to establish new norms of equipment and behaviour which would be appropriate for their role as dwellers in a new house. Whenever a resident went out, or paused for breath in the garden, he could see neighbours engaged in the same activities, and glad to exchange a grumble or a tip.

The tenant role offered a second important potential link between families, for all came within the responsibility of the same local authority. This bond has usually been important in leading to the formation of a tenants' association to request and sometimes agitate for the rapid installation of important services; but in Berinsfield the situation was more complex. The history of the hutted camp had been marked by sporadic and sometimes open conflict with the RDC, and by intervals of sullen non-cooperation. In July 1958, only half the respondents believed that the council's allocation policy would be fair and open. In November 1958, about 70 per cent of the rehoused families thought that the council had been fair; but very few of the families still in huts retained this view.

In the first set of interviews, references to the tenant role were mostly concerned with the problem of finding the extra rent for the new house. For most families the increase was between 30s and 40s (£1.50 and £2) per week. Later, when most families had adjusted to the increase, this problem received references only from the most recent arrivals. There was little spontaneous suggestion of a cooperative campaign for lower rents, or of help for families who had difficulty in meeting the extra commitments. The rent issue was quickly overshadowed by references to the open front gardens; and to the desire for a tenants' association which would ensure a prompt response to tenants' complaints.

The 'open fronts' were the major point of conflict in November 1958 between the council and the rehoused families. The council's insistence on this feature of the plan meant that most families had no separate front gardens, and little defence against any children who chose to stare through their windows. This threat to privacy was reinforced by a fear that the standard of maintenance applied by the RDC to the open fronts would fall below the tenants' aspirations. Our tape recordings of the tenants' association meetings for this period illustrate the importance of the open fronts controversy in the later months of 1958. The open fronts still gave rise to quite a few complaints in the following July:

> They should have put proper fences up in the beginning.
> They should give us front gardens, more privacy.
> They should do the front gardens; have a little wall in front, or railings.

One family went further, and expressed the view that: 'Half the rent you pay should be for privacy.'

The neighbour role was also crucial at first, and of diminishing importance subsequently. The 'respectables' voiced the fear that the new houses might be allotted to 'scruffy' families; and some wished that families had been grouped according to this standard:

> They tried hard to put people who were in bad conditions into a house. The only thing I think is wrong is to put all those rough people in. They should have been put all together – I don't think they will change.
> If they wanted a model village, they got the wrong people – people who do not care how they live.

Rehousing gave every family a new pair of next-door neighbours; most families had previously been acquainted only superficially with their new neighbours. As the neighbour role is usually of crucial significance on a new estate, it was to be expected in the first two sets of interviews that neighbour roles would be critical. Satisfaction with the neighbours consistently implied satisfaction with the residential community; while dissatisfaction with the neighbours almost always meant dissatisfaction with the residential community.

The importance of the neighbours was not, however, as striking on this analysis as had been expected. Since most families were previously acquainted, less status competition was necessary to crystallize the village's social structure. Prior acquaintance reduced the importance of nearness and unavoidable contact in determining relationships; from this point of view, Berinsfield was not a normal housing estate.

When families are tied to their homes, their range of acquaintances is very limited. They will tend to expect the immediate neighbours to fill the roles of both neighbour and friend. These two roles, however, may be interpreted in a variety of ways. If the families' expectations are compatible, they will generally play both roles towards each other, and the primary social relationships of phase one will then develop. These two roles are not completely compatible, however; if families' expectations are different, they will tend to play a narrow range of roles towards each other, and the secondary relationships of phase two will develop. When two families are already acquainted, the first exploratory phase may be unnecessary. This argument would account for the lack of evidence of obvious 'phase one' behaviour at Berinsfield, especially among the locals; for there was no indication that mutual help, borrowing and lending increased as families tried to adjust to their new environment.

The fourth common bond was the parental role. Unlike the first three, this tended to grow in importance with the passage of time. Respondents quickly noticed the lack of amenities for the children, and the need for cooperative action to discipline the more unruly ones. These were complementary, for it was hoped that good amenities would alleviate and in the long run remove the nuisance which the children represented to some residents. Many of the children from Field Farm had grown accustomed to roaming and playing wherever they chose; protests were largely futile: 'My children are getting out of hand since we moved up here: I want to get out.'

Many respondents hoped that this behaviour would not persist in the new village, for they regarded tidiness and the preservation of trees and grass as the most important means of making Berinsfield beautiful. There were also requests for a bus to take the younger children to their school, about two miles from the village. This request was met, through the efforts of the tenants' association, at the beginning of the 1959–60 school year; previously the children had had to walk along a very muddy path, or along the edge of a fast and dangerous main road.

The role of the children in determining the nature of the contacts between neighbours was also important. Their behaviour and needs may produce either cooperation or conflict: much will depend on the adjustment which the parents have already made to each other. The age of the children is important in determining the radius of their influence as a common bond. When they are young, it tends to operate within the neighbourhood. As they grow older, it tends to move to the residential community, and then farther afield. Disciplinary action at the community level was accordingly sought in relation to the older children; while trouble with the neighbours was the main threat represented by the younger ones.

Residential community roles represented the fifth common bond. References were mainly to social events for the adults and to the need for amenities, and occasionally a parish council, for the whole village. These references tended to become of greater importance as families adapted themselves to their new homes and neighbours. Social events were offered regularly by the social centre during the year of our survey; yet in spite of the relative success of bingo and jumble sales, the organizers felt that the centre attracted little sustained interest and support. At the time of the move, they assured us that attendance by the locals had become negligible; and very few of the strangers ever attended. In this respect, too, the phase hypothesis applied only weakly to Berinsfield.

Residential community roles had nevertheless become the most important category by the end of the research, and social events for the adults were one of the principal manifest needs of the village. There was thus a contrast between the expressed need for residential community roles and the limited use made of the available opportunities. This may reflect simply the absence of facilities to perform desired roles, such as those of shopper, church member and drinker. In part, it may be due to ignorance of the opportunities available. It may also, however, be related to the community centre's normal function of crystallizing differences within the residential community, which will alienate some groups and lead to a demand for activities which the centre cannot provide, or for existing activities in more congenial company. Finally, since the centre, like the general store, was still housed in a dilapidated hut, it may have lost status through its inability to acquire a new home.

Common Bonds 2
R. Durant

Reprinted with permission from Ruth Durant, *Watling, A Social Survey*, P. S. King and Son, 1939, pp. 42–9

At the end of this early period, in the summer of 1931, the Estate had acquired much of the likeness of a town and had lost much of its earlier resemblance to an intimate community of people. The people themselves had become more like strangers to each other. In other words, a housing estate which is faced with its specific problems is more likely to develop social consciousness and keenness for local unity than a modern town pursuing its daily routine.

But it has to be remembered that a housing estate will never exactly resemble an ordinary town; a number of important differences remain which at least offer the possibility of its being favourably distinguished by the intensity of local social life. Indeed, so far as Watling is concerned, this seems to have been achieved. Its development was positive as compared, firstly, with the institutional bareness of Watling's early life, and secondly, as compared with the dreary social existence of suburbia. It was negative when its temper and tempo are set against Watling's early keenness on its own behalf. Whilst new instruments of corporate activity had been created, the old communal enthusiasm had markedly waned.

One set of causes had been primarily responsible for this result: forces inherent in the development of the Estate itself were destructive of community life. Growth of local organizations necessarily means decline of ambition to secure them. This is an obvious fact which needs no elaboration. Moreover, at first the desire to equip the Estate with amenities was common. There was no difficulty in getting various groups of people to agree on a plan of campaign. Later, it was more difficult for them to agree on the administration of existing amenities especially since new residents had arrived who had not shared the failures and successes of the early struggle. Moreover, there was no institution whose authority was recognized by all people and to which a final appeal could be addressed.

Economic and social differentiation was a further result of Watling's growth. In the early period the major difficulties were common to all people. For many, however, adjustment to their environment meant to become acutely aware of their individual worries. The financial burden of higher rent, more fares and instalment fees on furniture weighed heavily. The weariness of long train journeys made itself felt. Poverty loomed larger than loneliness. People were too worried to develop social interests, and often too tired to seek entertainment. Just when communal life was most in need of their support, when local societies were in their infancy, the economic crisis set in and endangered the existence of innumerable households. For at least one-quarter of all families the margin of comfort was extremely small. That means that illness or unemployment, or the loss of a wage-earner, completely upsets their carefully balanced budgets. Hence the crisis not only enhanced the difficulties of needy families but it also pushed more households into that category.

Simultaneously, it sharpened the cleavage between poor and well-to-do people on the Estate. There were amongst the small families of the civil servants, transport workers and other people in secure positions, a considerable number who were not immediately affected by external influences, such as the crisis. In fact, they profited from the fall in prices and felt richer, whilst the others became poorer. Thus complaints about snobbishness and also apathy were repeatedly heard during the same period. None of these tendencies was very beneficial to social development.

A further factor created and accentuated differentiation. From 1928 immigration to the Estate slowed down; it became subject to vacancies only. Although large in total, immigration henceforth became an individual event, problems of adjustment to the Estate an individual experience for each particular family, and their solutions became extremely individualistic too. People either completely shut themselves up in their homes or they went to one of the existing local societies which competed for their favour. Each of these, whether it provided politics, garden seeds or nursing services, was now a closed unit. Hence, by joining, the newly acquired member was not hindered from himself becoming self-contained.

Moreover, it became increasingly difficult for the residents to identify this place with their existence. They realized that, sooner rather than later, they would have to leave it again: the individual family was so mobile. During the ten years which have passed since the first houses were occupied the total number of families who have lived on the Estate is nearly twice its maximum capacity. One out of every two families which have ever come to the Estate moved elsewhere before the end of ten years. Almost half of all families stayed there less than five years. Watling belonged to only one part of their day, and merely to a passing period of their lives.

Subcultural Conflict and Working-class Community
P. Cohen

Reprinted with permission from Phil Cohen, *Subcultural Conflict and Working-class Community*, Working Paper in Cultural Studies, Centre for Contemporary Culture, University of Birmingham, 1972, pp. 9–21

Since the very beginning of the industrial revolution the East End has provided a kind of unofficial 'reception centre' for a succession of immigrant communities, in flight from religious persecution or economic depression. First came the Huguenots, spinners and weavers, at the end of the seventeenth century, and still today their presence survives in surnames, and place names in the area. Then, throughout the nineteenth century there was a constant immigration of Irish, mostly labourers, and small traders from Central Europe, and in the last two decades of course Pakistanis, and to a lesser extent West Indians and Greek Cypriots. Today the East End is indeed like 'five parts of the world, put in one place'.

Each subcommunity brought with it not just specific skills, but also of course its own traditions, and cultural values. There was no question of assimilation into a dominant indigenous culture – either that of the 'native' dockland community, or of the English ruling class. What in fact happened, until recently, was that each new subcommunity, in turn and over time, became an accepted, but differentiated part of the 'East End' by allying itself with the longer established sections of the community against another, later subcommunity. The outsiders become established, become insiders, by dissociating themselves from an even more conspicuous set of outsiders. Perhaps it is a natural human tendency to draw the line under one's own feet; at any rate in the East End integration has proceeded by means of conflict, rather than by dissolving it.

There are three main social factors underpinning this pattern of integration: the extended kinship structures which regulate socialization in each subcommunity; secondly the ecological structure of the working-class neighbourhood; and finally the structure of the local economy. In reality these factors interact and reinforce each other – but it is important to understand them, because it is precisely the elimination of these factors, the transformation of these structures which has caused the present state of tension in the area. So let's look at them briefly, one by one.

Extended kinship networks

This is a system by which the family of marriage remains linked by an intricate web of rights and obligations to the respective families of origin, and serves as a link between them. Based in the first instance on maintaining the close relationship between mother and daughter, so that when she gets married the daughter will continue to live as close as she can to 'mum', and extending in widening circles to include uncles and aunts, grandparents, nephews and nieces, and their relations, this system virtually turns the family into a micro-community, and in fact provides for many of the functions of mutual aid and support that are elsewhere carried out by agencies in the community. Obviously such a system makes for cultural continuity and stability; it reduces generational conflict to a minimum – leaving home and getting married do not become life and death issues as they do in the nuclear family. Firstly because the extended family constitutes a much richer and more diversified human environment for the child; secondly children tend to stay at home until they get married, or to put it another way, only leave in order to do so; thirdly getting married does not involve any divorce between the young couple and their families, but rather recruits new members into the kinship network. And although the extended family preserves historical traditions of the subcommunity, handing them on from generation to generation, it does not serve to insulate it from the 'outside world'. On the contrary it serves as the basis for eventual integration. For the family both becomes firmly anchored in a given locality (matrilocal residence as it's technically called) and the network is continually expanding outwards; the net result is that over time the ties of neighbourhood are extended into ties of kinship and vice versa. If everybody knows everybody else in traditional neighbourhoods it is not because they are related through interlocking kinship networks, but that schoolmates, workmates, pubmates while they may or may not be related to relatives of one's own, will tend to be related to other mates, or mates to other relatives of one's own. But this can't be explained simply in terms of the internal dynamic of kinship, the ecology of the neighbourhood also plays a part.

Ecology of the working-class neighbourhood

The close-packed back to backs, facing each other across alleyways or narrow streets, corner shops and local pubs, the turning, all this helps to shape and support the close textures of traditional working-class life, its sense of solidarity, its local loyalties and traditions. And this in turn is underpinned by the extended kinship networks of the traditional working-class family, which have been so well observed in Bethnal Green.

But how does the ecology of the neighbourhood work in practice? Let's take the street as an example. In these neighbourhoods the street forms a kind of 'communal space', a mediation between the totally private space of the family, with its intimate involvements, and the totally public space, e.g. parks, thoroughfares, etc., where people relate to each other as strangers, and with indifference. The street, then, is a space where people can relate as neighbours, can express a degree of involvement with others, who are outside the family, but yet not as strangers; it maintains an intricate social balance between rights and obligations, distance and relation in the community. It also serves to generate an informal system of social controls. For where the street is played in, talked in, sat out in, constantly spectated as a source of neighbourly interest, it is also policed, and by the people themselves. Nothing much can happen, however trivial (a child falling, a woman struggling with heavy parcels, etc.), without it becoming a focus of interest and intervention. The presence of corner shops and pubs in the turning also serves to generate social interaction at street level, as well as providing natural settings for 'gossip cliques', which if they do nothing else constantly reaffirm the reality of neighbourhood ties!

The net result is that neighbours as well as relatives are available to help cope with the day to day problems that arise in the constant struggle to survive under the conditions of the working-class community. And in many areas, including the East End, institutions such as loans clubs, holiday clubs and the like developed to supplement family mutual aid, and formalize the practices of 'neighbouring'.

The local economy

Perhaps the most striking feature of the traditional East End economy is its diversity; dockland, the many distributive and service trades linked to it, the craft industries, notably tailoring and furniture making, the markets. This diversity meant that people lived and worked in the East End – there was no need for them to go outside in search of jobs. The extended family remains intrinsic to the recruitment of the labour force and even to the work process itself; son followed father into the same trade or industry while many of the craft and service trades were organized into 'family concerns'. As a result of this, the situation of the work place, its issues and interests, remained tied to the situation outside work – the issues and interests of the community.

There was a direct connection between the position of the producer and the consumer. The fierce pride of being an East Ender was often linked to the equally fierce pride of craftsmanship and skilled labour. And it was from the section of the working class – sometimes called the labour aristocracy – that the indigenous leadership was drawn; politically conscious and highly articulate in defence of local interest, both at the community level and at the point of production. This elite group was also the most socially mobile, tending to re-emigrate from the East End to the outer ring of the middle-class suburbs; as Jewish people used to put it: the distance from Bethnal Green to Golders Green was two generations. Yet their ranks were continuously replenished as new subcommunities established themselves as part of the respectable working class. There were also those less fortunate who, for a variety of reasons, fell by the wayside, and remained permanent 'outsiders' *vis-à-vis* the 'established'. They were relegated to the ranks of the labouring poor caught in a vicious circle of poverty, ill-health, unemployment and lack of education. This residual group was doubly excluded – unskilled and lacking union organization they had little or no bargaining power on the labour market; and stigmatized as 'pariahs' by the rest of the community, the scapegoat for its problems, and denied any effective voice in their solution.

At any given time, then, the social structure of the community as a whole, and of the subcommunities within it, tended to be polarizing into three distinct strata: the socially mobile elite who monopolize leadership; the respectables, who form the 'staple backbone' of the community; and the lumpen (so called) who are often driven to petty criminal activity to survive. And incidentally there is not a better example of the overriding importance of the extended kinship structure on the pattern of East End life than the fact that when this lowest strata began to evolve a kind of lumpen aristocracy, based on criminal activity, it was the small family 'firm' that was taken as the model for its social organization!

The future perfect versus the historical present

The social structure we've described held until the early fifties; and then, slowly at first, but with gathering momentum it began to change, and the pattern of social integration that had traditionally characterized the East End began, dramatically, to break down. Without going into a long argument about cause and effect, it is possible to say that this breakdown coincided with the wholesale redevelopment of the area, and the process of chain reactions which this triggered. The redevelopment was in two phases, the first spanning the decade of the fifties, the second from the early sixties to the present; let's examine the impact of each in turn.

The fifties saw the development of new towns and large estates on the outskirts of East London, Dagenham, Greenleigh etc., and a large number of families from the worst slums of the East End were rehoused in this way. The East End, one of the highest density areas in London, underwent a gradual depopulation. But as it did so, certain areas underwent a repopulation, as they were rapidly colonized by a large influx of West Indians and Pakistanis. One of the reasons why these communities were attracted (in the weak sense of the word) to such areas is often called 'planning blight'. This concept has been used to describe what happens in the take-off phase of comprehensive redevelopment in the inner residential zones of large urban centres. The typical pattern is that as redevelopment begins, land values inevitably rise, and rental values fall; the most dynamic elements in local industry, who are usually the largest employers of labour, tend to move out, alongside the migrating families, and are often offered economic incentives to do so; much of the existing dilapidated property in the area is bought up cheaply by property speculators and Rachman-type landlords, who are only interested in the maximum exploitation of their assets – the largest profits in the shortest time; as a result the property is often not maintained and becomes even further dilapidated. Immigrant families, with low incomes, and excluded from council housing, naturally gravitate to these areas, and their own trades and service industries begin to penetrate the local economy. This in turn accelerates the migration of the indigenous community to the new towns and estates. The only apparent exception to planning blight, in fact proves the rule. For those few areas which are linked to invisible assets – such as possessing houses of 'character', i.e. late Georgian or early Victorian, or amenities such as parks – are actually bought up and improved, renovated for the new middle class, students, young professionals, who require easy access to the commercial and cultural centre of the city. The end result on the local community is the same; whether the neighbourhood is upgraded or downgraded, long-resident working-class families move out.

As the worst effects of the first phase both on those who moved, and on those who stayed behind, became apparent, the planning authorities decided to reverse their policy. Everything was now concentrated on building new estates on slum sites within the East End. But far from counteracting the social disorganization of the area, this merely accelerated the process. In analysing the impact of redevelopment on the community, these two phases can be treated as one. No one is denying that redevelopment brought an improvement in material conditions for those fortunate enough to be rehoused (there are still thousands on the housing list). But while this removed the tangible evidence of poverty, it did nothing to improve the real economic situation of many families, and those with low incomes may, despite rent rebate schemes, be worse off. But to this was added a new poverty – the impoverishment of working-class culture. Redevelopment meant the destruction of the neighbourhood, the breakdown of the extended kinship network, which as we've seen combined to exert a powerful force for social cohesion in the community. I now think perhaps I've overstated the extent to which the community structures have broken down, as this paper was originally the basis of a proposal for funding the Project.

The first effect of the high density, high rise schemes, was to destroy the function of the street, the local pub, the corner shop, as articulations of communal space. Instead there was only the privatized space of the family unit, stacked one on top of each other, in total isolation, juxtaposed with the totally public space which surrounded it, and which lacked any of the informal social controls generated by the neighbourhood. The streets which serviced the new estates became thoroughfares, their users 'pedestrians', and by analogy so many bits of human traffic, and this irrespective of whether or not they were separated from motorized traffic. It's indicative of how far the planners failed to understand the human ecology of the working-class neighbourhood that they could actually talk about building 'vertical streets'! The people who had to live in them weren't fooled. As one put it – they might have running hot water and central heating but to him they were still prisons in the sky. Inevitably the physical isolation, the lack of human scale and sheer impersonality of the new environment was felt worst by people living in the new tower blocks which have gradually come to dominate the East End landscape.

The second effect of redevelopment was to destroy what we have called 'matrilocal residence'. Not only was the new housing designed on the model of the nuclear family with little provision for large low-income families (usually designated as problem families!) and none at all for groups of young single people, but the actual pattern of distribution of the new housing tended to disperse the kinship networks; families of marriage were separated from their families of origin, especially during the first phase of the redevelopment. The isolated family unit could no longer call on the resources of wider kinship networks, or of the neighbourhood, and the family itself became the sole focus of solidarity. This meant that any problems were bottled up within the immediate interpersonal context which produced them; and at the same time family relationships were invested with a new intensity, to compensate for the diversity of relationships previously generated through neighbours and wider kin. The trouble was that although the traditional kinship system which corresponded to it had broken down, the traditional patterns of socialization (of communication and control) continued to reproduce themselves in the interior of the family. The working-class family was thus not only isolated from the outside, but undermined from within. There is no better example of what we are talking about than the plight of the so-called 'housebound mother'. The street or turning was no longer available as a safe playspace, under neighbourly supervision. Mum, or Auntie, was no longer just round the corner to look after the kids for the odd morning. Instead the task of keeping an eye on the kids fell exclusively to the young wife, and the only safe playspace was the 'safety of the home'. Feeling herself cooped up with the kids, and cut off from the outside world, it wouldn't be surprising if she occasionally took out her frustration on those nearest and dearest! Only market research and advertising executives imagine that the housebound mother sublimates everything in her G-plan furniture, her washing machine or non-stick frying pans.

Underlying all this however there was a more basic process of change going on in the community, a change in the whole economic infrastructure of the East End.

In the late fifties, the British economy began to recover from the effect of the war, and to apply the advanced technology developed during this period to the more backward sectors of the economy. Craft industries, and small-scale production in general were the first to suffer; automated techniques replaced the traditional hand skills and their simple division of labour. Similarly the economies of scale provided for by the concentration of capital resources meant that the small-scale family business was no longer a viable unit. Despite a long rearguard action many of the traditional industries, tailoring, furniture making, many of the service and distributive trades linked to the docks, rapidly declined, or were bought out. Symbolic of this was the disappearance of the corner shop; where these were not demolished by redevelopment, they were replaced by the larger supermarkets often owned by large combines. Even where corner shops were offered places in the redevelopment area often they could not afford the high rents. There was a gradual polarization in the structure of the labour force: on the one side the highly specialized, skilled and well-paid jobs associated with the new technology, and the high growth sectors that employed them; on the other the routine, dead-end, low-paid and unskilled jobs associated with the labour intensive sectors, especially the service industries. As might be expected, it was the young people, just out of school, who got the worst of the deal. Lacking openings in their fathers' trades, and lacking the qualifications for the new industries, they were relegated to jobs as van boys, office boys, packers, warehousemen, etc., and long spells out of work. More and more people, young and old, had to travel out of the community to their jobs, and some eventually moved out to live elsewhere, where suitable work was to be found. The local economy as a whole contracted, became less diverse. The only section of the community which was unaffected by this was dockland, which retained its position in the labour market, and with it, its traditions of militancy. It did not, though, remain unaffected by the breakdown of the pattern of integration in the East End as a whole, *vis-à-vis* its subcommunity structure. Perhaps this goes some way to explain the paradoxical fact that within the space of twelve months, the dockers could march in support of Enoch Powell, and take direct action for community control in the Isle of Dogs!

If someone should ask why the plan to 'modernize' the pattern of East End life should have been such a disaster, perhaps the only honest answer is that, given the macro-social forces acting on it, given the political, ideological, and economic framework within which it operated, the result was inevitable. For example many local people wonder why the new environment should be the way it is. The reasons are complex; they are political in so far as the system does not allow for any effective participation by local working-class community in the decision-making process at any stage or level of planning. The clients of the planners are simply the local authority or commercial developer who employs them. They are ideological in so far as the plans are unconsciously modelled on the structure of the middle-class environment, which is based on the concept of *property*, and *private ownership*, on individual differences of status, wealth etc.; whereas the structure of the working-class environment is based on the concept of community, or collective identity, common lack of ownership, wealth etc. Similarly needs were assessed on the norms of the middle-class nuclear family, rather than the extended working-class family. But underpinning both these sets of reasons lie the basic economic factors involved in comprehensive redevelopment. Quite simply – faced with the task of financing a large housing programme, the local authorities were forced to borrow large amounts of capital, and also to design schemes which would attract capital investment to the area. This means that they have to borrow at the going interest rates, which in this country are very high, and that to subsidize housing, certain of the best sites have to be earmarked for commercial developers. A further and perhaps decisive factor is the cost of land, since very little of it is publicly owned and land values rise as the area develops.

All this means that planners have to reduce the cost of production to a minimum, through the use of capital intensive techniques – prefabricated and standardized components, allowing for semi-automated processes in construction. The attraction of high rise developments (tower blocks outside the trade) is not only that they meet these requirements, but they allow for certain economies of scale, such as the input costs of essential services, which can be grouped around a central core. As to 'non-essential' services, i.e. ones that don't pay, such as playspace, community centres, youth clubs and recreational facilities, these often have to be sacrificed to the needs of commercial developers, who of course have quite different priorities. Perhaps the best example of this happening is the notorious St Catherine's Dock Scheme. This major contribution towards solving the East End's housing problem includes a yachting marina, a luxury hotel, luxury apartment blocks, and various cultural amenities for their occupants plus – a small section of low-income accommodation, presumably to house the families of the low-paid staff who will service the luxury amenities. And lest anyone becomes too sentimental about the existing site, Telfords warehouses etc., it should be mentioned that the original development was by the East India Company in the early nineteenth century, involved the destruction of the homes of thousands of poor families in the area, and met with such stiff opposition from them that it eventually required an Act of Parliament to get the scheme approved!

The situation facing East Enders at present, then, is not new. When the first tenements went up in the nineteenth century they raised the same objections from local people, and for the same very good reasons, as their modern counterparts – the tower blocks. What *is* new is that in the nineteenth century the voice of the community was vigorous and articulate on these issues, whereas today, just when it needs it most, the community is faced with a crisis of indigenous leadership.

The reasons for this are already implicit in the analysis above. The labour aristocracy, traditional source of leadership, has virtually disappeared along with the artisan mode of production. At the same time there has been a split in consciousness between the spheres of production and consumption. More and more East Enders are forced to work outside the area; young people especially are less likely to follow family traditions in this respect. As a result the issues of the work place are no longer experienced as directly linked to community issues. Of course there has always been a 'brain drain' of the most articulate, due to social mobility. But not only has this been intensified as a result of the introduction of comprehensive schools, but the recruitment of fresh talent from the strata below – i.e. from the ranks of the respectable working class – has also dried up. For this strata, traditionally the social cement of the community, is also in a state of crisis.

Social Conditions in Brixton

Lord Scarman

Reprinted with permission from *The Brixton Disorders, 10–12 April 1981*, Report of an Inquiry by the Rt Hon. the Lord Scarman, HMSO, Cmnd. 8427, 1981, pp. 7–11, 14–16

The people of Brixton

(1) POPULATION

Like many other inner city areas the population of Brixton is falling. The population of the Borough of Lambeth as a whole dropped by 20 per cent between the 1971 and 1981 census. It stands now at some 246,000. The major cause of this decline has not been natural change but the movement of people away from the inner city. More importantly for the health of the area, those leaving the borough have been predominantly in the twenty-five to sixty age range, that is to say the working population, and there has been a net loss of professional and skilled workers and a net gain of clerical and manual workers. The net figures also apparently mask a high rate of population movement: the 1971 census showed that 20 per cent of Lambeth's population had moved into the borough during the previous five years.

The population of Lambeth therefore tends to be relatively young, working-class and transient. The borough has a higher proportion of children of school age than London as a whole, though lower than England overall, and a higher proportion of people in their twenties. Fewer Lambeth people are in professional or managerial occupations than in London as a whole, although the proportions of other non-manual, skilled or semi-skilled workers are similar. Other important features are a strikingly high figure of children in local authority care (2.3 per cent of the population aged eighteen or less) and an incidence of single-parent families which, at one in six, is twice the national average. There is evidence of a higher rate of mental illness and of physical or mental handicap in the borough than nationally. Social services expenditure by Lambeth Borough Council in 1979/1980 at £117.39 per capita was the highest in England, and over twice the average for all London boroughs. Total revenue expenditure per capita by the local Area Health Authority in the same period was also among the highest in England at £243, compared to an average of £230 for Inner London Area Health Authorities.

The features of Lambeth's population I have mentioned are to be found accentuated in the inner area of the borough, which includes Brixton. There is a generally higher rate of population decline than in the borough as a whole; a higher proportion of clerical, semi-skilled and unskilled workers; a larger proportion of low-income households; greater proportions of young and elderly; more one-parent families; and a higher incidence of mental illness and mental and physical handicap.

There is also in Brixton a higher proportion of black people. Overall, some 25 per cent of Lambeth's population were estimated in 1978 to belong to non-white ethnic groups. West Indians were the largest black group (12.5 per cent of the borough's population), followed by Africans (3.4 per cent), Indians, Pakistanis, Bangladeshis (2.4 per cent) and other non-white or mixed-origin people (6.5 per cent). The overall percentage of non-white people in the borough's population is similar to that in a number of other London boroughs, such as Ealing (24 per cent), Hackney (28 per cent), Haringey (26 per cent) and Newham (23 per cent), though less than Brent (33 per cent). In Brixton – which may be considered as being made up of five wards, Ferndale, Tulse Hill, Town Hall, Angell and Herne Hill – the percentage of non-white people in the population is higher than for Lambeth as a whole, at about 36 per cent: in two wards – Ferndale and Tulse Hill – it is 49 per cent. Within the overall population of the borough, those of non-white origin are disproportionately represented among the younger age groups. In 1978 about 39 per cent of those aged under fifteen and 29 per cent of those aged between fifteen and twenty-four belonged to non-white ethnic groups. Together the non-white groups provide more than 40 per cent of children of secondary school age. Again, in the Brixton area, the percentage of young black people is even more pronounced. In the Tulse Hill and Herne Hill wards, which provided the focus of the April disorders, black people form 30 per cent of the overall population, but 40 per cent of the nought to eighteen-year-olds and 50 per cent of the nineteen- to twenty-one-year-olds.

(2) THE BLACK COMMUNITY IN BRIXTON
(a) The family
The older generation of black people in Brixton largely came to Britain as immigrants in the late 1940s, and in the 1950s and 1960s. They came in response to the demand from Britain for unskilled workers and in a search for better economic and social conditions. As immigrants to a strange country, they undoubtedly experienced problems in adjusting to a different culture and way of life, as well as, on occasion, hostility and discrimination from the host community. Their aspirations for themselves and for their children were eloquently put to me in evidence by, among others, the Brixton Domino and Social Club, as were the difficulties of adjustment they faced. One particular difficulty mentioned was that which

the relatively permissive attitude of British society towards the disciplining of children presented for at least some West Indian parents in bringing up their families.

In raising their children, the older generation of black people had to do without the support of the extended network of kin which is a feature of traditional West Indian society. Though recent years have, no doubt, witnessed changes in the pattern of Caribbean society, it was, and largely remains today, the custom for women – mothers, grandmothers, and aunts – to hold the extended family together. They offered security to the young, the old, and the disabled members of the family; and they imposed a strict discipline upon the children. The role of the man was at best supportive, but seldom dominant. At worst, he was an absentee of little or no significance. It is no cause for surprise that the impact of British social conditions on the matriarchal extended-family structure of the West Indian immigrants has proved to be severe. Mothers, who in the West Indies formed the focus of the family, became in many cases wage-earners who were absent from the family home. Some idea of the destructive changes wrought in their family lives by their new circumstances can be got from a few statistics. The percentage of children in care and of single-parent families in the black community is noticeably higher than one would expect in relation to the proportion of black people in the community as a whole. Fifty per cent of single-parent families in the Borough of Lambeth in 1978 were non-white. The two wards where the April disorders were centred – Tulse Hill and Herne Hill – contain some 22 per cent of all the single-parent households in Lambeth and 2.1 per cent of the nought to eighteen age group in those wards are in care. Of the 185 children in care in those two wards on 10 September 1980, 112 (61 per cent) were black. In addition, the Melting Pot Foundation, which provides hostel accommodation for young black people, has estimated that 200–300 young blacks are homeless, sleeping rough or squatting in the Brixton area.

(b) Education

The children of the first generation of West Indian immigrants were in many cases born in this country. They (the second generation, whether born in this country or not) and the third generation which is now emerging share, for the most part, the aspirations and expectations of other British young people. There is overwhelming evidence, however, that they have failed to benefit from our society to the extent that they might reasonably have expected. In particular, the underachievement of West Indian children at school has been well chronicled recently in the Rampton report. Though the extent and causes of their underachievement remain a matter of controversy, I have received evidence from many organizations and individuals pointing to the failure of black youths to acquire sufficiently early the skills of language and literacy, and to the sense of disappointment and frustration which at least some black parents and children feel in the education system. But, while the existence of complaints about schooling is in no doubt, it is clear from the evidence I have received from the Inner London Education Authority, which my own visit to Tulse Hill School has confirmed, that much dedicated work is being done in the schools. The problems which have to be solved, if deprivation and alienation are to be overcome, have been identified – namely, teaching a command of the English language, a broad education in the humanities designed to help the various ethnic groups (including the 'host community') to understand each other's background and culture, and the basic training in the skills necessary to obtain work in the technological economy of the modern world; and methods, including a revolution in curriculum, to deal with these problems are being developed and put into operation. Nevertheless, it is clear that, to quote the careful words of the House of Commons Select Committee on Home Affairs in its recent report on Racial Disadvantage, 'it has long been evident that we have not got ethnic minority education right . . .'

(c) Unemployment
As the Select Committee in the same report wisely say, 'Disadvantage in education and employment are the two most crucial facets of racial disadvantage. They are closely connected. Without a decent education and the qualifications which such education alone can provide, a school-leaver is unlikely to find the sort of job to which he aspires, or indeed any job. Conversely, pupils who learn from older friends of the degree of difficulty encountered in finding employment may well be discouraged from striving to achieve at school. In other words, there is no point in getting ethnic minority education right if we do not at the same time sort out racial disadvantage in employment, and vice versa.'

When the young people of Brixton leave school, many of them, white and black, face unemployment. This reflects both the general economic recession from which the country is at present suffering and the contraction in the economic and industrial base of the inner city. In early 1981, unemployment in the area of Brixton Employment Office stood at 13 per cent. For black people, the percentage is estimated to be higher. The level of ethnic minority unemployment as a proportion of total unemployment at Brixton Employment Office in May 1981 was 25.4 per cent. Over the year to February 1981, total unemployment in Great Britain increased by nearly 66 per cent, compared with 82 per cent for the ethnic minorities alone. There are indications in the evidence I have received that unemployment among members of the ethnic minorities is of longer duration than that among the white population. Most significant, blacks are without doubt overrepresented among the registered and unregistered young unemployed, as a study by researchers from Liverpool University confirms. In the area of the Brixton Employment Office the rate of registered unemployed among black males under nineteen has been estimated at 55 per cent. According to the Manpower Services Commission:

> Unemployment among young people aged 16–18 in Lambeth has risen faster over the past year than for older age groups. This is true both for total and for ethnic minority unemployment . . ., and young people form an increasing proportion of those on the unemployment register.

(d) Discrimination
The reasons for the higher level of unemployment among young black people are, no doubt, many and various. Lack of qualifications, difficulties arising from unrealistic expectations, bad time-keeping, unwillingness to travel and, most important of all, trouble with the English language are factors which, it has been suggested to me, play a part. It seems clear, however, that discrimination – by employers and at the work place – is a factor of considerable importance, and one for which the sustained efforts of the local authority, the Careers Service and the Manpower Services Commission to place young black people in work cannot easily compensate. Much of the evidence of discrimination is indirect rather than direct; but I have no doubt that it is a reality which all too often confronts the black youths of Brixton.

Discriminatory and hostile behaviour on racial grounds is not confined to the area of employment. There is evidence that it occurs not only among school children and in the street but, unintentionally no doubt, in the provision of some local authority services, principally housing. It was alleged by some of those who made representations to me that Britain is an institutionally racist society. If by that is meant that it is a society which knowingly, as a matter of policy, discriminates against black people, I reject the allegation. If, however, the suggestion being made is that practices may be adopted by public bodies as well as by private individuals which are unwittingly discriminatory against black people, then this is an allegation which deserves serious consideration, and, where proved, swift remedy.

(e) The young people of Brixton: a people of the street
Many of the young people of Brixton are therefore born and raised in insecure social and economic conditions and in an impoverished physical environment. They share the desires and expectations which our materialist society encourages. At the same time, many of them fail to achieve educational success and on leaving school face the stark prospect of unemployment. Many of these difficulties face white as well as black youngsters, but it is clear that they bear particularly heavily on young blacks. In addition, young black people face the burden of discrimination,

much of it hidden and some of it unconscious and unintended. Without close parental support, with no job to go to and with few recreational facilities available, the young black person makes his life on the streets and in the seedy commercially run clubs of Brixton. There he meets criminals, who appear to have no difficulty in obtaining the benefits of a materialist society. The process was described to me in evidence by the Railton Road Youth and Community Centre as follows:

Young people around in the streets all day, with nothing to do and nowhere to go, get together in groups and the 'successful' criminal has a story to tell. So one evil has bred another, and as unemployment has grown in both older and younger generations crime has become more commonplace and more acceptable. This is a vicious circle to which there is no present end in sight.

Many young black people do not of course resort to crime. Nor, recent research has suggested, would it be correct to conclude that young black people are wholly alienated from British society as a result of the deprivations they suffer. But it would be surprising if they did not feel a sense of frustration and deprivation. And living much of their lives on the streets, they are brought into contact with the police who appear to them as the visible symbols of the authority of a society which has failed to bring them its benefits or do them justice. . . .

Conclusions

The social conditions in Brixton – many of which are to be found in other inner city areas – do not provide an excuse for disorder. They cannot justify attacks on the police in the streets, arson, or riot. All those who in the course of the disorders in Brixton and elsewhere engaged in violence against the police were guilty of grave criminal offences, which society, if it is to survive, cannot condone. Sympathy for, and understanding of, the plight of young black people, which I would expect to find in British society now that the facts are widely known, are a good reason for political, social and economic aid, and for a coordinated effort by Government to provide it, but they are no reason for releasing young black people from the responsibilities for public order which they share with the rest of us – and with the police.

Nor should it be assumed that nothing is being done for young black people in Brixton and elsewhere, or that Brixton is an area in which deprivation and decay are unrelieved by any hopeful features. It is clear from their evidence that Lambeth Borough Council are acutely aware of the problems of the community and of its black members in particular. In

October 1978 they adopted a comprehensive policy to promote equal opportunities and combat racial or other disadvantage, and they also set up a Race Relations Unit within the Office of the Borough's Chief Executive to develop and advise on such matters. They have taken particular steps to improve their housing allocation and employment recruitment policies. Substantial funds have been made available by Central Government through, for example, grants pursuant to Section 11 of the Local Government Act 1966, under the Urban Programme and, most recently, through the Inner City Partnership: about £9 million of funds have, I understand, been allocated to the Partnership in the financial year 1981/82.

There is much in Brixton, and it is a tribute to its people that this is so, which is positive and creative: one only has to walk the streets to appreciate the vigour and the liveliness of its multiracial society. Many people who live in Brixton have emphasized to me its positive features – not least the generally amicable relations between its black and white inhabitants – and their pleasure in living there.

At the same time, the disorders in Brixton cannot be fully understood unless they are seen in the context of the complex political, social and economic factors to which I have briefly referred. In analysing communal disturbances such as those in Brixton and elsewhere, to ignore the existence of these factors is to put the nation in peril.

The social and economic plight of the ethnic minorities in the United Kingdom has been researched in great depth and is now well known; and I have had the advantage of a great volume of evidence researching, exploring and explaining it. The foregoing outline (for it is no more) of the relevant conditions has drawn heavily on this evidence. Although there is evidence to suggest that the position of the ethnic minority groups has seen some improvement relative to the rest of the population in recent years, overall they suffer from the same deprivations as the 'host community' (i.e. the white population), but much more acutely. Their lives are led largely in the poorer and more deprived areas of our great cities. Unemployment and poor housing bear on them very heavily: and the educational system has not adjusted itself satisfactorily to their needs. Their difficulties are intensified by the sense they have of a concealed discrimination against them, particularly in relation to job opportunities and housing. Some young blacks are driven by their despair into feeling that they are rejected by the society of which they rightly believe they are members and in which they would wish to enjoy the same opportunities and to accept the same risks as everyone else. But their experience leads them to believe that their opportunities are less and their risks are greater. Young black people feel neither socially nor economically secure.

In addition they do not feel politically secure. Their sense of rejection is not eased by the low level of black representation in our elective political institutions. Their sense of insecurity is not relieved by the liberty our law provides to those who march and demonstrate in favour of tougher immigration controls and 'repatriation' of the blacks. Rightly or wrongly, young black people do not feel politically secure, any more than they feel economically or socially secure.

The accumulation of these anxieties and frustrations and the limited opportunities of airing their grievances at national level in British society encourage them to protest on the streets. And it is regrettably also true that some are tempted by their deprivations into crime, particularly street crime – robbery, car theft and the pick-pocketing offences: in other words, some of them go 'mugging'. They live their lives on the street, having often nothing better to do: they make their protest there: and some of them live off street crime. The recipe for a clash with the police is therefore ready-mixed: and it takes little, or nothing, to persuade them that the police, representing an establishment which they see as insensitive to their plight, are their enemies. If not 'anti-police', they are against the policemen whom they see as pursuing and harassing them on the streets.

None of these features can perhaps usefully be described as a *cause* of the disorders, either in Brixton or elsewhere. Indeed, there are, undoubtedly, parts of the country which are equally deprived where disorder did not occur. But taken together, they provide a set of social *conditions* which create a predisposition towards violent protest. Where deprivation and frustration exist on the scale to be found among the young black people of Brixton, the probability of disorder must, therefore, be strong. Moreover, many of them, it is obvious, believe with justification, that violence, though wrong, is a very effective means of protest: for, by attracting the attention of the mass media of communication, they get their message across to the people as a whole.

The Disturbances in Manchester
M. Venner

Reprinted with permission from Mary Venner, 'The Disturbances in Manchester',
New Community, vol. IX, no. 3, Winter 1981–Spring 1982, pp. 374–7

*The Hytner report (Report of the Moss Side Enquiry Panel to the Leader of
the Greater Manchester Council, Manchester, 30 September 1981)*

The Hytner report on the Moss Side riots in Manchester was published a
month earlier than Lord Scarman's report on the Brixton disorders, but
many of its conclusions about the background conditions and the more
immediate causes of the riots foreshadowed what Scarman was to say. On
some points the similarity between these independent investigations is
striking, especially in their discussions of the hostility of young people
towards the police. The Manchester report, for instance, describes the
attack on the Moss Side police station on the night of 8 July as 'a
spontaneous eruption of hatred against the police by young people',
echoing not only the ideas but also the language of Scarman.

But the Manchester report also points out the differences between what
happened in Moss Side and what happened in Brixton. These differences
exist not only because Moss Side is different from Brixton, but because
the disturbances in Manchester occurred well after the first outbreaks of
trouble in Brixton, Southall and Toxteth, and were largely an imitation of
them.

Background to the enquiry

The five-member enquiry panel, chaired by Benet Hytner QC, was set up
by the Greater Manchester Council (GMC) at the end of July 1981 to
examine the circumstances leading up to the disturbances in Moss Side on
8 and 9 July 1981, the way the trouble was dealt with by the various
bodies concerned, and the steps which should be taken to ensure that it
does not happen again.

The panel had no statutory powers to call witnesses or grant immunity
from prosecution, and the proceedings were fairly informal. The report
admits that this limited the effectiveness of the enquiry in some ways and
the panel decided that it was therefore unable to answer some of the
questions posed in its terms of reference. The Introduction to the report

also explains the difficult relationships that arose between the panel and the Manchester City Council and the Chief Constable of the Manchester Police, Mr James Anderton, and also with some community groups who decided to boycott the investigation. The enquiry was in progress at a time when the Police Committee of the recently elected Labour-controlled GMC was in dispute with the Chief Constable, and the report is very careful not to cause any further difficulties, while at the same time expressing its disappointment over the information with which the Chief Constable provided it, apparently with some reluctance. The panel also specifically avoided making any recommendations on matters outside the jurisdiction of the Greater Manchester Council and so says nothing about unemployment and current economic policies.

The report is written with clarity, tact and some humour (especially with reference to local football clubs). In outlining the environment of Moss Side, it emphasizes that the area is no worse, and is in some respects better than other parts of Manchester, or any other inner city area. Almost the entire district has been redeveloped by the council fairly recently, and no matter what criticisms can be made of the architecture of modern council estates, the quality of the housing is high and there are few slums. The area is well endowed with schools and its youth club facilities are probably better than elsewhere in the city. The Moss Side shopping centre is criticized for being poorly designed, underutilized and depressing, and the report makes suggestions for structural alterations to improve security and provide for evening activities. It concludes, however, that although the environment of Moss Side could be improved there is no evidence that it contributed significantly to the disturbances.

The Manchester City Council comes in for some criticism for being inefficient and overly bureaucratic, and for failing to consult local residents on development plans. It is suggested that some form of ombudsman is needed to monitor the relationship between the Council and the Community.

The panel was presented with much evidence that there is no friction between the various ethnic groups in Moss Side, although it feels that this view may be a little exaggerated. A very small proportion of white residents resent and fear blacks, while there are also some blacks who are jealous of Asians and feel resentful towards whites. In general, however, relations between ethnic groups are healthy and friendly and the panel sees this harmony as the result of years of hard work by many people.

The average age of Moss Side residents is lower than elsewhere, meaning that there is a preponderance of teenagers, and unemployment among these under-nineteen-year-olds appears to be as high as 60 per cent. The rate is even higher for black teenagers, and the report emphasizes the devastating effects of this unemployment on young people.

Police-community relations

When the Manchester report was released the media were surprised to find that it was not critical of Chief Constable Anderton. In fact, the report heaps praise on him for his hatred of racial prejudice and his efforts to promote harmony between the police and the ethnic minorities. It is not, however, so complimentary towards other members of his police force, who are described as preponderantly young, inexperienced, and driving around in panda cars. These officers are contrasted with the Community Contact Police who visit schools, organize activities for young people, and consult with ethnic minority groups. Moss Side teenagers know and like the Community Contact Police, but they most definitely do not like the operational police, and they distinguish clearly between them.

This hostility to the police force in general is based on what the young people regard as harassment. The enquiry heard unconfirmed allegations of capricious use of 'stop and search' powers, illegal detentions and racial abuse of young people by police officers. The number of teenagers in the district, their habit of congregating in the streets or shopping centre, and their enforced idleness due to unemployment, would be bound to lead to friction with the police at times, but not on the scale uncovered by the enquiry. The report suggests that the allegations which were made to the panel should be investigated, even if there is insufficient evidence to lay specific charges against any police officer.

The report also discusses the police complaints procedure and criticizes its lack of independence, and the small number of complaints successfully investigated. The public feels that there is no redress if they are mistreated by the police and suggests an independent mediator is required to pass complaints on to the police for investigation.

The panel largely dismisses suggestions of outside involvement from the ultra-right or ultra-left in the disturbances. The National Front is not active in Moss Side and, although the (ultra-left) Workers' Revolutionary Party and the Socialist Workers' Party are both thriving in the climate of disaffection and hostility to the police existing among Manchester's young unemployed, the enquiry felt that their success had been exaggerated. The report argues that extremists are not as much of a threat to society as the conditions on which they feed, and that Rastafarians and other peaceful 'black consciousness' groups are not 'extremists' and should not be treated as such by the police.

How the riots began: the 'myth of Moss Side'

After this thorough and serious analysis of the background to the Moss Side disturbances, and the factors which did *not* contribute to the trouble, the actual description of the outbreak of violence and its immediate causes reads more like a comedy.

The committee considers that what it calls the 'myth of Moss Side' was largely to blame for the fact that the riots occurred where and when they did. In the years before its redevelopment, Moss Side had been a slum and was associated with prostitution and crime. By the 1960s it had also become known for its West Indian population, drugs and illegal drinking. These widely held notions about the area were once based on reality, to a certain extent, but today they are no longer true. Slum clearance has removed most of the brothels, the illegal clubs and criminal hangouts, and expectations of racial tension have diminished. Yet the popular image of Moss Side lives on and, when riots occurred in Brixton, followed by Southall and Liverpool, people believed that if it happened in Manchester it would happen first in Moss Side. This turned out to be a self-fulfilling prophecy. The committee is convinced that the first bricks were thrown at about 2.30 a.m. on Wednesday 8 July, after a few white youths leaving a club in Princess Road had taunted their black friends that Manchester blacks were slower than their Brixton and Toxteth brethren. This incident was almost certainly spontaneous, and the rapid appearance of petrol bombs did not indicate any conspiracy or foreplanning, as they are easy to make, and had been used in other criminal disturbances in Manchester before this.

Although the young people who took part in the three nights of rioting that followed had genuine grievances against the police, and many reasons for feeling alienated from society, the immediate causes of the disturbances did not lie in such abstract realms. It all started because a few young people 'who had not much respect for the property of others or the law of the land . . . decided on the instant to copy, in Moss Side, conduct which had occurred elsewhere and which they felt was expected of them' (para 33.9). From then on a number of differently motivated groups of people joined in, some with criminal intentions, some looking for excitement, some simply to loot, and some expressing frustration and hostilities which would have remained unexpressed if they had felt they had some stake in society or if they possessed respect for authority or the law. Those who looted were mostly middle-aged and white.

During the Wednesday that followed, the committee believes, many people came into the Moss Side area from other parts of Manchester and possibly also from Liverpool and London, but they do not believe there was any significant involvement by outside organizers and troublemakers. Undoubtedly a few people tried to exploit the events to their own political advantage, but evidence suggests that the rioters took little notice of them.

The report finds it more worrying that the behaviour of some members of the Manchester police force during the disturbances was less than commendable, especially on the third night, when young officers were alleged to have driven around the area 'actively spoiling for trouble with young blacks', shouting racial insults and taunting them to come and fight. The committee points out that most of the police involved were not very much older than the rioters, and that they had been attacked with firebombs and bricks, so a certain amount of overreaction was not surprising. They conclude that there is no effective way of policing a riot once it reaches a certain size. They also point out that many young people seem unable to appreciate the consequences of their actions, and suggest that educationalists and youth workers should consider ways of impressing on school children and young people the fact that kicking someone in the head, using a flick knife, or throwing a petrol bomb can kill.

Conclusions and recommendations

The report concludes that the riots started mainly because they were expected; that people of all colours and ages took part for many different reasons; that a number of older white men and women joined in primarily to loot, whereas older West Indians and Asians did not; and that there is not necessarily a relationship between the riots and the number of West Indians in the area, although both may be related to the level of youth unemployment.

The panel approves of the Chief Constable's 'low profile' approach to policing on the second night of the disturbances. It would have been unrealistic to have expected the police to control the rioting and, although the level of property damage was high, there were very few police casualties and no loss of life. It recommends that allegations of overreaction by the police should be investigated, either to take action to prevent their recurrence, or to clear the reputation of the police force in the eyes of the significant section of the Moss Side community which believes these allegations. The report's main recommendations concern compensation claims for riot damage, reforms to the police complaints procedure, and an investigation into allegations of police harassment of young people.

The Hytner report is a comprehensive historical record of the events in Moss Side, and of the social background to them, but the two are not necessarily causally related. The immediate cause of the violence, as it is described in the report, was the example set by earlier riots elsewhere in the country, combined with opportunism, the quest for excitement and the expectation that the violence would happen. The motives of everyone involved are suspect. In uncovering the apparently trivial origins of the disturbances, however, the report sheds light on pre-existing conditions which cannot with certainty be said to have caused the riots, but which have been revealed by them.

Manchester Pakistanis

P. Werbner

Reprinted with permission from Pnina Werbner, 'Manchester Pakistanis: lifestyles, ritual and the making of social distinctions', *New Community*, vol. IX, no. 2, Autumn 1981, pp. 216–28

Urban lifestyles and distinctions

The portrayal of radically different urban lifestyles, pioneered by the Chicago School, had its counterpart in studies showing the varying lifestyles within immigrant communities. In recent years a renewed interest in black urban lifestyles in particular has been based on a polar contrast between 'mainstream' and 'ghetto specific' lifestyles. The 'mainstream' pole, representing the preferred lifestyle of the wider society, is sometimes viewed as dominant, with other lifestyles as a continuum evolving partly as rejections of unachievable mainstream ideals. A somewhat analogous contrast is often drawn between 'traditional' and 'Western' lifestyles, led by immigrants. Studies of Asians in Britain, for example, regularly assume a clear polar contrast in the lifestyles of 'traditional' Asian villagers and 'middle-class' Asian townsmen.

In the present paper, however, I attempt to show that both the transposition of culture from Pakistan to Britain, and the adoption of 'Western' practices by local Pakistanis, can only be understood in the light of variations in several fundamental lifestyle parameters, rather than through a single basic contrast. The analysis is indebted to studies by Bott of conjugal role variations in English families, Mayer and Jacobson of variations in the behaviour of labour migrants in town, Hannerz of black ghetto lifestyles, and Cohen of transformations in urban lifestyles.

An examination of these studies reveals the shared attempt to relate several, apparently disparate, social aspects of urban living:

1. the existence of distinctive, 'exclusive' cultural beliefs and practices among different groups and categories of urban dwellers;
2. the 'shape' of their members' social networks, and especially whether they are 'close knit' or not;
3. the bases for recruitment to these networks, and particularly whether they lead to 'closed' or 'open' networks;
4. the domestic division of labour, especially whether conjugal roles are segregated or not;

5. the economic behaviour, economic circumstances and occupational status of urban dwellers;
6. the effect of geographical mobility, and the management of social relations spanning geographical distance in town and beyond it.

That such social dimensions have repeatedly been related to each other is due to the central concern of these studies with the interdependence of cultural beliefs and values, economic behaviour, and patterns of social association, as these are manifested in towns. How is the 'culture' of townsmen to be defined, and is it a determining force, or merely an epiphenomenon of economic and political factors? Does an understanding of interpersonal relations provide insights into urban 'social structure', neglected in an exclusive focus on factors such as occupation, class, or the organization of the city? Underlying these questions is an attempt to explain the persistence of shared, distinctive ways of life in town, even among persons of different occupations and income. The present study attempts to argue that, within ethnic communities in town, sameness is often asserted in the face of difference, while at the same time internal forms of discrimination are signalled defying this uniformity. . . .

Modes of behaviour can be used by actors to signal moral approval or disapproval, as well as social superiority or inferiority. Very generally, the messages that urban dwellers convey through their choices of lifestyle appear to fall into three categories: (1) messages of dominance and superiority: (2) messages of sameness and conformity; (3) messages of 'independence', often containing moral reflections on more 'conventional' lifestyles (as in the case of currently familiar 'alternative' lifestyles).

Hence, lifestyles relate to actors' perceptions, and acceptance of underlying power relations in the society, and are an integral and vital aspect of the economic strategies they pursue. The messages conveyed are greatly complicated by townsmen's cultural biases, on the one hand, and by their prior and current levels of income, on the other hand. At any given level of income, townsmen may choose to convey different messages – of dominance, conformity or independence. Moreover, at any given income level townsmen may choose to signify their income or to hide it, sometimes with the aim of achieving an even higher level of income (through saving, investment, etc.) in the future. Paradoxes in the meanings of objects and modes of behaviour may also emerge at the extreme ends of the income scale. Among Pakistanis, for example, it is often the case that in Pakistan both rich and poor do not observe strict purdah or expect women to wear *burqas* (outer gowns with veils); whereas observance of purdah is typical of lower-middle-class behaviour.

Such paradoxes derive partly from attempts by established high-income groups to distinguish themselves from the *nouveau riche*. The message conveyed by these long-established groups appears to deny the full value of their wealth and its purchasing power, although in reality their discreet lifestyle is often costly, and they continue to control the centres of power and finance in the society. Their more subtle lifestyle is, however, also a subject of emulation. Lifestyle meanings are thus built around transformations and negations of prior meanings and, in the cases discussed below, these all occur within the framework of a capitalist, and basically consumer-orientated society.

The lifestyles of immigrants

The lifestyles pursued by immigrants and labour migrants follow a predictable pattern which is explicable in just such transformational terms. The initial period in town is usually one in which single men share lodgings and expenses. This migrant lifestyle is commonly found throughout urban centres of migration: indeed, it is a typical 'alternative' lifestyle, associated, in the case of migrants, with a virtual absence of attention to the values held by the host society. In practical terms it allows migrants to live frugally, at little expense, and is thus primarily a practical means of saving. They care little about the messages their poor living conditions convey, for the audience is absent, since their strategy is one of deferred social 'dominance' – on their planned return home. Apparently, sheer efficiency is here emphasized at the expense of symbolic differentiation. Religion, if practised at all, is fittingly puritanical and abstemious in nature. However, reports by researchers on this phase of migration indicate that the self-denial and sharing associated with such a 'sensible' strategy for saving often assume, in themselves, moral and symbolic meaning for migrants.

The decision to remain in town on a semi-permanent basis, and the arrival of wives and families, signal the end of this early phase of migration, and the beginning of acquisitive behaviour with its associated encoding of symbolic differentiation. New-old codes develop, shared within the migrant community but often remaining only marginally integrated into the codes of the host society. Among Pakistani migrants in Manchester, rapid social mobility as well as prior social status before migration have soon become factors signalled through variations in lifestyle; and, as the lifestyles of the wealthy have become more flamboyant and extravagant, some – but not all – of the lower income groups have devised new strategies of economic behaviour to enable them to emulate these lifestyles. In the process the old values and customs have been compromised, or revived, prior relations rejected or renewed, and a new social dynamic set in motion. During this period rituals and ceremonials have emerged as important foci of interaction, while religion – where it exists – has become more demonstrative and assertive.

The lifestyles developed among Manchester Pakistanis, as among other townsmen, stem in part from deliberate messages which they wish to convey about themselves. These messages, however, are often at variance with the interpretations made by a sceptical audience: thus, the highly mobile are scrutinized according to a subtle code of distinctions recognized by Pakistanis of urban, high-income families. In decoding, they also demystify. In this sense, actors' choices are limited. Moreover, choice is also, and more importantly, restricted by historical circumstances and by the economic or social priorities which migrants set themselves. In particular, their choice of associates – their personal network – determines the patterns of social exchange and expenditure pursued, while the choice of economic goals and paths of mobility determines the domestic division of labour.

Constraints on urban behaviour

A discussion of lifestyles cannot, therefore, remain at a level of codes and meanings: the analysis requires an understanding of the social constraints affecting migrants' behaviour and the opportunities open to them.

A major hypothesis put forward in the literature, following Bott's and Mayer's works, is that townsmen who are 'embedded' within a long-term 'close-knit' network of kinsmen or friends retain distinctive modes of behaviour setting them apart from other townsmen. Relations of trust and mutual support within the network are associated with an insistence on the upholding of group values. The expectation that such relations will indeed be continuous or renewable over a long period is crucial for retaining the individual's loyalty to group norms, as is the economic protection afforded. It should be remarked here that the protection is not merely in terms of possible future risks: the network also provides a prescription of economic aims and aspirations. It sets its aims and their means of achievement simultaneously. Interest is thus defined by the group and achieved through loyalty to it.

Not all labour migrants are, however, part of such close-knit networks. Some choose to be free to seize economic opportunities and remain highly mobile, while others live in highly transient areas or go through different career phases. An important question is whether prior background or current interests determine the variable tendency towards encapsulation, and the emphasis on cultural distinctiveness by migrants in town. While Mayer argues for the primacy of cultural background, Cohen has argued for a *process* of encapsulation stemming from a current competition for scarce resources between ethnic groups. He observed what he called an 'intensification' of religiosity in this process of competition, and his argument is, as I shall show, pertinent, but to be modified on the basis of variations in Pakistani lifestyles found in Manchester. These relate not merely to the intensification of ritual but to the role that women play in ritual and exchange relations, and in the family economy, with consequent implications for their domestic roles and position within the family.

Ritual and geographical mobility

An important contrast between the organization of ethnic groups and the host society rests on the ritual behaviour of migrants. . . . Bott argued that residential and occupational mobility amongst English families usually results in more loose-knit networks, or networks with a number of separate clusters. Among Pakistanis transactional relations of a ritual or ceremonial kind are important in counteracting tendencies towards the disintegration of close-knit networks. Occupational and residential mobility does not necessarily 'scatter' networks of friends, who continue to be gathered on ritual occasions. Such occasions are also a means of incorporating newcomers into an existing circle of friends, thus sustaining a relatively dense network despite changes in personnel.

The continuing density of migrants' networks must also be understood in relation to the type of network maintained by certain pivotal members of the community. These 'men of reputation' tend to have a far greater 'range' in their personal networks, spanning people of different status and lifestyles. Through the mediation of such men and women, who are commonly invited to most ceremonials within their circle and are often also active in voluntary associations, most Pakistanis living in Manchester can be contacted via a limited number of intermediaries, following well-tested avenues of communication.

Hence, convening of domestic and life crisis rituals in town serves not merely to superimpose 'moral' bonds where prior 'economic' or 'political' bonds exist. It also serves to sustain relations over time and to mobilize people who are otherwise residentially scattered. Voluntary organizations serve a similar purpose and they too add a further dimension to the already complex (or multiplex) relations between members of a 'close-knit' circle of friends and kinsmen.

Exchange relations and ritual

The mosque is a central ritual meeting place for those men who attend it regularly. But the mosque is also the great equalizer. Its ritual emphasizes the equality of men rather than their differences. Distinctions are obliterated, as the congregation stands or prostrates itself, foreheads touching the ground, like a tidal wave rising and falling. Instead of the mosque, it is in the domestic rituals and ceremonies celebrated in the home that distinctions and variations emerge. Rituals vary not only in their figurative elaboration but in the size of the congregations gathered, the quantities of food served, the cost of gifts exchanged, the frequency of events convened and attended. Weddings may last for several weeks and cost thousands of pounds. Birthday parties for young children may gather dozens of adults and include a full meal. *Eid* gatherings may be large or intimate. Furthermore, in addition to life crisis rituals or ceremonials and festive dinners, communal Koran readings (usually known as *khatam koran*) may be convened relatively frequently to fulfil personal vows or when embarking on a trip or venture, and may vary in size and cost.

Rituals and ceremonies are thus marked by crucial variations in the form of ceremonial exchange relations which they generate. Particularly significant is the degree to which the norm of 'excessive' giving prevails in ceremonial exchanges between kin and friends. This notion refers to an almost competitive, potlatch-like form of transactional behaviour, to the giving of more than can be consumed, to overreciprocating. It contains the idea of providing more than is strictly needed or is normally consumed on secular occasions. Hence, among the families of Pakistani businessmen networks are large, and competition for both reputation and status proceeds through large-scale feasting events. Weddings in particular are costly and elaborate affairs. Professionals, too, follow a norm of excessive reciprocation, but their networks of friends are smaller than those of the businessmen.

Related to the mode of exchange is the extent to which a system of ceremonial prestations is transposed – with or without changes – from Pakistan. An examination of the contrasting lifestyles of Pakistanis in the city shows that they vary in the mode and intensity of ritual and ceremonial performance, in the density of their social networks and in the multiplicity of contexts in which their relations coincide. The problem is one of explaining why it is that some Pakistanis in Manchester spend much of their time in a seemingly endless round of weddings and funerals, parting dinners and birthday parties, communal Koran readings and Muslim festivals. This round of ceremonial and ritual events is, perhaps, what most strikingly distinguishes their lifestyle from that of other Pakistani migrants who actively avoid frequent and overcostly exchange relations with their fellow migrants. They prefer to perform most important rituals at home, in Pakistan, sending money for the performance of the rituals to home-based kinsmen. They also prefer to bury their dead at home, and spend a great deal of money on the repatriation of bodies. In some senses, they still remain 'rooted' in Pakistan.

The performance by migrants of domestic rituals and ceremonies in Manchester is given a central place in my discussion because the transposition of such rituals is one mode enabling migrants to emphasize the distinctive culture uniting them with their fellow migrants, and separating them from other groups in the society. Such transposition is therefore not only indicative of the establishment of local roots, but also results in the drawing of a cultural-cum-social boundary around those who convene the rituals. At the same time *domestic* rituals and ceremonies draw social boundaries internal to the ethnic group as a whole, around select categories of people. Such rituals and ceremonies are therefore both inclusive and exclusive. They are 'inclusive' in the sense that the symbols in the rituals are shared and understood by all Pakistanis, sometimes by all Muslims. They are 'exclusive' in the sense that the convener is able to select the congregation attending the event, to include some and exclude others from it. Such events are therefore 'indexical' (indicative of social distinctions).

Ritual and social status

Variations in lifestyles relate to the perceptions that migrants have of their social 'status'. Pakistanis, like other South Asian people, are extremely conscious of status differentials and attach great importance to preserving and, if possible, advancing their status; however, the strategies which they pursue towards this end differ.

Hence, like 'Red' migrants in East London, South Africa, some Pakistanis seem to be concerned primarily with their status advancement in their home of origin in Pakistan, or in competition with kin residing in Britain (an extension of the home network). Others are far more concerned with their current status in Manchester Pakistani society as it has evolved in the city, although they still attempt to raise their status at home as well. It should be stressed that, for most migrants living in Manchester, their social networks locally are not mere extensions of those at home. Moreover, the great majority invest money both in Britain and in Pakistan, sending remittances home even in cases where families there are well off, or where most of their members are already in Britain. And, in addition, most migrants perform some rituals in Pakistan and some in Manchester. They also go on prolonged visits to Pakistan, laden down with costly gifts. In other words, most migrants are 'double-rooted'. The value placed on *local* relations, however, and with it the location and frequency of ritual performance, varies a great deal.

The ranking of priorities adduced in making allocations of limited resources lies at the heart of this variation. Status may be proved through the acquisition of material goods, but it is displayed in the process of ongoing exchange relationships. Migrants must allocate the resources at their disposal to a number of different forms of investment and social exchange, expressing their commitment to, and long-term involvement in, different sections of their personal networks. Allocations must be made for capital investment in Pakistan and remittances to family there, mutual aid and capital investment locally, ritual and ceremonial exchange in Pakistan, and ritual and ceremonial exchange locally. Customary ceremonial exchange, known as *vartan bhanji* or *lena dena* ('take and give'), is practised mainly during *rites de passage*, but forms an integrated part of a more general system of loans and exchanges. Hence, both are relevant to the allocational pattern. It is in relation to the choice of allocations that the tensions in the processes of upward mobility emerge, between the desire to achieve local status within a recognized ranking system, and local 'reputation', measured as a focal position within a social network.

Among Pakistanis a 'reputation' is largely achieved through the convening of large-scale ceremonials and extravagant giving, which are considered a mark of generosity but are regarded as financially 'wasteful' by many migrants. An alternative possibility, especially among lower-income families, is to achieve a reputation for willingness to extend long-term loans and mutual aid, while at the same time avoiding costly ceremonial exchanges if possible. Although entailing present self-denial, mutual aid does not deplete migrants' capital resources, and yet it upholds their reputation for being trustworthy and reliable. For migrants avoiding ceremonials, investment in property and furniture then become a further sign of their 'respectability'. While this strategy is achieved at the expense of extensive sociability, it does allow for capital accumulation.

Constraints on migrants dictate that not all of them are able to avoid extending the largesse of ceremonial events. In the central residential cluster where lower-income Pakistani families predominate, intense sociability between neighbours often develops, and with it a greater frequency in the performance of domestic rituals. Costly gifting and extravagant hospitality have become the norm, despite the families' low incomes, as they emulate the lifestyles of the wealthy. 'Peripheral' residents who live in greater isolation and lack these frequent contexts for sociability are better able to save and invest. The 'spenders' in the central cluster usually save through rotating credit associations known as 'Kommitti' rather than by extending long-term, interest-free loans to one another as the 'savers' do.

Lower-income migrant families may be contrasted, therefore, according to the 'inclusiveness' or 'exclusiveness' of their networks. The 'savers' tend to have small, exclusive networks. They pick and choose friends very carefully, on the basis of select criteria and gradually increasing trust. They make a clear distinction between 'true' friends (*pakka dostan*) and mere acquaintances. By contrast, the low-income 'spenders' have large and 'open' networks and vast numbers of 'friends'. They are constantly caught up in rituals, ceremonials, and public events. Their networks are characterized by a constant turnover of personnel, with neighbours often predominating in day-to-day interaction.

A somewhat similar contrast may be drawn between wealthy business-men and professionals, including among the latter the more educated Pakistanis in blue-collar occupations. The wealthy are able to sustain large and wide-ranging family networks, by convening grandiose and costly ceremonial events. Professionals do not spare their largesse, but distribute it in smaller, and more exclusive networks.

Migrants' avoidance of, or participation in, intense ceremonial ex-changes is also constrained by past historical developments. Early migrants initiated a long 'chain of migration', which has resulted in high concentrations of previously known or connected people in Manchester. The close-knit networks emerging through chain migration appear to encourage the generation of internal competition and extravagant hospitality, as minor status discrepancies assume great significance within such networks. In the early days, the networks formed a support system which enabled migrants to venture successfully into trading. Their achievement of wealth has been uneven, generating the background for intense competition through extravagant giving.

To understand this requires insight into the paradoxical nature of friendship. Overgifting on ceremonial occasions, with its competitive overtones, is an intrinsic aspect of the balanced and equal nature of Pakistanis' friendships. The equality that friendship implies is thus a precarious one, since excessive overgifting may lead to a breakdown in relations. The paradox lies in the fact that it is through overreciprocating and the retention of outstanding debts that trust is generated, and trust is essential for migrants as they struggle to succeed as entrepreneurs in a strange country.

What, then, can be said regarding the role of domestic rituals and ceremonials in town? The evidence suggests that performance of ceremo-nial events occurs where townsmen, and especially townswomen, already have 'close-knit' networks, and these ceremonials in turn generate an *increase* in network density. Moreover, ritual relations come to be super-imposed on neighbourhood and business relations, creating multiplex relations and a multiplicity of contexts in which migrants interact. This leads to a possible explanation of how highly stratified ethnic communities in town express their internal differentiation while at the same time remaining encapsulated and distinctive.

Competition and normative behaviour

In their studies, Mayer and Bott both emphasized that close-knit networks generate greater moral control, and this, they argued, leads to normative *agreement*, and encourages the upholding of in-group cultural ideas and values. Close-knit networks are, however, also characterized, as I have argued above, by fierce internal competition, and this too must be taken account of in the explanation of the normative uniformity prevailing in such groups.

In the case of Manchester Pakistanis, internal competition within close-knit groups has led to an intensification of ritual and ceremonial behaviour and thus, in effect, to a greater emphasis on culturally distinct forms of activity. Clearly, competition here takes place within an agreed cultural code and the values that it establishes validate the continuing significance of the code for the competitors.

Internal competition amongst Pakistanis does not, however, generate only an emphasis on distinctive cultural values. It embraces also a tendency to acquire status 'emblems' such as consumer goods or higher education, in a system of values shared with the host society – and with urban society in Pakistan.

Hence, while Cohen focuses on the boundaries of the whole ethnic community, and Mayer emphasizes the upholding of cultural orthodoxy, the evidence from my research suggests that ritual and religiosity become vehicles for the display of social differences within an ethnic group, even as they continue to uphold the distinctiveness of the group as a whole. At the same time such internal competition leads to a breakdown of cultural exclusiveness, as material values shared with the host society come to signal status differences in the migrant community as well.

Women, networks, and conjugal roles

A move towards consumerism and ritual intensification is thus a change which the arrival of wives precipitated. But the status of women in some Pakistani families has itself undergone a marked transformation. The variations in conjugal roles between Pakistani families arise from families' perceptions of their relative local status in the community, in conjunction with their perception of their *expected* or rightful status. Where a family has entered fully into the fray of local competition a wife usually elects to work, for this increases the ability of her family to maintain an extravagant lifestyle. Once this choice has been made and a woman works, there is usually a great deal more equality in the relationship between the sexes, and a more flexible domestic division of labour. By contrast, where wives work very little or not at all, men tend to dominate the choice of friends and there is greater segregation of conjugal roles.

The flexibility of conjugal roles among Pakistani migrants is all the more remarkable because almost universally migrants come from backgrounds where strict conjugal role segregation is the rule. The factors bringing about this change can be summed up as follows:

Local competition for status plus low incomes	→	*Working women*	→	*Equality in conjugal role relations and a joint division of labour*	→	*Non-segregation of networks according to sex*

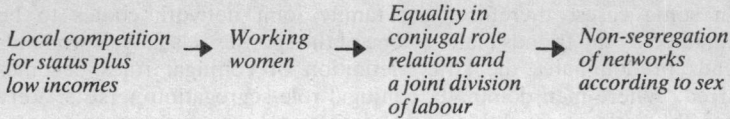

The processes of conjugal role transformation must be sought in the structure of the family social network. In an article reanalysing the 'Bott hypothesis', Kapferer argues that segregated conjugal roles stem from the separateness of husband and wife's network clusters, the absence of overlap between these clusters. He thus challenges Bott's proposition that the overall density of the family network determines conjugal role segregation.

Variations between Pakistani families point to the resolution of these two apparently conflicting hypotheses. The evidence suggests that conjugal role segregation is most crucially determined by 'primary' network associations, which are, or are not, restricted by sex, either male or female. Pakistanis sustain close friendships between couples, but often wives are primarily friendly with each other, just as husbands associate with one another. Their networks thus have a high density overall, yet can be split into two separate clusters, male and female (this pattern is typical, of course, of conjugal relations in rural societies).

Such a finding, however, simply removes the problem a step away. For why is it that a segregation of social networks by sex occurs? Clearly, immigrants are inclined to accept a view of male authority and a clear division of labour between the sexes: men act as chief breadwinners, women as mothers responsible for the domestic household. Islam dictates female purity, seclusion and separation between the sexes outside the immediate family circle.

What has occurred in the Manchester context is a modification of these ideas in practice, rather than their elimination in items of etiquette or in professed ideology. Sex-specific networks have developed because men are the breadwinners, and therefore there is a differential allocation of time available to men and women for developing close-knit networks. Such differences in time-allocation thus arise from occupational factors: men develop close friendships in factories during long hours of work together. During this time their wives may remain at home. If they take in home sewing, women in the central residential cluster often spend some hours socializing in each other's company, and they also accumulate the resources for sustaining elaborate ritual and ceremonial exchange relations. This allows them to develop large, female-centred networks, and they come to dominate the choice of family friends.

Where women do not work, or live removed from other women, they both lack independent resources and contexts of association. Their husbands' factory friends then dominate the family joint network.

In some cases, therefore, the family joint network comes to be dominated by the friends made by one of the spouses. Usually, if women's friends predominate, the strict definition of conjugal roles becomes blurred. Where men dominate, conjugal role segregation persists. Very generally, the spouse who is in the position to initiate the creation of a denser cluster of friends is more influential in shaping the joint network. Among professionals and some market traders separate clusters are not developed by spouses, for husbands and wives associate with other Pakistani friends mainly during their joint spare time, or run businesses jointly. In these cases relations between the sexes are much freer and the domestic division of labour extremely flexible. The argument can be summed up comparatively:

Women are affluent, or they work by taking in → *home sewing – and often live in the central cluster*	*Women have time and resources to develop denser female networks than husbands have* →	*Women determine joint family network.* → **Spenders**	*Not very strict conjugal role segregation, but* → *rituals segregated by sex*
Women don't work, or live isolated, while men work in factories with other Pakistanis →	*Men develop denser male-based networks than their wives* →	*Men determine joint family network.* → **Savers**	*Highly segregated conjugal roles, emphasis on* → *female modesty, few rituals convened*
Women and men work together, or in non-Pakistani work contexts →	*Spouses develop a network together (after work).* →	*Joint family network.* → **Spenders** *(but more are affluent and able to afford this)*	*Flexible division of labour, friendships not* → *restricted to the same sex, rituals usually held jointly, with men and women attending*

The 'traditional'/'modern' dichotomy

Interpersonal competition together with close friendship links are thus the inner force shaping different lifestyles, changing past values, increasing the possible behavioural models for consumption, domestic role arrangements, ritual customs, religiosity, and so forth. Yet throughout these changes, stereotypical mutual definitions by migrants of each other persist, hiding a multitude of changes, contradictions and situational interpretations. At this point the question raised in the introduction to this paper regarding the coded meanings signalled by variations in lifestyles can be dealt with.

'EDUCATED' AND 'VILLAGERS'

Particularly illuminating are the perceptions which Pakistanis from educated backgrounds have of the migrants around them. Many of these educated migrants tended at the time of the research to be in the ambivalent position of earning lower incomes than the very affluent, yet feeling superior to them in terms of their backgrounds and pedigrees. Thus an acceptable candidate for a professionals' circle was supposed to be 'educated' as opposed to a 'villager'. Yet the two concepts, which are employed as opposites, do not refer to the actual distinction between village and urban origin, nor do they measure accurately the amount of schooling that a person has. Rather, they refer to an attitude towards things Western and to a total mode of conduct in society. An 'educated' woman is one who wears Western-style clothes, or Indian-style *saris*, at least outside the house, who can speak English, who can hold a conversation with men, or indeed, with strangers, both men and women. A 'village' woman, by contrast, tends to wear traditional Pakistani baggy trousers and tunic, to know little or no English, to stick mainly to the company of women and to behave in an awkward way towards strangers – either ignoring them altogether or gossiping with them as though they were old acquaintances. As far as the men are concerned, 'educated' men must have poise so that they can hold their own in conversation with other men. Their suits should sit easily on them and be fashionable in cut and length. They should be able to talk of matters of general interest like politics or history, and not only to gossip or discuss business. Their English should be fluent and they should be knowledgeable about the customs of the English around them. They usually also have one or two English friends, although their closest friends are always Pakistanis.

The categorial ambiguities were evident in the discussion of a woman who, it was said, had been 'very educated' when she first came to Manchester. Her sisters-in-law, on the other hand, were more 'like villagers'. She had told my informant: 'Do you understand what they are saying' (referring to the 'deep' village 'Punjabi' the women spoke)? 'When I first came to Manchester I didn't understand a word they were saying.' But my informants both agreed that the acquaintance had herself become more 'like a villager'. In fact one of them told me, the sisters-in-law are all educated, but they seem more like villagers. When they get together they gossip in front of strangers, and if one of them leaves, they immediately begin gossiping about her. My informants agreed that this was not the right kind of behaviour, and they particularly disapproved of the way family affairs were aired in front of strangers. When I inquired about another member of the circle, a man who did not have a university education, whether they thought he was educated, they both responded that he was 'very educated'. This was so, they explained, because he had 'confidence'.

Labour migrants come from a variety of backgrounds and many of them have been extremely mobile – they have become wealthy and have also, in some cases, learnt to speak fluent English and to behave according to English etiquette. In Manchester a migrant has to establish his status both in relation to his present position and in relation to the position of his family in Pakistan. As one informant told me of a past friend: 'Here we are all the same, none of us are rich. He is proud because his family in Pakistan is very rich, but my husband's family is rich there too.' Of the businessmen of village origin, members of the circle point out that they know their families in Pakistan – they are just simple people. Some professionals see themselves as superior in terms of pedigree and education. On the other hand, many of the successful businessmen in Manchester admit themselves that they came from a 'simple' village origin – and the most successful of them are proud of the fact. The story of rags to riches is apparently a source of pride as long as the riches are sufficiently large and tangible. The mutual assessment of current statuses tends, therefore, to be fraught with ambiguity because of the discrepancies between background and current circumstances. A man from a village landlord family without much education who works in a factory in Manchester complained to me that few people in Manchester appreciated who his family was. This was, indeed, correct – his status was assessed largely in terms of his current achievements. Ultimately, it seems, most migrants accept that unless they establish their status locally, their family background will bring them little esteem.

Internal competition, especially among some businessmen, has led to a high emphasis on religiosity and an intensification of ritual and social closure. These two characteristics – parochialism and 'traditionalism' – are perceived by professionals to be somewhat 'backward' and 'village-like'. They, the professionals, who as a category display far less internal cohesion, place a high value on urban attitudes: on sophistication, worldliness, tolerance, discretion and modernity. They cultivate these attitudes which set them apart in their own eyes from other members of the community – more wealthy than they by far – and also emphasize their superior background despite their current moderate incomes. Yet they continue to have extensive links with businessmen.

Modes of 'Westernization' and 'conservativeness'

The 'modern' Pakistanis are 'Westernized', but in an oriental (Pakistani) way established among the elites in India and Pakistan during and since the British Raj. Many of the Western fashions adopted in Manchester, like blue jeans, were adopted even earlier in Pakistan. Members of the Pakistani elite living in Manchester can thus be 'modern' while having very few close social relationships with other English people. However, when the opportunity for establishing such relationships arises – with neighbours in the suburbs or with people at work – they are able to bridge the cultural gap with greater ease than members of other sections of the community.

The process of 'Ashrafization' has its counterpart in processes of 'Westernization'. The difference is emblematically displayed in veiling practices. An 'educated' villager told me that, in the villages, illiterate people do not bother to wear a *burqa* (outside gown with veil) and only sometimes wear a *chagga* (large white scarf). Among those who wear *burqas*, some wear ones with an old-fashioned, tent-like design, while the 'most educated' wear fashionable *burqas* made of silky material, which are elegantly cut. But the 'educated' women of the large cities, as I was told by a member of this category, have given up *burqas* altogether: 'Nobody wears a *burqa* any more, only villagers do that.' The subtleties of background and class conveyed through such items of clothing indicate the complexity of the notions of hierarchy and religiosity. The most 'illiterate villagers' and the 'educated townswomen' both do not bother with *burqas*.

Thus, there is a range of possible interpretations of the notion of 'conservativeness' which makes it a polysemic or multireferential term: it may refer to an emphasis on strict purdah or on traditional dress, to a high degree of scholastic and intellectually based religiosity or to a constant performance and attendance of domestic rituals and *rites de passage*, some of them highly elaborated. Ritualism and religiosity are not the same, and are even considered by some to clash, for Islam forbids ostentatious celebrations, and many customs – especially those associated with weddings – are considered to be of 'Hindu' origin and are disapproved of by the very pious.

On the other hand, unlike the situation in Pakistan, certain Western lifestyle items, and especially consumer goods, are within the reach of all, even of factory workers of village origin. Conversely, the emphasis on traditional ways of living has been revived most dramatically among some sections of the business elite as they have established themselves locally. This elite is, it must be noted, mainly of village origin, but many now have an urban domicile in Pakistan. But even among those of urban and educated background some have become extremely religious. The concepts of 'conservative' and 'modern' do not, therefore, cover the full range of lifestyles led by migrants, nor do they allow for a combination of different cultural modes of behaviour – Western and traditional – and for situational behaviour. Pakistanis do not hold a clearly consistent set of morally opposed categories of behaviour such as 'traditional' and 'modern'. Common stereotypes, offered by the more educated migrants as explanations of differences in the behaviour of fellow migrants in Manchester, relate primarily to an urban-rural dichotomy, while a modern-traditional dichotomy is given as a secondary explanation. Thus, to be classified as a 'villager' implies that a person is also 'uneducated' and 'traditional' and this explains his current lifestyle, mode of dress, etc. By contrast, 'townsmen' are considered to be people who are 'educated' and 'modern'. This tends to bring about an association between ritualism (traditional) and rural origin. Religiosity (traditional) divides townsmen, however, for it is more common in towns. It is impossible for the totally uneducated, usually of village background, to be highly religious practitioners, for religiosity requires a good knowledge of the Koran (which is read in Arabic). It is an optional path only for the better educated migrants.

In Manchester, however, religiosity and ritualism are often practised by the same people, thus cutting across the rural-urban dichotomy. The contrast, 'townsman-villager', is also an ambiguous one, despite its superficial clarity, particularly with regard to migrants who were once villagers but who now, as Mancunians, are townsmen, or have changed their domicile in Pakistan. The stereotypes used by migrants to explain other migrants' current behaviour in terms of these contrasting categories are inconsistent and can only be used situationally, depending on the issue at hand.

Conclusion

Finally, it should be asked how migrants fit into the threefold model of lifestyle 'messages' suggested in the introduction. Which groups of migrants signal messages of 'dominance', 'conformity' or 'independence' through their lifestyles?

It has been almost impossible to do justice to this question here. Very generally, I have indicated that wealthy traders clearly signal their dominance and superiority through ostentatious ceremonials, as well as the constant purchase of costly consumer goods. Among lower-income groups, the 'spenders' emulate this lifestyle and are, indeed, highly aware of it, for their extensive sociability brings them into contact with the more affluent Pakistanis in the community. They are thus 'conformists'.

The 'savers', on the other hand, signal their 'independence': they do not pretend to have resources to be 'thrown away' on ritual or ceremonial occasions. Their narrow circle of sociability means they rarely have contact with the affluent, unless they reach their aim of becoming traders themselves. Yet 'savers' are also conformists: they invest in consumer goods, such as conventional furniture and wall-to-wall carpeting, just as the 'spenders' do, emulating both their English neighbours and their Pakistani friends and kinsmen. They too compete within their narrow circle of friends, and spend at the rates currently accepted amongst them. Nevertheless, their shared, and fundamental, attitude appears to be one of deferred competition; their options are left open, they remain 'independent'.

So also do the 'professionals' convey their dominance and superiority by means of dress, sophistication and occupation, yet remain to some extent 'independent'. They avoid interacting extensively with the very affluent, as social relations with them would generate, they know, high rates of ceremonial exchange, and thus deplete their limited resources. They wish to leave their options open. They are highly mobile and thus not fully committed to the local competition stakes.

Differences in lifestyles are to some extent a matter of degree. Most 'spenders' attempt to make some investments, most 'savers' get caught up in competitive spending within their small circle of friends. Moreover, in times of major crisis, all migrants appear to turn to a few select friends or kinsmen for support. However, while lifestyle traits may be placed on a continuum between two extremes (of economic strategy, ritual behaviour, domestic division of labour, etc.) the lifestyle of any particular family is internally coherent, systematic and rational within its own terms. This is ultimately the great theoretical difficulty underlying a comparative discussion of lifestyles.

Soft City
J. Raban

Reprinted with permission from Jonathan Raban, *Soft City*, Hamish Hamilton, 1974, pp.112–23

People often complain of metropolitan life that it coarsens thought, that the intellect is held cheaply, that serious issues degenerate into trends of the moment and the coterie. From the judicious distance of a provincial university town, London and New York often look like circuses, their intelligentsias as sleek as performing seals. So much of talk is fashion and frippery; its buzz of new ideas is brazenly decorative, there to adorn the talker and to protect him from the incursions of the world. When an idea becomes a commodity, readily transmittable and exchangeable in the bazaar of society at large, it takes on the characteristics of other commodities. It may be unpalatable to think of ideas as if they could have the same function as housefronts, cars or handbags but it is surely true that they very often do so. People gather behind them, for private and highly partial reasons. The inexpensive synthesis, of the kind that can be extracted from ecology, or structuralism, or *The Gutenberg Galaxy*, or *One Dimensional Man*, comforts and assuages those who embrace it. It makes the world simpler, gives a thrust of direction and authority to the individual living in a prolix and confusing city. We are not so far here from Gissing's Thomas Bird, picking himself out from the crowd with his treasured private knowledge of the geography of Polynesia.

These narrow, passionate *cognoscenti* bolstered by received ideas, given to clubs and cliques and intense sectarian debates, are part of the essence of city life. For the member of an urban guerrilla cell, or an ecological watchdog organization, or a neo-mystical commune, or one of the countless coffee-and-discussion groups that are always springing up in big cities, his ideology is a *route*, a consecrated path through the unintelligible scatter of city streets. A sense of community, and the perspective which we acquire as one of the privileges of belonging to a community, are hard to come by in the city. Neither the street nor the neighbourhood (except in some of the leafier suburbs and odd clusters of besieged roads of working-class terraces) confers a sufficient sense of membership on its residents. The turnover of owners and tenants is too rapid, and the sheer physical density with which metropolitan space is occupied makes for a warren of private cubicles in which people jealously and secretively protect their own patches. Ideas, unlike neighbours, are chosen; and a community of people who share an idea, a craze, a belief is perhaps the most precious of all the associations which a man may make in a city. There is a café around the corner from where I live which is a nest of coteries in the long dull middle of the afternoon. Italian *au pair* girls go there, so do folk music enthusiasts and loitering record collectors. But there is also a curious group of young men in fishermen's jerseys who have the activist's look of glinting, mildly fanatical anaemia. One day I learned how to make a bomb; and the technical jargon of revolution spills from their table in single overheard phrases. I am not a party to their beliefs, nor do I know what they are (Trotskyists . . . anarchists . . . People's Democracy . . . midnight slogan painters . . . colourful fantasizing about the lives of other people is a chronic urban habit); and this very quality of unknownness scares me. But there is a real resemblance between this tableful of revolutionaries, if that is in fact what they are up to, and some of the less exotic coterie-milieux which I know better. I sometimes go to a pub in Soho with a corner full of book reviewers, and one catches the same note there: the same pitch of voice, the technical talk, the possessive hunch over the table of people making a close, improvised, temporary community in the middle of a city of strangers. Communities like this, which come to life around an idea, are constantly dissolving; they are not fixed in place or time, although membership of them is a permanently defining feature of one's identity.

A large city is a honeycomb of such groups. To the outsider, they are likely to seem silly or sinister, and certainly evanescent. For every group which establishes itself with capital and property in a quarter, there are many whose outward and visible signs are known and valued only by their members. Their most important possessions are their ideas, and these are preserved for fellow-initiates, not exposed to the hostile examination of the world outside. They communicate by rumour and the telephone; they meet in public places – in halls, in parks, in pubs and cafés, and on streets and squares. Like their members, they are in a state of constant locomotion in the city. One or two established organizations – the Salvation Army is the prime example – have borrowed the motile structure of these groups; grasping, as General Booth grasped, that the most effective institutions in a big city must keep on the move with the people.

Sometimes such a group will suddenly move into visibility and claim the attention of outsiders in the crowd with its extreme and bizarre public symbols. In New York, Los Angeles and London, there is a wandering tribe of street folk; they live in Radha Krishna temples, their heads are shaved except for a scrubby tuft on their crowns, they process through the streets in sandals and saffron-dyed sheets, chanting the 'Hare Krishna' mantra and beating on tambourines. On Oxford Street, motorists caught in the continual traffic jam yell cheerful obscenities at these outlandish communards. They seem indifferent. Their vegetarian diet and life of indoor meditation have pulled the skins of their faces away from their lips and eyes so that they have a curiously protuberant, root-vegetable look. Yet they are not without dignity: their voices are gentle, hazed, their accents invariably English urban, and patches of Manchester and Stepney show through their stiff, devoted impersonation of the mystic east. They are keen to evangelize, and methodically explain themselves with the rehearsed precision of a telephone answering service. I sat in my socks in a basement, sharing their bowl of grated oranges and vegetables, as they talked at me earnestly, not expecting to be believed, knowing, I suspect, that many of their visitors only come to smirk and peer. They are solemn, courteous, and extremely ugly: their scraped turnip faces nod slowly under the naked 200-watt bulb, which itself looks rather like another communard. Each word and gesture is reverently drawn out; everything here is ritual theatre – self-consciousness is elevated to mystical consciousness of the self, and everyday life turns into a studied allegory.

The International Society for Krishna Consciousness promotes a rural peasant culture as a spiritual antidote to and romantic release from city life. It recruits the disaffiliated young from the streets, offering them spartan communes and a simple, hokum-scientific doctrine of mind power. Like nineteenth-century spiritualism, of which it is a less sophisticated replica, it preaches an ethic of impoverished literalism. The movement's *swami*, in a characteristic booklet called *Easy Journey to Other Planets*, invites you to join a bargain coach-trip to the spiritual world:

> The material world is only a shadow representation of the anti-material world, and intelligent men who are clean in heart and habit will be able to learn, in a nutshell, all the details of the anti-material world from the text of the *Gita*, and these are in actuality more exhaustive than material details . . .
> . . . The gross materialist may try to approach the anti-material worlds by endeavouring with spaceships, satellites, rockets, etc., which he throws into outer space, but by such means he cannot even approach the material planets in the higher regions of the material sky, and what to speak of those planets situated in the anti-material sky, which is far beyond the material universe . . . Master *yogis* who control the anti-material particle within the material body by practice of mystic powers can give up their material bodies at will at any given moment and can thus enter the anti-material worlds through a specific thoroughfare which connects the material and anti-material worlds.

This is a sad piece of writing; barely literate twaddle in which the jargon of popular science is treated with a superstitious reverence. Reading it, one suffocates in the appalling intellectual constriction of its vision of the world, and senses, too, in its ramshackle and reduced vocabulary and grammar, some of the sheer difficulty which its intended audience must experience when they try to think about the world at all. (A more unpleasant, because more grandly commercialized version of the same style, may be found in the work of Ron L. Hubbard and the Scientologists – another group of urban evangelists who operate in London from a shop in the Tottenham Court Road, and have had some success in converting people off the streets of the city.) The liberation of spirit which it purports to offer is a liberation into chains; it drops one into a mental abyss in which the simplest of ideas, the most elementary of rational processes, is impossibly large, foreign and unwieldy.

But when the *swami* writes of a 'thoroughfare', he indicates a route for believers which goes not so much to the stars as through the city streets. For the devotee, London becomes legible by being relegated to a plane of inferior consciousness. It turns into a chimera: the 'material' city is there to be transcended by homemade mysticism and holy gobbledygook. The chanting, the amazing dress, the razored skulls of these young men are there as a fierce announcement – they have seen through the illusory life of shops and automobiles; for them, the city we inhabit does not exist. In their city, the stars are under their feet, and the cosmos has blacked-out Bourne and Hollingsworth; they process through the chimerical void to the unearthly tinkling of their tambourines.

Krishna Consciousness presents its ideas as uniquely expensive commodities: but they are freely available to anyone who is prepared to pay for them with self-abasement, discipline, and by wearing the proud stigmata of robes and tonsure. One of the most significant features of the movement is the way in which it embraces the caste system; it promises the status of a *brahmana* to the believer. 'The caste system', writes the *swami*, 'is very scientific'; but the castes of which he writes are fundamentally different from real castes in that anybody may elect himself to the caste which he considers himself fit to belong to. We are instructed to search our hearts for signs of 'spiritual advancement', and if we find ourselves qualified, then, automatically, we become brahmans. Status is a matter not of external circumstances but of the deliberate exercise of will over consciousness. It is inside our heads that we are aristocrats; the impersonal world, represented by the judgements and deferences of society at large, is, in the rhetoric of Krishna Consciousness, an irrelevant delusion.

It might be consoling to see the beliefs of the Krishna people as merely grotesque or dotty – the extreme responses of faddish, undereducated, underemployed young people to the unassimilable scatter of the city. But there is something more to them than that. Every western metropolis is at present swarming with bands of devotees, some flying political colours, some resurrecting or inventing exotic religions, some committed to eccentric hobbies and crazes. Some are as harmless as the radio-controlled model glider enthusiasts who foregather every Saturday on a corner of Richmond Park, cocooned from public inquisitiveness by their impressive technicalities, their talk of thermals and wavelengths and launching-ropes, mightily oblivious of the dogs and children who scamper among their balsa wood aeroplanes. They have a weekend world of their own, a private city which is invisible to the uninitiated. But at the other extreme, there are the revolutionary cells, and gangs like the Envies; people who have – like the members of the Hare Krishna Temple – concocted elaborate philosophies to prove that the city is a bead-curtain of illusion. The convicted conspirators of the English 'Angry Brigade', who had been accused of planting bombs in a number of public institutions and in the London house of a cabinet minister, subscribed to the theories of the Paris Situationists – who speak of the 'spectacle' or 'façade' of capitalism, and of revolution as imagination liberated from hierarchical modes of thought and behaviour. There can surely be no doubt that the unreality of the city, its prolixity and illegibility, its capacity to exceed all the imaginative shapes we try to impose upon it, enables its citizens to treat it with a terrifying arbitrariness. Georg Simmel, the nineteenth-century German sociologist, identified the characteristic urban habit of mind as *blasé*; Engels saw the city's major evil in the lack of curiosity shown by members of the crowd for each other. When the city becomes a mere façade, when Oxford Street ceases to exist, when violence can be casually inflicted by one metropolitan group upon another, then realism – a respect for detail, objects, independent and various lives – becomes the most pressing of all necessities.

At the Radha Krishna temple near the British Museum in Bloomsbury, a pale communard with a Glaswegian accent pointed to a man with a droopy moustache who was sitting next to me. 'Telex operator, right?' said the communard. The man stopped turning the pages of *Krisna Consciousness: the Topmost Yoga System*, and nodded slowly, reverently. 'To me', said the communard, 'he is pure consciousness. We do not see a person's job, or his clothes, or his house and family. We see his soul.' The man with the soul looked grateful, few other telex operators can visit distant planets or turn, like magic pumpkins, into brahmans, the ultimate aristocrats of the world-soul. He was leaving the street outside far behind; its dense puzzles, its intricate social networks, its inequalities, its confusion of noises and smells, were, he had learned, just dull impediments from which he could liberate himself at a blink.

Such subjective inspirational clairvoyance is a hallmark of these isolated groups within the city. It is shared by Weathermen, Diggers, Sufists, Envies, by moralistic thugs and by placid vegetarian contemplatives. Each holds an idea, an idiom and a uniform in common; and each believes that the city is a 'façade', easily transcended by an act of will, a trick of the mind, or the lit fuse of a bomb. The word 'consciousness', whether employed by the revolutionary or the religiomane, is a shorthand-notation: it conveys the notion that the intuitive self might actually come to replace the edifice of society – that the world on the ground might be moulded into the shape of a totalitarian world inside the head.

It is a dangerous kind of dreaming, this solemn, simple mentalism. It releases the dreamer into a domain of total possibility in which his reality is as inventive, psychotic or banal as his own imagination. He imagines himself a brahman . . . he is a brahman. If a toolmaker's apprentice from West Ham wants to turn into an Asian mystic, he may do so simply by rigging himself out in the appropriate uniform and chanting the prescribed abracadabra. If one shifts from group to group, one watches London dissolving; from a paddy field of disembodied souls, to a systematic capitalist conspiracy of banks, police stations, court-houses and monuments, to a range of Cuban hills where fellow guerrillas squat in waiting wearing patched jeans and ex-W.D. windcheaters, to the gothic, magical city of signs prophesied in the writings of Nostradamus.

In a television interview transmitted the day after her conviction in the 'Angry Brigade' trial in 1972, Anna Mendelson talked in what is increasingly becoming a characteristic idiom of our time; a style in which familiar words are pronounced as if they were components of an arcane code. She spoke distractedly in a dream-monotone: phrases like 'working-class', 'conspiracy', 'change of consciousness' came out rounded as pebbles, but what they meant to me was clearly not what they meant to her. When she was asked whether the bombings had had any tangible effect on the progress of the revolution in England, she stared mildly, apparently incomprehendingly at her interviewer and said, 'I suppose they must have . . . yes . . . they must have, mustn't they . . .' so vaguely that one felt that one had trespassed illicitly over the far side of her dream.

These intense, private groups, compacted around a core of symbolic objects and ideas, are very serious symptoms of a metropolitan condition. They may or may not be politically important in themselves; and when they take a religious turn they may indicate nothing about the spiritual awakening which fond members of the clerisy enjoy forecasting. But the club, the clique, the cell, the commune, the code are proliferating forms in the city. Huddled, defensive, profoundly complacent in their indifference or hostility to the rest of the city, they are the foxholes for all those whom the city has isolated, for whom no larger reality is habitable. Mayhew saw the illegible mass of the nineteenth-century city as a network of tight castes, each one operating independently of the others and of society at large. Money, education and social welfare provisions have largely released the castes of the modern city from thraldom to their occupations. Just as the poor can render themselves invisible in cheap fashion-styled clothes so they can acquire ideas and identities of a much wilder and grander kind than could Mayhew's costermongers and mudlarks. In our city, it is easy to drift into a privacy of symbols, a domain of subjective illusions made concrete by the fact that two or three people have gathered together to conspire in them.

It is impossible to miss the crackle of tribal hostilities in London and New York today. What is most worrying is the subtlety, narrowness and parochialism with which the lines are drawn. The fierce antagonism between blacks and whites, between haves and have-nots, is tragically comprehensible. What is not so easy to understand is the continual barrage of explosions from wars so small that only the participants can explain which sides are fighting them. *Gay News* reports vicious factional quarrels between opposed groups of London homosexuals, with smashed typewriters and bloody noses. A party for the opening of the Women's Lib magazine *Spare Rib* ended in an internecine brawl. Like the cross-hatching of bitchery which keeps literary coteries (themselves highly developed examples of self-conscious caste groups) alive, the malevolent buzz of city life is a way of marking boundaries of taste, staking out the ever-more-questionable frontier between us and them. People in one postal district despise those in the next; the owner of the baby Renault reproves the driver of the expensive Jensen; the revolutionary dismisses the Buddhist, the Buddhist the revolutionary. It is a war of ideas and epigrams, in which objects are called on to play the parts of ideas, to express the ideologies of their owners; and its local battles are passionately territorial in nature. Each party has its own city, its own version of the self, its own route through that other, endlessly malleable city of fact.

Leadership
N. Elias and J. L. Scotson

Reprinted with permission from N. Elias and J. L. Scotson, *The Established and the Outsiders*, Frank Cass and Co., 1965, pp. 130–2, 152–3, 155–9

For a very long time groups of families could only acquire the sociological quality of 'oldness' if they rose above the lower orders who had no or little property to transmit. The 'village' of Winston Parva seems to indicate that property is no longer as essential a condition of sociological 'oldness' as it used to be. Old peasant families based on the inheritance of land have of course been known in the past; so have old craftsmen families whose 'oldness' was based on the monopolized transmission of special skills. 'Old' working-class families appear to be characteristic of our own age. Whether they are a freak or an omen remains to be seen. Because sociological oldness in their case is not noticeably connected with inheritance of property certain other conditions of power which are normally to be found in other cases too, but which in other cases are less conspicuous, stand out more clearly in their case, particularly the power derived from the monopolization of key positions in local institutions, from greater cohesion and solidarity, from greater uniformity and elaboration of norms and beliefs and from the greater discipline, external and internal, which went with them. Greater cohesion, solidarity, uniformity of norms and self-discipline helped to maintain monopolization, and this in turn helped to reinforce these group characteristics. Thus the continued chance of 'old groups' to stand out; their successful claim to a higher social status than that of other interdependent social formations and the satisfactions derived from them, go hand in hand with specific differences in the personality structure which play their part, positive or negative as the case may be, in the perpetuation of an 'old families' network.

That 'old families' are known to each other and have strong ties with each other, however, does not mean that they necessarily like each other. It is only in relation to outsiders that they tend to stand together. Among themselves they may, and almost invariably do, compete, mildly or wildly according to circumstances, and may, often by tradition, heartily dislike or even hate one another. Whichever it is, they exclude outsiders. A good deal of common family lore is floating in the air of every circle of 'old families' enriched by each generation as it comes and goes. Like other aspects of the common tradition it creates an intimacy – even between people who dislike each other – which newcomers cannot share.

'Oldness' in a sociological sense thus refers to social relationships with properties of their own. They give a peculiar flavour to enmities and to friendships. They tend to produce a marked exclusivity of sentiment, if not of attitude, a preference for people with the same sensibilities as oneself, strengthening the common front against outsiders. Although individual members may turn away and may even turn against the group, the intimate familiarity of several generations gives to such 'old' groups for a while a degree of cohesion which other less 'old' groups lack. Born from a common history that is remembered it forms another strong element in the configuration of chances they have to assert and to maintain for a while their superior power and status in relation to other groups. Without their power the claim to a higher status and a specific charisma would soon decay and sound hollow whatever the distinctiveness of their behaviour. Rejecting gossip, freezing-out techniques, 'prejudice' and 'discrimination' would soon lose their edge; and so would any other of the manifold weapons used to protect their superior status and their distinction.

Thus, concentrated in the form of a model, the configuration found at Winston Parva in miniature shows more clearly its implications for a wider field. The task is not to praise and to blame; it is rather to help towards a better understanding and a better explanation of the interdependences which trapped two groups of people in Winston Parva in a configuration not of their own making and which produced specific tensions and conflicts between them. The tensions did not arise because one side was wicked or overbearing and the other was not. They were inherent in the pattern which they formed with each other. If one had asked the 'villagers' they would probably have said they did not want an Estate at their doorstep, and if one had asked the Estate people they would probably have said they would rather not settle near an older neighbourhood such as the 'village'. Once they were thrown together they were trapped in a conflict situation which none of them could control and which one has to understand as such if one wants to do better in other similar cases. The 'villagers' naturally behaved to the newcomers as they were used to behave to deviants in their own neighbourhood. The immigrants on their part quite innocently behaved in their new place of residence in the manner which appeared natural to them. They were not aware of the existence of an established order with its power differentials and an entrenched position of the core group of leading families in the older part. Most of them did not understand at all why the older residents treated them with contempt and kept them at a distance. But the role of a lower status group in which they were placed and the indiscriminate discrimination against all people who settled on the Estate must have early discouraged any attempt to establish closer contacts with the older groups. Both sides acted in that situation without much reflection in a manner which one might have foreseen. Simply by becoming interdependent as neighbours they were thrust into an antagonistic position without quite understanding what was happening to them and most certainly without any fault of their own.

This, as has already been said, was a small-scale conflict not untypical of processes of industrialization. If one looks at the world at large one cannot fail to notice many configurations of a similar kind though they are often classified under different headings. Broad trends in the development of contemporary societies appear to lead to situations such as this with increasing frequency. Differences between sociologically 'old' and 'new' groups can be found today in many parts of the world. They are, if one may use this word, normal differences in an age in which people can travel with their belongings from one place to another more cheaply under more comfortable conditions at greater speed over wider distances than ever before, and can earn a living in many places apart from that where they have been born. One can discover variants of the same basic configuration, encounters between groups of newcomers, immigrants, foreigners and groups of old residents all over the world. The social problems created by these migratory aspects of social mobility, though varying in details, have a certain family similarity. Sometimes they are simply conceived as geographical aspects. All that happens it seems is that people move physically from one place to another. In reality, they always move from one social group to another. They always have to establish new relationships with already existing groups. They have to get used to the role of newcomers who seek entry into, or are forced into interdependence with, groups with already established traditions of their own and have to cope with the specific problems of their new role. Often enough they are cast in the role of outsiders in relation to the established and more powerful groups whose standards, beliefs, sensibilities and manners are different from theirs.

If the migrants have different skin colour and other hereditary physical characteristics different from those of the older residents, the problems created by their own neighbourhood formations and by their relations with the inhabitants of older neighbourhoods are usually discussed under the heading 'racial problems'. If the newcomers are of the same 'race' but have different language and different national traditions, the problems with which they and the older residents are confronted are classified as problems of 'ethnic minorities'. If social newcomers are neither of a different 'race', nor of a different 'ethnic group', but merely of a different 'social class', the problems of social mobility are discussed as 'class problems', and, often enough, as problems of 'social mobility' in a narrower sense of the word. There is no ready-made label which one can attach to the problems that arose in the microcosm of Winston Parva because there the newcomers and the old residents, at least in the 'village', were neither of a different 'race', nor, with one or two exceptions, of different 'ethnic descent' or of a different 'social class'. But some of the basic problems arising from the encounter of established and outsider groups in Winston Parva were not very different from those which one can observe in similar encounters elsewhere, though they are often studied and conceptualized under different headings.

In all these cases the newcomers are bent on improving their position and the established groups are bent on maintaining theirs. The newcomers resent, and often try to rise from, the inferior status attributed to them and the established try to preserve their superior status which the newcomers appear to threaten. The newcomers cast in the role of outsiders are perceived by the established as people 'who do not know their place'; they offend the sensibilities of the established by behaving in a manner which bears in their eyes clearly the stigma of social inferiority, and yet, in many cases, newcomer groups quite innocently are apt to behave, at least for a time, as if they were the equals of their new neighbours. The latter show the flag; they fight for their superiority, their status and power, their standards and beliefs, and they use in that situation almost everywhere the same weapons, among them humiliating gossip, stigmatizing beliefs about the whole group modelled on observations of its worst section, degrading code words and, as far as possible, exclusion from all chances of power – in short, the features which one usually abstracts from the configuration in which they occur under headings such as 'prejudice' and 'discrimination'. As the established are usually more highly integrated and, in general, more powerful, they are able by mutual induction and ostracism of doubters to give a very strong backing to their beliefs. They can often enough induce even the outsiders to accept an image of themselves which is modelled on a 'minority of the worst' and an image of the established which is modelled on a 'minority of the best', which is an emotional generalization from the few to the whole. They can often impose on newcomers the belief that they are not only inferior in power but inferior by 'nature' to the established group. And this internalization by the socially inferior group of the disparaging belief of the superior group as part of their own conscience and self-image powerfully reinforces the superiority and the rule of the established group.

The 'bad behaviour' of a minority of Estate youngsters which reinforced again and again the 'villagers'" stereotyped image of the Estate was not confined to branches of sex morality. One of the standard complaints of the 'village' people was that about the bad behaviour of the 'swarms of children' from the Estate. Tales were constantly repeated about the 'masses' of children who grew up to be delinquents and criminals and who destroyed the 'old peace' of the 'village'.

Complaints about the 'swarms of children' who disturbed the peace of the 'village' were not entirely unjustified, but it was not so much the actual number of children on the Estate which mattered as the conditions under which they lived. The children who roamed the streets and disturbed the peace of the 'villagers' came from the minority of 'notorious' families which has already been mentioned. Living as they did in relatively small houses, children from these large families had nowhere else to go but the streets after school or work. Those who tried to join the older youth clubs were soon shown that they were not welcome. They had learned a certain reserve on the Estate and applied it, as it seemed, quite easily to their relations with 'village' youngsters. But a minority of youngsters from the Estate, mostly children of the problem families, reacted differently. They enjoyed embarrassing the people who rejected them. The vicious circle, the see-saw process, in which the old and new neighbourhoods, the established and the outsiders, were involved ever since they had become interdependent, showed its full force in the relations between their young people. The children and adolescents of the despised Estate minority were shunned, rejected and 'frozen out' by their 'respectable' contemporaries from the 'village' even more firmly and cruelly than were their parents because the 'bad example' they set threatened their own defences against the unruly urges within; and because the wilder minority of younger people felt rejected, they tried to get their own back by behaving badly with greater deliberation. The knowledge that by being noisy, destructive and offensive they could annoy those by whom they were rejected and treated as outcasts, acted as an added incentive, and perhaps, as the major incentive, for 'bad behaviour'. They enjoyed doing the very things for which they were blamed as an act of revenge against those who blamed them.

Some groups of this type, mainly composed of boys aged between fourteen and eighteen, 'got a kick out of' trying to enter one of the church or chapel clubs. They would enter the club noisily, shouting, singing and laughing. When a club official approached them one of them would ask to join the club while the others stood around grinning. The boys knew beforehand that they would be asked to agree to attend church services regularly. When this provision was put to them they would begin to groan and to shout in protest. Then they were usually asked to leave, though in some instances they were allowed to stay for one evening in order to see what advantages club life had to offer them. The request that they should leave was the anticipated climax of the performance for the group. They expected to be asked to conform to the established standards of behaviour as laid down by the churches; they expected to be rejected or to be accepted only on terms of their complete acceptance of 'village' standards. When this stage was reached the group would leave noisily, shouting abuse, slamming doors and then gathering in the street to shout and to sing for a while. Sometimes a group might agree to stay for the evening and would then 'make a nuisance' of themselves by knocking over chairs, by 'being rough with the girls', or by making loud obscene comments about club activities.

Rural Life: Locals and Newcomers
H. Newby

Reprinted with permission from Howard Newby, *Green and Pleasant Land? Social Change in Rural England*, Penguin, 1980, pp. 164–72

Today the lowland English village as an occupational community has virtually disappeared, except in a few very remote areas, destroyed by the twin assaults of the drift from the land of agricultural labour and creeping urbanization. Both have been accelerated since the war by the widespread application of the internal combustion engine. On the farm the introduction of tractors and combine harvesters has brought about a vast decrease in the number of employment opportunities and an added stimulus to the rural working population to move to the towns in search of jobs. They have been replaced in many areas by an urban, overwhelmingly middle-class population which has been attracted by a combination of cheap housing (until the late 1960s) and by an idealized view of rural life which their ownership of a car has at last allowed them to indulge. The arrival of this 'adventitious' rural population goes back further than is often assumed, and is by no means a purely postwar phenomenon. For example, George Bourne was writing about its effects in the villages of Surrey in his *Change in the Village* as early as 1912, by which time the railways had enabled a commuting population to inhabit the rural parts of the inner Home Counties. Since then the transformation of rural villages into non-agricultural settlements has taken place in a series of waves out along the lines of transportation from the major urban centres, particularly, in the first instance, London. During the interwar years commuting was encouraged by the railway companies and by speculative builders and it was only after the Second World War that the more widespread use of the car and the continuing electrification of the railways allowed the commuting zone to be extended further. By the end of the 1960s the motorway network had linked up most of the commuting areas between the major conurbations and the in-filling of commuter villages between such radial transport routes had virtually been completed. Only a few rural areas, isolated by bad roads and non-existent railways, remained relatively untouched, but even these, by virtue of their isolation, were often gobbled up by the equally voracious demand for holiday homes and weekend cottages.

There are now few villages without their complement of newcomers who work in towns. These new 'immigrants' have brought with them an urban, middle-class lifestyle which is largely alien to the remaining local agricultural population. Unlike the agricultural workers in an occupational community, the newcomers do not make the village the focus of all their social activities. The possession of a car enables them to maintain social contacts with their friends elsewhere, and if necessary, to make use of urban amenities while living in the countryside. Their entertainment, their socializing, even their shopping, tend to take place outside the village. This influx of strangers can, therefore, quite rapidly affect the nature of village society: suddenly, so it appears to the locals, everybody does *not* know everybody else. The newcomer, moreover, does not enter the village as a lone individual who has to win social recognition among the locals in order to make life tolerable. Instead, particularly during the 1950s and 1960s, the newcomers arrived in such large numbers – perhaps due to the building of a new housing estate by a local speculative builder – that the individual 'immigrant' found himself one of many others whose values, behaviour and lifestyles were similarly based upon urban, middle-class patterns of sociability. Although these are noticeably different from those of the local agricultural population, the newcomer does not always feel it is necessary to adapt to the hitherto accepted *mores* of the village. This, however, depends on what brought the newcomers to the village in the first place. If the incentive was a utilitarian one like cheap housing, then the newcomers will have little interest in observing the niceties of village life. They can, if necessary, establish social contacts among themselves or continue to seek them outside. On the other hand, those newcomers who wish to 'belong' may try to ingratiate themselves with the local population, sometimes – because of their misconceived expectations of village life – with disappointing results.

In either case, a new social division arises in the village which cuts across the class antagonisms of the former occupational community. On the one hand there are the close-knit locals, who are the rump of the old occupational community, and on the other the ex-urbanite newcomers whose arrival in such relatively large numbers over a short space of time cannot help but be disruptive. Some newcomers have been indifferent to the sensibilities of the local population; others, as we shall see, have been oversensitive to what *they* believe the needs of the village to be. In each case the effect has been the same: members of the former occupational community, faced with an invasion of 'their' village by outsiders, have tended to retreat in upon themselves and form a community within a community, cutting themselves off from the separate world of the newcomers. The occupational community becomes what can be called an 'encapsulated community', a village within the village, suspicious of and resistant to any intimate social contact with the commuters and second-home owners who now comprise a substantial proportion of the population. When farmers and farm workers refer to the 'loss of community' in their village it is usually to this kind of change that they are implicitly referring, for there are bound to be changing patterns of sociability developing in the village to which they are unaccustomed or from which they feel excluded. This new element in the village population also tends to create new dimensions of social conflict to replace the rural class antagonisms of the occupational community. Farmers and farm workers find that they have common interests as 'locals' which can be at loggerheads with those of the newcomers. From the farm workers' point of view, farmers therefore become 'one of us' to be counterposed to 'them', the rural immigrant population. As the recent experience of many English villages shows only too well, there are ample opportunities for conflict to arise between *both* farmers and farm workers on the one hand and the newcomers on the other.

Since the urban middle-class exodus to the countryside began in earnest in the 1950s there have typically been two issues over which such conflict has been generated: housing and the environment. . . . Here we may note how each issue has contributed to the initial polarization of the village population. Housing is obviously a crucial resource and one for which, moreover, the whole rural population – farmers and farm workers, locals and newcomers, agricultural and non-agricultural families – are competing. In general, this does not apply to local employment, because the newcomers either retain their employment in nearby towns and commute to work or they have come to the countryside to retire. Both they and their children are also more mobile and, typically, more highly educated, so they compete in an entirely separate – usually professional and managerial – labour market from the local population. Housing, however, is another matter. Here, newcomers do compete with the locals, contributing to a higher demand for rural housing which, together with the restricted supply, has led to extensive changes in the nature of the rural housing market. Although rural housing . . . has never been in plentiful supply, the newcomers provide an easy scapegoat for the otherwise 'hidden hand' of the housing market. Resentment among the locals grows at their inability to find housing for their children in their village. Farm workers find themselves more dependent upon tied cottages and both farm workers and the non-agricultural locals join the queue for council housing. Yet here they have found that the newcomers are also opposed to the construction of further council housing in the village on the grounds that it is 'detrimental to the character of the village' and detracts from the rural environment.

The provision of council housing therefore links up the second basis of local-newcomer conflict, which relates to broadly environmental issues. The newcomers often possess a set of stereotyped expectations of village life which place a heavy emphasis on the quality of the rural environment. . . . Many newcomers hold strong views on the desired social and aesthetic qualities of the English village. It must conform as closely as possible to the prevailing urban view – picturesque, ancient and unchanging. The expectation that the countryside should conform to a certain idea of the picturesque and that it should present an unchanging spectacle to the appreciative onlooker has, for example, led many newcomers to be bitterly critical of the changes wrought by modern farming methods. It is they who are in the forefront of conservation societies, who complain about uprooted hedgerows in the lowland farming areas and who resent the destruction or diversion of footpaths. This is because the newcomers regard the countryside in primarily aesthetic and recreational terms. For the same reason they have been known to treat surrounding farmland as though it were a vast municipal park across which their dogs can roam or their children can ride their ponies without much thought for the consequences. The problems that this can cause, which are often unintentional and the result of a lack of knowledge about modern agriculture, are sufficient to annoy any farmer already unhappy about what he considers to be unwarranted interference in his legitimate farming operations by busybody environmentalists. An already wary relationship between the farming population and the newcomers can easily become strained by such encounters, reinforcing the divisions between the two sides.

Individual petty conflicts therefore easily accumulate to add to the differences already apparent between locals and newcomers in terms of background and lifestyles. Because each side is personally unfamiliar with the other there is a tendency for stereotypes to emerge and for behaviour to take place on the basis of these stereotypes, making relationships even more difficult. Quite quickly the contact between the two sections of the rural population can become limited to the activity of a few 'go-betweens', whose employment requires them to relate to both sides. Shopkeepers and local tradesmen often carry out this role – indeed, surviving rural craftsmen, such as thatchers and blacksmiths, discover a rejuvenated demand for their skills among the newcomers. Other significant 'go-betweens' are the domestic workers hired by the more affluent newcomers

– the 'little woman' who comes in to 'do' twice or three times a week, and who is often the wife of a local farm worker grateful for the money. As scouts sent out by the locals to reconnoitre the otherwise mysterious lifestyles of the newcomers such people are terribly influential in defining the image of the newcomers among the locals – and of the locals among the newcomers. Gossip which is reported back easily becomes magnified in order to contribute further to the stereotypes.

For farm workers in particular the sense of loss which the influx of newcomers has prompted can be quite severe. Many newcomers share the prevailing urban view of the farm 'labourer'. They tend to be unappreciative of the farm worker's skills, not out of malice, but because they simply lack the detailed knowledge of agriculture on which to base a judgement. As they drive around the countryside the newcomers cannot distinguish between those fields which have been ploughed with a supreme exhibition of the farm worker's skills and those which have not; nor are they able to appreciate the beauty of a faultlessly drilled seed-bed, healthy stock or clean weed-free fields. The criterion by which a farm worker could once obtain high status – skill at work – is therefore threatened with being overthrown. Instead the newcomers tend to evaluate the farm worker and the other villagers on the basis of urban criteria for allocating prestige. This usually means conspicuous consumption in one or all of its varied forms – the size of the house, the size, age and make of the car, the possession of other consumer durables, the quality of furnishings, and so on. Even the garden, which can be used for the conspicuous display of flowers and shrubs rather than the more utilitarian purpose of growing food, may become part of this. Whatever form it takes, however, such conspicuous consumption – and hence the allocation of status – depends upon income and farm workers, on low wages, simply cannot compete in this league. The agricultural worker, however, reacts to the possibility of being deprived of his former status in his own village by changing the rules of the competition. Since non-acceptance on the basis of length of residence is one of the few ways in which local workers can retain any of their old status in the village, they restrict their social contacts to those who share these judgements with them.

For those newcomers who seek the social intimacy of a happy and integrated community life in the village, the reserve (and worse) of the locals can be mystifying and even upsetting. Many arrive full of goodwill and good intentions, but fail to perceive the often unanticipated consequences of their arrival on the lives of the local inhabitants, and even an oversensitivity of the need to spread goodwill around the village can appear to the locals to be both patronizing and unnecessary. For example, while the newcomers may fail to understand the skill and local status of the farm worker, they do not wish to treat him as a social outcast – this would run counter to the notion of community with which many newcomers strongly identify. Moreover the newcomers do like to see farm workers around the village since this serves as a reminder that they do indeed live in a 'truly rural' village, as opposed to a kind of rustic suburbia. However, the farm worker is allotted his 'place' in the grand, and somewhat idealized, design to which the village is expected to conform. He can be a 'character', a source of quaint rustic humour or homespun rural philosophy on such matters as the seasons and the weather, but he is rarely expected to be either forward-thinking or 'forward' in his demeanour. What are demanded are pet farm workers who cause no trouble but who form part of the landscape along with the fields and the trees.

This tendency to treat the local population as an adjunct to the scenery is a problem to which even the rural *aficionados* among the newcomers can fall prey and by which they can unwittingly cause offence. For example, the following expression of sympathy, taken from a letter to *The Times* in January 1977, at first sight appears unexceptional. The writer, who was troubled that the Lake District was losing its local population, put her case as follows:

> The Lake District is one of the most compactly beautiful regions in England and so much of its intrinsic attraction lies in the way of life led by native Cumbrians. Do people who buy second houses . . . in the Lake District realize that eventually they will destroy the very appeal of the area which they have always enjoyed? Do they for a moment consider that most visitors to the Lake District want to feel surrounded by natives of the fells and not middle-class accents and protocol?

Such comments show not so much an insensitivity to the problems of the locals, but reduces them to cyphers, tourist attractions almost, along with the surrounding scenery. In this case the native Lake District population becomes what one writer on this theme, R. E. Pahl, calls 'props on the rustic stage', which help to round off the picturesque vision of the countryside. To the farm worker sentiments such as these, however well-intentioned they may be, seem patronizing and, although in this particular instance the underlying attitudes were made unusually explicit, they are usually present in the assumptions of many newcomers.

In the light of these considerations it is perhaps not surprising that new social divisions and conflicts have arisen in the English village in recent years, nor that the local population has preferred to turn in upon itself in the face of these changes. This encapsulation of the locals in their own village has also been reinforced in many cases by a physical separation of the two sections of the community. Because of the workings of the housing market the local working population tends to congregate on the village council housing estate (where one is available), where the closely knit patterns of neighbourly association which were part of the occupational community are retained. Where villages contain more than one pub these, too, usually reflect the split between locals and newcomers, or, in the case of villages with only one pub, the bars may be socially divided – the locals to the public bar, the newcomers to the lounge, often 'modernized' in rustic mode for this purpose. The whole village therefore meets socially on only rare occasions, such as the parish meeting or the village fête, but even here socializing is often highly ritualized and rudimentary, as much symbolic as real. Village fêtes in particular often show up the divisions in the village rather well. To many newcomers they can seem a celebration of village conviviality, but closer inspection often reveals that who actually speaks to whom depends very much on background and lifestyle. Newcomers concentrate on the winemaking and the flower arrangements, while locals head single-mindedly for the beer tent and the equally serious business of the vegetable show, a forum in which husbandry skill is still subject to public competition. It is doubtful whether such social occasions bring about any lasting reconciliation between the two groups.

It is by no means clear that many newcomers are even aware of the feelings that they arouse from time to time in the local population. Having come to the village with certain expectations they may only see what they expect to find and, since the local working population has long been used to avoiding overt conflict in the face of those who have the capacity to create trouble for them, the superficial calm of village life may remain. The civilities of politeness and social etiquette may ensure that the locals' resentment is voiced only in their own social circle. It therefore becomes easy for the ideal of village life to remain among the newcomers, even though the reality for the locals may be very different. Nevertheless, in the contemporary English village it is this feeling of having been 'taken over' by outsiders that usually prevails among the agricultural population and with it not only a sense of 'loss of community', but an inevitable animus against the invasion of 'furriners'. This is not to suggest that English villages are currently hotbeds of social unrest – far from it. But when a suitable issue presents itself these underlying feelings easily become manifested, often to the surprise and consternation of the new village-dwellers.

Further Reading: **Community**

P. AMBROSE, *The Quiet Revolution*, Chatto and Windus, 1974.

C. M. ARENSBERG and S. T. KIMBALL, *Family and Community in Ireland*, Harvard University Press, 1939

C. BELL and H. NEWBY (eds.), *The Sociology of Community*, Frank Cass, 1974.

M. Bulmer (ed.), *Working-class Images of Society*, Routledge and Kegan Paul, 1975.

S. Chibnall, *Law-and-Order News*, Tavistock, 1977.

S. Cohen and J. Young (eds.), *The Manufacture of News*, Constable, 1973.

P. Evans, *Publish and Be Damned*, Runnymede Trust, 1976.

S. Field *et al.*, *Ethnic Minorities in Britain*, Home Office Research Study No. 68, HMSO, 1980.

M. Fitzgerald *et al.*, *Crime and Society*, Open University, 1978.

R. Frankenberg, *Communities in Britain*, Penguin, 1966.

S. Hall *et al.*, *Policing the Crisis: Mugging, the State, and Law and Order*, Macmillan, 1978.

P. Hartmann and C. Husband, *Racism and the Mass Media*, Davis-Poynter, 1973.

J. Klein, *Samples from English Cultures*, Routledge and Kegan Paul, 1965.

C. Moore and J. Brown, *Community versus Crime*, Bedford Square Press, 1981.

R. Plant, *Ideology and Community*, Routledge and Kegan Paul, 1974.

J. Rex and R. Moore, *Race, Community and Conflict*, Oxford University Press, 1967.

Royal Commission on the Distribution of Income and Wealth (Diamond Commission), HMSO, 1977.

J. Rushton and J. D. Turner (eds.), *Education and Deprivation*, Manchester University Press, 1975.

M. Stacey *et al.*, *Power, Persistence and Change*, Routledge and Kegan Paul, 1975.

R. Warren (ed.), *Perspectives on the American Community*, Rand McNally, 1966.

J. L. Watson (ed.), *Between Two Cultures*, Blackwell, 1975.

J. Whale, *The Politics of the Media*, Manchester University Press, 1977.

P. Willmott, *The Evolution of a Community*, Routledge and Kegan Paul, 1963.

3. Socialization

In general the term socialization is used to describe the ways in which the individual learns the values, beliefs and roles which underwrite the social system in which he participates. The child living in Britain learns to be not only a performer of roles which are applicable to his age and sex but also to his position in the society to which he belongs. Crucial to socialization is the idea of culture which may be defined as learned behaviour which is socially transmitted. The idea of culture involves 'the distinctive way of life of a group of people, their complete design for living'. From certain points of view culture may be seen as a set of rules.

Since socialization is concerned with preparation for roles in society, it begins in the relationships which develop between those with whom the child is in a position of subordination, principally the parents, and those with whom he or she is in a position of equality, principally, in the early stages, brothers and sisters. By degrees the child takes over standards from the parents and others with whom he or she is in contact. There are many differences according to social class background in the way in which this develops. These were illustrated graphically a generation ago in the comparison between a group of children living in slums and children going on to public schools in B. M. Spinley's *The Deprived and the Privileged*. The differences in early experience, she suggested, 'seem to be numerous, important and fundamental'. Little overlapping was found in this study between the experiences of the groups. Two of the most significant differences arose in the ways in which children were brought up. In the case of the slum children there was said to be no interference with the physiological satisfactions of feeding or excretion in the first year, but this period of indulgence ceased at the birth of the next child in the family. In the case of the children of higher social status there was a consistent attempt to improve performance in all respects, and this was also true in the second significant area of difference, that of attitudes towards the future. The high-status child was taught to think consistently in terms of deferring immediate gratifications whereas the slum child had no consistent set of values presented to him. While more recent studies have changed the picture somewhat, the distinctions are still widely used.

The middle-class model of socialization involves a great concern by parents for the performance of their children and training geared ideally to 'independence of action and a show of initiative'. Competitive behaviour is rewarded and success is acclaimed. For parents in many social groups the child is typically the hope of the future, especially where parents have not themselves gone as far as they had hoped.

Some of these issues arise in the readings concerned with relationships between parents and children to be found in Chapter 1. Later, other processes of socialization become important. For a considerable period of time before maturity the individual is socialized by the formal processes of the educational system. Contacts with the peer groups to which the individual belongs are also of considerable importance, particularly during the time when the 'youth culture' begins to become more influential as the influence of the parents and the school wanes. All three of the sources of socialization are considered in the readings which follow, together with that of the media and popular culture.

Reference has already been made to different patterns of childrearing in social groups. The **Newsons** undertook a sustained and intensive study of the development of a large cohort of children, and their work in this reading is largely concerned with differences in attitudes towards childrearing. Parental behaviour was seen to vary considerably towards children. Among the underprivileged, its forms may compel the children to become independent and turn from their parents to the peer group, and brings them to distrust authority and, to some extent, hardens them emotionally. The future-orientation of middle-class children, their more protected lives and the reciprocity built into their relationships with their parents differs markedly from this. Growing affluence is often assumed to lead to the adoption of specifically middle-class attitudes and ideas but it does not follow from the evidence presented here that there will be a rapid shift in this direction.

The relationships between school and the wider society are considered in the reading of **Bernstein**. He criticizes a term such as 'compensatory education' with its implications that school has to 'compensate' for something lacking in the family whereas the children in question have not been offered an acceptable educational environment. Labelling children as 'culturally deprived', referring to their 'linguistic deprivations', suggests that parents are inadequate and the consequences are lower expectations of children by their teachers. The focus needs to be upon the deficiencies of the school and, ultimately, the potential for change within the educational setting. The social experience of the child should be the starting point and the validity and significance of this experience should be clear.

Kogan considers why education might seem to be artificial, in that schooling involves tasks remote from the world, but also why, more than most human activities, it is tied up with what people want to do and want to be rather than with what they must do and are compelled to be. The purposes of education involve individual as well as social objectives. He points out that education's content and form appear to be far more open to dispute than other social provisions. For this reason it is to be seen as political. During the last generation there has been an enormous change in mass expectations, as well as in the political and administrative system as a whole. Between the main parties there are conflicts of view about the role of education. Conservatives emphasize individual objectives geared to the Opportunity State, and social objectives aiming to produce greater order and discipline among the work force and in society generally. The Labour Party put out a version of egalitarianism, which, by the creation of comprehensive schools, could heal the divisions between classes in society.

There has been a critique from a variety of sources which challenges many of the assumptions of orthodox education and introduces more radical elements into what has been training to maintain an existing society and learn traditional skills and attitudes rather than preparing pupils for change.

The kind of education which is provided for particular groups within the population reflects in part the historical development of the system and the needs of society as these are perceived by the policy-makers. **Glass**, in the reading on 'Education and Social Change', looks at the different levels of provision and the assumptions which underlie them. In place of the view of a relatively static tradition he presents one which has experienced a considerable number of changes in consequence of new priorities being established but which remains in general strongly elitist in the distinctions made between middle classes and the rest, in terms not only of potential but of educational opportunities.

Lacey examines the changes in commitment to the school of boys entering a particular grammar school in a northern area over a period of time. Two examples are given of boys whose careers, for reasons to do with the situation in the form, did not conform to the established relationship between social class and academic achievement.

Evidence shows that there are continuing differentials between the sexes, as there are indeed between the social classes. At primary level the findings published by Douglas twenty years ago have been reaffirmed in a survey showing that the advantage girls had in reading at eight years old grew less, while boys had a larger vocabulary throughout. The effects of subject specialization are examined for older children, with differences between boys and girls being apparent, and figures of entry into higher education are provided which show that women are still only just over a third of the total undergraduate population, despite the fact that it rose during the 1970s. The evidence about attainment and more particularly the destination of school-leavers links with the reading from **Blackstone and Weinreich-Haste**. The authors look at evidence from British and American researchers and educationists. The ways in which girls remain less successful than boys are examined in detail, as are the reasons for girls failing to reach their potential and opting out of particular areas of activity. Expectation affects this, and the link with gender is explored.

The authors point out that the variation in the proportion of women working in technology, medicine and law in different countries shows differences in 'stereotyping' and the norms of women's work. Subjects in some countries remain largely male or female domains, but this does not appear to be because of sex differences in ability. Role models and teachers' expectations are examined, and finally changes in provision to tackle the issues are presented.

The paper on 'Issues of Importance to Young People', originally prepared for those involved in youth work, covers a wide range. The parts which are reproduced here focus upon the aspects of socialization that have to do with schooling, education and social education, and in particular *compulsion*, *control* and *curriculum*; leisure and recreation, unemployment and employment, housing and accommodation, and finally environmental location. On every aspect **Smith** makes points which are general in character but provide perceptive insights into the situation of young people and their position in society. The reading includes a wide range of information and an agenda for thought and discussion.

The education and general socialization of girls is the subject of the reading by **Brake**. (It is complemented by the readings in Chapter 1, particularly those of Bott and Oakley.) Brake focuses upon the signals that girls receive from the mass media and popular fiction about the cult of femininity. He suggests that the socialization at school and home that most girls experience is backed up by what the media put out about femininity, and this adds a sense of fatalism about marriage and motherhood. There are subcultures such as those of young men where girls are pushed to the fringe of male activity because they are much more tied to home. Accepted behaviour, including relationships, and low job aspirations, lead to adaptations and particular courtship practices. The section on girls in male-dominated subcultures indicates the passive situation in which they are placed, and in some collusion with male chauvinism and their involvement in fighting. It also emphasizes the problems of creating a more acceptable feminine role within working-class culture, involving more autonomy and independence, when in fact what exists now seems to provide for most girls a solution.

Already some attention has been given in this chapter to parts of the media, in the discussion of the socialization of girls (Brake). The next reading is taken from a book by **Golding and Middleton** which examines press and public attitudes to poverty and the images that appear about them in the media. What emerges is the continuing stigmatization of the poor and the part played in reinforcing this, through what the authors describe as a shrill and mounting antagonism to the welfare system, by the news media. It is worth following the particular case described in detail because of the light it throws on the ways in which the onus for their plight is thrown back on the poor at a time of recession and of rapidly rising unemployment. In the authors' view, the case illustrates most of the themes that echoed through the ensuing 'scroungerphobia' period (to use Deacon's term). These are still present and look certain to continue to be important throughout this decade. It also 'reveals the mechanics by which a single event is translated by a series of institutional manipulations into a general cultural obsession'.

The reading raises many issues, both about the ways in which public concerns are presented and defined, and the effects of these in helping to form attitudes and reinforce policies that take us back, in part at least, to nineteenth-century concepts of the distinctions between 'undeserving' and 'deserving' poor.

Since the media are main sources of enjoyment, information, ideas and attitudes for the majority of people, after the experience of socialization in family, school, peer group, and through friendship, their importance is enormous. The issues that are raised are numerous (and the majority are outside the scope of this volume). They include the patterns of ownership of the media, which show increasing concentration; there is the question of the 'bias' which occurs and the motives for it. The extent to which this may be seen as a deliberate underwriting of the 'ruling ideology', or as the by-product of the search for whatever will sell newspapers or cause people to watch television, and so on, or the unavoidable consequences of the pressure of assimilating, reducing and simplifying enormous amounts of information, the greatest number of which may have no wider political or attitudinal implications, is open to question. It is certainly a vital subject for consideration. An implication of the Deevy case may be that it is the defenceless, or the vulnerable, and not the powerful, who are most at risk from the style of operation of the press in Britain.

Friendship is of a different order from relationships within the family and kin structure. This is the subject of the reading by **Allan**, which includes not only data on previous sociological studies about what friendship comprises but also material drawn from his own research in a small commuter village in East Anglia. Allan maintains that there is an emphasis in the literature on extreme forms of friendship and he stresses the need for clarity about what friendship comprises in studying and researching its forms. This is a consideration of a significant, most widespread but non-institutionalized relationship to which, like those in the readings by Macdonald and Mars, and Lake, in Chapter 1 and Henry in Chapter 7, sociologists have not so far directed a lot of attention.

Most writing about socialization is concerned with the effects of the family on the orientations and attitudes of children; **Dowse and Hughes** are concerned in the reading taken from their work with the extent to which the political ideas and attitudes of parents are transmitted to their children. Their sample of children (from eleven to seventeen years of age) and parents was drawn from Exeter. Earlier theorists stressed the primary importance of the family as an agency of political socialization but, in a large proportion of the families studied, there appeared to be 'no strong politically communicative interaction between parents and their offspring'.

Changes in the Concept of Parenthood
J. and E. Newson

Reprinted with permission from John and Elizabeth Newson, *The Family and its Future*, J. A. Churchill, 1970, pp. 142–51

Whatever interpretive framework we choose to adopt it is fairly clear that, moving down the socioeconomic scale, we are more likely to encounter a tradition-oriented, or 'old-fashioned', style of child upbringing. In the first place, sex roles between husband and wife are ever more rigidly differentiated as one moves away from the professional class, through the white-collar and skilled manual to the unskilled manual group. Work-roles in particular show this pattern; while most professional and white-collar occupations are open to women as well as men, and carry equal pay, there are a great many manual jobs which are exclusively reserved, by tradition, for men alone, and women at the manual level tend to be grossly under-valued. The degree of sex differentiation in the work-role tends to spill over into the division which is drawn at home between 'mother's role' and 'father's role'. Further down the scale, the father is less likely to take a share in feeding and tending the baby or in putting the toddler to bed. Perceived differences in maternal and paternal roles are also reflected in the ways boys and girls are differentially treated: parents' expectations of behaviour are more closely dependent upon the child's sex as one descends the class scale.

Other kinds of parental behaviour can similarly be seen as approximating more nearly to older traditions at the lower end of the scale. The father is more likely to be described by his wife as 'stricter' than herself, and accorded greater prestige as an authority figure. He is less likely to participate in story-telling, or to share an interest with the seven-year-old. Parents in the unskilled manual class more often resort to smacking as a disciplinary technique, and rely heavily upon their inherent status as adults, exerting as such an inalienable right to respect and obedience, and thus deliberately creating a social distance between adults and children. In line with this, they also appear to suffer less anxiety over what methods to adopt in dealing with their children, and are less inclined than other parents to be self-critical with regard to their own attitudes and behaviour.

Although, in common with other investigators, we have found in this group a preference for non-verbal methods of controlling children, we have also shown that there is a simultaneous readiness to use a verbal technique of teasing or threatening the child, in ways which depend for their effectiveness upon his immaturity of understanding. In direct contrast to mothers at the other end of the social scale, who show an almost superstitious respect for words as the agents of truth, lower-working-class mothers on the whole accept as normal the use of deliberate distortions of fact, often exploiting the child's natural fears and anxieties, in order to instil in him a salutary sense of their own power. It is perhaps significant how often such idle threats consist of a backing-up of the mother's own authority by some outside authority figure, which, being a more unknown quantity to the child than the mother herself, is perhaps presumed to retain its effectiveness rather longer. Examples of idle threats and teases follow; they are representative.

'I say, "A policeman will come and take you away, and you'll have no
   Mummy and no Daddy".'
'I often say, "If I have to keep shouting at you, I'm going to the
   doctor's, and if I don't get any better I'll have to go away".'
'I tell her God will do something to her hand if she smacks me.'
'I've told him I'll have to put him in a home if he's naughty.'
'She picks her nose – I tell her it's dirty and her nose will fall off.'

The following account is an example of how a chance occurrence may be deliberately used both to tease the child and to tighten control; similar examples have been reported from other cultures.

After I got your letter, mester asked what it was for; so my girl, naturally enough (*sic*), she said to Freddie (aged 4), 'Oh, it's to take you away, a lady's coming to take you away'. He said 'I don't want to go away'; so I said 'Well, you'd better be a good lad, then – or else she will'. (Do you often say that sort of thing?) Yes.

On the whole, the parental attitudes and group trends that we have so far discussed are those which differentiate most sharply between different working-class groups at the lower end of the social scale; which, in fact, characterize the unskilled worker's family from those of other manual workers. They suggest a traditional pattern of childrearing which would these days be condemned by most middle-class commentators and experts, and by a majority of parents generally, as at best uneducated and lacking in psychological insight, and at worst unkind and extremely undesirable. We must, however, remind ourselves that this style of parent-child relationships has a long history and deep cultural roots. The pattern would appear to share many features with patterns adopted by economically underprivileged parents in urban communities all round the world, and in societies which are, in many other respects, very different from our own. It has probably evolved in such a way that it allows parents and their children at least to survive and cope at a certain level; and whether or not this method will be successful in producing children who are reasonably well adapted to the kinds of conditions they are liable to face as young adults, at the least privileged end of the social spectrum in our decaying city centres, is still rather an open question. It could be argued, for instance, with some cynicism but also with some force, that a socialization pattern which compels children to independence; which turns them, at an early age, away from their parents and towards the peer group; which teaches them to distrust as unreliable all adults in positions of authority; and which, to some extent, hardens and desensitizes them emotionally, will continue to serve a function in making a hard life at least tolerable for the exceptionally underprivileged. It may also, of course, make them irreclaimable to such opportunities as exist.

However, it is necessary to emphasize that the pattern of childrearing which we have been describing is nowadays only to be found, in its essential form, in a small minority of families in our sample. Nottingham is a prosperous city with a low unemployment rate and a vigorous policy of slum clearance and rehousing on new estates. The old densely packed terraced housing in the central districts is steadily being eroded and replaced. For the majority of children, even within the working-class group, the socialization pattern has already changed. Father has come down from his erstwhile pedestal to be a friend to his children and a help to his wife. Relationships between parents and children have already become a good deal more egalitarian and democratic. And parents pinpoint the change by their pleasure at their children's willingness to talk to and share confidences with them with a freedom that they found so much more difficult, or even impossible, to attain with their own parents. In the context of a culture in which the major attitude changes over time have already affected all socioeconomic groups except the lowest, much of our work has been to attempt a description of the skilled and semi-skilled working-class style of upbringing, and to show how it still differs in more subtle ways from middle-class modes of behaviour.

Let us consider a whole variety of interlocking ways in which the experience of middle-class children differs from that of working-class children; in other words, we will switch our attention away from differences between groups at the bottom end of the social scale, and towards a consideration of differences between middle-class children and working-class children as a whole. It is convenient to do this in terms of a number of propositions which can be backed up by both qualitative and quantitative evidence drawn from the results of our study of seven-year-olds and their mothers. Briefly to define our terms, we take the middle class to comprise white-collar workers and upwards, and the working class to include all manual workers with the exception of foremen.

(1) Middle-class children are *future-oriented*. Their parents tend to marry somewhat later, on average, than those of working-class children, and this is often quite deliberately planned in order to allow the middle-class father to establish himself vocationally in some career which will have a rising income-curve through time. The middle-class child is thus born into a family which can look forward to considerably improved standards in the future – not because everyone in the country will gradually get richer, but because middle-class workers expect to benefit from a promotion system which brings them to their peak in middle age, whereas manual workers know that their earning power is likely to fade proportionally to their failing health and strength. This is what lies behind what Brian Jackson has succinctly described as 'the middle-class ethic of postponed pleasure'; and it is nowhere more strongly evident than in the way children in different social groups are taught to handle their pocket money. We have calculated, taking all different sources of income into account, precisely how much pocket money is at the disposal of the seven-year-old child in the course of a week; oddly or significantly, depending on one's viewpoint, there is a perfect inverse correlation between this average figure and the social class affiliation of the child: that is to say, the lower down the class scale, the more money the child is given to spend each week. It must be remembered, of course, that the middle-class child is probably enjoying rather more luxurious living-standards, and may be receiving considerable benefits in kind such as plenty of fruit, drawing materials, outings etc.; however, the fact remains that the working-class child has more immediate spending power. His mother is also more likely to give him extra if she happens to have it, without making conditions as to its sensible use. What is more, once the money has been put into his hands (often in small daily amounts), there is considerable tolerance of his spending it at once, although there is a tradition of saving up as a holiday approaches; whereas middle-class children are generally expected *on principle* to save a proportion of their smaller sum.

(2) Middle-class children – particularly the boys, compared with working-class boys – appear to lead *more sheltered and protected lives* than their working-class counterparts. Sometimes this is the result of parents actively discouraging their children from 'playing out' in the neighbourhood or forbidding their wandering off beyond their own road into an area where the children might be less 'nice'; but in practice it is seldom necessary for the middle-class mother to make such blatant restrictions, since middle-class areas tend anyhow to be geographically distinct and insular. It is also broadly true that the catchment areas of the state primary schools tend to reflect such social divisions. When house-hunting, middle-class parents are often strongly influenced to choose a particular area because of the reputation of the local primary school; and, even when they live outside the normal catchment area of a favoured school, they will tend to exercise

the right of parental choice (allowed for by the education act, but rather seldom invoked by working-class parents) so as to allow their child to attend a 'better' school some distance from their home. Alternatively, they may opt out of the state system altogether and send their children to private schools.

When we first began to look into the question of protection, our original intention was simply to obtain some measure of children's independence at the age of seven years. To this end, we endeavoured to form a scale based on answers given to a number of different specific questions, which could be rated and then summed to yield a composite index or independence score for each child. When, however, the separate questions were analysed as a function of social class, the results were not at all consistent from one question to the next. For instance, when we asked whether the child was permitted to go to the park or recreation ground alone, we found a clear class trend indicating that, as we move down the social class scale, more and more children are permitted to do this; when we asked about children going shopping alone, there was no consistent social class trend; and when we asked about travelling alone by bus, there was a significant trend showing that a greater proportion of middle-class children are expected to cope with this. Again, whereas more middle-class children are taken and collected to and from school, it is also true that fewer working-class children ever have the experience of staying away from home overnight, for pleasure, without their parents. Thinking in terms of some global concept such as 'independence training', these divergent results are not easy to reconcile. The evidence instead suggests that middle-class and working-class children are taught to be independent in somewhat different ways. Taking into account a good deal of additional evidence, one arrives at the conclusion that the working-class child is taught to be independent in the sense that he must learn to fend for himself *among other children* in a variety of situations where adult supervision is likely to be minimal. He is allowed to wander further, through very much more crowded streets, in order to reach a recreation ground where, again, he is likely to have to cope with large unsupervised groups of children; and he is expected to make his own way on foot to his local school. By contrast, the middle-class child is encouraged to be independent of his own parents by learning to rely on other *adults* for help and support. Parents expect some control over his choice of companions, by selecting both his school and the location of his play. Selection of school gives rise to problems of distance; these they solve either by ferrying or by teaching him to use public transport, an adult-supervised activity. He may stay a night away from home with a friend, but it is fully understood that the friend's mother is in charge. Thus the middle-class child is introduced to independence by degrees and in a highly protected context.

At first sight, this tendency on the part of middle-class parents to protect and supervise their children so closely might appear to restrict the range of experiences to which the middle-class child has access. It is true that the middle-class child grows up without much acquaintance with a busy street life, the hurly-burly of traffic, hostile and friendly adults and a mob of neighbourhood children. Adult memories of back-street childhoods evoke a richness of mingled delights and fears: the parents of back-street children often express considerable anxiety as to the unfortunate influences from which they are powerless to shield the child effectively. The middle-class child's experience is very different, but probably no less rich. Intellectually, his parents expect to provide opportunities for his own self-expression as well as for learning; socially, they provide the formal opportunity to play both guest and host. Outside the home, there is a deliberate widening of the child's experience, again under supervision. As one might expect, middle-class seven-year-olds are more likely than their working-class counterparts to be taken on visits to theatres, concerts, exhibitions, art galleries and historic buildings; but it is interesting that it is the middle-class children who also more often attend sporting events such as football matches with their parents, and also the cinema. A higher proportion of middle-class children also go to church with their parents, belong to Sunday School and are members of organized clubs or church groups.

(3) This leads to a further broad generalization: that middle-class children are expected to *learn communication skills* of many different kinds as early as possible. We ourselves have shown how, as early as four years old, the middle-class child is effectively rewarded for his skill in verbally stating his case for arbitration; and Bernstein has made an especially important contribution by his emphasis of the difference between an explicit and a context-bound use of language. The point at issue is whether the child is able to use language to communicate meaningfully, without recourse to gesture and pronominal indications of the context; such gestures in fact restrict him to communicating his thoughts only in contexts which his listener already shares. For example, the child who normally sees no need to be more explicit than 'You know him, out there, well he pushed her just here all like that' is entirely dependent for communication upon his listener's ability to watch his gestures and look out of the window to see to whom these gestures refer. He is more likely to have difficulty in putting his thoughts across in situations where the context is not available than the child who has the habit of being explicit: 'That boy in next door's yard, he twisted his sister's arm right up behind her back.'

It is, of course, precisely this comparative lack of familiarity with the context-free use of language which makes it difficult for many working-class adults to use the telephone effectively. Conversely, the telephone for most middle-class people, in work and at play, is an indispensable tool of communication. In perhaps the majority of middle-class households, its possibilities are taken for granted; middle-class children need little encouragement to learn its use from an early age, in order to take messages for their parents, and quickly discover its advantages to further their own social enjoyment, and indeed to break through the geographical restrictions still imposed on them at the primary-school age. Every middle-class parent of reasonably sociable children becomes irritably aware of the telephone as a successful medium for children's conversations with their peers. The working-class child, however, even if his father's job atypically demands a telephone, finds that very few of his friends have access to one, and that therefore his own use of the facility is negligible. The situation is a good example of a technological innovation which offers a specific if unlooked-for training in a communication skill, and it is interesting that the use of telephones is now encouraged as a deliberate pedagogic technique in schools for underprivileged children.

This is, of course, not the only way in which middle-class children acquire more opportunity to learn and practise the skills of explicit language. They are also read to more often from story books, frequently full-length books taken on a serial basis. They more often 'say their prayers' at bedtime. They are encouraged to communicate their private fantasy life to their mothers, who have more welcoming attitudes to fantasy and imagination than working-class mothers, and therefore reward the child by their interest and approval for describing to his mother what only he *can* describe. Middle-class children are also more likely to prefer imaginative, role-playing games to the play of the rough-and-tumble variety which is the first choice of more working-class children; while it is not altogether clear why this preference should exist (factors may be parental encouragement and greater privacy and space in the home), certainly imaginative play provides a much more powerful stimulus for the explicit use of language, whereas rough-and-tumble play is well enough served by purely implicit forms.

When we turn to other communication skills such as the child's developing ability in reading and writing, we of course find enormous social class differences in the extent to which parents expect such activities to spill over from the school setting into the child's home life. That parents look upon reading and writing as a normal part of *anyone*'s life, not just something one learns at school, must inevitably determine in part the child's ability to use such skills as flexible tools rather than as some kind of trick unrelated to real life. The writing of letters by children, story writing for their own pleasure, membership of public libraries and ownership of books all correlate dramatically with social class. To state the obvious, the skills of literacy are virtually indispensable to adults in middle-class occupations; and it is largely through writing letters and memoranda to one another that the professional and managerial classes exert power and influence over events and hence earn their livelihoods. Inevitably, then, middle-class parents are hypersensitive to any difficulties their children may have in learning to read and write; what is more, a knowledge of this fact brings a subtle but strong and effective pressure to bear on all teachers in primary schools within middle-class catchment areas.

(4) Turning finally to the ways in which parents attempt to control their children, the differences between the two major class groups are not simple. When the children in our sample were only a year old, there was a substantial group in all social classes, albeit a minority group (38 per cent overall), who felt that it was totally inappropriate to smack a baby of that age for any reason; and there was also a clear difference between the professional/managerial class, for whom this was a majority opinion, and the rest. By the time the child had reached four, the situation had changed somewhat: four is an age when, in all sorts of ways, the child comes into conflict with his mother, while at the same time he is still highly egocentric and not particularly amenable to his mother's reasoning. At this age, smacking is rather widely seen as appropriate, even if an unfortunate necessity, and there is no class difference in approval or disapproval of its use, although the top and bottom classes smack significantly less and more often respectively. By the age of seven, rather more parents see smacking as inappropriate, and smacking has in fact decreased over all classes; but class differences in frequency of smacking retain the same pattern.

There are also interesting divergences in the kinds of things for which smacking is thought to be a suitable punishment: for instance, at seven, middle-class parents are less likely to smack their children for un-truthfulness and for rudeness; and in fact it is rather typical of these mothers that they do not like smacking for matters which they regard as serious. In our view, however, it is a mistake to place too much emphasis upon smacking as such. The discipline of the human child is accomplished primarily by means of language. Acts of physical punishment are not generally important in and of themselves; they act merely as punctuation marks in a continuing dialogue between the parent and the child. On their own admission, nearly all parents in our culture are at times driven to smacking their children; but smacks are almost invariably accompanied by a barrage of verbal pressure, and it is not without interest that in Nottingham it is this verbal 'telling-off', rather than the hitting, which goes by the name of 'chastisement'.

Is there, then, any essential difference between the social classes in their handling of discipline generally? We have shown elsewhere how the middle-class mother tries to use verbal reasoning methods in attempting to influence her child, and we have linked this preference for verbal control to her democratic intentions in her style of discipline. The ordering of family behaviour on a democratic system immediately involves a high degree of verbal interaction as disagreements are talked out and every voice is heard; whereas the authoritarian system preferred further down the scale has no need of more talk than a firm 'Do this!' Basically, the democratic ethic boils down to a *principle of reciprocity*, and this is the most important idea that middle-class parents try to teach their children: that they should have respect for the rights and wishes of other persons *as individuals*. In the end, this principle can only be taught by example, backed up by endless verbal persuasion and reiteration: 'Don't do that to me, I wouldn't do it to you'; 'I know you don't want to share your bike with Jane, but she's your visitor, and you'll be *her* visitor when you go to her house'; 'Answer Mrs Brown when she speaks to you, you wouldn't like it if someone didn't answer you'. Middle-class parents consciously want their children to realize how other people feel when they are at the receiving end of thoughtless behaviour; they expect their children to make an imaginative effort to put themselves in the place of others, and thereby to become sensitive to the impressions which they create. The whole process is a painfully slow one, dependent as it is upon the gradual growth of self-awareness and social empathy. It is a necessary part of this orientation towards an integrated rather than piecemeal socialization, that the child himself is valued as a person whose wishes and desires must be respected, and is accorded status in his own right.

With this in mind, it is worth looking at class differences in what we may call 'child-centredness'. From a number of different areas of interaction between the mother and the seven-year-old, it has been possible to draw certain indicators of a child-centred attitude, and to construct an index of child-centredness on this basis. Briefly, the responses were scored as positively child-centred, as follows: the child has a place to keep his own possessions, if only a cardboard box; his friends are allowed to play inside the house most weeks; his mother shows sympathy if he does not want to go to school (not necessarily to the extent of allowing his absence); she shows sympathy if, to escape school, he pretends he is not well; she takes complaints of school seriously, i.e. does not ignore them; she keeps or displays some of his drawings; she shares a special interest with the child; she does not punish but only rebukes or ignores rudeness to her; she is prepared to say 'sorry' sometimes when she has been cross with him; she lets him have some say in plans for holidays or outings. On this index, mothers who score 7+ out of a possible 10 are considered highly child-centred, while those who score 4 or less are rated as low on child-centredness. Class differences are in fact very marked: 51 per cent of middle-class, compared with 25 per cent of working-class, mothers rate as highly child-centred on this criterion, while 15 per cent of middle-class mothers and 40 per cent of working-class mothers score low. It is possibly of interest that working-class mothers are significantly more inclined to child-centredness where girls are concerned, while middle-class mothers reverse this trend, though not to significance level. Clearly, the overall results show that the middle-class mother, in contrast to her working-class counterpart, accepts her stated principle of reciprocity as a practical way of life.

We have attempted here to outline and illustrate just a few of the characteristic differences in attitudes towards childrearing which sharply distinguish middle-class from working-class parents. We have argued in general terms that such divergences are to be expected because different social class groups have their own expectations and their own outlook on life, and these in turn lead them to attach importance to different qualities in the upbringing of their children. It is sometimes assumed that, as material living standards rise, people will instantaneously adopt specifically middle-class attitudes and ideas. Obviously working-class families want to share the good things which a modern technological society has to offer, and quickly acquire a taste for better clothes, more varied foodstuffs and consumer durables which were hitherto only available to a middle-class minority. It does not follow from this that we should expect a very rapid shift towards middle-class ideals and values generally.

Education Cannot Compensate for Society
B. Bernstein

Reprinted with permission from Basil Bernstein, 'Education Cannot Compensate for Society', *New Society*, 26 February 1970

I find the term 'compensatory education' a curious one for a number of reasons. I do not understand how we can talk about offering compensatory education to children who in the first place have not, as yet, been offered an adequate educational environment. The Newsom report on secondary schools showed that 79 per cent of all secondary-modern schools in slum and problem areas were materially grossly inadequate, and that the holding power of these schools over the teachers was horrifyingly low. The same report also showed very clearly the depression in the reading scores of these children, compared with the reading scores of children who were at school in areas which were neither problem nor slum. This does not conflict with the findings that, on average, for the country as a whole, there has been an improvement in children's reading ability. The Plowden report on the primary schools was rather more coy about all the above points, but we have little reason to believe that the situation is very much better for primary schools in similar areas.

Thus we offer a large number of children, both at the primary and secondary levels, materially inadequate schools and a high turnover of teaching staff; and we further expect a small group of dedicated teachers to cope. The strain on these teachers inevitably produces fatigue and illness and it is not uncommon to find, in any week, teachers having to deal with doubled-up classes of eighty children. And we wonder why the children display very early in their educational life a range of learning difficulties.

At the same time, the organization of schools creates delicate overt and covert streaming arrangements which neatly lower the expectations and motivations of both teachers and taught. A vicious spiral is set up, with an all too determinate outcome. It would seem, then, that we have failed to provide, on the scale required, an *initial* satisfactory educational environment.

The concept, 'compensatory education', serves to direct attention away from the internal organization and the educational context of the school, and focus our attention on the families and children. 'Compensatory education' implies that something is lacking in the family, and so in the child. As a result, the children are unable to benefit from schools.

It follows, then, that the school has to 'compensate' for the something which is missing in the family, and the children are looked at as deficit systems. If only the parents were interested in the goodies we offer, if only they were like middle-class parents, then we could do our job. Once the problem is seen even implicitly in this way, then it becomes appropriate to coin the terms 'cultural deprivation', 'linguistic deprivation', and so on. And then these labels do their own sad work.

If children are labelled 'culturally deprived', then it follows that the parents are inadequate; the spontaneous realizations of their culture, its images and symbolic representations, are of reduced value and significance. Teachers will have lower expectations of the children, which the children will undoubtedly fulfil. All that informs the child, that gives meaning and purpose to him outside of the school, ceases to be valid or accorded significance and opportunity for enhancement within the school. He has to orient towards a different structure of meaning, whether it is in the form of reading books (*Janet and John*), in the form of language use and dialect, or in the patterns of social relationships.

Alternatively the meaning structure of the school is explained to the parents and imposed on, rather than integrated within, the form and content of their world. A wedge is progressively driven between the child as a member of a school. Either way the child is expected, and his parents as well, to drop their social identity, their way of life and its symbolic representations, at the school gate. For, by definition, their culture is deprived, and the parents are inadequate in both the moral and the skill orders they transmit.

I do not mean by this that in these circumstances no satisfactory home-school relations can take place or do not take place; I mean rather that the best thing is for the parents to be brought *within* the educational experience of the schoolchild by doing what they can do, and this with confidence. There are many ways in which parents can help the child in his learning, which are within the parents' spheres of competence. If this happens, then the parents can feel adequate and confident both in relation to the child and the school. This may mean that the contents of the learning in school should be drawn much more from the child's experience in his family and community.

So far I have criticized the use of the concept of 'compensatory education', because it distracts attention from the deficiencies in the school itself and focuses upon deficiencies within the community, family and child. We can add to these criticisms a third.

This concept points to the overwhelming significance of the early years of the child's life in the shaping of his later development. Clearly there is much evidence to support this view and to support its implication that we should create an extensive nursery-school system. However, it would be foolhardy indeed to write off the post-seven-years-of-age educational experience as having little influence.

Minimally, what is required *initially* is to consider the whole age period up to the conclusion of the primary stages as a unity. This would require considering our approach, at any *one* age, in the context of the whole of the primary stage. This implies a systematic, rather than a piecemeal, approach. I am arguing here for taking as the unit, not a particular period in the life of the child – for example, three to five years, or five to seven years – but taking as the unit a stage of education: the primary stage. We should see all we do in terms of the sequencing of learning, the development of sensitivities within the context of the primary stage. In order to accomplish this, the present social and educational division between infant and junior stages must be weakened, as well as the insulation between primary and secondary stages. Otherwise gains at any one age, for the child, may well be vitiated by losses at a later age.

We should stop thinking in terms of 'compensatory education' but consider, instead, most seriously and systematically, the conditions and contexts of the educational environment.

The very form our research takes tends to confirm the beliefs underlying the organization, transmission and evaluation of knowledge by the school. Research proceeds by assessing the criteria of attainment that schools hold, and then measures the competence of different social groups in reaching these criteria. We take one group of children, whom we know beforehand possess attributes favourable to school achievement; and a second group of children, whom we know beforehand lack these attributes. Then we evaluate one group in terms of what it *lacks* when compared with another. In this way research, unwittingly, underscores the notion of *deficit* and confirms the status quo of a given organization, transmission and, in particular, evaluation of knowledge. Research very rarely challenges or exposes the social assumptions underlying what counts as valid knowledge, or what counts as a valid realization of that knowledge. There are exceptions in the area of curriculum development; but, even here, the work often has no built-in attempt to evaluate the changes. This holds particularly for educational priority area 'feasibility' projects.

Finally, we do not face up to the basic question: What is the potential for change within educational institutions as they are presently constituted? A lot of activity does not necessarily mean *action*.

I have taken so much space discussing the new educational concepts and categories because, in a small way, the work I have been doing has inadvertently contributed towards their formulation. It might be, and has been, said that my research – through focusing upon the subculture and forms of family socialization – has also distracted attention from the conditions and contexts of learning in school. The focus on usage of language has sometimes led people to divorce the use of language from the substratum of cultural meanings which are initially responsible for the language use. The concept, 'restricted code', to describe working-class speech, has been equated with 'linguistic deprivation' or even with the 'non-verbal' child.

We can distinguish between uses of language which can be called 'context-bound' and uses of language which are less context-bound. Consider, for example, the two following stories which the linguist Peter Hawkins constructed as a result of his analysis of the speech of middle-class and working-class five-year-old children. The children were given a series of four pictures which told a story and they were invited to tell the story. The first picture shows some boys playing football; in the second the ball goes through the window of a house; the third shows a man making a threatening gesture; and in the fourth a woman looks out of a window and the children are moving away. Here are the two stories:

(1) Three boys are playing football and one boy kicks the ball and it goes through the window the ball breaks the window and the boys are looking at it and a man comes out and shouts at them because they've broken the window so they run away and then that lady looks out of her window and she tells the boys off. (Number of nouns: 13. Number of pronouns: 6.)

(2) They're playing football and he kicks it and it goes through there it breaks the window and they're looking at it and he comes out and shouts at them because they've broken it so they run away and then she looks out and she tells them off. (Number of nouns: 2. Number of pronouns: 14.)

With the first story, the reader does not have to have the four pictures which were used as the basis for the story, whereas in the case of the second story the reader would require the initial pictures in order to make sense of the story. The first story is free of the context which generated it, whereas the second story is much more closely tied to its context. As a result, the meanings of the second story are implicit, whereas the meanings of the first story are explicit.

It is not that the working-class children do not have, in their passive vocabulary, the vocabulary used by the middle-class children. Nor is it the case that the children differ in their tacit understanding of the linguistic rule system. Rather, what we have here are differences in the use of language arising out of a specific context. One child makes explicit the meanings which he is realizing through language for the person he is telling the story to, whereas the second child does not to the same extent.

The first child takes very little for granted, whereas the second child takes a great deal for granted. Thus, for the first child, the task was seen as a context which his meanings were required to make explicit, whereas the task for the second child was not seen as a task which required such explication of meaning. It would not be difficult to imagine a context where the first child would produce speech rather like the second.

What we are dealing with here are differences between the children in the way they realize, in language use, what is apparently the same context. We could say that the speech of the first child generated universalistic meanings, in the sense that the meanings are freed from the context and so understandable by all; whereas the speech of the second child generated particularistic meanings, in the sense that the meanings are closely tied to the context and would be only fully understood by others if they had access to the context which originally generated the speech. Thus universalistic meanings are less bound to a given context, whereas particularistic meanings are severely context-bound.

Let us take another example. One mother, when she controls her child, places a great emphasis on language, because she wishes to make explicit, and to elaborate for the child, certain rules and reasons for the rules *and* their consequences. In this way the child has access through language to the relationships between his particular act which evoked the mother's control and certain general principles, reasons and consequences which serve to universalize the particular act.

Another mother places less emphasis on language when she controls her child and deals with only the particular act; she does not relate it to general principles and their reasoned basis and consequences.

Both children learn that there is something they are supposed, or not supposed, to do, but the first child has learned rather more than this. The grounds of the mother's acts have been made explicit and elaborated; whereas the grounds of the second mother's acts are implicit, they are unspoken.

Our research shows just this. The social classes differ in terms of the *contexts* which evoke certain linguistic realizations. Many mothers in the middle class (and it is important to add not all), relative to the working class (and again it is important to add not all by any means), place greater emphasis on the use of language in socializing the child into the moral order, in disciplining the child, in the communication and recognition of feeling. Here again we can say that the child is oriented towards universalistic meanings which transcend a given context, whereas the second child is oriented towards particularistic meanings which are closely tied to a given context and so do not transcend it. This does not mean that working-class mothers are non-verbal, only that they differ from the middle-class mothers in the *contexts* which evoke universalistic meanings. They are *not* linguistically deprived, neither are their children.

We can generalize from these two examples and say that certain groups of children, through the forms of their socialization, are oriented towards receiving and offering universalistic meanings in certain contexts, whereas other groups of children are oriented towards particularistic meanings. The linguistic realizations of universalistic orders of meaning are very different from the linguistic realizations of particularistic orders of meaning, and so are the forms of the social relation (for example, between mother and child) which generate these. We can say, then, that what is made available for learning, how it is made available, and the patterns of social relations, are also very different.

Now, when we consider the children in school, we can see that there is likely to be difficulty. For the school is necessarily concerned with the transmission and development of universalistic orders of meaning. The school is concerned with making explicit – and elaborating through language – principles and operations as these apply to objects (the science subjects) and persons (the arts subjects). One child, through his socialization, is already sensitive to the symbolic orders of the school, whereas the second child is much less sensitive to the universalistic orders of the school. The second child is oriented towards particularistic orders of meaning which are context-bound, in which principles and operations are implicit, and towards a form of language use through which such meanings are realized.

The school is necessarily trying to develop in the child orders of relevance and relation as these apply to persons and objects, which are not initially the ones he spontaneously moves towards. The problem of educability at one level, whether it is in Europe, the United States or newly developing societies, can be understood in terms of a confrontation between (1) the school's universalistic orders of meaning and the social relationships which generate them, and (2) the particularistic orders of meaning and the social relationships which generate them, which the child brings with him to the school. Orientations towards 'metalanguages' of control and innovation are not made available to these children as part of their initial socialization.

The school is attempting to transmit un-commonsense knowledge – i.e., public knowledge realized through various 'metalanguages'. This knowledge is what I have called universalistic. However, both implicitly and explicitly, school transmits values and an attendant morality, which affect the contents and contexts of education. They do this by establishing criteria for acceptable pupil and staff conduct. These values and morals also affect the content of educational knowledge through the selection of books, texts and films, and through the examples and analogies used to assist access to public knowledge (universalistic meanings). Thus, the working-class child may be placed at a considerable disadvantage in relation to the *total* culture of the school. It is not made for him; he may not answer to it.

The universalistic functions of language – where meanings are less context-bound – point to an 'elaborated code'. The more particularistic functions point to a 'restricted code'. Because a code is restricted it does not mean that a child is non-verbal, nor is he in the technical sense linguistically deprived, for he possesses the same tacit understanding of the linguistic rule system as any child. It does not mean that the children cannot produce, at any time, elaborated speech variants in *particular* contexts.

It is critically important to distinguish between speech variants and a restricted code. A speech variant is a pattern of linguistic choices which is specific to a particular context – for example, when talking to children, a policeman giving evidence in a court, talking to friends whom one knows well, the rituals of cocktail parties, or train encounters. Because a code is restricted it does not mean that a speaker will not in some contexts, and under specific conditions, use a range of modifiers or subordinations, or whatever. But it does mean that where such choices are made they will be highly *context-specific*.

It is an accepted educational principle that we should work with what the child can offer; why don't we practise it? The introduction of the child to the universalistic meanings of public forms of thought is not 'compensatory education'; *it is education*. It is not making children middle-class; how it is done, through the implicit values underlying the form and content of the educational environment, might.

We need to distinguish between the principles and operations that teachers transmit and develop in the children, and the contexts they create in order to do this. We should start knowing that the social experience the child already possesses is valid and significant, and that this social experience should be reflected back to him as being valid and significant. It can only be reflected back to him if it is part of the texture of the learning experience we create. If we spent as much time thinking through the implications of this as we do thinking about the implications of Piaget's development sequences, then it would be possible for schools to become exciting and challenging environments for parents, the children themselves and teachers.

We need to examine the social assumptions underlying the organization, distribution and evaluation of knowledge, for there is not one, and only one, answer. The power relationships created outside the school penetrate the organization, distribution and evaluation of knowledge through the social context. The definition of 'educability' is itself, at any one time, an attenuated consequence of these power relationships.

We must consider Robert Lynd's question: 'knowledge for what?' And the answer cannot be given only in terms of whether six-year-old children should be able to read, count and write. We do not know what a child is capable of, as we have as yet no theory which enables us to create sets of optimal learning environments; and even if such a theory existed, it is most unlikely that resources would be available to make it substantive on the scale required. It may well be that one of the tests of an educational system is that its outcomes are relatively unpredictable.

Why Education is Political
M. Kogan

Reprinted with permission from Maurice Kogan, *The Politics of Educational Change*, Fontana Paperbacks, 1978, pp. 15–22

Politics are those processes of discourse through which members of society seek to assert and ultimately reconcile their wishes. So those people who wish to make education non-political are either failing to understand that the purposes and procedures of education reflect what people want, or they are trying, perhaps unconsciously, to restrict the rights of fellow citizens to participate in decisions of deep and abiding importance to them. That is not to say that teaching should be politically biased. The fact that education brings into conflict so many different values makes it all the more important that pupils and students should be taught how to make their own choices.

Education, more than virtually any other social activity, is concerned with what *ought* to be rather than with what *is*. People become educated in order to promote changes in themselves or others. Some political actors, including Hitler and Lenin, hoped it would help them to change the world. All the major religions have tried to use education to mould the morals and beliefs of the young. The changes desired in people are as various as the whole range of human desire and feeling, and may conflict with each other even within a single school or school system.

This emphasis on change is not contradicted by education's socializing aims. Education acts powerfully to train pupils to maintain an existing society, and to learn traditional skills or traditional attitudes. Those processes will themselves have changed the pupil into a member of society even if they have not encouraged him to change that society. The unit of discussion is, indeed, important. Individual and collective benefit are not the same thing. Nor are individual and collective change and development. Personal development may be compatible with the collective good. Quite often, however, they are in conflict.

Now education is a highly artificial business in the way that building houses, making roads, mending limbs, or defending one's family and property are not. There are innate desires to learn but education, as Europeans have universally come to understand it, involves schooling. Schooling causes societies to select and train adults to work as teachers who then spend most of their working lives in specially built and equipped school buildings where they work on tasks that might seem quite remote from ordinary living. Education is also artificial in the sense that a world without it is not only conceivable but possible; the world has been without organized education for most of its history.

It does not follow that the British citizen is wrong to spend so much of his total earnings on education. (About 3.2 per cent of the gross national product between the mid-1950s and -1960s went into it. By 1969 it was 6 per cent.) It does follow, however, that education is, more than most human activities, tied up with what people want to do and want to be rather than with what they must do and are compelled to be. As Julia Evetts has written in *The Sociology of Educational Ideas*, 'The changes in educational outlook parallel the changes which a nation undergoes in the course of its history.' Education is the most volatile of collective activities because it incorporates simultaneously so many aspirations. It contains the hope that man may change himself so as to be happier, more productive, a good neighbour; and the hope that social arrangements can incorporate both the best of the past and the promise of the future.

If, then, education responds to both social demands and individual aspirations, an examination of the main educational issues since 1945 will also entail an inquiry into some of the most important arguments about politics and society during that period.

Before looking in more detail at the issues with which educators and their children have been concerned, it will be well to be clear as to how controversies about educational policies are in fact controversies about man's individual and collective present and future wants.

Men wish to improve themselves, and for several reasons. The first is an innate desire to be more powerful and competent, and more in control of their own powers, for the sake of psychological comfort, of self-esteem. In that sense education is not artificial. It is a prime purpose of education to help a pupil to develop a sense of his own worth. This becomes particularly important in the middle years of secondary education when adolescence causes a surge of both optimism and uncertainty. Teaching a pupil to express himself clearly, to work competently, to attend to personal appearance and style, has an 'internal' or individual purpose as well as more socially instrumental or external purposes. This purpose of education, of giving pupils a sense of control over themselves, constitutes the *autonomy* or *freedom objectives* of education and relates quite closely to those of enabling pupils to be economically self-sufficient and to contribute their share to the formation of family or national wealth. Lack of economic self-sufficiency and an inability to contribute a share to the economy is a major component of lack of self-esteem and is thought to be 'stigmatizing'. It is this *individual* objective of education that gives a fierce dynamic to education as a political force. The individual objective of education is that most strongly espoused by conservative policy-makers though their critics maintain that traditional systems are instrumental in creating elites and dutiful work forces rather than enhancing personal freedom. It comes into conflict with the more collective aspirations of the left who see education as a way of causing social change and social cohesion.

These individual objectives of education are closely tied to the *social* objectives with which they may conflict. Individuals need relationships with their family, peer groups, neighbourhood and work place if they are to function well as individuals. Interpersonal relationships, which are affected so deeply by a sense of self-esteem and adequacy, are learned socially, and the school is an important centre for such social learning. Social learning is an overt purpose of both primary and secondary education as both the Plowden and Newsom reports (on primary and non-selective secondary education respectively) stated. It is also a traditional purpose of elite university education, as is obvious from the biographies of, for example, the leaders of the Bloomsbury group. This objective is pursued when nursery pupils learn to play in groups, primary pupils undertake projects together, and university students share seminars in which the conventions of social interplay have as much weight as rigorous demonstration of logic and power of argument.

In another and wider sense, education has social objectives. It transmits the dominant culture to new generations by inculcating norms of language such as those of 'received' English, or what Basil Bernstein has called the 'elaborated code', imparted by education and society and by drawing attention to the accepted glories of the culture, such as the works of Shakespeare, eighteenth-century architecture and parliamentary modes of debate. Education also makes plain the acceptable standards of behaviour as laid down by law and by social convention: such as the correct behaviour between weak and strong, male and female, what attitudes towards personal property are acceptable, the need to make a contribution to society, to behave as a good democrat, and so on. In Britain this socializing process is often implicit. Most observers of the process consider it as part of an intuitive and natural consensus that exists among the great mass of reflective people in the country. Others reckon the socializing process to be part of a sort of slave owners' conspiracy to condition the mass of the people into doing what they are told. The reader might care to reflect on his own life history and see which account seems most true. But because education is held accountable for socialization, its assumed failures to teach young people how to behave and how to work productively keep education central to the main discourse that constitutes politics.

The socializing process is implicit rather than overt in Britain. Its more explicit components, though hard to find, can be discovered in those curiously mummified residues of established religion known as 'religious education' and the 'act of worship', which are the only elements imposed by law on the British school curriculum. When they were written into the 1944 Education Act their authors must have had the same intentions as the Soviet educational planners who insist on the teaching of compulsory Marxism. That, too, we understand from Nigel Grant's authoritative *Soviet Education,* is a ritual 'like compulsory chapel', boring and unreal to most.

Indeed, the cases of religious education and the act of worship, as an example of compulsory socialization from which unbelievers have to opt out, serve to remind us again of how education responds to social change. At one time, no statement of educational objectives could have omitted the intention of society to teach its young to believe in God and the consequential tenets of a true faith in Him.

The single major point made so far is that education and the schooling through which it is carried out are an artefact. Into that artefact is poured a wide range of human aspirations. Since human beings seek to be autonomous, free and self-respecting but are at the same time social, gregarious and potentially loving of others, and since they have to act collectively to defend, feed and house themselves through an economic system, it follows that education, too, offers a menu which has some sections à la carte but others consisting of compulsory dishes. Social policy generally never fails to incorporate ambiguity or conflict about underlying values. The tension between social needs and private wants, the balance between freedom and control, between individual independence and collective effort, are present in discussions of who should get what in housing, health, social services, income reinforcement, or town planning. But because education is a desired artefact, rather than a self-evidently valued set of procedures, its content and form are far more open to dispute than other social provisions. Only, perhaps, town planning – which, too, expresses, or fails to express, what people want more than what they definitely need – is reactive so much to fashion and to the range of human endeavours.

For these reasons education is political. It is volatile. It strongly reflects the often conflicting and wide-ranging preferences of a society which it also helps to sustain, improve, embellish and from which it draws resources. If politics are the way in which individuals assert their claims and have them reconciled with the claims of others, education reflects and clarifies and expresses those claims in the society, though it cannot of itself reconcile them.

Some of those claims changed radically between 1945 and 1976. There were dramatic changes in mass expectations to which the education system had to respond. The mechanisms and modes of those responses are the stuff of educational politics. In this book, the politics of educational change has two meanings. It is first the actions and belief of the main political parties. More important, however, the politics of educational change entails the study of changes in the total political and administrative system as reflected in, and precipitated by, changes in education.

Some changes were caused by and reflected by the political parties. But the reader will notice that the main political parties, as opposed to a few leading individuals within them, do not appear in this book as prominent actors in change. Both the political system of parliament and the party activities themselves, reflect, articulate and, to some extent, affect issues. They are not, however, prime movers although the main political parties both affected and were affected by the changes recorded in this book.

The Conservatives made education a component of the Opportunity State and thus have increasingly come into conflict with the Labour Party view, which took far longer to clarify, that education is an equalizing force. Conservatives thus emphasized the individual objectives of education and concentrated on those social objectives which aim to produce an efficient work force and a strong social fabric. Both of these assumptions explain their strong support for the expansion of higher education in the 1960s. The Labour Party first confused greater opportunity with greater equality but increasingly moved towards the 'strong' version of egalitarianism which argued for the creation of comprehensive schools. They hoped that the schools could heal the divisions of a class-ridden society. They have not yet resolved the concomitant problems of freedom of choice for those who want particular and privileged forms of education and who can either win it through competitive examination or pay for it.

These remain important issues of educational policy. But education in the last decade has moved beyond its traditional boundaries. The interplay between the larger political parties and the working out of solutions by the schools, colleges and public authorities are no longer the only sources of change. Important new attitudes and policies have started at the fringe of politics and have increasingly entered the main fabric of the system. The testing of authority has affected educational policies and interactions. The power of schooling and scholarship to refine and pass on knowledge as validated material, the assumption that schools and colleges are specialist institutions performing a professional function have been severely attacked by deschooling, free schools, and the radical student movements. Starting in part with fringe groups but also entering into the more serious framework of academic philosophy and sociology there is a strong critique which challenges the ability of the educational system to safeguard individual rights or those forms of the collective good which they regard as the most important.

In these changes of attitude we see symptoms of many of the moods and movements which affect British politics and social relations at large. The right to choose to work or not, the right to have access to social good without clear statements of responsibilities to society, the assumption that authority and institutions are no more legitimate than those who remain outside them, all of these 'fringe' assumptions can be found in all walks of life. Education is therefore not alone in responding to ideas from outside its own doors.

Education and Social Change
D. V. Glass

Reprinted with permission from M. Ginsberg (ed.), *Law and Opinion in the Twentieth Century*, Stevens and Sons, 1959, pp. 322–7

In the late nineteenth century England was still educationally a very underdeveloped society. It would, of course, be both incorrect and unjust to minimize the part which religious and philanthropic bodies had already played in establishing schools. The incidence of illiteracy could not have been as high as it is in some underdeveloped countries today. Even so, a third of the men marrying in 1840 in England and Wales, and half of the women, signed the registers by a mark; the proportions in 1870 were still 20 per cent and 27 per cent. The rate of change in the provision of education since 1870 has been so rapid that it must be taken into account when considering present-day educational deficiencies.

It must be equally clear that the phrase 'the English tradition of education' not infrequently used in arguing against further rapid change in the character of secondary education, has a very limited validity. It can scarcely apply to the public system which, even during its brief history, has greatly altered in respect of objectives, structure and methods of selection. Nor, in the sense of a centuries-old persistence of character, is the term really applicable to the private sectors, whether secondary or university. It is true that, as an institution, the grammar school 'has a thousand years of history behind it'. But the present character of grammar schools derives from action taken during the nineteenth and twentieth centuries, action originally taken because, however deeply rooted the grammar school idea may have been, the schools themselves had ceased to be effective as educational institutions. In any case, most grammar schools today are not private. They are maintained by the local education authorities; they are thus part of the public system; and they have been exposed to powerful pressures for change in the curriculum, in the universe from which pupils are drawn, and in the qualifications of teachers. The public schools, too – the schools belonging to the Headmasters' Conference and the most firmly imbedded and 'traditionalist' part of the private system – bear little resemblance to their original form. They were, on the contrary, the first schools to be reconstructed in the nineteenth century. Indeed, it was the reforms introduced by Arnold and others which, as G. M. Young has said, 'reconciled the serious classes to the public school', and which encouraged the establishment of additional schools; fifty-one out of the present one hundred and sixteen independent public boarding schools were founded in the nineteenth century. The curriculum has also changed, though more slowly, and half the present public schools specialize in science and mathematics. The process of change has applied equally to the universities. The history of university reform is too well known to need documenting here. But it is evident that Trevelyan's description of Oxford and Cambridge in the days of decay as 'little more than comfortable monastic establishments for clerical sinecurists with a tinge of letters' would scarcely apply now. Moreover, the larger part of the university complex is itself the creation of the nineteenth century, and almost two-thirds of today's university students are studying in institutions established since the 1830s.

Much of the present educational system is thus not traditional. Moreover, many of its characteristics are not particularly English. Even during the first half of the nineteenth century, once the memory of the French Revolution had become a little clouded, educational reformers in England drew markedly upon the experiments which were being conducted on the Continent. And this was just as well, for the new influences helped to replace the more specifically British contributions of Lancaster's mutual system and Bell's 'Madras' system, which appeared to require a school to be a combination of factory and of Bentham's Panopticon. Later in the century Matthew Arnold imported from France the term 'secondary education' and with it the objective of a reorganized and comprehensive system. Technical education, too, especially in its shifting emphasis from craftsmanship to general principles and their application, was influenced both by foreign competition and by foreign models. All this has clearly been to the good. But along with these innovations there has been one underlying continuity – the influence of the class structure on the images of education and its function. It is this continuity and its consequences which I should now like to discuss.

During the nineteenth century, educational developments reflected two fairly distinct sets of considerations, one relating to the mass of the population and the other to the middle classes. Public concern with elementary education was in large measure concern to meet certain minimum requirements in a changing society – the need to ensure discipline, and to obtain respect for private property and the social order, as well as to provide that kind of instruction which was indispensable in an expanding industrial and commercial nation. Though many individuals and groups showed a far broader vision, these minimal considerations are evident in the very limited objectives of the system which grew up at that time. In the earliest period, the Bible and the catechism were sufficient, Hannah More thought; she would 'allow no writing for the poor'. Later, the sights were set a little higher. Speaking of the working-class child, James Fraser, subsequently Bishop of Manchester, told the 1858 Newcastle Commission that: 'we must make up our minds to see the last of him, as far as the day school is concerned, at ten or eleven . . . and I venture to maintain that it is quite possible to teach a child soundly and thoroughly, in a way that he shall not forget it, all that is necessary for him to possess in the shape of intellectual attainment, by the time that he is ten years old'. The Commission accepted the fact that most children would go to work at the age of ten or eleven. A similar assumption underlies the 1870 Act. It is not surprising that H. G. Wells referred to it as 'an Act to educate the lower classes for employment on lower-class lines, and with specially trained, inferior teachers'.

To gentle the masses was another explicit purpose. 'A set of good schools civilizes a whole neighbourhood', said the Newcastle Commission; and Forster, when he introduced his 1870 bill in Parliament, spoke of 'removing that ignorance which we are all aware is pregnant with crime and misery, with misfortune to individuals and danger to the community'. And he continued, 'I am one of those who would not wait until the people were educated before I would trust them with political power. If we had thus waited we might have waited long for education; but now that we have given them political power, we must not wait any longer to give them education.' Some of these notions were changed when the 1902 Act provided a framework for both elementary and secondary education. But the civilization motive had a longer currency, and even in 1929 Sir Cyril Norwood argued that it was largely elementary education which had prevented 'Bolshevism, Communism, and theories of revolt and destruction from obtaining any real hold upon the people of this country'. 'I hope', he added, 'that those who attribute the scarcity of domestic servants to the unreasonable institution of elementary education, by which they are made to pay for the teaching of other people's children, will lay in the other scale this other service, which has made of Bolshevism only a bogy which sits by their pillows and frightens them in the night.'

Concern with secondary education sprang from different motives. The effectiveness of the public schools and the endowed grammar schools as educational institutions for those groups who could afford to make use of them was the main issue. In the early part of the century an attempt had been made to compel the public schools to give the local poor the rights to entry provided by the founders' statutes. But the attempt failed, and the place of the public schools in the national system of secondary education was not again discussed by a Government committee until 1942. Instead, in 1861 a Royal Commission was appointed to study the quality of the education in what have ever since been known as the 'Clarendon schools' – nine schools with 2815 pupils. And the Clarendon Commission was immediately followed by the Taunton Commission, which inquired into the education given in the endowed grammar schools. Though expressing some disquiet at existing class distinction in education, the Taunton Commission in the main accepted the situation as they found it, and their recommendations were drawn up for the benefit of the middle classes by whom the schools were being used. What is particularly interesting is the emergence at this stage of a fresh criterion of the effectiveness of secondary education, the criterion of providing an avenue to the universities; and there were unfavourable references to the fact that 550 grammar schools sent no boys to universities, in sharp contrast to the large numbers now going from the nine Clarendon schools and from some of the recently founded proprietary schools.

For university education, like secondary education, was coming to have a new meaning. The changing society needed individuals of greater educational maturity and tested qualifications. The old and the new middle classes needed avenues of employment which would provide both prestige and relatively high income for their sons. Considerations of both scientific and social status were causing the existing professions to raise their standards of entry, and additional professions, including the higher civil service, were beginning to develop, also demanding considerable educational attainments.

Institutions and Teachers
C. Lacey

Reprinted with permission from Colin Lacey, 'Schools and Academic Streaming', *British Journal of Sociology*, vol. XVII, no. 3, September 1966, pp. 245–62

The Local Education Authority of Hightown sends about 15 per cent of its eleven-year-olds to grammar schools each year. This clearly does not imply that 15 per cent of the pupils in *any* junior school in the town will find themselves in the same grammar school. There are six grammar schools in Hightown and these are specialized in a number of ways; there are two Roman Catholic grammar schools (one for boys and one for girls) which serve the separate RC education system in Hightown and the surrounding area; and four LEA grammar schools (two for girls and two for boys) which draw their pupils almost exclusively from Hightown. For non-Catholic, eleven-year-old boys in Hightown there are then three possible grammar school avenues; entry to a direct grant school outside the town, Hightown Grammar School and Hightown Technical Grammar School. (A very small fraction attend public schools.)

The boys entering Hightown Grammar are selected from a large number of junior schools, and the selection test tends to scoop a few pupils from each school. Over half the boys come from schools that send six or less pupils. Evidence from a variety of sources (junior school reports, autobiographies and the statements of junior school teachers etc.) clearly shows that these contingents include the vast majority of top scholars, team leaders, school monitors, head boys and teachers' favourites. In short they are the 'best pupils'.

When the boys arrive at Hightown Grammar they are divided at random into four classes. The classes are also House Groups. The pupils in them remain together for prayers, school meals and registration as well as lessons.

A more comprehensive picture of the degree of isolation of the first-year boy, on his arrival at Hightown, must therefore take into account the effect of the school organization: 58 boys out of 118 questioned had no friend from the same junior school in their class. Thus almost half of the first-year intake spend the great majority of their time at school in a class in which they are isolated from their previous friends.

It can be seen from the foregoing analysis that any batch of new boys assembling at Hightown Grammar School are likely to make up a highly selected and homogeneous group. The annual intake being about 120, they represent under 4 per cent of their age group in the community and all are boys who have ostensibly been selected on the basis of their sex, religion and academic achievement.

The homogeneity of the intake and the relative isolation of individual new boys from their junior school friends are both important factors affecting patterns of behaviour in the first-year classes. The first-year pupils show a high degree of commitment to the school. School uniform is rigidly adhered to; caps and blazers are proudly displayed, school functions and clubs are attended disproportionately by first-year boys. Their behaviour in the classroom is characterized by eagerness, cooperation with the teacher and a high degree of competition among themselves. 'Please, sir, Willy Brown is copying my sums' is a remark that could only come from a first-year boy. I once tried to measure the response rate to a narrative and question-and-answer lesson given by a History teacher. So many responded to each question that I could not record them. As the tension mounted boys who did not know the answers looked around apprehensively at those who did. These were in a high state of excitement and they smiled triumphantly at those who did not know the answers; they stretched their arms and bodies to the utmost as they eagerly called, 'Sir', 'Sir', 'Sir', every time the master glanced in their direction. When the master said, 'All right, Green, you tell us', there were quiet sighs and groans as those who had not been called upon subsided into their seats. The whole performance was repeated as soon as the next question was asked.

During such spells the desire to participate was so great that some boys would put up their hands and strain for notice, even though they had no idea of the answer. And, if asked to give the answer, they would either make a gesture suggesting that they had suddenly forgotten, or else subside with an embarrassed and confused look, to the jeers and groans of the rest of the class who would then redouble their efforts to attract attention.

The type of enthusiasm characteristic of a first-year class was occasionally found in second- or third-year forms but there were a number of observable differences. The second and third forms were more likely to 'play dead' and to allow five or six people to 'do all the work'; and, even if the master succeeded in getting a larger proportion to participate, there was always a residue of boys who hardly participated or who only did so by giving obviously wrong or funny answers. Finally there was the possibility that the form would use any excitement of this kind to sabotage the lesson or to play the fool. For example, a boy will stretch so hard that he falls out of his desk, another will accidentally punch the boy in front as he puts up his hand and the form's 'funny man' will display his wit in response to an ambiguous question – sometimes isolating the teacher from the class by referring to a private class joke.

On one occasion, for example, a master asked three boys to stay behind after the lesson to help him with a task calling for a sense of responsibility and cooperation. The master called 'Williams, Maun and Sherring'. The class burst into spontaneous laughter, and there were unbelieving cries of 'What, Sherring?' The master corrected himself. 'No, not Sherring, Shadwell.' From the context of the incident, it was clear that Sherring's reputation was already inconsistent with the qualities expected of a monitor. On another occasion, Priestley was asked to read and the whole class groaned and laughed. Priestley, a fat boy, had been kept down from the previous year because of ill health (catarrh and asthma) and poor work. He grinned apprehensively, wiped his face with a huge white handkerchief and started to read very nervously. For a few moments the class was absolutely quiet, then one boy tittered, Priestley made a silly mistake, partly because he was looking up to smile at the boy who was giggling, and the whole class burst into laughter. Priestley blew his nose loudly and smiled nervously at the class. The teacher quietened the class and Priestley continued to read. Three lines later a marked mispronunciation started the whole class laughing again. This performance continued with Priestley getting more and more nervous, mopping his brow and blowing his nose. Finally, the master with obvious annoyance snapped, 'All right, Priestley, that's enough!'

This short incident, one of several during the day, served to remind Priestley of his structural position within the class and to confirm the opinions and expectations of the class and the teacher towards him. Priestley's behaviour was consistent with his performance in the examinations at the end of the Autumn Term when he was ranked twenty-ninth out of thirty-three.

During this period of observation I also noticed the significance of the behaviour of another boy, Cready. Cready first attracted my attention because, although his form position was similar to Priestley's (twenty-sixth) he habitually associated with a strikingly different group. He behaved very differently in class, and had a markedly different reputation.

A sociogram for the class showed an apparent inconsistency. In class Priestley was frequently in the middle of a group of mischievous boys. If there was trouble Priestley was in it. I expected him to be fairly popular with some of the boys who led him into trouble, but none of them picked him as a friend. He chose five boys as his friends but the only boy to reciprocate was the other Jewish boy in the class.

The other boys used Priestley to create diversions and pass messages, and because he was so isolated he was only too pleased to oblige. He could never resist the temptation to act as if he were 'one of the boys'. However, when he was caught out they deserted him and laughed at him rather than with him. He was truly the butt of the class.

These incidents, seen in the context of the structure of the class, show

how Priestley had fallen foul of the system. He was not in control of his own situation, and anything he tried to do to improve his position only made it worse. His attempts to answer questions provoked laughter and ridicule from his classmates. His attempt to minimize the distress this caused, a nervous smile round the class, a shrug of the shoulders; pretending either that he had caused the disturbance on purpose or that he did not care, served to worsen his position with the teacher.

He compensated for his failure in class and lack of academic success by learning the stocks and shares table of the *Financial Times* every week. This enabled him to develop a reputation in a field outside the sphere in which the school was competent to judge. He would emphasize the *real* importance of this in his future career and thus minimize the effect of his scholastic failure. Even this did not improve his standing in the school, especially with the staff. It served only to explain his laziness, his bad behaviour and lack of concern with school work.

It is interesting to note the family background of these two boys. Priestley is Jewish, second in a family of three and lives in an area of expensive detached houses. His father is a clearance stock buyer. Cready on the other hand lives on a council estate, is fourth out of six in the family and his father is a quality inspector in an abrasives factory.

Cready and Priestley do not, therefore, conform with the established correlation between academic achievement and social class. Cready, a working-class boy from a large family on a council estate, is making good, while Priestley, an upper-middle-class boy from a smaller family, is failing academically. However, this negative case highlights the point I want to make; there was a measure of autonomy in the system of social relations of the classroom. The positions of Cready and Priestley are only explicable in the light of an analysis of the system of social relations *inside* the classroom. This system is open to manipulation by those who are sensitive to its details. Hence Cready, who had all the major external factors stacked against him, was able to use the system of social relations to sustain and buoy himself up, while Priestley, despite all the advantages that he brought to the situation, had fallen foul of the system and was not only failing but also speedily losing any motivation to succeed in the sphere in which the school was competent to judge him.

I reiterate that this is not an attempt to disprove the general established trend but to highlight the fact that there are detailed social mechanisms and processes responsible for bringing it about, which are not completely determined by external factors. By studying these mechanisms it will be possible to add a dimension to our understanding of the general processes of education in our schools.

Learning to Underachieve

T. Blackstone and H. Weinreich-Haste

Reprinted with permission from Tessa Blackstone and Helen Weinreich-Haste, 'Why Are There So Few Women Scientists and Engineers?', *New Society*, 21 February 1980, pp. 383–5

A national newspaper is advertising its job-finding pages with a poster which shows a 'representative' range of professional job-hunters. There is a woman nurse, a female secretary, and then a scientist and various other suit-clad men whose images exude success, power and decision-making. The ad has been criticized for its sexist assumptions, and rightly. Yet it does reflect where men and women stand in the professions.

Things are changing: but there remains a problem of 'under-achievement' among girls and women. The first conference in Britain on sex differentiation in schooling was held in Cambridge recently. Here we look at some of the material presented there by British and American researchers and educationists, and raise general questions about the origin of educational inequality between boys and girls, and its possible cure.

Concern about this inequality has grown. There has long been a tradition of commitment to girls' education. But there has now been added the broader political issue of sexual equality. People also realize what a large reserve of skill is being wasted, especially in science and technology.

Girls are less successful than boys in a number of ways. They are not much more likely to drop out of the education system after sixteen; but they set their sights lower. There are more girls than boys in further education; but (though the gap is narrowing) girls choose the easier courses and are less likely than boys to take enough A-levels to qualify for higher education (Table 1).

Table 1a. Educational attainment of school leavers

| | 1974-5 | | 1975–6 | |
	Boys %	Girls %	Boys %	Girls %
5 or more O-levels	7·4	9·7	5·4	7·4
2 A-levels	4·0	4·2	4·1	4·5
3 A-levels	9·3	6·8	9·9	7·0

Table 1b. Destination of school leavers, 1974–5

	Boys '000s	Girls '000s
Universities	24·7	14·2
Polytechnics	4·1	2·0
Teacher training courses	2·9	11·9
Other full-time education	31·7	57·3
Employment	289·9	252·5

(Source: *Social Trends*, Table 4.7, 1977)

The girls' performance depends on the subject. Girls do better in arts, boys do better in the sciences. An international study by Alison Kelly showed that boys consistently do better than girls in a standard science test in all the industrial societies studied (though girls in some countries, notably Japan and Hungary, do better than boys in others, notably Italy and Belgium). In Britain at least, unequal opportunities for training – especially apprenticeships – increase the skill gap further (Table 2). This particularly goes for science and technology.

Table 2. Destination of school leavers, 1974

	Boys '000s	Girls '000s
Apprenticeships	118·2	15·5
Professional	3·5	2·2
Clerical	19·2	96·3
Employment with planned training of		
over 12 months	26·4	13·5
8 weeks to 12 months	20·5	27·5
Other employment	86·9	80·9
Total	274·7	235·9

(Source: *Careers Service Statistics*)

But subject choice is crucial. Boys get more instruction in science than girls do, because the two sexes choose different subjects. Girls are far more likely to choose arts, and boys science. So girls are excluded from a range of possible careers for which science is required. They are ill-prepared for living in a high-technology world. Their clerical and service jobs are less well-paid than technically skilled work.

So concern about the attainment difference between girls and boys is twofold. Girls tend to fail to reach their potential; and they tend to opt out of particular areas of activity. How can we intervene to do something about this? Several European countries are trying to cut out obvious sex differences in curricula – particularly in crafts. West Germany, for example, is training girls in non-traditional skills. In Britain, the Engineering Training Board has set up a similar scheme.

Such efforts deal with specifics. In the long run they should gradually change the attitudes of both managers and potential recruits. But we also need a better understanding of the causes. Burgeoning research on sex differences and sex roles, particularly in America, is beginning to isolate the variables. It undermines some traditional assumptions about sex differences. The findings do not immediately provide blueprints for action, but they do indicate key areas for attention.

Sex differences in cognitive abilities have no biological or physiological base. By the age of eleven and sometimes earlier, boys and girls show different levels of language skills and spatial reasoning. But it is becoming clear that this is susceptible to training. Practice helps, and so does play. Lisa Serbin reported at the Cambridge conference that 'feminine' and 'masculine' interests, expressed through the toys they play with and irrespective of the actual sex of the child, were important variables in verbal and spatial skills. Four years ago now, Hugh Fairweather reviewed a large number of studies and noted that sex differences in cognition had been overstated and had no physiological basis. Differences within each sex are greater than between the sexes. Spatial reasoning seems to correlate with scientific ability and interest. But the conclusion must be that differences in the eventual capacities of teenage boys and girls to do science must be traced to environment and motivation.

However, it is wrong to blame parents and teachers in any very obvious sense. Feminist writers, especially, have claimed that boys and girls are conditioned through being treated differently by their parents and, later, their teachers. This has not been fully substantiated. Some evidence suggests that parents do not treat their children differently in any deliberate way. However, boys and girls do *behave* differently, and this elicits different reactions from both parents and teachers. Preschool boys already show a pattern of non-compliant, demanding, attention-seeking behaviour. They therefore get punished more than girls, both by parents and by teachers. They also get more attention than girls. Early on, and through school, the effect of the interaction between adult and child is to give boys more attention in general, but particularly for 'bad' behaviour.

The powerful agent appears to be expectation. Children learn early that gender matters. They learn the stereotype behaviour-patterns, and the appropriate lifestyle and careers, of men and women. Several researchers have reported that children have sharp categories of appropriate adult roles which may fly in the face of their experience. They may be convinced that only men are doctors, though their own doctor or even their mother may be a counter-example.

The anxiety associated with gender may be a consequence of indirect conditioning. There is some evidence that fathers react with anxiety when their sons, but not their daughters, engage in play that they think inappropriate to their sex. Children know the gender rules, and impose them among themselves, though not when they are alone. There is a process of self-socialization which probably works better than any external pressure. The mechanism of expectation can operate subtly. Parents and teachers may not be aware that they react differently to boys and girls, but their expectations affect the kind of behaviour they notice. This in turn may strengthen the different conclusions which boys and girls come to about their own abilities.

If boys are punished more than girls, it is not for poor school performance (Carol Dweck reported), but for non-academic things like neatness and conduct. Girls are rarely punished; when they are, it is specific and likely to be for academic mistakes. By contrast, they are frequently praised for conduct and neatness.

Girls and women attribute their success to luck or extra effort, their failure to lack of ability. Boys and men attribute their successes to ability, and their failure to bad luck or lack of effort. These attributions do not apply only to the self: they are general stereotypes held by both sexes about men and women in general. Carol Dweck found that teachers behave in accordance with these attributions. They are probably transmitting the attributions to the children, and reinforcing the motivations associated with them.

If you think your poor performance depends on external factors, you retain the confidence to change things next time. So, not surprisingly, boys are more likely than girls to find failure a challenge, and to respond to setbacks with resilience.

If you think your performance is due to external factors, then this induces a sense of helplessness. Dweck argues that many girls learn 'helplessness' in order to avoid challenge and to escape repetitions of situations in which they have failed. They lower their aspirations according to their achievement. Many studies have found a similar pattern right through the education system. Even women undergraduates modify their goals and career plans according to their year-to-year results. Men, on the whole, do not.

Girls' caution and lower aspirations show up in their career choices. You could argue that girls are more 'realistic' in their choices than boys. For twelve-year-olds, teaching, nursing, office work and hairdressing are more 'sensible' aspirations than test pilot, astronaut or pop singer. A recent study by one of us in two London schools found that, even at fifteen, boys were still more likely than girls to have unrealistic or fantasy expectations of their future lives. When asked to write about their future, the boys spent more time than girls in writing about what their career would be like. The girls focused more on training for their careers, and on family and marriage.

'Realistic' aspirations are not necessarily a bad thing. The London schools study suggests that, at fifteen, girls are already well prepared for a life which will include training, a career, marriage and a family, whereas many boys are far from that state. But career aspirations are heavily affected by ideas of what is appropriate for one's sex. Girls seem to opt for a narrow range of careers. These reflect assumptions about 'women's work'; on the whole, too, they make less training and skill demands than the range of jobs chosen by boys of comparable ability.

Some research has suggested that girls and young women 'fear success', especially success in a task traditionally regarded as a male province. The combination of success and sex-inappropriateness creates a powerful anxiety. In America in the late 1960s, university students were asked to continue the story: 'At the end of her first year at medical school, Anne found she had come top of the class . . .' This demonstrated anxiety in girls about the idea of women doing well in medical school.

For a while, the 'motive to avoid success' seemed a neat explanation of girls' underachievement. But later work indicates that it is neither so widespread nor so simple as it first appeared. In Britain it seems to be a minor problem. Perhaps British undergraduates are already so highly selected that they are the ones who lack this fear.

In the London schools study, this was examined through stories of a boy nurse and a girl engineer. In the more middle-class of the two schools, at least, it was the boys rather than the girls, who generally expressed negative attitudes about success. On the whole, the girls had positive attitudes but saw discrimination as an obstacle.

The complex interaction between sex-appropriateness, achievement and role expectation is evident if you look at the tendency for girls to choose arts and boys science. One explanation may be that language-based disciplines are incremental (i.e., you build on what you have already learnt); but maths and science continually involve new concepts. So language-based disciplines do not expose the individual to constant challenge and the risk of failure, but maths and science do.

A further explanation may be stereotyping. Learning foreign languages was thought to be the right thing for Victorian middle-class girls, partly as an extension of the art of conversation; science and engineering were not. Some subjects have remained either male or female domains. But the fact that Japanese and Hungarian girls, although they did worse than their male compatriots, did better on the standard science test than practically all *other* boys indicates the size of the difference between countries. The variation in women's representation in technology, medicine and law between countries shows the difference in stereotyping and in norms of 'women's work'. It also casts doubt on the fundamental nature of any sex differences in ability.

In a recent study with schoolchildren and undergraduates, one of us found that there is a definite cluster of science subjects which are perceived as masculine. This cluster is seen as having various characteristics which are associated with masculinity in our culture: hard, intellect-based, complex, concerned with things rather than people. This suggests that the masculine image of science is more complicated than just a matter of excessive male representation. For example, biology does not fit in with the masculine image of science. In a study some time ago Margaret Mead and Raoul Métraux commented on the aridity and 'non-life centredness' which many girls associated with science.

Boys' and girls' expectations and motives seem to be the key area for strategies of intervention. The evidence is that the process of acquiring these takes some time. Children's stereotypes are still malleable in middle childhood. So the school can help reduce sex inequalities. But how?

The first key issue is *role models*. Children do imitate and identify with parents and teachers, especially those of the same sex. Several studies demonstrate that having a working mother, or a mother who doesn't just concentrate on being a wife and a mother, is a factor in a girl's independence and her later motivation to enter a career, especially a non-traditional one. Senior posts in mixed-sex schools still tend to be held by men, and the type of work done by teachers of each sex tends to reflect traditional patterns. Immediate change may be hard, but schools should more directly welcome the increased number of working women as a direct benefit to daughters and become more conscious of the implications of a male-dominated power structure.

School textbooks, like films and television, provide important role models. Several critics have demonstrated the sexist biases of children's books, in both the underrepresentation and stereotyping of female characters. Science textbooks, in particular, need to give a balance of female and male examples of work and characters. Boys and girls ought to know about female scientists, both those in routine work and at the top of their profession.

The second key issue is *teachers' expectations*. These operate in various indirect ways. They are often unconscious and subtly expressed. Boys are asked to carry heavy things, girls to do more social tasks like taking messages. Boys help with technical aids. Girls are given more help with mechanical tasks, or are excused them. Study examples may be drawn from the interests of one sex only. Carol Dweck's study showed that a teacher may bring out the stereotypical characteristics of boys and girls as much by what he or she does not comment on as by what is directly rewarded or punished. Teachers need to gain insight into their own perceptions and expectations, and be aware of the subtle interaction process. Elizabeth Fennema's work on maths teaching in American high schools suggests that teachers give a disproportionate amount of time to high-ability boys. She has developed a video-tape to show teachers the evidence. Similar work needs doing here.

The third key issue is *pupil motivation*. Caution and low aspirations among girls seem to arise partly from their feeling that failure springs from lack of ability, rather than lack of effort. It may help if girls are given tasks where they can monitor their own performance and gain a sense of their own mastery, rather than be exposed to public praise or blame. But 'independence training' – to free girls from reliance on approval by adults and other children – is a long-term process; it is also double-edged.

The early reliance of boys on approval by other children of their age diminishes their performance and their attentiveness in class during their early years. But it may contribute to their later independence and sense of mastery. Girls' early reliance on adults benefits them in general school performance, but it sustains their dependence and ultimately makes them more vulnerable to pressures to conform.

One way to tackle this issue could be to remove choice from the curriculum in some areas. It is partly through curriculum choice that the science-arts split occurs so early and is so limiting. Eileen Byrne proposes a 'core curriculum' of science and languages for every child up to sixteen, in addition to English and maths. She also advocates, for both boys and girls, social education (including history and social studies) and education for parenthood. This differs from the core curriculum proposed earlier this year by Mark Carlisle, the Education Secretary – to some degree in content, but considerably in intent. The case for a core curriculum is supported by those researchers who consider that the present freedom of subject choice diminishes, rather than enhances, girls' freedom of career choice.

Pressures from other children are important in reinforcing the stereotypes of male and female domains. One way to tackle this could be single-sex education in the most vulnerable years. This is contentious. But there is clear evidence that in mixed schools boys are more polarized into science, and girls into arts, than in single-sex schools (Table 3). And though boys' achievement is comparable in single-sex or mixed schools, girls do less well in a mixed school.

Are the benefits in terms of social development in mixed schools greater than the costs to girls' performance in maths and science? This is an open question. Perhaps we should wait to see whether attempts to change the attitudes of teachers, parents and children in our current

Table 3. Type of school by A-level course

	All boys %	All girls %	Boys in single-sex %	Boys in mixed %	Girls in single-sex %	Girls in mixed %
Mathematics	41	15	37	41	19	12
Physics	41	9	36	43	12	7
Biology	16	21	16	18	21	21
English literature	23	53	28	21	48	55
French	8	24	11	5	23	25
Geography	27	22	23	29	24	20

(Source: *DES Education Survey 21*, Table 8)

schools are successful. In doing this, we must concentrate on how similar boys and girls are. Only then can we break down the stereotypes.

Issues of Importance to Young People
D. I. Smith

Reprinted with permission, this is a revised and updated version (1984) of an article by Douglas Smith which first appeared in *Young People, the Youth Service, and Youth Provision*, the submission of the National Youth Bureau to the Department of Education and Science Review Group on the Youth Service, 1981

By virtue of their age and their position in the transitions which they are undergoing, young people suffer a variety of legal and social disqualifications and disadvantages. These render the young legally, socially, politically and materially disadvantaged and vulnerable with respect to adults. This gives them a range of problems which they possess as *young* people.

Intersecting this division of young people and adults are these features which divide and stratify society in different ways and along different dimensions. It is the intersection of age with class, gender and ethnic origin which gives different groups of young people differing degrees of advantage, disadvantage and vulnerability. In this way the divisions in the wider society are reflected in comparable divisions among the young people themselves and in this respect different groups of young people have quite different sets of life-chances ahead of them. From this perspective degrees of vulnerability and disadvantage are theirs by virtue of their position as young *people*.

Social class is of primary importance for understanding the social position of young people in Britain today. Children of working-class families suffer disadvantage in respect of access to education, employment, income, wealth and a wide range of other social resources. Class disadvantage is far-reaching and permeates almost the totality of their lives.

Gender, in turn, is of primary significance and young women are disadvantaged in many ways. This can be at the personal level where girls experience and suffer from a covert and overt sexism which undermines their sense of personal worth and inhibits their chances of personal development, or at the more institutional level which leads to highly restricted opportunities for access to resources such as education, employment or an independent income.

Ethnic origin lends a further dimension to disadvantage. Young blacks particularly experience a discrimination which restricts their access to housing, education, and employment. They are confronted daily by discrimination and rejection and they now face a developing and violent racism emerging from certain sections of the white population.

It can be seen from this discussion that young people share certain problems and have many things in common as *young* people. In other ways, however, young people are highly heterogeneous, being divided by class, gender and race. And these are the very social and political factors which determine the nature of the essential conditions within which young people undergo individual growth and personal development. It follows from this that the concern with the individual, and the concern with the social and political, are not alternative perspectives at odds with each other. For in order to have an understanding of the individual development of young people, it is necessary also to have an understanding of the conditions of life which they collectively face and experience. Some of these essential life conditions, mediated by class, gender and race, can be seen in the following issues of importance to them.

Schooling, education and social education

Schooling and education are a central feature of all young people's lives up to the age of sixteen. Some of them stay on beyond the age of sixteen and their contact with school or education continues up to the age of eighteen or even further.

The key to understanding young people and school in contrast to young people and youth work lies in the three issues of *compulsion*, *control* and *curriculum.* These in turn influence both the direct relationship of young people to school and education, and also the nature of educational outcomes for young people in the context of the relationship of education to later life.

For the great majority of young people under sixteen years of age attendance at school is compulsory. Young people are obliged to attend school, or their parents, and the young people themselves, suffer the consequences of not doing so through a range of sanctions which the authorities can employ. Over time the period of compulsory schooling has been extended with the last change raising the minimum leaving age from fifteen to sixteen years in 1973. Following that change there has been considerable debate over the success of the additional year at school and the educational purpose it should serve.

In addition to being compelled to attend, young people have little or no *control* over their own schooling or education. Partly as a consequence of its compulsory nature, there is little incentive to allow young people to participate in decision-making processes within schools or within the education authorities. There is little incentive for schools and young people to arrive at *agreed* rules and procedures in respect of the running of schools or the provision of education.

Similarly the *curriculum* of the school is determined by others and young people have little influence over what is taught. Yet many young people, and many others, would question the value and appropriateness of the curriculum both in terms of the lives of the young people when still at school and in terms of its relevance to later life. Many curricula are still narrowly academic, linked primarily to the taking of examinations and the securing of qualifications.

In addition to the formal curriculum, however, there are what can be called the informal curriculum and the hidden curriculum which may be more open to the influence of young people. On each of these three issues, compulsion, control and curriculum, formal education and schooling stand in contrast to the provision of social education through the contribution of youth work. Social education through youth work is noncompulsory, relying on the individual decision of young people to take part. The philosophy of youth work is one which encourages and promotes participation and control by young people. And finally parts of the curriculum of social education are more geared towards the immediate position of young people and the satisfaction of their needs. Although clearly divided on these three issues there is contact between social education through youth work and formal education in the form of youth wings in schools or increasingly through projects drawing on youth work philosophy and youth work methods.

The contrast between youth work and formal education should not be overstressed, however. Notwithstanding the distance between the philosophy of youth work and its actual practice, schools themselves have increasingly adopted a social education role. This has occurred both through the linking of youth work directly to schools and alternatively by teachers arriving at social education practices by different routes. Much valuable work is done by teachers and this should not be neglected in the examination of the provision of social education.

The experience of school by young people is highly variable. On the one hand the social experience of schooling, the creation of friendships, and the membership of groups all contribute greatly to the personal and social development of young people. In other ways, however, school experiences can be quite different. Girls tend to follow a different curriculum from boys in a number of respects and schools are influential in reinforcing gender-typing. The children of working-class families tend not to stay on beyond the minimum leaving age and show considerable signs of underachievement. Similarly young blacks underachieve and recent reports have shown this to be a function of the schools and the teachers rather than being due to characteristics of the young people themselves.

A number of consequences for young people follow from the nature of the direct relationship to school and the relationship of education to later life and these are largely consequences of compulsion, control and the curriculum.

First, many young people feel a profound sense of dissatisfaction with school and this leads to various forms of school resistance. This ranges from simply a failure to pay attention when required through to different types of misbehaviour and possibly non-attendance. The response of the authorities is to invoke sanctions of punishment, suspension or the provision of education in special units. The young people are termed 'disruptive'. The relevance of the school experience is seldom questioned.

Second, many young people see schooling as irrelevant to their later lives and are anxious to leave at the earliest opportunity. This feeling has been intensified by high levels of youth unemployment, which can result in a competitive advantage for those first into the labour market, and further encouraged by changes in the provision of benefits which disqualify school-leavers from social security entitlement until the end of school holidays. In addition it is widely thought that high levels of unemployment amongst school-leavers has led to increased problems of discipline within schools.

Third, schooling and education in many respects perpetuate and reinforce existing social positions. For many young people their experience of education does not promote far-reaching changes in their lives but instead confirms them in their existing position.

Leisure and recreation

Outside the constraints of school and work young people have *free time* in which they can pursue a range of leisure and recreational opportunities. These opportunities may be made up of commercial provision such as discos, clubs or professional football matches; non-commercial provision such as youth clubs or voluntary associations organizing games or hobbies; they may listen to the radio, watch television, make music and play organized sports; or the opportunities may be made up of young people using the resources of an area to follow individual or group activity whether that be hanging around a shopping centre or playing football on a field. In this way the focus of leisure activity amongst young people often differs from that of adults. Often denied access to leisure provision for financial or other reasons young people will use non-leisure resources to engage in leisure pursuits. Through this, the leisure activities of young people can be highly visible and concentrated in public areas such as shopping centres, bus shelters or street corners.

The ability to take part in leisure activities of different kinds is governed by area, transport and income. Areas differ in the facilities they offer; transport gives access to facilities over a wider area; money is needed to gain access to facilities and to enjoy leisure time. This last point is of increasing importance as leisure becomes more commercialized and it no longer makes sense to speak of leisure without also considering work, the potential to earn an income, and the problem of enforced 'leisure' through unemployment.

Not all young people have equal access to leisure facilities. Girls have less free time than boys through them being expected to perform domestic duties in the household. In addition girls are differentiated from boys in terms of what others see as acceptable leisure pursuits in which girls can engage. Young blacks experience direct discrimination in access to leisure facilities and also a more indirect form of discrimination arising from the characteristics of the areas in which they live. Similarly, young people from working-class families are less likely to have access to financial resources for leisure use and may experience certain cultural predispositions which lead them to use certain facilities but not others. In many cases, though, it may be those other facilities which are the ones provided by the authorities or commercial organizations.

In consequence, young people can find that opportunities for leisure and recreation do not exist, are inappropriate, too expensive, too distant, or seen as illicit or illegal.

Unemployment and employment of young people

Probably the single greatest issue facing young people now and through the 1980s is youth unemployment. From being of negligible importance in 1974, by the summer of 1981 around 535,000 of the 910,000 school-leavers of 1981 were unemployed and 550,000 places on the Youth Opportunities Programme were made available to accommodate them. Official projections for the years 1982 and 1983 showed a rapidly worsening situation in which *the great majority* of school-leavers were not expected to find employment, and the longer-term economic projections suggested that high levels of youth unemployment would be a continuing feature of the 1980s. In fact, 1981 could well have been the year in which youth unemployment changed from meaning a delayed entry to work for young people to the position where a high proportion of school-leavers faced a future of long-term unemployment.

The years 1982 and 1983 confirmed the trend of the earlier projections. In the summer of 1983 there were 511,000 unemployed school-leavers and the number of places on the Youth Opportunities Programme had been expanded yet again to 630,000 for the year 1982 to 1983.

Not all young people are affected equally by unemployment. Those most likely to be excluded from the labour market are the poorly qualified and the untrained. Ethnic minority groups are particularly vulnerable to unemployment whilst in recent years the evidence shows that unemployment amongst girls has increased faster than amongst boys and the rates of unemployment of girls and boys are now similar.

The initial official response to youth unemployment was through the rapid expansion of the Youth Opportunities Programme which claimed to provide a range of different opportunities for young people. However, it would appear that some young people showed increasing resistance to these programmes and as the job placement rate rapidly fell young people became more disillusioned about the effectiveness and value of the government schemes.

The Youth Opportunities Programme, which was always intended as a temporary measure and was inadequate for dealing with mass youth unemployment, was replaced in September 1983 by the Youth Training Scheme. This scheme is planned as a *permanent* bridge between school and work and is intended to provide education and training for unemployed sixteen- and seventeen-year-olds. The provision of this permanent scheme is recognition of the fact that youth unemployment can no longer be regarded as a temporary phenomenon.

In the last quarter of 1983 460,000 places were made available through the Youth Training Scheme. There has been, however, a 25 per cent shortfall in the number of places taken up. Although it is too early to say what the precise reasons for this are, it seems very likely that the experience of the Youth Opportunities Programme has led to a lack of confidence in government schemes amongst young people. And what is clear is that, if given a choice, young people overwhelmingly want a 'real job' rather than a place on a government scheme. This leads on to two very important points.

First, youth unemployment has not arisen as a consequence of poor education or low levels of skill. As the problem intensifies, more young people with qualifications are unable to find work and more young people with qualifications have gone through the Youth Opportunities Programme only to return to the ranks of the unemployed. Youth unemployment is caused, quite simply, by the shortage of jobs for young people. And this leads directly to the second point. Youth unemployment is not the responsibility of young people themselves. There is little evidence to support the assertion that young people have priced themselves out of work by demanding too high wages. Indeed, all the evidence points to the fact that unemployment is due to factors entirely outside of their control such as the condition of the overall economy and the job opportunities in the local area in which they live. However, although not their personal responsibility, young people do suffer the consequences of unemployment, and some of these and the ways in which they affect those concerned are listed below.

The most immediate consequence of unemployment for young people is that they have either a low income, or no income at all if they choose not to register as unemployed. This, in turn, places severe constraints on the extent to which they can participate in society, and limits their access to consumer goods, independent accommodation, transport, and a whole range of leisure activities and opportunities. The feeling of constraint is intensified by the exposure of young people to advertising stressing the importance of a wide range of consumer goods which, of course, unemployed young people cannot afford. They are compelled to remain dependent on either the family or the state, and in this way the financial deprivation of unemployment stands at the centre of a whole range of other issues and is of paramount importance to the young people affected.

A second consequence of unemployment is its influence on the ability of the young person to achieve individual development and personal growth. To be denied access to employment is to be confined to an uncertain and precarious position in society with little opportunity to develop a security of personal status, or a developed concept of self, self-worth and personal dignity. This is reinforced by the negative experience of unemployment as their introduction to adult life. For although there is little information on the psychological consequences of prolonged unemployment for young people, a wide range of documentary information indicates a widespread feeling of apathy, non-involvement, depression and quiet despair on the part of the young unemployed. Of even greater concern must be the fact that recent research has indicated that the young unemployed suffer from higher rates of mental instability, mental illness and suicide than do their employed counterparts.

On a wider scale, there is a growing body of information pointing to the relationship of unemployment to crime and deviance by young people; to the connections between unemployment and large-scale social disorder; and to the susceptibility of the young unemployed to recruitment by extremist right-wing political organizations intent on sowing the seeds of racial conflict and encouraging attacks on minority groups.

Finally, it is important to draw attention to conflict within the family created by unemployment. Many of today's parents have themselves grown up in an era in which unemployment was almost non-existent. It can be difficult for them to understand the situation which confronts their sons and daughters. Other families, of course, have long histories of unemployment in which young people grow up in poverty. Whatever the family history, there are now many examples of family tension in which, eventually, the young person becomes expelled from the family home. It is perhaps paradoxical that at a time when young people need the most support from their family the situation is created in which they probably receive the least.

Although the main concern is with unemployment, it is also important to remember that some young people still do get jobs and do eventually get the opportunity to earn an independent wage. However, even during periods of full employment there are problems here for young people, and these are intensified during a recession. Many jobs entered by young people are badly paid, with poor training opportunities, no career opportunities and, indeed, often short-term. Many of these jobs offer the poorest conditions and the poorest return for their labour in sectors of industry without any form of effective employee representation or participation. Under these circumstances young people are highly vulnerable in the work place and often at the mercy of employers and adult workers alike.

Housing and accommodation

Access to adequate housing and accommodation is a basic issue facing everyone but within which young people are especially vulnerable. Although there are few reliable data about the housing conditions of young people, there are thought to be a significant number without accommodation and very many more living in poor housing, temporary housing or constrained to live in the parental home in difficult circumstances. These numbers are thought to be increasing and it is recognized that access to adequate accommodation is a growing problem amongst them.

The problem of housing for young people is the product of two sets of circumstances. On the one hand they are excluded from the non-market housing sector, and on the other hand they occupy a weak position in the free-market sector of housing.

In the non-market council housing sector there is usually little or no housing provision for single young people. They are not specified in the provisions of the recent housing Acts which place obligations on local authorities to provide housing for certain categories of homeless people. These restrictions can be circumvented by early marriage or tactical pregnancy by young people although this must be seen as constituting a weak foundation for adult life amongst young couples. Similarly, many local authorities will not allow single young people to register on council waiting lists, and such housing as is set aside for young people is very often housing which the authority cannot let to other tenants – high-rise blocks, substandard older housing, and housing on remote council estates.

Accompanying this exclusion from the non-market sector is the weak position of young people in the competition for housing in the free-market private rented sector. The private rented sector has been declining for many years and this has increased competition for housing in a contest in which young people are disadvantaged largely through the lack of an adequate income to secure accommodation, and increasingly so as unemployment becomes widespread. Very many young people simply cannot afford the rents which are charged for private accommodation.

The housing problems of young people show every sign of increasing in the future. There is a continuing trend towards a desire for independent housing amongst young people, yet this rising demand is occurring at the same time as financial policy decisions have reduced significantly the supply of new accommodation as house building goes into decline. The young people most likely to suffer from housing shortage are those from working-class families with a low income and no access to family capital, young blacks who still face discrimination in the search for accommodation, and young women who are less likely to have an adequate income through their restriction to lower-paid jobs. Additionally, young women are more likely to experience restrictions imposed by the family if they wish to seek independent accommodation.

A number of conclusions follow from the position of young people in the competition for adequate housing which have important consequences for the young people concerned.

Young people are often denied access to independent accommodation and thereby denied the opportunity to have their 'own place' and experience the independence that accompanies it, or they only have access to housing of the worst kind. They are often obliged to continue living in the parental home in difficult and unhappy circumstances and this is particularly true as rising youth unemployment contributes to increasing tension within families. Under these circumstances, family crises may result in young people running away from home for a time, pending the resolution of the conflict and an eventual return home. However, the absence of temporary or short-term accommodation often denies them the 'space' they need to do this successfully.

The inability of young people to secure accommodation limits the extent to which they can move to seek work. In these circumstances young people have no option other than to remain unemployed. And this sets in motion one of two linked vicious circles. The first of these is that without employment young people have a low income which means they cannot find accommodation. Without accommodation they cannot find employment. The second circle is that without accommodation young people become ineligible for certain kinds of state benefit. Under these circumstances their income remains too low for them to secure their own accommodation. There is no easy way for young people to break out of these circles.

Love and Marriage
M. Brake

Reprinted with permission from Mike Brake, The Sociology of Youth Culture and Youth Subcultures, Routledge and Kegan Paul, 1980, pp. 140–8

Girls receive from the mass media and from popular fiction distinct signals about the cult of femininity. Reading primers reinforce sexual roles, and comics are divided strictly along sex lines from the age of seven or eight. The themes in girls' comics are often related to isolation, competition, loneliness and emotional problems. The market aimed at the pubescent girl and the adolescent have a central theme of romanticism. Romantic attachment, and dependence on men is emphasized and advice on emotions, make-up and fashion is given as well as glamorous hints of the lives of pop stars. These are succeeded by glossy fashion magazines, aimed at specific age groups, again with advice about romance and sex, with more adult stories, but nevertheless presenting an escapist unproblematic world. Appearance is stressed, and fashion is used to construct a self which indicates to the world that the girl is from a world of fashionable femininity, where she has a relation not to class, but to a mythical world inhabited by a fashion hierarchy based on popular media figures. As girls grow older they seem to seek magazines which emphasize fashion rather than romantic stories. De Beauvoir has put this well:

to care for her beauty, to dress up, is a kind of work that enables her to take possession of her person, as she takes possession of her home through housework, her ego then seems chosen and created by herself.

Girls then have two sources of socialization for their future, school and at home, backed up by a media interpretation of femininity which adds a sense of fatalism about marriage and motherhood. For many girls, in particular working-class girls, these are attractive and seemingly fulfilling goals. It is only after marriage that women realize its isolation and emptiness. The reality is that the average age of marriage for a woman is twenty-two, and the woman's age at the birth of the last child is twenty-six,' and 42 per cent of all married women work. Schools, particularly in poorer areas where opportunities for women are restricted, prepare girls for the marriage market as much as for the job market. The future work prospects are belittled as temporary and unimportant. As Shaw suggests:

> The meanings and consequences of sexual divisions in our society are translated into educational terms so that the different subcultures of boys' and girls' schools are but specialized versions of a wider culture, in which female futures are still defined in essentially domestic terms – a stereotyping which our educational system does little to undermine.

The organization and form of girls' subcultures remain very much a matter of empirical investigation. As has been suggested, a prominent feature of male-dominated subcultures has been its exploration of masculinity, and its imagery, whether it is the ambiguity of mods and freaks, or the heavy machismo of greasers. Girls are present in male subcultures, but are contained within them, rather than using them to explore actively forms of female identity. The subculture may be a social focus, something to dress up for, and an escape from the restraints of home, school and work, but as yet no distinct models of femininity, which have broken from tradition, have evolved, although this may well happen when female-dominated subcultures evolve. This is unlikely at present, especially among working-class girls, because of the demands of adolescent heterosexuality and the female role. For working-class women, marriage is a role of primary importance, and economically essential. Marriage mediates against the starkness and drabness of work, it provides acceptable evidence of maturity and adulthood, and it is an important investment for the future. Its attraction may fade away with familiarity, but it is still strong enough to structure girls' choices. Working-class respectability has to be paid attention to: a girl is permitted sexual relations with her steady boyfriend, but she must guard against a reputation which will relegate her to the role of 'slag'. She develops a cynicism about boys who demand a sexual relationship without emotional commitment with a view to permanence. Girls are located in differing contradictions, as McRobbie and Garber suggest. They may be peripheral in one sphere, such as work, but they can be central in another, such as the home. Consequently, when they are mentioned in subcultural theory, they are seen as peripheral to the boys:

> Women were usually accompanied by a man and they did not speak anything like as much as the man. There was a small group of unattached females, but they were allowed no real dignity or identity by the men.

This, however, is because the largely male investigators accepted the masculinist definition of the girls' roles in these subcultures.

McRobbie and Garber argue that girls are not marginal, but structurally different, pushed by male dominance to the periphery of social activity because they are centrally into a different set of activities. Girls spend more time at home, according to Barker, Crichton *et al.* and McRobbie. Frith suggests three reasons for girls' absence from subcultures – first, parents control girls' spare time much more closely. Second, girls have to assume an apprenticeship for domestic labour which begins at home. In fact, girls often have to earn their pocket money by helping in domestic tasks. And third, girls spend a lot of time in preparation for out-of-home leisure activities. Frith in fact argues that:

> marriage is a girl's career and the source of the constraints on her leisure. This argument can be pushed further: a girl's leisure is her work. It is leisure activities that are the setting for the start of her career, for the attraction of a man suitable for marriage.

Where low job aspirations exist, as they do for most girls, then there is a commitment to early marriage. It is a way out, and a socially acceptable one, from educational failure and work dissatisfaction, and girls' job decisions tend to be made in terms of a short-term commitment and secondary to the long-term commitment of marriage. Romance is certainly central to girls' perceptions of the future and it is seen as a precursor to marriage. Sarsby found for a sample of fifteen-year-olds that girls sought partners who would be sensitive to them, whilst boys stressed physical attraction. Her working-class girls stressed the importance of security and support in marriage. E. Figes quotes a batch of essays written by London grammar school girls which reveal their thoughts are very centrally on marriage, and Sharpe found 82 per cent of her sample wanted to marry – three-quarters of them by the age of twenty-five. McRobbie and Garber suggest that one of the most important forms of subcultures amongst girls of the seventies was the Teeny Bopper (although this phenomenon was certainly present since the early 1960s). However, it became a centre for market focus during the seventies for the ten- to fifteen-year-old girl. It requires only the use of a bedroom, a record player and a friend. There are no exclusion rules, entrance qualifications, no risk of sexual or social failure. Frith agrees:

> girl culture becomes a culture of the bedroom, the place where girls meet, listen to music and teach each other make-up skills, practise their dancing, compare sexual notes, criticize each other's clothes and gossip.

This is the place that other girls are allowed to visit by their parents. Frith brings marketing evidence to show that the focus of this Teeny Bopper culture is usually a pop star, and what are purchased are magazines, then records and symbols such as T-shirts, posters and pictures. This fades as the girls go out and dance and date, but their magazines still feature pop stars rather than pop music. Attacks on Teeny Bopper idols are a cause of friction, and they are passionately defended. Robins and Cohen note:

> Osmond baiting was, in fact, one of the most familiar weapons used by older brothers in their continuous bickering with their younger sisters. A fourteen-year-old boy told how 'we went by the Rainbow [Theatre] once and we started screaming out of the window "Osmonds are bent, all queers" and they were lobbing everything that come in sight. You should see one of them, she's in a state crying over the railing, going "You bastards" and the next minute she picked up a bottle and threw it at the bus.'

It is worth noting that many pop idols who are ambiguously male in this subculture are sexistly reduced to 'poofs' by males more involved in other elements of rock culture. The Teeny Bopper subculture is a retreat and a preparation for young girls. They can relate to their best friend (girls often emphasize the importance of their best friend, whose friendship they see as continuing after marriage) and together practise in the secrecy of girl culture for the rituals of courtship, away from the eye of male ridicule.

There is a not dissimilar pattern for boys outside of the more dramatic subcultures, and who have the luxury of their own or a friend's room. They are more focused on rock music, and other masculine pursuits. The emphasis on romance in the culture of femininity leads to courtship practices. Dancing is important in this, and Mungham describes well the dance-hall scenario, with its heavy heterosexual machismo masking the fear of the independent woman. Girls in this setting learn an important area of their lives: that of waiting. They cannot directly initiate social encounters, but can only reject or accept what is offered. This is sometimes crudely and effectively done. One respondent told me how he went down a line of waiting girls to be brushed off with a crude 'Piss off – Dracula!' Girls become obsessed with romance in this context, realizing that the only exciting event in their bleak lives may be marriage, and they have no intention of blowing this by unseemly independence. They prepare carefully for dances and discos, arrive immaculately dressed with friends, and dance well. They then have to manage the courtship rituals, from boys trying to 'split a pair' of girls, to getting off, to going steady, which means being sexual with one boy, yet guarding one's reputation against boys who, it is accepted, are after only one thing.

Girls in male-dominated subcultures

In the more dramatic forms of male-dominated subcultures girls are in a structuredly passive situation, but this can be complicated. During the period of the Teds, girls would be present during the social activities but absent from the street corner culture. With the Mods, girls were subordinate but the mod 'cool' style allowed them to go out in groups or alone. With bikers, they never penetrated the central masculine core, riding or owning a bike: they were always a pillion rider. In the hippy subculture, they were still contained within the sphere of traditional femininity, even though it allowed a moratorium which suspended marriage (but not steady relationships). Hippy girls were long-haired, wanton, wild flower-children or, as McRobbie and Garber suggest:

> The stereotypical images we associate most with hippy culture tend to be those of the Earth Mother, baby at breast, or the fragile Pre-Raphaelite lady.

As early as school subcultures, sexual exploitation and the subordination of women is stressed. The boys in Sarsby's study who mentioned personal qualities sought in a girl stressed obedience, respect and virginity. The relations with girls in school means they must be sexually inviting but not sexually experienced; sexually attractive enough to raise the boy's status, but not experienced so that there is no kudos in having a relationship with her. They are expected to service the boy domestically; to be a surrogate wife. They are reduced to being the receiving end of masculine desire, and so have to operate within a framework of passivity. Willis sums this up:

> Although they are its objects, frank and explicit sexuality is actually denied to women. There is a complex of emotion here. On the one hand insofar as she is a sex object, a commodity, she is actually

diminished by sex, she is literally worthless, she has been romantically and materially partly consumed.

There lies under this a fear that if a woman's desire is awakened then she may become independent, and the male himself reduced to an object of comparison. A loyal domestic partner is sought, the 'good woman' based on the boy's image of his own, or an idealized mother.

With girls involved in delinquent subcultures, Wilson suggests interestingly that they may be in rebellion against their traditional role. The deviant or delinquent behaviour of girls tends to be sexualized both in the literature and in the popular mind. Wilson's sample of thirteen- to fifteen-year-olds followed the cult of femininity in that they saw themselves as one-man girls, and for them love was essentially involved in a relationship before sex. Their future jobs were seen merely as a step towards marriage, and they regulated their behaviour so as to avoid contact with 'easy lays' who might contaminate their own reputations. The girls were able to be sexually active without defining themselves as 'bad'. Because girls who are deviant or delinquent tend to have their offences sexualized, a latent function of control, care and protection orders is to reinforce conventional sexual morality. L. S. Smith investigating a sample of girls aged fourteen to sixteen in the Bristol area including those involved with skinheads and greasers found that court records revealed that in no way was female delinquency restricted to sexual misconduct, but also included the usual delinquent acts of boys of a similar age cohort. Terry found in America that girls suspected of sexual offences are more likely than boys to be charged, and Chesney-Lind found three times as many girls as boys institutionalized for sexual offences, running away from home and incorrigibility (again the care, control and protection areas), even though these offences are committed more by boys. Interestingly enough, Smith's girls tended to react to being stigmatized as 'sluts' or 'common' by aggression rather than promiscuity. They suffered a double rejection: first as delinquents, secondly stigmatized as 'sluts'. The girls rejected this latter view, and indeed they condemned promiscuity. They developed self-images as tomboys: tough, dominant and willing to join in fights on equal terms with boys. Sharpe notes that in one London school it is common for girls to fight each other until they are fourteen or fifteen, yet still remain fashion-conscious. Smith's girls found themselves isolated, as bad examples, from other neighbourhood girls, which pushed them into increased dependence upon the delinquent group. They became involved in more fighting, shop-lifting and drinking. The girls were seriously involved in the subculture, and showed group solidarity and active participation during group fights. Because of this they seemed to be treated as equals. This can be contrasted with reports from other sources about skinhead girls (*Schools Bulletin*, West Riding, July 1970):

Skinhead girls admire the way their boys treat them. They treat them as if they weren't there. . . . They never include them in their conversation, they have no manners and are disrespectful, but the girls respect them for being this way. It is all part of the understanding that goes with being a skinhead and being a true one. . . . All skinheads are big headed . . . he will make a small fight sound like a massacre . . . before a skinhead can carry a tool, he must be able to fight with his fists. A tool is no good if someone can knock you out with one blow. The girls take as much part in the fighting as the boys and will be ready to have 'aggro' at any time.

These reports from two different essays by girls illustrate the varied response: firstly the collusion with male chauvinism, and secondly the involvement with fighting. These girls dissociated themselves from the respectable working-class image of femininity, yet remained contained within the ideology of male supremacy. They were still sexually 'respectable'. Their fights were with other girls, but their relation to the culture of femininity is complex. In biker groups there is a fetishized image, a feminized counterpart of the male, but again the girl is the property of the male. As with skinhead girls there is the drawing on of an image found in working-class lesbian cultures: that of the 'diesel dyke' or 'stomping dyke', not so much a development of possible new feminine imagery but feminized interpretations of working-class male imagery. These girls must be seen, as Smith notes,

in contrast to the males whose delinquent behaviour is often seen as an extension of their role, they were seen to have offended against their own sex role and the traditional, stereotyped conceptions of femininity.

It is very difficult for girls to draw on any alternative concepts of femininity, because of their intimate interaction, especially in working-class culture, with traditional familial roles. Any homology sought in youth culture is ruled out because popular culture is itself sexist. Whilst the explicitness of rock and roll struck an important blow against small-town puritanism, from Presley's pelvis onwards, rock and roll nevertheless is a celebration of macho male sexuality which has a traditional notion of women's place, whether it is the sexuality of Rhythm and Blues, woman's need for a man in blues, or the ideology of country music. Rock and roll is still 'screw and smash', screw the girls and smash the opposition. Musicians are mainly men, except for esoteric exceptions like Alice Coltrane, and women are presented as lyricists, singers of sensitive work, or sex objects. Punk has at least attacked this image, although fetishization remains, at least it has elements of shock and self-satire. The sexism of popular culture, especially music, is that it is rooted in an industry which is correctly called show 'business'. Its aim is to make money, and not to criticize itself or society. Any women's band which challenges programmed femininity usually works outside of the industry. Mass-produced popular culture is important because it reaches a very wide audience, but it is dominated by the ratings, airplay and output all open to commercial and often corrupt manipulation. Despite this, and perhaps because of it, women's rock has taken a firm stance against sexism, and involves a different relationship from the audience than the sexual domination of male 'cock rock' bands.

McRobbie has argued, as has Willis for boys, that their own culture is itself the most effective agent of social control for girls. Their anti-school subculture stresses having a good time, not academic achievement. They are like Nell Dunn's heroine in *Up the Junction* who says, 'Time enough for night school, and all that, when you're an old bag.' Marriage is a fascination for them which, given their alternatives, is hardly surprising. It continues to be a major economic and emotional goal despite their knowledge of its problems. School for working-class girls relates to them contradictions in their class position, but home offers a less competitive position. The traditional female role is problematic but concrete, and their knowledge of it is not abstracted theory but direct and experiential. Like her brother, the working-class girl moves from one family to another on marriage. There is no room for a working-class single woman in traditional working-class culture, except on the margins of sexual failure. One is not prepared in the working class to live alone. There is an antidote to this in family life: a bad marriage is seen as preferable to loneliness (at least during the first marriage although work on women's aid centres suggests when alternatives are possible, the hold of marriage is considerably less strong). As Rowbotham reminds us, the drudgery of housework is lumped together with the more rewarding task of child care, although there is no reason why one person should do this all the time.

For middle-class girls, the problems of femininity are basically the same. However, whilst their education prepares them for the dual role, there may be a period between school and marriage which is a moratorium in the sense that they have some time for reflection. It is hardly surprising that the women's liberation movement originated amongst women in higher education. It is amongst these women that sexual politics has been considering relations to men and to other women, in the political, economic, ideological and sexual spheres. It is from this political context that a culture is developing which is examining the role and style of the new feminist woman. Important in this are the attitudes, behaviour and image involved. These are important if they are to have any effect on working-class girls. There is evidence from attempts by feminist teachers, social workers and youth workers to suggest that this can meet with considerable response amongst working-class youth. It is through these spheres that new concepts of femininity will percolate but it has to contend with the culture of traditional femininity and its class reinforcements to succeed. It can expect little assistance at this stage from popular culture or from masculinist subcultures. Working-class girls may well rebel against male supremacy, but even the aggressive subcultures do not direct their toughness against their men; instead toughness is a move to get themselves accepted by macho men. The major problem is that the feminine role is at present a solution for working-class girls especially.

Exorcizing Demons
P. Golding and S. Middleton

Reprinted with permission from Peter Golding and Sue Middleton, *Images of Welfare. Press and Public Attitudes to Poverty*, Martin Robertson, 1982, pp. 59–67

The media do not invent social concerns, nor do they deliberately organize the priorities in public debate. But in particular periods of real social change they cut through popular uncertainties with a display of the political eternal verities around which social consensus is sustained. The period we examined in particular detail, 1976, was 'the year of the cuts' – a label applied without the benefit of prevision. Major reductions in public services were announced in February, July and December, the earliest of these reducing previously planned programmes by £4595 million. It became orthodoxy that the social services should 'share the burden' at a time of national economic misfortune.

Against this background, and the growing unemployment figures, the increasing evidence of recession needed explanation, a task for which the news media are strategically placed. The period produced a shrill and mounting antagonism to the welfare system and its clients, focused in particular on what Deacon has aptly termed 'scroungerphobia'. The period seemed to fit well into the pattern Cohen has called a 'moral panic', in which 'a condition, episode, person, or group of persons emerges to become defined as a threat to societal values or interests'. The notion of a moral panic suggests a sudden and novel eruption of demonology. We are arguing that, at least in the context of poverty and welfare, the process is much more the recurrent refurbishing of a series of images and beliefs that have a historical continuity and that lie very shallowly below a veneer of apparent 'welfare consensus'.

We have identified three stages by which this exhumation of ideologically functional images occurs. In the first, a precipitating event sensitizes the media so that their surveillance procedures and journalistic categories are sharpened to capture similar subsequent events and give them considerable prominence. Second, the ensuing period evokes a steady stream of previously latent mythologies about the 'social problem' thus dramatically 'uncovered'. Third, the legislative, administrative and possibly judicial responses to this cultural thrust reinforce its potency and provide a real shift in the structure of state responses to the definitions provided by the moral panic. These responses in turn provide news material and confirmation of the arrival of a new matter of concern on the political agenda. In the period we examined this led an initial orchestrated indignation about welfare abuse to be broadened into a general scepticism about the purposes and extent of social security, and in turn to a strengthening of the role of the welfare apparatus itself as a mechanism for policing the poor.

The unveiling of latent belief systems is led by an initial precipitating event of sufficient dramatic power to orchestrate a number of the themes that become the leitmotivs of ensuing debate. In an examination of crime news, Chibnall locates such an event in the shooting of three policemen in Shepherd's Bush in London in August 1966. The consequent concern with the increase in criminal violence in British society, and more generally what Chibnall calls 'the Violent Society theme', gave a cultural homogeneity to news coverage of a range of subsequent events, linking the Krays with football hooliganism, student protest, teenage violence and political activism. Hall and his colleagues have described a similar sequence, setting the career of the label 'mugging' in its origins from transatlantic import to its precipitation as a scene-setting theme by the coverage of a lethal attack on an elderly widower in London in August 1972, and a similar violent robbery of a man walking home from a pub in Birmingham in November the same year. The precipitating event in our period was the trial of a forty-two-year-old unemployed Liverpudlian, Derek Peter Deevy, at Liverpool Crown Court in July 1976.

Precipitation: the crowning of 'King Con'

Deevy's was the case that launched a thousand clippings. He was charged with three specimen indictments of obtaining supplementary benefits by deception, the three charges totalling about £57. The total overpayment mentioned in the charge was £500, and it is worth remembering that this was the only figure substantiated in the trial, although Deevy's claims of £36,000 frauduently claimed, which may or may not have been extravagant exaggeration, came to exert a hypnotic effect over Judge and media alike. Deevy pleaded guilty and was sentenced to two years for each of the three indictments, to be served consecutively.

Media coverage of the case was extensive and hysterical. We obtained a copy of the transcript of the trial proceedings to compare with this coverage. What we expected to find was a systematic and selective distortion of a kind familiar to media researchers under the label of unwitting bias or 'inferential structures'. That is to say, journalists will view an event through the prism of their knowledge of previous, apparently similar events, and their expectations act as a template in producing news about the later event. This is normally explained in terms of the demands of journalistic routines, and the exigencies of production and presentation of news. In fact, when we looked carefully at the trial transcript, we found the trial to be quite accurately reported. Media and court alike had shared in borrowing prevailing and dominant beliefs about the welfare state, and in so doing had amplified and relayed them through the reinforcing system of the media. Five such beliefs appeared frequently in the trial proceedings. First, like the social explorers of the last century, the lawyers in the case showed a distaste mixed with righteous ignorance of the world of welfare institutions. Second, the social security system was repeatedly attacked for its ineptitude as a watchdog of the public purse, while Deevy was elevated into the role of a social benefactor for his boastful revelations of the soft, open-hearted and lax system he had exploited. Third, a major refrain was the notion that Deevy was, as the Judge put it, 'the tip of a national scandal', though the court had it both ways by also insisting that this was an outrageous case, the like of which had never been seen. Fourth, despite confusion about the actual sums involved, Deevy's luxurious lifestyle was lengthily discussed and illustrated. Finally, there was anxiety that welfare was too easy to get, expressed in concern that publicity for the trial might encourage imitation and reveal Deevy's methods. We can follow the story as it picks up these themes.

LUXURIOUS LIFESTYLES
Every story made sure to mention cigars, suits and indolent comfort. For some time this was paramount. The *Daily Telegraph*, which had two separate stories the same day, headlined one '£10,000-a-year lifestyle for Dole Fiddler', opening its coverage by noting Deevy's life of splendour. The *Sun* front-page headline, '£36,000 Scrounger', was followed by an underlined sub-headline, 'Six Years for Dole Cheat Who Spent £25 a Week on the Best Cigars'. The *Daily Express* coined the epithet King Con, and above their front-page headline 'Incredible Reign of King Con' was a strap, '£200-a-week tycoon on social security'. The story gave great prominence to the Judge's remarks about people asking 'what's the good of working?' The *Daily Mail* front-page story, 'Biggest Scrounger of the Lot', also drew attention to Deevy's Corona cigars and expensive suits. The *Daily Mirror* lead story 'King of the Dole Queue Scroungers' (a phrase clearly implying a host of like followers) began: 'Nothing was too good for Derek Deevy. His weekly cigar bill came to £25 and he regularly

bought expensive suits. The fact that he was out of work didn't spoil his life at the top.' There is little doubt that however little the average reader knew about the real extent of social security abuse, or about the size of unclaimed benefits, he certainly knew the cost of Derek Deevy's Corona cigars.

Cartoons are an especially effective and economical way of capturing stereotypes and injecting them firmly into popular demonology. The luxurious life of claimants like Deevy was a rich vein for the cartoonists. Giles in the *Daily Express* (15 July 1976) had an irritated but clearly well-fed elderly patron at an opulent garden party retorting to a smirking fellow-guest, 'I resent that remark, Harry! I do NOT do it all on Social Security.' Franklin in the *Sun* the same day had five dishevelled merry-makers gorging themselves on champagne and caviar in a Rolls-Royce labelled 'Social Security Beano for Fiddlers'. They are singing (a rare moment of humour) 'Oh you Beautiful Dole, You Great Big Beautiful Dole'. In case we miss the point the car is being driven between a doorstep-scrubbing housewife and two astonished, sweating, road-labourers.

The *Daily Express* editorial the next day pointed the moral: 'It is no use inviting people to work harder for the country if they feel, with justice, that the product of their effort, in part, is going to cigars and drinks and a good tax-free life for bums.' A week later in the *Express* this had been generalized. Below an editorial commenting on the latest unemployment figures (1,463,456, though 'many of these people are not unemployed in any serious sense') another editorial recalled the Deevy case and repeated the demand for a thorough investigation. But now it was a demand that went beyond investigation of illegality: ' . . . there is a strong case for the view that the whole system needs to be looked at again. Even the perfectly legal largesse looks excessive.'

HOW MANY MORE?

Deevy was immediately enthroned as King of a teeming population of scroungers and spongers. His trial and conviction were confirmation of the suspicions voiced earlier by Conservative MP Iain Sproat. The question, 'how many others?', seemed always to be rhetorical, inviting the reader to nod knowingly in affirmation of the suspicion that prompted the question.

The *Daily Express* (14 July) carried a centre-page feature by Iain Sproat headed, 'I believe we have seen only the tip of the iceberg', which recounted the by now familiar tales from Mr Sproat's postbag to illustrate his point that the Deevy case exploded 'the myth that abuse of the welfare system is some minimal problem'. The *Daily Mirror* began to gather in the evidence in a story (15 July) headed, 'Doing the Scrounge Rounds'. This featured four cases (three in Manchester) of people 'On the Scrounge'.

Given this massive evidence it was no surprise to learn in the first line of the story that 'Britain's army of dole-queue swindlers were on the run last night as a Government Minister warned he was going gunning for them'.

A variant on this theme derived from the trial is the contribution Deevy had made in shedding light on this unsavoury den of parasites and their cunning manipulations. Cartoons are again best at distilling this cultural brew. Cummings in the *Daily Express* (16 July 1976) had a queue of bowler-hatted gents from top companies waiting outside Deevy's cell. The jailor (whose colleague's newspaper is studded with Deevy's references, 'inventive', 'brilliant with figures', and so on) is telling them, 'You'll have to be patient! He's now being interviewed by Denis Healey for a job at the Treasury when he leaves prison . . .' Waite in the *Mirror* had a related idea. An anxious Deevy is sitting at a desk worriedly working on piles of claim forms and files, while his tea-bearing wife warns him, '141 Social Security false names and addresses – why don't you get a job and take things easy?' The *Sun* characteristically got the domestic view of Deevy the hero, quoting his wife on 'the frustrated genius' of her husband. The *Daily Telegraph* was equally complimentary in its editorial of 15 July: ' . . . the full inquiry into the Social Security system obviously carried out by DEEVY, the Fiddler of Genius, was a timely, if expensive, public service.'

SOCIAL SECURITY IS A SOFT TOUCH

Not only had our welfare state been shown to be distributing largesse on a mammoth scale, but was obviously doing so with a minimum of control. Staffed with naive bureaucrats who have none of the worldly cynicism of the press to protect them from the guile of men like Deevy, the social security system is an open treasure house without a doorkeeper. A *Sun* editorial gasped that 'The men from the Ministry (alias the taxpayers) didn't even seem to look up as they shelled out the cash'. The *Daily Mail* story (14 July) headed 'Biggest Scrounger of the Lot', described how Deevy 'milked' the system. The cartoon by Mac in the *Mail* the following day had a cigar-chomping claimant, dolly bird by his side, standing impatiently at the DHSS counter while his chauffeur-driven car waits outside. He is telling the counter-clerk, who is counting out piles of banknotes for him, 'Do hurry up – I've got twenty-six other labour exchanges to get to today y'know.' It is, in fact, extremely rare for cash to be handed over counters in either Employment Exchanges or Social Security offices, and has been so for many years. The image of banknotes being 'shelled-out' is a powerful one, however.

TIME TO CLAMP DOWN: THE POLITICIANS SPEAK

If we are dealing with 'A National Scandal', then the shift to the political arena will not be far behind. Ministers are forced to defend the existing arrangements, thereby confirming the need for control mechanisms rather than denying the extent of abuse. If the problem is defined, not as inadequate provision or complex administration, but as undue liberality, the solution automatically must lie in further policing of potential abuse.

Most media shifted their attention quickly away from the unseemly practices in the homes of the poor or the DHSS offices they plagued, to the more familiar battle-ground of party politics. In the *Daily Express* (14 July) it was, 'Crack-down on Scroungers Call by Angry MPs'; in the *Sun* (14 July), 'Angry MPs Demand a Big Probe'; in the *Telegraph*, 'Tory Storm Over £36,000 Dole Fiddle'. The demand for a public inquiry was almost universal, though there was almost no mention of the Fisher Committee, which only three years earlier had concluded its extensive report on social security abuse with the view that the problem was relatively negligible. The shift from the trial, via an unquestioned generalization that here was an instance of a general problem, to the arena of public debate in party politics is a routine of news production. It is familiar to students of news in other areas like race relations or trade unions, or of news in general. In transferring the attention of news consumers to the terrain most central to routine news collection and production, it confirms the existence of a general phenomenon as 'a national scandal' or as a problem to be solved, and equally legitimizes the solution of that problem in the actions of the state – tightening up, clamping down, and so on. The next two themes illustrate further how this appears.

THE DESERVING MUST BE SORTED FROM THE UNDESERVING
Much of the post-Deevy debate involved a public reclarification of the classic distinction between the deserving and the undeserving poor. By extension this becomes a redrawing of the boundaries of citizenship, inside which reside the honest, the taxpayer and the deserving poor, while outside reside the undeserving, dishonest spongers and scroungers, as well as other deviant or suspect groups.

In coverage of the Deevy case this theme appeared mainly in editorials and the quoted speeches of politicians. The Social Services Secretary, David Ennals, hard-pressed and defensive, was widely quoted in this vein: 'The ordinary taxpayer is entitled to insist that benefits go to those they are intended for, and not swindlers and criminals.' Iain Sproat's claim that half the people claiming unemployment benefits were not in fact unemployed, nailed the label firmly on this group in particular – the cigar smoking, liquor swigging good-life bums of the *Express* editorial.

Lynda Lee-Porter in the *Daily Mail*, in a column that frequently gives voice to populist cries of righteous indignation, illustrated the deserving/undeserving divide (14 July): 'The philanthropic social security have after all cushioned and accustomed out-of-work labourer Derek Deevy to a life of luxury for seven years.' Lynda's dad, it appears, used to walk three miles to collect her grandad's pit pension. As her dad is a proud man who would starve rather than take social security, '. . . I feel I've got the right to condemn the scroungers'. To show the heart beneath the stern exterior Lynda tells us she disagrees with Sir Keith Joseph – people *do* live in 'slummy slutty conditions' and there really is poverty. 'The ordinary decent kindly majority of us know there are people who need help. We want them to have it. We only get resentful and bitter when we see it going to the able-bodied, parasite, malingerers.'

FIGHTING THE GOOD FIGHT: THE ARMIES LINE UP

Prominent and recurrent among the imagery of the post-Deevy coverage was that of armies, fighting and battles. This is an important part of the rhetoric that establishes the claimant as outsider, or even enemy, of the nation. The most spectacular battle-cry was in the *Daily Express* on 15 July. Blazoned across the front page in huge capitals was the headline 'Get the Scroungers'. The report, based around Secretary of State David Ennals's promise to 'crack down as hard as we can on all forms of Social Security fraud', reports on fraud statistics and suggests 'Civil Service union leaders are angry that Social Security investigators will be hit by coming Government cuts'. (In fact the union had protested about the cut in officers available for house visits. Special Investigators have consistently been one of the few areas of expansion.) A week later, in the *Express*, readers were writing to complain about 'The King Con Brigade' (20 July). As the battle-dust died down the lines of the ensuing campaign had been clearly drawn. The fight was to draw on a lot of old battle manuals and war-cries as it progressed.

. . . A final footnote to the Deevy case bears mentioning. On the same day as the main Deevy coverage (14 July) came the news that the general manager of the Wakefield Building Society had been suspended from his post, while police were called in to investigate a previously undiscovered loss of £600,000. The fraud, for such it was, disappeared beneath the enormity of Derek Deevy's outrages. It made page nine in the *Daily Express*, page five in the *Daily Mirror*, page fourteen in the *Daily Mail*, and page seven in the *Sun*. The case was ironically parallel to Deevy's. The fraud had given the manager an income of £10,000 per year, most of which had gone on gambling. The sentence was six years. Yet all of this information could only be found on an inside page of *The Times* at the time of sentencing, where it was one of eighteen stories on the page (17 January 1978).

We have discussed the Deevy case in considerable detail for two reasons. First, it illustrates most of the themes that echoed through the ensuing scroungerphobia period. Second, it reveals the mechanics by which a single event is translated by a series of institutional manipulations into a general cultural obsession. Authoritative sources, here the courts and parliament, are the original definers of popular concern and a national sense of right and proper attitudes. The media selectively relay, simplify and colour these in the light of historically derived popular mythology and demonology. Thus does a ruling ideology become popular indignation.

Friends
G. A. Allan

Reprinted with permission from Graham Allan, *A Sociology of Friendship and Kinship*, Allen and Unwin, 1979, pp. 34–45

The term 'friend' is only applied to people who have a personal relationship that is qualitatively of a particular sort. It is the actual relationship itself that is the most important factor in deciding whether someone can or cannot be labelled a friend. Thus as well as locating people in the social structure, the term friend also implies something about the relationship between those so labelled. Thus it is a *relational* label rather than a categorical one. To express this more graphically, if one imagines gathering all a person's kin together, or all his neighbours or all his colleagues, there is no way of knowing what type of relationship (if any) he actually has with any of them. If all his friends gathered together, on the other hand, certain rather general assumptions could be made about his relationships with them. Indeed this is tacitly recognized in some of the sociological research into friendship. In these reports, the specification of the nature of the personal relationships between friends is often less important than an analysis of who these friends actually are: colleagues, neighbours, workmates, fellow club members or whatever. But in kinship studies, for example, the opposite applies; these studies are almost always concerned with analysing the nature of the on-going relationship between people who happen to have been defined as kin.

If this were the end of the matter, the analysis of friendship patterns would be comparatively simple. On this basis, all friend relationships should be of a similar kind, so all that needs to be done is to specify what that kind is. Unfortunately there are further complications. While the concept 'friendship' refers to a particular kind of sociable relationship, it is one whose definition is by no means precise. The range of relationships that can be covered by the term is great. Various connotations, not all of which occur in concert, can be brought into play at different times and on different occasions. So in everyday speech the concept is used to express different aspects of what we take being a friend to mean. In one context we may use the term to signify someone we are very close to, a 'true' or 'real' friend; elsewhere someone we have only interacted with in a handful of sociable or leisure situations may, in passing, be referred to as a friend.

A number of sociologists and anthropologists have recognized the difficulty there is in defining friendship. Julian Pitt-Rivers, for example, responding to his own question 'But what is a friend?' wrote: 'The range of interpersonal relations between Aristotle's axioms and the jejune imperatives of Dale Carnegie lead me to wonder.' Naegale, too, has recognized the wide variation there can be in friend relationships. What is surprising is the number of sociologists who either fail to recognize the variation there can be in the meaning of the term, or who, having recognized it, fail to take it into account in their analysis. After reviewing a selection of sociological literature on friendship, Edgell is quite right to reflect that: 'In none of the studies referred to so far has the meaning of friendship been adequately conceptualized by the investigators. It is a case of making excuses or measuring the extent of a social phenomenon without giving prior thought to what is being measured.'

The difference between 'being friends' and 'being friendly' is recognized readily enough: the former involves some degree of personal knowledge and some sense of mutual communion, and the latter merely assumes a form of attitude that follows from acknowledged rules of propriety and allows interaction to proceed smoothly and without risk of upset. (Indeed, Burns pointed out that one can even be friendly with people one dislikes, calling this the 'polite fiction'.) However, having made this distinction, many writers assume that being friends is an invariable, and therefore unproblematic, state of affairs. Frequently only the most intense forms of friendship, those between 'real', 'true' and 'very close' friends, are considered. If a relationship is not characterized by strong emotional attachment, feelings of empathy, mutual sympathy and understanding, it is immediately classified as something other than full friendship and removed from consideration. This is most evident in much of the quasi-philosophical writing on friendship. In this, the dictates of Aristotle are taken as the defining criteria of any friendship worthy of the name. Unfortunately the same is true of some of the sociological 'theorizing' about friendship.

However, within sociology the tendency to treat 'real' friendships as *the* form of friendship is more pervasive in another guise. In empirical studies respondents are often asked to name their 'best friends' or those to whom they feel closest. Various questions are asked about these friends and from the answers the researcher extrapolates and analyses friendship in general. Obviously in such cases the range of relationships that will be included in the analysis is severely limited because of the paucity of the sample of friends about whom questions are asked.

Examples of this process are prevalent in the research literature. Lazarsfeld and Merton base their influential discussion of value and status homophily in friendship formation on the results of an interview in which respondents were asked questions about their 'three closest friends'. Robin Williams, in his study of friendship and social values, recognizes clearly the problems there are with the category 'friend', but nevertheless proceeds in his analysis on the basis of questions about: (1) his respondents' best friend in their immediate residential area; (2) their best friend in the larger urban area; and (3) their best friend living anywhere. From these questions it is surprising that Williams is able to distinguish two types of friendship, one being 'marked by diffuseness, collectivity-orientation, norms of affectivity, and a relatively high degree of affective involvement' and the other tending 'to be specific, self-interested, oriented to norms of affective-neutrality, and low in affective involvement ("commitment")'. Babchuk and Bates asked their respondents – middle-class married couples – to name their 'very close mutual friends'. Similarly Zena Blau lists three questions she asked of her elderly respondents in order to ascertain 'the extent of [their] friendship participation'. The first asked them how many 'really close friends' they had in the town; the second how often they saw 'the friend that [they knew] best here in town'; and the third whether they thought of themselves as '[going] around with a certain bunch of close friends'. As a final example, Booth and Hess, for their analysis of cross-sex friendship, asked their respondents to think of those non-kin people they thought of as friends and then asked them to list those 'persons you would consider to be your very closest friends'.

These examples – and others can be found to support them – all illustrate the emphasis there is in the literature on extreme forms of friendship. Although a lot of what has been written generalizes about friendships of all forms, the data it is based on usually pertain to a restricted set of very close friends.

There is a further consequence which follows from friendship being a concept that is imprecise and variable which also has important bearing for research into friendship patterns. This relates to the way in which respondents use the term. To put the matter simply, if the concept 'friend' has various connotations and strands of meaning, it is important to know exactly which of them a respondent is using when he discusses his relationships with his friends. If there can be a degree of conceptual variation, the researcher must come to understand the ways in which each of his respondents uses the concept in the interview situation. At an everyday level the meaning may be taken as obvious, but for research purposes the obvious must be treated as problematic. It is particularly useful to discover why someone is not regarded as a friend, especially in those numerous cases where respondents are not quite sure whether the person they are discussing can or cannot be regarded as one. The point to make here is that in common usage terms like friend (and mate, pal, chum, etc.) are only vague means of analysis; they serve as resources as well as restraints. People use them as labels and devices for conveying meaning in particular situations, not as rigorous and precise analytical tools. This must be borne in mind when we come to interpret what respondents report.

Aspects of friendship in Western culture

I want to explore some of the main elements involved in our concept of friendship. The 'data' I shall use in doing this come from two sources: (1) previous sociological analyses of what friendship comprises; and (2) the accounts of their friendships given by the Selden Hey respondents. These sources will be used interchangeably. It is legitimate to use other researchers' writings in this way because not only have they expended time and energy in analysing the concept 'friendship' as their own informants have used it, but also they (like myself) are members of Western culture and, thus, to a fashion, 'experts' in the meaning of the term. It is of course equally legitimate to use other cultural material as data in this way (e.g. novels, plays, advice columns, diaries etc.). I restrict myself to the sociological literature on friendship because in this the analysis of what friendship is is most explicit. Following Schneider's lead many of the themes I develop below have been refined through discussing them informally with various 'informants' who, as above, are 'experts' on the meaning of the concepts friend and friendship.

The first point to make about friendship is that it is taken as a *personal* relationship in three connected senses: (1) that it is a relationship between individuals; (2) that it is a private relationship; and (3) that it involves the person as the person he really is (itself a cultural construct).

In the first sense friendship is a personal relationship in that it is seen as involving individuals as individuals and not as members of groups or collectivities. In other words, belonging to a particular group of people or being affiliated to them in some formal way does not lead to any other group of people being called friends. Nor does it lead to those in your own group necessarily being regarded as friends, although there is nothing to stop a group of people all being friends with one another. This follows from what was written above about friendship not being based on criteria external to the personal relationship between people but referring to the quality of that relationship.

Two points are directly related to this: first, friendship scores low on what McCall *et al.* term 'formality'. That is, friend relationships are not structured by the formal role position of those who are friends, for friendship is seen as independent of a person's formal role position. Most important, friendships do not develop between people *solely* because of the role positions they fill in any organizations or institutions. Secondly, following from the idea that friendships occur between individuals as individuals, a friend is valued as a unique person and cannot be replaced as can a person occupying a formal role position (e.g. a doctor or a lift attendant). Of course friends change, with new ones taking the place of old ones, but the new friends, like the old, are interacted with on the basis of their individuality and are not (or at least should not) be thought of as particular examples of a general interchangeable set of others. In Paine's phrase, friends are not considered to be 'mutually substitutable persons'.

Friendship is also a personal relationship in the sense of it being a private one, of concern only to those who are the friends. Thus friendship follows what Simmel calls 'the principle of excluding everyone who is not explicitly included'. Within legal limits, what is involved in a particular friendship, what friends do together, even how they treat one another, is for them alone to decide. As Suttles points out, friends can afford to ignore the normal 'rules of public propriety' when with one another. Even if what they do together upsets the moral or legal sensibilities of outsiders, this is not a ground for criticizing the friendship as a friendship.

It follows from this that, unlike blood brotherhood and some other relationships that anthropologists tend to translate into the term 'friend', friendship in English culture is not institutionalized. Although others may try to influence a person's friendship choices, there are few societal conventions governing who can and who cannot become friends. (Normally any pressure exerted over friendship choice is informal, e.g. gossip and ridicule, rather than formal, and usually only occurs when the friends differ markedly in sex, age or class.) Nor is there any ritual or public performance attached to friendship. Friendships are not formally made nor broken; there are no symbolic activities connected with these processes. Thus friendship just happens as you get to know someone, so cannot be created through ritual. And as it is of concern only to those who are friends, public demonstration of its strength is unnecessary. Friends may in fact create ritual in their friendship, for friendship is an open relationship subject to 'private negotiation'. They may also develop their own argot of 'shorthand' speech patterns, but neither ritual nor argot is necessary to any friendship.

The third sense in which friendship is personal stems from the notion that ideally in friendship people should 'be themselves', the people they 'really' are, with all pretence and pretension wiped away. (Whether or not this is actually possible is not relevant here. What is important is the cultural belief that this is how things should be between friends.) Someone who is truly a friend is not meant to put on a front or an act, he is taken as someone who is genuine; who, while with friends, is natural. To get to know someone as a friend involves getting to know the 'real person'. To like them is to like this 'real person'.

Now some friends will (that is, will be allowed to) get to know and understand a person's 'real self' better than others. This will make them better or closer friends. This aspect of being *allowed* to get to know the real person is important, for, referring back to Simmel, it is the means by which the individual has control over who is explicitly included. Only those whom he allows an opportunity to witness and view part of the (presumed) unadulterated natural self will be considered, or will consider themselves to be, friends.

Thus friends should be admitted to what Goffman terms the 'back-stage' or 'back-region' of one's performances, for ideally friends can be trusted not to reveal to others what they learn there. In many ways Bates's analogy of the person's self occupying a series of rooms which he allows others to view is more apt here. Not only are some friends allowed to see more of the dwelling/person than others, but also in practice 'rooms' may be revealed to different friends in a different order. In other words, Bates's analogy more fully captures the potential variations and processes involved in revealing one's 'real self' to others. To claim that some friends are allowed to discover the 'real self' more than others is to say that some are trusted more than others. This is the major difference between those people labelled 'real' or 'true' friends and the remainder. 'Real' friends appear to be trusted totally and can be relied on to protect their friend's interests. It is recognized that they will not reveal or use revelations of the self meant for their ears alone. Other friends not labelled real or true ones are likely to be treated more cautiously, only being permitted to visit some rooms, and then perhaps for only brief periods. They are people who are found interesting and with whom one is sociable, but they are not people to whom one reveals innermost fears or worries. As Suttles develops at length, an important way in which people become friends, and 'everyday' friends 'real' friends, is by breaking the normal 'rules of public propriety'. This serves to reveal the 'real self' and for the friends symbolizes the strength of their friendship bond.

A second characteristic of friend relationships is that they are defined as voluntary. They are seen as consequent on the free choice and selection of each friend by the other. To put this another way, they are achieved rather than ascribed. Where there is a personal relationship with another based on criteria other than free choice, or when a person's choice is consequential to a greater or lesser extent on factors for which he perceives he is not responsible, then the relationship is unlikely to be considered one of friendship.

This brings us back to a point made earlier. Relationships which arise from people's formal role positions are unlikely to be thought of as friendships if those concerned see their interaction as being consequent more on their formal role position than on the exercise of free choice. To say this is not to deny that friendships can, in fact, occur between people who occupy formal role positions *vis-à-vis* one another. Indeed this is one of the most common sources of friendships and, as Suttles remarks, in formal organizations friendship plays its part by providing 'a means of going beyond prescribed institutional or organizational affiliations'. It is to assert that whether a friendship is made or not is up to the individuals involved and is never a *necessary* consequence of their interaction in their respective role positions.

That ties of friendship and kinship are often seen as mutually exclusive in Western culture would also appear to be related to the notion that friends are achieved rather than ascribed. I have suggested above that friendship refers to a quality of the personal relationship existing between individuals whereas kinship is based on criteria external to that relationship. Consequently it would be reasonable to assume that a kinsman could be a friend, just as a colleague or a neighbour can, as there is nothing contradictory or mutually exclusive in the terms. However, such analytical distinctions are generally not made in everyday life nor in much of the sociological literature, so that in practice kin tend to be seen as distinct from friends. Only when people are asked specifically about the nature or quality of their relationships are they apt to describe kin as friends (and then as 'best friends'). Thus C. Turner reports that 'Kinsfolk . . . are never recognized as merely friends', and similarly Naegale, on the basis of discussions with high school students, points out that kin and friends occupy different spheres of activity. Schmalenback goes so far as to suggest that kinship and friendship have an entirely different basis, the former being an example of 'community' and the latter of 'communion'. At a more mundane level, kin and friends are often treated separately in empirical research, not least in community studies. Babchuk and Bates, Babchuk, and Booth and Hess amongst others similarly operationalize friendship in such a way that kin are explicitly excluded. The same distinction is tacitly assumed by many anthropologists when, for want of a more appropriate term, they equate relationships found in other cultures in which kin are explicitly excluded with friendship as it exists in our culture.

An assumption entailed in the idea that friendship is voluntary is that it is a relationship based on enjoyment. A friend is someone with whom you enjoy spending time and sharing activities. That is, a friend's 'real self' is appreciated and enjoyed for its own sake. Conversely if you do not enjoy interacting with someone, they are unlikely to be considered a friend. In some ways, though, to say friendship is a relationship of enjoyment overstates the case, for the enjoyment is implicit rather than explicit. It could be described as a relationship characterized by 'enjoyment by default'. Usually it is only over specific activities – a dinner party, an outing together – where a particular effort has been made by one or both sides that friends actually express enjoyment. For more mundane everyday interaction, it is unusual to do so. Because in our culture friendship is entered into voluntarily it is reasonable for those involved to assume that the other(s) are party to the interaction because they enjoy it.

The matter is complicated by the fact that enjoyment in interaction can come from two analytically distinct sources, only one of which is directly tied with friendship. First of all interaction may be enjoyed because the people involved like each other and, quite simply, enjoy interacting with each other no matter what the activity in which they are engaged. The relationship is enjoyed for its own sake. But interaction may be found enjoyable for another reason. The enjoyment may stem from the activity more than from the relationships those involved have with one another. For example, one may enjoy playing football or singing in a choir, but does this make one's fellow football players or choristers friends? In part the answer depends on how well they (their 'real selves') are known. Ambiguity arises when some are known quite well within a particular social context, but are not interacted with outside that setting. On the one hand, not only have such people been selected from the rest of the group present, apparently for their personal qualities, but further the activity itself is freely chosen, defined as social and presumably found enjoyable. On the other hand, in McCall *et al.*'s phrase, these relationships are none the less 'embedded' in a given social structure. To this extent they are not chosen freely but are almost equivalent to the more formal role positions the individual occupies. It just happens that these people are in the choir too, or in the football team or whatever. Frequently in the interviews, the Selden Hey respondents were unsure whether someone could be called a friend because of the basic contradiction. Similarly Naegale's groups of high school students created the concept 'just a friend' to cover this ambiguity, i.e. to describe people who were more than acquaintances but with whom interaction only took place within the structured, given (and therefore not freely chosen) setting of the school.

In general, the reasons why people become friends are treated as unproblematic in our culture, except in that branch of it known as psychology. It is something that just happens, and apparently just happens naturally. It cannot be forced or contrived. It may be encouraged, with an effort being made to develop it – in the words of one respondent who was beginning to get to know a colleague as a friend: 'We're working on it' – but to be thought of as genuine it must not be forced. Interestingly there are virtually no myths prevalent in our culture to 'explain' friendship attractions. There is no equivalent to what may be called the 'we-were-made-for-each-other' syndrome or to the mystical 'chemistry of sexual attraction' that are sometimes found in accounts of relationships of love. Nor is chance given as a reason for friendship because friendship is a relationship over which the individual is accepted as having some control. While it cannot be contrived it has to be facilitated. The individual could stop the process before it became friendship. You meet people by chance, live near them by chance, even work with them by chance, but you do not form a friendship by chance. If you ask a respondent why X or Y is a friend, the most common answer is 'I don't really know'. Occasionally more positive answers are given, such as: 'Well, we share the same interests.' But such answers are recognized as insufficient as clearly others who also share the same interests are not regarded as friends. More rarely other, apparently fuller though in fact equally vague, answers are given. For example, one respondent replied to such a question about one of his friends: 'Our characters seemed to mesh like two cogs.' In English culture, then, friendship is taken as not needing explanation. There just happen to be some people whom you come to regard as friends. Why this should be so, why you in fact get on with them, is not questioned.

Another important aspect of friendship that is emphasized in the research literature is that it should be non-exploitive. It is not a relationship *formed* for instrumental reasons, but one that exists simply because it is found to be enjoyable. It should be undertaken for its own sake rather than for some ulterior motive or as a means to some other end. Unlike Reina's portrayal of friendship among the Ladinos, for example, in our society friendship is not a relationship created solely for the favours that can be obtained through it. Its *raison d'être* is not to gain political or economic advantage nor to secure oneself against possible future misfortune. Indeed little is more likely to destroy a friendship than one person perceiving that another is using their relationship solely in order to obtain some extraneous benefit from himself.

This does not mean, of course, that friends do not exploit their friendships, nor that they get nothing out of them. As Paine points out, Wolf is wrong to assume that a friendship is *either* expressive *or* instrumental. This is illustrated nicely by the work of Burridge and Pitt-Rivers, even though both are dealing with friendships in other cultures. Friends can quite legitimately make use of one another in instrumental ways without threatening the relationship, provided that it is clear that they are being used because they are friends and not friends because they are useful. Thus a friend would expect to be used if he could help in some way but would feel less charitable if he discovered the other only treated him as a friend so that help could be obtained from him. One way in which the image of the relationship as one not being *based* on instrumental or exploitive interests can be sustained is by an effective or putative *equivalence of exchange*. That is, if A asks his friend B for help in some task, he does so on the implicit understanding that B in turn could use him at some future time. It is so that friendships can be seen to be non-exploitive that the ideas of reciprocity and symmetry are so important to them. The idea is best captured by Naegale when he talks of 'infrequent reciprocity', for in friendship the reciprocity must remain implicit and this is achieved best when it is an informal, almost casual, reciprocity.

A major means by which reciprocity is maintained in friendship is by the person who last benefited seeking to redress the balance. It works out as a case of the 'debtor' seeking to repay more avidly than the 'creditor' seeks to claim, for in this way the former can show that their relationship is not one of exploitation but one of friendship. Individuals find it embarrassing to be continually asking for assistance or receiving services of one form or another but never getting a chance to repay them. For example, a number of Selden Hey respondents reported that they did not like asking a friend X to babysit as X never needed their services as a babysitter in return. Perhaps X was childless or had a mother who babysat for her. The consequence was the same. The respondents did not want to put themselves in continual debt to their friends even though the friends themselves might not mind.

Closely tied to the idea of reciprocity is the notion that friendship is a relationship between equals. In Edgell's terms, it is a symmetrical relationship with the parties to it not being differentiated in a hierarchical manner. Within the context of the friendship no side has more authority or greater status than the other. It is a relationship typified by *communitas* rather than structure. This is one reason why friends tend to occupy the same status in the wider society as one another, a theme developed by Lazarsfeld and Merton and one as true for the Selden Hey research as for previous studies. Friends tend to be of similar age, sex, class and marital status. Blau has shown the importance of these structural variables in her analysis of friendship amongst the elderly. Rosow also emphasizes such variables, writing: 'Status similarities generally provide a strong basis for solidarity because they join persons of like social position who have the same relation to the larger society and who share a common set of life experiences, problems, perspectives, values and interests.' In other words, not only are people with similar status in society likely to find this consonant with treating each other as equals but further their 'real selves' are more likely to have things in common as a consequence of their similar structural position.

A final way in which friendship is a reciprocal relationship is that, in general, a friend is only regarded as a friend to the extent to which he considers you a friend. In other words, friendship must be reciprocal in terms of both sides' labelling of the other. This is a rather different kind of reciprocity from that discussed above. It refers not to the activities involved in a friendship – though it ultimately depends on these – but to the definition each person has of their relationship. The principle was spelt out clearly by one respondent who, while considering whether he regarded any of his former colleagues as friends, said: 'No, I don't think they were. I got on with them very well at work, but it was just at work . . . I'm trying to think whether any of them would call me a friend. I don't think they would, no.' Other respondents, though not stating the matter as plainly as this, recognized that people who did not regard them as friends could not be regarded as such either.

The Family, the School and the Political Socialization Process
R. E. Dowse and J. Hughes

Reprinted with permission from Robert Dowse and John Hughes, 'The Family, the School and the Political Socialization Process', *Sociology,* vol. 5, no. 1, January 1971

A major enterprise of political socialization studies is to assess the relative influence of the various socializing agencies with which the young come into contact. An early claim was that the institution most crucial in shaping the basic political orientations of each new generation was the family. Hyman, in his survey of work in the area of political socialization, recognized the importance of other institutions, but concluded that, 'Foremost among agencies of socialization into politics is the family.' This view was consistent with ideas developed in social psychology and sociology which stressed both the direct and indirect roles of the family in forming the basic general social orientations of its members. Accordingly, it seemed reasonable to infer that the family would also be critical in forming a subset of these general orientations, namely, orientations to politics. It was recognized, of course, that the formative influences at work within the family context were various and complex and might have only an indirect connection with political life as usually understood. Apart from any direct transmission of values which might take place between parents and their children, other important processes might include those shaping basic personality which, in turn, could conceivably play a part in determining the content and style of political beliefs and behaviour. But, whatever the processes at work, earlier theorizing stressed the primacy of the family as an agency of political socialization.

Closer to traditional political science, studies of adult political behaviour provided evidence which, on the face of it, was consistent with the thesis of family dominance. It had been noted with certain variables, especially party choice, that there were high levels of agreement between parents and their children. To quote the conclusion of one such study,

Campbell and his associates claimed that '. . . an orientation to political affairs typically begins before the individual attains voting age and . . . this orientation strongly reflects his immediate social milieu, in particular his family.'

Unfortunately, from the point of view of providing evidence relevant to the thesis of family primacy in the political socialization process, such studies suffer from a number of difficulties. First, they ignore parent-child similarities on political attitudes other than party choice; this is the characteristic most firmly fixed in adults and hence a poor guide to the levels of intergenerational agreement to be found on other, perhaps less stable, attitudes. A second difficulty is the reliance of these studies on retrospective reports by adults of their parents' beliefs and attitudes. It is not known to what extent the respondents' recall is accurate. Thirdly, allowing accurate recall, similarity on such variables as party preference between a group of adults and their parents is not, by itself, evidence that it is the family which causes the similarity. For example, where parents and their offspring are exposed to similar occupational milieux this could lead to similar views of the social order which might be reflected in similarities on more specific characteristics such as partisan loyalties. But to acknowledge the possibility of intergenerational similarities as a product of extra-familial agencies entails the possibility that family socialization may be only temporary and subject to modification by experiences intervening between child and adult statuses. Schools, mass media, occupation, may all expose the individual to attitudes and values other than those experienced within the family context.

Thus the assessment of family influence on the political socialization process cannot be undertaken by relying on adult samples. More recent data based on studies of children provide stronger evidence to build an assessment of family influences on the developing political orientations of pre-adults. Hess and Torney, in a study of American school children, provide evidence which questions the thesis of the family's overriding importance. They conclude that family efficacy in transmitting political attitudes and values may have been overstressed in previous research and that only certain kinds of political attitudes may be the result of specifically family socialization. These were party preference, an early attachment to country and government, and general attitudes towards 'authority, rules and compliance'. In a later American study by Kent Jennings and Richard Niemi, this time on a systematic parent-child comparison, it was found that apart from party preferences the associations between parents and their children on a series of political attitudes were low. On the basis of this evidence the authors conclude that 'any model of socialization which rests on the assumptions of pervasive currents of parent-child value transmissions is in serious need of modification'.

Apart from the family, one possible institution which might have some marked impact on the political orientations of the new political generation (since it is an institution in which the pre-adult is involved for a considerable period of his life) is, of course, the school. A conclusion of Hess and Torney's study is that in the United States the 'public school appears to be the most important and effective instrument of political socialization . . .'

In Britain the connection between education and social class has been observed and recognized for many years. Numerous studies have shown the strong relationship that social class bears to educational selection and the relationship of such selection to social mobility and occupational status. This selection plays a large part in determining adult occupation and, consequently, social class position. Grammar school children, regardless of their social origins, are much more likely to obtain non-manual employment of some kind than those children who have attended secondary modern schools. Given the strong relationship between social class and differential party support to be found in Britain the effects of social mobility are likely to be politically consequential.

It becomes obvious, then, that the process of political socialization is complex and one which, in industrial societies, cannot be attributed to one prime agency, whether the family or the school, or whatever. The main purpose of this paper is to assess the relative weight of the family and the school in shaping some attitudes and the political knowledge of a group of English school children. We do this with a matched parent-child sample, a technique which has not hitherto been employed at all in studies of socialization in Britain and has only been utilized in a very few cases in the USA.

The data

The data are taken from a study of a sample of school children between the ages of eleven and seventeen plus years from Exeter, Britain. The sample was drawn from a girls' grammar school ($n=148$), a boys' grammar school ($n=146$), two girls' secondary modern schools ($n=193$), and a boys' secondary modern school ($n=140$). The number of children in each school sampled represents a randomly selected 20 per cent of all children in each school. This sample constitutes a good cross-section of the state secondary education sector of the town. Each child in the sample was asked to complete a paper and pencil questionnaire under the supervision of one of the investigators. After completion of the questionnaire, each child was asked to take home to his parents an envelope containing a further questionnaire to be completed by the child's father. The completed parent questionnaire was to be returned in a sealed envelope to the school within a few days. In this way we obtained questionnaires from 627 children and from 327 parents.

The technique of gathering and matching information from both children and parents has a clear advantage over techniques which place reliance on recall by asking either children or adults to report parental attachments and attitudes without any independent check on the accuracy of such reporting. In our study this advantage was only partially realized. First, incomplete return of the parent questionnaires meant that a systematic parent-child comparison could only be undertaken with 52 per cent of the sample. Within both grammar and secondary modern schools the pattern of parental response/non-response was more strongly associated with parental class than with any other factor; but the relationship is not a significant one. Even less significant were the observed differences on other variables, such as political knowledge, political efficacy, frequency of political discussion with parents and so on. Hence, we do not feel that the low parental response vitiates our results, but it is a factor to be borne in mind. Secondly, although the children had been told most specifically that we wished their father (where available) to complete the parent questionnaire, we found, nevertheless, that in some cases wives rather than husbands had completed the questionnaire. We have, nonetheless, used the responses in an undifferentiated manner taking them simply as 'parent responses'. To what extent we can assume in this sample similarity between husbands and wives on political attitudes is unknown. At any rate, it is undeniable that it does introduce a possible margin of error.

The direct transmission of attitudes from parents to children

In this section of the paper we shall examine our evidence relevant to the proposition that there is a *direct* transmission of politically relevant values and attitudes from parents to children. If the thesis is correct, then one would expect strong similarities in attitudes and values between parents and children.

PARTY IDENTIFICATION

As mentioned earlier one of the main arguments produced to support the thesis that the family transmits political values was the coincidence of intergenerational partisan preferences. Party preference is perhaps *the* variable that might be expected to be transmitted by parents to children since it is probably the known political characteristic most firmly fixed in adults. Also, for a majority of adults, voting for a party is their most salient political act. Accordingly, if children are aware of any of their parents' political attitudes or beliefs, it is likely to be party preference. Furthermore, if parents are the major political role models available for their children to 'imitate', then one might expect high levels of inter-generational similarity on party preference.

In the questionnaire each child was asked to state whether he or she 'supported' a political party and, if so, to name that party. In addition, each child was also asked to state which party his or her father voted for in the last general election, that of 1966. This meant that we could measure the extent to which the child's preference, if any, corresponded to their perception of parents' preference. The difficulty here is the possibility of a spuriously high level of intergenerational agreement due to the child interpreting the parents' party preference in terms of its own. So, as a check on the accuracy of the children's perceptions of parents' vote, the parent questionnaire contained an item asking for which party, if any, the parent voted in the last three general elections, including that of 1966. As far as the political socialization process is concerned, this question of accuracy is important in interpreting the link between parents and children. For, if the perceptions of the parents' party preferences are accurate, this is reasonable evidence to suggest that some political facts, at least, are a feature of parent-child interaction. If, on the other hand, the children's perceptions are inaccurate this would not only cast doubt on the use of offspring's report as an indicator of parental party preference – a characteristic technique of many adult studies – but would also suggest a fairly low level of direct political communication within the family.

As will be seen, the picture is complex. In Table 1 the biggest category (30 per cent) are those children who state neither a parent nor a personal

Table 1. Child's preference and perceived parent's vote

			Totals
Children whose own party preference and their perception of their parents' party preference is identical	*A*	25%	159
Children whose own party preference is different to their perception of their parents' party preference	*B*	6%	38
Children who report a parent party preference but state no self preference	*C*	22%	138
Children who state no parent party preference but who state a self preference	*D*	17%	104
Children who state neither a parent nor a self party preference	*E*	30%	188
		100%	627

party preference. Of those children stating *both* a parent and a personal party preference, the majority preferred the party which they report for their parents (see Table 2). But perhaps the most interesting cases are the 39 per cent of the children who state either a self preference or a parent preference, but not both (Table 1 rows C and D). Although in fact fuller knowledge of these cases may reveal higher levels of actual agreement than is shown by these data, the interest about these children is what is represented by the one-sided reporting. Though they state either a self preference or a parental preference, they do not see their parents' preferences as underpinning or determining their own party choice.

Table 2. Relationship between children's party preference and perception of parents' vote in 1966 general election*
Children's party preference

Children's perceptions of parents' vote	Labour	Conservative	Liberal	Any other party	Totals
Labour	75%	15%	8%	2%	100% (95)
Conservative	4%	90%	6%	0%	100% (82)
Liberal	5%	15%	70%	10%	100% (20)
Total	(75)	(91)	(27)	(14)	197

gamma = 0.79 $x^2 p < 0.01$

* This table is taken from a total sample of children who both perceived a parent vote and stated a self party preference. The equivalent gamma association for the group of children whose parents had not returned questionnaires was 0.78; $x^2 p < 0.01$.

Similarity of party preference between parents and children was not strongly associated with sex, social class, or education. Boys were slightly less likely than girls to give the same party preference as their parents, as also were grammar school children as compared with secondary modern school children. On social class there was no significant difference at all.

For those children reporting a parental preference, the accuracy of their perceptions was fairly high, as shown in Table 3. Although this is a high level of accurate reporting, it must be remembered that fully 47 per cent (Table 1, rows D and E) of the total children sampled did not know what their parents' vote was in the relevant election nor did they guess. This suggests that for a large proportion of the families, political discussion is not a marked feature of family interaction. This is supported by the finding that where there *is* interaction in terms of fairly 'frequent' political

Table 3. Accuracy of children's perceptions of their parents' vote in 1966
General Election

Parents' vote in 1966 general election

Children's perception of parents' vote in 1966	*Labour*	*Conservative*	*Liberal*	*Total*
Labour	86%	10%	4%	100 (81)
Conservative	18%	67%	15%	100 (55)
Liberal	22%	33%	45%	100 (9)
DK/NA	42%	58%	0%	100 (89)
Totals	(119)	(100)	(15)	$N = 234$

The gamma association, excluding those parents whose vote was not
known, was 0.83, x^2p <0.01.

discussion between parents and children, these children are more likely to
perceive a parental party preference and to perceive it accurately,
although the associations are small.

The figure of 53 per cent (Table 1, rows A, B and C) of the sample of
children who could report a parental party preference puts the British
family (on the basis of this study, at least) on a point mid-way between the
American and the French family as an agent of political communication.
Converse and Dupeux report that less than 30 per cent of French adults
were able to report what their parents' party preferences were when they
were children. In the United States, on the other hand, between 75 per
cent and 80 per cent of children have been found able to report their
parents' party preferences.

It might be expected that the accuracy of the child's attribution of
parental vote would improve with the child's age, but in fact this was not
the case. It might also be thought that the coincidence of child and
parental preference would increase with child's age, and to a marginal
extent this was so. The association was, however, a weak one
(gamma=0.13, x^2p>0.10). Nor was it the case that older children were
more likely than youngsters to state a party preference of their own
(gamma=0.037, x^2p>0.10). Finally, younger children were only slightly
less likely to state a parental preference than were older children
(gamma=0.11, x^2p>0.05). Hence, it seems that the level of parental
transmission is *not* materially affected by developmental factors within
our age range.

The lack of any overwhelming similarity between parents and children
on party preference is not necessarily inconsistent with adult studies

showing much higher levels of intergenerational agreement. It may be that a greater correspondence between parents and children occurs later in life when such experience as work and the playing of a more direct, adult political role can shape more meaningful political orientations. But these later experiences have little direct connection with family transmission of political preferences as such.

Clearly these findings are not definitive. For one thing there is missing in this study a more direct measure of party identification than a vote for a party. Vote, the measure of party identification used here, is by no means an adequate indication of the meaning of party identification to the respondent. The problem is compounded when it is realized that the election of 1966 showed a strong swing to the Labour Party, and it may be that during this election a number of people may have changed their vote, thus displaying only weak partisan attachments.

There is a further problem to which attention must be paid if one is to interpret these findings fully. Although only a minority of the children report a party preference similar to that which they report for their parents, this association does not conclusively establish that it is the child's perception of parents' party preference which determines its party preference. Such a level of intergenerational agreement might be that expected from any group matched for relevant socioeconomic characteristics. Accordingly, we tried to assess the relative influence of variables such as parents' social class, child's education, and sex to see whether they were as strongly associated with the child's party preference as was the child's perception of his parents' preference. The association between the perceived parents' party preference and the child's self preference was 0.79. On social class the association ranged from a maximum – that between manual social class and Labour preference – of 0.58 to a minimum – between manual social class and a Liberal preference – of 0.02. On education the associations ranged from a maximum 0.50 for grammar education and a Labour preference to a minimum of 0.24 for grammar education and a Conservative preference. On sex there was no perceptible association on party preferences. In all cases, none gave an association stronger than that given by the child's perception of parental preference.

So, on the basis of this evidence, it would seem that if the child states a party preference and also has some perception of his parents' party preference then this perception is likely to shape his own party preference, and certainly has more effect than social class, education, or sex. But for a large proportion of the families there would seem to be no strong politically communicative interaction between parents and their offspring.

SOCIAL CLASS AND POLITICS

The strongest of all findings in voting studies is the correlation between social class position and voting for a particular political party. And, according to Alford, Britain, of all Anglo-Western democracies, shows the highest index of class voting. But, it is not known to what extent this link between class and voting preferences is a function of family socialization. In other words, do children, prior to any occupational experience, develop an awareness of the political dimension of social class, and is it parentally transmitted?

Parents and children were asked whether they thought that Britain was divided into classes. Parents were much more likely to respond affirmatively than were their children. Eighty-eight per cent of the parents claimed that Britain was divided into classes contrasted with 58 per cent of the children. There was no significant association between parents and their children's responses (gamma=0.01, $x^2p>0.10$). But slightly more of the children (18 per cent to 6 per cent of the parents) gave a 'don't know' response to this item. Among the children 29 per cent of those attending secondary modern school gave a 'don't know' response compared with 8 per cent of the grammar school children. This suggests that the responses to this item were likely to be cognitive. (The association between grammar school and a 'yes' response to the question was gamma=0.59, $x^2p>0.01$.) Only 19 per cent of the children replied positively to a question asking them whether they thought that class was important. In other words, though a majority of the children 'knew' about social class very few felt it was important.

Although the children's awareness of social class is relatively limited and seems to have little direct bearing on parental transmission of ideas about social class, nonetheless the children showed some knowledge of how social class related to electoral politics. In response to a question asking which party they thought people who held certain jobs would probably vote for, the children were, overall, well able to make accurate discriminations at the top and the bottom of the social scale. The children claimed, for example, that company directors and doctors mainly supported the Conservative Party, and lorry drivers and bricklayers mostly supported the Labour Party. There was less firmness in the responses to the less easily graded occupations such as schoolteacher, clergymen, farmers (see Table 4).

There is evidence here that a good proportion of the children see aspects of the political world as involved in some way with the notion of social class. Specifically, that occupational position implies certain partisan preferences; that the occupants of 'high' social class positions tend to be Conservative while 'low' class positions tend to Labour preferences. We are unable to offer any substantial evidence concerning the rationale children would use to explain this link, but in view of other evidence

Table 4. Children's responses to predominant voting preference of particular occupations

		Political parties				
Occupations	Labour	Conservative	Liberal	Vary	DK/NA	Totals
Company director	23	45	6	17	9	100% (627)
Clergyman	13	20	15	35	18	100% (627)
Doctor	21	32	11	22	14	100% (627)
School-teacher	23	25	10	29	13	100% (627)
Policeman	23	18	9	32	18	100% (627)
Lorry driver	50	14	7	17	12	100% (627)
Bricklayer	50	12	8	17	13	100% (627)
Shopkeeper	28	23	12	26	14	100% (627)
Roadmender	47	13	8	19	12	100% (627)
Garage mechanic	39	15	8	24	15	100% (627)
Farmer	23	22	16	22	16	100% (627)

mentioned earlier it is more than likely that the perceived connection between social class and political preference is little more than a cognitive framework not really associated with strong feelings about the importance of the link. Perhaps what we are seeing in these children is a trend noted by other writers who have pointed to the declining importance of social class in British politics. Continuing increases in the standard of living, the growing similarity between classes in terms of lifestyle could mean a gradual erosion of the class basis of political choice. This might suggest that the parents, brought up in a political context where class and politics had some crucial social meaning, communicate class perspectives which have less meaning to their children. Certainly, few of the children's attitudes to class could be traced to similar feelings on the part of their parents. Another possible explanation lies in the particular political culture of this part of Britain. Exeter is a non-industrial, relatively small town, and it is possible that class feelings are not supported by socioeconomic structures. Alternatively, it may be that whatever the attitudes of the parents concerning class, such topics are never or rarely part of parent-child interaction.

At this stage, then, the burden of the evidence provided by our data is that, apart from party preference, there seems to be little similarity between political values of parents and their children. Even party preference, overall at any rate, is not strongly transmitted to the children, although, among the children who do report a party preference, their perception of their parents' preference is more strongly associated with the children's self preference than either social class or education.

Why is it, then, in spite of the fact that parents are believed to have a crucial role in the general socialization process, there should be this lack of transmission of political values from parents to children? The first and perhaps the most obvious reason is the generally low salience of politics as a focus of parent-child interaction. Only 16 per cent of the parents in the sample reported that they were 'very interested' in politics, whereas 29 per cent claimed that they were 'not very interested'. It is quite likely that this latter figure underestimates the lack of interest since a number would on an item like this tend to overrate their real level of political interest, especially since the questionnaire was so clearly about politics. Also, the possibility is that it was the less interested parents who failed to fill out the questionnaire, further underestimating the low level of political interest. So given this generally low level of political interest it is not surprising that little political communication takes place between parents and children. Only 7 per cent of the parents reported that they 'often' discussed politics with their children. Forty-two per cent said that children should be encouraged by their parents to take an interest in politics, yet other evidence suggests that this, by and large, was merely verbal acquiescence to the norm and had few behavioural consequences. In any event, the fact that non-manual parents and parents of high education were more likely to affirm that children should be encouraged to take an interest in politics suggests that the earlier response is indicative of a general tendency of this group to encourage a broad social awareness in their children rather than a focused attempt to awaken any specifically *political* interest.

The second reason why there are few resemblances between parents and children is that there are developmental factors which influence the form and the content of the child's ideas about politics (and, of course, the world generally). Greenstein, Hess and Torney, Easton, and Dennis in their studies of American children all show the developmental pattern of children's ideas and thinking concerning the political world. Such studies suggest that young children more than adults tend to take a benevolent and trusting view of political figures. Certainly the children in our sample took a rather uncritical view of aspects of the political system. For example they tended to see the party system as satisfactory, only 27 per cent saying that the country would be better off without political parties. There is also evidence to suggest that such an uncritical perspective tends to decrease with age. The affirmative responses to a question, 'Do you think good men go into politics?' did so. Of the eleven- to twelve-year-olds, 57 per cent said 'yes' to the question, while only 38 per cent said 'yes' among the fifteen-year-olds and over.

Both the foregoing arguments may go some way to explaining the relatively low attitudinal similarity between parents and children. A third possible reason is concerned with the fact that children are in contact with other potential political socializing agencies, especially the school, which may modify any effects of parental influence, such as they are. In other words, to reiterate a point made earlier, familial influence, whether direct or indirect, is not likely to operate in isolation from other possible socializing influences. And compared with very young children, this is truer of the children of the age group studied here whose contact and interaction with other potential socializing agencies is much broader.

Conclusions

Although the secondary modern children are cognitively at a lower level of political awareness than are children in grammar schools, it is not the case that they differ very significantly in their evaluations of political life. For example, on a question asking about the effect of politics on everyday life, grammar school pupils were only marginally more likely to say it had a 'great effect' (72 per cent against 67 per cent). Again, on the 'cynicism towards politicians' questions, secondary modern pupils were not much more likely to be cynical (57 per cent cynical as against 49 per cent). On a question which asked respondents to choose between the sons of a clerk, a duke, a managing director, and a scientist as potential PMs, the secondary modern children chose the duke's son (38 per cent) rather more than did grammar school children (27 per cent) but in the spread of choices there were no really significant variations. About the same order of difference also emerged in the answers, divided by school, on the political efficacy scale. We have shown above that children in both grammar and secondary modern schools were quite accurate in assessing voting potentials of various occupations, but only a small minority regarded class as 'important'. Perhaps a few more examples will clinch the point: 29 per cent of grammar school children thought the country would be 'better off' without political parties whilst 35 per cent of secondary modern pupils agreed. Both groups agreed that for the opposition to win the next general election would not be a 'disaster for the country'. Finally, 62 per cent of grammar school children thought 'good men go into politics' and 67 per cent of secondary modern children thought the same.

Table 5. Child's political knowledge as a function of child's education, parents' education and class

Row	Parents' education (H) High (L) Low	Parents' social class (H) High (L) Low	Child's education (H) High (L) Low	Child's rank on political knowledge based on percentage high scorers	Percentage high political knowledge scorers	Totals
A	H	H	H	1	87% (42)	48
B	L	H	H	2	69% (27)	39
C	H	L	H	3	63% (10)	16
D	L	L	H	4	59% (30)	51
E	L	H	L	5	18% (7)	38
F	H	L	L	6	13% (1)	8
G	H	H	L	7	12% (2)	17
H	L	L	L	8	7% (6)	91
					$N =$	308

It was only on knowledge and interest that very clear and significant differences emerged – both are items structurally supported in the grammar school – and it is probably the case that these constitute the crucial differences between the two groups. Such differences are significant in the sense that they may well account for, or at least underpin, the known differential rates of political involvement amongst adults. However, if the differences are important the affective resemblances are quite clearly crucial, assuming that our data are generalizable for the UK, since they tap important elements of the political culture. There appears to be general satisfaction and support of the political regime, the community and the authorities. The support is clearly not a very participatory one, especially amongst secondary modern pupils; it seems, indeed, one of general acquiescence in the system. But it should be remembered that in the grammar schools the foundations of potential involvement are laid.

Marginal but consistent differences emerged between the two groups on the affective level; grammar school children consistently appeared less cynical, more potentially participatory in the sense of believing that power and influence are relatively widely distributed in the political system and of attaching more importance to policies than leaders. But it should be stressed that the differences *are* marginal and despite the academic differences between the two school types they do not lead to, or obviously support, very different political subcultures.

Our findings indicate, in a context other than the American, that the process of political socialization amongst children can be looked at as complex interaction between many agencies but especially school and home. We have explored a number of dimensions of this interaction in order to demonstrate that the 'traditional' emphasis on the home is misplaced. Our study strongly suggests that the school is the more significant agency, although it does not work in isolation from the home. This points to the need for further exploration of the relationship between these and other institutions in the formation of children's political attitudes and values.

Further Reading: **Socialization**

J. Boissevain, *Friends of Friends*, Blackwell, 1974.

S. Cohen (ed.), *Images of Deviance*, Penguin, 1971.

S. Cohen, *Folk Devils and Moral Panics*, MacGibbon and Kee, 1972.

P.Corrigan, *Schooling the Smash Street Kids*, Macmillan, 1979.

M. Craft (ed.), *Family,Class and Education*, Longman, 1970.

S. J. Eggleston (ed.), *Contemporary Research in the Sociology of Education*, Methuen, 1974.

N. Evans (ed.), *Education Beyond School*, Grant McIntyre, 1979.

L. Gow and A. McPherson, *Tell Them From Me*, Aberdeen University Press, 1980.

A. H. Halsey, J. Floud and C. A. Anderson (eds.), *Education, Economy and Society*, The Free Press, 1961.

A. H. Halsey, A. Heath and S. M. Ridge, *Origins and Destinations: Family, Class and Education in Modern Britain*, Oxford University Press, 1980.

A. Little and R. Willey, *Multi-ethnic Education: the Way Forward*, Schools Council, 1981.

B. Showler and A. Sinfield, *The Workless State*, Martin Robertson, 1981.

M. A. Smith, S. Parker and C. Smith (eds.), *Leisure and Society in Britain*, Allen Lane, 1973.

D. Thorns, *Suburbia*, MacGibbon and Kee, 1972.

4. Work

When we want to describe someone, we characteristically do it in terms of their occupation. Words like 'miner', 'chemist', 'shopkeeper' and so on are more than convenient labels; they indicate and illustrate aspects of a whole way of life. This is perhaps even truer in the negative, for when we describe someone as 'out-of-work', 'retired', 'under age', and so on, we indicate that the person so described is in some way *out* of the mainstream of social life. Just as these shorthand descriptions of a person illustrate the way 'jobs' are deeply woven into the language we use to interpret everyday social events, so occupational roles have significance for the whole social structure.

There are many different ways of studying the phenomenon of work in contemporary society. We have tried in this chapter to pay particular attention to the subjective experience of work and to the significance of work for the individuals who are directly involved in it. But it is obviously important not to lose sight of the institutional framework within which work takes place. Moreover, we should bear in mind the specific historical experience of a particular industry or occupation when attempting to interpret and explain behaviour at the present time.

Salaman argues that employment relations have a crucial general significance for social structure, and that the nature of control in the organization can be illuminated by close study of the exchange of effort for reward. This is by no means an original insight, but it is in some ways, as Salaman argues, a neglected one, for this process of exchange has important and indirect effects on the structure of social relations at the work place and the moral basis of that structure. Employers accord legitimacy to managerial expectations over quite a wide range, and although there is a logical conflict built into the very notion of employment relations, in practice these relations exhibit a considerable degree of stability over time and geography. But the precise structuring of these relations is conditioned by historical and cultural factors, as the studies by Dore of Japanese and Gallie of French industrial organizations show.

The research on which the paper by **Goldthorpe** was based was carried out in Luton between 1962 and 1965 as part of a study of affluent workers. A more complete account is available in the book by Goldthorpe, Lockwood, Bechhofer and Platt referred to in the list of Further Reading for Chapter 5. To quote the authors, 'The main objective of this study was to test empirically the widely accepted thesis of working-class embourgeoisement: the thesis that, as manual workers and their families achieve relatively high incomes and living standards, they assume a way of life which is more characteristically "middle class" and become in fact progressively assimilated into middle-class society.' They interviewed over two hundred 'affluent' car assemblers, machinists, setters, chemical process workers, and maintenance men. They show that these social meanings given to work, based on previous experience, can largely determine the *content* of experience within the factory itself, and play a more important role in developing work-place attitudes and behaviour than the organization of work or technological imperatives. In other words, 'assembly-line man' may be largely a fiction, which obscures the extent to which the labour force attracted to and entering a specific field of employment may be 'preselected'.

This approach emphasizes the importance of subjective experience in 'creating' a work environment, within certain limits set by the production technology, and the administrative structure of the organization through which the work activities of individual participants are controlled.

Curran and Stanworth are concerned, not with employees in large organizations which are organized on bureaucratic lines, but with workers in small firms. This is a category which has been neglected by sociologists in the United Kingdom until quite recently. They suggest two reasons for this comparative neglect: first, that the sociological and historical analysis of the 'founding fathers' concentrated on large-scale organization, and were, consciously or unconsciously, oriented towards an evolutionary perspective which saw small-scale enterprise as an early or embryonic phase in the development of industrial capitalism. Moreover, the practical problems of undertaking research into smaller enterprises were greater, relative to the chances of research 'pay-off' in terms of numbers of interviews or the representativeness of the results obtained. One may suspect also that the shifts in political emphasis in the late 1970s and 1980s deriving from the publication of the Bolton report on Small Firms in 1971 have induced a greater realization among sociologists of the significance of this category in the occupational structure. This is not to imply any crude political time-serving on the part of those writers and researchers who recognized the *sociological* significance of this problem. But it is salutary to note how often events determine the framework of analysis. Sociologists are concerned in the last analysis with what does happen, rather than with what did not or should not have happened, according to some meta-empirical framework of theory.

Curran and Stanworth's findings are important, therefore, because they illuminate the limitations of the theory of self-selection. Thus they set bounds on the overarching nature of explanations in terms of worker orientations to employment: at least as far as workers in small firms are concerned.

Lupton indicates the relevance of this approach to the problem of 'restriction of output'. He shows that what appears at first glance to be 'irrational' behaviour in economic terms on the part of workers in fact makes good sense when considered as part of rational strategies of action developed to cope with *real* conflicts of interest between management and workers. Focusing on the problem of controls exercised by workers on output and earnings, he lists the various factors – some 'internal', some 'external' to the structure of the firm – which may be associated with differences in the behaviour of workers on the shop floor. This study compares two firms, one ('Wye') in the rubber-proofed garment industry, the other ('Jay's') an electrical components manufacturer. Lupton did not use survey methods, but gathered his material by the intensive method of 'open participant observation', which involved his working in the two firms for a considerable period.

Lockwood (recommended in Further Reading) analyses the work situation of the clerk, as it has developed from the nineteenth-century 'counting house' to a more rationalized, large-scale type of office. Relying mainly on documentary and historical materials, he traces the increase in 'rationalization' and the growth in the average size of the office, during this period in this country. The ratio of non-manual to manual workers in manufacturing industries has increased, as has the proportion of workers in 'white-collar' industries generally. But the physical concentration of large numbers of 'blackcoated workers' has been counterbalanced by an increase in specialization so that the actual working group remains rather small in size.

Lockwood discusses the forms of organization and conditions of work which are conducive to the development of class consciousness. He argues that the chain of command between 'management' and 'clerical staff' is rooted in personal contact, which leads to cooperative social relationships and a tendency to perceive the aims and ends of management and clerks as essentially similar, so that no fundamental conflicts of interest are felt to be present.

Vinnicombe develops the themes in Lockwood's analysis in her study of the managing director's private secretary, and analyses one 'female' job. The secretary acts as the 'gatekeeper' in the communication network of the boss. Thus her power depends not merely on her own position in the organizational hierarchy, but, more importantly, on his. Conversely, the boss effectively delegates, formally as well as informally, power to his secretary, as she structures communication to and from him. So the secretary's experience and command of organizational resources becomes a crucial facility for the boss to implement the demands of his own role. There is a high element of skill and personalization in the relationship.

As newer technologies are introduced to the office, and in particular word processing, it is probable that the secretarial role becomes polarized between its 'organic' and 'mechanistic' elements. This distinction was introduced by Burns and Stalker in their important study *The Management of Innovation* (recommended in Further Reading), which analysed the impact of technological factors on the structure of organizations and work roles. Woodward, in an analysis which continues to be highly influential, had earlier shown that organization structures in manufacturing industry varied according to the demands of the production technology. Later research has modified this view, indicating that organizational structure is to a great extent 'contingent' on a large number of factors, historical as well as structural, which would have to be examined empirically in order to ascertain their contribution to a specific situation.

The work situation of the coalminer described by Dennis, Henriques and Slaughter in *Coal is Our Life* (recommended in Further Reading) is different from that of the clerk in many ways, two of which have particular relevance. While the clerk is in the mainstream of society, working in acceptable conditions, and only rarely involved in shift-working or any major disruption of conventional working routine, the miner is a representative of an 'extreme' occupation. He works under conditions of unpleasantness and physical danger, and is isolated from society by the nature of the work he does and the social relations of the community in which he lives. Moreover, he may typically perceive relations between management and workers in terms of a conflict of interest, rooted in the economic wage-nexus and reinforced by the historical experience of depression and deprivation. Here again, as in Lupton's study, participant observation was the major research method, and two of the three research workers lived for some time in the small Yorkshire town that was the subject of the study.

While the precise details of the organization of work have changed since Dennis, Henriques and Slaughter undertook their study, the confrontation between management and workers is still endemic in the social relations of mining. In this field, as in much of sociology, a good deal of research has been undertaken into aspects of social behaviour which, taken in isolation, may appear to be unusual, abnormal or irrational. However, analysis of the context in which such behaviour takes place, and of the typical explanations and justifications advanced for it, can enable us to interpret the apparently 'irrational' by elucidating its 'subjective rationality' in terms of the norms and values of the appropriate social groups, and its 'objective rationality' in terms of the networks of relationships which being a member of such a group involves.

Thus Tunstall in *The Fisherman* explains the apparently irrational resentment felt towards the radio operator by deck-hands on a deep-sea trawler, which makes him a scapegoat for the crew although he provides an essential function and role in the fish-catching team. The radio operator 'is isolated from the deck-hands by the nature and place of his work, by social origin and style of life, and by his closeness to the skipper'. Moreover, 'he does not do a physically demanding job', which conflicts with the deck-hands' conception of fishing as a job requiring a good deal of strength, toughness and physicality. A scapegoat is required to absorb the tensions produced by the demanding conditions of the job. 'Being an object for their combined hostility, the sparks helps to cement the unity of the deckmen.' Hollowell's book *The Lorry Driver* examines the subculture of another group whose working conditions tend to isolate its members from 'conventional' society.

Another theme of general relevance is that caused by the need to set boundaries to analysis and explanations of aspects of social behaviour. Both Goldthorpe and Lupton stress the importance of features of the social situation 'external' to the work place for understanding behaviour that occurs within it. Dennis, Henriques and Slaughter place their analysis of the work-place relations of coalminers in the context of the historical experience of the social class of wage-earners, who sell their labour power to owners of capital in return for the opportunity of utilizing the facilities of employment to earn a wage.

That the confrontational style of industrial relations described by Dennis, Henriques and Slaughter is not restricted to coalmining is emphasized by **Beynon**'s study of motor car manufacturing. The instability of the industry and its susceptibility to short-run fluctuations of the market have combined to produce a history of insecurity for the workers. Periods of boom, with a high demand for cars that could only be met by systematic overtime, were typically followed by a recession in which short-time working was the norm. But wherever the management pointed to external factors beyond their direct control as the cause of the fluctuations in employment, the workers tended to point the finger at the failure of management to predict market demand and thus to plan in advance for continuity of employment.

Beynon's study builds on Lupton's analysis when he points out that the market directly affects relationships in the plant. As Beynon points out, 'In a situation ridden with latent conflicts, the decision to lay men off can be likened to a declaration of war, and it is not only the workers who attempt to exact reprisals against the other side in this situation.' Within this broad context, there are important links between work and the family and community. The particular occupational group may largely determine patterns of leisure also.

Beynon points out that 'the life of a working man without work is often desperate. What most working men want of a job is that it offers them some security.' As we write, Britain is experiencing the most devastating economic recession for half a century. Unemployment, or at least intermittent employment, is becoming part of the pattern of expectations of almost all elements in the labour force. Whether the causes are political or economic, due to structural rigidities in the British economy, or to global factors beyond the control of government, employers or unions, the impact on the individual who experiences an interruption of employment may be considerable.

Daniel's careful analysis shows that the labour force can be conceptualized not as a set of static pools of labour, but as a complex and mobile process of flows. Thus 'for most of those who lose their jobs, unemployment is not, and does not become, a state or condition, it is a hiatus'. However there may be real, and even less tractable circumstances affecting those young people who have yet to enter the labour market. For them the pattern of expectations may be entirely different. Despite optimistic speculation in the 1960s of the impending demise of work and the imminence of the 'leisure society', no alternative mechanism for allocating social rewards and maintaining a structure of roles and expectations has thus far emerged in industrial society. Watch this space.

Employment Relations
G. Salaman

Reprinted with permission from Graeme Salaman, *Class and the Corporation*, Fontana Paperbacks, 1981, pp. 180–9

The employment relationship itself, involving the exchange of effort for financial reward, constitutes a form of control in that management can manipulate levels of reward in order to encourage employees to vary their input of effort, can threaten to terminate the relationship, or hold out the promise of careers, promotion. More than this, management frequently makes efforts to influence employees' perception of their place in the firm. If successful, these efforts constitute a form of control; if, for example, they persuade employees to commit themselves to management's goals, or to see the enterprise in terms of a functionally based division of labour, with each party playing his or her allotted function in the achievement of a *shared* organizational goal.

Despite the obvious centrality of the wage-effort exchange to organizational life and organizational control, few sociological analyses have paid much attention to this relationship, preferring, presumably, to regard this exchange as 'normal' and given. Yet as Baldamus, in his important work, *Efficiency and Effort*, shows, a thorough understanding of this relationship illuminates much of the organization. In particular it draws attention to the various aspects of effort control exercised by management, and the ways in which the whole exchange is based upon cultural notions of what constitutes a fair day's work. For Baldamus, employing organizations are firmly based upon an exchange of employees' *effort* – with all its implications for tedium, fatigue or danger – for money. From the employees' point of view, the salient question is their assessment of the 'reasonableness' of the rate of exchange, as measured against some implicit notion of fairness. Nevertheless, the relationship itself is only viable, from management's point of view, so long as the reward for employees' efforts is less than the value of these efforts on the market. The employer purchases effort, but in order to make it profitable and useful, this effort must be controlled in two major ways. It must be *stable*. There can be no wild fluctuations in levels of effort. If there are, the delicate integration and coordination of the enterprise is jeopardized. And they must be at a required level of *intensity*. The greater the (stable) level of intensity, the more productive the enterprise.

Baldamus emphasizes that the wage-effort bargain involves an integral conflict: there is a disparity between effort and reward. Management seeks to increase this disparity; employees seek to reduce it. On this reality of employment is built industrial conflict. However, as Hyman and Brough point out, this is not to deny that the employment relationship is also based upon a moral basis – on the whole most workers accept some degree of managerial legitimacy, hold to some agreed standards of effort. Indeed, these authors argue that: 'The very fact that contemporary economic organizations function at all is an indication that workers' orientations to their employment are not merely instrumental but contain important value-attachments . . . it would appear that employee norms of performance *do* in most (even if not all) cases prescribe a minimum as well as a maximum level of effort.'

Etzioni suggests that organizations employ three distinct types of reward – material (financial, fringe benefits etc.), symbolic (receiving superiors' or peers' approval, conforming with accepted and valued standards) and coercive (physical force and constraint, or the threat of these). Most work organizations use the first very widely; the second is used mostly by organizations with some strong and pervasive ideological basis – churches, political groups; the third is used in prisons, mental hospitals. Etzioni also suggests that organizational employees or members can vary in their orientation towards the power the organization exercises over them – and the form of reward used. Three sorts of orientation are distinguished: moral (which involves some strong commitment to the control and the reward); instrumental (when obedience is seen as a direct exchange for a satisfactory level of recompense, with little moral element); and alienative (when members will seek to avoid the controls, and will deny the justice of the control system entirely). These orientations vary in the amount of involvement shown by employees or members in the organization's control structure and the rewards utilized. Furthermore, Etzioni suggests that different forms of reward are directly associated with specific forms of orientation: coercive rewards generate alienated responses; symbolic rewards have little impact on employees with an instrumental orientation but relate to moral involvement. Instrumental orientations require material rewards.

However, though it is possible to isolate forms of organization in which these different reward/orientation combinations are fully demonstrated, it is also true that many organizations employ more than one form of reward, and are characterized by more than one form of involvement. Sometimes rewards vary over time with the same group of employees. More frequently one finds that different groups within the same organization are involved in different forms of control and rewards, and demonstrate different forms of involvement. Finally, of course, it is not unusual for employers to utilize material rewards; but they also attempt to generate some moral involvement through exhortation.

Many aspects of employees' definitions of work obligations demonstrate a commitment to work and employment as having a moral character of some minimal sort. Hyman and Brough also emphasize how workers' assessments of the *value* of their efforts are restricted and partial. Just as effort is constrained by work norms, so assessments of the worth of the effort are limited. The 'choice of pay comparisons is typically unambitious and powerfully shaped by custom: major inequalities which form an established part of the income hierarchy are rarely a focus of contention, the choice of comparative reference groups is structured by an acceptance of prevailing norms of the "proper" rewards and status of different socio-economic groups; or at least by a belief that inequalities are "natural" and inevitable.'

These attitudes are formed by a number of factors: the experience of work itself and of subordination; managerial ideologies stressing the legitimacy of organizational structure, and of persons' positions within it; notions of individual differences in intelligence and ability; the realization of the limited power of disruptive groups; the inability to imagine an alternative social order. What is at issue here, ultimately, is the role and origins of the ideological assumptions which back up notions of fair pay, of a fair day's work. As Hyman and Brough emphasize, these crucial underpinnings of the employment relationship, without which it would hardly be viable, at least in its current, highly differentiated inegalitarian forms, must be understood in the light of an analysis of the nature and origin of work and class ideologies within capitalism.

Precisely because the employment exchange relies upon workers' unambitiousness, their acceptance of their position, and of the order within which they work and on their limited wage aspirations, management strives to structure workers' conceptions, to encourage their view of the wage-effort exchange as based on a harmony of interests. Such efforts have always characterized the employment relationship. But there is evidence that increasing worker 'de-subordination' occasions management concern for the increasing problems of motivation. An important aspect of this problem in the UK is reflected in the almost continuous series of incomes policies since the Second World War. Incomes policies, as Tarling and Wilkinson point out, are used to lower 'real wages relative to productivity, as part of a total package aimed at attacking inflation'. Yet these authors note that the actual operation of these policies has created an *impasse*: each wave of pay policy meets increasing resistance; each period of enforced restraint results in a catching-up process post-policy, but fails to achieve increased investment in the private sector. The result is the increasing resistance of the trade union movement to income control, and the increasing politicization of the relations between manager and worker. Questions of remuneration and control become, through the operation of incomes policy, irrevocably interconnected. Indeed, from the management point of view, incomes policies can *increase* the problem of worker motivation by restraining limits of remuneration.

One proposed solution to the problem of motivation is to alter (or appear to alter) the costs incurred by employees in the exchange. By enlarging jobs, enriching or humanizing work, it is hoped to reduce worker alienation and re-engage their commitment. Such efforts are described and analysed by Nichols and Beynon. The contradiction at the heart of such efforts is obvious: if jobs are genuinely altered so as to allow incumbents some degree of control, of autonomy, then the employees must be likely to use this control to bring into question the overall organizational hierarchy of the enterprise. If they cannot, their discretion must be more apparent than real. This point is argued by Zimbalist who shows that work 'humanization' promotes labour's identification with management control – but only as long as the capitalist remains in control. Soon the workers demand more: at this stage the experiment must be curtailed. Capitalist organizational forms, argues Zimbalist, are ultimately incompatible with substantial worker input into the decision-making process in industry.

There is a danger that such arguments ignore the room for manoeuvre which exists within capitalist forms of control. Of course, 'ultimately', Zimbalist's assertion holds. But before that point is reached, capitalism is capable of displaying a variety of control strategies, as we have seen. One common option, for example, is to delegate responsibility and authority, but to guarantee the reliability of the delegatee through various measures. . . . To argue that different forms of work organization – bureaucracy, Scientific Management, job- enlargement, professionalism – are strategies of control and regulation within the context of capitalism, and the pursuit of profit, requires analysis of the factors responsible for such dramatic variations in rewards and autonomy. The most obvious explanation is in terms of functions of different categories of employees within the capitalist system, and their class position. . . .

Certainly cross-cultural studies by Dore and by Gallie lend support to the importance of different strategies of control and employment in achieving worker acquiescence and commitment. Dore, for example, after describing and comparing Japanese and British employment relations, argues that arrangements in the two countries are sufficiently different to justify being regarded as different *systems*: the Japanese is made up of lifetime employment, a seniority plus merit wage system, an intra-organizational career system, a high level of enterprise welfare, and of enterprise consciousness; the British system is composed of mobility of employment, market-based wages, self-designed careers, more state welfare, less enterprise consciousness, but greater professional, craft or class consciousness. One major difference between the two systems is that the Japanese employment relationship accords to manual workers – at least those lucky enough to achieve full membership of large corporations – those employment privileges which in Britain are restricted to middle-class employees. Dore applies to this system the term 'welfare corporatism'. He notes that this system has definite advantages for the employer. It encourages identification with the enterprise and its goals, it permits the more ready management of industrial conflicts; and while he agrees that the Japanese system could be seen simply as a manipulative strategy: 'To say that the Japanese system is manipulative and the British is not is presumably to suggest that while both Japanese and British managers would like to diminish distrustful antagonism among their workers, the Japanese do it better.'

Of course, Dore does not argue that managers can choose any strategy they like. The emergence of different patterns in Japan and Britain is the result of cultural differences, and, most importantly, of the different timings of industrialization in the two countries. Japanese managers and politicians have, as it were, been able to avoid the pitfalls Britain, as an early developer, has experienced. Between 1850 and 1920 'the world had changed in significant ways . . . the objective structure of opportunities and constraints, and hence the means by which profits and growth can be maximized can never be the same for the late developer, as they were for the early developer.' History, however, applies an inertia to organizational innovation, previous patterns of worker-manager relations exert constraints. Nevertheless, Dore notes that some tendency within British organizations to apply some 'Japanese' employment practices is evident. Gallie's study of French and British organizational structures also reveals contrast in managerial strategies, the French managers regarding organizational structure as part of managerial prerogative, the British managers seeking some measure of consent to proposed changes. These two strategies were related to markedly different levels of union militancy, which are themselves the products of historical/cultural differences in the two countries.

This chapter has been concerned with characteristic theories of organizational control which derive directly from the classic theories of Durkheim, Weber and Marx. Each theorist can be seen to have initiated an approach to organizational structure and control which still exerts considerable influence.

The theories discussed here differ not so much in their analyses of the mechanisms of organizational control – bureaucracy, technology, forms of work design etc. – but in their analysis of the *origins* of these mechanisms and strategies. Within the Durkheimian tradition, organizational structure and mechanisms of control originate in the organization's goals and the technology employed to achieve these. The neo-Weberian approach, which often involves a one-sided interpretation of Weber's theory, emphasizes the variety of organizational forms, and seeks to relate these to variations such as organizational environment, size or market. The significant variable determining these empirical relationships is efficiency. However, to regard Weber's analysis of bureaucracy, and his emphasis on bureaucracy as articulating in institutional form the increasingly pervasive value of rationality, as an emphasis on the determinant role of *efficiency* is naively to misunderstand Weber. What Weber attempts, in fact, is an analysis of bureaucracy as the 'institutional prototype for the emerging rationalized society'. In such a society, science, calculation, technology and measurement serve the achievement of ends. Such priorities and methods of analysis are reflected in rational-legal bureaucracies, established to achieve, by established, explicit, calculable impersonal principles, the goals of capitalist employers. As numerous commentators have noted, Weber saw a close relationship between capitalistic priorities and bureaucratic, i.e., rational, means. For Weber, then, the key variable is the increasing application of rationality.

In contrast, for Marx, and later Marxists, the key variable is capitalism, with all that this implies for classes, class relations, and the pursuit of profit by the utilization of alienated labour. Within a capitalist economy enterprises are constantly subject to competitive pressures, and to pressures emanating from employees. These result in the limited number of very specific work design strategies, the most obvious of which is Taylorism. Marxist theorists regard the design of work within enterprises, and the choice of technology with which it is closely related, as reflections of the capitalists' efforts to maintain profitability and control. Externally, these arrangements are supported by the differentiation of the work force into primary and secondary labour markets, and by the pervasiveness of a technocratic ideology which upholds and mystifies organizational structure and decision-making. Furthermore the design of work and organizations is supported by various efforts to incorporate the working class into the objectives and forms of thinking characteristic of, and conducive to, capitalism. Partly this is achieved by a considerable degree of agreement over objectives – profits – associated, of course, with continuing disagreement over distribution. Partly it results from the fact that the capitalist economic system and its detailed elements and exchanges appears to the worker as relations between things. Value is determined by exchange. Employment relations become depersonalized. The system as a whole which so depersonalizes work activities, employment relations and individual value, itself appears as beyond human agency, or prospect of alteration.

Attitudes and Behaviour of Car Assembly Workers

J. H. Goldthorpe

Reprinted with permission from John Goldthorpe, 'Attitudes and Behaviour of Car Assembly Workers: a Deviant Case and a Theoretical Critique', *British Journal of Sociology*, vol. XVII, no. 3, September 1966, pp. 227–40

In the literature of industrial sociology since the Second World War studies of workers in car assembly plants have almost certainly outnumbered those of any comparable industrial or occupational group. The essentials of the characterization are by now familiar. The car assembly line is 'the classic symbol of the subjection of man to the machine in our industrial age'; the assembler 'approaches the classic model of the self-estranged worker'; he is 'the blue-collar prototype of "the mass men in mass society"' and, often, he is 'the prototype of the militant worker as well'.

In this paper, our first aim is to present results obtained from a study of workers in a British car assembly plant; results which, in certain respects, differ fairly clearly from the pattern which has emerged from previous investigations. The nature and extent of the differences are not such that they would lead us to challenge in any comprehensive way the 'image' of the car assembler which is generally accepted. However, the 'deviant' aspects of our findings do indicate certain *theoretical* weaknesses in the sociology of the assembly-line workers as this has so far progressed: specifically, they suggest that (a) too great a weight has been given to technology as a determinant of attitudes and behaviour in the work situation; and that (b) too little attention has been paid to the prior orientations which workers have towards employment, and which in turn influence their choice of job, the meaning they give to work and *their definition of* the work situation. The second objective of this paper is, thus, to substantiate this argument and to point to the theoretical developments which would appear to be necessary.

The study on which we report was based chiefly on interviews with workers in six assembly departments of the Luton plant of Vauxhall Motors Ltd. Our sample was a random one of men in these departments who were: (i) Grade I assemblers; (ii) between the ages of twenty-one and forty-six; (iii) married; and (iv) resident in the town of Luton itself. The number in the original sample was 127; and of these exactly 100 (79 per cent) agreed to be interviewed at work. In connection with the wider purposes of our research project, 86 of these men were then re-interviewed in their homes and together with their wives. The data from this study which we wish to consider here can be advanced under the following three heads: (1) the assembler and his job; (2) the assembler and the shop-floor group; (3) the assembler and the firm.

The assembler and his job

In this respect, our findings were closely comparable with those produced by earlier inquiries.

(1) Assemblers appeared to derive little intrinsic satisfaction from their jobs; rather, in performing their work-tasks they tended to experience various forms of deprivation: primarily monotony (reported by 69 per cent), and to a lesser degree physical tiredness (48 per cent) and having to work at too fast a pace (30 per cent).

(2) These deprivations were directly related to characteristic features of assembly-line jobs: the minute subdivision of tasks, repetitiveness, low skill requirements, predetermination of tools and techniques, and mechanically controlled rhythms and speeds of work. Of the men in our sample 63 per cent said that they would prefer some other shop-floor job to their present one; and of these men, 87 per cent said they would have liked to move off the 'track' altogether, chiefly into jobs such as inspection, maintenance, rectification and testing. Moreover, among the reasons given for favouring such a move, those relating to the content of work were paramount. Jobs off the 'track' were seen as offering more opportunity to exercise skill and responsibility, greater variety and challenge, and more freedom and autonomy.

(3) Consequently, the workers we studied were for the most part attached to their present employment chiefly through the extrinsic economic rewards which it afforded them. Thirty-one per cent stated that the level of pay was the *only* reason why they remained in their present work, and, in all, 74 per cent gave pay either as the sole reason for this or along with others. The reason next most frequently mentioned was that of 'security' (25 per cent), and this, it was clear, was thought of far more in relation to long-run income maximization than to the minimum requirement of having a job of some kind. On the other hand, in contrast to this emphasis on economic considerations, only 6 per cent of the sample said that they stayed with their present employer because they liked the actual work they performed. In other words, then, our assemblers defined their work in an essentially *instrumental* way; work was for them primarily a means to ends external to the work situation. More specifically, one could say that work was seen as a generally unsatisfying and stressful

expenditure of time and effort which was necessary in order to achieve a valued standard and style of living in which work itself had no positive part.

These findings are, we repeat, in all respects markedly similar to those of other studies of car assembly workers. To this extent, thus, our results tend to confirm the idea that the responses of men to the work-tasks and roles of the car assembly line are likely to vary little more, from plant to plant, than does the technology itself.

However, to our last point above – concerning the assembler's instrumental view of work – we would wish to give an emphasis which differs rather significantly from that of most previous writers. Generally, the 'devaluation' of work which is implied here has been taken as perhaps the clearest symptom of the car assembler's alienated condition. For Blauner, for instance, this concentration on the purely extrinsic rewards of work is 'the essential meaning of self-estrangement'; and in Chinoy's view, the alienation of the auto worker basically results from the fact that this work has become, in the words of Marx, 'not the satisfaction of a need but only the means to satisfy the needs outside it'. It is not our aim here to dispute this interpretation. But, at the same time, we would wish to stress the following point: that, at least in the case of our sample, the predominantly instrumental orientation to work was not simply or even primarily a *consequence* of these men being car assemblers; rather, one could say that most had become car assemblers *because of* a desire, and an eventual decision, on their part to give priority to high-level economic returns from work at the expense, if necessary, of satisfactions of an intrinsic kind. In other words, their instrumental orientation had led to their present employment, rather than *vice versa*.

These data would suggest, then, that the workers we studied had for the most part been impelled, by their desire for higher incomes, into taking work which was in fact better paid than most other forms of employment available to them largely to compensate for its inherent strains and deprivations. If, therefore, these workers are to be considered as 'alienated', the roots of their alienation must be sought not merely in the technological character of the plants in which they are now employed but, more fundamentally, in those aspects of the wider society which generate their tremendous drive for economic advancement and their disregard for the costs of this through the impoverishment of their working lives.

Furthermore, it also follows that in seeking to explain the industrial attitudes and behaviour of these workers generally, one must always be prepared to treat their essentially instrumental orientation towards their employment as an *independent* variable relative to the work situation, rather than regarding this simply as a product of this situation.

The assembler and the shop-floor group

In most previous studies of car assembly workers, attention has been given to the way in which assembly-line technology inhibits the formation of cohesive work groups. Although the majority of men work in fairly close proximity to others, the fact that they tend to be strung out along the length of the 'track' means that the development of specifically *group* relations is usually impeded; that is to say, workers are prevented from sharing in *common* networks of social relationships, set off from others by more or less distinct boundaries.

Findings of this kind have, without exception, been interpreted as evidence of yet further deprivation in the working life of the car assembler.

The results of our study which relate to the shop-floor situation at Vauxhall go contrary to the findings, and perhaps still more to the interpretation, of previous studies of car assemblers in two main respects.

It was apparent from observation in the assembly departments that the nature of technical organization did in fact largely rule out the possibility of the formation of cohesive work groups. Most workers were close enough to others to be able to exchange words fairly easily: 59 per cent of the men we interviewed said that they talked to their workmates 'a good deal', and 29 per cent 'now and then', as against 11 per cent saying 'hardly at all'. But there was little to indicate that shop-floor relations amounted to more than a generally superficial camaraderie. Thus far, our findings conformed entirely to the established pattern.

However, not only did we find no evidence of a high degree of group formation within the assembly department, but we were equally unable to find evidence that the majority of men in our sample were actually *concerned* with 'group-belongingness' in work, or felt deprived because this was not to be had. Rather, our data pointed to the opposite conclusion. For example, we asked our respondents: 'How would you feel if you were moved to another job in the factory more or less like the one you do now but away from the men who work near you? Would you feel very upset, fairly upset, not much bothered, not bothered at all?' The result was that only 4 per cent answered 'very upset' and 25 per cent 'fairly upset'. The remainder were almost equally divided between 'not much bothered' (34 per cent) and 'not bothered at all' (36 per cent). And those men who talked to their mates 'a good deal' were as likely to fall into the latter two categories as were the others. Moreover the further comments which respondents typically made on this question confirmed the obvious implication of these data: that maintaining stable relationships with workmates was not generally regarded as a very important aspect of the work situation.

Moreover, this interpretation is corroborated by further data we have on the extent to which, among the workers we studied, work relations formed the basis of friendships outside the plant. Like an earlier investigator of the Vauxhall labour force, we found that for most men, work and non-work were largely separate areas of their social life. When asked: 'How many of the men who work near to you would you call close friends?' 63 per cent of the sample did in fact claim at least one such friend. But the answers to further questions revealed that only in a small minority of cases (18 per cent of the total sample) were these workmate friends actually seen outside the factory in other than a more or less casual way; and that in fact 40 per cent of those claiming 'close friends' among their mates saw these men outside the factory either not at all or only by pure chance. These findings were subsequently confirmed by data from our 'home' interviews which showed that workmates made up only a relatively small proportion of the persons with whom our respondents spent most of their leisure time and whom they entertained in their homes.

Most studies so far made have in fact revealed that assemblers express a relatively high degree of dissatisfaction with their firms and tend to show hostility towards their policies and management. Furthermore, it is clear from statistical evidence that in Great Britain and the United States, at least, the car industry is among the most strike-prone of all and suffers in particular from a high rate of 'unofficial' disputes.

In choosing Vauxhall as the basis of our study, we virtually ensured that, so far as workers' relations with their firm were concerned, our findings would in some degree diverge from those that have come to be regarded as characteristic of car assembly plants. For, as is well known, Vauxhall is conspicuous among major car manufacturing firms in Great Britain for its success in maintaining an almost strike-free record. However, our findings would in fact indicate that Vauxhall's atypicality goes some way beyond this low incidence of overt conflict, and in ways which again give rise to significant theoretical issues.

Our data point, in fact, to the possibility that, given a prior orientation to work of a largely instrumental nature, car assemblers may well see their relationship with their firm in a generally positive way; that is, as centring on a bargain that provides, better than most others available to them, the high-level economic returns which, for the present at least, they wish to derive from their work. Thus, in spite of the deprivations which their jobs on the line may entail, these men will be disposed to maintain their relationship with their firm, and to define this more as one of reciprocity and interdependence rather than, say, as one of coercion and exploitation. And furthermore, if among these workers' wants and expectations from their employment such 'social' satisfactions as 'belongingness' and 'togetherness' do not have high priority, then the impersonality and anonymity of the car assembly plant are no longer likely to give rise to discontent and resentment of a generalized kind. In conclusion, then, the several specific criticisms which we have levelled at the theoretical basis of earlier studies of car assemblers may be summed up in a single more general argument. Most previous writers, we would suggest, have tended to oversimplify the problem of workers' response to the stresses and constraints of assembly-line technology (and have tended to assume greater uniformity in this respect than proves to be the case) because they have left out of account an important *variable*; that is, the orientations which men *bring* to their employment and which *mediate between* the objective features of the work situation and workers' actual experience of, and reaction to, this situation.

The approach which we have found necessary, in order to make intelligible the attitudes and behaviour of our Vauxhall assemblers, entails a 'social action' perspective. The starting point is not with assembly-line technology, but rather with the ordering of wants and expectations relative to work, and with the meaning thus given to work, which result in men taking up and retaining assembly-line jobs. And the key explanatory notion to which we have then referred is not that of the enterprise as a production system, but that of the definition of work and of the work situation, dominant among the assemblers we studied; that is, as we have shown, a definition of work as an essentially instrumental activity – as a means to ends external to the work situation, which is not itself regarded as a milieu in which any worthwhile satisfactions of an immediate kind are likely to be experienced. In this approach, therefore, technology and formal organization are treated not as the direct determinants of shop-floor attitudes and behaviour but rather as constituting a set of limiting factors, the psychological and social implications of which will vary with the significance which workers attach to them. In brief, we reject the idea that workers respond or react in any automatic way to features of their work situation, objectively considered; and we emphasize the extent to which the 'realities' of work are in fact created through workers' own subjective interpretations.

Self-selection and the Small Firm Worker
J. Curran and J. Stanworth

Reprinted with permission from James Curran and John Stanworth, 'The Small Firm Worker', *Sociology*, vol. 13, no. 3, September 1979, pp. 427–32, 439–42

Although manual workers generally have received a great deal of attention from industrial sociologists, small firm workers have received comparatively little. This is surprising in that the vast majority of economic establishments in Britain could be described as 'small' and although it is true that only a minority of workers are employed in small firms, this minority remains substantial. There are a number of possible reasons for this neglect of the small firm worker but two may be suggested as of some importance.

First, the founding fathers of sociology were consistently more interested in the emergence of large-scale organizations in modern society and, either explicitly or implicitly, saw the small enterprise as characteristic of an early phase of the development of industrial society, destined soon to disappear. This is perhaps most apparent in the works of Weber and Marx. Weber saw the large bureaucracy as a defining characteristic of modern industrial society and argued that this kind of organization would increasingly permeate all spheres of social life, displacing smaller, more particularistic, organizations. Marx, even more explicitly, argued that the small enterprise associated with early capitalism would give way to an ever increasing concentration of ownership and the development of large-scale enterprise as a result of the inexorable operation of capitalist market forces.

A second reason for this neglect of the small firm concerns the more practical problems of research. Access to the small firm is often difficult for research purposes and the 'pay-off' from each successful entry tends, by definition, to be a rather small sample or a case study whose representativeness may be questionable. Small firm owner-managers are much less likely than managers in large firms to have received a higher education or to have been exposed to the 'behavioural science' perspective which forms an integral part of most modern management training. Further, the world-view of the owner-manager has been repeatedly found to stress independence, antipathy towards large external organizations, and a dislike of theory as opposed to practice. He tends, therefore, not to share the vocabulary of the social scientist or be particularly sympathetic to requests for cooperation in academic research.

Problems of defining the small firm

Defining the small firm for research purposes is no easy task. The most influential recent discussion of this problem is that offered in the Bolton report. At a general level, the Bolton Committee argued that the small firm had three principal defining characteristics:

> Firstly, in economic terms, a small firm is one that has a relatively small share of its market. Secondly, an essential characteristic of the small firm is that it is managed by its owners or part-owner in a personalized way, and not through the medium of a formalized management structure. Thirdly, it is also independent in the sense that it does not form part of a larger enterprise and that the owner-managers should be free from outside control in taking their principal decisions.

This definition is relatively easy to criticize, but its most serious weakness, as the Committee itself admitted, was that it could not be operationalized since insufficient data is available on the management styles, organizational structures and market shares of British firms. Instead, arbitrary statistical definitions were selected by the Committee for each of nine economic sectors examined. In several instances, such as retailing and motor trades, the definition was based upon annual sales turnover. In others, such as road transport, it was based on numbers of vehicles used. In manufacturing the Committee adopted a definition based on work-force size, '200 employees or less'.

Sociologically, a definition based on one simple criterion is unlikely to be satisfactory for it takes no account of organizational structure which may vary considerably for organizations of a given size or of the meanings and definitions of those who participate in the enterprise. The dominant role in the small firm, for example, is often, as noted above, filled by an individual with a highly distinct world-view which, in turn, is likely to impinge sharply on the meanings and definitions of other participants.

Sociological studies of the small firm worker have, however, usually adopted similar simple statistical definitions generally based upon work-force size. Almost all have been studies of workers in manufacturing industry but typically they have adopted a lower upper size limit than the Bolton Committee with 100 employees or less being most favoured. Other studies which are indirectly relevant, appear to be consistent with this kind of approach. The research upon which the present paper is based initially adopted a definition of 200 employees or less but as fieldwork proceeded, reservations developed and a lower upper limit would now be probably suggested for the two industries investigated.

Self-selection and the small firm worker

In the literature on occupational placement among manual workers there is little relating size of firm to decisions on occupational choice. But it is widely believed that some workers make a positive choice to work for small rather than large firms and *vice versa*. Ingham in particular argues strongly for this view and supports it with research findings. Essentially, he argues that, over time, workers build up a stable set of orientations which are central to the process of occupational choice and closely related to factors associated with size of firm.

Ingham's interpretation of the small firm worker occupational identity and world-view is a development of the argument offered by Goldthorpe *et al.* in the *Affluent Worker* studies. The complex of orientations Ingham attributes to the small firm worker he terms *non-economistic-expressive*. Workers with this kind of orientation place a relatively low emphasis on economic rewards and high emphasis on non-economic rewards. Small firms tend to pay less well than large firms but, because of lower levels of bureaucratization, greater variety within work roles, and greater opportunities for moral involvement, offer a good 'fit' with the *non-economistic-expressive* orientation. Provided, therefore, that workers with such an orientation can exercise a reasonably free choice they will gravitate towards employment in small firms.

Manual workers with the above orientation may be contrasted with those studied by Goldthorpe *et al.* who manifested what Ingham terms an *economistic-instrumental* orientation. This orientation involves an emphasis on economic gratifications and a relative indifference to non-economic rewards. Large firms provide an environment most congruent with this orientation and, given relatively full employment, workers with this orientation may be expected to choose to work in such firms.

Ingham's argument and research findings have, rather surprisingly, been subject to few criticisms. However, besides the smallness of his sample (forty-seven small firm worker respondents) his interview questionnaire was not well designed to establish patterns of continuity amongst respondents' orientations. Only six questions sought information on previous jobs and only three concerned motives for taking or leaving jobs. But, further, the idea of self-selection linked to strongly developed, stable orientations among small firm workers may be seriously questioned on several wider grounds.

First, the argument goes very much against the main body of sociological literature on occupational placement. In study after study, a central finding has been the seemingly haphazard and aimless character of occupational decisions among manual workers. They appear to have a very incomplete knowledge of the labour market and rarely investigate more than a limited range of available jobs even where a wide choice exists. Once the influence of social class, the local employment market, sex, age, and ethnic group membership are taken into account, the individual worker's positive influence seems relatively unimportant.

Some recent trends and theories of occupational placement go further and argue that the notion of freedom of occupational choice is largely a myth and that occupational placement is best understood in terms of individuals being channelled into jobs. Individual workers, at whatever point in their adult work experiences, are limited in the kind of job they can take not only by a lack of knowledge and the influences identified above, but also by immediate situational influences such as a shortage of money and relatively low expectations about finding jobs they would actually *like* to do. (This argument is, of course, strongly reinforced by generally higher levels of unemployment in the 1970s as compared to previous decades.)

The self-selection thesis also underestimates the involuntary character of much job changing among manual workers in other ways. In an examination of the reasons given by respondents for leaving jobs in the research upon which the present paper is based, involuntary reasons (redundancy, dismissal, the firm closing down or moving location etc.), sometimes comprised over one in four of all reasons given. In periods of economic recession, the proportion of job changing affected by such involuntary influences may be expected to be even higher.

Second, like a great deal of earlier research employing a social action perspective, Ingham's argument fails to devote sufficient attention to the network of social relations in which the focal group participates. The orientations and behaviour of others are a powerful constraint on manual worker choices and behaviour. Occupational placement involves not only a choice on the part of the worker but also a choice on the part of the employer. An overconcentration on worker orientations implies that employers are relatively indifferent to the kind of worker they employ and that there is little difference between the employee selection practices of small and large firms. Previous research and the research upon which the present paper is based support neither of these assumptions.

The small firm owner-manager normally has a decisive or near-decisive influence on employment policies in the firm. Over the last decade, a good deal of research has accumulated suggesting that the small firm owner-manager is a distinct social type with a world-view quite different to that of the large firm manager. This world-view is, in many respects, closer to a nineteenth-century *laissez-faire* ideology stressing independence, the absolute right to manage with a minimum devolution of authority, paternalism, and a dislike of trade unions. In selecting workers, small firm employers frequently place considerable emphasis on their judgment of the worker as a *person* rather than simply on qualifications and previous experience. Large firm employers, on the other hand, are more likely to have a personnel department whose specialist staff place greater emphasis on universalistic selection criteria and bureaucratic procedures. Chief among the latter criteria are evidence of having completed an apprenticeship or equivalent training and evidence of a relevant and stable employment record. Since large firms are also more likely to be unionized than small firms union membership will also frequently be a prerequisite for employment.

The small firm, as the Bolton report pointed out, has to exploit any possible advantages open to it in an economy dominated by large firms. One such advantage is comparatively cheap labour. This is possible because the small firm employer can, by backing his personal judgment rather than trusting paper qualifications, employ workers with different characteristics to those employed by large firms. One clear way in which this occurs is in the employment of younger workers. As other research has shown, the difference in the average age of workers in small and large firms may be substantial. In the present study, the average age of respondents in small firms was twenty-eight as compared with thirty-seven in the large firms.

Small firm employers in the present study not only found younger workers cheaper to employ but also tended to believe that older workers were less flexible in their work attitudes. Small firm employers who discriminate in this way are less visible to outsiders who might criticize such practices than a large firm would be and, probably more important, trade union pressures in the large firm would tend to reduce such discrimination.

One further way in which the greater freedom of small firm employers is shown is in the positive seeking of suitable workers through personal contacts and the discarding of 'unsuitable' workers. In the present research, small firm workers were much more likely than their large firm counterparts to have taken jobs after being contacted directly by an employer. Equally, small firm executives stressed that they actively sought to get rid of 'unsuitable' workers arguing that a small firm could not afford to carry any 'dead wood'. Workers in large firms are again more likely to be protected from dismissal on such grounds by trade union membership.

A third ground on which the existing view of small firm worker self-selection may be questioned relates to criticism of the whole notion of developing orientations towards work. Such criticisms have been levelled against the *Affluent Worker* study by several writers, particularly in the form of an alleged overemphasis on previous experiences as against current work and non-work experiences. These criticisms apply equally to Ingham's arguments concerning the small firm worker. In addition, it is Ingham's view that life-cycle influences are of little importance in the formation of, and changes in, worker orientations.

The importance of life-cycle influences on worker orientations has previously been demonstrated in several studies, and Goldthorpe *et al.* suggested that it was probably an important factor in the instrumental orientation found among their sample of manual workers. In the present study, younger, unmarried workers were more likely to stress intrinsic aspects of work as important in thinking about work than older, married workers and, since small firms employ a higher proportion of the former, this partly helps to account for a greater emphasis on intrinsic aspects among small firm workers as compared to large firm workers.

It appears, therefore, that there are good reasons for suggesting that worker orientations are considerably more volatile than is implied by Ingham's argument. More generally, it seems highly questionable anyway to suggest that, in a rapidly changing society where the individual's work life may span half a century, considerable reformulations of occupational identity will not occur.

A sample of small firm workers in two industries

The data presented in the present paper are based upon tape-recorded interviews with a sample of 145 male shop-floor and supervisory workers from eight small firms in the printing and electronics industries. An additional control sample of 88 respondents was drawn from two large firms, one in each of the two industries. All interviews were carried out in respondents' homes (or other suitable non-work venues) during the period late 1974 to early 1976. Response rates of over 73 per cent were achieved in all firms. In addition, 40 open-ended interviews were conducted with executives in the firms studied.

All the firms and respondents were located in or around Surrey, mainly in the northern half of the county. The two industries selected for study were chosen because of the sharp contrast they offered. Printing is a traditional, craft-based industry which, until comparatively recently, has experienced only a slow rate of technological change. It is predominantly a small firm industry with over 95 per cent of workers located in establishments employing less than 100 people. It is also, unusually for an industry dominated by small firms, highly unionized. The electronics industry, on the other hand, is a much younger science-based industry with a higher proportion of its labour force employed in large firms. It also has a much lower level of unionization and has experienced an especially high rate of technological innovation since the end of the Second World War.

The reason for choosing such contrasting industries was to allow an examination of the influence of industrial subcultures on the formation and development of worker orientations. Previous research on small firm workers has tended to mix samples drawn from different industries apparently assuming such differences were of little consequence. Printing, however, has a highly developed industrial subculture, and a major finding of the present research was the existence of a distinct industrial subculture in the electronics industry. In the event, industrial subcultures had an important bearing on both small and large firm worker orientations.

The main research instrument used was an interview schedule containing a mixture of both structured and open questions supported by probes; each interview lasted, on average, 1¼ hours. Respondents' views were sought on three main areas: (1) previous work experiences, (2) attitudes towards the job held at the time of interview, and (3) non-work life and world-views. The present paper concerns mainly the first of these areas. . . .

Occupational placement, industrial subculture and size of firm

A distinct pattern of differences in the emphasis placed by respondents on intrinsic and extrinsic considerations – the cornerstone of the self-selection thesis – was revealed in the data on successive job changes. However, this pattern appeared more related to *industrial subcultures* than to size of firm. By industrial subculture is meant the distinctive meanings and institutions shared by those who work in a particular industry which concern work and the social relations connected with work.

Over the series of job changes examined, it emerged that small printing firm workers were by far the most extrinsically minded of the four subsamples, regardless of size of firm. Equally, the small electronics firm workers were by far the most intrinsically minded of all subsamples. (It should be stressed, however, that this is not to say that such reasons *predominated* amongst those given by either of the relevant samples. In each job change situation examined, intrinsic and extrinsic reasons, even when *combined* usually accounted for only about half of all reasons.) This pattern of differences in intrinsic and extrinsic mindedness, much greater between industries than between firms of differing sizes, was repeated consistently for each job change examined.

The analysis of workers' answers to questions on job changing and other aspects of work suggested that the patterns of extrinsic and intrinsic mindedness found were related more to industrial subculture than size of firm. In printing, up until the end of the 1950s, the worker had a level of earnings and job security which placed him in a very superior position compared to other manual workers. Since then, however, levels of earnings in general printing have fallen relatively and radical technological change has reduced levels of autonomy and security. In particular, the shift away from traditional letter-press technology has made it possible for many firms to set up using semi-skilled, non-union workers. Respondents in the present study were very aware of these changes and their effects on earnings and job prospects.

A further reason for the high level of consciousness of extrinsic job aspects – and especially of earnings levels – among printing workers is the presence of an earnings elite in the industry. These are the small proportion of workers involved in national and local newspaper production who normally work in large firms. They form a positive reference group for many workers in general printing and are a reminder of the continuing prosperity of at least some printers.

The fact that printing is a highly unionized industry is also relevant. The unions negotiate standard earnings and conditions for a wide variety of firms and greatly influence earnings in non-trade union firms. The unions are also a major means by which information on earnings is communicated throughout the industry, again even to non-trade union members.

These factors combine, therefore, to make the printing worker much more extrinsically minded than might otherwise be the case. But, equally, the craft character of printing, strongly emphasized in some previous studies and thought to be reflected in intrinsic mindedness among workers, was found to be overstated. Much modern print work involves routine, repetitive tasks with little intrinsic appeal for workers whether in small or large firms. The small printing firm worker, often less well paid than the large printing firm worker and with fewer prospects of joining the industry's earnings elite is, therefore, not surprisingly very earnings conscious and this appears to account for the strong emphasis on extrinsic factors in their occupational identities.

The industrial subculture in electronics, on the other hand, emerged as very different to that in printing. First, the close connections between science, scientific research and the industry were frequently mentioned by respondents. They felt they shared, in some way, in the status and public recognition of the benefits of electronics for modern living. This was probably related to the fact that respondents in the present research were involved in small batch production of high quality products, more or less closely related to recent research developments. Strikingly, the electronics industry respondents were much more craft minded than the printers. Frequently, they were involved in building whole products, testing them and ironing out problems before they left the factory. Often also they clearly viewed the product as highly worthwhile. All these influences, therefore, led to a heightened consciousness of intrinsic aspects of the job, especially in the small firm which displays these conditions more frequently than the large firm where longer production runs are more common.

A knowledge and consciousness of earnings levels was much lower among electronics workers, overall, than among printing workers. Partly, this was because of a relative absence of trade unions in the industry and hence a lack of communication about earnings levels. Partly, also, it was due to the greater variation in work-role content in the industry. In printing there is a limited range of fairly well-defined tasks – some with unions organized specifically around them – while in electronics there is a much wider range of products which leads to greater task variation. Further, difficulties involved in defining the exact boundaries of the industry make reference group comparisons more difficult.

However, there *is* an earnings elite in the electronics industry – contract workers. This elite does not, however, form such a positive reference group as newspaper workers in printing. First of all, they are a relatively recent phenomenon, whose existence could be threatened by reductions in labour shortages or changes in the tax laws. But, secondly, ordinary workers often resent contract workers because they get paid a higher hourly rate for exactly the same job. Contract workers themselves often made it clear that they regarded non-contract workers as either less skilled or less enterprising than themselves. In short, the high earnings group in the electronics industry was rather more of a negative reference group – 'money grabbers' – in an industry where workers put a greater emphasis on intrinsic aspects of work than in printing.

Overall, therefore, aspects of the industrial subculture appeared more important in influencing patterns of intrinsic-extrinsic orientations to work than influences associated with size of firm. However, it is worth stressing again that extrinsic-intrinsic orientations by no means dominated respondents' reported thinking on job changing.

Conclusions

The view that small firm workers differ from their large firm counterparts in terms of orientations leading to self-selection in occupational placement, seems highly questionable. Not only does such a view go against the main thrust of previous theorizing and research on occupational placement among manual workers but is not supported by the research reported in this paper. The latter points, instead, to an alternative interpretation of occupational placement and size of firm.

The range of influences involved in occupational placement patterns among small firm workers was found to be much wider than that implied in the self-selection thesis and involved a greater emphasis upon social relations with others and upon involuntary influences. Among the social relations found to be important were those with significant others, for example, parents at the beginning of work experiences and especially employers. The latter might best be seen as 'gatekeepers' controlling entry into firms of differing size through their adoption of rather different criteria of employee selection.

Involuntary influences on workers' behaviour in occupational placement comprise a range of less obvious influences whose impact tends to be cumulative as the period of work experience lengthens. The most important of these influences appears to be whether the worker completes a period of recognized formal training, typically an apprenticeship. This is important because it is likely to be positively correlated with greater employment stability, a lower propensity to switch industries and greater opportunities of trade union membership. In terms of market situation – the possibilities of selling one's labour to a range of buyers plus a choice of employment alternatives allowing a trade-off between earnings and other rewards – the worker with such a training finds himself in a different position compared to the worker who has not.

It would, however, be wrong to assume that the worker with a cumulatively superior market situation has a choice of working in either small or large firms while the worker with a poor market situation can work only in a small firm. The fully experienced, formally trained, skilled manual worker may be not entirely attractive to the small firm employer except in limited numbers. Some small firm employers take on a small number of such workers but otherwise staff the firm with less skilled workers so that, overall, labour costs are lower while difficult jobs are nevertheless satisfactorily completed. In short, there may be fewer opportunities in small firms for workers with a superior market situation. Further, such workers may be seen by small firm employers as having a lower degree of loyalty simply because they can leave more easily than other employees. If they also have a trade union card this may make the small firm employer less keen to employ them if he is antipathetic to trade unions since they may be the agency for pressures for the subsequent full unionization of the firm.

Equally, the worker with a poor market situation may still try to work for a large firm rather than a small firm. The small firms in the present study employed relatively few workers aged over forty-five. It might be suggested, therefore, that some workers at least move over to work for large firms with increasing age. Possibly they accept jobs with lower status than they might obtain in a small firm because they seek the security of a large firm or because they can no longer retain or obtain a job in a small firm due to small firm employer age discrimination. It may be also that some manage, by one means or another, to obtain a union card which would also help in making this transition.

The present paper shows, however, that not only does the self-selection theory of occupational placement fail to take into account a whole range of situational influences outside the field of worker orientations but that even where the latter are considered, differences in orientations may be related more to industrial subculture than to size of firm. The data indicate that, even where just two industries are considered, the influences of industrial subcultures may be such as to reverse the expected relationship between size of firm and workers' emphasis on intrinsic aspects of work. It may be suggested that an extension of the study into other industries would almost certainly provide further cases of this relationship. In addition, the analysis of the links between industrial subculture and emphasis on intrinsic or extrinsic aspects of work indicates that this might well change over time. In other words, the relationship here is a dynamic one, and we should not replace size with industrial subculture to suggest some fixed relationship with worker orientations.

On the Shop Floor
T. Lupton

Reprinted with permission from Tom Lupton, *On the Shop Floor*, Pergamon Press, 1963, pp. 187–8, 195–9.

The expression 'restriction of output' is commonly used to describe the behaviour of workers who set standards of output below those which management considers that it can reasonably expect from them. The question 'why do workers restrict output?' has produced various answers. The most widely accepted of these is that which stresses the incompatibility of the rationally contrived controls over workers' behaviour which are imposed by management, and the controls which are to be found in the spontaneous social relationships which workers enter into at work. According to this interpretation, management formulates an expected level of output which is based upon considerations of technical efficiency. The behaviour of workers is then directed towards the achievement of this level of output. The social groupings in the workshops, which are based upon sentiments of friendship and sociability, and which adhere to values which are traditionalistic rather than rational, develop their own norms of what constitutes a 'proper' level of output and impose their own controls upon behaviour. The workshop norm may be well below what management expects. This interpretation of 'restriction of output' is attractive because it does not imply laziness, malice, or deliberate planning by workers to defeat the purposes of management. Its widespread acceptance is due largely to the influence of the work of Elton Mayo and his followers. It suggests that workers do not restrict output deliberately so as to safeguard themselves from exploitation, but to protect what they believe to be their best interests.

There are at least three questionable assumptions implicit in this interpretation of 'restriction of output' which I have thus summarized. The first of these is that there exist methods which allow of accurate prediction for assessing the expected performance of productive units. Secondly it is assumed that the main impediment to the fulfilment of management expectations lies in informal relationships in the workshops. It is not admitted that expectations may not be fulfilled because of lack of ability by management to translate plans into actual output. Thirdly, the possibility is ruled out that there may exist real conflicts of interest and viewpoint between managers and workers. If such conflicts could be shown to exist, then it would be entirely reasonable to explain fears of rate-cutting and the like in terms of a rational and realistic appraisal of their interests by the workers.

There is no doubt that the market for electrical transformers is much more stable, and that there are no severe seasonal depressions. It is also clear that competition between the firms in the industry is not intense: indeed there is a good deal of cartelization, and there are many collusive marketing arrangements. The firms are very much larger and certainly the amount of capital required to enter the industry would not encourage any workers to expect to become an owner.

Thus there is, in the electrical components industry, more stability and less downward pressure on wage rates. One does not hear from managers at Jay's the kind of remark we heard from a sales manager in the rubber-proofed garment industry: 'A halfpenny on the price might mean the difference between getting an order and losing it.' Neither does one hear in the garment industry the kind of remark heard from workers at Jay's: 'When you are sitting around waiting for work the firm just passes the cost on to the customer, and the consumer pays through the nose for the special jobs we do, so why should the firm worry.'

Trade unionism is highly developed in heavy electrical engineering and its organization is highly effective at workshop level. Thus at the same time as the structure and the economics of the industry create the 'elbow room' for manipulation, the existence of trade union power in the workshops provides workers with one of the means to control their situation. Since management is not pressed by competition continually to seek to 'trim' piecework prices they can accept 'fiddling' as a reasonable way of adjusting their relationships with the workers and their unions. And this is further made possible because labour cost is a much lower proportion of the total cost of the product than it is in the garment industry, 8–10 per cent as against 13–15 per cent. Thus, if market conditions are adverse, savings can more easily be effected elsewhere. It would seem that the hypothesis suggested by me in an article based upon the Wye study emphasizing the importance of 'external' factors is consistent with the material from Jay's.

The difference in behaviour which I observed between the two workshops would seem to be explained if it can be shown that both management and workers made a realistic appraisal of their situation, and then acted according to their interests as they saw them. The material suggests that they did this. This is not to say that everyone always behaved rationally in the light of his or her interests. Much of the behaviour we observed can be interpreted in terms of 'Mayoism'. But a great deal of the field material ceases to make sense unless one admits of a realistic appraisal of interests, and of discrepancy – even conflict – between the goals of workers and managers in many situations.

I do not claim of course, that all the workers in the workshops I studied were aware in detail of all the factors which affected their interests. Obviously they were not, although I was often struck by the extent and accuracy of their knowledge. Sometimes their behaviour appeared to be directed against their own best interests. But lack of knowledge does not necessarily imply lack of realism. One acts on the knowledge one has. This applies to management too. For all the techniques of modern management it is not possible to predict production targets exactly, or so I found. Nor are the controls which management exercises perfect in their application. And this is because management also acts on incomplete knowledge. Although partly one of communications, the problem is greater than that. Knowledge which is in the nature of things incomplete, is communicated, and upon this knowledge people must act. It is in this area of incomplete knowledge and understanding that the social adjustments which I have described are made. I conclude that in Jay's, where there was security, and 'elbow room' to make adjustments, the 'fiddle' was a quite stable adjustment of the discrepant goals and interests of management and workers. In Wye, 'looking after No. 1' seemed a logical sensible policy in the circumstances.

I have checked my findings with previous work in the field, and I have enquired about the state of affairs in other parts of the electrical components industry. In Roy's work, which describes a 'fiddle' closely resembling that at Jay's, there is not much reference to what we have called 'external' factors. His study was carried out in the steel industry, and it is reasonable to suppose that the complex of external factors closely resembles that which I found at Jay's. Enquiries made at a large electrical firm in the same area as Jay's making a similar product, and with a similar wages structure, revealed that an almost exactly similar 'fiddle' operates. A manager there told us that this firm had lately taken on some foreign labour. The story is now being told in the firm that the first English phrase that the newcomers learned was 'one hundred per cent'.

My analysis has taken me some way towards a definition of the conditions under which restrictive and non-restrictive behaviour may be found. It is now possible to list the factors I have been discussing under the headings 'external' and 'internal' with the object of discerning whether any particular combination, or clustering of factors seems to be associated

Table 1. 'External' and 'internal' factors

	A *Situation at Wye*	B *Situation at Jay's*
External		
Market:		
(a) Stability	Unstable	Stable
(b) Size	Small, differentiated	Large, undifferentiated
Competition	Intense, lack of collusive arrangements	Weak, collusion and pricing arrangements
Scale of industry	Small with small firms predominating	Large, small numbers of large firms
Location of industry	Concentrated in one area	Widely dispersed
Trade unions	Local, weak in workshops, poorly developed shop steward system	Nationally organized, powerful, strong in workshops, well developed shop steward system
Cost ratio	High labour cost	Relatively low labour cost
Product	Consumer goods	Capital goods
Internal		
Method of wage Payment	Straight piecework Simple	Bonus system Complicated
Productive system	Minute breakdown of operations. Batch production. Individual as unit in work flow. Short time span	No minute breakdown. Batch production. Section as unit in work flow. Long time span
Sex of workers	Women predominate	Men predominate
Workshop social structure	Sociable grouping not co-extensive with productive groupings	Sociable groupings are also productive groupings. Collective attitude to output and earnings 'Comfortable'.
Management-worker	Economic interests tend to converge. Personal relationship, but values divergent. Worker control has no part in adjustment	Stable. Worker control plays part in adjustment. Economic interests diverge but large area of value convergence

with certain kinds of worker behaviour in relation to controls over output and earnings.

When one compares the situation at Wye and at Jay's, it is seen that with regard to all the factors listed there are significant differences. And these differences are associated in each case with differences in the pattern of shop-floor behaviour. Thus we may define the situation in each workshop in terms of a 'cluster' of the characteristics listed in Table 1, and state the hypothesis that when the cluster of characteristics in column A is found one will find behaviour in the workshops which resembles the behaviour which I found in the workshop at Wye, and that when the Jay's type of cluster is found, one would expect to find Jay's type behaviour. I would also suggest that these two kinds of cluster are those which would be most commonly found. For example, it is in industries with small firms and intense competition that one would probably find lack of mechanization, high labour cost, women workers and weak trade union workshop organization. In an industry with large firms and little competition one would probably find mechanization, low labour cost, men workers and strong trade union workshop organization. But these are obviously not the only possible clusters. For example, one might find an industry which is composed of a large number of small firms which are not locally concentrated but widely scattered, but with trade unions that are strong at workshop level in such an industry. Or one may find that trade unions are strong in the industry in one area and weak in another. Or one might find a competitive industry of small firms which is highly mechanized. It is also true that some items in any 'cluster' may be very influential in relation to other items in the cluster and to shop-floor behaviour. I have myself suggested already in the Wye and Jay's cases, that some items seem to have more weight than others.

On the whole I consider that the Wye and Jay type of cluster will be commonly found, and one could consider them as lying at either end of a continuum, with all sorts of combinations making up the clusters in between, but with similar clusters themselves clustering at each end of the continuum. Those clusters at either end are in a sense definitions on the one hand of situations where there is much collective worker control over output and earnings, and on the other of those where there is little control of this kind.

The Secretarial Role

S. Vinnicombe

Reprinted with permission from Susan Vinnicombe, *Secretaries, Managements and Organizations*, Heinemann Educational Books, 1980, pp. 8–15, 104–8

The secretary's job has a long history, for until relatively recently, the skill of writing was possessed by only a few people. The word 'secretary' derives from the Latin *secretum*, and in medieval times a secretary was the person who dealt with the correspondence of the king, or other high-ranking person, and consequently with confidential and secret matters. Although a variety of tasks are associated with the secretary today, the original notions of confidentiality and skill in correspondence are still the elements most traditionally linked with the occupation.

While shorthand and typing skills are essential to the position of a private/personal secretary, they may, by no means, be the clerical skills exploited by the employer. Fiore elaborates on this point. He suggests

Table 1. Functional characteristics of the secretary's position

Mechanistic (typing activities)	*Organic (administration/non-typing activities)*
1 Job description easier	1 Job description more difficult
2 Input/output more controllable	2 Input/output less controllable
3 Problems more predictable	3 Problems less predictable
4 Task elements largely psychometric	4 Task elements largely cognitive
5 Independent activity more vital to productivity	5 Dynamic interaction more vital to productivity
6 Creativity/innovation areas circumscribed	6 Creativity/innovation areas less circumscribed
7 Development more visible	7 Development less visible
8 Peer competition visible	8 Peer competition less visible
9 Multi-channel communication less essential to effectiveness	9 Multi-channel communication more essential to effectiveness
10 Success relatively independent of particular boss supported	10 Success relatively dependent on particular boss supported

Source: Fiore, M., 'The Secretarial Role in Transition', *Supervisory Management*, November 1971, p. 22.

that the activities of the private secretary may be perceived from a dual functionalist perspective. There are those allied to word processing which Fiore regards as 'mechanistic' in nature, and those allied to general administration which he regards as 'organic' in nature (see Table 1).

The distinction between mechanistic and organic activities is best brought out by relating them to specific secretarial jobs. At one end of the scale is the pool typist. She works alongside other pool typists and her work consists wholly of copy typing, which has been given to her by a number of junior managers, or allocated to her by a pool supervisor. Her job is thus totally routine with immediate visible results which are easily measured. Her success is entirely dependent on her speed and accuracy of typing and thus communication with other people is not only unimportant but in most cases is disruptive to performance. Even work originators tend not to brief her personally on the typing; they will merely leave her some written instructions. The pool typist characterizes a secretarial position where activities are wholly mechanistic.

At the other end of the scale is the senior executive secretary or personal assistant to the managing director. She may spend little or no time typing since she may have her own junior secretary to whom such tasks can be delegated. Instead, most of her day is spent in a supportive administrative capacity carrying out a variety of tasks, from making the coffee to taking her boss's place at a meeting. This kind of secretary works very closely with her boss, and indeed, her success depends vitally on maintaining this coordinated team approach. The personal secretary not only undertakes anything required of her by her boss but also, and importantly, initiates many work-based activities herself.

Again, the effectiveness with which she carries out the latter depends on how well she knows her boss and can anticipate his needs. Often such secretaries have spent many years, in some cases a working lifetime, with one boss. Such secretaries frequently pride themselves on being able to predict precisely what the boss's reaction is going to be in any given situation. It is not surprising that they are often used as the boss's barometer in decision-making. Whereas in the situation of the pool typist it is easy to control work and measure performance, with the personal secretary work-loads are contingent on the boss's work-loads, and performance is difficult to gauge since outcomes are not always immediate or quantifiable. Also, the pool typist may be very successful in terms of carrying out her duties, in adopting a very calculated interest in her work, illustrated by, for example, strictly adhering to office hours. This would be a formula for failure with the personal secretary who, unless she is prepared to work late and take jobs home with her, would never be successful. She has to let her work demands define her day. Such a private secretary occupies a secretarial position where activities are largely organic.

Needless to say, the above two descriptions typify opposite ends on a continuum defining a secretary's position. Once an individual is no longer a pool typist it becomes difficult to define her job accurately, since it tends to be a blend of mechanistic and organic activities. The relative proportions which make up any one secretary's job are primarily determined by her boss, with the secretary bringing to bear a certain amount of influence. The nature of the boss's position and the industry in which he is located will also affect this situation.

If the personal/executive secretary stands at the 'top' of the female hierarchy in the office, in between her and the pool typist is the departmental or group secretary (sometimes referred to as a shorthand typist). They possess both typing and shorthand skills, like the top secretaries, but rather than working exclusively for one boss they tend to work for a group of managers. Thus they are unable to build up the same degree of personal identification with a boss as the personal secretaries, and they are likely to undertake less administrative duties than do personal secretaries. It is quite common for group secretaries, for instance, neither to take bosses' telephone calls nor to control their diaries.

The secretarial hierarchy may be defined along a number of general characteristics common to any other organization's hierarchy, e.g. status, salary, size of office, autonomy. What particularly distinguishes movement up the secretarial hierarchy, however, may be reduced to two factors:

1. The degree to which the boss-secretary relationship becomes personalized.
2. The degree to which the dependency relationship between boss(es) and secretary shifts from being one where the secretary is totally dependent on her boss(es) to one where the boss becomes almost totally dependent on the secretary.

The second factor needs some elaboration. At the bottom of the hierarchy the typist relies totally on the boss to determine her work-load, define her activities, and check her work, whereas at the top of the organization it is the secretary who plays a significant and visible role determining her boss's work-load, defining his activities, and checking that he has completed all his tasks (see Figure 1). The nature of the dependency relationship has thus effectively been totally reversed. On the whole, the degree to which the boss-secretary relationship becomes personalized and the dependency relationship alters are not independent; generally, secretaries who work closer with their bosses and identify with them are the ones whose bosses rely on them totally in order to carry out their jobs effectively.

Recent developments in the structure of offices have probably tended to widen the differences between the three levels of this hierarchy. There

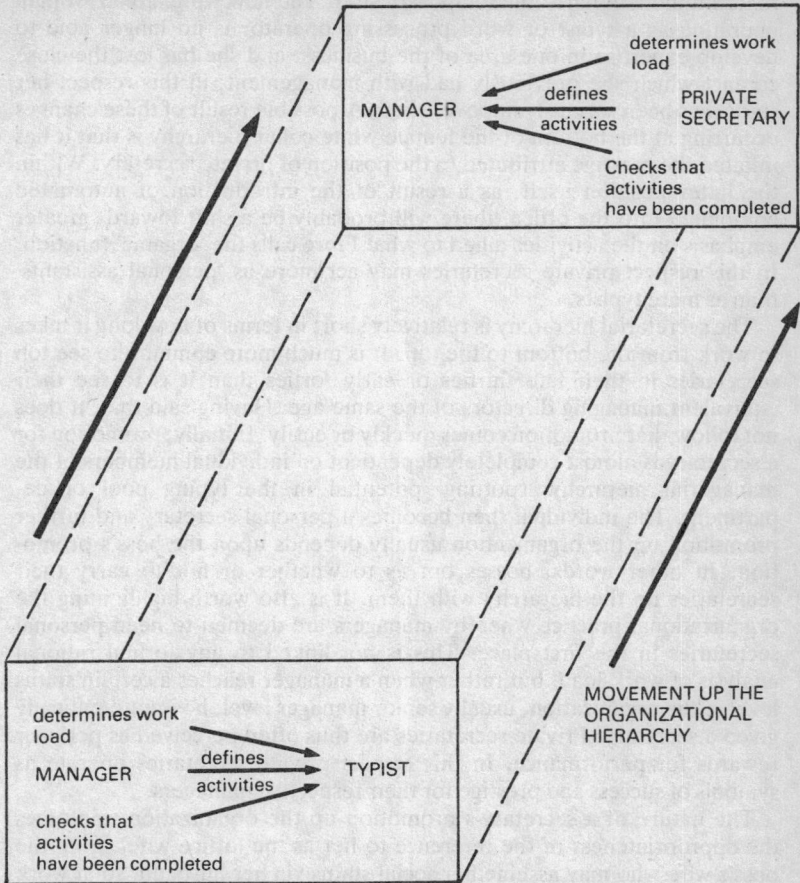

Figure 1. *Secretarial movement up the organizational hierarchy*

is a tendency to 'pool' typists and shorthand typists together in order to increase the efficiency of the service. One advertising and marketing company in London estimated a saving of £17,000 a year through adopting a centralized dictating system in the office. The consequences of this move are that the skill of shorthand is becoming obsolete (having been replaced by dictation machines); the tasks have become more routinized; and the white-collar woman in this situation has become easily replaceable. The widespread implementation of word processing units will exacerbate this gap. Within this context it is easy to see why the occupation has been able to accommodate part-time temporary staff. The new white-collar woman operating as a typist or word processing operator is no longer able to develop expertise in one area of the business, and she has lost the close contact which she previously had with management; in this respect her status has been seriously impoverished. A possible result of these changes occurring at the bottom of the female white-collar hierarchy is that it has inflated the prestige attributed to the position of private secretary. Within the latter position itself, as a result of the introduction of automated equipment into the office, there will probably be a shift towards greater emphasis on the activities allied to what Fiore calls the 'organic' function. In this respect private secretaries may act more as 'personal assistants' than as mere typists.

The secretarial hierarchy is relatively short in terms of how long it takes to work from the bottom to the top. It is much more common to see top secretaries in their late thirties or early forties than it is to see their equivalent managing directors of the same age. Having said that, it does not follow that promotion comes quickly or easily. Initially, promotion for a secretary is almost completely dependent on individual members of the managerial hierarchy 'spotting' potential in the typing pool or department. The individual then becomes a personal secretary and further promotion up the organization usually depends upon the boss's promotion. In other words, bosses opt as to whether or not to carry their secretaries up the hierarchy with them. It is also worth highlighting the organizational practice whereby managers are deemed to need personal secretaries in the first place. This is not linked to any formal rational analysis of work-load, but rather when a manager reaches a certain status level in the organization, usually senior manager level, he is automatically given a secretary. Private secretaries are thus often perceived as perks or rewards for performance. In this respect private secretaries operate as symbols of success and prestige for their respective managers.

The nature of a secretary's promotion up the organization reinforces the appropriateness of the reference to her as the 'office wife'. Like the boss's wife who may assume her social status via her husband, so at work the secretary acquires her position and status through her boss. On account of the lack of any standard job descriptions, rational criteria for allocating secretaries, or performance appraisal schemes for secretaries, the latter are often in a relatively powerless position to manipulate their careers. It is paradoxical that while the secretarial position came through the bureaucratization of organizations, it goes contrary to all the principles of bureaucracy: namely, rationality, depersonalization of relationships, and the application of universal standards. The boss-secretary relationship represents the most striking example of the retention of patrimony within the organization.

One of the key contributions perceived of private secretaries is the way they operate as a 'system of cliques' within and between formal lines of authority, thus facilitating the handling of issues which might have taken much longer had they gone through the regular channels of communication. Eccles suggests that the importance of the secretary in handling issues on the boss's behalf is particularly pronounced when the boss is working on assignments away from the home office. He suggests that secretaries act as 'interpreters, guides, fixers, filters, negotiators and organizers of the debates about important problems'. The relationship between boss and private secretary is, then, necessarily a supportive one and one in which there is a reciprocation of influence and prestige. Roman elaborates on this point: 'A secretary . . . is a skilled executive and interpreter of her boss's thinking and she is often the executant of their thinking, especially so in the absence of the boss.'

There may, however, be certain problems. Bensaher highlights a critical one which deserves far more attention than it receives. Since the secretary so frequently acts as the boss's surrogate/substitute, it is essential that the boss and secretary have some 'mutually agreed framework within which she is to operate'. If this framework is not worked out it is possible that the secretary is not acting within the interests of the boss. This point relates to the fact that the boss and private secretary must think, plan, and act as a team. Just as the success of a doubles partnership in tennis critically depends on the ability of each player to anticipate the shots of the other, to complement one another's style and to synchronize their game, so also the boss and private secretary should work hard at developing their team strategy. In this respect it is a great shame that management and secretarial training programmes persist in training the partners separately, thus reinforcing this rift.

In conclusion, then, the importance of the private secretarial role lies in its symbiotic relationship to its parallel managerial position. This manifests itself in two ways. First, a high status is conferred on the private secretary through her close working relationship with her boss. Secondly, and this is the one which forms the focus of this book, an important function is fulfilled by the private secretary in terms of the way she acts as an 'extension' to her boss, and on occasions even as a surrogate to him.

The executive has turned his secretary into his gatekeeper. She can filter, certainly deter, maybe veto the importunings of the would-be visitors. Is there any reader who doesn't know of situations where it is more important to be well-in with the secretary than with the executive himself? Are there no cases where the enquirer gets better, more useful, information from the secretary? The gatekeeper secretary is performing a managerial function.

The executive depends on her for the receipt of authentic information. She is adjacent to the circulation of people in the corridor and may well see more of them than he does. In his absence she has to take decisions for him. She may have much greater contact with the day to day network in the organization. (A. Eccles, 'Wanted: a Personnel Manager, Preferably with Typing Skills', *Top Secretary*, May 1974)

The importance of the gatekeeper role of the personal secretary has been demonstrated in a large organizational communications study in Florida. In the project the researchers analysed the frequency with which individuals communicated with other individuals; the direction of the communications (i.e. who initiated contact); and the nature of the communications. The results indicated that it was one of the directors' secretaries who had greatest access to information, and information sources, in the company. What is especially interesting here is that a top secretary not only emerged as a more important liaison than other lower-level secretaries, but that she was more important than all the directors. This must rank as a critical observation in appreciating how organization communication systems really work. With this in mind it is not surprising that Sorensen sums up the private secretarial position in these terms: 'the key member of the manager's team should be his secretary', and MacKenzie states: 'Of the many resources contributing to the manager's effectiveness, none is more critical than his secretary.'. . .

At a general level it is evident that many organizations give little or no attention to analysing their real secretarial needs (that is, on the basis of managerial work-load, as opposed to managerial status), and considering how these are best satisfied. The lack of any strategic plans and standard personnel polices, together with a noticeable absence of any management training on using secretaries, help to precipitate a situation in which secretaries are underutilized and treated in an arbitrary, and occasionally demeaning, way. As a result, organizations suffer from excessive secretarial costs, low productivity, and high labour turnover; managers suffer from their secretaries' lack of interest in the work and lack of commitment to their bosses; and secretaries suffer from low job satisfaction and the absence of any planned career development.

Looking more closely at the actual nature of secretarial activities, it is apparent that as secretaries move up the hierarchy they tend to undertake significantly more administrative tasks than mechanistic ones. The extent to which secretaries carry out administrative duties, however, could be greatly increased if managers were more willing to delegate to their secretaries. It is probably no coincidence that it was found that as secretaries became more self-initiating in their work activities so they tended to become more efficient in terms of time lost 'waiting for work'. In addition, as secretaries became more self-initiating in their work activities so they also tended to be more internally motivated and satisfied with their jobs. A crucial spin-off for managers is that they are relieved of some of their low-level tasks and so in turn can also be more productive.

At the top of organizations, where secretaries traditionally operate in the one-to-one working relationship with their managers, secretaries carry out a variety of administrative tasks. These tasks all tend to stem from the secretary's gatekeeper position in her boss's communication network. Theoretically, this position gives the secretary almost complete control over the boss's communications. It also means that she has the opportunity to wield a great deal of influence. The extent to which she can influence matters, while primarily connected to the gatekeeper position she occupies, is also related to her personality and the number of years she has worked in the organization. The last point is important and frequently underestimated. Many top secretaries have well-developed personal contacts throughout the organization and have an extensive knowledge of the organization's activities – and sometimes even its secrets.

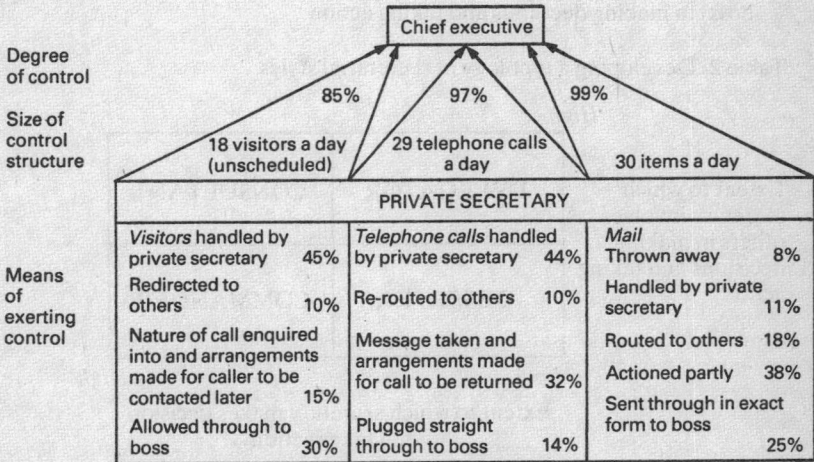

	Chief executive	
Degree of control		
	85% 97% 99%	
Size of control structure	18 visitors a day (unscheduled)	29 telephone calls a day	30 items a day

PRIVATE SECRETARY		
	Visitors handled by private secretary 45%	*Telephone calls* handled by private secretary 44%	*Mail* Thrown away 8%
Means of exerting control	Redirected to others 10%	Re-routed to others 10%	Handled by private secretary 11%
	Nature of call enquired into and arrangements made for caller to be contacted later 15%	Message taken and arrangements made for call to be returned 32%	Routed to others 18% Actioned partly 38%
	Allowed through to boss 30%	Plugged straight through to boss 14%	Sent through in exact form to boss 25%

Figure 2. *An empirical analysis of the top private secretary's gatekeeper position in the managing director's communication structure*

The amount of influence wielded by top secretaries in their gatekeeper positions is considerable. In my study it was shown that they had 85 per cent control over their bosses' visitors, 97 per cent control over their telephone calls, and 99 per cent control over their mail (see Figure 2). Interestingly, there were no significant relationships between the amounts of influence wielded in each of the three communication systems. This finding was also forcibly borne out where five private secretaries in different kinds of jobs were studied. These five secretaries differed quite markedly in terms of their perceptions of their primary roles, varying from allocator of the boss's time to filterer of the boss's information. This prompts the question of secretarial styles of working. Over the past twenty or thirty years a great deal of time and effort has been channelled into developing appropriate instruments for diagnosing managerial styles, and of confronting managers with their profiles as an aid to improving performance.

Perhaps now is the time to think of developing the concept of secretarial styles. In my own research it became increasingly evident to me that secretaries varied considerably in terms of how they dealt with their bosses' communications, particularly so in the bosses' absence. The two main dimensions along which secretaries differed were:

1. The degree to which the secretary herself makes decisions and takes action.
2. The degree to which the secretary involves others (i.e. apart from her boss) in making decisions and taking action.

Table 2. Developing a typology of secretarial styles

	High	
Extent to which secretary involves others in making decisions and taking action	DELEGATOR	CONSULTANT
	DESERTER	COMMANDER
	Low	
	Low	*High*

Extent to which secretary makes decision
and takes action

In Table 2 four styles can be identified and defined:

1. *Low* on the extent to which secretary makes decisions and takes action. and
   Low on the extent to which secretary involves others in making decisions and taking action.

This is the *deserter* style of managing. This type of secretary neither makes a decision herself nor allows others to make it for her. Her strategy is to 'shelve' decisions until the boss is in a position to make them himself. This style is exemplified by the secretary who acknowledges her boss's letters but leaves to him all the action to be taken on them.

2. *Low* on the extent to which secretary makes decisions and takes action.
   and
   High on the extent to which secretary involves others in making decisions and taking action.

This is the *delegator* style of managing. This type of secretary recognizes that decisions should be made quickly and delegates them to other executives. The reasons for delegating decisions to others may be that she does not want the responsibility for making the decision, she feels that other executives will make 'better' decisions, or she may feel that the decision is more appropriately handled by another executive. The responsibility of this type of secretary is to decide to whom to delegate the decision.

3. *High* on the extent to which secretary makes decisions and takes action.
   and
   Low on the extent to which secretary involves others in making decisions and taking action.

This is the *commander* style of managing. This secretary recognizes that decisions must be made quickly and feels that it is 'right' for her to make them. She turns to nobody for advice. This secretary may be seen to exert the most influence since decisions are kept entirely within her domain. This style is best exemplified by the secretary who attends meetings on behalf of her boss.

4. *High* on the extent to which secretary makes decisions and takes action.
   and
   High on the extent to which secretary involves others in making decisions and taking action.

This is the *consultant* style of managing. This type of secretary recognizes that decisions should be made quickly and feels that other executives can valuably contribute to the decision-making situation. Thus this type of secretary does not relinquish responsibility for the decision, like the delegator, but does consult other directors and executives in order to elicit advice or information. This style is exemplified by the secretary who sets up a retirement dinner in terms of choosing a hotel and menu in consultation with the personnel manager, who arranges the Press release with Public Relations, and when everything is tentatively decided sends memoranda to everyone involved to keep them informed as to what has happened.

Shifting from the main results of my research and my interpretations of them to the implications for organizations, I think four are worth highlighting. First, I think many managers (and possibly secretaries also) are unaware of their secretaries' potential. This will become all the more important when word processing has taken over the traditional mechanistic tasks associated with secretaries. Secondly, following on from that point, once new opportunities have been recognized whereby secretaries can operate more effectively (and more happily), then individual managers and secretaries need to work closely together to ensure they synchronize working styles. This means that the secretary should be aiming to complement her boss, rather than supplement or substitute for him. Training can play an important role here in developing such teamwork.

Thirdly, this analysis raises the issue as to how organizations use the secretarial role. The irrational bases of the role have been highlighted. At the top of organizations this is particularly true where secretaries, for example, may become 'redundant' when their bosses retire. Much more attention needs to be focused on strategically planning for secretaries and developing personnel policies in relation to them.

Lastly, this research prompts the issue of sex roles in organizations. As more women rise in the managerial hierarchy it is interesting to speculate as to whether the boss-secretary relationship on a female/female or female/male situation is the same as a male/female one. Discussions with a number of managers suggest that it is the female/female one that is likely to be the most problematic; perhaps this is because there is a sexual identification, which in turn poses threats to the relationship. The whole subject of the roles of the sexes needs to be surfaced and exposed in the light of the recent legislation and changing attitudes towards women in organizations.

These four implications, stemming directly from my own study of secretaries, are sufficient arguments for reappraising the role of secretaries. When consideration is given, however, to the radical repercussions of the introduction of word processing systems, then it is indeed timely to shake up the secretarial world.

Insecurity and Struggle in the Car Industry
H. Beynon

Reprinted with permission from Huw Beynon, *Working For Ford*, Penguin, 1973, pp. 153–9

In spite of publicity to the contrary, and talk of easy times on the dole, the life of a working man without work is often desperate. What most working men want of a job is that it offers them some security. Married men with children value a regular wage above all else in their work. Such men dominated the labour force at Halewood, and their stewards, we remember, consistently mentioned security as the most important aspect of a job.

The significance attached to job security becomes all the more important when placed alongside the fact that the production of motor cars has been characterized, almost above all else, by instability. The interdependence of the car plants, the proliferation of small, independent suppliers and market fluctuations have synthesized in the lay-off and short-time working. All of the Halewood workers I talked to had experienced a period of lay-off in the time that they had been employed in the PTA, and eight of the stewards and fifteen of the members mentioned instability of wages as a major drawback to working in a car plant. The Ford Motor Company in its move to Halewood attempted to handle fluctuations in the demand for cars through regulating the hours worked by a stable labour force, rather than by seasonal recruitment and lay-off. As a personnel officer put it: 'This has been a hire and fire industry for too long. What we have tried to do in this plant is to keep a stable labour force. Not to kick them out at the drop of a hat, but to try to give continuous production. That's the way to build up a loyalty to the Company.' Ford's operation of this policy made overtime for the workers on the line almost obligatory during periods of peak demand. The shop steward organization grudgingly accepted this, provided that 'proper notice' was given. However, the policy was no safeguard against the market. Market recession brought with it short-time working.

In the summer of 1965, for example, the Company introduced a period of short-time working in which the hourly paid employees in all its British plants were put on a four-day week. The joint steward committee of the three Halewood plants met to consider the situation and produced a three-page leaflet on short-time working which was distributed throughout the trade union movement. In this they explicitly attack the meaninglessness of 'continuity of employment' at Ford's – a concept which had been one of the keystones of management's negotiating position within the Halewood plants. To quote from the leaflet at length:

The trade unions agree to commit their members to a policy of a high amount of overtime during the peak spring and summer periods when schedules are running high, as opposed to the hiring of extra labour who would be fired when schedules drop. They also agree to 'mobility of labour', whereby men are constantly redeployed to maintain efficiency of plant operations, often with great inconvenience to the men concerned. Both these measures are patiently endured, and much cooperation is given. The reward for this is labelled 'continuity of employment', virtually a guaranteed five-day week, and yet the Ford Motor Company, the only company to have secured such agreements, is the first of the motor car manufacturers to cast its employees on to short-time working and imperil their livelihood with redundancy tactics.

The trade unions are also angry at the complete lack of prior consultation and ultimate refusal of negotiation. This, despite the case that can be made by ourselves for the non-necessity for the Ford Motor Company to resort to the drastic measure of introducing short-time working. Had the desire been great enough, here was a splendid opportunity for the Ford Motor Company to make a magnanimous gesture to its workpeople and at the same time reap tremendous benefits for its Halewood plant. This plant, so stricken of late with quality problems of the highest magnitude, from a multiplicity of sources, also in the throes of a mighty expansion programme, could have set its house in order and benefited immensely by merely cutting back its production schedules, at an estimated negligible cost to this wealthy company of some £300,000. This measure could have presented the Company with valuable time and an excess of labour which could have been utilized to successfully clear the back-log of defective vehicles in the selling line area, which at the time of writing, number a daily growing congestion of approximately 1300 cars. The workers in this plant are aware that schedules not intended for production until the October, November period, have already rolled off the production lines, the reason being that for some fifteen weeks prior to the annual summer shutdown, this plant had obviously greatly overproduced. During this period men were actually disciplined for failing to comply with excessive fifteen hours per week overtime demands, in addition to Saturday, which in the main were readily adhered to. Now we are callously confronted with 'short time'. After impressing upon us for months the importance of building 'quality' into the job, which responsibility we have readily accepted as it is our 'bread and butter' at stake, the Company now choose to ignore our suggestions to improve the situation. We are now facetiously informed that it is not Ford's intention to attempt to build Rolls-Royces thus indicating that once again it is the sole prerogative of the Ford Motor Company, to the exclusion of the trade unions, to determine the future of Halewood and its workers.

It has long been our contention that any move taken by this devious company, backed by the money, brains and resources it commands, has at least a double-edged benefit for itself in the outcome. In light of the above facts, therefore, we are more than suspicious that one of these benefits could be the new models or 'facelifts' as they are termed. Unlike its competitors, it is not the practice of the Ford Motor Company to stockpile unsold vehicles. The cutback in production effected by the reduction in the working week would therefore alleviate the problem of producing vehicles which would shortly become obsolete with the advent of the new models at the Motor Show. Instead of using a cutback then to rectify the atrocious quality of jobs currently produced and at the same time give value to the consumer, the Company choose the 'new model' benefit, to the detriment of its employees.

The committee then was severely critical of management's failure to enter into consultation with them before arranging the short-time working. In this, and in their treatment of quality and overproduction, the stewards raise the questions of market forces and managerial prerogatives. This strikes at the heart of power and politics within a car plant; and the history of the Halewood stewards' committee, and of motor car production generally, is played upon themes such as these. Again and again they occur. During the last six months of 1967 the production was halted in the PTA plant on two occasions and the workers were laid off and sent home. One of these lay-offs occurred in the middle of the night, the other at a more civilized hour. This one occurred at 2.30 on a Wednesday afternoon and lasted until the following Monday. During the previous weeks the number of cars in the storage parks around the estate had been increasing gradually. The plant was overproducing. The cars that were being produced weren't being sold and so on the Wednesday production was brought to a halt and five thousand men were laid off.

On that day I was in one of the material handling sections talking to the steward and a few of his members. After the dinner break several of the men reported a rumour that the plant was to shut down. The steward asked me if I had heard anything about a potential lay-off. I told him that I had been in the Personnel Department that morning and had talked with the convener during the dinner break but had heard no mention of a lay-off. By two o'clock the rumour was confirmed by the section supervisor and by half past two production was halted and the plant was empty and silent.

The men in the material handling section were angry about being laid off. They considered it to be wrong and unjustifiable that they should lose half their wages for the week.

It's always us. We *make* the fucking cars, we chase around here all day like fucking morons and as soon as anything goes wrong it's us who get the shit. They'll be all right up there in the office. They'll get their wages. It's always the same, we take the knocks for their stupidities. We've got kids and mortgages as well. They don't seem to consider that.

They didn't consider the lay-off to be unavoidable or a logical consequence of large-scale production. Rather that it was the fault of management. The management had made faulty predictions and had planned badly, but it was *they* (the workers) who suffered. Furthermore it was felt that once management had created the situation by way of their own errors, or inconsideration, they then proceeded to manipulate the situation to their own advantage.

All you've got to do is to watch the car park. You watch the car park and you'll get a pretty good idea of what will be going on inside this plant. When the park starts filling up a bit they start to push a bit. Little things like, but you haven't got to be a genius to work out what's happening. Whenever we have a strike here we have it when it suits Ford's. Never when it suits us.

The market then affects relationships in the plant. Economic fluctuations reveal themselves in the balance of power on the sections. Given this the actual decision to shut the plant becomes one of a number of strategies in the power game, and the game isn't over once the decision has been made. The men's biggest complaint was that they weren't given more than half an hour's notice of the lay-off.

They take a terrible attitude to the men on the shop floor here. I don't know how they behave as they do. They tell you nothing. Look, we've been laid off this afternoon and we haven't even been told that officially. They tell you nothing. All your pay can be stopped and they tell you nothing. That's typical of this firm.

Members of the Personnel Department explained the shortness of the notice by the fact that the decision didn't become inevitable until after the dinner break, and that right up to that time it was hoped that a lay-off could be avoided. Even if there is some truth in this explanation – even if the Halewood management were hoping for a reprieve from Warley – it doesn't adequately explain why the possibility of the lay-off was kept as such a closely guarded secret. The reason given for this secrecy by the stewards and several of the members I talked to, was simply that management was afraid of the consequences.

> They see it like this see: they're going to shut the plant down at 2.30 and by that time they'll have produced so many cars. Then they'll know how many cars they'll have to get rid of, they'll be able to work their numbers out. So what they're afraid of is what the blokes will do once they know that the plant is stopping. Nobody trusts anybody in this place. What they're afraid of is the lads saying 'sod you' and either going home or doing bad jobs. It happens you know. When there's trouble like this you often get lads going down the lines with pennies or knives, scraping the paint off the cars.

In a situation ridden with latent conflicts, the decision to lay men off can be likened to a declaration of war, and it is not only the workers who attempt to exact reprisals against the other side in this situation. Often a depressed demand for cars encourages a supervisor to settle some old scores with his steward or with men on his section who have given him trouble. On the material handling section, for example, a skeleton crew was to remain in the plant during the shutdown. The decision on the manning of the crew was left in the hands of the supervisor who announced that he intended to 'draw up a list'. The shop steward and several of the men on the section opposed this violently. One of them remarked that 'that bastard wants to fill the place with his "blue eyes"'. A group of the men wanted to crowd into the supervisor's office and 'have it out with him'. Jeff the steward persuaded them against this, arguing that it would be playing straight into his hands. Instead he went to see the supervisor and after a long furious argument it was agreed that the names of the skeleton crew would be picked out of a hat. Jeff said:

> That's what we've got to put up with here see. Big Joe wants to run this section his way all the time. He'd have us saluting if he could. We've managed to get it through to him that we're not having it, that we want some say in what goes on here, by standing up to him. But it only takes something like this for him to think he can start waving the whip again.

The men objected strongly to being laid off; they had children, hire purchase debts and mortgage repayments to make, and to lay them off with half an hour's notice wasn't right. The lay-off can be seen to produce a heightening of the critical attitudes that these men held towards the company. Turner in fact attributes the industry's strike record and the militant demands of its workers to the fact that men who possess a low moral commitment to their employer and who tend to be more like 'economic men' than other workers experience a very considerable instability of earnings. This example clearly reveals how the lay-off is structured into the world of the assembler, how the elements of instability, monotony and conflict over the wage-work bargain all cohere to produce situations of heightening conflict.

There seems to be some evidence that members of management in the motor industry are aware of the significance of insecurity of earnings. To quote Bob Ramsey, the Ford Motor Company's Director of Labour Relations:

Men have been too easily bounced out of this industry in the past. We have been much too inclined to lay people off. We don't lay people off now unless it's absolutely necessary. You've got to draw the line at some point. But we don't do it if we can help it. We feel that the track shouldn't be stopped by either side. If we keep laying people off they are quite right to say 'why should I worry about production?' We want to get away from all that.

It seems likely that statements such as these, if carried into practice, would have a considerable effect upon work relationships. Nevertheless, it is important to remember that it is not so much the lay-off *in itself* that has given rise to conflict in car plants, but the coherence of other elements in the work situation around the insecurity of employment. Furthermore it should also be remembered, as Ramsey indicates, that the market sets very definite limits upon the extent to which any motor car company in Britain can guarantee security of employment to its workers. Given the instability of motor car production and the severe dependency of the assembly plants upon the supply of components, it seems likely that even where fall-back rates have been negotiated, the assembly-line worker will continue to experience insecurity of earnings during the seventies.

This leads to a second, more general point. Apart from administering the selection of skeleton crews on sections where such crews are required the shop steward is virtually helpless in the face of a lay-off. Job insecurity brings home very clearly the fact that while a degree of job control may be established by workers through the shop stewards' committee, to work in a factory means to work, to a very large extent, on management's terms. While a shop steward may well find himself in a situation where he has to challenge management's authority on the shop floor, he is more often in situations where he is forced to play the game management's way. Another senior executive of the company saw it like this:

It's difficult to say what type of steward does best for his members. A militant may well force a few concessions, but we'll always be waiting to get them back or to make life a bit difficult for him. While a quiet, more reasonable bloke may be less dramatic he'll probably get more for his members because if he's in any trouble we'll help him out. We make concessions to him that we wouldn't make to the other bloke.

In the face of a powerful, prestigious adversary, the soft-sell is often the best form of attack and self-defence. This is particularly the case if you're meeting him on his home ground. It takes a lot of courage, conviction and confidence to stick out a confrontation with a manager in a posh office, desk, carpet, good suit. And you in your overalls. It's even more difficult if he flatters you and appears reasonable. Many stewards rarely get over this. For most of the time they play negotiations management's way. They learn the limits of the game and in the routine of their lives in the plant tend not to step outside them: 'You can't fight a battle every day.'

But sometimes they've got to. And this is what makes nonsense of most public debate on industrial relations. Too often it is assumed that if only the shop steward and his members had the 'right attitude', strikes and industrial conflict generally would be tremendously reduced. The only attitude that would ensure this is one of subservience and stupidity. For what the pundits fail to recognize, or choose to ignore, is that we live in a world dominated by capital and a capitalist rationality. In this world decisions are understood as 'investments', what makes a thing good or bad is the 'return' on it. Not it in itself. A good becomes a commodity valued not for what it can do, so much as the price it can be exchanged for. People too become commodities for the commodity world has men's labour at its centre. Spun round by capital and transformed into charts on office walls. 'Labour costs' – that sums it up. Production based upon the sale of labour power. By men, putting themselves at the disposal of other men for over half their lives. In order to live they preserve capital and their bondage. It is not perversity that makes assembly-line workers claim that they are treated like numbers. In the production of motor cars they *are* numbers. Numbers to be manipulated by people who are trained and paid to do just that. To cut costs, increase output. And lay men off. As a commodity, so is their power to labour treated. This is not to say that managers are necessarily inhumane people. Many managers, and employers, deeply regret the need to lay men off, to make them redundant. But they recognize that it is a need, a necessity dictated by market forces, for this necessity applies to them as well.

There are real lines of conflict within a car plant. A conflict that will be more obvious at one time than another. But it can never be assumed away, for it runs deeper than the 'cooperativeness' or otherwise of the assembly-line workers and their union representatives. It is underpinned by the very existence of wage labour and the market. While a shop steward may well attempt to play the game management's way, in many circumstances this attempt will be fraught with severe tensions.

Why is High Unemployment Still Somehow Acceptable?

W. W. Daniel

Reprinted with permission from *New Society*, 19 March 1981, pp. 495–7

The image that permeates general discussion of unemployment and the unemployed is the image of the rubbish dump.

Unwanted workers are discarded onto the tip. With each new wave of redundancies, more valuable workers are rejected. Each layer in the tip is of progressively higher quality. The discards quietly rot in the sump until 'an upturn in the economy' – when employers, their firms expanding, may come and see if any in the upper layers are still fit to work.

Different types of fear are expressed. Some people fear that those at the *top* of the pile of unemployed will rebel against their fate, and that increasing unemployment will result in extremist political action or general disorder. Indeed, they are surprised that the levels of unemployment we have already reached appear to have been so readily accepted.

The other main fear is that those at the *bottom* of the pile will lose any skills, habits of working or motivation to work, that they ever had.

This rubbish-dump image of unemployment contains a number of blatant misconceptions. These are:

1. That unemployment rises as a result of more people *becoming* unemployed.
2. That the rise in the number of people who are becoming unemployed is due to redundancies like those that will follow the closure of the Linwood car plant in Scotland.
3. That as unemployment rises, so the less able are joined by the more able among the unemployed 'stock'. (The 'stock' is technically defined as those people who are out of work at a particular moment, such as the day when the monthly count is taken.)
4. That the unemployed are an identifiable social and economic group which has permanence. This is the most fallacious and dangerous of these four misconceptions.

Reality is, in each case, the opposite of those propositions, and it is better to see unemployment as a *flow* of people into or out of work, rather than as a rubbish dump. It is more like a stream. For most people, unemployment is temporary; even now, they are back in work within three months. The *number* of people entering unemployment contributes little to the total: what matters is *how long* they stay unemployed. Three months, rather than two or one, makes an enormous difference. Most people become unemployed for reasons other than redundancy, the bankruptcy of their firm, or its closure.

Table 1. 1973 and 1980: the unemployed flow, stock and long-term unemployed

	1973	*1980*
Average monthly flow onto register	284,000	316,000
Average monthly flow off register	304,000	266,000
No. unemployed*	476,000	2,045,000
Rate of unemployment*	2·1%	8·7%
No. out of work for over 12 months (men only)	143,000	295,000

* Great Britain; seasonally adjusted; December
Note: Figures for the long-term unemployed are given for men only because, while the male figures are unsatisfactory, the female figures are meaningless.
Source: *DoE Gazette*; totals rounded

Let us look back over time. 1973 was the year of the Barber boom. It had the lowest level of unemployment in the 1970s: the December 1973 rate was 2.1 per cent. 1980 had the highest level of unemployment since the war: 8.7 per cent in December. And yet the monthly number of people entering unemployment in each of the two years was remarkably similar (see Table 1). In 1973, the average monthly influx in round figures was 284,000. In 1980, it was 316,000. The number of unemployed more than quadrupled, but the flow into unemployment went up by only 11 per cent.

Of course, increasing unemployment *is* associated with rising numbers of redundancies. But the increase in redundancies and more unemployment tend both to be consequences of a third influence – a fall in the demand for labour – rather than being directly and causally linked.

It is true that as unemployment rises, so a larger number of people become unemployed because of redundancy. But, at the same time, there is a fall in the number of people entering unemployment for other reasons. The other reasons are chiefly people quitting (though that notion is complex, and they often jump before they are pushed), and to a lesser extent dismissal for reasons other than redundancy. The total number flowing into unemployment is kept fairly constant over time because quitting is more frequent at times of low unemployment, and redundancy is more frequent at times of high unemployment.

Even with unemployment at its present level, however, only about one third of the people who enter unemployment do so as a result of redundancy. Many of those are technically redundant, in the sense that their jobs cease to exist; but they are not redundant in the common understanding of the term – which is represented by the Consett steelworks closure, the British Leyland rundown, and the reduction of manpower at Times Newspapers. A substantial minority come to the end of a fixed-term contract, or to the end of a job that they knew was not permanent when they took it.

Only about one in every four or five people now become unemployed because of classic redundancy. And even those are more likely to be because a small firm gets into trouble, rather than major corporations, nationalized industries or established employers having to close plants or cut their work force. Hardly any are displaced from the public services, despite much talk of cuts in public expenditure.

An important implication of the extent and form of redundancy among the unemployed is that, contrary to popular myth, very few have big redundancy payments. Less than one in every ten men who become unemployed gets a redundancy payment of £500 or more. Among the one in every twenty-five who get £2,000 or more, the bulk are nearing retirement age. So much for Mrs Thatcher's latest wheeze that the unemployed should start new businesses with their redundancy pay.

How long out of work?

The fall in the demand for labour affects the length of time people spend out of work when they become unemployed. Indeed, it is best to see the stock level as really a (rather unsatisfactory) measure of the length of time it takes people to find work. The current record level of unemployment is primarily due to record lengths of time out of work. All the same, about one third of the unemployed leave the register within about one month. (An accurate figure is impossible. We have no regular information on the length of time all those who join the register spend out of work.)

Obviously, the figure for the 'stock' of unemployed – which is the figure that the press headlines every month now – very heavily overrepresents the longer-term, relative to their number among the flow. Someone out of work for one year is certain to be included in a stock count on any day of that year. Someone out of work for six months has a 50:50 chance of being included. Someone out of work for only a week has only a 50:1 chance of being included.

Historically, we have had two sources of information on what are called 'completed flow durations' – i.e. the length of time it takes all those becoming unemployed to find a job. Neither has been satisfactory. One source has been estimates undertaken on an actuarial basis (i.e. assessing probabilities, as in insurance work). The second has been the experience of employees displaced by major redundancies: there have been about twenty separate studies of such people in Britain over the past quarter-century.

In the 1960s, actuarial estimates done in those years of low unemployment suggested that about half of those who became unemployed left the register within two weeks of joining it. The findings of empirical studies of the redundant were consistent with this. Another important finding was that a large proportion found work *before* they became unemployed.

By the mid-1970s, actuarial estimates suggested that about half the people becoming unemployed left the register within a month, and 90 per cent within six months. The 'stock' level of unemployment had doubled between the 1960s and the mid-1970s: but the median length out of work had only gone up from a fortnight to only a month.

At present, the best guess is that the median has risen to three months or so. We are facing record lengths of time out of work; hence record stock levels. But the bulk of people who become unemployed probably leave the register within three months. Combine that pattern with the characteristics of those who remain out of work longer, and you begin to see why the current level of unemployment appears to be so 'accepted' by the country at large.

Traditionally, the unemployed have been distinguished by their lack of skill, their low level of pay while in work, their age, and their poor health and physical fitness. Thus, nearly half of the men among the unemployed stock have tended to be classified as unskilled, but only 7 per cent of working men do unskilled jobs.

The rubbish-dump view of unemployment assumes that, as unemployment rises, so the more difficult to employ are joined by people who are readily employable, because they were in work before the increase in unemployment. In practice, that change does not occur; or, rather, it does not occur anything like as much as the simple model assumes.

The composition of the unemployed stock is the result of two processes of selection. The first determines *which* people become unemployed. The second determines *how long* they spend out of work.

At present, for instance, it remains the case that the unskilled and semi-skilled, and the low-paid, are markedly more likely to become unemployed than other categories. It is still true, too, that the unskilled, the low-paid, the older worker, and the less fit, spend longer out of work. So the long-term unemployed – and hence the unemployed – consist disproportionately of the unskilled, the low-paid, the older worker and the less fit.

Two mechanisms assist this outcome. The first is the scope to 'trade down', enjoyed (if that is the word) by younger, fitter, more skilled people who lose their jobs. That is to say, they can remain in employment by accepting jobs at lower levels. The skilled begin to accept semi-skilled and unskilled jobs – thereby, of course, further aggravating the position for semi-skilled and unskilled job seekers.

Secondly, there are changes in the definitions of old, unskilled and unfit on the part on employers. They begin to see people as being older workers at fifty-five, rather than at sixty; as being unskilled at a higher level of ability and aptitude; and as unfit when in better physical condition.

The rubbish-dump view of the unemployed leads to the expectation that, at higher levels of unemployment, the out-of-work will rot or rebel. It has led to all sorts of elaborate explanations why record levels of unemployment have so far proved acceptable. These have included suggestions that the work ethic and the inclination to work have been dying; that redundancy payments and benefits have made unemployment tolerable; or that the informal or 'black' economy has been taking over from the formal one.

But if you focus on the facts of the unemployed flow up to very recent times, the question hardly arises as to why present levels have been accepted by the public. There is no need for implausible and unsupported explanations.

For most of those who lose their jobs, unemployment is not, and does not become, a state or a condition. It is a hiatus. Their attention, activities and efforts are focused on one goal: getting back into work as soon as possible. In most cases, the length of time spent out of work has not yet reached the point where people stop concentrating on finding work, and start thinking about what else they might do to change a more permanent condition. Where unemployment does become a more permanent condition, the people affected are not the stuff of which rebels or rebellions are made. They tend to be old, unskilled or unfit.

All this, of course, is not to argue away the problem of unemployment; or to suggest that, if durations continue to increase as they have, they will still be tolerated.

The chief arguments against unemployment as a tool of public policy are that it is a waste of human potential, and that its costs as a policy are concentrated on the poorest and weakest sections of the community. Unemployment makes the wretched more wretched, and rising unemployment increases their number.

The growing extent of long-term unemployment is some measure of the extent of that wretchedness. The official figures are bad enough (as Table 1 shows). But they greatly understate the number of people who have been out of work for over a year, because of a technical quirk. Where periods of unemployment are interrupted by sickness, the official duration is counted from the point of re-registration afterwards. The number of people among the unemployed stock who have not worked for over a year, could be as much as a third higher than the official total of long-term unemployed.

The other point about present policies is this. The general level of unemployment has increased over the past fifteen years because the median length of time between, or before, jobs has risen from two weeks to three or four months. And for many people it can be much longer.

If present trends continue, it cannot be long before, in some places, what has traditionally been a hiatus, has to be faced as a lasting condition for a substantial number of younger and abler people. 'Acceptability' may not survive that.

Further Reading: **Work**

P. ABRAMS, *Work, Urbanism and Inequality*, Weidenfeld and Nicolson, 1968.

P. D. ANTHONY, *The Ideology of Work*, Tavistock, 1977.

W. BALDAMUS, *Efficiency and Effort*, Tavistock, 1961.

D. L. BARKER and S. ALLEN, *Dependence and Exploitation in Work and Marriage*, Longman, 1976.

T. BURNS and G. M. STALKER, *The Management of Innovation*, Tavistock, 1961.

B. CHIPLIN and P. SLOANE, *Sex Discrimination in the Labour Market*, Macmillan, 1976.

N. DENNIS, F. HENRIQUES and C. SLAUGHTER, *Coal is Our Life*, Eyre and Spottiswoode, 1956.

G. ESLAND and G. SALAMAN, *The Politics of Work and Occupations*, Open University Press, 1980.

M. FOGARTY, I. ALLEN and P. WALTERS, *Women in Top Jobs, 1968–79*, Heinemann, 1981.

A. FOX, *Beyond Contract: Work, Power and Trust Relations*, Faber, 1974.

P. HOLLOWELL, *The Lorry Driver*, Routledge and Kegan Paul, 1968.

E. JAQUES, *A General Theory of Bureaucracy*, Heinemann, 1976.

B. JONES, *Technology and the Future of Work*, Oxford University Press, 1982.

D. LOCKWOOD, *The Blackcoated Worker*, Allen and Unwin, 1958.

M. MANN, *Workers on the Move*, Cambridge University Press, 1973.

J. NICHOLS (ed.); *Capital and Labour*, Fontana Paperbacks, 1980.

J. M. PAHL and R. E. PAHL, *Managers and Their Wives*, Allen Lane, 1971.

R. SCASE and R. COFFEE, *The Real World of the Small Business Owner*, Croom Helm, 1980.

S. TERKEL, *Working*, Penguin, 1975.

J. TUNSTALL, *The Fisherman*, MacGibbon and Kee, 1962.

T. VEBLEN, *The Leisure Class*, Unwin, 1970.

A. WARMINGTON, T. LUPTON and C. GRIBBIN, *Organizational Behaviour and Performance*, Macmillan, 1977.

D. T. H. WEIR, *Men and Work in Modern Britain*, Fontana Paperbacks, 1973.

M. WEIR, *Job Satisfaction in Modern Britain*, Fontana Paperbacks, 1975.

J. WOODWARD, *Industrial Organization: Theory and Practice*, Oxford University Press, 1965.

5. Class

Almost all societies are stratified in some way; divided, that is, into strata such as 'castes', 'estates', 'classes', 'status groups', the members of which possess certain characteristics in common, which serve also to mark them off from members of other strata.

However, a stratification system is not an inevitable and unalterable feature of all societies, but is associated with the historical development of particular societies, and not therefore with underlying 'natural' or biological characteristics of the members of the strata. In fact a good deal of sociological research has been devoted to analysing the lack of concordance between distinctions of 'ability' or 'fitness' and the divisions · of rank and reward which form part of the structure of society.

Thus while stratification of some sort is a nearly universal feature of all societies, its particular forms vary from one society to another, and do not, therefore, guarantee any 'natural' or 'proper' division into ranks.

For Marx, social classes were rooted in the system of production, by the fact that different groups stood in different relations to the means of production, and had different interests in it. Thus economic factors were paramount in determining class membership and class interest. The two most clearly distinguished classes were the bourgeoisie and the proletariat. The former both owned and controlled the means of production, and had the opportunity to accumulate surplus wealth; the latter had only their labour power to sell.

Weber further distinguished stratification by social status, honour and prestige, and treated political power as an independent influence on stratification, rather than as a mere product of the class system. But the core of Weber's reformulation was to widen the notion of the economic basis of class formation, to include any situation where a market for scarce resources operated. **Dahrendorf** points to the emergence of other bases of social conflict, in particular the distribution of authority within 'imperatively coordinated associations'.

Within this broad framework a number of major themes have engaged the attention of sociologists.

Marx predicted that the class system would tend to polarize, and that the relative gap between bourgeoisie and proletariat would grow, leading to an exacerbation of class conflict and eventually to a revolutionary situation in which the ruling class would be overthrown. However, the last hundred years has seen the growth of many intermediate groups of salaried and professional workers – bureaucrats, managers, technicians and office workers, for instance – who are neither clearly bourgeois nor clearly proletarian, but represent a sort of 'new middle class'. Some of the possible consequences of this are examined by C. W. Mills in *White Collar*.

Again, although the wage levels and standards of living of manual workers have risen a good deal in absolute terms during this century, there is doubt about how the extent to which wealth has been redistributed from rich to poor.

There are many summary treatments of 'class' and 'stratification' in textbooks, and students will be familiar with these. A good general account is given in Noble's textbook *Structure and Change in Modern Britain*. Noble describes social stratification as 'the pattern of relationships which systematizes the inequalities of opportunities and reward between groups and tends to perpetuate these inequalities from one generation to the next'. He points out that many of the points of reference on which we tend to base our understandings and perception of the class structure are derived from studies of communities which have been affected, possibly altered irrevocably, by the historical processes of social change. Thus 'Westrigg', the community described by Littlejohn, may or may not be found by an observer today to be as Littlejohn described it. However, there is very little doubt that the analytic schema of class will be an essential part of that new report.

Social stratification, then, is connected with inequalities of opportunity and reward. The clearest expression of those inequalities comes from comparisons of income and wealth. It is tempting to believe that economic 'facts' are somehow separable from social structures, but this is not so. Economics are a consequence of the operation of a market for goods and services, and as such are conditioned by expectations, norms, wants, values and activities which are rooted in the social structure. So Goldthorpe and Lockwood analyse inflation in sociological terms, as does Gilbert later in this book. For these commentators inflation is primarily a phenomenon of rising expectations rather than of the autonomous operation of change in the money supply or price levels.

Since 1945 real incomes in the UK have doubled: there has been some redistribution, and the share of income achieved by the top 1 per cent fell from 11.2 per cent to 5.5 per cent. The redistribution, however, has not been from top to bottom. The share of the bottom 50 per cent has not changed dramatically. The distributional structure has become 'flatter', however: the ratio of the pay of a senior manager compared to that of a skilled worker has declined from 11 times to 2.4 times, and to that of an unskilled worker from 23 times to 3.2 times.

It is sometimes argued that there has been a 'levelling down' of incomes: certainly the structure of income inequality has altered since the Second World War. Fringe benefits and payments through the 'black economy' do alter the picture somewhat, but there is possibly less warrant for seeing these as class associated in the same way.

Wealth may be a different matter. It is still almost impossible to build wealth through savings from income. Most wealth is inherited. Income can only be readily translated into wealth through house-ownership; in particular, through taking advantage of the beneficial effect of inflation on mortgage debt.

Nonetheless, substantial inequalities between members of different social classes undoubtedly persist and can be measured. One of the most striking features of contemporary British society is that mortality rates and morbidity rates have not merely *not declined* as much as in other advanced industrialized societies, but may even be relatively deteriorating. Townsend writes, in his introduction to the **Black** report: 'Among the countries of the world having the lowest infant mortality Britain ranked eighth in 1960 but had slipped to fifteenth by 1978. In the latter year, the infant mortality rates for Hong Kong and Singapore were slightly lower than the rate for Britain.'

This is a disturbing enough picture, thirty years after the creation of the National Health Service, but from a sociological perspective, what is equally as significant is the persistence of the social class gradient which makes the standardized mortality rate twice as high for unskilled workers in social class V as for professional workers in social class I.

One of the dominant and widely accepted indicators of the effect of social class on health is the infant mortality rate, and it is here that the class effect is most striking. Moreover, 'The most marked class gradients are for deaths from accidents and respiratory disease, the causes . . . closely related to the socioeconomic environment.'

The diffusion of property-ownership, through shareholding, and the growth in size of many economic enterprises have provoked rethinking about the nature of the link between ownership and control. Burnham argued that the managers were destined to become a new ruling class because of their control of the means of production and their crucial position in governmental administrative organizations, but this notion is radically questioned by others who examine the interlinkages between shareholding and managerial power. The thesis that the 'logic of industrialism' inevitably produced a 'convergence' between the class structure of communist and non-communist societies at a similar stage of development is examined critically by Goldthorpe.

However, empirical analysis of the class structure depends on the availability of data relating, for instance, to the distribution of wealth or income.

Goldthorpe and Lockwood, in a classic statement, examine the consequences of the idea that the general improvements in the standard of living of manual workers, greater economic security and the underpinning provided by the Welfare State may have tended to produce an 'embourgeoisement' of the working class. The suggested consequences of this are, for instance, that 'affluent manual workers' would aspire to middle-class status, and become assimilated to it, would adopt middle-class patterns of consumption and recreation, and would tend to vote Conservative rather than Labour. The authors distinguish between the 'economic', 'normative' and 'relational' levels of stratification, and indicate that it is fallacious to argue a point at one level with data drawn from another level. Their overall conclusion is that 'middle-class' and 'working-class' patterns of life are clearly distinguishable and that it is thus premature, if not simply inaccurate, to talk of Britain being a 'middle-class' or 'one-class' society, or to argue that class is no longer a useful category for the sociological analysis of an affluent capitalist society.

The Marxist tradition of class analysis has always emphasized the distinction between classes as mere interest groupings (or 'class-in-itself') and classes as coherent groups which are coordinated and united for class action and conflict (or 'class-for-itself'). In order for differences of interest over the distribution of the surplus value created in the system of production to be transmitted into class action, two conditions have to be met. The group concerned had to generate a political structure which would transcend particular grievances and agitation and it had to achieve an understanding of its historical destiny and of its position in the class struggle as a whole. This consciousness of class becomes the basis of an ideology which supports and sustains the group.

Class consciousness implies a common awareness of exploitation among individuals who occupy a similar position in respect of the systems of control and distribution, of solid resources, and in particular of industrial property.

But this analysis has not always proved easy to interpret, in particular in relation to those who occupy intermediate positions in the industrial hierarchy, and especially clerks and other 'blackcoated workers'. Some sociologists have classified clerks as members of the propertied class, while others have argued that their interests are more akin to those of the proletariat, the group who neither own nor control societal resources.

Roberts and his co-authors produce further evidence which shows that, even among blue-collar workers, the components of class consciousness are by no means simple and straightforward. The workers in their study are not unaware of differences in class interest or of the facts of the authority structure at the work place, but nor do they necessarily subscribe to the ideology of the upper or managerial classes. Their perceptions of the communal basis of class consciousness may be limited to their own factory, area, or skill grouping, and their conceptions of alternative future may be constrained by a pragmatic reflection that, after all, tomorrow is more likely than not to be organized on lines similar to today's.

Braverman's book, recommended in Further Reading, has been quite influential in promoting a revised view of the changing class structure, in some ways closer to the original Marxist analysis. He agrees that the bourgeoisie has strengthened its hold over the proletariat because the increased sophistication of the technological basis of the organization of work has resulted in a deskilling of the work force as the qualities of skill, craft, endurance and initiative are transferred from men to machines. As the worker becomes deskilled, so his bargaining power is reduced and the cost of labour relative to other factors of production regresses. This process obtains for office workers equally as for manual workers.

Braverman's analysis is directed chiefly at the USA, but it is important to consider its implications for Britain also. He directs attention to the fact that the 'bourgeoisie' and 'proletariat' are not fixed aggregations of occupational groupings, but are analytical categories, and that 'classes are not fixed entities but rather ongoing processes, each in change, transition, variation'. Class is a historical process.

Mallet, like Braverman, writes from a Marxist perspective, but his conclusions are different. He sees the emergence of a new basis for class conflict as increasing automation strengthens the power of technicians and operatives in sophisticated plants. As this control over the actual technology of production is increased, so the possibility of conflict with the owners and financial managers is intensified.

Gallie's empirical study of workers in the French and the British oil refineries throws up basic differences between the French and British workers in the sample, associated with the historical and cultural experience of the working class in the two nations. Thus the French managers were confrontational, paternalistic and authoritarian, the British semi-constitutional, participative and cooperative. The union response to authority differed also, French unions perceiving themselves as agents of revolutionary change, the British as representatives of the interests of their members. Gallie concludes: 'The emergence of new forms of technology occurs, not in some form of social vacuum, but in societies with well established institutional arrangements, and with distinctive patterns of social conflict.'

It may be helpful in this context to refer to Bernstein's work reprinted in Chapter 3, in order to consider the way in which class factors actually work in concrete social situations. By conditioning and modifying the style of language which children develop and use, whole modes of apprehension of the external world and ways of relating to it are in fact determined. Thus a working-class child, brought up in what Bernstein calls a 'public language' style, may have a much more limited range of possibilities of relating to social situations and other people than has a middle-class child, who is equally fluent in a language style which encourages abstractness, symbolization and analysis, rather than description and personalization. Thus Bernstein draws attention to the importance of language in the process of the definition of social situations, and as the medium for the maintenance of distinctive class cultures.

Social mobility is often seen as an important feature of industrialized societies, and particularly of capitalist ones (although downward social mobility is only rarely studied). However, at any point in time in contemporary British society, most people remain throughout their careers in their class of origin. But changes in occupational structure, involving the expansion of professional, managerial and white-collar work and the decline of many traditional occupations, have led to an increase in the number of people in non-manual jobs, many of whom have parents who were themselves manual workers.

During the 1950s and 1960s it was widely believed that British society was becoming progressively more affluent and that class barriers were being consequentially eroded. As living standards rose, the chances of moving upwards in the social status hierarchy were improving. Every issue of the colour supplement seemed to carry a story of a hairdresser or fashion designer of lowly origins having been accepted, even lionized, in polite society. Is this pattern broadly correct?

Heath reviews a number of studies of social mobility. He points out that not all sociologists who have studied the problem have actually been looking at, or for, the same phenomena. He points out that 'how a sociologist decides to categorize occupations will reflect his own beliefs about the nature of the social world, his theoretical preferences and objectives, and his own moral or political attitudes and values . . .'

Despite these ambiguities, and the gross difference in approach between the functionalists who tend to favour a 'prestige' model of occupational hierarchy and the Marxists who see classes as real historical groups linked by relations of antagonism, some conclusions are possible.

Heath's review of the evidence is cautious and guarded: '. . . the data dispel any notion that Britain is a society in which an individual's class position is fixed at birth. . . . Does this mean that Britain has now become a relatively mobile, open society? The short answer is No.' This topic is, however, both technical and complex, and it is necessary to modify this summary judgement considerably. In the light of international comparisons, Britain appears to be similar to 'Canada, Denmark . . . Norway and the USA as middle-of-the-road societies with Australia and Sweden as relatively open, and Spain as relatively closed, given their levels and rates of industrialization'.

In interpreting these findings, we are led once again to the conclusion that society cannot easily be decomposed into bits, discrete entities with predictable causal effects on other parts of the structure. For societies comprise national political and cultural systems with an evolving history. This – more than the level or stage of industrialization – may condition the ensuing rates of social mobility.

Jamieson's paper further develops the theme. There are some important non-technical differences between the British and the American companies in his sample, the latter being more informal and employee-centred, and these differences relate to cultural rather than technological development.

Increasingly the crucial nexus in the process of social mobility is the educational system, and Turner, in a comparative study of the USA and Britain, reprinted in the previous edition of *The Sociology of Modern Britain*, shows how differences in the definition of the 'organizing norms', concerning the way in which upward social mobility should take place, are related to other features of society, and may predetermine which categories of the population are 'eligible' for mobility. Thus the USA exemplifies 'contest mobility' while the UK exemplifies 'sponsored mobility'.

It is often argued that the conditions of modern industrial organization, the growth in size of the enterprises, and the necessity for aspiring executives to move from place to place to obtain promotion have produced a class of managers who are highly mobile in geographical and social terms. This has consequences for social affairs as the 'spiralists' tend to withdraw from the local community, and to leave local leadership to the shopkeepers and small businessmen and others described by Watson as 'burgesses'.

Payne looks critically at some of these typologies, comparing Watson's burgesses and spiralists with Gouldner's 'locals and cosmopolitans' and Stacey's traditionalists and immigrants.

Finally, **Littlejohn** illustrates from a study of a rural parish in the south of Scotland how the factors of economic class, language style, and opportunities for social power operate in a concrete situation to produce a local class and status system. Although this system has several 'objective' features, it remains flexible and open to definition in different ways by its members, so that no single value is seen as predominant, or fundamental.

A social class is neither a mere category arbitrarily defined by myself on the basis of one or two 'characteristics' such as property-ownership, nor is it a group in the strict sense of the term as implying clear-cut boundaries and a constitution laying down a limited set of relationships among its members. 'A class is rather for its members one of the major horizons of all social experience – an area within which most experience is defined' (Littlejohn).

The Authority Structure of the Industrial Enterprise
R. Dahrendorf

Reprinted with permission from Ralf Dahrendorf, *Class and Class Conflict in Industrial Society*, Routledge and Kegan Paul, 1959

One social institution to which Marx devoted a great deal of attention has survived capitalist society: the industrial enterprise. Trivial as this statement may sound, there is no reason to avoid it. There can be no doubt that many changes have occurred in the century between 1850 and 1950 both outside and inside the industrial enterprise. It may appear meaningless to identify the small factory of a capitalist entrepreneur in 1850 with the large corporation of 1950 in terms of productive capacity and number of employees, technical perfection and spatial extension, complexity of organization and conditions of work. However, although these changes are by no means irrelevant for conflict analysis, we have to start with a more fundamental relation which remains, or has remained so far, unchanged. In capitalist as in post-capitalist society, in the Soviet Union as in the United States, the industrial enterprise is an imperatively coordinated association. Everywhere it displays those conditions of social structure which give rise to social conflict in terms of class theory. Wherever there are industrial enterprises, there are authority relations, latent interests, quasi-groups, and (industrial) classes.

In dealing with the formal organization of the enterprise, a distinction is usually made between the 'functional' aspect of the division of labour and the 'scalar' aspect of super- and subordination. Both are functionally necesssary; they are complementary aspects of industrial organization. One of the secrets of the increase of productivity by mechanized factory production lies in the subdivision of the total process of production into cooperative detail processes. Every one of these is equally indispensable for the accomplishment of the total process. From a strict functional point of view, the unskilled labourer, the foreman, and the executive stand on one level; the enterprise cannot function if one of these positions remains vacant. However, for purposes of the organization, coordination, and leadership of such subdivided detail processes a principle other than the division of labour is needed. A system of super- and subordination guarantees the frictionless operation of the total process of production – a system, in other words, which establishes authority relations between the various positions. The incumbents of certain positions are endowed with the right to make decisions as to who does what, when, and how; the incumbents of other positions have to submit to these decisions. Nor are the commands given and obeyed in the industrial enterprise confined to technical work tasks: hiring and firing, the fixing of wage rates and piecework systems, introduction and control of disciplinary regulations, and other modes of behaviour are part of the role expectations of the incumbents of authority positions in the enterprise and give rise, therefore, to its scalar or authority structure. For the industrial worker, the labour contract implies acceptance of a role which is, *inter alia*, defined by the obligation to comply with the commands of given persons. Industrial authority does not, of course, involve the subordination of total persons under other persons; it is restricted to persons as incumbents of given, limited roles; but it is therefore no less authority, i.e., a 'probability that a command with a given specific content will be obeyed by a given group of persons'. Although, in other words, the foreman cannot legitimately command his workers to collect stamps in their leisure time, there exist in the industrial enterprise, within a definable range, authority relations in the strict sense of class theory.

Since the industrial enterprise has an authority structure and is therefore an imperatively coordinated association, we are entitled to assume that the incumbents of positions of domination and subjection within it are united in two conflicting quasi-groups with certain latent interests. This inference follows from the model of class formation. If the theory of group conflict proves useful, its validity is as universal as the imperative character of the enterprise itself. Wherever there are industrial enterprises, there is a quasi-group of the incumbents of roles of domination, the latent interests of which are in conflict with those of a corresponding quasi-group of incumbents of roles of subjection.

In disputes between trade unions and employers, an argument is often put forward by the employers which has found its way into sociological literature also. Employers like to assert that they represent the interests of the total enterprise whereas the unions merely stand for partial interests. It might appear that there is no convincing refutation of this argument. However, in the light of the theory of group conflict it becomes apparent what the basis of this argument is and why it is ideological, i.e., demonstrably false – a fact which is of considerable significance for class analysis. We have seen earlier that the interests of a ruling group assume, as ruling interests, the character of accepted values in a unit of social structure. They are a reflection of the real structure, the existing conditions, although these are upheld and guaranteed by the rule of but one class. They might therefore appear as binding for all elements of a unit of social structure. Yet the theory of class exposes the fact that the existing conditions are themselves in a sense merely 'partial', that they exist by virtue of the authority of one part, or class. As the prime minister is both representative of the whole nation and exponent of the majority party, the entrepreneur is both 'the enterprise' and one partial interest in the conflicts generated by its structure – depending on the image of society underlying our analysis. In this sense, 'conservation' and 'modification' of a *status quo* are, from the coercion point of view, strictly equivalent 'partial' interests the conflict of which can be conceived as one of the determinants of the dynamics of social structure.

Two objections are frequently raised these days against the universal reality of conflicting latent interests in industry. They are easily disposed of, yet it may further clarify the issue to discuss them briefly. The first of these objections is based on the thesis that what is often called the 'bourgeoisification of the proletariat', i.e., the improvement of the economic situation of industrial workers, makes the assumption of continuing conflict unreasonable and, indeed, nonsensical. If, it is argued, the workers are no longer proletarians, if they do not live in poverty and suppression, they no longer have reason to revolt against their employers. The public of post-capitalist societies realizes, with baffled surprise, the continued reality of strikes and yet insists, at the same time, on the theory that industrial conflict has lost its causes and issues where the standard of living is high. This paradox testifies to a remarkable consistency of conviction, if not to insight. The theory of group conflict does not postulate any connection between class conflict and economic conditions. For the emergence of social conflicts the standard of living of their participants is in principle irrelevant, for conflicts are ultimately generated by relations of authority, i.e., by the differentiation of dominating and subjected groups. Even if every worker owns a car, a house, and whatever other comforts of civilization there are, the root of industrial class conflict is not only not eliminated, but hardly touched. The fact that economic demands may provide the substance (a substance situationally specific and in that sense incidental) of manifest interests must not give rise to the erroneous notion that satisfaction of these demands eliminates the causes of conflict. Social conflict is as universal as the relations of authority and imperatively coordinated associations, for it is the distribution of authority that provides the basis and cause of its occurrence.

A second objection against the assumption of the persistence of a latent conflict of interest consists in the thesis that the replacement of capitalists by managers has removed the basis of industrial class conflict. Upon closer inspection, this thesis, too, proves untenable. As we have seen, latent interests can be conceived of as quasi-objective role expectations. They are held not by persons, but by positions, or by persons only insofar as they occupy certain positions. If a person occupies a position of domination in an enterprise, it is irrelevant in principle whether his authority is based on property, election by a board of directors, or appointment by a government agency. For the latent interests of the incumbents of positions of authority, their incumbency of these positions is the sole significant factor. Although, therefore, their modes of recruitment and bases of legitimacy make for significant differences between capitalist and manager in other contexts, their authority positions in the enterprise are alike, and their places in conflicts of interest identical. For the explanation of group conflict, the factual relations of authority are the crucial factor. To this extent I agree with Burnham's thesis and with Marx's and Renner's analysis of joint-stock companies; the replacement of functioning owners or capitalists by propertyless functionaries or managers does not abolish class conflict, but merely changes its empirical patterns. Independent of the particular personnel of positions of authority, industrial enterprises remain imperatively coordinated associations the structures of which generate quasi-groups and conflicting latent interests.

The Pattern of Present Health Inequalities
D. Black, J. N. Morris, C. Smith and P. Townsend

Reprinted with permission from the *Black Report*, HMSO, 1980, pp. 51–64

Inequalities in health take a number of distinctive forms in Britain today. This chapter examines the pattern of inequalities according to a number of criteria: the relationships between gender and mortality, race and mortality, regional background and mortality, plus a range of measures of ill-health. But undoubtedly the clearest and most unequivocal – if only because there is more evidence to go on – is the relationship between occupational class and mortality.

Occupational class and mortality

Every death in Britain is a registered and certified event in which both the cause and the occupation of the deceased or his or her next of kin are recorded. By taking the actual incidence of death among members of the Registrar General's occupational classes and dividing this by the total in each occupational class it is possible to derive an estimate of class differences in mortality. This shows that on the basis of figures drawn from the early 1970s, when the most recent decennial survey was conducted, men and women in occupational class V had a two-and-a-half times greater chance of dying before reaching retirement age than their professional counterparts in occupational class I (Table 1, page 329). Even when allowance is made for the fact that there are more older people in unskilled than professional work, the probability of death before retirement is still double.

What lies behind this gross statistic? Where do we begin to look for an explanation? If we break it down by age we find that class differences in mortality are a constant feature of the entire human life-span (see Figure 1). They are found at birth, during the first year of life, in childhood, adolescence and adult life. At *any* age people in occupational class V have a higher rate of death than their better-off counterparts. This is not to say that the differences are uniform; in general they are more marked at the start of life and, less obviously, in early adulthood.

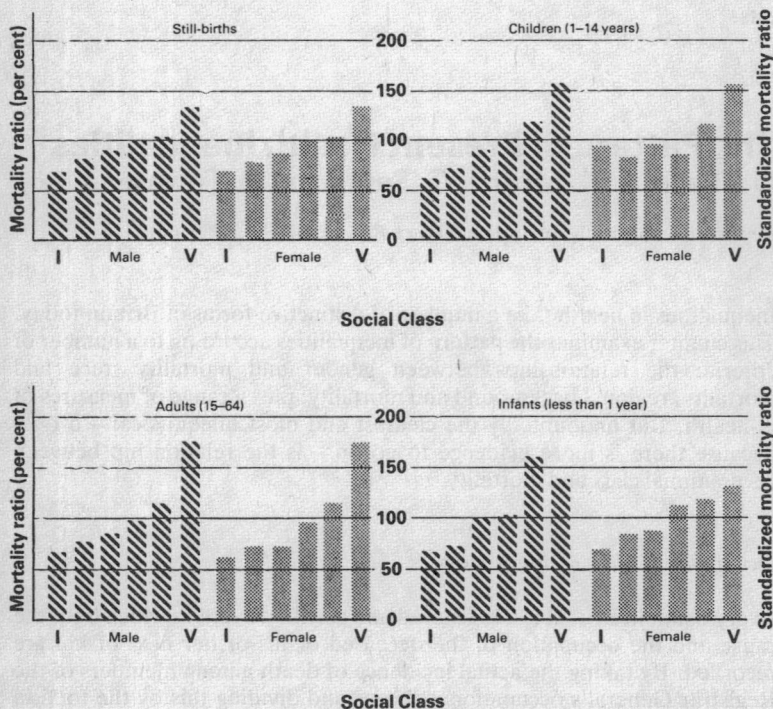

Figure 1. *Mortality by occupational class and age. Relative mortality (%) is the ratio of rates for the occupational class to the rate for all males (or females).* (Source: *Occupational Mortality 1970–72*, HMSO, 1978, p.196)

At birth and during the first month of life the risk of death in families of unskilled workers is double that of professional families. Children of skilled manual fathers (occupational class IIIM) run a 1.5 times greater risk.

For the next eleven months of a child's life this ratio widens still further. For the death of every one male infant of professional parents, we can expect almost two among children of skilled manual workers and three among children of unskilled manual workers. Among females the ratios are even greater.

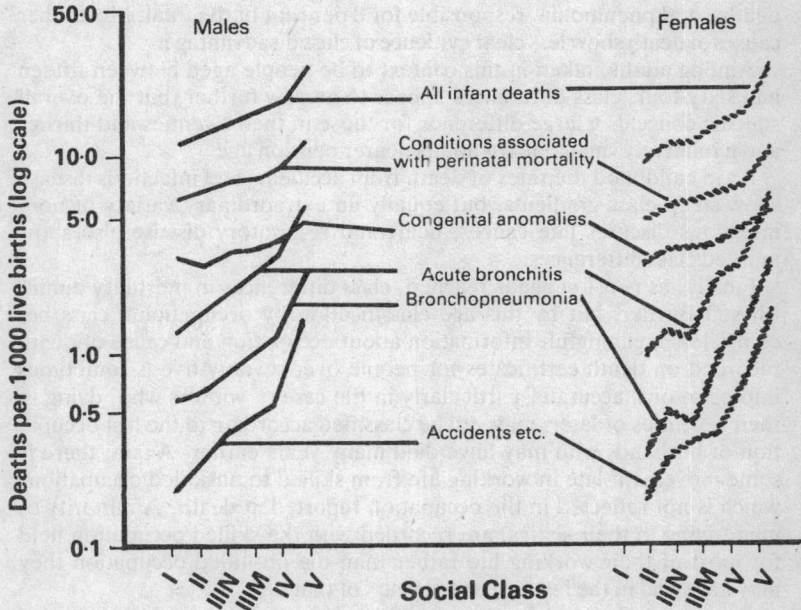

Figure 2. *Infant mortality by sex, occupational class and cause of death.* (Source: *Occupational Mortality 1970–72,* HMSO, 1978, p.158)

If we measure this against different causes of death – Figure 2 – we find that the most marked class gradients are for deaths from accidents and respiratory disease, two causes which we will show later to be closely related to the socioeconomic environment. Other causes, associated with birth itself and with congenital disabilities, have significantly less steep class gradients.

Between the ages of one and fourteen relative class death rates narrow, but are still clearly visible. Among boys the ratio of mortality in occupational class V as compared with I is of the order of 2 to 1, while among girls it varies between 1.5 and 1.9 to 1.

Once again the causes of these differences can be traced largely to environmental factors. Accidents, which are by far the biggest single cause of childhood deaths (30 per cent of the total), continue to show the sharpest class gradient. Boys in class V have a ten times greater chance of dying from fire, falls or drowning than those in class I. The corresponding ratio of deaths caused to youthful pedestrians by motor vehicles is more than 7 to 1. Trailing somewhere behind this, but also with a marked class gradient, are infectious and parasitic diseases, responsible for 5 per cent of all childhood deaths, and pneumonia, responsible for 8 per cent of the total. Most other causes of death show less clear evidence of class disadvantage.

Among adults, taken in this context to be people aged between fifteen and sixty-four, class differences appear to narrow further, but the overall statistic conceals a large difference for those in their twenties and thirties and a relatively small one for adults nearer pension age.

As in childhood the rates of death from accidents and infectious disease show steep class gradients, but equally an extraordinary variety of non-infectious diseases like cancer, heart and respiratory disease also show marked class differences.

Finally, as pension age is reached, class differences in mortality diminish still further, but by this age classification by occupational class becomes less meaningful. Information about occupation and cause of death recorded on death certificates for people over seventy-five is sometimes imprecise or inaccurate, particularly in the case of widows who, dying in their seventies or later, may still be classified according to the last occupation of husbands who may have died many years earlier. Again, there is some movement late in working life from skilled to unskilled occupations which is not reflected in the occupation reported at death. A minority of men, dying in their sixties, are recorded with the skilled occupation held for most of their working life rather than the unskilled occupation they may have had in the last five or ten years of that life.

Occupational class may therefore be a weak indicator of lifestyle and life chances over lengthy periods. Bearing this in mind, data about the mortality of men aged sixty-five to seventy-four in 1970/72 showed that there were very large differences between some groups of manual and non-manual workers. For example, the mortality ratio for former miners and quarrymen was 149, gas, coke and chemical makers 150, and furnace, forge, foundry and rolling mill workers 162, compared with administrators and managers with a ratio of 88 and professional, technical workers and artists with a ratio of 89 (OPCS, 1978, p. 107).

Now let us look at some other criteria for dividing the population which have a bearing on any attempt to describe the 'structure' of health among the population.

Sex differences in mortality

The gap in life expectancy between men and women is one of the most distinctive features of human health in the advanced societies. As Table 1 indicates, the risk of death for men in each occupational class is almost twice that of women, the cumulative product of health inequalities between the sexes during the whole lifetime. It suggests that gender and class exert highly significant but different influences on the quality and duration of life in modern society.

Table 1. Death rates by sex and social (occupational) class (15–64 years) (rates per 1000 population, England and Wales, 1971)

Social (occupational) class	Males	Females*	Ratio M/F
I (Professional)	3·98	2·15	1·85
II (Intermediate)	5·54	2·85	1·94
IIIN (Skilled non-manual)	5·80	2·76	1·96
IIIM (Skilled manual)	6·08	3·41	1·78
IV (Partly skilled)	7·96	4·27	1·87
V (Unskilled)	9·88	5·31	1·86
Ratio V/I	2·5	2·5	

* In this table women with husbands have been classified by their husband's occupation, women of other marital statuses are attributed to their *own* occupational class.
Source: *Occupational Mortality 1970–72* (microfiches and 1978, p. 37).

It is also a gap in life expectancy which carries important implications for all spheres of social policy, but especially health, since old age is a time when demand for health care is at its greatest and the dominant pattern of premature male mortality adds the exacerbating problem of isolation for many women.

Although attempts have been made to explain the differences between the sexes, comparatively little systematic work exists on the aetiology of the mortality and morbidity differences between men and women and much remains to be disentangled. Women suffer uniquely from some diseases and it would be wrong, for example, to assume too readily that all wives share the same living conditions or even standards as their husbands. Some men have the advantage, for instance, not only of a preferential diet at home but subsidized meals at work. Where both husband and wife are in paid employment, the meals they get in the day, as well as working conditions and the nature of the work, may be radically different. There is a great deal more research to be undertaken to sort out these various influences.

Regional differences in mortality

Mortality rates also vary considerably between the regions which make up the United Kingdom. Using them as an indicator of health, the healthiest part of Britain appears to be the southern belt below a line drawn across the country from the Wash to the Bristol Channel (see Table 2). This has not always been true. In the middle of the nineteenth century, the south-east of England recorded comparatively high rates of death, while other regions like Wales and the far north had a rather healthier profile.

Table 2. Regional variations in mortality

Standard region	SMR: standardized for	
	Age	Age and class
Northern, Yorkshire and Humberside	113	113
North-west	106	105
East Midlands	116	116
West Midlands	96	94
East Anglia	105	104
South-east	90	90
South-west	93	93
Wales I (South)	114	117
Wales II (North and West)	110	113
England and Wales	100	100

Source: *Occupational Mortality 1970–72*, p. 180.

Race, ethnicity and health

Another important dimension of inequality in contemporary Britain is race. Immigrants to this country from the so-called New Commonwealth, whose ethnic identity is clearly visible in the colour of their skin, are known to experience greater difficulty in finding work and adequate housing. Given these disabilities it is to be expected that they might also record rather higher than average rates of mortality and morbidity.

This hypothesis is difficult to test from official statistics, since 'race' has rarely been assessed in official censuses and surveys. Moreover it is far from clear what indicator should be utilized in any such assessment – skin colour, place of birth, nationality – and the most significant may depend on the precise issue of interest.

The pattern of social and economic disadvantage experienced by black Britons is connected with occupational class and is reflected in the working of the labour market. But other factors may also be important, and at least amongst adult males the variables of occupational class and race do not compound one another in a linear fashion as far as health is concerned, when place of birth is used as a means of measuring race. The age standardized mortality ratios of immigrant males compares favourably with their British-born equivalents in occupational classes IV and V, but less so higher up the scale in classes I and II (see Table 3). The interpretation of these ratios is made difficult at the higher end of the occupational scale because they are based on small numbers.

Table 3. Mortality by country of birth and occupational class (S M R) (males 15–64)

Country of birth	I	II	IIIN	IIIM	IV	V	All
India and Pakistan	122	127	114	105	93	73	98
West Indies	267	163	135	87	71	75	84
Europe (including UK and Eire)	121	109	98	83	81	82	89
UK and Eire (including England and Wales)	118	112	111	118	115	110	114
England and Wales	97	99	99	99	99	100	100
All birth places	100	100	100	100	100	100	100

Source: *Occupational Mortality 1970–72*, pp. 186–7.

In the poorer occupational classes, where the standardized mortality ratio is based on larger numbers of deaths, men born in India, Pakistan or the West Indies seem to live longer than their British-born counterparts. It should be remembered, however, that the percentage of workers in class V among the British-born is less than 7 while the equivalent percentage of those born in, for example, India and Pakistan is 16. In addition, of course, the average British-born male classified as an unskilled manual worker is likely to be older than his foreign-born counterpart and is more likely to have acquired this low occupational status after a process of downward social mobility associated with failing health.

This rather favourable comparison between immigrant and British-born males may also reflect the underlying tendency for migrants to select themselves on the grounds of health and fitness. Men and women prepared to cross oceans and continents in order to seek new occupational opportunities or a new way of life do not represent a random cross-section of humanity. A better comparison for exploring health inequality would ideally involve second- or third-generation immigrants, but these are the very groups that are difficult to trace for statistical purposes. What little evidence that has been accumulated, however, does suggest that the children of immigrants do suffer from certain specific health disabilities related to cultural factors such as diet or to their lack of natural immunity to certain infectious diseases. Studies based on small samples of immigrant children have pointed to the possibility of higher-than-average morbidity associated with material deprivation, but the evidence is scarce and somewhat inconclusive and needs to be augmented by further research.

Housing tenure and mortality

Because of its bearing on our discussion of explanations for inequalities in health, it should also be noted that when the population is divided into housing tenure groups – owner-occupiers, private tenants and local-authority tenants – class gradients vary considerably (Table 4). People who live in houses which they own have lower rates of mortality than those who rent their homes from private landlords who in turn have lower rates than those who are tenants of local authorities. Housing tenure is, of course, one possible measure of the accumulation by an individual or family of fixed property or assets; it also says something about familial attitudes and priorities. Here it can be shown that this variable shows a very close relationship with the risk of premature death.

Table 4. Mortality by tenure and class (S M R) (males 15–64 years)

Class	Tenure		
	Owner-occupied	Privately rented	Local authority tenancy
I	79	93	99
II	74	104	99
IIIN	79	112	121
IIIM	83	99	104
IV	83	100	106
V	98	126	123

Source: unpublished data, Medical Statistics Division, OPCS, preliminary results of the LS 1970–75.

Illness and class

Morbidity data provide a second way of looking at the pattern of class inequalities in health. Moreover there is a sense in which the extent of ill-health in a social group is a better indicator of its health *vis-á-vis* another group than is the relative mortality rate. Morbidity data are available from a variety of studies and *ad hoc* surveys and are of two kinds, though both are scant at the national level. The first is based on examination of, or symptom identification in, the social group as a whole or in a properly selected sample. An approach of this kind has sometimes been used in the attempt to assess the prevalence of specific diseases within research studies. Social or occupational class is sometimes noted.

The second kind of data derives from analysis of medical consultation and hospital admission rates. But not only do we have few data of this kind by occupational class, there is the disadvantage that rates reflect not only the incidence of disease but also the process by which an individual defines himself (or herself) as ill, seeks medical attention and has his (or her) definition confirmed or legitimated by medical authority. Since we know that there are class-related differences in the propensity of an individual with a given set of symptoms to go for treatment or attention, as well as in the subsequent medical response, we recognize that data of this kind cannot be interpreted clearly.

Nevertheless data from both these sources confirm, broadly speaking, the picture which mortality data have already indicated.

An example of the first sort of morbidity data is provided by a survey of the prevalence of chronic bronchitis in Great Britain. Ninety-two GPs, distributed throughout the country, were asked to select similarly sized age/sex-stratified random samples from their practice lists. All were to be aged between forty and sixty-four. In terms of GP diagnosis, the percentage suffering from chronic bronchitis rose with descending class from 6 per cent in class I to 26 per cent in class V. Bronchitis is diagnosed from symptoms and these can vary from doctor to doctor, but even when a more rigorous 'standard diagnosis' was used, the picture was broadly the same.

GPs have also recorded details of consultations. Results from one study showed that consultation rates for each of a wide range of conditions for males, females and children, classified according to occupational class, are of considerable interest though not easy to interpret. The findings were summarized in the following scheme, where + indicates morbidity above and − below average:

	agricultural occupations	non-manual occupations	manual occupations
psychoneurotic disorders	−	+	−
cardio-vascular disorders	−	+	−
respiratory disorders	−	−	+
gastric disorders	−	−	+
arthritis/rheumatism	−	−	+
injuries	−	−	+

Another way of looking at the results is by comparing mortality ratios (by class and disease) with consultation ratios, as in Table 5. If we compare the class gradients on the left-hand side of the table with those on the right-hand side we find that with some exceptions (for instance coronary disease and diabetes) the gradients on the right-hand side are steeper. This suggests more severe sickness or smaller likelihood of treatment with declining class.

Table 5. Comparison of distribution of standardized patient consultation ratios (males 15–64, May 1955–April 1956) and standardized mortality ratios (males 20–64, 1949–53) by class: selected conditions

	SPCR class					SMR class				
	I	II	III	IV	V	I	II	III	IV	V
Respiratory tuberculosis	102	85	105	102	91	58	63	102	95	143
Malignant neoplasms	75	111	94	91	111	94	86	104	95	113
Diabetes mellitus	89	123	100	108	74	134	100	99	85	105
Coronary disease/angina	89	108	102	89	93	147	110	105	79	89
Hypertension	120	127	99	70	89	123	106	103	83	101
Influenza	83	82	103	113	107	58	70	97	102	139
Pneumonia	70	87	90	121	132	53	64	92	105	150
Bronchitis	49	70	99	118	146	34	53	98	101	171
Gastric and duodenal ulcer	48	78	99	88	116	68	76	101	99	134

Source: *Logan and Cushion 1960*, p. 16.

This tends to be brought out too in more recent national studies of self-reported illness, like the General Household Survey. Thus, the rates of 'limiting long-standing illness' (as defined in the GHS) rise with falling socioeconomic status and are three times as high among unskilled manual males and females as they are among their professional counterparts (see Table 6).

It will be seen however that the comparable ratios for 'restricted activity' or acute illness are much smaller, and generally resemble the ratios for consultation rates. However, inequalities are smaller in childhood and larger in middle age. Rates of sickness absence from work are also widely unequal. Thus, a special inquiry into the incidence of incapacity for work found marked class gradients for a number of diseases. When the number of employed males beginning a spell of incapacity was expressed per 1000 in each occupational class, standardized for age, there were, for disease of the respiratory system, 91 in combined classes I and II and 177 in class V. For influenza the figures were 39 and 70, bronchitis 15 and 57 and arthritis and rheumatism 7 and 40 (Ministry of Pensions, 1965).

Table 6. Sickness and medical consultation in early adulthood (average rates per 1000 population 1971–1976)*

Socioeconomic group	Limiting long-standing illness		Restricted activity (in two-week period)		Consultations	
	males	*females*	*males*	*females*	*males*	*females*†
Professional	79	81	78	89	105	134
Managerial	119	115	74	83	113	137
Intermediate	143	140	83	95	116	155
Skilled manual	141	135	87	86	123	147
Semi-skilled manual	168	203	87	102	131	160
Unskilled manual	236	257	101	103	153	158
Ratio unskilled manual to professional	3·0	3·2	1·3	1·2	1·5	1·2

* England and Wales for 1971–2.
† 1972–6.
Source: *General Household Survey 1976*, HMSO, 1978.

Summary

There are marked inequalities in health between the social classes in Britain. In this chapter mortality rates are taken as the best available indicator of the health of different social, or more strictly occupational classes and socioeconomic groups. Mortality tends to rise inversely with falling occupational rank or status, for both sexes and at all ages. At birth and in the first month of life twice as many babies of unskilled manual parents as of professional parents die, and in the next eleven months of life four times as many girls and five times as many boys, respectively, die. In later years of childhood the ratio of deaths in the poorest class falls to between one and a half and two times that of the wealthiest class, but increases again in early adulthood before falling again in middle and old age.

A class 'gradient' can be observed for most causes of death and is particularly steep for both sexes in the case of diseases of the respiratory system and infective and parasitic diseases.

Other aspects of class than merely occupational category have an impact on health, although few data relating mortality to education and income, for example, are available. This is however illustrated by evidence that in all classes owner-occupiers have lighter mortality than those paying rent.

Available data on (self-reported) morbidity tend to reflect those on mortality, though inequalities between occupational classes are more pronounced, and the gradients more uniform, in the case of chronic sickness than in the case of acute or short-term ill-health.

Affluence and the British Class Structure
J. H. Goldthorpe and D. Lockwood

Reprinted with permission from John Goldthorpe and David Lockwood, 'Affluence and the British Class Structure', *Sociological Review*, vol. 11, no. 2, new series, July 1963, pp. 133–63

Until relatively recently, most discussion of change in the British class structure has been carried on in terms of (1) shifts in the occupational distribution of the population, (2) the reduction of extreme economic inequalities, and (3) the amount and rate of intergenerational social mobility.

(1) Writers such as Cole, for example, have documented the process whereby technological advance and economic growth have greatly increased the importance of clerical, administrative, managerial and professional employments, and it has often been noted how in this way the overall shape of the British class structure underwent significant modification from the mid-nineteenth century onwards. A broad range of 'intermediate' strata emerged to bridge the gap between the 'two nations', perceived alike by Engels and Disraeli, of the manual wage workers and the major property-owning groups.

(2) It has been shown how also from the mid-nineteenth century, and again largely in consequence of continuing material progress, the national distribution of income and wealth slowly became somewhat less skewed; and how, eventually, with the aid of developing social welfare services, the problem of mass poverty was overcome. In this way then, it may be said, the span of social stratification in Great Britain was reduced; in other words, the range of differentiation, in basic economic terms at least, became less extended.

(3) It has been frequently pointed out that as a result of the growing diversification of the occupational structure, the educational system, rather than kinship or 'connection', has come to act as the key agency in allocating individuals to their occupational roles; and further, that if for

no other reason than the need to utilize talent more efficiently, educational opportunity, in a formal sense at any rate, has been made less unequal. Consequently, the degree of intergenerational social mobility, in particular, has tended to increase and in this way the stability of social strata has been in some degree diminished.

On these lines, then, a picture has been built up – and it is one which would be generally accepted – of a system of stratification becoming increasingly fine in its gradations and at the same time somewhat less extreme and less rigid.

The chief sociological implications of the argument that the more prosperous of the country's manual wage workers are being assimilated into the middle class would appear to be as follows:

(1) That these workers and their families are acquiring a standard of living, in terms of income and material possessions, which puts them on a level with at least the lower strata within the middle class. Here one refers to certain of the specifically economic aspects of class stratification.

(2) That these same workers are also acquiring new social perspectives and new norms of behaviour which are more characteristic of middle-class than of working-class groups. Here one refers to what may be termed the normative aspect of class.

(3) That being essentially similar to many middle-class persons in their economic position and their normative orientation, these manual workers are being accepted by the former on terms of social equality in both formal and informal social interaction. Here one refers to what may be called the relational aspect of class.

One would have thought it obvious that in any discussion of the thesis of embourgeoisement distinctions on these lines would have been regarded as indispensable. What is necessary, in our view, is that the economic, normative and relational aspects of the matter should each be studied as rigorously as possible, and that any conclusions concerning embourgeoisement should be formed on the basis of research specifically focused on the problem in this way, rather than being merely ad hoc generalizations drawn from a shapeless mass of data.

So far as income levels and the ownership of consumer durables are concerned, comparisons can be made with a fair degree of reliability between the more prosperous section of the working-class and middle-class groups. Such comparisons have in fact shown that in these respects many manual workers and their families have achieved economic parity, at least, with many members of the lower strata within the middle class. However, the point that we would stress here is that incomes and consumption patterns do not constitute the whole of the economic aspect of class stratification. Such factors as security and prospects for advancement are also relevant; and in this connection the evidence at present available indicates that broad differences remain between manual and non-manual employments. In relation to security, for example, the manual worker is still generally more liable than the non-manual worker to be dismissed at short notice; he is also less likely than the latter to enjoy various occupational fringe benefits, such as sickness pay and pension schemes. In relation to advancement, not only are the non-manual worker's chances of upward occupational mobility significantly greater than those of the manual worker, but in any case the former can often expect his income to rise by calculable increments throughout his working life, whereas the income of the latter is likely to rise very little once he reaches adulthood – save, of course, as a result of general improvements in wage rates gained through collective bargaining.

So far as promotion is concerned, the chances of the rank-and-file worker rising above supervisory level are, on all the evidence, clearly declining in modern industry. For those who leave non-selective secondary schools at the age of sixteen for a manual occupation, this kind of work is becoming more than ever before a life sentence. The same factors that are making for greater intergenerational mobility – technological progress, increasing specialization and the growing importance of education in occupational placement – are also operating to reduce the possibility of 'working up from the bottom' in industry, and are thus indirectly re-emphasizing the staff-worker dichotomy.

The treatment of the economic aspect of class in the thesis of embourgeoisement is then unconvincing because it is incomplete. In regard to what we have called the relational aspect of the problem, however, the neglect is more or less total. A variety of studies carried out in different parts of Britain over the last ten years or so have pointed to a marked degree of status segregation in housing, in informal neighbourhood relations, in friendship groups, in the membership of local clubs, societies and organizations and so on. And in all cases the division between manual and non-manual workers and their families has proved to be one of the most salient. It may, of course, be held that very recently and in certain particular contexts – say the New Towns or the suburban areas of newly developed industrial regions – the extent of this segregation has begun to decline. But the point is that so far no evidence of this has been brought forward and, further, that the basic importance of such evidence to the argument concerning embourgeoisement has not, apparently, been recognized.

In fact, apart from the statistical data on incomes and consumption, it is on evidence of changes of an attitudinal and normative character that the thesis of working-class embourgeoisement largely rests. This evidence, which we must now examine, is of two main kinds: (1) evidence provided by enquiries – some of them field studies – into the changing patterns of the family and community life of manual workers; and (2) evidence provided by attitude and opinion surveys of manual workers, in particular those dealing with individuals' own estimations of their class position. We may say at the outset that in our view the arguments put forward on this basis are again generally unsatisfactory ones. The material in question, we believe, has been treated in a far too uncritical manner and does not adequately sustain many of the interpretations that have been placed upon it.

It is our view, then, that if questions of class identification and class norms are to be at all usefully investigated through interview techniques, the pollster's overriding concern with easily obtainable and easily quantifiable results must be abandoned and an effort made to do justice to the complexity of the issues involved. Research has in fact already been carried out which gives a promising lead in this respect. In particular, one would cite here the studies of Popitz in Germany, of Willener in Switzerland and of Bott in England, which, although conducted entirely independently of each other, are essentially comparable both in their approach and their findings. In each case it was in effect recognized that the problem of the 'meaning' of respondents' statements on class and cognate questions could only be overcome by interpreting these statements in relation to respondents' overall perception, or image, of their society. Thus, in all three studies the elucidation of these images became a central focus of interest. It was generally found that as an idea was built up of the way in which a respondent saw his society, and especially its class structure, the more clearly the rationale of his answers to particular questions would appear. One was dealing, in other words, with a Gestalt, not with a series of separate and unconnected responses. A close interrelationship was seen to prevail between the individual's perception of his society, his general value system and (insofar as these were investigated) the attitudes he took towards more specific social issues. Furthermore, it was in each case revealed that among groups of individuals occupying comparable positions within the social hierarchy, a broadly similar 'social imagery' tended to occur, together with a more or less distinctive normative orientation.

In the findings of these studies we have in fact probably the clearest indications that are available of the basic differences in the social perspectives of working- and middle-class persons and, thus, an important guide to the core distinctions which would be relevant to any discussion of their respective lifestyles. For this reason it may be useful to set out here – if only in a very simplified way – certain of the major conclusions which were arrived at in all three investigations.

(1) The majority of people have a more or less clearly defined image of their society as being stratified in some way or other; that is to say, they are aware of inequalities in the distribution of wealth, prestige and power.

(2) One 'polar' type of image is that of society as being sharply divided

into two contending sections, or classes, differentiated primarily in terms of the possession or non-possession of power (the 'dichotomous' or 'power' model). Contrasting with this is an image of society as comprising an extended hierarchy of relatively 'open' strata differentiated primarily in terms of prestige (the 'hierarchical' or 'prestige' model).

(3) The 'power' model is that most frequently approximated in the images of working-class persons – that is, wage-earning, manual workers. The 'prestige' model on the other hand, is that most frequently approximated in the images of middle-class persons – that is, salaried or independent non-manual workers.

(4) Those images, at least, which approach at all closely to one or other of the two polar types serve as the focus of distinctive complexes of social values and attitudes.

(5) The distinction between these two complexes is chiefly that between two basic themes which may be called the collectivistic and the individualistic (these being understood not as political ideologies, but rather as the raw materials of social consciousness which political ideologies may articulate).

The rationale of this linking of collectivistic and individualistic orientations to 'power' and 'prestige' models respectively is not difficult to appreciate. On the basis of the research in question, and of earlier studies of class values and attitudes, it may be illustrated in the schematic and, we would stress, ideal-typical manner shown on page 341.

One has here, thus, two sharply contrasting social perspectives, each of which comprises a set of internally consistent beliefs, values and attitudes. Whether the same degree of logic would be found in the case of any particular individual may well be doubted: so too may any exact correspondence between 'collectivism' and manual workers and 'individualism' and non-manual workers, especially in regard to occupational groups on the manual/non-manual frontier. However, in the light of the evidence available, it would seem likely that approximations to one or other of the ideal-type perspectives outlined do regularly occur among social groups with less ambiguous class and status positions.

In conclusion, we may attempt to pull together the threads of our argument by using the discussion of this paper as a basis for the following, necessarily tentative, views, concerning the probable effects so far of working-class affluence on the British class structure.

(1) The change which would seem most probable is one which may be best understood as a process of normative convergence between certain sections of the working and middle classes; the focus of the convergence being on what we have termed 'instrumental collectivism' and 'family centredness'. There is as yet, at least, little basis for the more ambitious thesis of embourgeoisement in the sense of the large-scale assimilation of manual workers and their families to middle-class lifestyles and middle-

	Working-class perspective	*Middle-class perspective*
General beliefs	The social order is divided into 'us' and 'them': those who do not have authority and those who do. The division between 'us' and 'them' is virtually fixed, at least from the point of view of one man's life chances. What happens to you depends a lot on luck; otherwise you have to learn to put up with things.	The social order is a hierarchy of differentially rewarded positions: a ladder containing many rungs. It is possible for individuals to move from one level of the hierarchy to another. Those who have ability and initiative can overcome obstacles and create their own opportunities. Where a man ends up depends on what he makes of himself.
General values	'We' ought to stick together and get what we can as a group. You may as well enjoy yourself while you can instead of trying to make yourself 'a cut above the rest'.	Every man ought to make the most of his own capabilities and be responsible for his own welfare. You cannot expect to get anywhere in the world if you squander your time and money. 'Getting on' means making sacrifices.
Attitudes on more specific issues	*(on the best job for a son)* 'A trade in his hands.' 'A good steady job.'	'As good a start as you can give him.' 'A job that leads somewhere.'
	(towards people needing social assistance) 'They have been unlucky.' 'They never had a chance.' 'It could happen to any of us.'	'Many of them had the same opportunities as others who have managed well enough.' 'They are a burden on those who are trying to help themselves.'
	(on trade unions) 'Trade unions are the only means workers have of protecting themselves and of improving their standard of living.'	'Trade unions have too much power in the country.' 'The unions put the interests of a section before the interests of the nation as a whole.'

class society in general. In particular, there is no firm evidence either that manual workers are consciously aspiring to middle-class society, or that this is becoming any more open to them.

(2) The groups which appear involved in normative convergence cannot be distinguished in terms of economic factors alone. Certainly, on the working-class side, affluence is not to be regarded as sufficient in itself to bring about the attenuation of solidaristic collectivism. The process of convergence must rather be seen as closely linked to changes in the structure of social relationships in industrial, community and family life, which are in turn related not only to growing prosperity but also to advances in industrial organization and technology, to the process of urban development, to demographic trends, and to the evolution of mass communications and 'mass culture'.

(3) Even among the 'new' working-class groups in which instrumental collectivism and family centredness are manifested, status goals seem much less in evidence than economic goals: in other words, the privatized worker would appear far more typical than the socially aspiring worker. The conditions under which status aspirations are generated may be regarded as still more special than those which are conducive to a more individualistic outlook. Thus, we return to the point that normative convergence has to be understood as implying as yet only a rather limited modification of the class frontier.

(4) Finally, it is consistent with the above views to believe further that the political consequences of working-class influence are so far, at least, indeterminate.

Impediments and Alternatives to Class Consciousness
K. Roberts, F. G. Cook, S. C. Clark, E. Semeonoff

Reprinted with permission from K. Roberts *et al.*, *The Fragmentary Class Structure*, Heinemann, 1977, pp. 96–103

Are hegemonic values the only crucial obstacles and would a genuinely revolutionary consciousness be the only authentic response to the predicament of the working class? Is a class-conscious proletariat awaiting the opportunity to appear given the necessary crisis situation coupled with the requisite ideological leadership? In our view this diagnosis oversimplifies a more complex situation and there are other obstacles that make the polarization of the British working class into a revolutionary force a most remote possibility.

To begin with, although there may be a daily class struggle in industry this is rarely more than but one ingredient in the situation. There are other equally authentic elements in the worker's social reality that compete for attention. As previous research has demonstrated, our own enquiry found that in different ways and to admittedly different degrees, nearly all respondents were positively attached to their jobs. Most employees like their work and are not eagerly awaiting a revolution that will rid their lives of this institution. It is misleading to think of the man on the assembly line as the typical manual worker. Only approximately 2 per cent of the labour force is engaged upon mechanized line or belt work. For those who are, the experience can be anything but pleasant; it can be boring and monotonous as the cheers testify when the track breaks down in car assembly plants. But there are skilled workers in particular whose jobs are intrinsically rewarding, while others find that the people they work with make doing the job pleasant. In addition to this, workers are not only workers but also have homes, families and leisure. They need not treat work as a central life interest but can develop an instrumental approach in which their expectations, as far as intrinsic job satisfactions are concerned, are modest and easily satisfied.

The idea of abolishing work even in a fantasy situation such as a pools win holds slight popularity. Furthermore, there is little more boring than being on strike, going slow or working to rule. Aside from any financial damage involved, for others, apart from the few activists who can be at the centre of affairs, waging the class struggle can be intensely depressing. So attitudes towards work are generally mixed. Work may be an arena of conflict but, at the same time, it can be a source of various satisfactions and individuals can psychologically disengage instead of pressing for change in response to whatever irritations are encountered.

Another impediment to class consciousness concerns the manner in which the working class is splintered by numerous cross-cutting internal divisions. Some are hierarchical, as between different levels of skill, while others are lateral as between different but equally skilled trades. From the sidelines these divisions can appear trivial when set against the common interests that all workers share but from the hub of the working class they look anything but petty. Particular crafts possess their own traditions and loyalties that have been harboured over generations and initiation may require a prolonged apprenticeship. The resultant occupational communities may foster a sense of 'us' and 'them', but the 'us' within which individuals are emotively bound need not encompass the whole of the working class. Indeed, rather than promoting it, intense craft loyalties can inhibit the growth of any wider class solidarity as, according to Brown and his co-investigators, has been the case amongst Tyneside shipbuilders.

Many employees are as concerned with differentials in status and earnings *vis-à-vis* other groups of workers as with pursuing a common struggle against employers. Hence the intractable problem of low-paid occupations. In principle everyone is in favour of helping the low-paid but, at the same time, other groups want to maintain their relative standing, so the low-paid continue on relatively low pay. Concern over differentials and relativities are as much part and parcel of shop-floor life and occupy as central a place in the history of trade unionism as the class struggle, and they cannot reasonably be dismissed as false consciousness. The factory, firm and trade are real entities with which ordinary workers can identify and ideas about a wider class struggle often cannot compete.

Yet a further obstacle to the development of working-class consciousness is the absence of a clearly defined other side. The existence of a well-defined enemy can always help bolster solidarity amongst an in-group but, for the working class, the 'them' in the us/them equation are not easily identified. The working class is not a caste and its boundaries are blurred. There is no single factor that decides whether or not a person belongs to the working class and this indecision is fully reflected in public opinion. Furthermore . . ., members of the working class often possess individual ambitions for themselves and their children. Many have relatives who have already 'got on'. So, against which opposition would a class-conscious proletariat side?

It is easy for theorists to name capitalists, bourgeoisie or property owners, but these are just names rather than social formations that workers encounter in their daily lives. In any case, there remains a huge cushioning middle ground between these proffered enemies and the strata who identify themselves as working class and it is with this soggy centre, largely occupied by bureaucratic officialdom, that the day-to-day class struggle is usually fought. It is also this middle ground into which many workers would like themselves or their children to rise. Individuals can be ambitious for themselves without weakening any desire to improve the conditions of their current strata and proletarian workers are as keen to get on as other sections of the population. This illustrates how far away even proletarian workers remain from genuine class consciousness. Attitudes towards superordinate strata are too mixed for the class struggle to become a whole-hearted occupation.

By definition, the working class is class aware but, nevertheless, the class-conscious worker is the exception. Workers are involved in a class struggle and perceive this aspect of their circumstances with varying degrees of clarity but rarely with total commitment. Notions of a class struggle and appeals to class loyalties strike a chord amongst most groups of working men, but it is only one chord amongst many that are being regularly triggered. This is why working-class organizations such as trade unions have a constant struggle to maintain interest, enthusiasm and solidarity and, to the extent that solidarity is intermittently achieved, its boundaries rarely cover the entire working class.

What this amounts to is that the failure of a revolutionary proletariat to surface cannot be entirely attributed to ideological oppression. This is only one part of the story for a more basic truth is that the class struggle is just one aspect of the manual worker's everyday reality. Class consciousness is one possible response but it is not the only authentic reaction. There are several features of the worker's situation that encourage other responses and this is why the polarization of the working class into a revolutionary force may remain a possibility but is very unlikely.

The future of the working class

The cleavage dividing the blue-collar strata from the rest can be made to appear deep or shallow depending upon the type of evidence introduced. The most marked disparities between the blue- and white-collar strata were subjective class identities, party political loyalties and trade union membership. Focus upon this information and the hiatus separating the blue- from the white-collar strata appears considerable. However, we are not entitled to overlook that in our own and other comparable investigations, on questions tapping individuals' views on specific issues such as public ownership and trade union power, most blue-collar workers endorsed the majority white-collar position.

In one sense, the whole of the above discussion has been an attempt to define the significance for modern society of there being a self-aware working class that tends to vote Labour and to organize itself in trade unions, so there should be little doubt that we consider this cleavage to be of continuing importance. But this does not justify playing tricks with survey data and forgetting the contrary evidence.

On specific sociopolitical issues dissent from the generally dominant point of view is certainly stronger amongst manual than non-manual workers. Taking individuals' attitudes on specific issues alone, however, although one would rightly conclude that the manual strata are a base for the development of oppositional values, it would be difficult to argue that the class structure is marked by a major cleavage dividing blue-collar workers from the rest. At the level of specific issues, many common values are found throughout the population with the working class being merely a section where dissent is relatively common but still the exception to the rule. This may be partly attributable to an ideological hegemony maintained by superordinate strata, but explaining the facts does not explain them away. In reality the working-class character of the manual strata is compartmentalized and sufficiently divorced from attitudes on specific issues to stultify its impact as an oppositional force.

The evidence implying a severe cleavage between the blue- and white-collar strata can be alternatively interpreted as suggesting that this particular division in society is recognized and effectively accommodated within the social system possibly even to the extent of being overinstitutional-ized. Oppositional values distinguishing the blue-collar strata may have ground more deeply during the historical period when alignments in politics and industry that persist to the present were originally taking shape. Today, however, much of the institutionalized opposition of the working class, apparent in its membership of trade unions and support for the Labour Party, resembles a hollow shell. Trade union membership was the norm amongst our manual respondents but it was only exceptionally accompanied by an ideological commitment to a working-class movement. The most common reason for joining a trade union, given by 49 per cent of our blue-collar members, was the operation of a closed shop. Similarly, the majority of our manual respondents voted Labour and sometimes explicitly accounted for their party loyalties in class terms. The Labour Party retains considerable electoral support because it is identified as a working-class party and, for this reason, to hold its 'traditional' vote the Party needs to maintain a distinctly working-class appeal. At the same time, however, when it comes to propagating and executing a programme of socialist reform including a frontal attack upon existing structures of economic power and privilege, such as by extending public ownership, the enthusiasm of Labour's working-class supporters can quickly evaporate, creating a dilemma of which the Party's leadership is well aware. The blue/white-collar schism is real and has been institutionalized to play a central role in political and industrial life, but it is a division that fails to penetrate grass-root attitudes in a thoroughly convincing manner.

Faced with this evidence it might seem obvious to infer that change must be imminent. Is there not a strain towards consistency built into the human psyche? Must we anticipate that before long manual workers will either abandon their 'nominal' working-class identities, trade union and Labour Party loyalties or else become a more solidly radical force?

Each of these prophecies has earned some support from analysts who have perused the seemingly contrary evidence just presented. However, it may be too easy for people who make an occupation out of intellectual pursuits to exaggerate the importance of intellectual coherence in social life at large. Others are not punished or rewarded to the same extent as sociologists depending upon whether the things they do, think and say are consistent. It is entirely possible for individuals to live comfortably with contradictory attitudes that are brought out and put away depending upon the prompts. People are not ordinarily under the pressure even to make them conscious of the inconsistencies in their outlooks, let alone to mould their beliefs into coherent wholes.

The working class, therefore, constantly puzzles investigators who find it difficult to make sense of their contradictory findings. In Brown's study of Tyneside shipbuilding workers, for example, the views expressed during interviews proved anything but militant but this did not prevent militant industrial action occurring during the period of the investigation. Depending upon the immediate situation, men will down tools and talk a militant language or feel favourably disposed towards their jobs and employers. One wonders which evidence gives the true picture and the answer is that both pictures are true. Different situations strike different chords and there are no pressures demanding overall coherence. It is mistaken to assume, therefore, that pressures are at work which, given time, will iron out inconsistencies in working-class attitudes and behaviour.

Researchers normally like their findings to fall into tidy patterns. Failure to discover statistical or otherwise meaningful relationships between variables is often considered an indictment of the research itself. Hence there is always a temptation to forget the evidence that does not fit. Michael Mann is one of the few investigators willing to face the inconsistencies in the results of his own research, and once the ambiguity is tolerated, then as Mann illustrates, many acute insights concerning the state of the working class become available. Following fieldwork amongst manual employees in Peterborough, Mann concluded that 'neither the workers as a whole, nor any identifiable sub-group possessed a coherent belief system'. Mann proceeded to observe that, together with those sharing in societal power, 'only those who seek to change society need to encompass it intellectually'. Ideological consistency is a luxury that the working class can manage without and, in order to understand the working class, this is a fact that must be squarely faced. As Mann argues, 'There is no need for working-class people to develop beliefs that legitimate or illegitimate society so long as they recognize the *factual* need to comply with its demands', meaning that individuals are quite capable of working for capitalist concerns without being ideologically committed to capitalism as a socioeconomic system – and similarly workers can vote Labour and join trade unions if their interests seem to be served by doing so without being committed socialists or subscribing to any other coherent, radical ideology.

The intention is not to portray working-class people as irrational, muddled and incapable of logical thought. Manual workers are as able to think coherently as anyone else. As we have shown, when blue-collar workers are appropriately questioned they are perfectly able to present coherent images of society and to give entirely rational accounts of their careers, hopes for their children and political loyalties. The argument is not that the working class is peculiarly incapable of intellectual coherence but that manual workers are rarely constrained to see society as a whole, decide upon the structural alterations they would prefer, and align their behaviour and more specific beliefs accordingly. There is nothing akin to the sociology seminar amongst popular working-class pastimes.

Although there may be only one working class, therefore, and even if its ideological tendency is proletarian, it does not follow and, indeed, there are pressures described above contending otherwise, that it must eventually become a class for itself. Perceptions of conflict in the work situation are only occasionally totalized and linked to a vision of an alternative society, and there is more than the awaited crisis combined with effective ideological leadership inhibiting such developments. On balance, therefore, it seems most unlikely that the working class will evolve into a revolutionary force liable to reshape society.

The historical trends are narrowing even that degree of proletarian solidarity and associated ideological precision that sections of the working class have achieved but this does not mean that the manual strata are going to become docile and acquiescent. Progressive embourgeoisement is as unlikely as polarization. There are no grounds for suspecting a movement towards a conservative coherence. A slackening of proletarian solidarity need not mean a decline in working-class dissent. What we are more likely to find is working-class dissent becoming increasingly fragmented and expressed outside the institutional framework that the Labour Party and trade unions have provided. Paradoxical though it may seem, any decline in working-class solidarity must necessarily undermine established procedures through which dissent has hitherto been channelled. So strikes are not withering away as was forecast in the 1950s but industrial disputes are now mostly unofficial and it is difficult for trade union leaders to guarantee any social contract on behalf of their members.

Given the continuing blue-collar predicament, being paid visibly and considerably less than managers and professional people, the flat career pattern and limited access to housing and related life chances outside the work situation, there is going to remain a working class that can never be organized into total acquiescence. For society at large, therefore, the working class remains an unstable and continuing challenge but not a revolutionary threat.

Social Mobility
A. Heath

Reprinted with permission from Anthony Heath, *Social Mobility*, Fontana Paperbacks, 1981, pp. 49–61

The most recent large-scale study of Britain was undertaken by a group of Oxford sociologists in 1972. The sample consisted of 10,000 adult males who constituted a representative cross-section of all males aged twenty to sixty-four and resident in England and Wales in 1972. These respondents were asked to give an outline of their own occupational and educational biographies as well as some basic biographical information about their fathers, mothers, wives, brothers and friends. As is usual in these surveys, the material is all of a 'factual' rather than attitudinal kind, although in a follow-up in 1974 some additional data were collected on the subjective experiences of a limited number of the original respondents.

The Oxford study has been sharply criticized for its omission of women, but there is fortunately another source, the General Household Survey conducted by the government statistical service, which we can use.

There is however another problem which we cannot postpone, namely that of classification. Any discussion of social mobility necessarily requires us to distinguish a set of categories between which mobility is to take place. This problem has received all kinds of treatments. Pareto was most interested in movement between the governing elite and the non-elite; Sorokin was more concerned with movement between occupational groups which were differentiated according to their social honour; Lipset and Bendix focused on movement between manual and non-manual occupations, which they tended to equate with movement between the middle and working classes (classes being seen as broad social groupings with shared identities, consumption patterns and political attitudes); Blau and Duncan in contrast saw the occupational structure as 'more or less continuously graded in regard to status rather than being a set of discrete status classes' and hence rather than looking at movement between discrete categories focused on occupational achievements as measured on a continuous scale of socioeconomic status; Glass and his co-workers looked at movement between seven 'status categories' distinguished in terms of their social prestige and based on the assumption that 'the community consists of strata arranged in the form of a hierarchy'; and finally John Goldthorpe, in his report of the Oxford project, looked at movement between seven social classes differentiated according to the market and work situations of their incumbents.

The classification of occupations exhibits more disarray that almost any other issue in professional sociology and provides endless ground for argument and confusion. How a sociologist decides to categorize occupations will reflect his own beliefs about the nature of the social world, his theoretical preferences and objectives, and his own moral or political attitudes and values (and all these will themselves be interrelated). We cannot say that one categorization is 'wrong' and another 'right'. There is no neutral, objective yardstick for deciding on the correct way to classify social reality. Even if we can show that, say, functionalism involves certain empirical assumptions that are unwarranted – for example, the claim that occupations' prestige and social honour vary according to their importance for the society – we still cannot say that it is 'wrong' to scale occupations according to their prestige. We may say it is uninteresting, or unfruitful, or even perhaps that the measurement has been badly done, but these adjectives do not really mean the same thing as 'wrong'.

Despite the diversity of sociologists' attempts at classification, they can in theory be regarded as variations on two extreme positions, or world views. At one extreme come writers like Pareto, Sorokin or Blau and Duncan who see society as composed of a hierarchy of occupations in which there are no sharp breaks. True, Blau and Duncan allow that there may be some kind of 'natural break' between farm and non-farm, and between manual and non-manual occupations, but they are more impressed by the overlap between these categories and the way one category shades into another. The basis of their ranking is the occupation's 'status' or 'prestige', horribly vague concepts in Blau and Duncan's treatment, but implying simply that some occupations are 'better' or 'worse' than others as judged by the overall rewards, both monetary and non-monetary, which their incumbents receive.

At the other extreme come variants on the Marxist world view. Society is seen as divided into social classes which stand in antagonistic relations to each other. The factor that creates 'class' is fundamentally economic interest, and it is held that the economic interests of, say, manual wage labourers are clearly distinct from those of the petty bourgeoisie or the landowner. The emphasis is therefore on the *cleavages* within society, not the overlaps. Instead of being ranked in a hierarchy of status or prestige, occupations are grouped into discrete categories on the basis of their distinct economic interests. And so we have 'class mobility' rather than 'prestige mobility'.

So much for the theory. In practice, the broad outlines of most classifications are quite similar, although the detail varies enormously. Thus Glass's team placed professional and high administrative occupations in the highest of their seven status categories; Goldthorpe places them in his 'top' class which possesses the most favoured market and work situation. Unskilled manual work comes at the 'bottom' in both classifications.

There is more disagreement in the 'middle' at the manual/non-manual borderline (which may in itself tell us something about the fuzziness of that border). Glass (or more accurately Hall and Jones) place routine grades of non-manual work in the *same* status category as skilled manual work, and place them *below* shopkeepers and foremen. Goldthorpe in contrast places clerical workers, foremen, shopkeepers and skilled manual workers in four distinct social classes, but which are in a sense at the same 'level': we would regard it as inappropriate to talk about 'upward' or 'downward' mobility between these classes.

We shall be using Goldthorpe's classification in the table which follows. The seven classes which it distinguishes can be set out briefly as follows:

Class I: higher-grade professionals (both self-employed and salaried), administrators, managers and large proprietors.

Class II: lower-grade professionals, administrators and managers, higher-grade technicians, and the supervisors of non-manual employees.

Class III: routine clerical workers, sales personnel and other rank and file non-manual workers.

Class IV: farmers, small proprietors and self-employed workers – the 'petty bourgeoisie'.

Class V: supervisors of manual workers and lower-grade technicians.

Class VI: skilled manual wage-workers who have served apprenticeships or other forms of industrial training.

Class VII: semi- and unskilled manual workers in industry, plus agricultural workers.

Goldthorpe sometimes groups these into three broader classes – the service class made up of Classes I and II (so called because it is the class of those who service, i.e., exercise power and expertise on behalf of, the corporate authorities); an intermediate class composed of Classes III, IV and V; and a working class combining VI and VII. Another useful division which we shall employ from time to time involves treating Classes I, II, III and IV as the white-collar classes, and V, VI and VII as the blue-collar classes.

Short-range and long-range mobility

From problems of classification let us move on to some results of the Oxford mobility study. Table 1 gives the conventional mobility table using Goldthorpe's classification of occupations. It is an 'outflow' table showing the destinations of men from different social origins. Thus, of the men who came from Class I social origins (that is, whose fathers had Class I jobs), nearly half had themselves secured Class I positions by the time of the 1972 survey whereas the remainder had in some degree suffered downward mobility compared with their fathers. We must note that respondents have been classified according to their *present* occupations while their fathers have been classified according to the occupation which they held at the time the respondent was aged fourteen. This point in the father's career was chosen because it does enable us to talk sensibly of the respondent's social origins. Present or last main occupation would not enable us to do that since, of course, most fathers carry on working, and many change jobs, long after their children have left home.

Table 1. Intergenerational mobility: outflow

Father's class	Respondent's class (%)								
	I	*II*	*III*	*IV*	*V*	*VI*	*VII*	*Total*	*N*
I	48·4	18·9	9·3	8·2	4·5	4·5	6·2	100·0	582
II	31·9	22·6	10·7	8·0	9·2	9·6	8·0	100·0	477
III	19·2	15·7	10·8	8·6	13·0	15·0	17·8	100·1	594
IV	12·8	11·1	7·8	24·9	8·7	14·7	19·9	99·9	1223
V	15·4	13·2	9·4	8·0	16·6	20·1	17·2	99·9	939
VI	8·4	8·9	8·4	7·1	12·2	29·6	25·4	100·0	2312
VII	6·9	7·8	7·9	6·8	12·5	23·5	34·8	100·2	2216
%	14·3	11·4	8·6	9·9	11·6	20·8	23·3	99·9	(8343)

Sample: men aged 25–64 in 1972.
Source: *Oxford Social Mobility Group.*

Let us now use Table 1 to see if we can shed some light on the received wisdom about the prevalence of long- and short-range mobility in Britain today. Since we must treat Classes III, IV, V and VI as being in a sense all at much the same level, we shall regard short-range mobility as any movement in or out of this group of four 'middle' classes, while long-range mobility is that from top to bottom – from Classes I and II to VII, and vice versa.

The first impression received from Table 1 is that the 1972 sample had indeed experienced a great deal of intergenerational mobility, more of it being upward than downward. We can apply Westergaard and Resler's comment to the new material: the data dispel any notion that Britain is a society in which an individual's class position is fixed at birth. Capitalism certainly does permit a fair degree of circulation. The figures on the diagonal (sloping from top left to bottom right) give the percentage of men from each class origin who were in the same class in 1972 as their fathers had been earlier. In most cases this is less than one-third, and for the sample as a whole only 28 per cent had been intergenerationally stable. The other 72 per cent had experienced class mobility of some kind. Even if we treat Classes III to VI as being on the same level so that movement between them involves a change of class positions but not one that can sensibly be termed 'upward' or 'downward', we still find that nearly half the sample had been mobile, 31 per cent moving up and 18 per cent down.

The surplus of upward mobility is not surprising, given the expansion of professional and managerial jobs and the contraction of semi- and un-skilled manual ones: 14 per cent of the respondents, but only 7 per cent of their fathers, held Class I occupations; 23 per cent of the respondents, but 27 per cent of their fathers, held Class VII occupations. Expansion at the top and contraction at the bottom means that there simply has to be some net upward mobility, and so there is. There is no 'logical absurdity and arithmetical impossibility' here of which Musgrove can accuse us.

There is an important caveat which we must enter here, however. Exactly how much mobility and stability we find will depend on the number, size and character of the categories we distinguish. We could, slightly maliciously, divide the sample into just two categories – say Class I in the first and all the other six in the second. This classification would not be altogether unlike Pareto's distinction between the elite and non-elite and would yield a non-elite containing over 85 per cent of the sample. Hardly surprisingly, we would find that few people had experienced intergenerational mobility across this particular boundary; only 14.6 per cent, in fact.

Lipset and Bendix's division of the population into manual and non-manual, or working and middle classes is another one of obvious interest, and again it is easy enough to regroup the categories. If we regard Classes V, VI and VII as manual ones, and the rest as non-manual, we find that total mobility across the boundary comes to 34.2 per cent – a somewhat higher figure than Lipset and Bendix found for any of the countries they studied. Does this mean that Britain has now become a relatively mobile, open society? The short answer is 'No'.

How much mobility and stability we find, therefore, depends to a large extent on the particular classification which we use. We cannot possibly take a single figure as 'the' rate of social mobility in a specific country. It would not be far-fetched to suggest that we can get almost any answer we want simply by fiddling with the categories. Fortunately, however, there are some conclusions (although not as many as some writers claim) which are going to survive any reasonably plausible rejigging of the classification. For example, no sane observer is going to doubt that there is more short-range mobility than long-range. This is pretty clear from Table 1. Less than 10 per cent of men from Class I origins had dropped to semi- and unskilled manual work in 1972, but over a quarter had dropped the shorter distance to Classes III–VI. There is a similar pattern if we turn to upward mobility from Class VII origins: 15 per cent achieved long-range upward mobility, but 50 per cent made the smaller distance to Classes III, IV, V and VI.

But do these figures allow us to conclude, as Westergaard and Resler did, that movement 'from rags to riches or riches to rags' is very rare? Rags, riches and rarity, like beauty, lie in the eye of the beholder. How much money do you need to qualify as rich? In the 1972 enquiry the respondents in Class I had an average annual income of £3251, over twice as much as the amount earned by those in Class VII. Will this do? And what is to count as rare? Do we draw the line at 1 per cent, 5 per cent, or 10 per cent? Westergaard and Resler's claim is one of those infuriating statements, so often found in sociology, in which the authors give no clear guide as to what would count as a confirmation or a refutation. All we can sensibly say are things like 'movement from rags to riches is rarer than that from rags to moderate affluence' – which is hardly going to make the headlines.

The manual/non-manual barrier

The notion of a 'barrier' between the middle and working classes is another that is almost as bad as 'rarity', but we can perhaps make a little more headway this time. Certainly, there is no barrier in any literal sense. If we say that Classes I, II and III are those unambiguously above the barrier, we can see from Table 1 that about a quarter of the men from working-class social origins (i.e. Classes VI and VII) succeeded in crossing this barrier. And the men who got across it did not collapse, exhausted from the effort, on the ground immediately beyond the barrier. Having crossed it, the working-class man was just as likely to carry on all the way into the higher-grade professional, administrative or managerial jobs of Class I as he was to end up in the routine clerical work of Class III.

True, rather fewer men from Class I were likely to cross the barrier in the other direction into the working class. This asymmetry, which has been found in other countries, has led writers like Blau and Duncan to talk of a 'semi-permeable membrane' or 'one-way screen' which it is easier to pass through in one direction than the other. They went on to say:

Some white-collar occupations require much less skill and command considerably less income than many blue-collar occupations. This makes it possible for men with inferior abilities who want to remain in the white-collar classes to do so. Men raised in white-collar homes are often strongly identified with the symbols of white-collar status. The unsuccessful ones among them are, therefore, willing to pay a price for being permitted to maintain white-collar status. The existence of relatively unskilled white-collar occupations, such as retail sales and clerical jobs, makes it possible for the unsuccessful sons of white-collar workers to remain in the white-collar class by paying the price of accepting a lower income than they might have been able to obtain in a manual occupation. The unskilled white-collar occupations tend to absorb most of the downwardly mobile from the higher non-manual strata, which makes these occupations a boundary that creates relative protection against the danger of downward mobility from the white-collar to the blue-collar class.

This is in many ways a plausible argument, but let us look at the actual evidence for Britain. Let us compare the occupations entered by 'unsuccessful' men with inferior abilities from different social origins. For the present purposes we can define the unsuccessful as those who went to elementary or secondary modern schools and left at the minimum school-leaving age without any formal academic qualifications such as School Certificate or O-level. The question we now have to ask is whether these unsuccessful men from white-collar homes were largely absorbed by unskilled white-collar jobs like retail sales and routine clerical work (jobs included in Goldthorpe's Class III).

The short answer for Britain is a firm 'No'. Some of these men (rather surprisingly perhaps) managed to get Class I and II jobs, but even if we put all the white-collar occupations together, they still absorbed only 24 per cent of these unqualified offspring of white-collar fathers. This is a bit better that the unqualified children of blue-collar workers managed – 15 per cent got into these jobs – but it is hardly adequate evidence for a boundary that 'creates relative protection against the danger of downward mobility from the white-collar to the blue-collar class'. The great majority of educationally unsuccessful men with 'inferior abilities' seem to end up in some kind of blue-collar work.

But did they jump or were they pushed? Did these educationally unsuccessful men enter blue-collar work because they were excluded from the white-collar work they would have liked, or did they actually choose manual work for its higher pay despite the absence of 'the cherished symbol of the white collar'? The answer may tell us something about the prevalence of status snobbery in Britain, a snobbery that is often asserted by commentators on British life but rarely demonstrated.

The kind of data that is available cannot tell us about the motivations of respondents, but there are two pieces of evidence which are quite instructive. The first is the income people get from the different jobs. Class III jobs – the routine clerical and sales ones – do not pay at all well for those educationally unqualified men compared with *skilled* manual work (Class VI). In other words there is a considerable price to be paid for the white collar – in 1972 it was about £150 per annum. *Un*skilled manual work, on the other hand, pays even worse. The man who is left with a choice between joining the unskilled white-collar labour force or the unskilled blue-collar one is not making a financial sacrifice if he opts for the former.

The other useful piece of evidence concerns apprenticeships. These typically lead, in the beginning at least, into skilled manual work; they are quite keenly sought after – you hardly drift into an apprenticeship; and they might be taken as indicating some kind of commitment to manual work – if only for the money. Men from white-collar homes were actually even *more* likely to get these apprenticeships than their educationally unsuccessful peers from working-class homes. And it is a good guess that getting one helped many to avoid the low pay and low status of the unskilled manual job.

The moral is simple. Qualifications improve your chances of getting a better-paid job (although they do not ensure it). If you miss out on the qualifications to be won at school, try for the vocational ones that can be obtained after leaving school. White-collar families tend to know this lesson; they are better at securing school credentials in the first place, and they seem better at using the 'alternative route' of technical and vocational qualifications if they miss out first time round. There is little sign that they allow snobbery to stand in the way of economic self-interest. It is a good bet that many of these 'downwardly mobile' men jumped into skilled manual work for the better pay and prospects which, compared with the alternatives, it offered them. But the men who ended up in unskilled manual work were pushed – or perhaps just slipped; it is hard to see what positive attractions they could have been offered.

Capitalism and Culture
I. Jamieson

Reprinted with permission from Ian Jamieson, 'Capitalism and Culture', *Sociology*, vol. 14, no. 2, May 1980, pp. 232–8

The strongest test of the hypothesis that American firms stress the values of universalism and achievement more than their British counterparts comes in the area of qualifications for the job. It was predicted that 'American' managers would be better qualified than British managers. Table 1 below summarizes the main data.

Table 1. Percentage of British and 'American' managers with stated qualifications

Qualification	US managers		GB managers	
	%	N	%	N
Managers with post A-level quals.	56·0	80	33·4	26
Managers with first degree or equiv.	36·5	53	29·0	23
Managers with management training	66·9	97	48·7	38

Some comments are necessary on this table. First, the figures are rather flattering to the British companies because of the contribution to the whole made by GB Pharmaceuticals, whose staff appeared to be particularly well qualified. If one discounted this contribution, then the difference becomes even more marked. Cross-tabulating qualification by function, it was found that production managers tended to be better qualified than the managers in the other functions; this is particularly true, as one would expect, for the high technology industries of pharmaceuticals and electronics. As it happens however, production managers were found to be overrepresented in the British sample, and once this variable is controlled for, the gap between the qualifications of the managers working for the American firms and those working for the British firms widens still further. Curiously enough however, it is in the production area that the difference actually reverses itself. The British production managers tended to be slightly better qualified than their 'American' equivalents: 64 per cent of 'American' production managers (n=21) had a first degree or equivalent, while 75 per cent (n=21) of

British managers had. In all other areas the 'American' managers were better qualified and dramatically so in the marketing area. The British marketing managers were worse qualified, using either post A-level qualifications, or first degree or equivalent, as a measure of qualifications, than the managers in any other function; they also had the second smallest amount of managerial training, after the managers in general administration. This picture is very different in the American firms: here the production managers were still the best qualified, but the marketing managers followed closely behind, 60 per cent (n=21) of these managers possessed a first degree or its equivalent, compared with only 14 per cent (n=2) of British marketing managers. Personnel managers in both sets of companies tended to be relatively well qualified, although better qualified in the American firms. Managers working in this function were also most likely to have had some form of management training in both the American and the British firms.

These findings, which showed the managerial personnel of the American companies to be better qualified than their British opposite numbers, are well supported by other research. Numerous studies have pointed out the comparative deficiency inside British managerial ranks, indeed several writers have insisted that the major gap between British and American industry is not a technological one, but a managerial one. The most interesting finding is not the general difference between British and American firms, which was perhaps predictable enough, but the nature of the observed differences. It could be argued that in the area of production the demands of a relatively sophisticated technology require well qualified managers, and thus the effects of culture are minimal. I would suggest that there are also other reasons operating in the case of the British companies. I have already shown that the production department was regarded as the most crucial area for most of the British firms and, if this is correct, it should follow that it was in this area that the firms were attempting to maximize efficiency. One of the ways of doing this would be to hire managers with obvious formal technical qualifications for the job. By contrast, an area like marketing was regarded by many of the British companies as something which did not require much, if any, *technical* expertise, certainly nothing that could be learned formally from the textbook or college. What it did require was a creative approach, and certain personality features like extroversion, flair, drive, 'feel for the product' etc. These features were not seen by the British companies as being necessarily correlated with academic qualifications – much better correlates were experience and the 'right type of person'. The American companies were in a rather different position. Production was regarded in most cases as being rather more routine, most of the processes were developed and perfected in the United States, and the American parent often issued strict instructions about the type of machinery to be used, exact product specifications, quality control etc. What was required at the British end of the operation was managers who could routinely manage the process, and this did not require men with the highest academic qualifications. This interpretation is reinforced by Steur and Gennard, who note somewhat similar findings in their comparative study of the electrical engineering industry. They observed that, 'The knowledge input into the subsidiary of a foreign parent company need not all be embodied in the men on the spot.' Just as the British companies tended to concentrate on production, so I have argued, the American companies tended to concentrate on marketing as the most important function. Marketing does not directly *require* highly qualified personnel in quite the same way as sophisticated technology might require qualified people to manage it, and so one finds, even in the American companies, that the qualifications of the marketeers are not so high as their fellow managers in production. Yet the American method of marketing does involve a whole range of sophisticated techniques which do require, at the managerial level, certain intellectual abilities, of which academic qualifications might be thought as good an index as any other.

One of the most often cited differences between British and American industry, is the fact that American managers exhibit very much higher rates of inter-firm mobility than the British. Certainly this prediction would follow from the theoretical analysis. As Burrage has argued, in the more ascriptive British culture one would expect to find rather less inter-organizational mobility, British firms preferring to recruit potential managers at an early age and retain them for a long period of service, loyalty being of crucial importance. Thus one would expect the more particularistic relationships in British firms to be far more permanent than the more universalistic relationships that allegedly pertain inside American firms, where anybody who fits the universalistic criteria could fill the role. This line of reasoning is also followed by Dubin. A study by Stewart and Duncan-Jones would appear to confirm this general view of greater mobility in the United States. Yet the data in general do *not* present a totally unambiguous picture; studies by Wright Mills, Newcomber, the editors of *Fortune*, and Brua all claim to show that one of the distinguishing features of top management in America has been its conspicuous *lack* of inter-firm mobility. It could be argued that this ambiguity is the result of differing definitions of top managers, and/or whether the studies bothered to count the number of 'exploratory' moves that many young managers make in the first few years of their business life. If one considers the mass of managers below the top ranks in both societies, however, the picture is just as confused. Granick declares that, 'The British managerial turnover between companies is even greater than the American after the first few years of the individual's total career.' The best study of differential inter-firm mobility rates of managers in British and American industry is probably the Ohio/Midlands study of Inkson *et al.* They concluded that there was only a 'fractional difference between the two managerial samples'. There is then considerable confusion in the literature, heightened by the fact that impressions are often taken for evidence and that much of it is self-citing. My own findings are detailed below in Table 2, and I conclude that the evidence is not consistent with the view that the managerial employees of American firms had experienced greated mobility than the similar group employed in the British firms.

Table 2. Number of firms in the career of managerial respondents

No. of firms	US managers		GB managers	
	%	N	%	N
1	17·2	25	15	12
2–4	56·6	82	62	48
5+	26·2	38	23	18
Total	100·0	145	100·0	78

There are other sorts of managerial mobility besides inter-firm mobility in which one might have expected to find differences between the two samples. Not only can managers move between firms, but they can also move between functions during their careers and between jobs within the same firm. Table 3 below summarizes the data on the number of jobs that managers have held within their present firm. These findings, which show some differences in intra-organizational job mobility, were predictable enough from an earlier finding that whilst all the American firms were operating some form of management development programme, only two of the British firms were. These management development programmes involved, amongst other things, making sure that each manager went through a programme of different jobs. This finding is supported by other workers, cf. Granick, Novotny, Inkson *et al.*, and Ellis and Child. Although several writers, notably Granick and Sofer, have suggested that there might be more movement between functions inside American firms, I could find no evidence of this in my study, exactly the same percentage of managers (44 per cent) in both populations reported that they had changed functions during their careers.

A popularly held view of the differences between British and American managers, and one that can be grounded in my theoretical framework, is the view that American managers are more committed both to their organizations and to the business world in general, than their British

Table 3. Number of jobs held in present firm, British and 'American' managers

No. of jobs	US managers		GB managers	
	%	N	%	N
1	19	28	29	23
2–4	60	87	61	47
5+	21	30	10	8

counterparts. This was a complex hypothesis to test and one that required considerable disentangling before one could operate with it. In the questionnaire the managers were presented with four statements about their relationship to their job and were asked to indicate which came closest to their views. The statements were: 'A dominant factor in my life and as a primary source of satisfaction'; 'A distinctly interesting and important part of my life'; 'An activity separate from the rest of my life and one which must not be allowed to dominate'; 'A source of demand and pressure that threatens other activities'. Roughly 75 per cent of both populations opted for the second response and although rather more 'American' managers indicated that their job was a dominant factor in their lives, it is the overwhelming *similarity* of the responses from the two populations that represents the main finding. Another way of testing the general hypothesis was to compare the opinions of the two groups of managers on what qualities they thought necessary for success in business. Yet when the question is phrased in this way, the literature itself reflects an ambiguous view of the American business manager. On the one hand, one has a body of material tracing its descent from the protestant ethic. This historical legacy, the hypothesis states, can still be seen in the 'inner-directed' American businessman devoting most of his energies to the pursuit of economic success. This view is challenged, in general terms, by David Riesman in his celebrated essay, *The Lonely Crowd*, and developed more specifically in the business environment by W. H. Whyte in his treatise *The Organization Man*. Here the thesis is advanced that individuals are becoming increasingly 'other-directed'. In order to test for the presence or absence of these characteristics amongst the two samples of managers, ten traits relating to business success were derived from the Riesman-Whyte hypothesis (following the work of Porter). The managers were asked to rate them on the basis of how important they thought they were for success in business. The traits are listed below:

Inner-directed	Other-directed
Forcefulness	Tactfulness
Imagination	Agreeableness
Independence	Cautiousness
Self-confidence	Adaptability
Decisiveness	Cooperativeness

The results of this exercise were as follows: first, the responses of the British and 'American' managers could have been drawn from the same population. Although the 'American' managers did rate 'forcefulness' rather more highly than the British, whilst the British rated 'cooperativeness' rather more highly than the 'Americans', the results do not lend support for the hypothesis that managers working for American firms felt that they had to adopt a more aggressive strategy to be successful. Secondly, the items did *not* fall neatly, as far as the respondents were concerned, into packages of 'inner' or 'other' directed items.

Finally to two hypotheses about the differences between British and American industrial companies that are prominent in the literature. First, that those working for American firms would work harder and longer. Certainly more managers working for the American firms complained of the pressure of work compared with those working for the corresponding British firms. I think this was partly because some of the American firms, particularly those that were using schemes like 'management by objectives' had put a greater structure on managerial jobs, had set targets and deadlines where none had previously existed. These feelings of work pressure mentioned by the 'American' managers were backed by the answers to the question on how many hours they worked on company business per week. Controlling for managerial level and the function of managers, those working for American firms worked longer hours, although the differences did not reach a level of statistical significance. The average hours worked per week by 'American' managers on company business was 50.85 hours, whilst the corresponding figure for the British managers was 47.91 hours. The second hypothesis was that the American firms would be more ruthless than the British in dealing with managerial 'failures'. This hypothesis gains considerable support in the literature. Chruden and Sherman talk of the 'hire and fire' reputation of American firms in Europe, and Sofer in his comparative study of the American firm 'Autoline' with the British firm 'Octane Ltd', notes the 'unusually high risk of becoming a casualty at some point' in the American firm, and the propensity to 'retain dead wood' on the part of the British firm. These features are supported by the observations of Farmer and Thomas. I attempted to test this hypothesis by asking the personnel managers about their policies on this matter, and the 'American' personnel managers did by and large give the impression of greater ruthlessness. Analysis of the managerial labour turnover figures for the two groups of companies, however, did not appear to substantiate their claims.

Conclusion

The research design of this study has been rigorous in that it has compared American firms operating in England with similar British firms. I have argued that if American firms operating in England and employing English managers still manage to exhibit differences from their British counterparts then this would have been strong evidence in favour of cultural values influencing business structure and behaviour. The study design is not perfect however, because it does admit of the possibility of one other factor accounting for the reported differences between the British and American firms, the fact that the American firms were *overseas* subsidiaries. In order to control for this factor the British and American firms would have had to have been located in a third country so that all the firms were overseas subsidiaries.

In fact the number of differences discovered between the two groups of firms was rather small, and this is surprising in view of the popular stereotypes about American firms and their employees. It is worthwhile summarizing the differences that were detected and considering their causes. The view that American companies would reflect the more open culture of American society, and would be more willing to disclose information about themselves, was confirmed. It is difficult to see how this could be a function of being an overseas subsidiary. Four major differences were noted in the structure and operation of the two groups of companies. First, the American firms tended to give greater importance to the human capital of their organization than did the British firms. They took more care in the selection and appraisal of managers and were more inclined to train their personnel. It is difficult to see this result occurring because the American firms were *overseas* subsidiaries, and this interpretation is reinforced by the fact that the personnel area was not one that was much subject to formal controls by the parent companies in the United States. Secondly, the American firms made far greater use of a wider range of techniques for managerial control, this was particularly true in the area of personnel, marketing and finance. This finding is consistent with either the culture hypothesis or the overseas subsidiary hypothesis. Thirdly, the American firms tended to possess an organizational climate that was more informal and employee centred, status distinctions were less evident in most of the American organizations. This finding seems much more consistent with the culture hypothesis. Fourthly, whereas the British firms were inclined to stress production as being the most crucial area of the firm, and the ethos and methods of this function tended to influence the whole structure, in the American firms the stress was more likely to be placed on marketing. This result is consistent with either of the two hypotheses, although it was certainly true that because the American parents tended to control the production process rather tightly, then from the point of view of the American subsidiary, their emphasis tended to be placed in that area where they felt that their own efforts would be crucial, and this tended to be marketing. The four areas of difference mentioned above all refer to the organization of the company; interestingly enough, fewer differences were found amongst the managers in the two groups of companies, and perhaps this indicates that it was easier to mould company structure from across the Atlantic than it was the management personnel, especially when they were the nationals of another country. Only two major differences were observed between the British and 'American' managers. The outstanding difference relates to qualifications; the managers working for the American companies were significantly better qualified than their British counterparts. The difference relates both to formal academic qualifications and management training. Although such a stress on qualifications would be consistent with controlling the subsidiary from overseas, particularly perhaps the management training finding, such training being required to manage the more formal systems of control found in the American firms, one has to place this interpretation in the context of the finding that the personnel area was one of the least affected by policies and instructions issuing from the American parent. The second difference observed was that the 'American' managers had experienced significantly more internal job mobility in their companies.

It has been a common practice in cross-cultural management research to separate cultural values from other variables that might be thought to influence business structure and behaviour, e.g. economic variables, technology. In this tradition I might have counterposed capitalism with culture in the explanatory framework of this study. It is important to realize however that the economic system always exists inside a sociocultural system and both systems are historical products. One of the gravest errors that has been made by those writers who have attempted cultural explanations of economic behaviour is to have treated culture as a separate causal factor which needs to be entirely distinguished from economic factors. The sociocultural stock of any society has been formed over a long period of time in interplay with the economic system and the two are inextricably bound together. The stock of 'solutions' to the economic problems faced by the controllers of the nation state or the individual firm have to be found within the context of the sociocultural structure of their own society. One example from this study will I hope make this point: is the more informal, employee centred structure of American companies to be explained by reference to the lack of status distinctions inside American society, themselves a reflection of the values of achievement, universalism etc., which had certain historical origins? Or alternatively, is one to argue that such an organizational strategy is adopted by many American firms, particularly perhaps the most 'progressive' ones, because it is believed to be more efficient and profitable? i.e., the explanation is couched in terms of the demands of capitalism. I hope that this example demonstrates the futility of counterposing culture *or* capitalism.

Typologies of Middle-class Mobility
G. Payne

Reprinted with permission from Geoff Payne, 'Typologies of Middle-class Mobility', *Sociology*, vol. 7, no. 3, September 1973

Our ideas about the mobility process are drawn from a number of studies but here I wish to deal with three of the most important: the work of Merton on locals and cosmopolitans, the work of Mrs Stacey on traditionalists and non-traditionalists, and Watson on burgesses and spiralists. Each of these widely accepted dichotomous typologies has been treated as expressing established laws of social behaviour, and together they have formed the basis and inspiration for several recent works. But very little has been done to demonstrate exactly what are the intrinsic strengths of these similar dichotomous typologies which explain their acceptance as sociological commonplaces.

For example, Bell enthusiastically adopts Watson's concepts as

the most important advance in stratification theory since Lockwood's concept of work situation.

Although he later suggests three new subtypes of spiralist (depending on expectations of future mobility and whether they work for bureaucratic organizations) there is no discussion of the basic processes involved, and the subtypes are not used in the rest of the book to explain other data. But more important, Bell confuses three sets of terminology: spiralist/burgess, cosmopolitan/local, and non-local/local. For instance he says on page 47 that his respondents 'can be spiralists and burgesses, or in Merton's (1957) terminology cosmopolitans or locals', a confusion he repeats on pages 6 and 19. Subsequently in 'Community Studies', he and

Newby compound the error by equating Stacey and Merton in at least two places (a mistake first made by Frankenberg).

More recently Edgell has been equally uncritical, quoting Bell's high regard for Watson's advance in stratification theory, defining spiralism, and then using it with no further discussion. While he is concerned to relate spiralism to family life, so extending the idea of spiralism by looking at its consequences, he nowhere considers whether the spiralist/burgess dichotomy is the most useful typology in the first place.

Even Pahl, who has been the major contributor in recent studies of mobility, has added to the confusion in an article which first appeared in 1966 and has since been reprinted. Indeed, in much of his work, there seem to be two implicit assumptions; not only are spiralists real people (not just types) but their behaviour in local milieux can be typified as clearly as their career behaviour. However, this typification is not a simple one. Around London, the spiralists from outside the South East 'find these outer metropolitan estates convenient transit camps' and therefore live insulated from their locality. But in a Hertfordshire New Town, while both husbands and wives of the mobile 'new radical middle class' favour part-time voluntary or paid work for the wife, and meetings and entertaining are popular activities, some other middle-class newcomers are isolated and lonely, and still others (more Conservative) have already migrated to nearby villages. In the villages the spiralists are 'joiners' – 'the village is defined in terms of the quality of its social life'; the spiralists 'have defined for themselves a village-in-the-mind'.

So there are a number of different typical spiralist adaptations to local social milieux which are not only unexplained by the type 'spiralist', but which must also raise the question of how far spiralism can be used to refer to anything more than specifically *career* behaviour. Certainly, when Pahl has to explain aspects of behaviour in local milieux by saying that some spiralists are localistic cosmopolitans, the time has come to reconsider the basic terms of the typologies.

This is not to say that typologies in general have no uses in sociology. But as Pahl has argued in 'Managers and Their Wives', knowledge about patterns can easily become a substitute for understanding the processes which give rise to those patterns. Unfortunately he does not go on from there to reconsider the basic mobility typologies in the light of his understanding of the dynamics of managerial careers and local behaviour. It is in an attempt to shift the focus from the currently used (and abused) typologies to these underlying processes, that this paper considers the work of Merton, Stacey and Watson. In each case, the comments below seek to emphasize certain aspects which have been since overlooked, thereby showing that none of the studies should be treated uncritically as suitable bases for generalization.

Locals and cosmopolitans

Merton was concerned with 'influentials', a term which refers specifically to a mode of interpersonal communications behaviour and has nothing to do with power, status, or structure. His data were collected from the American Small Town culture tradition as it existed thirty years ago. The sample was very small, and Merton himself makes few claims about his data. In two footnotes he reminds the reader:

Although figures summarizing our case study are cited from time to time, these are merely heuristic, not demonstrative in character. They serve to indicate the sources of interpretive hypotheses which await detailed, systematic enquiry.

Merton himself is quite clear that his is only a pilot-study, but it is a pilot-study which has in fact not led to the detailed, systematic enquiry which is needed.

Therefore the widespread acceptance of Merton's concepts is not based on any rigorous empirical groundings. This is not to argue that his concepts are totally wrong: even without solid research behind them or flowing from them for that matter, it could be the case that as ideal-typical constructs, they serve a useful function in conceptual mapping for other sociologists. But in fact Merton's dichotomy has limitations at this level as well, as a brief consideration of his work will show.

The two types can best be described by the ways in which they differ. For instance the cosmopolitan discussed international affairs (that is to say the War) at an international level, while the local talked about the repercussions international affairs would have on the local community. The local was more likely to be interested in Rovere people, to be involved in local politics, and to read the local newspaper. The cosmopolitan was more concerned with friends at a distance, with social services rather than politics, and was more likely to subscribe to several national periodicals. There is considerable variation within types, but a contrast between the ideal-typical cosmopolitan and local shows that the former is younger, significantly more educated, and is a 'newcomer' who has lived in a number of communities, unlike the local influential.

Here he is relying too heavily on his 'heuristic' figures. What he misses is that the career patterns of the two groups are different, and that the cosmopolitan has a wider and more varied life experience outside the town and fits less well into the community because of his recent arrival, as Merton's own data show. It can be argued that because of more extensive ties (of kinship and friendship) outside the community, he is *held back* from joining: because he is alien, he is *pushed back* by the community.

If Merton's data are treated from this point of view, different patterns of previous experience are seen to explain modes of influence, not *vice versa*. In the same way, differences in associational membership are explained not by community orientation, but by the previous experience. It follows that immigrants need not necessarily be cosmopolitans, as this depends on the range of their life experience and the extent to which they can integrate into the community.

The popularity of the local/cosmopolitan typology does not lie in its empirical strength, nor in its heuristic utility. Indeed it could be argued that it does not lie in Merton's original work at all. Rather it arises out of Gouldner's manipulation of the concepts. Gouldner applied the local/cosmopolitan dichotomy to academics in a small liberal arts college, and not surprisingly, the sociological profession was quick to appreciate its narcissistic potential. Among others, Glaser and Kornhauser explained the position of the highly educated professional in the bureaucracy, in terms of these orientations. But while this usage may be valid to describe a narrow category of professionals and their occupational values, this is not the same as a blanket application to the rest of the middle class and their *community* behaviour. With a slight modification of terminology, it is this blanket usage which has been accepted into current urban sociology.

Traditionalists and non-traditionalists

One of the principal sources of ideas about mobility and orientation to local social milieux in Britain is Margaret Stacey's study of Banbury, 'Tradition and Change'. Like Rovere, Banbury twenty years ago was a small town isolated in a rural area, and not typical of the operation of local milieux generally. Few areas suffer such abrupt and massive invasions by outsiders, and few are so isolated and established in the first place. It might be reasonable to generalize from Banbury to other settlements which are experiencing similar influxes such as the development of new towns around cores of older villages. But it would be less plausible to generalize from Banbury to all new estates, and less so to individual families moving house. In these cases, which are far more common social phenomena, the ratio of newcomer to established resident is less likely to be disturbed, and the balance remains much more heavily weighted towards the established residents.

Nevertheless it might be argued that 'Tradition and Change' does provide a suitable theoretical starting point for a general typology. Unfortunately, this is not so, because there has been a confusion of three separate concepts; previous life experience (immigrant and non-immigrant), value orientation (traditionalist or non-traditionalist), and social class.

Stacey rejects actor-based estimates of what a 'Banburian' is, because 'estimates depend on the individual, upon his age, his occupation, his politics, his attitude to life, and his readiness to conform to and accept the ways of the town' and apparently, despite the later dichotomous picture, no clear pattern was perceptible. Instead four categories were used, depending on place of birth and residence to the age of seven. These migration categories are constructed in a way which ignores the fact that social relationships accumulate over lifetimes.

In dealing with the second component of the typology, the traditionalist/non-traditionalist concept, it is easier to quote Stacey:

> traditionalists: those who are part of the traditional social structure and who live by the traditional values and customs of old Banbury. There are others, the non-traditionalists who do not belong to the traditional social structure and do not accept its values and customs; they do not share any common social system or system of values and customs for they are composed of many different and sometimes opposed groups; they include those who have come in with quite other systems of values and customs and those who are developing new ways to meet the changed circumstances of their life and work.

Thus the non-traditionalists appear to include those who refuse to accept the local society and those who *do* accept it, and are attempting to integrate into it or compromise with it: two very different things. Stacey does discuss

> people who have come into the town from similar social backgrounds to follow traditional occupations, or who have accepted enough of Banbury's traditions to fit into it or to make their life in the locality with Banbury as their principal frame of reference. They, as much as the Banbury-born traditionalists, rely on the local papers as essential sources of information about the fortunes and misfortunes of local people and families or of the clubs and societies.

But is this further category as traditional as other Banburians, lacking informal gossip networks and local kinship networks, particularly as

> traditional society is made up of a network of face-to-face groups based on family, neighbours, occupations, associations, and status?

Even if the traditionalist/non-traditionalist and Banburian/immigrant definitions can be clarified, their application leads to a complex typology, in which there are twenty-four possible cells if we include three social classes. While some of these combinations are less common than others, all are logically possible. Stacey concentrates on examples for eleven of the twenty-four types, principally non-migrants who are traditionalists, and immigrants who are non-traditionalists. She says at one point, 'Perhaps the majority of non-traditionalists are immigrants', in other words, at best a large minority of non-traditionalists are *not* immigrants, but throughout 'Tradition and Change' the respondents are discussed as if the traditionalist/immigrant attributes can be coalesced into a dichotomy for each social class. On Stacey's own evidence, this is not true at an empirical level, and there is certainly no heuristic value in such a confusion. As she has since pointed out, her perspective at the time was to extend the idea of traditional and non-traditional *systems* to traditional and non-traditional *individuals*. It is not surprising that no clear picture emerges from the data, beyond a basic polarization.

It is impossible to tell how far this class polarization would continue to be more important than migration and orientation, had these last two been kept separate in the analytical framework. Integration into a local social milieu is not just a matter of attitude and length of residence, as both can vary independently. Of course we have here concerned ourselves with only one aspect of the Banbury study, not with the study as a whole. But for our narrow purpose, it has neither the empirical groundings nor the analytical framework on which to build and support the generalizations about middle-class mobility which have been hung upon it.

Burgesses and spiralists

Our third major source of ideas is Watson's work which is explicitly concerned with the generation of theories. In the case of his concepts of 'burgess' and 'spiralist', there is little to be said about the methodology as he himself says very little. Once again the original study was carried out around 1950; it concerned a small coal-mining community on the East Coast of Scotland.

In contrast to Merton and Stacey, Watson's concepts concentrate on the career structures of the middle class. The 'spiralist' works for national or international organizations, moving within and between them, from place to place and from job to job, in the course of his career. The 'burgess' remains anchored in one place, and therefore his identification with the local social milieu is different and more complete. As settlements become increasingly enmeshed in national economic and social organizations, so the presence of spiralists becomes more important.

Watson makes a number of distinctions between spiralists according to education, occupation, stage of career, and policy of employer, but he suggests that there is a common ethic of spiralism which largely depends on the experience of university education. While

the product of Eton and Oxford is a different social person from the product of Grammar School and Redbrick, [they both] share the general spiralist culture acquired through their higher education and prolonged training,

a culture which is different from that of each local community. Thus to Watson, education and training are important, rather than the subsequent events of interaction with the local system or the particular wider perspective acquired through a mobile career. Here Watson is treating both career and education as being broadly homogeneous for all the spiralists, but this does not explain his other concept of the blocked spiralist, a spiralist who decides to 'go local', stops spiralling, and settles into a local community. Only if we consider the modifying influence of successive residential periods (or changes in family cycle, or career values and so on) can Watson be adapted to explain the 'spiralist dropout'. Cumulative career experience is worth more attention than Watson gives it, for it is the degree to which successive local milieux succeeded or failed to meet his changing social needs that helps to shape the spiralist's consequent actions.

His second subcategory is based on the potential mobility of the particular job that the spiralist does. He points out that the difference between fee-paid and salary-paid professionals is that the former have been less integrated into modern bureaucratic systems and so are less open to mobility. Predominantly salary-paid professions depend on large-scale units of production, expensive capital plant, bureaucratic hierarchies administering centralized directives, and large numbers of people. Fee-paid professionals are either an occupational elite (consultants to an industry as a whole, a relatively new hybrid) or individuals who are self-employed in small units of production needing relatively smaller populations to provide the cases which require the application of their skills.

A corollary to this which Watson does not develop is that those in the last category have different relationships in the local social system. The local inhabitants are largely irrelevant to the spiralist as far as his job goes: but the general practitioner, the family solicitor, the private tutor, the priest, the small shopkeeper, the social worker, and to a slightly lesser extent the bank manager and the estate agent, whatever their occupational contract with national organizations, all depend much more on the goodwill of the local residents. The local inhabitants are highly relevant to the non-spiralist *and* to the typical fee-paid professional in the very nature of their jobs. The essence of being a GP is not the practising of medicine, but the practising of medicine on the local inhabitants.

Similarly while clergymen do have a 'flat' occupational spiral, it entails a different integration into the local milieu than most other spiralist professions. In these others, the spiralist is selling his skills indirectly to the community (and through the organization, on a national scale) rather than to the local residents. Thus the case of the priest, bank manager, and to some extent the teacher, fall between the pure burgess and the pure spiralist; the personnel officer may have closer links with the local system than the research physicist, and line managers have closer links than staff managers.

Another ill-fitting category is the 'pseudo-local'. On the one hand he may be Pahl's spiralist (or immigrant), who has the village-in-the-mind and who is therefore committed to the social life of the locality: his rootlessness generates a 'Need for Place', apparently at a psychological level. He is unlikely to be accepted as a local by his own local class equivalents. Alternatively he may be a blocked spiralist who is adjusting his orientation. A third possibility are the wives of spiralists who use up their spare time in community activities out of commitment or out of boredom, pending their husbands' next move. In 'democratic' households, the husband is likely to be involved as an adjunct to his wife's self-presentation.

Watson also raises the issue of company policy. Some employers encourage mobility with removal grants, furnishing allowances, explicit training policies and so on. Others, such as ICI, combine this with entertainment grants to staff personnel for the first two years of residence in a new area, precisely to increase social intercourse with neighbours and presumably in the hope that new contacts dispel loneliness and improve morale among employees and their families, and are a good form of public relations with local residents. This modifies the social relations which arise out of the nature of occupations themselves. Conversely, other firms discourage local involvements so that personnel have no ties which hinder the efficient mobilization of all available talent at the time and place the company decides (the army barracks are an extreme form of this). Finally some firms encourage mobility within the organization, while others do not make this an explicit policy.

Conclusions

This review of the three core studies shows that while all relate migration to integration in local social milieux, they cannot be subsumed as one conceptual unit. Frankenberg, Edgell, Pahl, and Bell and Newby all treat these studies in an oversimplified way, without first considering the status of the basic concepts that they employ interchangeably. There is nothing wrong in using mobility as a starting point in the analysis of local social behaviour, but in doing so there are better strategies on which to base research than typologies, as a more flexible social action approach indicates.

Thus if typologies, or twin-poled continua, are rejected, the way is open to study underlying processes: this will include the actor's experience before he arrives, and his subsequent reactions, both within the social milieu under study, and beyond it. As this widens the range of investigation, the next step must be to start to codify the factors involved.

Thus the response of the migrant is a function of his own previous experience of occupational and family life, and the features of the local milieux he enters. On his part, there is the dislocation, the severing of past ties and the search for new ones, the forgetting of inappropriate old values and customs, and the acquisition of new ones. There is also the needs which his family situation creates. Most studies of mobility have not given sufficient attention to family life-cycle. Children raise problems of care and education which can determine place of residence and interactions in that place. At the same time, dual career families have different problems from those where only the husband works.

It follows that migration and local orientation are complex subjects, covering a variety of processes. Rather than imposing a typological order, it is more useful to consider the clusters of related variables involved. The 14 areas for investigation listed below are a starting point in an attempt to conceptualize the process by which the mobile middle class take up their role and identity in local social milieux.

(1) *Orientation to the local milieu*: The migrant (or young local) may treat the local milieu as a 'staging post' and thus have no desire to integrate, or he may be eager to enter into the social life of the area. Previous life experience is particularly important here in explaining values and attitudes. It may be useful to know how the migrant integrated in his previous place of residence.

(2) *Orientation to other communities*: As well as retaining external reference groups in status terms, the migrant may well be 'held back' from joining his new social milieu because of previously acquired social relationships, particularly kinship ties. The adolescent period is important in this connection, as is social mobility in the conventional sense.

(3) *Orientation to the occupation*: The individual may have a commitment to his local occupational organization, or to his profession in general, or something in between. Alternatively, he may value his occupation to such an extent that he isolates himself from the local milieu because of the time he gives to his occupation.

(4) *Occupational need of the local milieu*: Some occupations relate directly to local residents like clergyman, head teacher, doctor, or even personnel officer. Other jobs, like research scientists (or sociologists?), are not intrinsically involved with local residents. This involvement may be informal, or at an institutional level such as social security, employment exchanges, other forms, welfare services, etc.

(5) *Need to use the local milieu as a (status) reference group*: Individuals

define themselves in terms of other people: thus house, garden, furnishings, etc., are seen as appropriate to a certain status. This may work by limiting social interaction (a big house removed but visible from the road) or by interaction (entertaining at home, conspicuous 'pseudo-local' use of a public house, etc.). Such a need for a status referent is an acute problem for the migrant, who is by definition isolated, especially at first. To some extent the answer is to use a non-located community: geographically distant professional colleagues, friends from previous places of residence, etc.

(6) *Need to join the local social milieu*: Whatever the migrant's orientation or need for a reference group, he and his family are to some extent forced to interact with other residents as an answer to routine problems like baby-sitting and shopping, and emergencies such as illness, childbirth and accidents, which can only be solved by cooperation with others or with formal (often voluntary) agencies. Stage in family life-cycle is most important here.

(7) *Skills in joining local milieu*: Experience of mobility makes the migrant familiar with the techniques of adaptation and the problems that must be overcome if he is to participate fully in the local milieu.

(8) *Extent of change*: The migrant's values and attitudes may be more or less inappropriate, depending on his previous experience. He may be exchanging a commuter village for another commuter village, or a village for an inner suburb; the degree of dislocation will vary.

(9) *The recency of the migration*: It is necessary to know not only how long the migrant has been resident but also how his orientation and needs have changed since his move. Changes in the local social milieu must also be allowed for, in order to obtain a complete picture.

The remaining factors are not so much of the migrant, rather they are more conditions of the local milieu in which he finds himself.

(10) *Availability of occupational facilities*: An individual may be able to achieve promotion or change his employer without moving house if there are suitable occupational opportunities perceived as being within range. Alternatively he will have to move (as ultimately his children will probably need to do). When the wife also has a career, this is an acute problem, for the two careers are seldom in harmony, and priorities have to be assigned, usually to the husband's career.

(11) *Availability of commercial facilities*: The highly educated and affluent migrant demands a special range of shopping and public entertainment which may not be available locally. Wide experience allows comparison, and acquired tastes for the consumer styles of 'colour supplement life' may be the cause of considerable discontent, particularly in the case of wives. A subcategory of this is the availability of suitable housing (in a status sense) which helps to determine the geographical location of the migrant, with consequences because of the friction of space

for his local activity. It is thus necessary to know something of the migrant's expectations and his perception of the locality, as well as the actual availability of these facilities.

(12) *Availability of social facilities*: The move will leave the migrant with relatively fewer kinship and friendship ties in the locality. If there are no personnel with whom to cooperate (as in (6) above) and no associations (or lack of numbers to support such associations which provide for the specialist interests of the migrant) then integration is harder as the voluntary association is an important mechanism of integration for the migrant. This is not to assume anything about the migrant's *need* to integrate; at this point the concern is the solution of any such need.

(13) *Availability of transitional roles*: The local subculture may include the role of recent immigrant and mechanisms to integrate him, or his arrival may be resented and resisted. The overall balance between locals and immigrants will probably influence this.

(14) *Extent of cohesion in the local social milieu*: At the start of this article attention was drawn to the range of social relationships which can comprise a social milieu. In some highly integrated and visible milieux, joining one association or making one friendship labels the migrant as a particular 'type' for the residents, and so restricts his further interactions. In other milieux the migrant can remain invisible: compared with the ideal-typical village the city provides a greater resource of groups with which to associate – each of which is independent of the other groups.

With minor changes of syntax, the same areas of interest apply to the non-migrant, or 'native'. By using this term and the word 'migrant' attention can be focused on a single attribute of any person under study, his geographical mobility; it is then possible to discuss his orientations and needs separately, and also to see the relative effect of dislocation due to mobility as opposed to lack of integration due to orientation and needs. At the same time, an understanding of particular milieux can be obtained. This is something which the studies above have failed to achieve.

The reason for discussing these ideas about middle-class migration was not merely the migrants' intrinsic interest or significance within modern capitalist society, although that is important. Rather, they can throw light on the operation of local milieux, a problem which in its various disguises has dominated urban sociology. The list of areas for investigation not only deals with the migrant, it forms a provisional framework with which to investigate the behaviour of any middle-class resident in any area, as part of a general social action approach to the analysis of local social milieux.

Local Class Structure

J. Littlejohn

Reprinted with permission from John Littlejohn, *Westrigg; the Sociology of a Cheviot Parish*, Routledge and Kegan Paul, 1963, pp, 1, 2, 7–9, 81–4, 90, 111–12, 117–21, 223–9

Westrigg is an upland parish in a mainly rural county in the south of Scotland.

Settlement is of the dispersed type. There is no village in the parish, no shops or pubs; dwellings and the few public buildings are scattered along the valley floors with here and there a small cluster, the two most compact being forestry settlements. The two nearest towns are fifteen and seventeen miles away. Near the junction in the parish of the two roads from these towns are a post office, school and smiddy. This, the centre of communication, is thought of by parishioners as the centre of the parish, though the geographical centre is two miles north from it. By common agreement a Public Hall was erected at the geographical centre in 1922.

The scattered settlement pattern is partly due to the requirements of large-scale sheep farming. Almost every cottage is tied, i.e., is part of the property of a farm (or the Forestry Commission now) and can be rented only if one is employed by the farmer (or Forestry Commission).

However, the settlement pattern cannot be explained simply by reference to the environment and the requirements of sheep farming. The present pattern took shape under an organization of the farm in which the farm worker and his family belonged to the farm in a more strict sense than is the case now.

In everyday conversation parishioners categorize each other into three classes by using the terms 'gentleman farmer', 'working farmer' and 'working folk'. There are differences in the frequencies with which persons of these categories employ the terms; those designated 'working farmers' and 'working folk' use all three terms much oftener than those designated 'gentleman farmer'. The 'gentleman farmers' rarely use the term to refer to themselves, and do not often speak of 'working farmers' either, preferring the term 'small farmer'.

The local terms, gentleman and working farmers, and working folk, obviously imply a classification of the agricultural population and of forestry labourers.

That the classes are viewed as superior and inferior to each other is soon apparent in conversation. When identifying a third party for me informants would say, e.g., 'he's not a working farmer, he's *only* a working man' or 'he's not a gentleman farmer, just a working farmer'. An upper-middle-class man once remarked of agricultural labourers 'of course some of these people are hardly better than animals in intelligence and way of living'. Sometimes irritation at one provokes sweeping condemnation of the class as when a farmer exclaimed *à propos* some minor lapse on the part of a shepherd, 'they're all alike these people, they just can't think'. A lower-middle-class woman remarked of a working-class neighbour, 'you can see the lower element coming out even in her'. A view of the working class widely held among both the middle classes is that they are 'childish'. Direct remarks like these are not very common: more common is the indirect and quite unmalicious reference like this by a farmer, 'This morning a stranger passed by the field where I was working and said "good morning" to me as if I were just a labourer. I was quite pleased, in fact a lifelong ambition of mine has been to be treated as if I were nobody.'

Employers of labour obviously wield power in the sense of being in the position to hire and fire, and in addition a farmer's power of influencing a workman's chances of employment in a district are by no means negligible. Farmers in any one district are in an informal compact as over against workmen, shown in this farmer's description of hiring. 'You advertise in the papers and wait and hope someone will answer. Then when you get an answer you ring up his employer and ask "are you finished with this man?" – "yes" – "is he any good?" – "wouldn't touch him with a barge pole" – "all right, thank you". Eventually you meet a man and tell him the conditions he'll work under . . .' When a workman leaves a job he is given a written testimonial containing no adverse judgements, which he knows to be worthless. A shepherd said, 'You only ask for the testimonial because if you don't get one your neighbours would think there was something far wrong. But the bosses talk about you on the telephone to each other. That's where they have you.' Several workmen cited cases of alleged victimization, in which a farmer prevented an employee he had sacked from finding another job.

The sociological problem of determining how class status is allocated cannot be solved solely by pointing to so many factors, all of which are already known, or by an arbitrary decision that one or other is 'fundamental'. What is important is that at different points in the system different factors become of crucial importance in the allocation of status. This again was clear from comments of informants while making class placements. An area where there was much hesitation in judgement (among informants of all classes) was the distinction between craftsmen and the smaller working farmers. A craftsman may own no more property than a bag of tools and a motor car, yet his income can be as sizeable as a small farmer's. A craftsman may be in a position of authority over an apprentice or may hire a young assistant, and though in such a relationship the teacher/pupil note will often sound, the craftsman has ultimate sanctions at his disposal not greatly different from those a small farmer has *vis-à-vis* an employee. In this area too it is often difficult to make a distinction between craftsman and farmer on the basis of 'standard of living' or style of life. Yet all informants eventually did draw a distinction solely on the basis of the sheer fact of land ownership (it being understood that 'land' meant a holding large enough to be an independent business enterprise). 'After all,' they would say, 'he does own a farm, and (X the craftsman) doesn't.'

Higher up the system neither the sheer fact of property ownership nor its amount distinguishes between one class and another, the professional people having none and several upper-middle-class farmers having holdings as small as those of lower-middle-class farmers. The point in landvalues where factors other than size of farm come into play (in this community) seems to be at about 2000 acres. Above this size farmers are all of the upper-middle class, and sheer size is an important qualification; of one farmer a class peer remarked 'he gets in (to our class) of course just because his farm's so big'. Below this size the farmer may be of either class. The other factors brought to bear on status judgements at this point with regard to both farmers and professionals are education and 'background', 'style of life' and estimate of relative income. Though I call these 'factors' as if they were four clearly distinguishable variables, informants did not in fact separately specify them as such. None used the actual term 'style of life', though women informants obviously meant this when they stressed the importance of good manners, eating customs and size of house as determinants of status.

It is implicit in the data presented above that the class system of the parish cannot be represented as three distinct groups sharply demarcated one from another so that boundaries are clearly apparent between adjoining classes. There is obviously a certain indefiniteness about it – a feature of class systems in industrial society which has often been commented upon. The area of indefiniteness in the system calls for some explanation but first it must be described. Briefly, the position is that while the uppermiddle class is sharply distinguished from the lower-middle class there is not the same clarity of boundary between the latter and the working class. Taking the criterion of association this means that while members of the upper-middle class do not associate with members of the other two classes, some members of the lower-middle sometimes associate with some members of the working class.

This feature of the system is closely connected with another already discussed, namely that the class status of a person or a family is not necessarily determined by reference to one single value; and since the values used in allocating status are hardly commensurable on a single scale, in the area described status can be allocated or claimed on the basis of several values.

All informants agreed that speech and accent were the most trustworthy symbols in placing a stranger, with clothes and manners a fairly reliable second. That all these function as symbols of status is clearly seen in the treatment meted out to persons who attempt to display one of these traits as it is displayed by a class higher than the one they are known to belong to. They are ridiculed in a way which shows that they are held to be trying to claim a class status they are not entitled to. For example, recently some working youths bought a suit of clothing of the expensive sort worn in the upper-middle class. They were jeered at by their class peers and each given a nickname showing he was regarded as claiming illegitimate status – 'Lord Westrigg', 'Sir X', and so on. Similarly there is one working-class family whose speech is more like the middle classes than like the rest of the working class. The lower-middle class regarded this family with approval saying they did not speak so 'Scotch' as the others and were not 'rough' in manner, etc. To the rest of the working class the family is 'affected', accused of 'putting on airs' and 'thinking itself above us'.

The culture of the higher classes is officially defined as better than that of the lower. In the local school the language and manners taught are those of the middle classes. Though the majority of the children are of the working class they are discouraged from using their own normal speech. During one lesson, for example, the children were asked to name various sorts of buildings shown to them in pictures, of which one was a kennel. Asked to name it one of the boys replied correctly in dialect 'a dughoose'. He was somewhat chagrined to be told he was 'wrong'. In short the children are being trained to believe that their normal way of speaking is wrong and to imitate the dialect of the middle classes. The same applies to manners; the children are taught to address and refer to adults as 'Mr' and 'Mrs', to use handkerchiefs and to be circumspect in interaction with others. These are middle-class customs. Working-class men in particular demand of each other an immediate solidarity in interaction which seems to render middle-class manners superfluous.

This brief sketch of class culture I hope justifies the use of the term 'social milieu' to describe the nature of social class. A social class is neither a mere category arbitrarily defined by myself on the basis of one or two 'characteristics' such as property ownership, nor is it a group in the strict sense of the term as implying clear cut boundaries and a constitution laying down a limited set of relationships among its members. A class is rather, for its members, one of the major horizons of all social experience, an area within which most experience is defined. Encompassing so much, it is rarely conceptualized.

This does not mean that the concept of a local class system is a sociologist's myth; it only means that individuals, when asked about it, answer in terms of their own experience of it. That there is a system is I think shown by the fact that no informant placed him or herself wrongly, no one claimed a status higher or lower than that accorded by the majority of fellow parishioners. Each person knows his or her place in the system, can place accurately other people he has the requisite information about, but has no need to turn his experience of the system into a conceptual scheme.

The classes differ in the range and frequency of their association outside the parish. The norm here is that the higher a class the wider and more frequent are its contacts outside the parish; or to adopt the network image, the higher the class the more dispersed is the network of relationships in which it is involved, the lower the class the more contained is its network. The basis of the difference in scale is the former's relative freedom from having to work to a routine timetable, and ownership of private means of transport and communication, as opposed to the latter's being tied to a daily job and dependent on public transport.

At this point it may be asked whether in fact the middle classes have lost power in the parish over the last fifty years. The data suggest that the more frequent contacts, both formal and informal, of the upper-middle class outside the parish serve to maintain their position of dominance within the parish.

It is the family and not the individual that is the unit of social class. By family in this context I mean those members of a family living together in the same household. It is necessary to state this because an individual can alter his class status in his own lifetime; the child can come to occupy a different status from his parents, the sibling from the sibling. In such cases persons of different status do not live together as members of the same household. That the family, in this sense, is the unit was clear both from informants, class placements and their comments while making them.

Since a family begins with a marriage, and since a class system restricts association among the population stratified, a full account of the connections between family and class must deal with the process known as assortative mating. Social barriers of any sort limit the possibilities of random contact among people, and tend to foster marriages between persons with similar social characteristics. Social class barriers are among the most important in this process. Where a class system prevails there are three possible combinations of class status of the spouses. The two can be of equal status, the man higher than the woman or the woman higher than the man. The first combination is the normal one; of all marriages in the parish only eight were not of this sort. The second combination is much more frequent than the third, the ratio here being seven to one.

It may be asked why any sort of marriage across class lines is relatively rare. Numerous reasons can be adduced which, however, are merely implicit in the class system itself.

These 'reasons' are, however, only aspects of the class system itself. Perhaps a more cogent explanation is to be found in the incompatibility between kinship norms and those governing relations between classes. There is a warm and friendly relationship between grandparents and children, and between parents' siblings and siblings' children. In cross-class marriage the children are in a different class from the parents and siblings of one of the spouses. People of different classes do not associate in warm and friendly relations. It seems likely that if marriage between members of different classes became general either the kinship system or the class system would have to alter very much from their present form. While I have no data to prove this, it is clear that in the community there is incompatibility between the two sets of norms and that where they conflict class norms take precedence. Relations with kinsfolk of a lower class are either severed or become characterized by a certain reserve. In either case accusations of snobbery are made by the lower against the higher. For example, one lower-middle-class man has an uncle in the parish who is a farm worker, but the two never associate. The former and his wife regard the latter as a tiresome old man, though he is highly respected among the working class. The uncle and members of his household sometimes express resentment against the nephew and his household.

That too frequent marriage across class lines might destroy the present class system is suggested by the fact that marriage of a woman of higher status to a man of lower is very much rarer than the opposite. It is regarded as a more serious breach of the norm. Association outside of work relationships is not merely a sociologist's index of quality of status; it is what equality of status means in everyday behaviour in the community itself.

Further Reading: **Class**

R. M. BLACKBURN and M. MANN, *The Working Class in the Labour Market*, Macmillan, 1979.

H. BRAVERMAN, *Labour and Monopoly Capital*, Monthly Review Press, 1974.

M. BULMER, *Working-class Images of Society*, Routledge and Kegan Paul, 1975.

J. BURNHAM, *The Managerial Revolution*, Penguin, 1962.

C. CROUCH, *Class Conflict and the Industrial Relations Crisis*, Heinemann, 1977.

D. GALLIE, *In Search of the New Working Class*, Cambridge University Press, 1978.

A. GIDDENS, *The Class Structure of the Advanced Societies*, Hutchinson, 1973.

J. H. GOLDTHORPE, D. LOCKWOOD, F. BECHOFER and J. PLATT, *The Affluent Worker in the Class Structure*, Cambridge University Press, 1969.

A. H. HALSEY, A. F. HEATH and J. M. RIDGE, *Origins and Destinations: Family, Class and Education in Modern Britain*, Clarendon Press, 1980.

C. D. HARBURY and D. M. W. N. HITCHINS, *Inheritance and Wealth Inequality in Britain*, Allen and Unwin, 1979.

R. HYMAN and R. PRICE, *The New Working Class?*, Macmillan, 1983.

S. OSSOWSKI, *Class Structure in the Social Consciousness*, Routledge and Kegan Paul, 1963.

F. PARKIN, *Class Inequality and Political Order*, MacGibbon and Kee, 1971.

N. POULANTZAS, *Classes in Contemporary Capitalism*, New Left Books, 1975.

I. REID, *Social Class Differences in Britain*, Open Books, 1981.

M. RUTTER and N. MADGE, *Cycles of Disadvantage*, Heinemann, 1976.

R. SCASE, *Industrial Society, Class, Cleavage and Control*, Allen and Unwin, 1977.

A. STEWART, K. PRANDY and R. M. BLACKBURN, *Social Stratification and Occupations*, Macmillan, 1980.

E. P. THOMPSON, *The Making of the English Working Class*, Penguin, 1968.

J. WESTERGAARD and H. RESLER, *Class in a Capitalist Society*, Heinemann, 1975.

6. Power

In many ways this chapter forms a counterpoint to the themes which emerged in the section on class, while some selections take up topics which were raised in the section on community.

Power is a universal feature of societies of all types, but is possibly easier to recognize than to define. Its simplest and most pointed description is Lenin's 'Who? Whom?'. To Weber it represents the probability that one social actor will obtain his own goals, against the wishes of another. To Parsons it is a 'generalized facility', a property of systems of social action, while Wright Mills saw it as the outcome of a 'zero sum' game in which if one side wins, the other must lose.

The distribution of power is institutionalized in structures and processes: Westergaard and Resler comment, 'Power is to be found more in uneventful routine than in conscious and active exercise of power.'

Scott and Hughes examine the 'power elite' in Scotland and their study indicates the extent to which even the United Kingdom, small and compact as it appears to be by comparison with some other countries, in reality consists of a number of moderately well integrated regional, national and local subsystems. Scotland itself, in legal, cultural and psychological terms, is another country.

But the integration at the top is determined and thorough. The most powerful body in Britain is the senior grade of the home Civil Service, rarely seen *en masse*, immortalized only slightly unfairly in *Yes, Minister*. **Kellner and Crowther-Hunt**'s book is essential reading, but it is frustrating reading, too, because one senses that the very stuff of the reality of this power is too insubstantial to be measured, even in their careful description.

Few sociologists have been able or have wished to undertake research in this area. There is very little which helps to explain the actual dynamics of power, how power operates in specific situations, how it is handled by the various interest and pressure groups involved, and what the outcomes of decision-making are. We could have included in this reader some more impressionistic accounts of the experience of being involved with power and politics at first hand, but felt that these would not have been in tune with the remainder of this book.

Worsley indicates the ways in which a sociological analysis of politics involves a much broader definition of what is 'political' than does the conventional account in terms of 'what governments do'. He examines the reasons for the subordination of the power of the military and religious sectors of society to the political 'state', and for the close association between the political and the economic in Britain. Of crucial importance is the mechanism by which the ruling groups 'legitimate' their possession and exercise of power, by manipulating the symbols of authority. Clearly even an analysis in the simplest terms of 'who governs' involves explanations of 'why, and how are they allowed to govern?' – 'why is it felt appropriate, and by whom is it felt appropriate that they should govern?' Thus political sociology needs to go much further than the mere examination of the correlates of specific types of voting behaviour, into an analysis of the formation of political culture.

This involves a consideration of political socialization, of how certain symbols come to be regarded as legitimate and their possession vested in representatives of particular classes and interest groups – a theme which links this chapter to those on socialization, social class and the family.

Thus, Dowse and Hughes, in Chapter 3, examine the extent to which the political ideas of parents are transmitted to their children. While it may be the case that early experiences in the family are especially important in the development of political values and the determination of political identification, the type of school one attends and the socioeconomic status of one's parents may affect these issues also. Political attitudes and behaviour are not a matter simply of conscious cultural tradition, handed down from one generation to the next. But nor are they simply a function of the class position an individual occupies at a particular time. The relationship between social class as it may be 'objectively' determined by the outside observer, or as it is subjectively assessed by the individual himself, is a complex one and each viewpoint has to be taken into account.

It is certainly true as a very broad generalization that the middle class tends to vote Conservative and the working class to vote Labour. But when the 'working class', however narrowly defined, constitutes at least two-thirds of the population, how are we to account for the remarkable persistence of Conservative administrations, if the electorate is polarized on straightforward lines of social class? (In a thorough study of middle-class voting, admittedly published in the early 1950s, Bonham estimated that the 'middle-class vote' constituted 30 per cent of the electorate.) In practice, of course, there is a considerable minority of working-class voters who habitually support Conservative candidates. Most studies put the percentage of working-class Conservative voters at around one-third – or to put it another way, the Conservative Party normally derives half its support from working-class electors. While there are certain regional differences in support for the main parties – for instance, south-east Lancashire which has a tradition of working-class conservatism – the national pattern is fairly consistent.

Furthermore, the influence of class on voting is not entirely consistent in another sense too. Many studies have found that support for the

Conservative Party may be strongest, not among the most affluent or powerful, but in the lower middle class consisting mainly of clerical and white-collar workers. Perhaps it is because they are in the middle of the class struggle that they need to affiliate even more determinedly with the groups in society who hold the highest status and wield the most power. Another explanation, consistent with the studies of white-collar workers discussed in Chapter 5, is that it is the 'pragmatic acceptance' of the white-collar groups, rather than their involvement in what C. Wright Mills called 'the status panic', which underlies their recognition of the political facts of life. These, in terms of the political game as it has been played in Britain for most of this century, are that the Conservatives are the 'ins' while the Labour Party is the party of the 'outs'.

In a classic study of voting, undertaken in Greenwich in 1950 by Benney, Gray and Pear, the authors conclude that the way an individual thinks of the class structure and perceives his own position within it may be a more important influence on his voting than his 'objective' class position. There is probably an element of status aspiration too, in that people tend to identify with the middle class by the very act of voting Conservative. So the relationship is a reciprocal one.

Rose goes beyond the mere association of independent variables such as social class, age or sex with the dependent variable of voting behaviour. His study, recommended in Further Reading, looks at the association between 'working classness' and the Labour Party since 1900. As well as voting, he considers the policy of the party, the recruitment of political leaders, and the party's capacity to mobilize political support. He concludes that 'no consistent relationship between class and party on these three dimensions is found, nor is there any evidence of a trend towards or from convergence'. Class remains important in the explanation of political differences in British society (indeed, Alford concluded that class has a more significant effect on voting in Britain than in the United States, Canada and Australia). But Rose suggests that this may be for a rather negative reason – that is, the absence of stronger grounds of cleavage. One of the remarkable facts of British political life since the nineteenth century has been its stability and the persistent capacity of the regime to maintain its credibility and legitimacy. Traditionally in British politics, race, religion and nationality have not been important bases of political cleavage. Rose comments: 'It appears that non-class divisions are much more likely to lead to the repudiation of a regime than are class divisions. Without going so far as to argue that class-based parties help create and maintain legitimacy, one can emphasize that such divisions are entirely consistent with the existence of a fully legitimate regime.'

Nordlinger's book goes further into the phenomenon of working-class conservatism, as does the study by McKenzie and Silver (both works are mentioned in Further Reading). Nordlinger argues that the working-class

Conservative voter tends to perceive high-status individuals as possessing leadership quality and skills which their social backgrounds have developed. One group, the 'deferentials', prefer to be ruled by representatives of high-status groups because they do not believe themselves or their peers to be capable of undertaking the tasks of leadership. Another group, the 'pragmatists', argue that the high-status leaders have in practice done a better job of leadership and that this is because they have in general achieved their elevated position in life through their own efforts. So this tends to go along with a perception of the class structure as being relatively permeable and allowing scope for the talented individual to get to the top. McKenzie and Silver's study, though based on a more intensive and sophisticated sample, comes to broadly similar conclusions. Like Nordlinger, they find some working-class Conservatives to be 'deferential', but Nordlinger's 'pragmatists' are replaced by 'seculars'. Members of the latter group prefer leaders who have risen to high office without the benefits of inherited wealth or social standing, tend to evaluate their party's record in office in terms of policies and achievements, and support the Conservative Party on the basis of what they perceive to be its proven competence at governing the nation. Moreover, unlike the deferentials, they tend to have a pragmatic view of the House of Lords, and not to see the Conservative Party as a national institution, quite different in kind from other contenders for government.

Another kind of explanation of working-class conservatism is given by Parkin in an article in the *British Journal of Sociology* in September 1967. In this paper, Parkin suggests that because the dominant institutions – the established church, the public schools, the universities, the military and governmental elites, as well as landed capital and private business enterprise – are inextricably bound up with Conservative values and the Conservative Party, it is the working-class Labour voter who is deviant rather than his Conservative workmate. The long-settled, urban working-class community represents a specific type of institutional setting in which the normative commitment to 'deviance' – that is, Labour-voting – can be maintained and supported. Moreover, members of the 'working class' who are not so continuously sustained in their symbolic rejection of the core values of British capitalist society will lack this 'normative protection' and may provide the basis of working-class support for the Conservative Party. Parkin's analysis of these issues is curiously prophetic in the light of the continued attenuation of support for the Labour Party.

Bogdanor's book is an important contribution to the revisionism which has overtaken political sociology since the advent of the Social Democratic-Liberal Alliance. Until the mid-1970s it was a commonplace that the class basis of British politics and the nature of the electoral system together militated against the emergence of third parties. Indeed, one textbook of sociology published in 1970 doubted 'whether the Liberal Party could survive another General Election'.

Bogdanor argues that 'during the period of mass suffrage, parties have been central to democracy . . . the basic form through which political representation has taken place . . . created the political agenda and . . . secured the adherence of voters to political programmes'. Thus the *loose* attachment of the two great parties to the middle and working classes respectively and their continued existence each as a 'broad church' reconciling a divergence of views internally, as great or almost as great as that between them externally, has proved a facilitating feature in national politics. However the power of party ultimately derives from the electorate, which can prove unwilling to extend this mandate in the case of repeated political failure or ineptitude in government. The incapacity of the traditional parties to solve the problems of Britain's diminished place in the world political system, or even to achieve the kind of successful management of the economy attained by its industrial competitors, has led not to apathy but to an unwillingness to trust parties to deliver the goods: 'Even in Britain, party identification is no longer sufficiently strong for the parties to be able to rely upon the loyalty of a stable and relatively immobile segment of the electorate willing to place party allegiance before a pragmatic conception of the public interest.'

The SDP is too new a feature of the political scene for sociological analysis to have been brought to bear to any considerable extent; however Bogdanor concludes that 'the prospects for either a stable three-party system or a stable political realignment in Britain look almost equally remote. Instead Britain seems likely to enter a period of volatility and uncertainty where the guidelines of the past will become almost wholly irrelevant.'

It would be a serious mistake, however, in a discussion of power in British society, to focus attention exclusively on the electorate and their political attitudes and behaviour.

In coming to grips with the realities of power in a modern institutionalized capitalist society, we have to face the questions posed by such writers as Mosca, Pareto, Michels and, more recently, C. Wright Mills. Their common point of interest is in the ruling elite, the class or group which is involved in making the most politically significant decisions.

In *The Power Elite*, Mills argues that in the complex interpretation of business, industry and government, power may appear to be much more widely diffused than in fact it is: 'Under the owners of property a huge and complex bureaucracy of business and industry has come into existence. But the right to this chain of command, the legitimate access to the position of authority from which these bureaucracies are directed, is the right of private ownership.'

This point is taken further in 'The Insiders' (reprinted in the first edition of *The Sociology of Modern Britain*), which looks critically at the thesis, propounded by Burnham, of 'The Managerial Revolution'. Burnham had argued that the wider spread of shareholding and the enormous increase in the complexity of modern business and industry has created a new group of powerful men – the managers – who owed their power to their control of the resources of vast corporations, while not being involved in share ownership to any great degree. But the authors of 'The Insiders' follow Mills in seeing the class interests of shareholders and corporate managers as being essentially similar for 'their personal wealth and power is intimately related to the power, stability and success of modern business enterprise'. While the large shareholder derives his wealth from dividends or from capital appreciation, the manager derives his from salaries, bonuses and fringe benefits.

Useem and McCormack examine the latest stages in the process in which intercorporate relations come to take over from upper-class relations in constituting a 'dominant segment' in British society. But the link is a complex one, and while, as Stanworth and Giddens put it, 'Britain made both gentlemen of businessmen . . . and businessmen of gentlemen', the interests of a specific industrial or commercial enterprise or sector are not necessarily easily reconciled with those of a particular class.

Likewise, Guttsman's analysis of *The British Political Elite* leads him to conclude that it is misleading to try and study this elite in isolation from the upper class in which it is rooted. This group tends to come predominantly from the major public schools and the prestigious universities of Oxford and Cambridge. Guttsman's study supports the view that the ruling elite is able to maintain its position over more than one generation and that this constitutes a ruling class, ' . . . if we mean by it a group which provides the majority of those who occupy positions of power, and who, in their turn, can materially assist their sons to reach similar positions'. The gateways to elite position, even for the outstandingly able person of working-class origin, tend to be through the educational system rather than through – for instance – business success.

One partial exception to this generalization is suggested by Richards's study of Members of Parliament, recommended as further reading. Some occupations requiring extensive education and training, such as solicitor and barrister, are overrepresented among members of the House of Commons but, by and large, the parliamentary elite is sufficiently distinctive from the civil service-business-educational elite identified by Guttsman to make it reasonable to characterize it as representing an alternative locus of power. Indeed, Richards observes that: 'Members share another attribute. Before election almost all of them were non-entities, at least in national terms . . . few men change over to politics after outstanding achievements in some other walk of life.' Many members do, however, share a common background and experience as representatives of the people in local government service.

Griffith is on more familiar ground, but his analysis is both simple and salutary. Not all positions in the elite are equally *available*. Arguably, members of the legal profession in general and of the judiciary in particular exercise power directly and unambiguously. Griffith's analysis indicates that the social background of members of the bench is likely to be of a specific, narrow, and limited kind. This inevitably conditions their perception of the reality as well as the morality of events rehearsed or transacted before them. To the extent that they are unaware of the constraining influence of their own perceptions, their failure to obtain 'objectivity' is a sociological as well as a social problem.

If parties do not represent, and neither businessmen nor judges are entirely what they appear to be, do governments, after all, govern? **Robinson**'s thesis is that central government control is an enterprise demanding considerable agility, timing and luck, certainly not easily achieved. In part this is because inertia and the decisions of the past, encapsulated in structures, provide a readier guide to events than do the intentions and aspirations of the present. Moreover British government lacks the machinery of scrutiny and review which can identify and regulate according to criteria of cost-effectiveness. So governments become caught up in a trap of promising to do what they are structurally incapable of performing.

Even at the local level, government and control are not easily wrested by elected politicians from the permanent officials, as **Saunders**'s analysis shows. Where the balance is tipped towards the politicians it nonetheless comes to be the prerogative of a 'political elite' centred around the leader of the majority party and his close retinue. There are therefore two bases for the critique that local government lacks legitimacy because it is undemocratic.

In Aneurin Bevan's autobiography, *In Place of Fear*, the author describes his political pilgrimage from colliery to union branch, to local government, parliament, and ultimately government, as a search for the real springs of power, which always lay one step beyond. So perhaps it is unhelpful to see this chapter as any more than a series of insights and partial accounts of a universal solid phenomenon.

Inevitably there is an open-endedness about all discussions of power, because the struggles continue. The year after the Portuguese revolution of 1974, the slogan *A Luta Continua* appeared on the walls indicating that even revolution *finishes* nothing, merely opens up some new possibilities. This emphasizes the optimism of Russell's celebration of the radical challenge to the 'old bands of authority': ' . . . men will no longer submit merely because their forefathers did so, a reason is demanded for abstaining from claiming one's rights. . . . This condition of revolt exists in women towards men, in oppressed nations towards their oppressors, and above all in labour towards capital. . . . It is a state full of danger, as all past history shows, yet also full of hope. . . .'

The Scottish Ruling Class
J. Scott and M. Hughes

Reprinted with permission from A. A. Maclaren (ed)., *Social Class in Scotland: Past and Present*, John Donald 1976, pp. 170–6

Problems in the study of sub-national elites

Britain is not a totally autonomous unit since it is subject to international political and economic constraints. This is even more the case for Scotland. The Scottish system is a 'sub-national' unit operating in the overarching British 'national' system. As such it too possesses only a *relative autonomy*: the exercise of power in Scottish society is seriously limited and constrained by the environment in which it takes place. These environmental constraints are even more significant for the Scottish system than they are for the British system and it therefore follows that certain modifications to the schema must be made if we are to conceptualize the realities of the situation. We make these modifications through the parallel conceptions of the centre-periphery thesis of political power and the metropolis-satellite thesis of economic power. Employing these ideas permits us to examine the question of whether sub-national elites are more or less autonomous centres of power or whether they are mere intermediaries between the national elites and the local community. The framework employed is presented in Figure 1.

	National leadership	Local leadership
Political level	Centre	Periphery
Economic level	Metropolis	Satellite

Figure 1

In an attempt to come to grips with the problem of the 'underdeveloped' nations of the Third World, André Frank developed the notion of studying the economic relationship *between* a developed metropolis and the underdeveloped nation, seeing the latter as a satellite economy of the metropolis. Rather than seeing the underdeveloped nation as an isolated 'traditional' or 'feudal' society, we must realize that the only reason why one society is underdeveloped in relation to the other is because of the exploitative relationships of appropriation existing between metropolis and satellite. Not only is this schema applicable to relations between developed and underdeveloped *nations*, it is also applicable to *regional* divisions within nations. It is our contention that Frank's framework is a useful way of viewing the relationship between the British and Scottish economies. We suggest that Scotland may be seen as a satellite of the London metropolis – and more specifically that the Glasgow-Edinburgh axis is the focus of the satellite and is, to a certain extent, a metropolis in relation to North-Eastern and Highland Scotland.

The centre-periphery thesis has a similar origin but is generally used in the context of the kind of theory that Frank is criticizing: it is used as a political counterpart to the 'dual economy' theory. For instance, Davies argues that the centre comprises the dominating mechanisms of urban politics whilst the periphery consists of the areas of society which are uninfluenced or unreached by the politics of the centre. It is thus generally used in studying 'modernizing' societies, and the periphery is equated with the traditional sectors – small communities lacking market mechanisms and based on ascriptive social relations.

We propose that the centre-periphery thesis be modified along the lines of Frank's schema. That is, any particular area may only be regarded as peripheral in relation to another, central, area: it is peripheral precisely *because* the other is central. We would argue that if this is *not* accepted then we cannot regard the two areas as parts of the same system – and if this is the case then the analogy of centre and periphery is inappropriate. We propose that Scotland may be seen, politically, as a periphery of the British centre.

Thus we are arguing that London is both political *centre* and economic *metropolis*, whilst Scotland is a *peripheral satellite*. The question then arises of the specific mechanisms which constitute this relationship: what is the exact nature of the relationship between social control in Britain and social control in Scotland?

Mackenzie recognizes this geographical and sectional division in social control when he writes that,

It seems . . . realistic to think in terms of a leadership sub-system based on the South Eastern 'heart-land', to which other sub-systems in part conceded their role of leadership, although they remained also partly in conflict with it.

Clearly we must examine the 'boundaries' of the various systems and their relative autonomy with respect to one another. Summarizing his discussion of the Scottish political system James Kellas remarks that,

The Scottish system is both dependent and independent within the British system.

If we are to approach adequately the empirical measurement of the relative autonomy of Scottish elites we must build this perception into our previously established framework. Now clearly any of our four kinds of control – ruling class, governing class, power elite, and leadership groups – may occur at either the national or sub-national level, but certain combinations are more likely than others. An overall cross-classification would yield sixteen logically possible relationships between national and sub-national elites. The available empirical evidence would suggest that social control at the British level takes the form of a ruling class. We are therefore concerned with only four of these possibilities. These are set out in Figure 2.

	National structure	*Sub-national structure*
1.	Ruling class	Ruling class
2.	Ruling class	Governing class
3.	Ruling class	Power elite
4.	Ruling class	Leadership groups

Figure 2

Is there a ruling class in Scotland?

Any attempt to consider the question of the existence of a ruling class in Scotland must be rather tentative at the present moment since the available data are of limited value only. Official statistics tend to cover narrowly defined 'economic' factors and are not easily related to the theoretical categories of sociological analysis. Since there are no explicitly *sociological* studies in this area, it is necessary to use the somewhat limited data available in directories, biographies, membership registers etc.

In order to relate these data to our conceptual framework, we must formulate a set of operational definitions which will, as it were, bridge the gap between data and framework. We propose to use the term 'economic notables' to refer to the whole cluster of economic elites, and we operationally define the category as referring to all those individuals who are directors of the top manufacturing and retailing firms, banks, insurance companies, and investment trust companies. Our sample of 'top firms' was derived by extracting *all* those Scottish firms in the relevant categories of *The Times 1000*. Our sample therefore includes such giants as Burmah Oil, Scottish and Newcastle Breweries, House of Fraser, The Weir Group, Anderson Mavor, The Distillers Company, The Scottish Amicable Life Assurance Company, The Scottish Widows' Fund and Life

Assurance Society, The Royal Bank of Scotland, and less well known firms such as The Scottish Western Investment Company, The Scottish Eastern Investment Trust, The Low and Bonar Group, The Titaghur Jute Factory, Scottish and Universal Investments, and The American Trust Company. In total, the category of top firms comprised 69 companies. We use the term 'economic elite' to refer to those economic notables holding two or more directorships in these top firms. Thus, in relating these operational definitions to our conceptual framework, we are interested in the structure and recruitment of the economic notables; since, in practice, adequate data are not available, we shall focus on the narrower economic elite.

Similar distinctions can be made, with respect to political participation, between political notables and the political elite. Unfortunately, the data are even less satisfactory in this area and so, without extensive research, it is impossible to use such distinctions. We shall therefore employ only the category of 'political notables'. In operational terms, then, our criteria for the existence of a ruling class refer to high integration and closed recruitment amongst both economic and political notables and a significant overlap of membership between the two.

The economic notables in whom we are interested are those in top positions in the commanding heights of the private sector of the economy. We wish to examine the connections within the industrial and financial sectors and between the two. We shall also examine the extent to which this 'functional' division is reflected in the geographical separation of Glasgow and Edinburgh – a question of great importance in examining the metropolis-satellite thesis.

The financial organizations upon which we shall focus are the major banks, insurance companies, and investment trust companies. We intend to show that the operations of these firms are shaped by the fact that there is no money market in Scotland – this is located in London, which exhibits both financial and commercial interests in close proximity to one another. Writing of Edinburgh, David Keir remarks that,

> Edinburgh can be called the financial capital of Scotland yet it does not qualify to be a true financial centre. Though it is the seat of government for Scotland, and houses many financial institutions, it has never been a centre where risk capital could readily be raised for industrial projects. In part this has come about because Edinburgh has no money market, that is for short term obligations.

Thus, any examination of Scottish financial firms is immediately concerned with the overarching 'British' system based on the City of London. The Scottish financial system can be seen as a differentiated subsystem of the British financial system, suited to the distinctive characteristics of

Scottish trade and industry. Nevertheless, as many writers have argued, and as would seem to be apparent from Scotland's recent economic problems, these financial institutions have not always been well-attuned to the needs of Scottish industry and have frequently preferred investments outside the country, particularly in North America – and more recently in Japan – to indigenous industrial development.

Banks, insurance companies and investment trust companies have all been of importance in providing industrial finance. Perhaps the most characteristic financial institutions of the Scottish scene are the numerous investment trust companies. These trusts developed during the nineteenth century in order to finance developments overseas. We estimate that today there are 49 such companies in Edinburgh, Glasgow, Dundee and Aberdeen, about half being located in Edinburgh. Our figures show that Scottish registered investment trust companies controlled assets totalling approximately £2000 million, compared with the £2600 million controlled by Scottish insurance companies. Clearly, the directors of the top investment and insurance companies warrant the designation economic notables.

The industrial and merchandising sector is very extensive in character, ranging from the heavy industries of the west – iron and steel, shipbuilding, machine tools, and textiles – to the more diverse industries of the east. Our category of economic notables includes all the directors of the major firms in this sector, regardless of the type of work carried out by the business.

Table 1. The distribution of directorships (1972)

Number of directorships held	Number of men	Total number of directorships
1	423	423
2	38	76
3	17	51
4	4	16
5	–	–
6	–	–
7	1	7
Total	483	573

Table 1 gives basic figures on the distribution of directorships in 1972 for the 69 top Scottish firms. It shows that a total of 573 directorships were held by only 483 men and that there were 60 multiple directors. That is, of

483 economic notables, 60 formed the economic elite. In total, 150 directorships were held by members of the elite.

When these figures are examined by sector they show that financial
firms are more likely to have multiple directors than are industrials. Of
the 38 top industrial and merchandising firms, just under a half (17) had
multiple directors; but amongst the top 31 financial firms, all but one are
interlocked.

Table 2. The distribution of interlocks (1972)

Number of interlocked directors per company	Industrial and merchandising	Financial	Total
0	21	1	22
1–3	16	15	31
4–6	1	11	12
over 7	0	4	4
Total number of interlocked companies	17	30	47
Average number of interlocked directors per company	1·9	3·9	3·2

The figures in Table 2 show the number of interlocked directors per
company and their distribution by sector. They show that whereas the
interlocked industrial and merchandising firms have between one and
three multiple directors (an average of 1.9 per company), financial firms
are just as likely to have more than three. The average figure of 3.9 for
financial firms covers up some significant differences within the sector:
whereas investment trusts have an average figure of 3.1, insurance companies have an average of 4.4 and banks an average of 7.5. Clearly, such
bald figures must be interpreted with care, since interlocks *between* investment trusts, for example, may result in a relatively small mumber of
people sitting on a large number of boards, and therefore producing a
greater degree of interlock than would appear from the figures in Table 2.
In order to investigate this possibility we carried out an analysis of the
directorships of *all* Scottish banks, insurance and investment companies,
and unit trusts.

Using the *Directory of Financial Institutions* (1973) as our source of
data, we compiled an inventory of the financial companies registered in
Scotland in 1972. This includes several companies which are subsidiaries

of English and overseas companies. Further research is intended to analyse the relationship between wholly Scottish financial companies and non-Scottish owned companies. At present, however, this requires more data on shareholdings. The resulting 80 companies had a total directorate of 535, held by 342 individuals.

Perhaps the first observation to make is that, of these 342 directors, 56 were also in the economic elite of the main sample. This means that 93 per cent of the economic elite were present as directors of financial companies. Similarly, 123 non-elite notables were on the boards of financial companies – 29 per cent of the non-elite notables. Thus, an overlap between the main sample and the financial firms is evident. By combining these figures, we find that 37 per cent of the economic notables held directorships in financial firms. Consequently, examining the presence of economic notables in the financial sector, we see that 52 per cent of the directors of financial firms figure in the main (as sample 16 per cent economic elite members, 36 per cent non-elite notables). This significant overlap supports and further exemplifies our discussion of the importance of financial interests amongst the economic notables, and supports the conclusion that interlocking of directorships in the smaller and subsidiary firms consolidates the position found amongst top companies. A more detailed analysis of the financial firms will, therefore, provide further information on the distribution of power in Scottish society.

A general picture of the directorships shows that 54 per cent were multiple directorships. These were held by 28 per cent of the directors, an average of three directorships per man. This indicates a high degree of integration between the financial firms, achieved through a significant minority of individuals holding multiple directorships. More detail on this integration can be gained from an examination of the various subsectors of the financial sector.

Investment trust companies are the most numerous, comprising 61 per cent of all financial companies, and containing 49 per cent of *all* directorships. They are tightly interlocked with one another and are extensively interlocked with other financial firms – contributing 57 per cent of all multiple directorships (31 per cent of all financial directorships). This propensity for investment trust companies' directors to hold more than one directorship gives the companies a central position in the interlocking of financial firms and the representation of their interests (63 per cent of investment trust directorships are multiple directorships. There is an average of 3.4 multiple directorships per company. See Table 3).

Insurance companies are the second largest subsector, comprising 20 per cent of financial companies and having 26 per cent of directorships. They are less well integrated than investment trusts, since they have fewer interlocks with other financial companies having 16 per cent of the multiple directorships (an average of 2.9 multiple directorships per

Table 3. Financial directorships (1972)

	Banks	Insurance companies	Investment trusts	Unit trusts	Unit trust management	Total
Single directorships	39	95	99	5	7	245
Multiple directorships	45	46	165	21	13	290
				GRAND TOTAL		535

company). Banks occupy a similar position with 16 per cent of the total directorships and 16 per cent of multiple directorships. However, since the number of banks is half the number of insurance companies, they are more tightly integrated and interlocked.

This brief overview of the situation indicates that investment trust companies play a key role in integrating the financial sector of the Scottish economy – but our data are not sufficiently detailed to assess the *precise* contributions made by the various companies, or the relative success they enjoy in representing their interests.

It is worth considering the size of funds controlled by the non-banking financial companies, although we do not have precise information on banking funds. Our figures suggest that funds are more thinly spread amongst the investment trusts than amongst insurance companies – approximately £2000 million (42 per cent of total Scottish non-banking funds) being held by 49 investment trust companies. The 16 insurance companies control approximately £2600 million (54 per cent). However, the differing degrees of integration characteristic of the two types of company imply that investment trust funds may not be any the less important as a resource, and that any analysis of economic power must take account of both size of funds *and* integration of firms with other firms. Unit trusts have a much smaller share of the cake with 4 companies holding £224 million (5 per cent of non-banking funds).

So far, the picture that emerges from our analysis is one in which an economic elite of 60 men bring about an integration of the industrial and financial sectors of the Scottish economy. Our analysis suggests that there is a remarkably high degree of integration within the financial sector, and that the elite members who sit on the boards of financial companies are frequently to be found on the boards of industrial companies. The picture is, therefore, one of a partial differentiation of the economic notables into industrial and financial elite groups with an overall integration of these notables through the activities of a relatively small economic elite, oriented primarily by financial interests.

Thus, we would argue that our evidence suggests the existence of either a solidary or uniform elite, i.e. an economic elite with a high degree of integration. It may be argued against this, that a large number of individuals sitting on only one board (423) indicates quite a low degree of integration; but our separate analysis of all Scottish financial firms has shown that if we go beyond the top 69 companies, we find a number of interlocks, involving these notables, amongst the smaller or subsidiary companies. We would conclude that our evidence gives reasonable grounds for the conclusion that the economic elite is either solidary or uniform.

Mandarins and Ministers
P. Kellner and Lord Crowther-Hunt

Reprinted with permission from Peter Kellner and Lord Crowther-Hunt, *The Civil Servants*, Macdonald, 1980, pp. 221–3

The Civil Service has, in recent years, been able to absorb or neutralize a whole series of rival power centres which might otherwise have weakened its power monopoly. This is at once an illustration of the extent of its power as well as being an example of the way that potential power is being still further increased. Four examples will suffice to indicate these octopus characteristics of our mandarins.

1. When potentially rival power centres have been set up within the Whitehall machine, the Civil Service establishment has quickly succeeded in absorbing or neutralizing them. Thus, in 1964, the Department of Economic Affairs was set up with a substantial contingent of 'outsiders' to act as a counterweight to the Treasury. It took the Treasury just five years to get it abolished. A similar fate is befalling the Central Policy Review Staff. This much-needed adjunct to government was set up by Heath in 1970. Serving the Prime Minister and the Cabinet directly, it was partly intended as a countervailing force to departmental or interdepartmental official advice that was coming to ministers collectively. Since it included a significant proportion of outsiders on its staff (indeed, under Lord Rothschild it was run by an outsider), it was expected to bring a broader and more independent view to ministers collectively than that hitherto produced by the traditional Whitehall machine. But what is happening to it? It is now being absorbed by the traditional machine. It is no longer run by an outsider. It no longer has any significant outsiders on its staff. In fact it is now not infrequently brought in at the top level as an allegedly quasi-

independent body to give added support to any crucial Civil Service recommendations which the Whitehall mandarins feel ministers might otherwise be bold enough to reject. This certainly was what happened as far as devolution was concerned.

2. When potentially rival power centres are set up outside Whitehall, the Civil Service quickly sets out to neutralize them. The creation of the office of the Ombudsman in 1967 is perhaps the best example of this. Here was an organization specifically designed to protect the individual from the Whitehall bureaucrats. But the Civil Service up to 1979 succeeded in ensuring that the Ombudsman himself was always one of themselves – a retired civil servant; his entire staff, now some ninety individuals, have been, and still are, all civil servants on temporary secondments from their parent departments. No doubt the Civil Service would seek to justify this on the principle of 'set a thief to catch a thief', but to many of us it is as if a Regional Crime Squad was headed by a retired convict and staffed by career burglars.

Another example of the same sort of Civil Service take-over of an apparently 'outside' power centre is the University Grants Committee. By intention, it is a body of independent academics to advise the Secretary of State for Education about the universities and it is there to act as a bulwark between the universities and the government, so maintaining the independence of the universities. But what has happened to it? One might well have thought that the universities themselves would have appointed the twenty or so academics who are the members of the UGC. Not so. The civil servants in the Department of Education advise the Minister of Education on which academics shall be appointed; for the most part they are academic second liners lacking the weight and authority of their respective Vice-Chancellors. Secondly, the 120 or so full-time members of the UGC's permanent staff are virtually all civil servants on temporary loan for a two to three year period from the Department of Education; and they are even posted by that Department between the Department and the UGC in the same way that the Department moves its officials round between its own individual branches. As if all this were not enough to ensure adequate departmental oversight of the workings of the UGC, when the twenty or so members of the UGC have their regular monthly meeting they almost invariably meet in the presence of senior officials from the Department of Education – the Permanent Secretary and the Deputy Secretary, for example.

3. Civil servants usually manage to dominate any apparently independent 'outside' advisory committees a department might set up. A good example of this was the Department of Education's Advisory Committee for the Training and Supply of Teachers. It was serviced by the Department's

officials. They provided the information and papers on which it worked and senior departmental officials were present at its meetings. But ministers were not normally there. I caused something of a stir by being present at one meeting to initiate face-to-face discussions on an issue on which I wanted the committee's views. And I insisted on being present because I believed my officials would otherwise introduce the question in a way which might slant the subsequent advice I received. If, on this occasion, I was trying to use this advisory committee to back me in a particular battle I was having with my officials, it is equally true that, for the most part, officials viewed it and sought to use it as a device for reinforcing the advice that they themselves were directly and separately giving their ministers. And if they are present much more often than ministers, they are much more likely to succeed.

4. The most recent example of the octopus qualities of the Civil Service was devolution. Here were two Acts of Parliament which sought to set up separate assemblies and governments for Scotland and Wales. But these separate assemblies and governments were not to have their own independent staffs. Their officials were to be members of 'Her Majesty's Home Civil Service' which meant that their basic loyalties would have been to Whitehall (which would have had the last word in transfers and certainly in promotion as far as the upper echelons were concerned). And as if this were not enough, the Westminster government would have had its own offices and directly employed staff in Scotland and Wales so Whitehall could keep a close watch on all that would have been happening there. The intended Whitehall embrace could not have gone much further. The frigid response of Scottish and Welsh voters did at least prevent such questionable plans from being implemented.

The Analysis of Power and Politics
P. M. Worsley

Reprinted with permission from Peter Worsley, 'The Distribution of Power in Industrial Society', *Sociological Review Monograph 8, The Development of Industrial Societies*, 1964, pp. 16–17, 20–6

Insofar as people's behaviour takes account of the existence of others, and is affected by expectations about others, we call it 'social'. Some of this behaviour is specifically purposive; it aims to produce effects. But not all of it is, and not all behaviour of interest to the social scientist is 'social', in Weber's sense of the term. Weber himself, indeed, emphasized that 'sociology is by no means confined to the study of "social action"; that is only . . . its central subject matter . . .' Causally determined action, as well as 'meaningfully' determined action, is part of the sociologist's subject matter. So, although 'meaningfully' behaviour may be 'non-social', causally it can never be without social consequences.

Restricting ourselves, however, to 'social' action, we can be said to act politically whenever we exercise contraint on others to behave as we want them to. The allocation of resources to further these ends is an economic allocation. The overall assertion of values entailed is an operation of political economy.

These conceptual departure-points imply a very wide conception of politics, what we may call 'Politics I'. By this definition, the exercise of constraint in any relationship is political. All kinds of pressure, from mass warfare and organized torture to implicit values informing interpersonal conversation, make up the political dimension. Looked at this way, there is no such thing as a special kind of behaviour called 'political'; there is only a political dimension to behaviour. Yet the vulgar (and often academic) use of the term 'politics' – what we shall call 'Politics II' – restricts the term to the specialized machinery of government, together with the administrative apparatus of state and party organization. To follow the implications of this usage through, strictly, would involve us in denying to simple undifferentiated societies the privilege of having a political system at all. Moreover, we also recognize that extra-governmental organizations within advanced societies dispose of power, and have their own constellations of power: we speak of 'university politics'. By this, we do not mean, merely and obviously, that organizations like universities or trade unions, either continuously or intermittently, bring pressure to bear upon government, and are thereby behaving 'politically' – and only on such occasions. Nor do we mean that party politics emerges from and intrudes into subcultures. We mean, rather, that these subcultural groups are, latently and constantly, organized power-groupings. They have an internal system through which this power is deployed: externally, their mere existence is a fact which governments, even the most authoritarian, have to take account of. Normally, too, such power-groupings make sure governments do take account of their interests; they are not merely passive.

Power does not exist 'in itself': it flows between people. And everybody has some of it, some area of choice, of ability to affect things his way. It may only be the power to be negative, to 'vote with one's feet'; in the extreme, only to choose death – but that is a choice, and, as the study of martyrology alone shows us, one which is by no means without social consequences. But some people have overwhelming and decisive power. Power is not randomly distributed, but institutionalized.

The identification of the rulers, therefore, must involve an examination of the distribution of power generally within civil society. In British society, there are only two institutional orders, however, within which very great power is concentrated: the political order and the economic order. This is not true for all societies. In some, for example, those in control of the means of violence are specially important. In the USA, organized religion is a far more potent force than in this country, especially at the community level. The identification of the power elite, the delineation of the distribution of power, are matters for empirical investigation. But a simplistic kind of political behaviourism does not carry us very far. It is commonly assumed, for example, that the role of the military in the USA is very much more considerable than in the UK.

Only in wartime has the military successfully and seriously obtruded itself into the formation of public policy – or even tried to – but at such times, military policy is the central issue in public policy. Viscount Montgomery's public pronouncements are striking in their atypicality – and are self-consciously 'deviant' and outrageous into the bargain.

The British military, then, has never become a caste – it is too closely woven into the culture of the ruling classes. It is no longer, however, one of the major magnetic power-centres attracting the enterprising and the ambitious, probably because, increasingly, it no longer makes the key military decisions. These are made abroad, and the military machine which once coped with the Indian subcontinent, to mention no other area, finds itself stretched in dealing with Cyprus and other backwaters of the world.

Many of these features are reproduced in another formerly central institution of British society, the Church of England, which has been recently described as 'by far and away the most important social institution in the land', and 'by far and away the largest organizer of youth in the country'. Yet, in quantitative terms alone, it now exercises direct and regular influence over less than three million adult members, plus a further 1,161,000 Sunday school children aged between three and fourteen. By contrast, the *Daily Mirror* had a readership of nearly thirteen million people in 1954 – one-third of the population aged sixteen and over and 'Granadaland' alone embraces some eight million adults.

The Army, the Church, and the Law are not what they were. But ordination still does not mean alienation: four Oxbridge colleges produced nearly one-quarter of the Church of England bishops between 1860 and 1960, and the public schools and older universities still dominate recruitment. The class connections of the lower clergy, however, have become less specifically tied to the upper classes (and 22 per cent of contemporary ordinands attended secondary modern and similar schools). Like the Army, as the Church has become less attractive to the upper classes, it increasingly finds its new recruits from formerly excluded social strata, and its senior leaders from within specifically churchly families. If the Church is no longer 'the Conservative Party at prayer', it is also still a long way from being 'that nation on Sunday'. Paradoxically, its democratization, which might well be a future source of religious strength, reflects its diminished social position. It no longer attracts those in search of decisive power; prelates have less to be proud about: education has long slipped from their grasp; morals are increasingly becoming the bailiwick of the BMA, and ideology of the mass media.

As serious centres of power, then, we are concerned predominantly with the political and economic orders. It is significant that Dahrendorf, who emphasizes, pluralistically, that all institutions carry their quantum of power, in fact only singles out economic and political power for special analysis. For Britain, the close association between the two elites at the apex of these institutional orders – the governing elite and the coalesced property-owning landed aristocracy and industrial bourgeoisie – has recently been very closely documented by Guttsman, together with the entry of 'new men' into the ranks of the governing elite (largely via the mechanisms for upward mobility presented by the Labour Movement and an extended educational system).

The uninterrupted, albeit modified, dominance of the property-owning classes, in a society which has long been the most highly 'proletarianized' in the world, is surely one of the most striking phenomena of modern times.

The answer does not lie in the possession of machine-guns by the ruling class. In this century, only in 1926 has armed force ever been in sight. The challenge of the masses – who created a whole series of instruments of self-expression and self-assertion, from the cooperatives and the trade unions to the Labour Party – has never been a revolutionary one.

The explanation of this continuity and stability involves examination of the modification of both the ruling class and of the ruled. The former were able to accede to the demands of the masses for the vote flexibly and gradually; in the economic sphere, concessions to the 'welfare' demands of the newly-vocal enfranchised masses were also made skilfully and gradually. In the process, the theory and practice of *laissez-faire* had to be thrown overboard. Gradually, the State assumed more and more responsibility for more and more areas of social life. In an age when the nationalized sector of the economy is responsible for half the investment spending, a third of the employment income, and a quarter of the national product, Herbert Spencer's resistance to state interference, whether in the shape of the Post Office, the public mint, poor relief, 'social' legislation, colonization, organized sanitation, or state education, seems remote indeed.

The extensions of the franchise in 1832, 1867 and 1884, were the crucial steps, politically. Yet the beginnings of reform produced no sharp polarization of forces. In the crucial period 1832–68, 'the classes were represented in almost the same proportions in each of the two parliamentary groupings' – 'left-centre' (Liberal) and 'right-centre' (Conservative). After 1867, the new middle classes gradually crept on to the governmental scene (normally holding offices of lower prestige and 'administrative' content). Not until 1923 did a non-aristocrat hold the office of Foreign Secretary, and not until 1929 was a British government elected on full adult suffrage.

The entry of the middle classes into the centres of political power was thus a long-drawn-out process; the emerging proletariat, in its turn, only very gradually distinguished itself from the party of the middle classes.

Much more was involved in the difficult enterprise of modernization than political changes alone. On their own these might well have led to the rule of the masses so feared by sections of the elite. The modernization of British society was a much more many-sided process, the rationalization and stabilization of a whole 'political culture'. This enculturation was not accomplished by some undifferentiated 'ruling class'; more specifically, many of the crucial reorganizations were the achievement of the Liberal Party, and bore the stamp of liberalism, even though that party, theoretically the repository of anti-bigness, anti-statism, and the cult of the individual, nevertheless had quite determinedly reorganized itself as a centralized, hierarchical machine, modelled on Chamberlain's Birmingham caucus system, and as a political party with a mass, extra-Parliamentary base. Self-rationalization was the climax to a long series of rationalizations of the wider society in the third quarter of the nineteenth century, a watershed between the society symbolized by Palmerston and modern mass democracy: reform of the Civil Service (the Northcote-Trevelyan reforms), of the Army (Cardwell's reforms, 1868–71), and of education, both for the elite (the development of public schools on the Rugby pattern) and for the masses (the development of primary education, 1870–80). For the newly literate, a special literature industry was founded. Via education, a proportion of the working class could find its way into the middle classes. Convinced by their personal experience of the reality of upward social mobility, they constituted, and constitute, an important reservoir of believers in the notion of *la carrière ouverte aux talents*; their consciousness is structured by their own experience of mobility in the 'middle levels of power', to use Mills's phrase, and generalized into a theory applicable to the society as a whole.

The persistence of patterns of deference and traditionalistic loyalty among other large segments of the lower strata cannot be documented here, nor has it yet been adequately documented anywhere. 'Deference', however, only explains part of the mass vote which the Conservative Party has been able to mobilize since modern politics began in the 1870s.

This solidarity was far more complex than any crude label like 'feudal', 'deference-pattern', or even 'traditionalism' would imply. The imperialist note, indeed, was strikingly untraditional, and was resisted for a long time in both Conservative and Liberal circles, as well as Labour. As Guttsman has pointed out, the feudal heritage was, in fact, a distant one (and had been profoundly challenged and modified via Civil War and industrialization): 'English romantic thought accepted the basic tenets of the Enlightenment: freedom of thought, equality before the law, but it reacted against the libertarian and egalitarian views of the French revolution.' The latter tradition was taken up and developed by the working class; it could not easily form a part of the self-legitimation of the ruling class.

Simple, 'objective' classification of occupations, then, or of the distribution of power, does not take us very far in explaining the success of British conservatism in attracting one-third of the trade union vote to this day. Counting heads is essential in order to establish some primary facts about who people are, but even in order to know what to count at this level, we operate with (often implicit) theoretical assumptions. To get any further, to explore deeper levels of behaviour, we have to move beyond this kind of classificatory activity into the field of 'political culture'. Of course, crude classification and correlation is analytically easier (if technically, perhaps, complicated enough) than more sophisticated exploration; it is also less controversial. The difficulties entailed in exploration arise intrinsically from the fact that human consciousness is involved, for we are dealing with attitudes, shaped by many variables. But the really fertile fields for sociological investigation lie precisely in the exploration of the interplay between the subjective and the objective. Class does not, metaphysically, mean anything 'in itself'. It is always acted upon, interpreted, mediated, by somebody, and it is the social agencies which inject meaning into class, and transmit these meanings to people, that must increasingly concern us. They concern us increasingly, both because this is the needed development in intellectual and analytical terms, and because, empirically, the mechanisms by which consciousness is manipulated are of growing importance in modern society.

Multi-party Politics

V. Bogdanor

Reprinted with permission from Vernon Bogdanor, *Multi-party Politics and the Constitution*, Cambridge University Press, 1983, pp. 56–66.

The birth of the SDP and the formation of the Alliance of course increase the chances of the centre in British politics. Yet the question which has to be answered is whether they change the character of electoral support for the centre. Is support for the SDP and the Alliance likely to prove as brittle as support for the Liberals has been; or, by contrast, is the Alliance likely to be the beneficiary of a new source of socioeconomic support, or a new constellation of political issues? Interestingly enough, when the negotiations between the Liberals and the SDP over the allocation of constituencies began in 1981, the SDP insisted upon its rightful share of winnable seats, defining as 'winnable' a seat where the share of the Liberal vote was high. This is an indication that, for its leaders at least, the SDP vote was likely to prove an addition to the Liberal vote, and unlikely to be able to tap any new sources of support. But, of course, such evidence is in the nature of things highly tentative.

Being a new party, it is impossible to determine the answers to questions about the nature of the SDP's support with the same degree of confidence as is possible in the case of the other parties; and indeed there have been hardly any academic studies of the nature of the SDP vote. Such evidence as is available must be treated, moreover, with very considerable caution since the SDP has not yet been in existence long enough for meaningful questions to be asked about the nature of its long-term support; and as the Party has not yet fought a general election, its supporters have only had the chance to display their allegiance in by-elections or local elections. The material, then, is simply not available to allow one to make assertions about the nature of SDP support with any degree of confidence.

Nevertheless, such survey evidence as is available seems to indicate that the SDP faces the same problems as the Liberals in creating a solid block of permanent adherents. We have already seen that the SDP shares the Liberals' lack of a distinctive socioeconomic base, and it will therefore find it difficult to secure electoral allegiance on any basis of group self-interest. In addition, being a new party, the SDP, unlike the Liberals, cannot even claim any inherited attachment; it has had no time to build up committed partisans; and, no doubt, even less of the electorate have an awareness of the content of social democracy than of liberalism. The very limited evidence available indicates that the SDP have, so far, been no more successful than the Liberals in creating a distinctive 'issue space' for themselves; for their appeal too seems based more upon the quality and style of their leaders, together with a distrust of the major parties, rather than upon support for SDP policies, of which the electorate may have only a hazy understanding. At the Warrington by-election fought by Roy Jenkins in 1981, references to the policies of the SDP came far behind more generalized sentiments as a reason for supporting the Party; while at the Glasgow, Hillhead by-election won by Roy Jenkins in March 1982, the SDP actually lay behind the Conservative and Labour Parties as the party which the electorate preferred for dealing with nine major issues.

It seems then that support for the SDP and the Alliance is no different in nature from support for the Liberal Party in the past. The Alliance, of course, can attract greater support than the Liberal Party since it contains leaders who have held high government office – Roy Jenkins is a former Chancellor of the Exchequer and Home Secretary, David Owen a former Foreign Secretary and Shirley Williams a former Education Secretary. The Alliance, therefore, gives the centre in British politics a much higher degree of credibility than the Liberal Party on its own could enjoy. On the other hand, because the SDP lacks committed partisans, its support may hold up less well than that of the Liberals in time of difficulty. There is in fact considerable evidence that Liberal support was less susceptible than that of the SDP to erosion by the so-called 'Falklands factor' which increased the support for the Conservative government in the local elections of 1982, and in by-elections and opinion polls from spring 1982. On the whole, however, the support which the Alliance has obtained shows merely that the SDP in combination with the Liberals has become a more effective vehicle of protest than the Liberal Party on its own could be. It has not yet succeeded in benefiting from any new electoral cleavage; nor has it been able to attach to itself any significant social interest, an advantage perhaps from the standpoint of policy-making, but less so for building up a stable coalition of committed supporters. There is no evidence as yet that the Alliance is near to achieving a fundamental realignment in British politics of the kind which the Labour Party was able to accomplish in the 1920s.

If that was the sum total of what could be said on the subject of the electoral prospects of the Alliance, its prospects would be far bleaker than in fact they are. For its chances of success may owe less to its own positive qualities than to the depth of disillusionment towards the two major parties, a product of the policy failures of successive governments. But there has also been a process of partisan dealignment which is occurring in British politics, a gradual unfreezing of traditional party loyalties from which the Alliance may benefit.

The traditional picture of voting behaviour in Britain is one of stability and geographical homogeneity with the majority of the vote being given to one of the two major parties. Between 1945 and 1970, neither of the two major parties won more than 49 per cent of the vote, or less than 43 per cent of the vote, while the share of the poll gained by the two parties never fell below 87 per cent. We have already noticed that the class basis of political allegiance gave considerable stability to the vote, and prevented too great a geographical diversity in voting patterns. Until 1974, it seemed as if the two major parties commanded two large and loyal armies of disciplined voters who would be likely to support them from one election to another, almost regardless of governmental performance. Elections, therefore, would be decided by the small number of voters who converted to, or defected from, one of the major parties.

This neat and tidy picture has become increasingly inappropriate. The low percentage of the vote secured by the two main parties in the 1970s was quite unprecedented. The Conservative share of the vote in February 1974 – 37.9 per cent – was the lowest which it had received since 1906; while in October 1974 its vote fell further still, to the lowest level in its history as a mass party, and although the Conservative vote recovered somewhat in 1979, its share of the vote was still lower than it had been in any of the other postwar elections – 1951, 1955, 1959 and 1970 – in which it had won a parliamentary majority. The Labour vote in February 1974, although sufficient to put it into government, was the lowest which that party had gained since 1931, and the fall in its share of the vote from 1970 – 5.9 per cent – was the largest drop in support for any Opposition since the war. In October the Labour Party's vote increased, but in 1979 it fell even below its level of February 1974. Moreover, by-election results after the formation of the Alliance in 1981, showed that Labour was unable to capitalize upon the economic difficulties facing the Conservative government, and that it was in danger of falling back even further from its already low base of 1979.

This decline in support for the two major parties seems to be accompanied by a fall in the proportion of the electorate willing to identify *strongly* with either of them, although the proportion of the electorate willing to identify in some manner with the two parties has not itself fallen by very much, and in any case remains remarkably high by the standards of Western democracies. Party identification fell only 3 per cent between 1964 and 1979 – from 93 per cent to 90 per cent – but the percentage with a 'strong' or a 'very strong' identification declined from 44 per cent in 1964 to 22 per cent in 1979. This decline seems to have been evenly spread amongst different social classes and age groups, but to have gone further and faster within the youngest age group, the newest cohort of the electorate. If it is really the case that the newest age cohort admitted to the electorate is more disillusioned than its elders, then the decline in strong party identification is likely to continue at an increasing rate. But the newest cohort generally has a weaker identification than its elders because it has had less opportunity to acquire strong party loyalties through the act of voting. It may be, therefore, that the lesser degree of identification displayed by this cohort is in large part a generational factor and has little wider significance.

The continuing high level of party identification is a salient warning against predicting a rapid collapse of the two-party system in Britain. Nevertheless, the fall in 'very strong' and 'strong' identifiers indicates that there are fewer party stalwarts. It means that the two major parties can no longer count on partisan loyalties automatically working in their favour. The same conclusion follows from a consideration of changing social patterns in Britain.

Table 1. The weakening of the class/party link

Class	1979				Difference Con. – Lab.		
	Con.	Lab.	Lib.	Other	1964	1970	1979
Middle	%	%	%	%	%	%	%
A Professional	70	13	14	2			
B Business	61	18	17	3			
TOTAL	62	18	17	3			
Total A + B					+53	+48	+44
					+19	+17	+25
C1 Office workers	53	28	16	3			
Working class							
C2 Skilled	41	42	13	4			
D Semi & unskilled	33	50	14	3			
E Welfare recipients	39	48	11	2			
TOTAL	38	45	13	3	−28	−13	−7

Source: Richard Rose, *Class Does Not Equal Party: the Decline of a Model of British Voting* (Studies in Public Policy No. 74, University of Strathclyde, 1980), p. 20.

Class, like party identification, has been a stabilizing factor in British politics in the past. Yet there is now considerable evidence that ties between class and party are weakening, and that a larger percentage of voters are no longer prepared to vote for their class-consonant party – Labour for working-class voters; the Conservatives for middle-class voters. The evidence is summarized in Table 1. It will be seen that in 1979, the Labour Party was supported by less than half of the working class, and that its lead over the Conservatives amongst the working class had fallen from 28 per cent in 1964 to 7 per cent in 1979. No similar trend is noticeable in the case of Conservative voters; yet there had been a fall of almost one-tenth in the Conservative lead over Labour in classes A and B, while only a little over one-half of the voters in class CI voted Conservative in 1979. Furthermore, the percentages willing to support their class-consonant party (that is, working-class Labour supporters and middle-class Conservative supporters) have also fallen, as the following figures show.

1964	1970	1979
57%	54%	49%

One reason for this weakening of the class-party link is that fewer members of the electorate conform to class stereotypes. We can list a series of class characteristics which would be possessed by an ideal-type member of the working class or an ideal-type member of the middle class, and then ask what percentage of the electorate conforms to the ideal-type picture. According to Richard Rose, 'An ideal-type British worker would be expected to have, in addition to a manual occupation, a minimum education, trade union membership, a council house residence and subjectively identify as working-class. Reciprocally, a middle-class person would be expected, in addition to a non-manual occupation, to have an above-minimum education, be a home-owner, not belong to a trade union, and subjectively identify with the middle class.' However, the percentage conforming to these stereotypes was only 23 per cent of the electorate in 1970, and by 1979 it had fallen to 14 per cent. The vast majority of the electorate, therefore, finds itself cross-pressured by conflicting class characteristics, and so the likelihood of voters supporting their class-consonant party is bound to decline. Moreover, fewer voters are willing to place themselves in class categories at all. At the 1979 election, survey evidence showed that less than 50 per cent of the electorate did so; despite the fact that the two major parties were closely associated with a class appeal, Labour's links with the trade unions being emphasized whilst the Conservatives, under Mrs Thatcher, appeared as more stridently 'middle class' than had been the case for many years. The class appeals of the major parties have, paradoxically, not been accompanied by a resurgence of class voting. And, given the social changes which have occurred, they could not have been seriously expected to do so.

Nor does it seem as if class has been replaced by any other social structural determinant of voting behaviour which can bind the voter to his party. Instead, the decline of the class-party link has left a space for other factors to influence voting behaviour. After the 1979 general election, many commentators noticed the divergence in swing between the North and South of England, and the standard deviation of constituency voting was by far the highest in that election than in any since 1945. The average swing to the Conservatives south of a line stretching from the Humber to the Mersey, including Wales, was 6.4 per cent; while north of this line the average swing was 2.9 per cent. This was not so much a locational effect as a result of differences in the perception of unemployment and inflation. Where unemployment was perceived to be the main issue of the election, the swing against Labour was less, even though the Labour government of 1974–9 had itself presided over a considerable increase in unemployment. Where, on the other hand, the control of inflation was judged to be the main issue, the swing to the Conservatives was larger. There were, in addition, genuine locational effects in voting behaviour. Cities with a large number of car workers, for example, swung heavily to the Conservatives, as did new towns and mining areas. Conversely, constituencies with a large number of immigrants and university towns showed swings smaller than average.

Thus, not only was there less support for the two major parties in the 1970s than in previous decades, but the nature of that support had changed. It was based less upon the stabilizing factors of party identification or class solidarity, and more upon short-term factors such as the record of the government or the electorate's perception of political issues. There seems indeed to have been a slow but steady decline in the influence of social factors upon voting behaviour, and it has been replaced by a much greater degree of issue voting.

One result of this shift from class solidarity to issue voting is to highlight the difficulty in which the Labour Party is placed because the main issues with which it is identified – nationalization, spending on the social services, and maintaining the power of the trade unions – are regarded with increasing hostility even by the Party's own supporters. Table 2 shows how opinion amongst *Labour identifiers* has moved against the Party's main policies. The Labour Party, then, must not only confront the consequences of the social changes discussed earlier. It also faces the problem that a majority, even amongst those who regard themselves as Labour Party supporters, disapprove of the main issues with which the Party is associated. Both its social and its ideological bases are under threat.

The evidence of studies of voting behaviour indicates that there has been a process of political dealignment since 1970. Instead of being able to rely upon solid blocks of support, the parties seem to be faced with an increasingly volatile and sceptical electorate. The attitude of the voter is no longer marked by a high degree of allegiance to the traditional landmarks of class, family or religion. Instead, the voter is sceptical of

Table 2. Labour Party identifiers and Labour Party policies

				Feb. *&* *Oct.*		*Change* *1964* *to 1979*
% of Labour identifiers	1964	1966	1970	1974	1979	
In favour of more nationalization	57	52	39	53	32	−25
Who do not believe that trade unions have too much power	59	45	40	42	36	−23
In favour of spending more on the social services	89	66	60	61	n.a.	(1964 to Feb. 1974) −28
Saying that more social services and benefits are needed	n.a.	n.a.	n.a.	43	30	(1974–9) −13

Source: Ivor Crewe, *'The Labour Party and the Electorate'*, in Dennis Kavanagh (ed.), *The Politics of the Labour Party*, p. 39.

the pretensions of the parties and disdains the crudity of the rhetoric used to cement party ties. The voter's judgment is based rather on a more hard-headed calculation of the merits of the different parties, founded mainly, although by no means exclusively, upon their success in resolving the major economic problems of the day. The parties, therefore, are now judged far more on performance than on their class affiliations; and they are judged more on performance than promise, for issue voting tends to be negative in character – a retrospective judgment on the policies which a government has pursued, rather than a belief in the promises of the manifesto. The vote is a verdict on the past rather than an aspiration for the future.

Because the governments of the 1970s have been seen as unsuccessful in coping with the major economic problems which Britain faces, they have gradually lost the confidence of the electorate. It is this factor rather than the process of social change which is responsible for the *rapidity* of changes in political attitudes; for changes in class feeling occur at a glacially slow rate. If governments had enjoyed more success, or faced less daunting adverse circumstances, they might have been able to counteract the effects of social change. In any case the extent of disillusionment should not be exaggerated; for, as we have seen, identification with the two major parties remains high in comparison with other leading democracies. It would be far too apocalyptic to imagine that the Labour and Conservative Parties are near to total collapse.

What does the evidence of studies of voting behaviour tell us about the possibilities for the Liberal/SDP Alliance and the future of multi-party politics in Britain? The evidence points to dealignment, but not realignment; dealignment from which the Alliance may conceivably benefit, but not to realignment, such as occurred when Labour replaced the Liberals in the 1920s. The gradual unfreezing of traditional loyalties offers a marvellous opportunity to a new political formation which it would not have enjoyed in the 1950s or 1960s. But the Alliance has not yet been able to take advantage of this opportunity to secure a solid core of loyal supporters so that it can take its place as a major party in the political system. For that to happen, it would either have to acquire the support of a new coalition of social forces, as Labour did in the 1920s; or it would have to become identified with a major issue which gave a new dimension to political conflict, and radically altered the cleavage structure. This was achieved by the Democrats in the United States after 1932 when they came to be seen by the electorate as the party best able to deal with the slump; and by the Gaullists in France in 1958 who were seen by the electorate as the party which could ensure governmental stability and national success. There is no sign as yet that the Alliance is anywhere near to emulating this achievement. For this reason, the formation of the Alliance may not lead to the rapid replacement of one major party by another as occurred in the 1920s; nor to a stable three-party system. The role of the Alliance need not be equated with that of Labour in the 1920s as a party about to take its place in a realigned political system. Rather its role may come to bear more similarity to that of some of the new parties which have arisen in recent years in many Western democracies.

In Western Europe, many of these new parties have been of the 'protest' variety – Democrats 66 and Democratic Socialists 70 in Holland, the Centre Democrats and Mogens Glistrup's Progress Party in Denmark, together perhaps with the Green parties in West Germany and France. None of these parties has yet been able to achieve an electoral breakthrough despite some initial successes. Moreover, the history of right-wing breakaways from social democratic or labour parties in Western Europe and Australia shows how difficult it is to supplant parties enjoying an institutional or organizational base and a solid core of party support. In France, the socialists who opposed the Common Programme between socialists and communists were routed in the Assembly elections of 1978, even though the Programme itself was a dead letter by then; in Italy the breakaway PSDI polls consistently less than the Socialists; while in Australia, the Democratic Labour Party (originally known as the Anti-Communist Labour Party) managed to secure 9.4 per cent of the vote in its first electoral test in 1958, but now maintains only the most tenuous political existence. In Denmark, Erhard Jacobsen's breakaway Centre Democrat Party succeeded in attracting 51,000 signatures of support in 1973 (equivalent to half a million in a country the size of Britain) but secured only 7.8 per cent of the vote in the legislative elections of that year.

Admittedly the Alliance is likely to perform somewhat better than these parties, and to remain as a third force in the political system. This is because dissatisfaction with the major parties is far deeper in Britain and therefore more voters will be willing to experiment with an 'unsound' alternative. Moreover, the leaders of the Alliance enjoy more credibility than the leaders of the new parties on the Continent, or past leaders of the Liberal Party, and they are more popular with the electorate than the leaders of the two major parties. For this reason, it is perfectly conceivable that the Alliance might be able to take advantage of short-term discontents so as to propel itself into government. But this would probably be the result of a high degree of alienation from the two major parties rather than enthusiasm for the Alliance itself or its policies. An Alliance government would represent a negative coalition of diverse discontents, rather than a positive desire to 'break the mould' of British politics. A government formed on such a basis would have difficulty in formulating a set of coherent policies equally satisfying to all of its supporters in an electoral coalition containing mutually incompatible elements.

Whether it succeeds in winning a place in government or not, the formation of the Alliance is likely to accentuate trends towards a more volatile and unstable political system. This volatility was, of course, already a feature of electoral reactions in the 1970s well before the formation of the Alliance. By contrast to the 1950s, when opinion between elections seemed to remain fairly stable, the evidence of the polls indicates rapid short-term swings in the popularity and unpopularity of the parties between elections; and this has been especially marked since the 1979 general election.

In such an uncertain situation, short-term factors, perhaps occurring in the election campaign itself, will increasingly come to influence voting decisions. Twenty years ago, the conventional wisdom among students of elections was that events occurring during the election campaign were unlikely to exert any significant influence upon the result. The same cannot be said today. As Ivor Crewe has noted, 'Between 1964 and 1979 the proportion of voters who left their final decision until the last week or two of the campaign jumped from 17 per cent to 28 per cent, and the proportion claiming to have thought seriously of voting differently in the course of the campaign rose from 24 per cent to 31 per cent.'

In a political system of this kind, parties may well secure election victories on essentially short-term factors which rapidly evaporate. The mandate argument will lose what little credibility it ever had; indeed, governments will find it increasingly difficult to mobilize an electoral coalition sufficiently cohesive and long-lasting to enable their policies to be presented with any degree of democratic legitimacy at all. The Commons will come to represent less a mirror of the opinion of the nation, than the result of a well-timed dissolution or the fortuitous exploitation of a campaign issue. In such a political climate, the argument for proportional representation so that a wide variety of interests may be more adequately reflected in the Commons, is likely to be heard with increasing insistence. Indeed the political system and the Constitution itself are likely to come under increasing strain.

The Dominant Segment of the British Business Elite
M. Useem and A. McCormack

Reprinted with permission from Michael Useem and Arlene McCormack, 'The Dominant Segment of the British Business Elite', *Sociology*, vol. 15, no. 3, August 1981, pp. 381–9, 398–402

Introduction

The directors of large British companies constitute the backbone of a capitalist class, a class whose distinct location in the economic system generates a correspondingly distinct way of participating in the political system. Yet if it is obvious that business leaders typically enter the political arena to defend free enterprise and its corollaries, it is less certain that their actions necessarily advance the general interests of business, rather than simply the position of their respective companies. Indeed, both structural Marxist and pluralist writings have generally argued that the parochial concerns of individual firms receive far greater expression in this process than does the collective welfare of capital. Competition among firms, sectoral cleavages, and directors' primary identification with their own enterprise all inhibit the formation of even class-wide political awareness, let alone an organizational vehicle for promoting their shared concerns. Capitalist class disorganization, it is argued, prevails. Pluralism and structural Marxism radically diverge, of course, in the implications they draw from the presumed disunity. For pluralism, the capitalist class is far too divided to be any more effective than any other interest group in imposing its views on the government, thus enabling the state to avoid capture by business. But for structural Marxism, it is precisely because of this disorganization of capital that the state can and does (for other reasons) assume the role of protecting the class-wide interests of business.

Counterposed to both arguments is the equally familiar thesis, advanced by instrumental Marxists and many non-Marxist writers alike, that the government is more responsive to the outlook of big business than of any other sector, and certainly of labour. The responsiveness is the result in part, it is suggested, of the social unity and political cohesion of the business elite. With such cohesion and coordination, business is able to identify and promote successfully those public policies that reflect long-term priorities shared by most large companies.

The following analysis departs from pluralist and structural Marxist theory by *not* necessarily assuming that the British capitalist class is largely disorganized. Rather, the nature and degree of internal unity is left an open question, to be resolved through direct study. But the analysis also departs from instrumental Marxist and other interpretations by advancing a specific thesis on how a degree of unity is achieved. The general purpose of the paper, then, in Giddens's framing, is to help 'specify the modes in which [upper-class] economic hegemony is translated into political domination'. This will be done by developing and then testing a thesis on an element of internal organization of the business elite which, if present, could facilitate the articulation and promotion of policies protective of the transcendent class interests of capital. It will be suggested that a 'dominant segment' has formed within the business elite, and that this segment has acquired the capacity to serve as a leading organizer of the capitalist class as a whole.

Though there are hundreds of thousands of companies in Britain, analysis is limited here to the thousand largest. This is partly a matter of empirical convenience, for the field of inquiry is narrowed to a manageable scale. But it is also analytically motivated, for the thousand largest enterprises are responsible for the bulk of economic activity, whether measured in market share, output, turnover, employment, or assets. This concentration of economic resources has generated a corresponding concentration of business influence. In assessing the political implications of the increasing centralization of British industry, for instance, Hannah observes that 'in recent years governments have . . . developed their relationship with large firms . . . as a means of achieving wider policy aims. Given the importance of large firms in the economy – we have seen that the largest 100 of them together account for almost one-half of manufacturing output – it is hardly surprising that they have become an important adjunct of government.' Thus, in searching for the ways in which business enters politics, large companies and their directors constitute a promising focus of inquiry. The business elite, or as will be used interchangeably, the corporate elite or capitalist class, is taken to consist of the directors of the thousand or so largest enterprises. Approximately two-thirds of the members of the typical company board of directors also serve as senior executives with the company; the remaining non-executive directors are usually employed as managers of other large corporations.

The dominant segment

Though nominally distinct entities, large companies in Britain (and most other capitalist economies) are drawn into encompassing webs of inter-locking ties. Among the most prominent are those of stock ownership and shared directorships, chief strands of two general webs usefully distin-guished as exchange and communication networks by Scott and Hughes. At least a third of the equity in large quoted companies, for instance, is held or managed by other companies, primarily insurance firms and other financial institutions; but even industrial corporations maintain substan-tial investments in one another. Overlaying this inter-corporate ownership network is another ownership lattice based on personal holdings, wherein family fortunes derived from land or early entrepreneurial success have been diversified to ensure continued growth. In some instances these types of exchange networks are reinforced by a parallel set of communica-tion network ties, but the latter are also subject to a logic of their own. The origins of the pre-eminent communication strand – the interlocking directorate – are the subject of an extended and yet unresolved debate. But whatever the factors that generate shared directorships among large companies, one consequence, anticipated or not, is the creation of an organizational foundation for an elite stratum within the capitalist class.

Two properties of the interlocking directorate are chiefly responsible for the special qualities of the foundation of this segment. First, the network is highly inclusive of large companies. Though historically far more diverse and divided, the progressive concentration and integration of not only manufacturing and finance but all major industries has generated a network of directorships directly or indirectly linking nearly every important company. Such a trend is evident in the time-series data compiled by Stanworth and Giddens. Of 85 large manufacturing and financial companies in 1906, fewer than half were united by shared direc-torships; but of a comparable sample of 85 firms in 1970, better than four-fifths were so joined. Moreover, bridges across the great divide between industry and the 'City' have grown as well. Directorship links between similar samples of large manufacturing firms and banks increased nearly seven-fold between 1906 and 1970. The resulting network is now virtually all-encompassing. Directorship ties among 40 large industrial and 27 large financial companies in 1970 were examined by Whitley, for instance: 56 of the 67 firms are linked to at least one other company in the set, and if indirect connections through other corporations are taken into consideration, 62 of the 67 companies are either directly or indirectly linked. A more recent study of the directors of 235 of the largest manu-facturing and financial firms for 1976 reveals comparable levels of network integration.

To this property of company *inclusiveness* is added a second crucial network characteristic: *diffuseness*. Some interlocking directorships are established to secure pre-existing exchange relations among pairs or small cliques of firms. As an instrument for reinforcing the inter-corporate exchange network, this part of the communication network is little more than an extension of it. There is substantial evidence, however, that many if not most shared directorships are formed for very different reasons. While these reasons have been traced variously to class strategies for controlling large corporations, managerial strategies for enhancing individual careers, and company strategies for gathering information on other corporate practices, they all lead to the same outcome – a diffusely structured interlocking directorate. What largely occurs is not the cementing of ties between trading partners, creditors and borrowers, or other pairs of exchange-related firms, but simply the formation of linkages between (from an exchange standpoint) arbitrarily paired large companies. Providing the firms are big, particular exchanges between them are of little moment in the forging of communication links. The interlocking directorate, then, diffusely links corporations, and it does so according to logics not reducible to specific exchange relations among them. A pattern prevails, then, that facilitates the flow throughout the network of highly generalized information about the problems and practices of nearly all major companies. These communication circuits are both inclusive enough to encompass the entire apex of the corporate pyramid, and diffuse enough to ensure movement of the broadest-interest information.

Those who serve as directors of two or more large companies constitute, therefore, a diffusely structured network overarching nearly all important companies. Though ancillary elements of this network have been little studied, friendship and kinship networks do appear to add an additional element of informal cohesion. To this social cohesion is added an important degree of political cohesion. Personal involvement of the multiple directors in the affairs of several corporations, often situated in highly divergent markets, ensures direct exposure to a broad range of company problems. Since interlocking directorships among firms operating in the same market are discouraged, multiple directors typically see the problems of several different sectors, and not infrequently their experience even transects the industry/City divide. Generalization of the directors' personal experience is further enhanced by the frequent contact with other multiple directors overseeing still different sets of firms. As a result, from the competing and at times contradictory problems faced by big companies, there is likely to emerge a shared understanding of their common, reconcilable needs, which is then likely to be gradually encoded into a distinct culture and political perspective widely shared within the multiple-director circles. The multiple directors, in short, are more prone than single directors to acquire a class-wide understanding of the shared interests of large capital (however imperfect this understanding may be relative to some ideally defined standard). Multiple directors and their network can be seen as constituting a distinct segment of the capitalist class. Here we follow Zeitlin *et al.*'s conceptualization of a segment 'as having a relatively distinct location in the social process of production and, consequently, its own specific political economic requirements and concrete interests which may be contradictory to those of other class segments with which, nonetheless, it shares essentially the same relationship to ownership of productive property'. And as a distinct stratum, the dominant segment can be expected to play a distinct political role.

Articulation of the general interests of capital becomes particularly important in the interface between business on the one hand, and government and various non-profit institutions on the other. If policies of government and non-profit organizations are to reflect the general needs of business, business leaders who understand such trans-corporate needs should take centre stage. And multiple directors, if the foregoing arguments are correct, would generally be better prepared to move forward than their single-director counterparts. Moreover, not only should their vision be more suitable, but it can also be reasoned that they should be more often selected to serve as representatives of business. From the standpoint of government and non-profit organizations intending to solicit the views of business, the multiple-director segment would be a particularly appealing source of advisers. The varied connections of their members lend them a special aura of stature, legitimacy, and influence that is but faintly shared by single directors, eminent as they may be within their own company. From the standpoint of the business community itself, multiple directors would also make better business ambassadors. Because of their greater visibility, connections, and presumed impartiality, multiple directors should be especially favoured, and therefore promoted, for appointment to the outside world. Bolstering this expectation are studies demonstrating that individuals and organizations that are highly central to a community's inter-institutional networks come to exercise an especially influential voice in community political affairs. Thus, members of the interlocking directorate can be expected to far more often serve as business representatives to government and non-profit organizations than the remainder of the corporate elite. It is hypothesized, then, that the British corporate elite contains a 'dominant segment' whose political visibility is especially pronounced. The division between this segment and the remainder of the elite, however, is not a sharply demarcated one, nor should the dominant segment be seen as a homogeneous entity, for even more influential circles within circles are likely to be found inscribed within the dominant segment itself.

The political prominence of the dominant segment in Britain is also anticipated if its role in America and elsewhere can serve as a suggestive guide. The centralization of American capitalism, Mills long ago observed, had created a set of corporate directors who not only transcend the parochial concerns of their own firms to embrace general industrial concerns, but also 'move from the industrial point of interest and outlook to the interests and outlook of the class of all big corporate property as a whole'. Assessing the significance of similar trends in the Canadian economy, Porter ascribes to the interlocking directors a unique political role: 'They are the ultimate decision-makers and coordinators within the private sector of the economy. It is they who at the frontiers of the economic and political systems represent the interests of corporate power. They are the real planners of the economy.' Direct study of the dominant segment's political role in America finds that, as anticipated, it is more active in electoral politics and more prone to support established Republican candidates than is the remainder of the corporate elite; and it is disproportionately active and influential in the affairs of a range of non-business institutions, including national and local government. The role of this segment is found to be significant even in less developed capitalist economies. Studies of Chile by Zeitlin and his colleagues reveal that the economically and politically most dominant families are those whose directorships and holdings span several companies or who are rooted in the two major and partially opposed forms of capital, landed and corporate wealth.

The dominant segment of the British business elite may well also have come to acquire a similarly distinct political role. Compared with other members of the business elite, it is expected that those of the dominant segment more often assume an active role in shaping the affairs of non-business institutions. Financial contributions and personal assistance are among the chief forms of such activity, but since systematic records of the former are not presently available, attention is limited to the latter. The predominant form of personal assistance is service on boards of advisers, trustees, etc., whose primary role is to guide or oversee the policies of the non-business institution.

Research procedure

The governance and advisory activity of 1972 directors of 196 large British companies in both the national government and a range of non-profit organizations is the subject of analysis. Most of the 196 companies maintained boards with fewer than 21 directors, and in these cases all of the directors have been selected for study. In the few instances of larger boards, one or more directors have been randomly excluded to reduce to 20 the total number of directors for a given firm in the sample. The companies themselves were selected according to the following procedure. From the standard sectoral rankings of the largest UK firms prepared by *The Times* for 1977, we drew the 60 largest industrial companies, 50 somewhat smaller industrials appearing in the middle range of the top 1000 list, the 7 clearing banks, the 23 largest life insurance companies, the 15 largest accepting houses, the 11 largest discount houses, 10 large investment trusts, 10 large property companies, the 5 largest retail firms, and the 5 largest finance houses. Foreign-owned corporations, subsidiaries of other enterprises, and a few companies for which the identity of the directors could not be determined after searching several standard sources, were excluded. The 196 companies can be considered a reasonably representative set of the largest British-owned firms spanning all major sectors of manufacturing and commercial activity.

A total of 2211 board positions were associated with the 196 companies, though these openings were filled by only 1972 individuals since some of the directors serve on two or more of the boards simultaneously. To establish the location of the directors in the internal organization of the corporate elite, four sources of information have been jointly utilized. The 1978 and 1979 editions of *Who's Who* and the 1978 edition of the *Directory of Directors* provided the identity of additional company directorships, if any, held by each director. Since the latter volume lists subsidiary along with main board memberships, use of a concurrent edition of *Who Owns Whom* was required to distinguish between them; only main directorships are included. The dominant segment consists of those who serve on the boards of two or more *large* enterprises. Large firms have been defined as consisting of all quoted UK industrial companies and all non-industrial companies appearing on the lists of large financial and property firms compiled by *The Times*. Of the 1972 directors, 1554 sit on only one large company board and are designated single directors. Multiple directors include 264 who serve on two large-firm boards (double directors), and 154 on 3 or more boards (many-board directors). Thus, slightly more than one-fifth (21 per cent) of the total set of company directors comprise the dominant segment. Not only is the involvement in governance roles expected to be greater for multiple directors than single directors, but the logic of the previous arguments would also imply that the rate of involvement is an increasing function of the number of directorships held. The many-board directors should constitute an innermost circle of the inner circle.

Participation in government advisory service

Hundreds of boards, commissions and advisory bodies are temporarily or permanently created to assist the national government. No less than 360 Minister-appointed public boards served the government in 1978. Their functions varied widely, from operation of quasi-autonomous agencies (e.g., the British Broadcasting Corporation) to the management of nationalized industries (British Steel Corporation), guidance of research and development programmes (Science Research Council), and oversight of social service delivery (Regional Health Authorities of the National Health Service). The general purpose of the boards, in the case of the nationalized industry for instance, 'is to provide the industry with the best possible collective leadership and not . . . to secure the representation of certain interests, such as those of workers and consumers'. Business presence on nationalized industry boards comes as no surprise, then, but company directors are found elsewhere as well. One study, for instance, of the occupational positions of the 272 members of 39 major public boards in 1956 (the British Transport Council, Central Electricity Authority, and Gas Council among others), found that two-fifths of the members were company directors and at least one company director was present on all but two of the public boards. The voice of business on such boards, however, is not expected to be a simple cross-section of business opinion.

Systematic assessment of the directors' advisory service with the national government has been undertaken here in two ways. Major government appointments are identified from information contained in the directors' entries in several standard biographical references. Two deficiencies of these data must be kept in mind, however. First, slightly more than half of the directors could not be located in the biographical directories. Second, for those who are listed and who do report a government appointment, the dates of service are usually absent. This is potentially problematic if we are concerned to show that the possession of multiple directorships heightens the probability of appointment, for this information would not allow us to distinguish cases of multiple company board appointments that have followed (and probably resulted from) visible service on a public board from the opposite sequence of events. Though reciprocal causation is arguably present, our concern here is to isolate the impact of a director's location in the corporate world on his or her chances of entering the world of quasi-autonomous government advisory committees. Both of these problems can be overcome if the membership rosters of the public boards are systematically checked against our set of 1972 directors. A comprehensive set of rosters could not be readily obtained, but they were located in one reference source for a large number of the most prominent government bodies in 1978 and 1979, and at least one of our directors appears on 37 of these boards (the British Broadcasting Corporation, United Kingdom Energy Authority, and the National Bus Company are among those represented). The rate of participation for the three groups of directors in national government advisory service is presented in Table 1.

Table 1. Percentage of company directors who served on a Government public board in 1978–9 or in a Government advisory position during career, by number of large company directorships

Number of large company directorships	Government public board, 1978–9	Government advisory position, career		(N for public board and B estimate)	(N for A estimate)
		A estimate*	B estimate*		
	%	%	%		
One	2·6	12·4	4·7	(1554)	(564)
Two	6·1	22·5	15·2	(264)	(169)
Three or more	12·3	35·1	29·9	(154)	(131)
Ratio of three + co. boards to one board	4·6	2·8	6·4		

* The B estimate percentages are based on all directors, while the base for the A percentages is only those directors who appear in one of the biographical directories.

The likelihood of service on a public board in 1978 and 1979 is a direct function of the number of large company directorships. The director of a single company bore a less than 3 per cent chance of selection, for double directors the probability increased to 6 per cent, and for the many-board directors it exceeded 12 per cent, or more than four times the prospects for those outside the dominant segment (bottom row of Table 1). The many-board company director cum public board member is well illustrated by the activities of one merchant banker, Edwin Philip Chappell. The bulk of his career has been with the sixth largest accepting house, Morgan Grenfell, where he is vice-chairman. But he also attends board meetings of Equity & Law Life Assurance Society (the fourteenth largest insurer), Fisons (approximately hundredth in manufacturing), Guest, Keen & Nettlefolds (the fifteenth industrial), and International Computers Ltd (the premier British computer manufacturer) of which he assumed chairmanship in 1980. His diverse banking, insurance, and manufacturing experience has proven an asset to the government as well, for Mr Chappell also serves on one of the Treasury's Economic Development Committees (for the food and drink manufacturing industry) and as a governor of the British Broadcasting Corporation. And recently he also had held positions as chairman of the National Ports Council and as member of the Department of Education and Science's Business Education Council.

For examining the differential rates of overall career service using biographical source information, two estimates can be calculated. These estimates place boundaries on the true rate which could not be extracted from available data. The likelihood of mention in one of the biographical directories depended both on whether the director was a member of the dominant segment and on whether he or she had served in a government advisory capacity. Among single directors, for instance, only 36 per cent were deemed worthy of feature by the directory editors, whereas attention was bestowed on 64 per cent of the double directors, and 85 per cent of the many-board directors. These figures themselves confirm one of the assumptions upon which the present thesis has been constructed, namely, that the dominant segment is far more prominent and visible than the remainder of the corporate elite. But the figures also imply that if we compare governance rates using only those directors who appear in a biographical directory, we will underestimate the actual differences between the dominant segment and the remainder of the corporate elite. On the other hand, if we base the rates on all of the directors in this study, using the tenuous though probably largely correct assumption that most directors who are not in a standard biographical directory have not served in a major advisory capacity with the government either, we will overestimate the actual differences. The true rate, thus, lies somewhere between the figure based on only the directors listed in one of the biographical directories (henceforth the A estimate) and the figure based on all directors in the sample (the B estimate), though we suspect the actual rate is far closer to the latter. Both figures, in any case, are reported in Table 1, and either way the results are consistent with expectations. As in the 1978 and 1979 patterns, procedure B suggests that the rates are a progressive function of centrality to the dominant segment; 5 per cent of the single directors report some major advisory contributions to the government, while 15 per cent of the double directors do so, and 30 per cent of the many-board directors record the same. The A estimates indicate a smaller gap in these probabilities (three-fold versus more than six-fold). Yet however these estimates are calculated or adjusted, the observed patterns remain compelling: when it comes to assisting the national government, it is to the dominant segment that Ministers and government departments most frequently turn when the counsel of business is sought. . . .

Implications and conclusion

The evidence suggests that it is incorrect to describe the capitalist class as intrinsically atomized, incapable of recognizing even its most elementary class interests. But equally misleading is the converse proposition that a unity of interest has been recognized throughout. Most company directors still find little reason to promote, let alone identify, the public policies that would best serve their companies in the aggregate. In fact, most British managers display the same widespread tendency found among their American counterparts 'to act irrationally from the point of view of the economic and political viability of the business system', since, in Vogel's assessment, 'what [is] rational from the perspective of the individual firm [is] irrational from the perspective of the economic interests of business as a whole'. Yet if the bulk of British directors are bound by enterprise rationality to produce system irrationality, and if, consequently, most 'big businessmen in Britain are not bound by a strong sense of common political purpose' or even 'social identity', not all are so encapsulated by purely local concerns. Economic concentration and corporate integration have unintentionally created the foundation for a fraction far more cosmopolitan in outlook. Uniquely positioned to transcend, however imperfectly, the narrowness of political vision imposed on most company directors, this fraction has assumed a political role on behalf of the class that the class as a whole is incapable of playing. The state may assist the 'liberation' of the general interests of business from the 'fragmented, stubborn, and shortsighted empirical interests of single capital units', but it does so with active guidance from a politicized leading edge of capital itself.

In this general form, the dominant segment thesis is clearly a working hypothesis rather than established fact. But its likely validity is suggested by the evidence offered here to support one of its most central elements: the representatives of business to the government and third sector tend to emerge from that section of the corporate elite most capable of acquiring a systemic awareness of and promoting public policies serving the long-range concerns of big business. Data from the representative cross-section of large British companies and their directors used here point to precisely that pattern. Core members of the dominant segment are, depending on the specific measure, three to six times more likely than other corporate directors to be invited by government to render advice on new employment legislation, operation of the BBC, and nearly everything in between. Cultural organizations, universities, and philanthropic found-ations utilize strikingly similar criteria when issuing their invitations for outside counsel. The inner circle of the corporate elite is overselected by ratios of two to six when non-profit organizations form their governing boards. It is this core of business leaders, then, 'with simultaneous con-tacts in industry, finance and government', writes Barratt Brown, who can thus 'provide some element of planning and control in an otherwise unplanned economy'. Thus, in Banks's succinct phrasing, 'the device of interlocking directorships succeeds in creating a form of unity in a situ-ation of diversity, without going all the way to a monopoly in a single organization'.

The dominant segment forms enduring relations with the governing circles through both formal and informal channels of access. Evidence presented here supports the view that the major business associations, with the Confederation of British Industry at the forefront, offer a decisive means of formal linkage. The leaders of the CBI are not a cross-section of the business community, nor, one might tentatively infer, are CBI policy initiatives representative of prevailing business opinion. Rather, those who shape CBI positions, who guide its deliberations, and who enter as CBI emissaries into regular meetings with government Ministers and senior civil servants, are a highly select lot, given to ideas that may promote the capital accumulation of all but are frequently antithetical to the momentary wisdom of most. To assert that the CBI is little more than an instrument for dominant segment politics would certainly be an overstatement, but there is no doubt that the CBI is closely guided by the concerns of this inner circle. Of the directors in our study who serve on the two most central governing bodies of the CBI, the President's advisory committee and the ruling Council, fully half are members of the dominant segment (only a fifth of the sampled directors are part of the segment).

We have found that the CBI also screens who shall be able to act further as a spokesperson for business during meetings of government oversight and advisory bodies of all kinds. Those with multiple corporate connections have their prospects for appointment to a public board radically improved if they also possess the qualities necessary to emerge as a luminary in the CBI. Multiple directors who have entered the leadership circles of the CBI are six times more likely than other multiple directors or single directors in the CBI leadership to receive an invitation to assist the government (and the odds are ten times greater than for directors with neither attribute). The British Institute of Management also appears to provide this gatekeeping function, and still other associations presumably contribute as well. From the standpoint of the individual industrialist or financier seeking to enter the inner sanctum of top-level contact with government, one of the surest paths is to join several other large companies as a non-executive director and then ascend the CBI leadership hierarchy.

Social networks, of which 'old boy' ties still remain a salient strand, informally extend what is more formally achieved through the business associations. Multiple directors are several times as likely as others to embody those qualities requisite for initiation into one of the foremost institutions of elite sociability, the select club. And club membership is, by a factor approaching two or better, associated with participation in the governance of non-profit organizations and in government advisory service alike. Moreover, entry into club-based social networks can compensate in part for the absence of network affiliations otherwise derived from appointment to several large company boards. Multiple direc-torships and business association leadership account for the greatest dif-ference in participation rates, but informal networks as indexed by club membership add a modest increment of their own. Taken together, these three factors go a long way towards identifying the politically active element of the capitalist class.

Although available evidence consistently corroborates propositions drawn from the dominant segment thesis, the overall thesis can still only be placed on a tentative footing, since important elements and im-plications await verification. First, the expectation that this elite stratum carries a distinct ideology into its outside political activities deserves special attention. The more forward looking perspective expected to be prevalent within the dominant segment has been described by many observers. Westergaard and Resler, for instance, identify two persistent 'clusters of capitalist opinion on the role of the state', with one tendency seeking to minimize all government involvement in the economy and to resist labour demands at all turns, and the other seeking to 'extend state activity in aid of business – for rationalization, coordination, and promo-tion of an economic climate favourable to growth and prosperity – and to secure the "partnership" of organized labour'. The former is in keeping with the defence of the individual firm's immediate prosperity; the latter is more consistent with promoting business's more general, long-term pros-perity. Tentative evidence suggests that partisans of the latter are especially to be found in the dominant segment, but definitive assessment is needed.

Second, the actual degree of influence of the dominant segment in public affairs remains to be seen. The positional power of this fraction relative to the remainder of the corporate elite is pronounced, but com-pared with other groups contending for favour, its influence is less certain. The inner circle's capacity to mobilize diverse corporate resources on behalf of policies it prefers makes it a formidable player. Nonetheless, its ability to defeat labour, public, bureaucratic and other opponents is still an open question.

Third, it is anticipated that the patterns observed here for participation in advisory and governance activity should be replicated in other channels of political activity as well. Purely informal contact and consulting with top government officials is common among dominant segment members, for instance, but far less so among other company directors. Similarly, compared with the typical company director's gravitation towards the centre of the Conservative Party, the elite fraction's contributions of time and money to the Conservative Party are likely to be both greater *in toto* and more concentrated on the moderate wing, and channels of communi-cation with Labour Party leaders should be more open as well.

Fourth, the relation of large companies to the dominant segment requires determination. Banks and other financial institutions are more central to the multiple-director network, for instance, and certain types of manufacturing firms are more connected than others. Since the precise political thrust of the dominant segment is a function of its company foundation, the composition of the leading companies underpinning the dominant segment deserves assessment. In addition, the extent to which companies are tied to the dominant segment is likely to have an impact on their behaviour. For example, firms whose directors are members of the dominant segment can be expected to make far larger charitable and political contributions than companies whose directors have few ties to the dominant segment. The present analysis has concentrated on the organization of the dominant segment at the level of company directors; examination of the organization at the level of the companies themselves is the next task.

Finally, it can tentatively be suggested that the structure of the corporate elite has come increasingly to shape relations between class and state. A company-based capitalist class would appear to have increased in political significance as the influence of the wealth-based upper class has declined. Despite a continuing cultural ambivalence about even the value of industry, the traditional aristocracy long ago evolved a working alliance, if not integration, with ascendant business elements, most obviously in the City but with important segments in industry as well. In Stanworth and Giddens's terse phrasing, 'Britain made both gentlemen of businessmen . . . and businessmen of gentlemen.' Given the wealth, connections, and esteem of the upper class, a more precise phrasing in light of the findings here may be that the mutual conversion was largely limited to those upper regions of the business world that we have dubbed the dominant segment. Indeed, evidence developed elsewhere supports the derivative prediction that multiple directors count among their ranks a highly disproportionate number of scions of long-established patrician families. But as the alliance has evolved, with the upper class the dominant partner at the outset in cultural if not economic terms, there is some evidence that inter-corporate relations have been gradually yet inexorably displacing upper-class relations in defining who constitutes the political leadership of the capitalist class. If location in the web of upper-class families was once a determining factor, location in the web of inter-company directorships may now be far more important. Relations with the third sector evince a comparable transformation: the declining contributions of the upper class to the arts are being more than compensated by the rising levels of company support. Inter-corporate rationality, it seems, is replacing upper-class rationality in defining how business pursues its broadest interests. And if so, surely at the forefront of the movement is the dominant segment.

The Politics of the Judiciary
J. A. G. Griffith

Reprinted with permission from J. A. G. Griffith, *The Politics of the Judiciary*, Fontana Paperbacks, 1977, pp. 24–31

From time to time in recent years, analyses have been made, based on information in reference books, of the social background of the more senior judiciary.

The most comprehensive in terms simply of social class origins covers the period from 1820 to 1968.

Period of Appointment	1820–1875	1876–1920	1921–1950	1951–1968	1820–1968	Number
Social class	%	%	%	%		
I Traditional landed upper class	17·9	16·4	15·4	10·5	15·3	59
II Professional, commercial and administrative upper class	8·5	14·6	14·3	14·0	12·7	49
III Upper middle class	40·6	50·5	47·3	52·3	47·4	183
IV Lower middle class	11·3	9·7	8·8	8·1	9·6	37
V Working class	2·8	1·0	1·1	1·2	1·3	6
Not known	18·9	7·8	13·2	14·0	13·5	52
	100	100	100	100	100	
Number	106	103	91	86	386	386

Over the whole period the dominance of the upper and upper middle classes is overwhelming. They account for 75.4 per cent to which may be added, proportionately, 10 per cent from those 'not known'. Moreover the total percentage of these first three groups in the most recent period is 76.8, which is higher than the overall percentage. Over the whole period covered by this analysis the dominance of the first three classes is unchanged.

Another survey, published in 1975, covers the period 1876–1972 and, with a few omissions, analyses the 317 judges who sat in the High Court, the Court of Appeal and the House of Lords during that period. The author does not, however, break down these 96 years into shorter periods so trends within the whole are not apparent. He considers school background and finds that 33 per cent attended one of the nine most famous public schools while 70 per cent attended Oxford or Cambridge Universities.

School education is a good indicator of social and economic class background, particularly as the relative cost of attendance at one of the independent 'public' schools has changed little, until very recently. It must also be remembered that university education at Oxford and Cambridge before 1945 (when those who are now judges attended) was also very largely a middle-class activity, within the first three groups of the table set out above.

In 1956 the *Economist* published a short survey. This covered 69 judges of the Supreme Court, House of Lords and Judicial Committee of the Privy Council and showed that 76 per cent had attended 'major public schools' (not further defined) and the same percentage had been to Oxford or Cambridge. In May 1970 *New Society* looked at 359 judges including those offices surveyed by the *Economist* but also, amongst others, county court judgeships and metropolitan magistrates. This found that 81 per cent had attended public schools and 76 per cent had attended Oxford or Cambridge. In 1969, Henry Cecil investigated the background of 117 out of 235 judges of the House of Lords, the Supreme Court, county courts and stipendiary magistrates. From a random group of 36 judges of the Court of Appeal and the High Court, he found that 31 had been to public schools (86 per cent) and 33 to Oxford or Cambridge (92 per cent). From a random group of 45 (out of 90) county court judges and 24 (out of 48) stipendiaries, he found that 52 had attended public schools (75 per cent) and 56 Oxford or Cambridge (81 per cent). In 1975 Hugo Young analysed the educational background of 31 appointees to the High Court during the previous five years. He found that 68 per cent went to public schools and 74 per cent to Oxford or Cambridge.

These figures have changed very little over the last thirty or more years. In 1940 about 80 per cent of the judges of the Supreme Court had attended public schools. In 1969, this was true of 79 per cent of Henry

Cecil's group of 117. A higher proportion of the earlier generation did not attend university at all – eight out of 35 in 1940 but only eight out of 135 in 1970. Of those who did attend, the bias in favour of Oxford and Cambridge has remained effectively unchanged. The *New Society* survey compared county court judges in three recent years. In 1947, in 1957 and in 1967, seven county court judges were appointed. Of these 21 judges, all but one in 1947, two in 1957 and one in 1967 had attended public schools; all but three in 1947, two in 1957 and three in 1967 had attended Oxford or Cambridge.

The decline in the number of 'political' judges is also shown. The *Economist*'s survey of 1956 recorded that 23 per cent of their 69 judges had been MPs or Parliamentary candidates. But fourteen years later, Henry Cecil could find only 10 MPs and 5 candidates out of his 117 judges (13 per cent).

The age of the full-time judiciary has remained constant over many years: the average on appointment has been about fifty-two or fifty-three and the average age of all those in office has been about sixty. Inevitably, given the system of promotion, the average age is highest in the Court of Appeal and the House of Lords, at about sixty-five and sixty-eight years respectively.

Since 1876 there have been 63 Lords of Appeal in Ordinary (Law Lords). An analysis of 49 of these showed that 18 had fathers who were lawyers, 16 had fathers of other professions (churchmen, doctors, teachers, architects, soldiers). Twelve fathers were in business (of whom one was working-class), and three fathers were farmers or landowners. Forty-six Law Lords had been to Oxford or Cambridge, seven to Scottish universities, four to Trinity College Dublin, two to London University (one of whom had also been to Cambridge) and one to Queen's Belfast. These facts and figures added relatively little to what was already known in outline. More interesting is the analysis of political background. The authors divided their period into three groups. Group A included 20 Law Lords appointed in the period 1876–1914; Group B had 21 appointed between 1918 and 1948; Group C had 22 appointed in 1948–69. Of the 20 Law Lords in Group A, eleven had been MPs and three Parliamentary candidates; of the 21 in Group B, five had been MPs; of the 22 in Group C, four had been MPs and two Parliamentary candidates. While these figures show the decline since the late nineteenth and early twentieth century of appointments of such politicians, they also show little change since 1918. It is, however, unwise to base generalizations on such figures. What matters more than prior political involvement is how far Law Lords consciously or otherwise are influenced in their judgments by their own political opinions, how far this is avoidable and how far it is undesirable. One highly 'political' Lord Chancellor – like Lord Hailsham of St Marylebone – can, if he chooses, make a considerable impact on judicial law-making at the highest level but, for this to be so, it is not necessary that he should have held political office or have been a Member of Parliament or a law officer.

All these figures show that, in broad terms, four out of five full-time professional judges are products of public schools, and of Oxford or Cambridge. Very occasionally the brilliant lower-middle-class boy has won his place in this distinguished gathering. With very few exceptions, judges are required to be selected from amongst practising barristers and until recently no one without a private income could survive the first years of practice. To become a successful barrister therefore it was necessary to have financial support and so the background had to be that of the reasonably well-to-do family which, as a matter of course, sent its sons to public schools and then either straight to the bar or first to Oxford or Cambridge. In the last three years, the need for a private income during the first years has to an increasing extent returned.

Nevertheless, some men and women have, since the middle 1960s, benefited from the expansion of university education, from the growth of law faculties in universities, and from the wider availability of this education and, with little private income, have been able (largely because of the increase in publicly financed legal aid) to make a living at the bar. By the mid-1980s some of these will move into the ranks of successful barristers from whom judicial appointments are made. Only then shall we be able to assess how far the dominance of the public schools and (what is of much less significance) of Oxford and Cambridge has begun to lessen. And not until the 1990s shall we know whether (as seems most unlikely) judicial attitudes have changed as a result.

Not yet however can the view of Lord Justice Lawton be accepted. Delivering the Riddell Lecture in 1975 he said that it was a common misconception that the judiciary were drawn from the moneyed classes and educated at leading public schools and at Oxford or Cambridge. In his view judges were 'drawn from all ranks of society' and were 'a microcosm of Britain today'. The learned Lord Justice did not support this view with any evidence.

Judicial independence means that judges are not dependent on Governments in any ways which might influence them in coming to decisions in individual cases. Formally, this independence is preserved by their not being dismissible by the Government of the day. This does not affect their promotion, which, like their appointment, is effectively in the hands of the Lord Chancellor with, nowadays, little or no Prime Ministerial intervention. In financial terms, such promotion is not of much significance. But life in the Court of Appeal and, even more, in the House of Lords is not so strenuous as in the High Court (or below), personal prestige and status are higher among the fewer, with a life peerage at the top. These are not inconsiderable rewards for promotion, and the question is whether there are pressures on, particularly, High Court judges to act and to speak in court in certain ways rather than in others. Are there decisions which could be classified as popular or unpopular in the eyes of the most important senior judges or the Lord Chancellor? Is a judge ever conscious that his reputation as a judge is likely to be adversely affected in their eyes if he decides one way, and favourably affected if he decides another way?

The answer is that such pressures do exist. For example, a judge who acquires a reputation among his seniors for being 'soft' in certain types of cases where the Lord Chancellor, the Lord Chief Justice, the Master of the Rolls and other senior judges favour a hard line is likely to damage his promotion prospects as he would if his appointment were found to be unfortunate on other more obvious grounds. But this does not amount to dependence on the political wishes of Governments or Ministers as such. In no real sense does such direct dependence or influence exist. How far judges consciously or unconsciously subserve the wider interests of Governments is another and more important question.

What is meant by saying that judges must be impartial and seen to be so? Judges themselves claim this as their great virtue and only occasionally is it seen to be departed from. Lord Haldane was a practising barrister in 1901 when he recorded:

I fought my hardest for the Dutch prisoners before the Privy Council this morning, but the tribunal was hopelessly divided, and the anti-Boers prevailed over the pro-Boers. It is bad that so much bias should be shewn, but it is, I suppose, inevitable.

D. N. Pritt in his autobiography told of his many political cases and of one which 'came before a judge of great experience and knowledge, so bitterly opposed to anything left-wing that he could scarcely have given a fair trial if he had tried'.

Are such phrases applicable today? Every practising barrister knows before which judges he would prefer not to appear in a political case because he believes, and his colleagues at the bar believe, that certain judges are much more likely than others to be biased against certain groups, like demonstrators or students, or certain kinds of action, like occupations of property by trade unionists or the homeless.

This however is to say little more than that, as we have already remarked, judges are human with human prejudices. And that some are more human than others. But if that were all we would expect to find a wide spectrum of judicial opinion about political cases. Instead, we find a remarkable consistency of approach in these cases concentrated in a fairly narrow part of the spectrum of political opinion. It spreads from that part of the centre which is shared by right-wing Labour, Liberal and 'progressive' Conservative opinion to that part of the right which is associated with traditional Toryism – but not beyond into the reaches of the far right.

The Myth of Central Control
A. Robinson

Reprinted with permission from Ann Robinson, 'The Myth of Central Control', *the Listener*, 17 June 1982, pp. 8–11

In 1979 we elected a government which promised, among other things, to bring public expenditure under firm control. Three years later this promise is unfulfilled. Public expenditure and taxation, in spite of much publicized 'cuts', are higher in real terms than they were three years ago.

Public spending is the acid test of any central government's capacity to exercise its powers. If a government cannot control its own expenditure, it cannot really be said to be in control of its own administrative machine. The present failure could spring from many causes: it could be the pressure of the current recession, or the wrong-headed ideas of the Government, it could be a lack of will, or perhaps a lack of suitably talented personnel. But, could another party do better? The fact that successive governments over the past twenty-five years have *all* failed to keep public expenditure within their own agreed limits seems to suggest that there may be some deeper underlying reasons for their continued failures.

In theory, British governments ought to be able to achieve their objectives better than most. It is widely believed that the most significant feature of the British political system is its strong, powerful and effective central government. In this talk, I want to explore the nature of our belief and trust in the capacity of our central government. And I shall then offer an alternative view which suggests that government in this country is now too fragmented and decentralized for effective central control. If my analysis is correct, central control is a myth, or at the very least it is an unwarranted assumption for voters and parties to act upon.

There is undoubtedly some evidence to support the theory of strong central government. First, there is legal centralization of power. Britain is a unitary state in which Parliament is the sole source of legal authority. All the powers exercised by local authorities, nationalized industries and quangos have been granted to them by Act of Parliament, and can be removed from them by the same means. If such bodies act beyond their legal powers, Ministers can always enforce the will of central government through the courts, or by imposing financial sanctions. The second feature of the theory of central control is that of centralized decision-making. The central government, it is said, determines the aims and objectives, and can effectively pass them down through the bureaucratic machine for implementation. By passing legislation, issuing notices and circulars and setting cash limits on expenditures, the central government can determine what is done in practice throughout the administrative machine. So the theory of central control can always be defended by calling upon the evidence of legal form, and by pointing to specific examples of successful ministerial action.

But is such legalistic evidence really adequate to sustain the theory of strong central government when we see, in practice, one government after another failing to control public expenditure? The constant failures seem to suggest that we should look beyond legal form to the actual political power relationships that operate in government today.

Although electors and some academics have continued to display trust in the capacity of British central government, events over the past twenty years have sown the seeds of doubt in the minds of many politicians with experience of office. They have watched control slipping away from the centre as government activities expanded and took on new forms. From the early 1960s, they struggled to re-establish their power by reforms in the machinery of central government. They invented devices to plan the future growth of public expenditure, and provide management links between the centre and those who carried out the day-to-day work. They set up committees and 'Super Departments' for better coordination, and 'Think-Tanks' for the clarification of central government objectives. But these reforms, based as they were on the belief that the machinery of government was designed to respond to directives from the centre, have had little effect. They failed because the underlying pattern of administration was changing.

As public expenditure rose, it was accompanied by great changes in the nature of the British administrative system. From a neat, closely organized system of central government departments, well suited to the limited functions of the nineteenth-century state, it has taken on features comparable to those found in many federal states. The statistics of government employment tell part of the story. By 1979, the public sector of the economy employed over seven million people out of a total work force of some 24 million. But only a small proportion of the seven million are employed by the central government. Today, less than 700,000 are classified as civil servants, and these are a mixed bunch, from Permanent Secretaries to ordnance factory workers. At the most generous estimate, there cannot be more than 30,000 or 40,000 people employed in a control function in central government departments. And the numbers engaged in this function have hardly increased at all during a twenty-year period which has seen an expansion of total public employment from five to seven million. Indeed, it is the present Government's intention to *reduce* the numbers at the top. Central government's capacity for scrutiny and supervision is consequently very small in relation to the total public service, and as the numbers at the centre decline relative to the whole, so too does the scrutiny and supervision.

At the same time, there have also been major structural changes in the British bureaucracy. As new functions of government have been added, they have, in many cases, been handed over to the local authorities or to newly created bodies, only loosely connected with their central sponsoring department. I can give but a few examples out of many. Local authorities have taken on many new tasks, including the expanded social services and higher education in the form of polytechnics. The expansion of the universities in the twenty years since the Robbins report has been in the hands of the largely autonomous University Grants Committee. Labour exchanges and training have been 'hived off' to the Manpower Services Commission, which employs 25,000 people and has a budget of over £1000 million. The important point to remember is that few of these bodies are staffed by civil servants as such, and, even where they are, they are not under the day-to-day managerial supervision of their sponsoring central government department. A recent Parliamentary Question on the regularity with which manpower reviews are carried out revealed that there may be gaps of seven years or more between these exercises. Managerial links between agencies and their sponsoring departments are infrequent, and are generally sustained at a relatively low level – certainly not between the Permanent Secretary and the agency's Chief Executive. So from a managerial point of view, the agencies are largely self-directing and self-regulating.

Perhaps these structural changes in the administrative system would not necessarily weaken the centre's capacity for control if the legal powers of the central department and its Minister were always sufficiently clear to ensure central government victory in cases of conflict. But Ministers who take agencies to court do not always win their cases. The final judgment rests on the Acts which grant powers both to Ministers and to the agencies of government.

For example, the Home Office lost its case against the Commission for Racial Equality when the Commission won its right to conduct a formal investigation into the operation of the Immigration Service. The Home Office, which is responsible both for the Immigration Service and for the CRE, contested the Commission's right to conduct an investigation into the work of a government department. But the court found for the Commission on the grounds that its statutory powers of formal investigation were not limited. This case established a legal authority vested by statute in a quasi-governmental body that allowed it to act in direct contradiction to the expressed wish of its own sponsoring department.

But, in fact, this sort of legalistic example hides the more common practices of government agencies. Since no one is looking over their shoulders, the agencies themselves are free for the most part to interpret the powers granted to them. They have devised subtle means of circumventing the wishes of Ministers and departments. One important ministerial power, we are told by the centralists, is that of issuing circulars and guidelines. But in practice this power is subject to many constraints.

There may be legal limits to the Minister's power to determine details. A recent research study undertaken for the Equal Opportunities Commission showed that the Minister of Education probably did not have the statutory power to issue circulars to local authorities with the aim of reorganizing schools to ensure equal educational opportunities for both sexes. A Minister attempting to issue such a circular might find himself challenged in the courts. But, the research revealed, even if such a circular were to be issued, the reaction of the local authorities would most likely be to ignore it. Ignoring, reinterpreting, and delays in implementation of ministerial circulars are common tactics employed by agencies. Only if agencies or workers persist in ignoring or delaying the requirements of notices or circulars in cases where there is a very high level of central government commitment to action, as in the case of comprehensive education, will a Minister move to the last resort and take an agency to court or introduce new legislation to enforce his will. Obviously, a Minister cannot resort to such drastic action on every subject and every detail. In any case, it is clear that Ministers cannot simply go ahead and issue circulars on any subject in the certainty that they will be complied with. And the constraints on this particular ministerial power are such that many circulars just never get sent out at all: the agencies are left to determine what actions they will take for themselves.

Finally, the centralists argue, the central government has the power of the purse. Through rigorous application of 'cash limits' the central government can determine what agencies do. But 'cash limits' are an extremely crude instrument of control. Certainly the central government can decide what shall be the total sum available to each broad function of government in any given year, but it has inadequate machinery to determine the details of how the money is spent. The Treasury is a very small department that can give only seconds of attention to each great block of spending. Parliament totally ignores the details of the estimates. The consequence is a *de facto* decentralization of spending decisions.

The effects can be measured by looking at the variation in expenditure from one area to another and from one institution to another within any given service. Education provides some vivid examples. Cost per pupil in secondary schools ranges from £536 to £959 a head; in primary schools the variation is from £362 to £703 a head. School books cost as little as £18 per pupil and as much as £58. Looked at in this way, the British education system does not provide strong evidence of 'central control'. Almost every service of government displays similar differences. The cost of educating a degree-level student or of keeping a child in care varies greatly from institution to institution, and so on. These differences do not reflect variations in need so much as real choices made by agencies.

The effect of the changes in structure and relationships has been to turn government upside down. Instead of objectives and financial targets being decided by the central government and then transmitted down to agencies for implementation, they filter upwards to the central government from the agencies and bureaux. They – not the handful of Ministers and Permanent Secretaries – have the policy initiative. They, after all, have the knowledge of how day-to-day administration works; they deliver the services direct to the public; they, not the central departments, have contact with the clients of the state and are, they consider, best placed to interpret their needs. They therefore become a source of financial claims upon the government. Ultimately it is the agencies of government, not the centre, who determine how much shall be spent on what.

A particularly well-documented example of this phenomenon is the Manpower Services Commission. An essay which won the Haldane Society Prize a couple of years ago described how the agency expanded very rapidly because central government Ministers wanted to be seen to care about the problem of rising unemployment. They displayed their care by allocating ever-increasing sums of money to Manpower Services, but they left the details of policy-making to the Commission itself. There was little policy direction from the top to determine what types of programmes should be established. And there was little machinery for assessing the cost-effectiveness of the programmes provided. The managers of the various sections of the Commission thus captured the policy initiative, and demanded more and more spending. And even after the money had been spent, there was little central control because the staff of the office of the Comptroller and Auditor General – whose job it is to scrutinize the spending of government agencies – were too few and too junior to ask the right questions.

Thus the pattern and levels of public spending on many services today reflect real choices made by agencies of government themselves over long periods of time, as much as they reflect policy decisions made by the Cabinet and in the Treasury. And the choices made by government agencies are perpetuated year by year because the amounts of money allocated to them are not subject to in-depth scrutiny. The British central government has no techniques for re-evaluation of programmes such as those used in the United States and other federal decentralized states. It has no machinery for making comparisons of cost-effectiveness between institutions. Because so much of public spending is ultimately determined by numerous individual decisions throughout the public sector, it has become unresponsive to demands for change. When governments, as in the 1970s and 1980s, are faced with the need to increase spending on some items because of changing needs and cannot rely on economic growth to supply a boundless source of revenue, they try to re-order priorities and restrict spending on other items. But the nature of the administrative machine today inhibits rapid response to central government decisions to reduce spending.

Governments themselves are fully aware, once in office, that central control is elusive. But they do not know how to re-establish their authority. They no longer trust in the reform of the machinery of central government. The reforms of the 1960s and 1970s proved ineffective. The present Government has avoided changes in the administrative machinery and it is cool on proposals for a stronger role for the office of Comptroller and Auditor General. It has recently made some political appointments to agencies, including the Commission for Racial Equality and the Manpower Services Commission, to achieve a closer political link between agency and government. But by the time the next election comes round, little will have changed in the underlying capacity of central government, even if a few public victories are scored by individual Ministers over particular local authorities and agencies. Over wide areas of their political responsibility, governments have no central control. Short of a massive effort to regain that control, an effort which would mean a dramatic increase in Civil Service numbers at the centre relative to the periphery, they are left with little choice but to accommodate themselves to the decentralized, loosely articulated nature of British government today. If the political accommodation does not take place, both electors and parties are headed for further disappointments as new governments promise what they cannot achieve.

Urban Politics: a Sociological Interpretation
P. Saunders

Reprinted with permission from Peter Saunders, *Urban Politics: a Sociological Interpretation*, Hutchinson University Library, 1979, pp. 210–23.

Social composition

Historically Britain's local government has always been dominated by people drawn from a higher social class than the majority of those they represent. As Prewitt and Eulau observe, 'Even in the most democratic society, the electorate does not choose from among all its members. It chooses from among a pool of eligibles disproportionately drawn from the higher social status groups in society.' This is not to suggest that local power has consistently been concentrated in the same hands. But such reshuffling as has taken place, largely as a result of the progressive democratization of local government and the rise of the Labour Party, has generally taken the form of a shift from upper class and big business domination one hundred years ago, to middle class and smaller business domination today, with an increase in some areas in the representation of skilled manual workers.

In Birmingham, for example, the traditional power of big business in the local council has given way to the increasing significance of 'professional-businessmen', and especially 'exchange professionals' such as estate agents and solicitors – men who own their own businesses and who have a substantial interest in the local property market. Similarly in Glossop, the old economic and social elite which ran the town in the nineteenth century is now virtually insignificant as regards direct representation on the local council. Traditional social and political leaders in these and other towns thus appear to have adopted an increasingly 'cosmopolitan' perspective, backing out of local affairs as improvements in communications and transportation over the last century have enabled them to sustain wide-ranging social networks with other members of their class, far beyond the confines of their communities of residence. But those who have replaced them in the command posts of Britain's towns and cities, while less socially conspicuous, are nevertheless still by and large a very different breed from most of those who elect them.

Much the same picture emerges in relation to Croydon where, at least since 1849, the town's governing bodies have invariably been controlled by varying types of businessmen. Before that date, the town had no single or unified system of local administration. Until 1780 it had been managed (to the extent that it was managed at all) by the benevolent hand of the Canterbury archbishopric which maintained a palace and estate in the town, and from then until the mid-nineteenth century the various minimal functions of government were administered by a variety of local trusts, boards and commissions. It was not until 1849 that these functions were brought together under the newly constituted Board of Health. Elected annually on a restricted suffrage, the membership of the Board was from the outset overwhelmingly comprised of local businessmen and upper-class benefactors, many of whom had considerable property interests in the town and surrounding area. For thirty-four years, these men used the Board both to provide some basic and much needed public amenities and to consolidate the privileged position which they and their class enjoyed. Ably combining altruistic ideals with the profitable pursuit of self-interest, they administered a town in which the disparities between the working-class west side and the middle-class east continued to grow while business prospered.

In 1883, some of the town's most prominent business and political leaders succeeded, against protests from various small traders in outlying areas, in gaining Croydon's incorporation as a borough, and six years later, following the 1888 Local Government Act, the town was designated one of the new County Boroughs. But although the name and the functions changed, the character of the membership did not, and the faces on the new council appeared little different from those on the old Board of Health. No less than 28 per cent of the members elected to the County Borough council were, on any definition, big businessmen – the owners of the town's largest stores, the biggest companies and so on. Total business representation stood at over 60 per cent, while a further 25 per cent of members merely described themselves as 'gentlemen'. It appears from the records that no manual workers gained election.

Croydon remained a County Borough for the next seventy-six years until the reorganization of London's local government system came into effect in 1965. At this time, Croydon became one of thirty-two London boroughs and lost a number of its responsibilities in the fields of planning, housing and roads to the newly formed Greater London Council. Even before this, the local council had been losing its powers – public transport was taken out of local hands in the 1930s, hospitals were handed over to the NHS after the war, and gas was similarly made the responsibility of the new nationalized regional boards – but the loss of both functions and autonomy under the 1965 reorganization was strongly resented in local political circles, and there is today still a legacy of hostility in Croydon towards the higher tier authority. Although it lost responsibilities, however, the council grew in size as the strongly middle-class and staunchly conservative Purley and Coulsdon Urban District was merged with Croydon under the boundary changes at that time.

This merger only served to reinforce the middle-class domination of the local authority which had gradually become established since the turn of the century. By 1971, of course, the big businessmen and local gentry who had been so prominent in the late nineteenth century had disappeared from the council altogether. The proportion of small traders had also dipped significantly from 22 per cent of the total membership in 1891 to just 6 per cent in 1971. But this decline of the old upper class and the traditional petty bourgeoisie only reflects the phenomenal increase in the representation of the new middle-class and professional businessmen. The working class is still, by and large, left out in the cold. Thus, while the rise of the Labour Party has usually led in other parts of Britain to a substantial increase in manual worker representation in local government, in Croydon it has resulted rather in an increased representation of professional workers. To some extent, this reflects the character of the social composition of the town itself, for unlike northern industrial towns such as Sheffield, Wolverhampton and Newcastle-under-Lyme where up to half of all Labour councillors are drawn from the manual working class, in

Croydon the figure is only 14 per cent, and this appears more in line with other southern commercial towns like Brighton. Nevertheless, even in Croydon the manual working class accounts for around 50 per cent of the total population, and it is clear that this class is thus considerably under-represented in the council chamber. The Labour councillors may or may not be for the working class, but very few of them are of it, although a considerable proportion appear to have been upwardly mobile in inter-generational terms.

The large increase in the representation of professional workers on the council over the last eighty years is thus accounted for in the main by Labour members, many of whom follow those 'liberal professions' such as teaching, journalism and social work commonly associated with middle-class radicalism. Twenty-eight per cent of the Labour group consists of these liberal professionals, the remainder comprising managers (14 per cent), professional businessmen (10 per cent), other professional groups (17 per cent) and skilled manual workers (14 per cent). The composition of the majority Conservative group, on the other hand, falls mainly into the three categories of professional businessmen, most of whom are exchange professionals (29 per cent), company managers and executives (27 per cent), and the traditional professions such as civil servants (24 per cent). This strong business representation in the ranks of the majority group is emphasized even more strongly at the level of the group's leadership, with no less than eight of eleven committee chairmen and five of the seven members of the powerful Policy subcommittee being company executives, professional businessmen or small traders. The dominance of big business in the County Borough council of the 1890s is thus mirrored in the dominance achieved by other sectors of business in the London Borough council of the 1970s.

The membership of the council is not only unrepresentative in terms of occupation, however. On the basis of replies received to a questionnaire survey, I estimate that around 40 per cent of all council members were privately educated and that approximately the same proportion received a state grammar school education. Again there are variations between the party groups with well over half of the Conservative group having attended fee-paying schools compared with around one in eight of Labour members. Furthermore, the sex distribution among council members is grossly distorted against women, males outnumbering females by more than four to one in both groups. There are, in addition, no women on the Policy subcommittee, and only one female committee chairperson. This bias against women in top positions cannot be accounted for in terms of differential lengths of council service, for three women have sat on the council for more than twelve years.

Compared with the social composition of the total population, and even with the composition of other local councils which have been studied, the

Table 1. Croydon council membership characteristics, 1973

	Years of service					Education			Occupation									Age					Position			Party		Sex
	under 3	3–5	6–8	9–11	12 or more	Fee-paying	Grammar	Other	Executives	Managers	Professional businessmen	Liberal professionals	Other professionals	Traders, etc.	Clerical	Manual	Other/Not Known	21–34	35–44	45–54	55–64	65 and over	Policy subcommittee	Committee chairman	Alderman	Labour	Conservative	Female
Male	23	8	5	4	17	26	21	10	7	6	14	4	14	4	3	4	1	13	12	11	14	7	7	10	10	24	33	
Female	8	1	–	1	3	4	9	–	–	2	1	5	1	–	–	–	4	4	2	5	2	–	–	1	–	5	8	13
Conservative	9	7	5	3	17	26	14	1	7	4	12	1	10	3	2	–	2	7	5	10	14	5	7	11	8	–	41	8
Labour	22	2	–	2	3	4	16	9	–	4	3	8	5	1	1	4	3	10	9	6	2	2	–	–	2	29	–	5
Alderman	1	–	–	–	9	6	2	2	1	–	2	1	4	1	–	1	–	–	1	2	3	4			10			
Committee chairman	–	2	1	–	8	7	3	1	2	–	5	1	2	1	–	–	–	–	–	3	5	3		11				
Policy subcommittee	–	1	1	–	5	4	2	1	1	–	3	–	2	1	–	–	–	1	–	–	6	–	7					
65 and over	–	–	–	–	7	5	–	2	2	–	–	–	2	–	–	2	1					7						
55–64	3	3	–	3	7	7	8	1	3	4	3	–	3	2	–	–	1				16							
45–54	5	3	1	2	5	6	6	4	2	2	3	1	5	1	–	1	1			16								
35–44	10	2	1	–	1	7	5	2	–	2	5	3	1	1	1	–	1		14									
21–34	11	1	3	–	–	5	11	1	–	–	4	5	4	–	3	–	1	17										
Other/Not known	2	–	–	1	2	2	2	1									5											
Manual	1	–	–	–	1	–	–	4								4												
Clerical	1	–	1	–	–	1	–	–							3													
Traders, etc.	3	1	–	–	–	2	–	2						4														
Other professionals	5	1	–	4	5	7	8	–					15															
Liberal professionals	7	–	–	–	2	1	8	–				9																
Professional businessmen	5	3	2	–	5	8	7	–			15																	
Managers	4	2	1	–	1	5	1	2		8																		
Executives	1	2	1	–	3	5	1	1	7																			
Other	7	–	–	–	3			10																				
Grammar	17	2	4	3	4		30																					
Fee-paying	7	7	1	2	13	30																						
12 or more					20																							
9–11				5																								
6–8			5																									
3–5		9																										
under 3	31																											

Sources: Croydon Council Year Book and questionnaire returns

 * Figures for education and age are based solely on questionnaire returns. These were incomplete (only 40 of 70 members replied) but appeared to be representative on all other variables. For the sake of clarity and comparability, therefore, data on age and education have been multiplied by a factor of 7/4 in this table. It is important to note, however, that on these two variables, the figures given only represent estimates based on a 56 per cent response rate.

 Where the information was available, figures on occupation have been calculated to include the last full-time occupation of retired respondents, and the husband's occupation of married women not themselves in full-time employment.

membership of Croydon council thus exhibits some marked peculiarities. The proportion of manual workers is much lower, and the proportion of privately educated members is much higher, than the norm, while the direct representation of business interests in the council (and notably at the higher levels) is very strong. Not that any of this, by itself, means very much, for as Giddens points out,

> We are surely not justified in making direct inferences from the social background, or even the educational experience, of elite groups to the way in which they employ whatever power they possess once they attain positions of eminence. Because a man emanates from a specific type of class background, it does not inevitably follow that he will later adopt policies which are designed to promote class interests corresponding to that background.

Positional analysis is only the starting point.

Nevertheless, this brief review of the social composition of the local council in Croydon does have two significant implications. The first is that it provides a pointer towards the sorts of beliefs and values which we may expect to find among at least some of the town's political leaders. If there is a tendency for each of us to view the world in a different way according to where we are standing, then it is clearly significant that so many of the men who fill the top local political positions appear to be standing in much the same position; a businessmen's council is likely to see things through businessmen's eyes. The second implication is that certain groups in the population – notably the middle class in general and the business community in particular – are vastly overrepresented in the town hall, and this may mean that their interests are more likely to be taken into account in the course of the decision-making process. Both of these point . . . rest on the assumption that local political leaders can and do have a significant say in local policy-making. We must now consider the validity of this assumption.

The local council: internal relations

The policy-making process in most local authorities in England and Wales has been 'rationalized' in recent years following various central government initiatives, the most significant of which have been the 1972 Baines report and the 1974 reorganization. This has produced two main consequences. First, there has been an increased vertical integration of local, regional and national levels of government. This has resulted in a fragmentation of functions between the levels (e.g., the division between local and structure planning), and in an overall increase in central regulation of local policy-making. Secondly, the internal organization of local authorities themselves has changed. This is not to suggest that before the 1970s local councils were controlled by the elected members while today they are controlled by the officers, for this would be too gross a simplification. Clearly there has been a shift, at least as regards the formal structure of management and policy-making, away from the members, and this is reflected in the development of corporate planning teams (consisting of the heads of all the main council departments) which tend to work closely with small 'inner cabinets' of leading members of the majority groups of the different authorities. But this is only the culmination of a long-term trend in local government – in 1967 the Maud report argued that the traditional distinction between making policies and implementing them had long since become blurred – and, more significantly, it is a formal change in organizational structure which may not be directly reflected in organizational practice. The point here is that it has become a sociological cliché that the formal structure of an organization does not necessarily indicate what actually goes on within it, and there is no reason to expect that local authorities constitute an exception to this. Both functionalist and interactionist approaches to the sociology of formal organizations have stressed the need to examine how members routinely accomplish their 'roles', and it follows that the analysis of the formal organizational framework of local authority decision-making can only be a first step in understanding how policies come to be made.

The formal decision-making procedure in Croydon is broadly similar to that followed by most other local authorities in the country, and it is summarized in the diagram opposite. It can be seen from this that there are certain strategic positions – notably membership of the Chief Officers' Group and membership of the Policy subcommittee – which would appear to provide the capacity for controlling virtually the entire policy-making process, for the lower-level participants are largely dependent upon them for both the original initiatives and for information about alternative proposals. However, we need to ask whether and how this potential control is exercised in practice. In other words, the formal model outlined in the diagram is little more than a 'script' which may guide to a greater or lesser extent what Gans has termed the decision-making 'performance'. As one Croydon Chief Officer observed, 'It's extremely difficult to describe the real decision-making practices. You can construct organization charts but these are only the theory and life isn't like that.'

From the perspective of the elected members of the council, the positions of greatest potential power are the seven seats on the Policy subcommittee and, to a lesser extent, the chairmanships of the major service committees such as education, housing and social services (although the chairmen of these committees are usually also members of the Policy subcommittee). All of these key positions, of course, are held

Table 2. Local authority decision-making: the formal structure

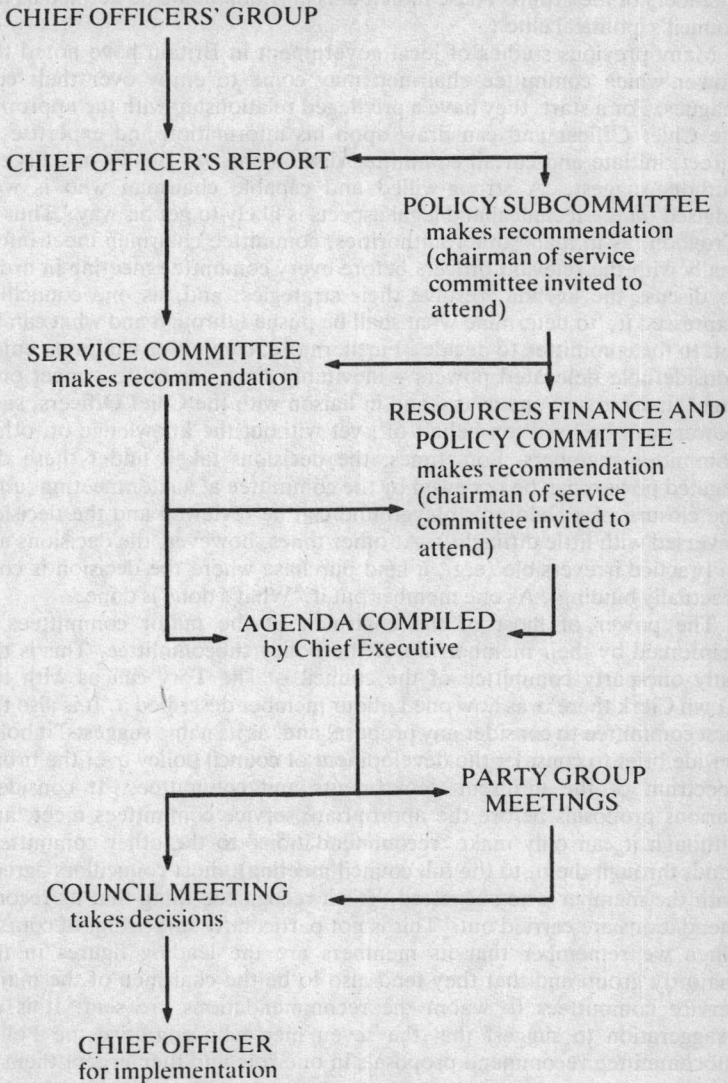

CHIEF OFFICERS' GROUP

↓

CHIEF OFFICER'S REPORT ←————————

    POLICY SUBCOMMITTEE
    makes recommendation
    (chairman of service
    committee invited to
    attend)

↓

SERVICE COMMITTEE ←————————
makes recommendation

    RESOURCES FINANCE AND
    POLICY COMMITTEE
    makes recommendation
    (chairman of service
    committee invited to
    attend)

AGENDA COMPILED ←————————
by Chief Executive

↓

    PARTY GROUP
    MEETINGS

COUNCIL MEETING ←————————
takes decisions

↓

CHIEF OFFICER
for implementation

by members of the majority party group, which in Croydon means the Conservatives, and they are filled by the leading and generally most senior members of the group. These individuals may nominally be defined as the council's 'political elite'.

Many previous studies of local government in Britain have noted the power which committee chairmen may come to enjoy over their colleagues. For a start, they have a privileged relationship with the appropriate Chief Officer and can draw upon his information and expertise to direct, initiate and curtail committee discussions. As Bealey and his co-authors suggest, 'A strong-willed and capable chairman who is well advised on the technical and legal aspects is likely to get his way.' Thus in Croydon, as in many other authorities, committee chairmen meet informally with the relevant officers before every committee meeting in order to discuss the agenda, resolve their strategies, and, as one councillor expressed it, 'to determine what shall be pushed through and what can be left to the committee to decide'. Furthermore, committee chairmen enjoy considerable delegated powers – inevitably since committees meet only eight times in any one year – and in liaison with the Chief Officers, such powers can be used 'on behalf of', yet without the knowledge of, other committee members. Sometimes, the decisions taken under these delegated powers can be reviewed by the committee at a later meeting (e.g., the closure of a children's playground can be reviewed and the decision reversed with little difficulty). At other times, however, the decisions are in practice irreversible (e.g., a land purchase where the decision is contractually binding). As one member put it, 'What's done is done.'

The power of most of the chairmen of the major committees is reinforced by their membership of the Policy subcommittee. This is the only one-party committee of the council – 'The Tory caucus with the Town Clerk there' was how one Labour member described it. It is also the first committee to consider any proposal and, as its name suggests, it holds a wide brief to consider the development of council policy over the broad spectrum of the different departments and committees. It considers various proposals before the appropriate service committees meet, and although it can only make 'recommendations' to the other committees (and, through them, to the full council meeting), most councillors agreed with the member who suggested, 'It's a recognized thing that its recommendations are carried out.' This is not particularly surprising, of course, when we remember that its members are the leading figures in the majority group and that they tend also to be the chairmen of the major service committees to whom the recommendations are sent. It is no exaggeration to suggest that the seven men who comprise the Policy subcommittee recommend proposals in one role and then accept them in another.

Even in the unlikely event of a service committee rejecting a Policy subcommittee recommendation, the 'political elite' still has two other strings to its bow. First, its recommendations, together with those of the various service committees, are considered by the Resources Finance and Policy committee, of which Policy is a subcommittee. In other words, all seven members of the Policy subcommittee sit on the very committee which considers the various recommendations which have been made, and its chairman and vice-chairman occupy the same positions on Resources Finance and Policy. Furthermore, this latter committee, which does include a minority of Labour members, always votes on strict party lines, and thus invariably endorses the recommendations of the Conservative group leaders. In short, service committee proposals are unlikely to be accepted where they conflict with those of the Policy subcommittee. Secondly, even where the Policy subcommittee is overruled by the decision taken in a full council meeting, it still retains an effective veto power since it controls the distribution of resources among the various departments of the council. In other words, the Policy subcommittee has the power to decide whether to allocate the necessary finance to a service committee which has resolved on a policy of which it disapproves. In 1972, for example, the council accepted a Health committee proposal for the introduction of a free family planning service in the borough. The Policy subcommittee, however, refused to allocate sufficient additional funds for the scheme to be put into operation, and the decision was therefore not implemented. Little wonder that one Labour councillor said of the Policy subcommittee, 'It lays down the policy of the council and what it says goes. Various attempts to resist it in the past have failed. . . . It's strong because it includes the men who can persuade and dominate their fellows.'

This ability to 'persuade and dominate' is not simply a reflection of the strategic location of the Policy subcommittee in the decision-making process, however, for it also reflects the relationship between the 'political elite' and the rank-and-file of the majority party group. Sherman has argued that, 'In local government today, the group is more powerful and demanding than the party whips in Whitehall', and although this may be something of an exaggeration, there is no doubt that, since the eclipse of the 'independent' councillor (which in Croydon can be dated effectively from the early 1960s although a handful of right-wing independents continued to gain election until the early 1970s), the party caucus has become a central element in the decision-making process. In Croydon, members of both party groups exhibited a marked reluctance to vote against group decisions; only 15 per cent of Labour members reported ever having voted against a group decision, the comparable figure among Conservatives being slightly higher at 20 per cent. Majority group decisions are thus tantamount to council decisions, and the power to control the majority group is thus crucial in determining the ability to control the council.

That the 'political elite' effectively controls the majority group in Croydon is beyond doubt. Conservative group meetings function mainly as a means of disseminating information on decisions which have already been resolved in committee, and as a way of determining voting strategies for forthcoming council meetings. The majority group meeting does not therefore serve as a vehicle for rank-and-file involvement in policy-formation, and in this respect, Croydon appears no different from many other authorities. Because it meets after the agenda for the council meeting has been compiled (i.e., after the 'political elite' has made its 'recommendations'), all that usually remains to be done is to ensure that the members formally fall into line behind their leaders. This they invariably do with little trouble. The ideological commitment and political zeal of most Conservative members is relatively low compared with that found in the Labour group – only one quarter of the Conservatives, compared with half of the Labour members, cited 'involvement in decision-making' as their major concern as councillors – and this is reflected in their high level of compliance with the decisions taken by their leaders. As Harris has pointed out, there is perhaps less excitability and passion on the right of British politics than on the left, and this certainly appeared the case in Croydon where the Conservative rank-and-file was, by and large, fairly content with the passive political role it was called upon to play.

This is not to suggest that there have never been conflicts within the majority group, nor that the rank-and-file members have no control over the leadership. One particularly acrimonious dispute, for example, took place over the leadership's decision to accept the government's call to reorganize secondary education in the borough in the 1960s. This issue resulted in the resignation of the chairman of the Education committee following the mobilization of a right-wing faction against him. However, three points need to be made about this. First, the issue was somewhat unique in that most internal dissension within the majority group occurs around questions of personalities or parochial loyalties (mainly northern against southern ward representatives) rather than on a left–right split. Secondly, even in this fairly unique case where Tory 'gut-feeling' was strongly opposed to the abolition of the grammar schools, the group leaders were still powerful enough to force the reform through. Indeed, the 'political elite' twice changed its policy on comprehensive reorganization, yet on both occasions was able to carry with it the support of the great majority of Conservative members. Thirdly, the successful coup against the Education committee chairman was only short-lived, and it resulted in 1974 in an important shift in the relations of power between the leadership and the rank-and-file. Until 1974, the major source of power for the rank-and-file members was their right to elect annually the chairmen of the different committees, but in that year the leader of the group announced that all chairmen would in future be appointed by him (although he was still to be elected by the group). 'It means', he explained, 'the leader having more political control of the council, and that the load is shared as the leader would wish it to be. It's no good having the chairman of a committee who's opposed to the leader all the time.' Armed with these new powers, the group leader then proceeded to reinstate the former Education committee chairman to his old post, and since then the majority group has been reduced to a state of virtual impotence in relation to the leader and his appointees.

Although it is now firmly in control of its own majority group, however, the 'political elite' still depends for its power on its ability to negotiate two other crucial potential limitations posed by the internal organization of the decision-making process. One of these concerns its relationship with the Chief Officers of the council; the other concerns its ability to avoid direct and open confrontation with the Labour group.

The Chief Officers represent the strongest potential limitation on the power of the 'political elite', for not only do they initiate policy discussion (often as a result of central government or internal departmental stimuli, but also sometimes in response to members' own suggestions) and implement them, but they are also involved in the third and more contentious role of actively resolving them. The close relationship between a Chief Officer and a committee chairman, for example, is a two-edged sword, for if the latter uses the expertise of the former, it is also the case that the former can influence the latter through the information he chooses to make available and the way in which he does so. As Heclo points out, information and expertise constitute crucial power resources in the increasingly complex world of local government. Or as Weber observed, 'The question is always who controls the existing bureaucratic machinery. And such control is possible only in a very limited degree to persons who are not technical specialists.'

Further Reading: **Power**

J. BLONDEL, *Voters, Parties and Leaders*, Penguin, 1966.

A. BUDD, *The Politics of Economic Planning*, Fontana Paperbacks, 1978.

D. BUTLER and D. KAVANAGH, *The British General Election of 1979*, Macmillan, 1980.

M. CASTELLS, *City, Class and Power*, Macmillan, 1978.

I. CREWE, *Elites in Western Democracy*, Croom Helm, 1974.

J. FIDLER, *The British Business Elite*, Routledge and Kegan Paul, 1981.

W. GUTTSMAN, *The British Political Elite*, MacGibbon and Kee, 1963.

R. JESSOP, *Traditionalism, Conservatism and British Political Culture*, Allen and Unwin, 1974.

P. KELLNER and N. CROWTHER-HUNT, *The Civil Servants*, Macdonald, 1980.

C. LAMBERT and D. T. H. WEIR, *Cities in Modern Britain*, Fontana Paperbacks, 1975.

R. LANE, *Political Life*, The Free Press, 1961.

C. LEYS, *Politics in Britain*, Heinemann, 1983.

S. LUKES, *Power, a Radical View*, Macmillan, 1974.

R. McKENZIE and A. SILVER, *Angels in Marble*, Heinemann, 1968.

G. A. NORDLINGER, *Working Class Tories,* MacGibbon and Kee, 1967.

G. PARRY, *Political Elites*, Allen and Unwin, 1969.

P. C. J. PULZER, *Political Representation and Elections in Britain*, Allen and Unwin, 1967.

G. RICHARDS, *The Backbenchers*, Faber and Faber, 1972.

R. ROSE, *Electoral Behaviour: a Comparative Handbook*, The Free Press, 1974.

W. D. RUBINSTEIN, *Men of Property*, Croom Helm, 1981.

B. RUSSELL, *Power: a New Social Analysis*, W. W. Norton, 1938.

M. STACEY and M. PRICE, *Women, Power and Politics*, Tavistock, 1981.

P. STANWORTH and A. GIDDENS, *Elites and Power in British Society*, Cambridge University Press, 1974.

7. Values and Social Change

According to Parsons, values are 'the primary connecting element between the social and cultural systems'. This definition portrays values in the context of the expectations which govern social behaviour in a particular historical society. The aim of this reader is to achieve some basis for an interpretation of the framework of British society. So it is of importance to pay attention to the values which inhere in British society. **Shils**'s 'British Society' may seem at first to be dated, but we believe the essential features of this analysis are very relevant today. When Shils refers to 'the constrictedness of imagination and aspiration' he points to some of the balancing features in British life and praises the institutional machinery for the public conduct of conflict, and the peaceful adjudication of contention. 'Civility remains high,' he says. However in the twenty years since Shils was writing, some of these balancing features themselves seem more questionable. Civility is no longer an obvious feature of public life. The political system is no longer a relatively peaceful alternation of the 'ins' and the 'outs', and is it any longer possible to argue that there is no political party committed to the subversion of the existing system?

Lupton is even more critical, judging that the social structure of Britain explains the perceived incompetence of the economy to maintain 'even a moderate rate of economic growth'. His wide-ranging analysis links education, class and politics to the organization of industry and the apparent failures of industrial relations.

Shils and Lupton conclude that British society has degenerated into a series of 'vicious cycles'. **Gilbert** contrasts the 'vicious cycle' with the 'virtuous cycle'. He argues convincingly that the British problem is not one of early maturation and the consequence of the initial *success* of Britain in the first stages of the industrial revolution. The problem is one of normative regulation. The norms are different and the structures of social control are different also. So what is seen as normal and inevitable in relation, for example, to styles of management in industry is in fact very different from the managerial practices and cultures which exist in other societies. Thus management in Britain is equally locked into its local cultural matrix.

Halsey is more optimistic, and sees in the rebirth of a fraternal ethic a possibility for social and communal revival. His analysis is especially

timely, however, where he argues that 'exhortation alone is futile. . . .
The problem is to discover . . . those social institutions that will
encourage and foster the kinds of relations between people that are
desired.' He looks back almost explicitly to the analysis of Kellner and
Crowther-Hunt when he points to 'the constant need for alert and
knowledgeable citizens . . . to prevent the public services from
degenerating into organizations which serve the private interests of public
servants'.

For **St John-Stevas** the main point of politics is pragmatism, but a
pragmatism rooted in a deep sense of balance in society. The
Conservative Party, like the nation, is for St John-Stevas 'a broad church'.
Stevas again points to 'the necessarily buffering and intermediate role of
institutions as protection against the tyranny of the majority' or 'the naked
and brutal exertion of power by bureaucracies or by strong but minority
interests'. The analysis is itself pragmatic, but rests on some basic
sociological assumptions when Stevas writes: 'Society's concern with
moral values springs . . . not only from their intrinsic worth but from the
perception of the connection between the moral and social orders. One
rests upon the other.'

Henry's extract is a brief and almost impertinent reminder of the power
of informal institutions. He points out that one of the reasons why
informal institutions and practices rarely feature in sociology core analysis
is that they are not so easy to study as the formal and institutional
structures. Informal institutions form part of a hidden social structure
which is none the less significant for being unobserved and none the less
influential for being covert.

One of the curiously invisible aspects of social structure is the position
of women. **Mitchell** attacks the institution of the family because of its role
in the systematic impression of women in industrial, capitalist society. The
family is 'a segmentary, monolithic unit largely separated off from
production and hence from social human activity'. It is woman's role in
the family as the provider of sexual satisfaction to her male partner, as the
principal agent of childrearing, which imprisons her in a restricted set of
routines and provides rigid limitations to what are socially acceptable
manifestations of personality. Moreover the exclusive identification of
female activities with procreation and socialization may ultimately be
harmful to the children as well. Mitchell quotes Riesman and his
counterpointing of work and sex as essential human activities. The
alienation produced in the former may be mirrored and distorted in the
latter arena of social competition and conflict.

The conflict at the work place itself is mediated through different values.
Crouch and **Goldthorpe** together identify the master structures of values
which influence this arena. Goldthorpe refers to the 'relatively neglected
problem of the implications of inequality for social integration'. The great

extent and variety of social inequality and its pervasiveness provide a master-matrix for social structure which is highly resistant to change. Goldthorpe concludes that social inequality poses no direct threat to the stability of the political order but militates seriously against stable normative regulation in the economic sphere. He does not find the British system of industrial relations in a state of 'anomie' in which disorder has developed because of a breakdown of previously accepted relationships.

In **Runciman**'s seminal analysis of social justice he quotes with approval Rawls's conception of justice as fairness. This conception is widespread and is found, for example, in the language of Yorkshire miners who refer not to a specific level of wage as appropriate but to 'fairation' as the guiding norm of the system of wage bargaining. Eliot Jacques indeed attempted to elevate this principle to being a master formula for job evaluation and wage determination. But what is fair – indeed, obvious and ordained – to one group is contentious and disagreeable to another. First-year students of sociology sometimes complain of research and theory that confirm their preoccupations as 'obvious', while dismissing that which challenges them as 'irrelevant' and 'biased'. **Spencer**'s calm and telling piece, originally published in 1873, still rings true in the clamant hubbub of sectional interest which generally passes for debate on issues of values.

Social change has been described as 'the most difficult and most fascinating problem in sociology'. It would be easy enough to dodge the problem by inclusion – for, after all, is not all sociology the analysis of social change? – but this would be evasion. We have prepared three editions of this book of readings over a period of some twenty years from its initial inception, and over that period have read almost all the empirical research undertaken into the sociology of modern Britain. The *relative* stability and change embodied in the major institutions in British society have varied considerably and not always predictably.

Heraclitus wrote two thousand years ago that one can never drink water from the same river twice; all is change, all is flux. The Britain of the 1980s is more like the Britain of the 1970s than it is like anything else, but in many ways new themes are emerging, new currents taking shape, new pools of turbulence forming. Wilbert Moore argued that social change is a principal feature of all advanced societies, and that the impact of planned and unplanned change is becoming more widespread, and thus 'virtually no feature of life is exempt from the expectation or normality of change'.

While, therefore, much of this book of readings deals with the 'normality of change', some extracts try to cope with the consequences of the breakdown of familiar institutions. In this respect, up-to-dateness and contemporaneity may be less important to the student than the development of the most helpful framework of analysis.

The Welfare State is now believed to be under attack from the right.

Titmuss, in a seductively simple presentation, asks some basic questions about the role of universalism and the justification for redistribution.

Marshall takes this argument further and links the moral justification of the Welfare State to the prime values of individualism and collectivism. For him, 'the Welfare State is the responsible promoter and guardian of the welfare of the whole community'.

Tawney echoes Halsey, or indeed it would be historically more apt to say that Halsey echoes Tawney, and the short extract from Tawney's immensely influential analysis leaves the question hanging. 'A nation . . . must have recourse to principles,' claims Tawney. But principles of what, and about what sphere of human and social action? Hopefully this chapter has provided some of the elements from which the reader may begin to piece together an answer.

They can, however, only be elements. Sociology cannot pretend to a comprehensive solution to the situation of modern Britain, but in its methodology, its theoretical traditions and its specific research findings, it exemplifies a fruitful and humanistic approach to understanding that is quite compatible with Karl Popper's dictum: 'Everything depends upon the give and take between ourselves and our task, our work, our problems, our world.'

Sociology itself can be evaluated in terms of Russell's outline of the task of a liberal education as 'to give a sense of the value of things other than domination, to help to create wise criticisms of a free community, and through the combination of citizenship with liberty in individual creativeness to enable men to give to human life that splendour which some few have shown it can achieve'.

British Society

E. Shils

Reprinted with permission from P. Hall (ed.), *Labour's New Frontiers*, André Deutsch, 1964, pp. 6–16

British society today certainly is no paradise. Yet as human societies go, its attainments, in recent decades, are very considerable. It has made great progress in the present century towards the moral equality which is a *sine qua non* of a good society. The level of material well-being of previously horribly impoverished strata has been greatly improved. The weak, the defenceless, the young, the failures are better cared for than ever before, and even where the actual care remains markedly insufficient, solicitous concern exists and promises real improvement in the future. Educational opportunity is diffusing more widely than ever before the capacity to share in the cultural inheritance, to broaden the range of intellectual and aesthetic experience and to acquire the skills and qualifications necessary for occupational and professional achievement. It has continued to remain in the front ranks of the pioneers of scientific research. It has renounced with relatively good grace its empire which was, until quite recently, among its greatest glories, and among the greatest creations of world history. The country has had stable government and the government has remained democratic. The institutional machinery for the public conduct of conflict and for the peaceful adjudication of contention is likewise fairly good by any realistic standard. Civility remains high. The manners of public life are relatively gentle and considerate. The political system, although far from meeting ideal standards, has at least not collapsed as it has in France. Public liberties have remained more or less intact. There are no large parties which are so alienated from the rest of the political system that they are committed to the subversion of the existing constitution, as in Italy and France. Its immunity from ideological fevers has not had to be acquired, as in contemporary Germany, by recuperation from a long bout of murderous madness.

Yet the situation in Britain today distresses many who contemplate it. They are, quite reasonably, not content that there should be no growth in virtues already acquired. Sometimes distress over present shortcomings blinds critics to the accomplishments, persisting and recent, of British society, but our awareness of their blindness does not invalidate their criticisms. There still remain, despite the transformation of the public appearance of the ancient regime, very deep strata of 'darkest England', of hierarchical harshness, of contemptuous hostility towards the weak and unsuccessful. There are still pockets of misery particularly among the aged. A 'race problem' is beginning to emerge in and at the edges of the Negro and Indian ghettoes in some of the larger cities. The educational system at nearly every level is unable to cope with the increased numbers who should be educated, and it is contorted by its inegalitarian inheritance. The inter-university hierarchy and the inferior dignity of technological studies, both of which are related to the class system of this country, are still alive and injurious to the fruitfulness in life and in society of those who suffer at the lower strata of these hierarchies. Much of the urban physical environment – especially housing accommodation and amenities – is inconvenient far past the point necessitated by modern technology, and it is hideously ugly. The major provincial centres are dreary and boring. Political and economical leadership, although generally virtuous and mild mannered, is unimaginative and inspires little confidence; it is lacking in initiative and self-confidence. The British economy, which must provide the wherewithal for the next necessary improvements, is encumbered by archaic practices and arrangements, and both at its top and at its bottom it shows the constraints and distortions of its hierarchical traditions. The enormous progress that has been made in the movement towards moral equality only makes more evident the crippling inequality and the powerful snobbery which still exist. The power of the aristocracy and gentry has been largely broken, but the aura of deference which attended that power still persists. This manifests itself in many ways, the most important of which is the inhibition of individuality and initiative.

One of the features of British society which impresses a foreign observer is its constrictedness of imagination and aspiration. There is a lack of vigour and daring in the conception of new possibilities of life and a too narrow radius of aspiration. In its older industries, there is an anxious adherence to past practices. Foreign models dominate the vision of those who would leave the British past behind. Those who try to break away into some new sphere seem to lack self-confidence and innovators are distrusted. Too little is expected of life and too little is expected from oneself and from others in the discovery of new ways of doing things. The demand for pleasure is too restricted; curiosity too confined to conventional paths.

It is true that there are variations in this picture of the situation. Certain industries do attempt to find better techniques through research; there are great scientists at the height of their power, at work in the country. Some new universities are trying out new syllabi; certain local education authorities introduce innovations. But on the whole, they stand out by their rarity. It is in the younger generation throughout British society that the compression of desire which the traditions of British society demand is less willingly accepted. The 'youth culture' which includes pop music, sartorial elegance, early sexual intercourse, motor-bikes and juvenile delinquency, is part of this refusal. These all express a new aesthetic sensitivity, a greater appreciation of more diverse experiences and a livelier contact with other human beings. Yet there too, in this most notable manifestation of spirit, one perceives a readiness to retract under the pressure of adulthood, into a more confined 'life-space', more like that in which the elders have been living.

The class system which took form in the nineteenth and early twentieth centuries in this country demanded a lot both from those who were its obvious beneficiaries and those who were its obvious victims. From those at the bottom, it demanded more than obedience, it demanded respectability. There were many who did not conform but they were outcasts; they were expected neither to 'get on' nor even to hold their own before the universal dangers of unemployment, dependence on charity and base impulse. An iron discipline which looked straight ahead and not very far and a steady attendance to obligation did not leave much room for the opening of imagination or sensibility. The religion of respectability and the religious beliefs of the respectable reinforced what was necessitated by private property, scarcity and the police. Respectability entailed not only self-restraint, it entailed deference to one's betters, which involved self-derogation.

The obvious beneficiaries had their own religion of respectability too. It was a respectability which was less confining but it was acquired by a discipline in institutions which restricted the range of experience and narrowed the imagination. It had the great advantage that those who survived it felt themselves qualified for anything. It was a discipline which was integral to ruling. Those who passed through it went on to the Civil Service, the Indian Civil Service, the Colonial Service, politics, the law, and the Anglican clergy which in those days was much closer to the atmosphere of ruling than it is today when it lives in miasmal depression. Those who followed none of these paths still inhaled the air which is breathed by rulers.

Had Britain been a rather rich, hierarchical society without an empire, like Sweden, those at the top might not have felt so ascendant. But having an empire meant that India and Africa, and parts of the Middle and Far East, were also in a sense the lower strata of British society, the peak of which was the destined inheritance of the successful survivors of institutional discipline. The 'effortless superiority of the Balliol man' or of any man who had successfully passed other parts of the institutional system was the product of a sense of confidence. Their mere 'being' qualified them to do what had to be done – to administer, to do research, to understand the essentials of any problem and to take the action called for.

The great changes within national societies and between them in the present century have eroded the ascendancy of the beneficiaries of the British system of stratification. Within Britain the continuous growth of democracy has almost obliterated the power of the aristocracy and it has especially diminished its symbolic grandeur; and the growth of trade union power and the nationalization of major industries has restricted the power of the plutocracy. The dissolution of the Empire and increasing real independence of the English-speaking dominions have contracted the size of the society over which the British elite – and British society as a whole – were superordinated.

These two simultaneous diminutions of the power of the British elite have had tremendous consequences for the life of present-day Britain. The elite have lost that sense of effortless superiority which came from 'being' what they were. Their diminution has laid them open to self-criticism and to criticism by those who shared in their glory. Those over whom they ruled at home are now no longer so impressed by the standard which they represented or by the ideal of respectability which was its immediate derivative. Humiliated pride and once repressed resentment both come forward now.

British society is no longer regarded by those who live in it as a repository of a charismatic quality which exalted its members and imposed itself on the world. Pride in being British is no longer what it was. There is little confidence that one's inherited pattern of institutions and culture or one's own party has the answers to important questions. There is a critical spirit abroad. Much of it is a nagging criticism and offers only archaic solutions to real problems.

The Culture is Wrong
T. Lupton

Reprinted with permission from Tom Lupton, 'The Culture is Wrong', *New Society*, 22 September 1966

Economic explanations of Britain's inability to maintain even a moderate rate of economic growth are nowadays frequently accompanied by reference to lack of moral fibre, absence of positive leadership, false ideologies, petty sectional interests, and latterday Luddism. Politicians refer nostalgically to the 'Dunkirk spirit'. We hear of 'wreckers' who promote class warfare and spread false economic doctrines. Managers are urged to show more initiative and to learn imported skills from Harvard professors at summer schools. Even a sympathetic observer like Edward

Shils can write of a 'construction of imagination and aspiration' in contemporary Britain.

All this shows a growing awareness that some obstacles to growth are non-economic. It would be wrong to conclude, however, in an excess of George-Brownism, that mass conversion to the doctrine of national salvation through individual effort is possible, or a solution. Since economic nostrums also have limited effect, it might be of use to attempt to identify sociocultural obstacles to higher productivity and healthy growth.

British social structure is demonstrably highly resistant to shifts towards greater equality of wealth, power, and educational career opportunity. Yet it is commonly thought that educational and career opportunities have greatly improved in the last fifty years. This gap between fact and belief could well be at the root of much of the dissatisfaction, frustration and cynicism which can be found in the 'lower' strata of British society, and which affect responses to appeals for greater effort, and attitudes to new machinery and administrative methods.

At the top of British society, access to key positions is based too much on family connection and type of school and university, and not enough on intrinsic merit and educational and economic achievement, irrespective of social background. This has often been stated and as often challenged. My own enquiries show there is more hard evidence to back it up than to contradict it. Its effect could be a plethora of polished duffers in seats of power, or of able men ill-equipped to run the institutions of a technically complex siege economy, or both. Traditional values perpetuated by educational exclusiveness, inherited leadership, amateur 'all-roundism', continuity, cultured leisure and leisured enquiry and what Tawney once referred to as 'the sentimental aroma of an aristocratic legend' – all these may be thought to suffocate the urge for radical reform and the growth of specialized professional competences.

The importance for economic development of having the right kind of elites has often been emphasized. Perhaps we have inherited the wrong kind. It is true that our traditional elites are highly absorbent, but so pervasive is the 'sentimental aroma' that it mellows the absorbed, and sours the rejected. The extent to which our economic performance has been inhibited by these factors merits closer enquiry.

The increasing traffic between Whitehall and the business world is usually thought of either as an example of pressure group activity, or as evidence of growing consensus – both healthy symptoms. In a persuasive article J. P. Nettl has thrown serious doubts on these interpretations. The facts he adduces, and the logic of the situations he describes, suggest rather that big business is infected by bureaucratic values and procedures and that business men are weaned from their proper concerns. They, too, play the Whitehall game and become amateur all-rounders. Another example, it would appear, of the propensity of our institutions, and the values which suffuse them, to blunt the qualities needed for highly special-ized performance, and to misuse talent.

Again, it would be difficult, on present evidence, to prove a direct causal connection in the wrong direction between the processes of economic decision-making in Whitehall and business efficiency, pro-ductivity and growth; but the idea is worth following up.

From a different perspective McLelland provides theoretical backing for the general line of argument pursued so far. Careful psychological experiments and thorough international comparisons together lead him to the view that economic development depends upon individuals with 'high achievement need' – which is, put crudely, a mental state which induces vigorous pursuit of self-generated standards of excellence, a kind of lay Puritan ethic.

Traditional values stifle it. McLelland's remedy is to arrange the primary socialization of children and subsequent social experience to increase the supply of persons with high achievement need, and to alter social arrangements to create opportunities for its full expression. It might be that Britain produces too many who complacently accept traditional standards, and discourages those who do not.

The sociological evidence about top people is thin, perhaps because sociologists, whose nosing around is an implied threat to the *status quo*, are unwelcome among them. Much more is known about the lesser folk. Little and Westergaard have recently reviewed the state of knowledge. They conclude that, though inequalities of access to secondary education have been (expectedly) reduced in the last half century, the reduction has been small. Increased opportunity has been given to working-class children, but many of them, for class-cultural and economic reasons, have been unable to benefit fully. For the same reasons many bright ones fail even to gain entrance. The significant increase in university places has been taken up mainly by middle-class children.

Over the same period, rates of social mobility have altered hardly at all. This indicates perhaps that what we have gained by a limited increase in educational opportunity has been lost by the closing up of extra-educational channels of mobility as some sectors of economic life have become increasingly bureaucratic and professional.

Plainly, at all levels, despite the movement of some individuals, the structure of our class system has remained so far impervious to radical reform. This is more than just a matter of occupational inertia. Class differences are also differences in life chances and styles of living. The classes are separated by social and geographical distance, by barriers of communication, by differences of speech idiom and techniques of culture transmission, of in-tellectual climate, in patterns of consumption, and in leisure pursuits. It is a moot point whether the mass media, reflecting and emphasizing as they do distinctions in the social structure, make a desirable impact.

A favourite theme of after-dinner speakers is the need in the interests of economic efficiency to end once and for all the talk of 'two sides' in industry. We are all in the same boat now, they say, and in a rough sea we ought not to rock it. A more refined version of the same theme says that the separation of industrial ownership and control has given rise to a new breed of professional managers, efficient and dedicated to the public weal. Entry to the new technocracy is open, it is said, to the humblest if the talent is there. No one wants to grind the faces of the poor any more for the sake of profit. So Marx was wrong, and Burnham was right, and trade unions are an anachronism and declarations by business men about industrial relations make sense.

It sounds good. Unfortunately, the facts do not point in that direction. In the first place, technological advance and increases in scale of business operation have emphasized career discontinuities between managers and non-managers – which are already implicit in the social structure, as Lloyd Warner showed long ago. The professionalization of the middling ranks of management, and the growth of large-scale national and international organizations has now produced what Watson has called the 'spiralist', a mobile man with no firm social roots, a very different animal from the working man tied by kin, occupation and lifestyle to the local community. There are few, if any, crosscutting ties between the two groups to moderate the conflicts between them which arise from division of function and cultural incongruence, and the quarrels over access to scarce power, cash and satisfaction at work.

The working class has not escaped the consequences of technical change. A more complex and minute division of labour has threatened many traditional occupational interests and allegiances, and hallowed working practices. For this reason, among others, the increased power and security brought by full employment has seen a tightening, rather than a relaxation of protective practices, and increasing conflicts of interest between occupational groups. It is misleading to consider that these processes, when taken together with the growth of technical and white-collar occupations, are evidence of the break-up of the working class and its cultures and institutions. Common patterns of residence and style of life, an oral tradition of culture transmission, and common experience of relative deprivation and the expectation of deference to one's 'betters' preserve solidarity and an egalitarian ethos. All this is in sharp contrast to the competitive culture of the career professional, and the ways of the traditional 'cultured' elite.

This analysis helps to explain the persistence of restrictive practices, and the alienation of union leaders from rank-and-file difficulties of geographical redeployment of the labour force and retraining.

It might be comforting if, in the middle ranks of society, the managerial revolutionaries were on the march – dedicated technocrats and super-organizers moving into the seats of power. But some evidence from a recent study reveals that if the separation of ownership and control has produced a new breed of trained salaried managers, they are strangely absent from the boardrooms of British industry, where the cult of the amateur still persists. It is not difficult to see why education for management is so difficult to get off the ground.

If our social class structure, with its fairly distinct and discrepant subcultures, stifles movement and change, and produces conflict, there is at least one positive goal the politicians and the advertisers have got us all to agree about – that to accumulate material possessions is good, and that a man is judged and socially categorized as much by these as by his intrinsic worth or proven achievement. This being so, barriers to accumulation arising from doubtfully legitimated social inequalities, may well channel energies into doubtfully legitimated means of accumulation in attempts to buy intangible signs of social prestige. This is a partial explanation of the increase in crime. Taken together with the boring and uninteresting work which technical progress brings for working men and women, it serves also as a partial explanation of fiddles, restrictive practices, 'instrumental' attitudes to work, and a resentment of technical and administrative pushes to higher effort and efficiency.

We seem, in short, to be suffering from severe cultural 'lag'. Our social structure and institutions and their values on the one hand, and our economic goals on the other, are strangely but perhaps understandably incongruent. We have no social regulators to prevent cultural hangovers, to compare with the post-Keynesian economic regulators we now confidently and hopefully deploy. Perhaps, as some suggest, drastic wage freezes and stiff central controls will force a change of attitudes and set off the required social changes. Experience does not bear this out.

Patient research, enlightened administration, better (or more appropriate) education and training, improved occupational selection, the encouragement of talent, and a campaign against snobbery, privilege and incompetence – all these combined might help. But one sometimes wonders whether we have been irrevocably entranced by the fatal charms of social continuity, tolerant and civilized incompetence, and a moderately growing material affluence.

A Sociological Model of Inflation
M. Gilbert

Reprinted with permission from Michael Gilbert, 'A Sociological Model of Infla-tion', *Sociology*, vol. 15, no. 2, May 1981, pp. 198–205

Dynamic aspects of the model

Until now, I have considered the four elements of the analytical model (normatively prescribed goals, normative restraints, power, and pro-ductive capacity) as if they were independent of one another. In practice, I doubt if this is likely to be the case. It seems far more likely that the presence or relative strength of one element will have implications for other parts of the model. In particular, actual societies are likely to have one of two particular configurations of the four variables. One configura-tion corresponds to a 'virtuous cycle' which is highly conducive to avoiding or restraining inflationary pressures. The other to a 'vicious cycle' which exacerbates inflationary pressures. The former is likely to be able to cope with inflationary shocks, such as higher import prices of commodities and raw materials like oil. The latter is not only unlikely to cope with such external disturbances, but very likely to generate its own inflation.

Consider first the implications of a productive system with a high and increasing productivity capacity. In the short term this can fuel rising material aspirations, although in the longer term these may be directed elsewhere. However, if productive capacity exceeds the level of material demands this will tend to enhance the legitimacy of the sociopolitical system and in particular to underwrite the authority of any normative system which restrains the pursuit of economistic ends. A structural basis for normative restraint is provided because the favourable substantive outcomes have implications for the support given to the formal pro-cedures which produced them. Conversely, societies with low or declining productive capacities may find that they experience some national sense of relative deprivation *vis-à-vis* other societies that figure more pro-minently in the international economic growth tables. This may heighten awareness of a gap between desired material goals and actual achievement and simultaneously undermine any existing system of normative restraint.

Consider further the implications of a relatively low level of material demands, or at least a level that is satisfied by the on-going economic system, and a legitimated normative system prescribing how such ends may be pursued. Firstly, these are likely to lead to an underutilization of whatever power resources are available to income-receivers because they have no need to look for such mechanisms. Secondly, because conflict is abated, they are more likely to be associated with harmonious and orderly work-place relationships and thereby facilitate productive investment and expansion. This is likely to be further reinforced, if, as is likely under these circumstances, the government's fiscal problems are relatively slight, thereby providing a favourable atmosphere, and appropriate interest rates, for stimulating business activity. Again, the converse situation may arise. Dissatisfied, unrestrained income-receivers will tend to seek out and create power resources. Disharmonious work-place relationships are likely to occur as claims are vigorously pursued. Under such circumstances the introduction of new production methods and procedures is likely to be resisted. In capitalist economies, particularly ones increasingly affected by multinational companies, this is hardly conducive to further investment and productive growth.

In short, as I indicated above, I believe it is possible to map out two plausible models with different, and opposite, configurations of the four variables and suggest that particular societies will tend to conform to one or other type. Thus, if we could measure each of the four variables: degree of economism; strength of regulatory norms; power dispersal and concentration; and capacity of the productive system in terms of their relative strength or weakness, societies would tend to correspond to one of two models: the former constituting a 'virtuous cycle'; the latter a 'vicious cycle'.

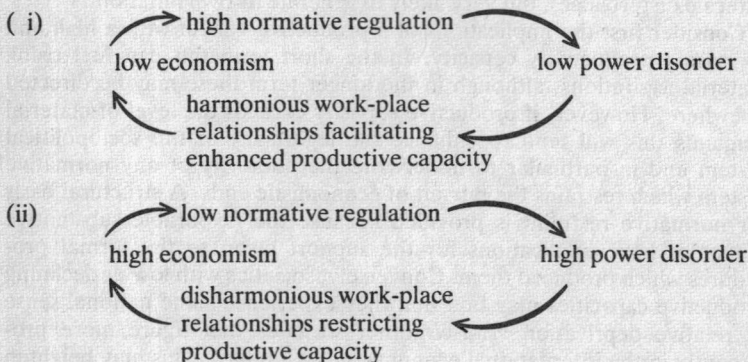

(i)　high normative regulation

low economism　　　　　　　　　low power disorder

harmonious work-place
relationships facilitating
enhanced productive capacity

(ii)　low normative regulation

high economism　　　　　　　　　high power disorder

disharmonious work-place
relationships restricting
productive capacity

Following Fox, the two cycles are respectively described as having a 'high-trust' and a 'low-trust' dynamic. In the first case starting with a productive capacity that might be high for chance reasons, such as Japanese or German postwar reconstruction setting off a high growth rate, material demands can be relatively easily satisfied. Consequently, authoritative normative systems restraining the way in which claims are advanced are given structural support. The established procedures work and minor dissident groups can be subjected to legal constraints underpinning such normative systems because they have wide support. That is deviant cases are readily recognized as deviant. Power equilibrium is preserved because a relatively satisfied population does not utilize the possibilities engendered by an advanced division of labour and industrial concentration. Finally, the stability engendered by the high normative restraint and low use of power encourages orderly work-place relationships, and thereby directly and indirectly steady investment and enhancement of productive capacity, thereby completing the cycle. Arguably, in different ways and for different reasons Japan, Sweden and West Germany have this high-trust dynamic.

The converse 'low-trust' cycle is almost identical with the British sickness. A low level and growth of productive capacity facilitates both unfilled material aspirations and low support for regulatory mechanisms. Witness the collapse of successive incomes policies under pressure from below. In the prevailing atmosphere groups of workers utilize bargaining advantages to drive home sectional demands, whilst employers use oligopolistic situations to press price increases. Further, governments are pressured both to provide a 'social wage' and to support the industrial infrastructure. Finally, in this situation, productive investment stagnates whilst disharmonious work-place relationships limit utilization of available technology.

These are, of course, only models, and their development depends on particular historical and cultural circumstances. In the last section of this paper I try to trace the development of the contemporary British situation, which, as I have said, bears a marked correspondence to the 'low-trust' dynamic.

The origins of the British sickness

At first sight Britain appears to embody the low-trust dynamic. In terms of all four elements of the model, Britain seems to correspond to the inflationary situation. Relatively high materialistic values coupled to sectional or individualistic ends are pursued by calculative bargaining strategies. Such strategies are increasingly used not only by manual workers but also by white-collar, managerial and professional employees. Although there have been a number of attempts to regulate incomes they have all been relatively short-lived. Arguably, this is both because the institutional arrangements for settling wage-bargains are highly anomic, based as they are on decentralized bargaining units and a multiplicity of different unions within the same company or plant, and because the overall structure of rewards is itself unprincipled based as it is on the relatively free play of past and present market forces.

Furthermore, the power of groups of income-receivers to push through claims is relatively strong. Labour is relatively highly organized and, as Goldthorpe has argued, has become increasingly mature and self-confident. Such power has been reinforced by two developments: the growth of the closed shop; and the increased concentration of postwar British industry. These two factors taken together have considerably enhanced the power of relatively small groups of workers to pursue their wage claims successfully. However, the increased concentration of industry also enables the controllers of large-scale business to exercise considerable power. As Scitovsky has argued, this means that both in labour and product markets power has become relatively concentrated amongst sellers and, accordingly, market mechanisms which might otherwise provide stability are weakened and the scene is set for a 'wage-price' spiral. In addition, attempts by the state to repoliticize economic life have themselves been used by organized labour as a bargaining tool to widen the areas over which they have influence, and, in particular, to maintain or expand public expenditure.

Lastly, Britain has experienced a low long-term rate of growth of productivity compared to most Western industrial countries. This has been heightened by a low level of investment itself linked to repeated government deflations of the domestic economy aimed at curbing inflation and/or rectifying an adverse balance of payments. As a result British economic growth has made it difficult for aspirations for a higher economic and social wage to be met. In addition, low economic growth is both cause and effect of the non-cooperativeness of organized labour in promoting economic advance. Changes in working procedures are resisted either as a bargaining tactic and/or because past experience has shown that the result will be maintained, rather than increased, production combined with a lower level of employment. But the consequence of these restricted practices and the industrial strife which accompanies much bargaining is to restrict investment, innovation and thereby economic growth.

Doubtless, this sketchy outline is exaggerated and oversimplified. Not all organized labour is powerful and prone to using its power to press sectional demands; not all product markets are oligopolistic; nor are all sections of the work force resistant to change. Yet, it does in general terms have considerable substance and, accordingly, goes a considerable way to explaining why the British economy, compared to most Western economies, seems to be peculiarly capable of generating its own inflation and has great difficulty in absorbing inflation generated overseas.

Whereas some of the factors underlying this process are a relatively recent development, others seem to be related to factors peculiar to

British industrialization and the emergence of industrial relations institutions in the nineteenth century. In particular, there is substantial evidence that from a very early period organized labour in Britain was highly economistic and sectional in its orientations and that the laissez-faire pattern of economic development had important implications for industrial relations.

Several writers such as Hobsbawm and Bauman have documented the sectional nature of nineteenth-century labour organization. Early craft unions were often formed on the basis of the old guilds. They were intended to preserve or enhance the economic advantages of their members over the labouring masses. One of the central mechanisms that they employed was manipulation of their labour market to keep the supply of labour down. Social cohesion was maintained by the forming of communities of occupational interest.

These processes were sometimes reinforced by the divisive tactics of employers. Foster has argued that in some industries such as cotton, working-class organizations were deliberately fragmented by the device of establishing particular groups of workers to control and organize the work of other sections of the work force. Not surprisingly, such groups received high pay. Thus economic, technical and authority divisions were superimposed on one another.

The sectional nature of working-class organization continued with the development of the New Model Unions. They operated primarily to protect group interests. They posed little challenge to the economic system but instead accommodated their behaviour to its functioning. They practised a form of economic competition against other groups, albeit competition which was far from perfect but one characterized by market control, job regulation and demarcating areas of practice. As Bauman points out one of the main charges made against skilled workers by the relatively unorganized unskilled masses was that of 'occupational egoism': self-interest exercised at the occupational group level regardless of how it affected the interests of other groups.

To the sectionalism of working-class organization can be added its economism and instrumentalism. Amongst others, Thompson has argued that the working class very quickly learned the rules of economic life. Union organizers soon learned to bargain cannily over time-rates and then piece-rates: bargaining aimed at maximizing economic returns without increasing work or effort. Thus a picture can readily be built of a highly economistic skilled working class which even by the late nineteenth century was already operating in ways not dissimilar to those caricatured as elements of the British sickness of the last part of the twentieth.

However, two further elements need to be stressed at this point. First, the conduct of industrial relations was itself pervaded by the dominant values of a laissez-faire economy. The relatively low level of government involvement in the industrialization process was mirrored in the sphere of industrial relations. Management-employee relationships were essentially voluntaristic in the sense that they were based on bargaining (mainly over economic matters) between the two parties 'freely' entering into contracts formed independently of external constraints. The terms of the contract were a matter for the two sides involved, and from this point of view a union basically acted as the collective representative of a group of workers in a common position. Any legal rights and responsibilities unions possessed were a reflection of the rights individual workers enjoyed summed to the group level. What was legal or illegal for an individual worker was legal or illegal for the union.

Lastly, as I have indicated, bargaining was essentially over economic matters: pay and conditions of work. Under what Crouch has termed the 'historic compromise', organized labour basically accepted management's right to manage in return for the ability to contend over economic matters. Adaptation to the conditions of a capitalist free market economy involved an economistic acceptance of the system. Organized labour, even by the end of the nineteenth century, was prepared to operate within rather than challenge the prevalent socioeconomic system. Not, of course, that such an adaptation was without its rewards particularly for the skilled working class. Part of the fruits of early industrialization and imperialism did go to the 'labour aristocracy'. Economism, apart from its consonance with the values of laissez-faire capitalism, was a pragmatic form of behaviour for both organized labour and the business class. For the former it brought economic advance; for the latter it bought a moderate and relatively quiescent labour force.

If one considers these elements together, it is clear that the processes of British industrial development were strongly linked to the creation of a work force that was organized on a sectional and economistic basis; that had adapted to a laissez-faire economy; and that was relatively unfettered by broader normative and legal constraints. Further it was one whose aspirations, limited as they were to materialistic ends, could be met by Britain's economically advantageous position. Once this position declined due to loss of empire and competition from more newly industrialized countries then even these economistic demands posed a challenge to the viability of the socioeconomic system. Put in terms of the model I have employed, initially the productive capacity of the economy could meet the materialistic demands placed on it. When it suffered a relative decline, then high economism coupled to low normative regulation was likely to have inflationary consequences, particularly if as in the postwar period changes in the structure and degree of concentration of the economy increased the power of organized labour.

Thus changes in the structural conditions have allowed pre-existent normative elements to have consequences which had hitherto remained dormant. It is particularly worth stressing that in Britain the legacies of the form of early industrialization and a laissez-faire industrial relations system may have produced a working class that was peculiarly sectional and individualistic in its orientations. In a recent work Currie has contrasted the 'individualism' of the British worker with the 'collectivism' of the German and Japanese worker. He traces the origins of these values to differences in the pattern of industrialization. However, what might be consequential on these differences is the extent to which particular work forces can have their materialistic aspirations subjugated to and controlled by an authoritative normative system. Arguably, the 'collectivism' of the Japanese and German work forces makes it more likely that new regulative systems can be introduced as older status orders decline. In particular one can think of the institutional developments of 'welfare corporatism' and 'co-determination'.

The implication of this argument is that Britain may be a special case not because it was the first industrial nation and therefore is a prototype for other advanced Western societies but because of the form of its industrialization. What initially provided a mechanism for dividing the work force and limiting its aspirations to economic factors rather than issues of authority and control, has subsequently formed the normative basis of inflationary difficulties. For it to come to fruition it was necessary that the pattern of behaviour spread to other groups than skilled craftsmen; that the structure of power allow these aspirations to be pursued; and that the productive capacity of the economy be relatively weakened. Thus, maturation both of the domestic and the international economy have played their parts. However, by themselves, they do not account for why Britain compared to most Western countries has had more difficulty coping with recent inflations. Instead, differences in norms and normative controls may be at least as important.

Fraternity as Citizenship
A. H. Halsey

Reprinted with permission from A. H. Halsey, *Change in British Society*, Oxford University Press, 1978, pp.160–9

The only way to meet the challenge of those who would dismiss any successful prospect for Britain is to turn from analysis of our present discontents to an attempt to chart the way to a brighter future. This does not mean abandoning objectivity. The determining of social ends should always be disciplined by study of the means to reach them. . . . Exhortation alone is futile, whether to altruism or to tolerance or to recognition of the equal claim of others to share in the bounty afforded by society. The problem is to discover, to establish, and to strengthen those social institutions that will encourage and foster the kinds of relations between people that are desired.

I have asserted that liberty, equality, and fraternity are the three fundamental values in terms of which societies are to be judged. None of these ideals is fully realized in Britain. The question, then, is how each may be more fully realized. Simultaneous maximizing of them is not possible. It is a matter of finding the best balance between the revolutionary triad. Yet I believe that advance towards all three is possible, and that the limits of that advance depend upon the development of fraternal institutions.

But fraternal institutions is an ambiguous phrase. I mean it to denote social groups whose members share the same essential ideals of conduct – recognition of, and care for, the needs of others – which are associated with our noblest conception of the family. I take the notion of fraternity in political discourses to be a metaphorical reference to this ideal of a moral community, covering all the relationships, conjugal and consanguineous, that are entailed in the family. Indeed, it has sometimes been argued, and with force, that the fraternal metaphor impoverishes this conception: that brotherhood is more diluted and more prone to enmity than any of the other relationships; and that, in the revolutionary creed, 'brotherhood has been selected as the image of perfection, not because it represents the family at its best, but because it is the family at its least familial'. Fraternity of this kind, in reality, rejects the family. But this is not my intention. On the contrary, while recognizing that family loyalties may limit or conflict with similar civic or community ties, I assume that the fraternal loyalty of the monk or the dedicated party member can and should be an overriding creed and code of conduct only for the few. Nor is this type of human association a necessarily superior expression of moral integration. The ethical value of such a fraternity, whatever the self-sacrifice which it may entail, depends upon the treatment it gives to those who by choice or circumstance are not part of the brotherhood.

Moreover, just as the harmonious family, nuclear or extended, bears value in its own right, so too can the limited political community, even though it restricts itself to something less than the ecumenical brotherhood of man. The United Nations, the United Kingdom, England, Scotland, and Wales, can surely exist together. Of course, against those who advocate or allow particularistic forms of fraternity, the charge of 'contradiction' may be laid. Restricted definitions of community inevitably leave problems of external relations. Bounded human groups, by definition, always set such problems. But the proper reply, appealing to experience, is that the smaller group can cultivate the values to be applied in the larger. If these values are liberty and equality, then a practical meaning is given to the idea of the brotherhood of man. It is in this sense that I see fraternity, even though, and indeed because, it is rooted in small-scale organizations, as the pre-condition of liberty and equality. But, by the same token, the forms of fraternal association which can make up a fraternal society can vary, and communities can remain integrated while attaching different importance to liberty and equality.

Modern history has offered two contesting alternatives for realizing the revolutionary ideals – capitalism and communism. Western industrial capitalism poineered the market as the central mediating institution in the development of wealth and its distribution. But the market promotes neither fraternity nor equality. It was historically the means of escape from feudal community and has been the target of Marxist criticism as the mechanism of class inequality and of the substantive restriction of liberty. Industrial communism substituted a state bureaucracy for the market. But here, and especially in the Russian case, the liberal critic can point to the repressive fraternity of the party which controls the state apparatus, and the sacrifice of political liberty in exchange for a far-from-perfect equality. Out of this contention the possibilities seem to be no more than a choice between two vast historical failures.

It there another way? I think so. The third alternative, for Britain, is to take its own traditions of citizenship and democracy seriously in all their richness and inspiration. They offer the basis for a new fraternity without which both liberty and equality are impoverished. They offer also the political and social means of progress towards a newly integrated society. They were pointed to in Durkheim's emphasis on local autonomy and respect for tradition in late nineteenth-century Britain. They are best thought of as a *radical tradition*: a willingness to change institutions under changed circumstances so as to realize more perfectly the values sought by past reform.

The relevance of capitalism and communism, in any event, has to be put in the context of actual and present British circumstances. These, briefly recapitulated, are the legacy of a 'first-world' development, post-imperialism, tentative integration with the European continent, and centrifugal movements within the United Kingdom. But they also include a tradition of fraternity which has supported the slowly developing institutions of civic, political, and social citizenship. In Britain, political fraternity is citizenship. Its seeds were sown in the civil liberties of the seventeenth and eighteenth centuries. Its roots grew in the social inventiveness of the urban working class of the nineteenth century, and in the traditions of public service which were developed by the liberal elements of the professional middle class. These have been the finest expression of British membership one of another, but the Labour Movement has faltered in its attempt to nationalize the local welfare societies of an exploited class, and the ideal of public service has been diluted in its transformation to an overpowerful bureaucracy. So the political organization of citizenship, which is democracy, and the social organization of citizenship, which is community, continue to be thwarted by class interest and bureaucratic subversions.

What, then, are the prospects for a third way, through fraternity as citizenship, between the first and second worlds of capitalism and communism? There is no simple answer. The forces of conflict and cohesion are complex: and they stem from the wider world as well as from within our own society. Salvation lies neither in European integration, nor in retreat to the more archaic native nationalism. These are conditions for successful solutions; they are not the solutions themselves. Nor is there any simple economic answer, whether through North Sea oil or a return to the market. Growth alleviates scarcity. But at our level of economic development, it stimulates appetite as much as it gratifies it. By fostering the positional good economy it lays up frustration as much as satisfaction.

Indeed, the greatest danger is precisely the offer of simple solutions to our complicated plight. We have an economy that does not release our energies, a polity that does not secure our trust, and a culture which does not sufficiently attract our affections. Simple solutions can only lead to political tyranny, whether from the Right or the Left. Either would destroy that fundamental element of our social life and tradition in which we can take pride – our long developed and tenaciously held civil liberty. Our essential predicament is that the historical conditions which allowed this liberty also permitted divisive inequalities of class and status, a stratified society held together by imperial might abroad and deference and respect for shared religious and cultural values at home. But external empire and internal social control have been losing their power to pacify without violence, leaving market success and political bureaucracy, in all their weaknesses, to justify a still markedly unequal society.

Past failures to achieve fair and equal social distribution have driven some to apathy, others to a belief in a violent seizure of power and the imposition of an authoritarian social order, and still others to denial of the possibility or even desirability of an egalitarian society. These are the roads to tyranny. Our experiences of industrial, nationalist, and racial conflict continually demonstrate the need for a new sense of equality to replace old class-restrictive liberties and status-crippled fraternities. We have still to provide a common experience of citizenship in childhood and old age, in work and play, and in health and sickness. We have still, in short, to develop a common culture to replace the divided cultures of class and status.

Our society cannot stand on such shifting foundations. To strengthen them, we need principles and practices of social distribution which are acknowledged to be just by the great majority. And in a world of growing visibility of reference groups, these principles will be seen as just only if they actually are just. The implication is that in a political democracy which secures our liberties, the paramount principle of distribution must be equality. Equality of opportunity is not enough. It is a state of affairs we have still not reached but which is, in any case, a step towards a society that could be more ruthlessly stratified than the one we live in now. Nor is it enough to eliminate all irrelevant discriminations of skin, colour, sex, cultural background, or family upbringing. We need full equality of the basic material conditions of social life. If poverty remains in Britain this is not because the technical means to its abolition are missing: it is because of an inadequate sense of moral implication in the lives of compatriots. It is a failure not of economic production, but of fraternal distribution. The guarantee of the material essential for freedom from want does not require even a radically egalitarian policy. The fraternity nurtured in the kind of family experienced by the majority, extended by standards of schooling that most parents expect, and embodied in the political definitions of citizenship which were proclaimed during and after the Second World War, would put an end to poverty, once and for all.

Beyond this readily attainable minimum of a fraternal society, R. H. Tawney's conception still stands: Because men are men, social institutions – property rights, and the organization of industry, and the system of public health and education – should be planned, as far as is possible, to emphasize and strengthen, not the class differences which divide, but the common humanity which unites them.

Unless they are shown to be relevant to needs, inequalities based on differences of personal quality are no argument against equality. Nor is the familiar argument that incentives necessitate inequality to be taken as a fundamental law of human economic nature. The incentives they assume are the products of present values and interests which arise from our existing institutions, and institutions can be changed. In a fraternal society it could reasonably be expected that any extra rewards to effort and capacity that might be necessary for an efficient division of labour would leave the basic structure of equal citizenship unimpaired.

The outstanding example of an established fraternal institution, one in which the most elevated familial ideal is extended voluntarily to the stranger, is the British blood donor system which R. M. Titmuss has compared with the marketing of blood in the United States and other countries to demonstrate that large-scale fraternity is a human practicality and not merely a Utopian exhortation. From his study of American practice, Titmuss concluded 'that the commercialization of blood and donor relationships represses the expression of altruism, evades the sense of community, lowers scientific standards, limits both personal and professional freedoms, sanctions the making of profits in hospitals and clinical laboratories, legalizes hostility between doctor and patient, subjects critical areas of medicine to the laws of the market place, places immense social costs on those least able to bear them – the poor, the sick, and the inept – increases the danger of unethical behaviour in various sectors of medical science and practice, and results in situations in which proportionately more blood is supplied by the poor, the unskilled, the unemployed, negroes, and other low-income categories of exploited human populations of high blood yielders.' We do not have to assume with Titmuss that, in social institutions, there is a Gresham's law of ungenerosity. But we can recognize the opposite and integrating principle, which is to seek fraternity as citizenship in all public organizations. To do so is to encourage, through public policy, those fraternal motives which the blood transfusion service brilliantly exemplifies.

From this point of view there is nothing more important than the policy pursued by the State towards the family. Families have unequal shares of material and cultural capital. The remedy is positive discrimination. The material base for parenthood does not measure up to democratic standards of fairness. It is true that, no thanks to government, babies now tend to be born rather more in the better-off and less in the worse-off homes. Fertility is coming to be positively correlated with family income – a reversal of the previous absurdity. But mothers, and especially working-class mothers, are still at once the most hard-worked and the least-rewarded members of our working population. They are an essential element of the social division of labour but, unlike nurses, teachers, social workers and the like, are excluded from the paid occupational division of labour. They deserve an income which reflects their service to society. They deserve publicly provided facilities in street child centres and play groups to relieve their isolated labours in raising the under-fives. The family is our best carrier of the basic education of each new generation of citizens. An enlightened social policy should recognize this and define the experts and specialists, the schools and the child services, as agents for the support, not the replacement, of family upbringing. The implication is that we must challenge the usurpation of authority by experts (whether they appear as teachers or as administrators) and grant full citizenship to the amateur parents against the professional pedagogues. This is what is meant, for instance, by the community school. Not parent governors as tokens in a ritual, but genuine parental and community government of schools.

I sketched the outline of an educational system giving balanced expression to the ideals of liberty and equality which would be a practical further development of the slow reform of the class-divided schooling bequeathed to Britain from liberal capitalism in the nineteenth century. The comprehensive primary and secondary school is its fraternal foundation, and could be the nursery of a fully democratic citizenship. The private market would have no place in it.

Political and industrial organizations could be refashioned to mirror the values cultivated in home and school. The twentieth-century trends in government and industry have made size and complexity into serious obstacles to effective citizenship and threaten to replace it by oligarchic and bureaucratic power. The increase of economic cooperation over larger areas makes all the more urgent the devolution of decision. Bold advances towards a more developed citizenship – in Scotland for the Scots, in the work place for workers, in the school for parents, in the locality for the neighbour, and so on – could evoke popular support. John Osmond's eloquent plea for Welsh devolution, pointing to the way in which democracy should be rooted in community, is a persuasive contemporary example:

> Man needs an anchor in a particular community. It is the source of that moral power which enables him to resist the monolithic State. The nation and the community in which he seeks his roots is not an end in itself: it is man's link with eternity. 'Cadw tŷ mewn cwmwl tystion', as Waldo Williams so movingly expressed it: man's relationship to the community is 'Keeping a home amidst a cloud of witnesses'.

Similarly, economic organizations, with their characteristic legacy of hierarchy, increasing scale, low discretion, and low trust, could be redirected towards industrial citizenship.

These familial, educational, and industrial examples cover only a small part of the total range of the institutions of production and reproduction, all of which need to be measured and reformed in the direction which leads to a society which is integrated, because it rests on an optimal balance of what is possible to make real our traditional revolutionary dreams. My review of past progress makes it all too clear that the journey to a society of fraternal citizens is no easy one. Stratification is stubbornly resistant to change: there is bound to be opposition. There are always those who place private interest above public welfare. Yet in a society of the kind I am advocating, patient persuasion has to be our principal weapon: for persuasion is democracy in action. Only if it is given constant priority can we both guard our freedoms and override the resistance of vested interest. Only then, but certainly then, democracy has the right to enforce its will.

The attainment of a new and sound basis for social order requires political will of a strength we have hitherto lacked. No one can guarantee that either the challenge will be accepted, or the response forthcoming. But I would certainly claim that what I suggest we need is also socially and politically possible. Its elements are in our social traditions and on our political agenda. Adversity itself is now sufficient to give social response to political initiative. Here again the initiatives have to be congruent with the end in view: and that means democratic politics. Democratic politics is essentially a system in which citizens actively mould the final decisions binding on all. It works only if liberty of thought and expression is ranked first among rights and the active exercise of citizenship first among duties. Political action is inevitably carried on by imperfect people in public office. Hence the constant need for alert and knowledgeable citizens, to defeat oppression and to prevent the public services from degenerating into organizations which serve the private interests of public servants.

That, all too briefly, is my view of our best way into the future. We have no paradise lost, no paradise to be regained. Yet we can, if we will, take heart from the ancient story of the departure of our primal ancestors from the Garden of Eden:

> Some natural tears they dropped, but wiped them soon;
> The world was all before them, where to choose
> Their place of rest, and Providence their guide:
> They hand in hand, with wand'ring steps and slow,
> Through Eden took their solitary way.

Tory Philosophy – a Personal View
N. St John-Stevas

Reprinted with permission from Norman St John-Stevas, 'Tory Philosophy – a Personal View', *Three Banks Review*, no. 134, June 1982, pp. 3–13

A pragmatic party like the Tory Party, holding in its hand as its strongest card its competence to govern, faces the real danger that its moral basis will not be sufficiently projected and understood. The Labour Party with its constitution, its doctrines and its clearly defined theoretical aims finds much less difficulty in getting over its ideals; yet the moral ethos of the Tory Party is equally strong although much more subtle and complex than that of its rivals on the left.

Tories and tradition

Of all the political parties in the state the Tory Party owes most to history. We have been around the longest and we are the custodians not of a dogma or doctrine but of a tradition. Those who argue that true Conservatism was born in May 1979 are obliged to reject not only the whole postwar Tory tradition from Winston Churchill onwards but the Party's prewar history as well. There is, in fact, a clear line of succession moving forward from Baldwin and Chamberlain to Butler and Macmillan and backwards to Salisbury, Disraeli and Bolingbroke. The Tory Party is an historical party or it is nothing. The experience of being born again is no doubt a psychological fact of considerable personal importance but you cannot base either a religious or a political structure on such an essentially private happening.

The Tory Party has, of course, had its dogmatic moments but they have been departures from the norm. In the end, dogma has always had to give way to the facts of life. Protection at one time appeared to be an article of faith but it was a Tory Prime Minister, Sir Robert Peel, who repealed the Corn Laws. Again for many years imperialism was an ascendant principle in the Conservative cosmos but it was always modified and held in check by other perceptions and commitments. The point was put admirably by the present Prime Minister when she declared: 'Free enterprise has a place, an honoured place in our scheme of things but as one of many dimensions. For Tories became Tories well before the modern concept of a free market economy meant anything, well before it became a matter of political controversy.' The richness and diversity of the Conservative tradition cannot be reduced to a single doctrinal principle. 'Monetarism', as Sir Keith Joseph has made clear in a pamphlet bearing the title 'is not enough'. It is not only not enough. Isolated from its political, social and moral context, it is positively misleading and dangerous as an indication of party attitudes. In isolation it lends itself to distortion and misrepresentation and to crude but politically damaging caricatures. If we are to counter the socialist projection of the party as the paradigm of hard-faced selfishness and callousness, monetary policy has to be set squarely in the wider setting of traditional Tory social concerns and traced to its roots in moral values.

Monetarism and morals

Britain may or may not be a nation of shopkeepers – the point has been argued since Napoleon's gibe – but we are certainly not a nation of economists. When practitioners of the dismal science descend on us, Lord Home is not the only one to reach for the matchbox. I do not believe that the average voter understands very much about the theoretical bases of monetarism in its several varieties and it is hard to blame him for that. When the high priests themselves are in dispute about the essentials of their faith a certain amount of agnostic confusion amongst the small fry is pardonable. Nothing is more difficult to communicate than an arcane creed on the tenets of which the custodians are in conflict. So let us turn from the hermeneutics to the facts, a course which, in moments of crisis and dispute, the Prime Minister has often wisely counselled. The Tory Party was returned to power at the last election not because a monetarist conversion of Pauline proportions swept across our suburbs and shires but principally because the Prime Minister, with her inspired gift for common sense, succeeded in articulating the thoughts, fears, anxieties and aspirations of the majority of the people. The nation had to come to the moral conclusion that we had reached the end of the road, that the excesses and abuses of union power could no longer be tolerated in a free parliamentary democracy, that inflation had become a deadly threat to our wellbeing, our institutions and our mode of life itself, and that a new way forward must be found. So from those bleak winter months of 1979, popular convictions and resolves emerged that the rake's progress needed to be halted, that public expenditure had to be reined back not as an exercise in masochism but to create room for the expansion of the wealth-producing private sector, that taxation needed to be reduced to provide incentive and encouragement to enterprise. This was not so much an advance to a new monetarism as a return to old values, to appreciation that life is a struggle, that for nations as well as individuals there is no escape from the necessities of thrift, hard work and change if happiness and prosperity are to be achieved.

Monetarism then is a means not an end. It is a technique not a moral objective. And it is one of a number of techniques not a panacea. The point of saying all this is to stress the intrinsic flexibility of government economic policy. It is not a mechanistic exercise in economic logistics. Great Britain is not the scene of a gigantic experiment to prove the truth or falsity of academic economists' controverted theories. We are in politics not in economics. The demands of economic theory have to be moderated by their application in the practical world of politics. Thus the Government accepts that during the period of readjustment of industry we will have to go through a period of high unemployment but that is quite different from accepting high unemployment as a permanent instrument of policy. There is no inconsistency between accepting reluctantly the need for a transitional period of unemployment and modifying its impact on those who are bearing the brunt of the burden by giving special help to hard hit areas and intervening with steps to help the young unemployed.

Inevitably, Britain's economic decline has meant that most political debate in the last two decades has hinged on economic issues. We have had to translate our principles into policies which specifically address our major economic problems – our poor record of productivity growth; our loss of markets at home and abroad; the increase in the proportion of our national product spent by the State; the destructive power of irresponsible trade unionism; high inflation; high marginal rates of taxation and high unemployment. It seems to me unlikely that there is one simple key which will unlock all these problems or that, even if there were, it would open the door to our entire political philosophy. Conservatism is not, therefore, synonymous with some technique for running the economy, however glitteringly fashionable it may be. A few years ago incomes policy, planned growth and tripartism were all the vogue. I did not think then, nor do I think now, that an outline of those policies amounts, 'tout court' to a statement of Conservatism. The same might be said of monetarism. I would not personally regard a description of someone as a monetarist, or even a Keynesian for that matter, as significant as a description of him as, say, a Christian or a Conservative.

A balancing act

So it is balance that should characterize Conservative economic policy and this has deeper philosophical roots. The need for balance arises from two Tory insights into the human condition: the unique worth of the individual and mankind's inherited mistake. Ultimately, these aperçus have a religious foundation. Christianity provides a theological basis for them both. The value of the individual arises from his relationship to God and his eternal destiny, but this bright picture is shadowed by his capacity for evil and the depth of his sin. Liberal economics is based on an appreciation of the value of the individual and accordingly possesses a profound truth.

There is no doubt that the societies which have relied on fostering man's self-interest have reaped great rewards in terms of freedom and high living standards. This is the justification for capitalism, namely that under it the ordinary person is freer and better off than under socialism. The case for the free market economy is reinforced because, in Reinhold Niebuhr's words, 'there is no one in society good or wise enough finally to determine how the individual's capacities had best be used for the common good or his labour rewarded'. The man in Whitehall definitely does not know best. Self-interest may not be normative but it constitutes a reality which has to be recognized and for which there is no substitute.

So far so good for the market economy. But there comes a point at which the good Conservative must part company with the liberal enthusiast and it comes with the theory that justice, harmony and the highest common good are automatically achieved by the operation of the free market.

The whole history of the nineteenth century in Britain and elsewhere refutes this assertion. So does the history of the 1930s both in Britain and the United States. Property, as the Fathers of the Church knew well enough, has a Janus face and can be a source of injustice as well as a defence of individual rights against exploitation by others. The intervention of the State is thus required to restrain individuals and promote justice. The art of Conservative politics is to strike the right balance and permit the fostering of self-interest without exposing weaker individuals to exploitation and the community to disruption. The equilibrium of the free market is a myth because it regards man as an economic rationalist ignoring such other motives as pride, ambition and self-aggrandizement.

Tory realism thus sets its face against the Utopian and sentimental politics of the liberal right and the socialist left. No doubt, if faced with a choice between evils, the right-wing alternative would be preferable since individual injustice is never as oppressive as the centralized authoritarian version, but the Tory path is a true *via media*. Faced with a clash of warring creeds the Tory response is to mix them and somehow synthesize Adam Smith with Karl Marx.

Conservatism, as Mr T. E. Utley has pointed out in his essay *Capitalism: the Moral Case*, is wider than capitalism. Central to Conservative thinking is the idea of community which moderates the rigours of the clash between individual and state. Conservatives have faith in social spontaneity and organic growth. They see society as a true *Koinonia*, the manifestation of a shared life of cooperation and reconciliation by those who hold certain ideas in common. The common good is a complex, not a simple, concept. Public order and civil peace, the security of the young, the protection of the weak and the old and the inexperienced, the maintenance of the civilized decencies of public behaviour are all included but it extends beyond these to other moral and social values. Together they constitute the wisdom of a great society transmitted over generations which furnishes the intuitional *a priori* of both the rationalities and technicalities of public and private law. These values are so widely accepted and tenaciously held that if they are challenged by the exercise of power public opinion, drawing upon them, is able to energize political action to defend them. This is precisely what happened in the winter of 1979 and in the subsequent general election.

A Church not a sect

A characteristic of the Conservative Party which flows from its synthesizing role is that like the Church of England it is comprehensive. It is indeed a Church as opposed to a sect. The party is based not on formulas or dogmas but on certain broad principles which precisely because of their breadth are capable of differing interpretations. Thus in their day, Mr Enoch Powell and Sir Edward Boyle had, and in our own day Mr Jim Prior and Sir Keith Joseph have, despite distinctive intellectual approaches, good and equal claims to describe themselves as Tories. This broadness of approach leads to a spirit of tolerance at every level of the party. The witch drives and heresy hunts on the left are happily unknown in Tory circles.

There is no means of withdrawing the Tory whip from a recalcitrant Member of Parliament although he may resign it if he wishes to do so. Other agreeable side effects are that dirty political linen is not laundered in public and that splits and fissures in the Cabinet have on the whole been healed or concealed in Tory administrations. Of course, should things change and the party become committed to a doctrinal system this harmony would be likely to become weakened or be replaced by dissonance and discord.

This comprehensiveness of the party is mirrored in its electoral support. I suppose that the majority of industrialists and the well-to-do are Tories but the party has never been the creature of the Confederation of British Industry in the way that Labour has been, at times, the puppet of the unions. The genius of the party has been to hold on to its traditional supporters like farmers and country folk while adding new recruits from the urban and industrial classes. This process was seen at work at the 1979 election. As every Conservative candidate knows, there has always been a nucleus of Tory working-class support on council housing estates but, at the last election, the swing to the Tories on the council estates was unprecedented in its sweep and strength. Doubtless this will be cemented by the opportunities to buy their own houses afforded in Mr Heseltine's Housing Act and strengthened still further by the extraordinary action of the Labour Party in insisting that councils be given the right in future to buy back houses sold at the selling price.

Patriotism

Furthermore, the Tory Party is the party of patriotism. I am not, of course, suggesting that Tories have a monopoly of this desirable quality but that the values of the party are pre-eminently those of Queen and country. You can see that at Conservative meetings in a hundred village halls, where it is the Union Jack and not the Red flag that swathes the table: you can hear it at the adoption of any Tory candidate where the meeting always concludes with the national anthem, not the Internationale.

The Tory Party is the party of national pride, the party that cares about Britain's role in the world, the party not of little England but of Great Britain. This was the impulse that led the party to support entry into the EEC and that keeps it faithful to its commitment. It is only from within a wider grouping that British influence can be effectively exercised today. Realism rather than idealism makes Conservatives pro-Europe. We accept a European framework as essential for Britain's economic prosperity and above all for her successful defence from external attack.

Realism dominates the Conservative approach to foreign policy which is seen primarily as a means of advancing and protecting British interests. This approach is not as narrow as it at first appears since, as a trading nation, we have a paramount need of peace and stability. The promotion of these benefits not only Britain but the rest of the world. Realism makes Tories cool about the United Nations, not because we do not believe in international organizations, but because we look at what these organizations are actually doing, not what they say they are doing, and hence see their limitations. This approach may at times appear cynical but a cynic's merit is to see the facts.

As to the internal politics of other countries whether South Africa or the Soviet Union, a Tory tradition which goes back to Castlereagh and Canning is based on the promise that the character of the regimes of foreign countries is not a primary concern of foreign policy. This attitude has its dangers but it spares the party the moral contortions which the Labour Party has to go through to reconcile its principles with common sense and it rules out crusades. Only a tiny minority of Tories approve of apartheid but an equally small number think that moral condemnation of apartheid entails a boycott of South Africa over trade and defence.

Preserve our institutions

Tory patriotism is expressed in pride in our institutions, especially those of the monarchy, Parliament and the courts. Tories are, however, animated by more than sentiment in this respect: there is a hard-headed assessment that it is these institutions which provide the necessary protection in a democracy against the tyranny – so feared by Mill – of the majority will, or the naked and brutal exertion of power by bureaucracies or by strong but minority interests.

Disraeli was fully seized of the point: in his constitutional reflections in his Crystal Palace speech in 1872, he referred not to defending our 'constitution' but to 'preserving our institutions'. Furthermore, he was urging not so much their maintenance as their restoration.

The only reforms of the Lords carried out in recent years have been by Tory governments, the most notable and effective being Mr Harold Macmillan's taking up of Bagehot's suggestion and making it possible to create life peerages. Equally, it has been a Tory government, the present one, which has set about a systematic reform of the House of Commons. This process must continue if parliamentary government is to be made effective once again. Not that Parliament in its septecentennial history has ever (save for the disastrous Commonwealth period) governed. Its function has been rather different: to subject the executive to limitation and control; to protect the liberty of the individual citizen against the arbitrary use of power; to focus the mind of the nation on the great issues of the day and, by remaining at the centre of the political stage, to impose what I believe Sir Ian Gilmour has called 'Parliamentary manners' on the whole system. The new and expanded committee systems which we have set up – the implementation of the reforms suggested by the procedure committee – our proposals for a new public bill procedure and our suggestions for a more effective exercise by Parliament of its historic prerogative of withholding or granting supply constitute the most important parliamentary reforms of the century. They will bring the Commons back into the centre of effective political life.

Conservatives are concerned not only with the country but with the individuals who make it up. Liberty as an abstraction has never had much appeal but the particular and traditional liberties of the subject are another matter. 'Law and Order' is an unfortunate phrase with particular racialist associations but what Conservatives are concerned about is something rather different, the preservation of liberties under the law. No law, no liberties is as true as no bishop, no king. Hence, there is nothing Eldonine about Tory distrust of demonstrations, no panic fear, but a hard-headed assessment of a position where extremists are using the right of demonstration not to reform institutions or to extend liberties but to destroy them.

One liberty to which Conservatives attach particular importance is freedom of choice. This principle can be seen at work in both social and economic policy. Conservatives would rather that individuals did the saving necessary for the nation than that the Government should do it for them, hence the emphasis on reducing direct taxation. They would rather see an individual making provision for his own old age than the Government. A basic Tory approach is that the State should do nothing for the individual which he is able to do adequately for himself.

The principle is balanced by a concern for the condition of the people which is an intrinsic part of the party's tradition. Unlike the Republican Party in the United States, the Tory Party in Britain has never had any difficulty in distinguishing between socialism and social welfare. The party can invoke not only the shades of Shaftesbury and Disraeli but those of Baldwin, Chamberlain and (if shade is the right word) Macmillan as well. Conservatives instinctively want to see voluntary service and self-help encouraged, but no Tory wants to see a dismantling of the welfare state. Perhaps some of the recent emphasis on cutting government expenditure has rather distorted the matter but the Government is in fact spending more not less on social welfare than its Labour predecessor.

Ultimately the basis of Conservatism is a recognition of both the possibilities and the limitations of human nature. Tories believe in original sin although not all would give it such a precise theological formulation. Belief in the perfectibility of man is a delusion of the left not of the right. Accordingly Conservatives have a lively appreciation of the value of limited government knowing that there is much that government cannot do and that individuals and families have to do for themselves. No Tory believes that politics can create the good life, it can only provide for its possibility. Variety, choice, freedom, enjoyment, these are the Tory watchwords and they correspond to deep needs in human nature. The Conservative Party is the middle party in the country where the middle principles matter.

Disraelian Toryism

The Conservative leader who best epitomized the Toryism which I am describing was Disraeli. Disraeli's Toryism with its national principles, its profound sense of the organic nature of society, its compassion for those in need – as evidenced by his almost lone championship of the Chartists – was sharply opposed to what he called 'the brutalitarians', 'the school of Manchester' (an original and intentionally uncomplimentary phrase), the Benthamites who would refashion England with their harsh logic and their pitiless economic doctrines, careless and possibly ignorant of basic human instincts and feelings. Disraeli knew about and therefore sympathized with the lot of the poor: his knowledge of their actual life was greatly superior to that of Dickens. He saw society in terms of a trust, drawing its cohesion from the observance of mutual obligation, and its rulers ready to employ where necessary the huge engine of government to promote the wellbeing of the people. Toryism needed to identify itself with the forces and feelings making for stability, the preservation of the national institutions and the enlargement of national prestige. Hence came the great Crystal Palace trilogy that the tasks of the Tory Party were to maintain our institutions, uphold the empire of England and elevate the condition of the people. They have been the lodestars of the true Tory ever since.

Disraeli saw these principles not only as being right but as making sound political sense. He had experienced for himself what happened to the Conservative Party when it identified itself with a single interest and that a declining one – land: he had seen an urban and industrial England emerge of which, apart from a redoubt in Lancashire, the Tory Party knew nothing: he had seen his party become that of the counties and small rural boroughs based primarily on southern and south-eastern England, resting on a shrinking base and identified with no future force: and he had reaped the bitter harvest of exclusion from majority office for thirty years. He was determined that this would not occur again. So were many of his successors, Baldwin, Chamberlain, Churchill, Butler and Macmillan who had read the signs of the times aright. The ability that the party has shown ever since Disraeli's day to capture a substantial part of the working-class vote has been a crucial element in its success. It certainly determined the issue against Labour in 1979.

Disraelian Toryism was never a political system of rational propositions, rather it was a series of images and ideals designed to move and inspire, to reinvigorate rather than to reconstruct society. Yet its practical achievements were remarkable. The Parliament of 1874 was the first in British history to devote a major part of its energies to the improvement of the condition of the people: it regulated the hours of work and legalized trade unions: it provided dwellings for the poor: it revolutionized public health: it protected friendly societies: it regulated commerce in food and drugs with a statute that remained in force until 1928.

Disraeli's *Sanitas Sanitatum omnia sanitas* had been transubstantiated into a political reality. The gulf between the two nations portrayed in *Sybil* of the rich and the poor had to a limited extent been bridged. We can be sure that Disraeli, had he been alive today, would have been the first to seek to bridge the chasm between the two nations of our own times, the employed and the unemployed.

Ethics and politics

A true Tory always stresses the connection between ethics or morals and political freedom. The threat of totalitarian and extremist ideologies, whether of left or right, still menaces free societies today but an even greater danger is a collapse into an anarchy which is amoral and valueless.

A generation could quickly grow up ignorant and uncertain of our ethical and cultural heritage. This I characterize as the threat of a new barbarism. Today's barbarian is not outside the city walls but within them. He wears no bearskin and carries no club and may be armed with nothing more lethal than a ball-point pen. The nearest he may get to the primeval forest is the quadrangle of an Oxford (or Cambridge) College but he is a barbarian none the less if he undermines the religious and moral values on which our traditions of civility are based.

This undermining may be done in a number of different ways. Moral and spiritual issues may be judged and resolved solely by their practical results, or they may be reduced to the status of linguistic problems and disposed of by an analysis of language, or they may be treated as being matters of wholly subjective feeling. All these approaches reject implicitly or explicitly what for centuries has been the foundation of Western society – the belief in an order of values both objective and universal, the following of which constitutes the good life and its rejection the bad. The rejection of reason as a sure guide in human affairs destroys not only liberty but equality and fraternity. There can be no liberty without self-restraint, no equality without recognition of others as being endowed with reason and rights like ourselves, no fraternity without a sense of shared values. Without brotherhood society is reduced to a conglomeration of warring atoms in which conflicts are decided by force not law. Warfare such as this destroys in the end the very idea of community – that form of society in which what is shared is more important than what divides and in which men remain locked in argument but not in battle or fratricidal strife.

Society's concern with moral values springs then not only from their intrinsic worth but from the perception of the connection between the moral and social orders. One rests upon the other. The State borrows from above and below itself: it looks upwards to religion and morality as well as downwards to history and sociology. An earlier age produced the aphorism 'No Bishop: No King'. Our own would do well to ponder on another, 'No morality: no law'. To deny or to lose sight of the ethical nature of political freedom is folly but it is a folly characteristic of our time.

The essence of a free society is that order is not imposed by force from the top but emerges spontaneously from within in obedience to restraints and imperatives that stem from inwardly possessed moral principles. Democracy is thus much more than a mechanism, more than a political experiment. It constitutes nothing less than a spiritual and moral enterprise. Those who would be politically free have constantly to control themselves. Without that self-restraint which springs from a sense of values internally assented and accepted freedom cannot survive. Emerging within society as a shared possession, this moral force alone has power both to discipline the destructive powers of men and at the same time to overcome the inertia, indifference, boredom and triviality which more and more seem to be the mark of our time. A paramount duty of the Tory Party as Labour disintegrates into a welter of fads and fancies, of faction and fratricide, is to maintain and renew the moral consensus of the nation on which ultimately our political institutions rest.

Can I Have It in Cash?

S. Henry

Reprinted with permission from Stuart Henry (ed.), *Can I Have It in Cash? A Study of Informal Institutions and Unorthodox Ways of Doing Things*, Astragal Books, 1981, pp. 1–9

We argue for a new perspective on social institutions. Until now those who have not theorized about the state or macrosocial structure have concentrated almost exclusively upon the formal institutions of society: marriage and the family, industry and employment, education, medicine, social services and the institutions of law. This attention is justified because most of our time and energy is spent within these institutions and it is through them that economic and political power flows. But what is missing from previous accounts is the implicit and hidden contribution of informal institutions. How can we look at marriage and the family, for example, and ignore extramarital affairs which may maintain the very existence of many families? How can we estimate the real economic activity of a country when as much as one fifth of its work force may have unregistered second jobs or be involved in informal trading networks? How can we judge the effectiveness of our health care services when the bulk of health care takes place in the family and local community? We need to know how these informal institutions operate, and also how they relate to their formal counterparts.

Although informal institutions and practices are, and have always been, shared and expected by people who are involved in formal institutions, they rarely feature in sociological, economic or political accounts and theorizing. One reason why informal institutions have been overlooked is not difficult to understand. Quite simply they are not easy to study. There are no records kept, nor figures published, on the number of people having intimate relationships outside marriage. Few people will admit to having unregistered second jobs. Most people would deny taking part in fiddles at work, and, while it is not difficult to examine economic exchanges taking place in the supermarket or corner shop, where does one go in order to locate amateur trading networks? Unlike conventional areas of social life, informal institutions do not readily lend themselves to research. There are no registered addresses to which letters can be sent, no information officers, secretaries or treasurers who are available to sit down and explain the ins and outs of what goes on. For obvious reasons, informal institutions are everywhere and nowhere, all about us but nowhere to be seen.

A second reason why there is an absence of material on this area is that sociologists and other social scientists are grounded in the same common-sense assumptions and share the same taken-for-granted understanding as everyone else, concerning what constitutes our social institutions. When a man is asked what he does for a living he will most probably describe his formal occupation. He might be a 'manager', 'dentist', 'plumber', 'lecturer', 'waiter' or 'factory worker', and such job descriptions have specific ideal-type characteristics which invoke similar pictures in our minds. What we do not picture are the informal but related practices of being in any one of these jobs. Waiters are seen as rushing between the kitchen and customer serving wine and food; they are rarely envisaged as fiddling bills, pilfering food and having second jobs in neighbouring hotels. How often does one think of a dentist being paid in fresh fruit and vegetables or a surgeon receiving a case of whisky for removing a patient's appendix? In short, a person's primary job and formal job description are augmented by a wide range of secondary activities which to the uninitiated might seem irrelevant. Outside their formal jobs people participate in other ways of earning a living such as doing 'odd jobs', 'part-time work', 'do-it-yourself' work and 'favours for friends'. None of these things would be apparent from a person's description of him or herself as a 'dentist' or a 'waiter'.

So, in order to appreciate more fully the functioning of social institutions, the implicit informal roles that people carry out must be given as much emphasis as the explicit formal ones. We need to know how the formal roles are modulated by informal customs and practices and how far they feature in the meaning structure of people's everyday lives. Social science has an obligation to reintegrate a study of the everyday practice of social life with the commonly expressed theory of it; to see the informal and formal institutions as complementary parts of a whole; and to acknowledge that official accounts given by conventional approaches exclude informal institutions. As James Cornford rightly points out, such institutions have *always* existed and have always been depended upon. In the context of a discussion on industry Graeme Shankland expressed the view that both informal and formal institutions are necessary and that:

In a healthy society these two sectors sustain each other and their relationship should be a symbiotic one of mutual support. The formal sector effectively controls the commanding heights of the economy and the political system, but the informal sector is essential not parasitic or residual . . . it operates rather in the interstices of the formal institutions of modern urban society; it cannot offer an alternative society but a complementary economic activity to the formal with a different, informal and more personal life style. Many industries thought of as formal are in fact deeply dependent on the informal sector . . . this has been a feature of the urban industrial landscape since the first industrial revolution.

The implications of adopting this new direction in our approach to the study of society will lead us to question the way in which levels of activity are measured. At present these are based upon people's contribution to formal institutions; but a large amount of informal activity is unrecorded. Therefore if official rates of say, unemployment, divorce or criminal offences go down, it might simply reflect *increasing* unofficial, informal activity such as more people taking part in unregistered work or 'moonlighting', more 'affairs' and more hidden crime. If governments are to make realistic planning and policy discussions they need to know about informal institutions, the way these institutions operate and their relationship to the process of change. In order to understand change in society it is necessary first to understand how formal institutions co-opt the parts of informal institutions that they see as useful and how those co-opted aspects then become part of the established institutions of society. For example, the health care industry has begun to offer services that informal self-help groups have shown to be of value. In America now that the Childbirth Education Association has developed and demonstrated a market for prepared childbirth, all the underutilized obstetrical units are busily engaged in developing educational programmes, hiring nurse-midwives and letting fathers into delivery rooms. As Jack Geiger cynically described it, 'when the counter-culture develops something of value, the establishment rips it off and sells it back'.

A typology of informal institutions

The idea that the whole of the activity of a society is not locked up in a total economic or social system, nor that any one mode of transaction or relationship dominates is not new. Polanyi, for example, argues that rather than having one economy, *most* societies have several systems of exchange and operate 'multicentric' economies with separate economies for different classes of goods. He argues that the system of market exchange which appears to be of overriding importance in money-based industrial societies is only one of many systems of exchange. Most non-industrial societies possess at least one and sometimes two non-market systems, such as the 'redistributive' and the 'reciprocal' spheres of exchange. Each of these has its own rules, its own reality and its own language consisting of words that are appropriate only to exchange in that specific economy.

A good example of this is shown in a study by R. Salisbury of the New Guinea Siane society which has three distinct economies, one for each of three different classes of goods: *valuables*, which are essentially pigs; *luxuries* such as palm oil and pandanus nuts; and '*things of no account*', comprising mainly vegetable food. The goods which circulate in each of these economies cannot be equated with goods in another and therefore cannot be exchanged: pigs, which are valuables, cannot be exchanged for vegetables ('goods of no account') because the two kinds of goods are in separate economies. When the Siane came into contact with the Western market economy and the labour market, they acquired cash in the form of pound notes, shillings and coppers. Rather than treat these as money, the Siane identified pound notes as valuables, shillings as luxuries and coppers as 'of no account'. Because of the separation between economies, a pound note could not be changed into shillings and coppers, neither could a shilling be changed for coppers. Similar studies by Bohannon of the Tiv of Northern Nigeria and by Firth in Polynesia have also demonstrated the presence of multicentric economies.

Applying this kind of analysis to our own society, Davis says that the United Kingdom has at least four sub-economies each distinguishable by the rules which govern transactions within it. The *market economy*, he says, is governed by laws of commercial trading, employment and labour relations. It includes all legal transactions in services and commodities. The *redistributive economy* is governed by laws of taxation, welfare and state expenditure. The *domestic economy* is governed by customs and expectations concerning the relationship between family members. It also includes all productive activities which are not mediated by a market such as making, mending and food processing. Fourthly, says Davis, there is a *gift economy* which is governed by rules of reciprocity and includes all those transactions which we call giving a present, making a gift and so on. He says that rather than talking of one mode of transaction predominating over the others we should be examining the relationship between the different sub-economies.

For our purposes Davis's typology has certain inadequacies. While it includes the domestic economy or household economy, it does not accommodate other informal economies such as the hidden economy or the black economy. Where in the typology would we place unofficial work done outside formal employment but not in the family context? Where would we put amateur trading networks that occur inside a community but not as part of the official economy? Where do we locate care which is independent of the state redistributive system? Neither does Davis's framework allow a distinction to be made between economies which are legal and those which are illegal or proscribed by the economic regulations governing a society. The insight in Davis's scheme is that it sees *our* society, and not just non-industrial society, as composed of different sub-economies rather than simply being dominated by the market economy, and he directs us to look at the relationships between those different economies. In order to accommodate the full range of informal economies and their social institutions it is necessary to develop Davis's typology further.

Rather than differentiate between informal institutions on the basis of the kinds of rules which govern the transactions and relationships within them, we can distinguish between them according to the degree to which they are integral to, or an alternative to, official institutions and also according to their legal status. Taking official institutions to be all those activities which are a recognized, regular feature in society's systems of accounting, we can identify two kinds of official economy. There is an official legal economy which we can term the *regular economy* which includes: all market economic activity, formal production, consumption and employment; all official redistribution through state benefits; formal marriage, education, housing, health and social welfare; as well as the administration of justice and government. The regular economy is characterized by being capital intensive, having a high technical content, being highly complex and being organized on a hierarchical, command basis. Participation in the regular economy's formal institutions confers nominal status upon individuals. This regular economy is paralleled by an officially recognized illegal economy or *criminal economy* that includes all those illegal activities which are measured by the official criminal statistics as 'offences known to the police' such as theft, robbery, burglary, handling stolen goods, and so on. The criminal economy is the mirror-image of the regular economy in so far as there would be no market for criminal enterprise unless there were a public restriction or ban. Without such illegal classification these activities would be little different from those of legitimate business.

Separate from the regular and criminal economies are four more economies, two of which make up a continuum of unofficial institutions – which are integral to the official economy – and two of which constitute an alternative set of institutions to the official ones. The unofficial legal economy which we can call the *informal economy* would encompass all those activities and institutions which occur within official institutional settings but which are not officially recognized as part of these formal institutions. Where unofficial activities and institutionalized practices were illegal or extra-legal these would constitute a separate economy which we might term the *hidden economy*.

The third pair of economies are distinguishable from their official counterparts on the grounds of being alternative ways of doing things. They comprise self-generated informal institutions in which people control things for themselves on a do-it-yourself or self-help basis. Unlike unofficial economies, alternative economies operate independently of, and outside the contexts of the regular economy's institutions, although . . . they are in many ways dependent upon the regular economy's existence.

Where such institutions are legal we can refer to them as constituting a *social economy*. Where the activities are extra-legal or illegal, we might describe them as a *black economy*.

Overall, as can be seen from Table 1, this gives a six-fold typology of economies and their institutions.

Table 1. A typology of informal economies and their institutions

	Official	*Unofficial*	*Alternative*
Legal	REGULAR ECONOMY marriage, employment, health and social services etc.	INFORMAL ECONOMY perks-payment, voluntary organizations, tribunals etc.	SOCIAL ECONOMY cohabitation, domestic production, barter and exchange, self-help groups etc.
Extra-legal or illegal	CRIMINAL ECONOMY prostitution, professional theft, drug trafficking etc.	HIDDEN ECONOMY extramarital affairs, pilfering and fiddling, amateur trading etc.	BLACK ECONOMY irregular work, 'moonlighting', some fringe medicine etc.

We can see how this typology applies if we take work as an illustration. A man might obtain official employment in a factory where he will be given a formal written job description detailing his functions and duties for his role in the *regular economy*. His work might comprise assembling pressed steel parts. Before long he may discover that following the officially laid down techniques it is not possible to align the holes in those parts that have been slightly distorted during pressing. More experienced workers in the plant might show him that his job *is* possible if he resorts to a special unofficial technique for retapping the holes. Thus he soon learns that it is only possible to do his job with a degree of additional, unofficial, *informal* knowledge and practice which has become institutionalized as part of the job. In another example, Ditton found that bread salesmen were expected to avoid any mistakes made when collecting their sales money and were penalized by having deductions made from their wages should mistakes occur. In practice shortages were impossible to avoid by legitimate means. During his sales training the novice bread salesman learns that shortages can be pre-empted by overcharging customers for their bread, thus fiddling the customer on behalf of the company and on behalf of himself. He therefore takes part in an *illegal hidden economy* in order to carry out his formal job.

The same process operates in nearly all occupations. Behind the official rule and theory exists the unofficial and hidden practice. In order to carry out the official job functions an employee must rely to a considerable degree on informal relationships and institutions, and he knows that many of his tasks could not be completed without these 'tricks of the trade'.

At another level informal institutions operate outside of the official system as an *alternative* way of providing income, goods and services, which might otherwise be unobtainable. When the official system fails to provide work or to deliver the basic commodities or services, or does so at too high a price or in too inhuman a way, people may resort to 'irregular' economic activity. Our factory worker in the example above, might prefer to employ a friend to do some plumbing and decorating rather than to take this work to an established firm in the regular economy. Should his car break down he might take it to the man on the corner who is known to fix them for cash. In so far as none of these skilled workers have registered their 'business' with the relevant authorities then they will be part of the *black economy*. Our factory worker might prefer to pay the black economy car repairman, plumber or decorator by supplying him with some specialist tools obtained 'cheap' from the factory where he works. Doing so would make him part of the *hidden economy* and he might find his assembly job meaningful largely in terms of its usefulness in enabling him to participate in a network of such informal activity. Finally, he might instead prefer to do his decorating or car repair work himself at the weekend. In this case his activity would become part of the *social economy*, but would not show up in the official economic regular measurements as work done.

But informal institutions are not restricted to production and consumption. They feature prominently in education, welfare, housing and law, and are as common to marriage as they are to medicine.

The Position of Women
J. Mitchell

Reprinted with permission from Juliet Mitchell, *Women's Estate*, Penguin, 1971, pp. 189–97

Production

Today, automation promises the *technical* possibility of abolishing completely the physical differential between man and woman in production. But under capitalist relations of production, the *social* possibility of this abolition is permanently threatened, and can easily be turned into its opposite, the actual diminution of woman's role in production as the labour force contracts.

This concerns the future; for the present the main fact to register is that woman's role in production is virtually stationary, and has been so for a long time now. In England in 1911, 30 per cent of the work force were women; in 1970, 37 per cent. The composition of their jobs has not changed decisively either. The jobs are very rarely 'careers'; when they are not in the lowest positions on the factory-floor they are normally white-collar auxiliary positions (such as secretaries) – supportive to masculine roles. They are often jobs with a high 'expressive' content, such as 'service' tasks. Sociologists can put it bluntly: 'Within the occupational organization they are analogous to the wife-mother role in the family.' The educational system underpins this role-structure. Seventy-five per cent of eighteen-year-old girls in England are receiving neither training nor education today. The pattern of 'instrumental' father and 'expressive' mother is not substantially changed when the woman is gainfully employed, as her job tends to be inferior to that of the man's, to which the family adapts. Thus, in all essentials, work – of the amount and type effectively available today – has not proved a salvation for women, quite the contrary.

Reproduction

Scientific advance in contraception could, as we have seen, make involuntary reproduction – which accounts for the vast majority of births in the world today, and for a major proportion even in the West – a phenomenon of the past. But oral contraception – which has so far been developed in a form which exactly repeats the sexual inequality of Western society – is only at its beginnings. It is inadequately distributed across classes and countries and awaits further technical improvements. Its main initial impact is, in the advanced countries, likely to be psychological – it will certainly free women's sexual experience from many of the anxieties and inhibitions which have always afflicted it. It will definitely divorce sexuality from procreation as a necessary complement.

The demographic pattern of reproduction in the West may or may not be widely affected by oral contraception. One of the most striking phenomena of recent years in the United States has been the sudden increase in the birth rate. In the last decade it has been higher than that of underdeveloped countries such as India, Pakistan and Burma. In fact, this probably reflects simply the lesser economic burden of a large family in the richest country in the world. But it also reflects the magnification of familial ideology as a social force.

Socialization

The changes in the composition of the work force, the size of the family, the structure of education, and other factors – however limited from an ideal standpoint – have undoubtedly diminished the social function and importance of the family. As an organization it is not a significant unit in the political power system, it plays little part in economic production and it is rarely the sole agency of integration into the larger society; thus at the macroscopic level it serves very little purpose.

The result has been a major displacement of emphasis on to the family's psycho-social function, for the infant and for the couple. I have discussed the vital nucleus of truth in the emphasis on socialization of the child. It is essential that it is acknowledged and integrated entirely into any programme for the liberation of women. It is noticeable that it was one of the first concerns of the Women's Liberation Movement. Yet there is no doubt that the need for permanent, intelligent care of children in the initial three or four years of their lives can (and has been) exploited ideologically to perpetuate the family as a total unit, when its other functions have been visibly declining. Indeed, the attempt to focus women's existence exclusively on bringing up children, is manifestly harmful to children as well. Socialization is an exceptionally delicate process which requires a serene and mature socializer – a type which the frustrations of a *purely* family role are not liable to produce. Exclusive maternity is often in this sense 'counter-productive'. The mother discharges her own frustrations and anxieties in a fixation on the child. An increased awareness of the critical importance of socialization, far from leading to a restitution of classical maternal roles, should lead to a reconsideration of them – of what makes a good socializing agent who can genuinely provide security and stability for the child.

The same arguments apply with added force to the psycho-social role of the family for the couple. The belief that the family provides an impregnable enclave of intimacy and security in an atomized and chaotic cosmos assumes the absurd – that the family can be isolated from the community, and that its internal relationships will not reproduce in their own terms the external relationships which dominate the society. The family as a refuge from society in fact becomes a reflection of it.

Sexuality

The major structure which at present is in rapid evolution is sexuality. Production, reproduction, and socialization are all more or less stationary in the West today in that they have not changed for three or more decades. Sexual repression, on the contrary, is proving less and less successful in regulating spontaneous behaviour. Marriage in its classical form is increasingly threatened by the liberalization of relationships before and after it which affects all classes today. In this sense, it is evidently the weak link in the chain – the particular structure that is the site of the most contradictions. I have already emphasized the progressive potential of these contradictions. In a context of juridical equality, the liberation of sexual experience from relations which are extraneous to it – whether procreation or property – could lead to true inter-sexual freedom. But it could also lead simply to new forms of neo-capitalist ideology and practice. For one of the forces behind the current acceleration of sexual freedom has undoubtedly been the conversion of contemporary capitalism from a production-and-work ethos to a consumption-and-fun ethos. This was already commented on in the early 1950s:

> . . . there is not only a growth of leisure, but work itself becomes both less interesting and less demanding for many . . . more than before, as job-mindedness declines, sex permeates the daytime as well as the playtime consciousness. It is viewed as a consumption good not only by the old leisure class, but by the modern leisure masses.

The gist of Riesman's argument is that in a society bored by work, sex is the only activity, the only reminder of one's energies, the only competitive act; the last defence against *vis inertiae*. The same insight can be found, with greater theoretical depth, in Marcuse's notion of 'repressive desublimation' – the freeing of sexuality for its own frustration in the service of a coordinated and drugged social machine. Society at present can well afford a play area of premarital *non*-procreative sexuality. Even marriage can save itself by increasing divorce and remarriage rates, signifying the importance of the institution itself. These considerations make it clear that sexuality, while it could contain the potential for liberation, can equally well be organized against any increase of its human possibilities. The new forms of reification and the commercial consumption of sexuality may void sexual freedom of any meaning. This is a reminder that while one structure may be the *weak link* in a unity like that of woman's condition, there can never be a solution through it alone.

What, then, is a possible revolutionary attitude? It must include both immediate and fundamental demands, in a single critique of the *whole* of women's situation, that does not fetishize any dimension of it. Modern industrial development, as has been seen, tends towards the separating out of the originally unified function of the family – procreation, socialization, economic subsistence, etc. – even if this 'structural differentiation' has been checked and disguised by the maintenance of a powerful family ideology.

In practical terms this means a coherent system of demands. The four elements of women's condition cannot merely be considered each in isolation; they form a structure of specific interrelations. The contemporary family can be seen as a triptych of sexual, reproductive and socializatory functions (the woman's world) embraced by production (the man's world) – precisely a structure which in the final instance is determined by the economy. The exclusion of women from production – social human activity – and their confinement to a monolithic condensation of functions within a unity – the family – which is precisely unified in the *natural part* of each function, is the root cause of the contemporary *social* definition of women as *natural* beings. Any emancipation movement must still concentrate on the economic element – the entry of women fully into public industry and *the right to earn a living wage*. The error of the old socialists was to see the other elements as reducible to the economic; hence the call for the entry of women into production was accompanied by the purely abstract slogan of the abolition of the family. Economic demands must be accompanied by coherent policies for the other three elements; policies which at particular junctures may take over the primary role in immediate action.

Economically, the most elementary demand is not the right to work or receive equal pay for work – the two traditional demands – but *the right to equal work itself*. At present, women perform unskilled, uncreative, service jobs that can be regarded as 'extensions' of their expressive familial role. They are overwhelmingly waitresses, office-cleaners, hairdressers, clerks, typists. In the working class, occupational mobility is thus sometimes easier for girls than for boys – they can enter the white- collar sector at a lower level. But only two in a hundred women are in administrative or managerial jobs, and less than five in a thousand are in the professions. Women are poorly unionized and receive far less money than men for the manual work they perform: this, among other things, represents a massive increment of exploitation for the employer.

Education

The whole pyramid of economic discrimination rests on a solid extra-economical foundation – education. The demand for equal work, in Britain, should also take the form of a demand for an *equal educational system*. In post-compulsory education there is no evidence whatever of progress. The proportion of girl university students is the same as it was in the 1920s. Until these injustices are ended, there is no chance of equal work for women. It goes without saying that the content of the educational system, which actually instils limitation of aspiration in girls, needs to be changed as much as methods of selection.

Only if it is founded on equality can production be truly differentiated from reproduction and the family; and the woman at work not bear with her the attitudes of the home. But this in turn requires a whole set of non-economic demands as a complement. Reproduction, sexuality, and socialization also need to be free from coercive forms of unification. Traditionally, the socialist movement has called for the 'abolition of the bourgeois family'. This slogan must be rejected as incorrect today. It is maximalist in the bad sense, posing a demand which is merely a negation without any coherent construction subsequent to it. The reasons for the historic weakness of the notion is that the family was never analysed structurally – in terms of its different functions. It was a hypostatized entity – just like its ideology in contemporary society. The abstraction of its abolition corresponds to the abstraction of its conception. The strategic concern is the liberation of women and the equality of the sexes, not the abolition of the family. The consequences of this demand are no less radical, but they are concrete and positive, and can be integrated into the real course of history. The family, as it exists at present, is, in fact, incompatible with either women's liberation or the equality of the sexes. But equality will not come from its administrative abolition, but from the historical differentiation of its functions. The revolutionary demand should be for the liberation of these functions from an oppressive monolithic fusion. This dissociation of reproduction from sexuality frees sexuality from alienation in unwanted reproduction (and fear of it), and reproduction from subjugation to chance and uncontrollable causality. It is thus an elementary demand to press for free State provision for oral contraception. The straightforward abolition of illegitimacy as a legal notion as in Sweden and Russia has a similar implication; it would separate marriage civically from parenthood.

The problem of socialization poses more difficult questions, as has been seen. But the need for intensive care in the early years of a child's life does not mean that the present single sanctioned form of socialization – marriage and family – is inevitable. Nor that the mother is the only possible nurse. Far from it. The fundamental characteristic of the present system of marriage and family is in our society its *monolithism*; there is only one institutionalized form of inter-sexual or inter-generational relationship possible. It is that or nothing. This is why it is essentially a denial of life. For all human experience shows that inter-sexual and inter-generational relationships are infinitely various – indeed, much of our creative literature is a celebration of the fact – while the institutionalized expression of them in our capitalist society is utterly simple and rigid. It is the poverty and simplicity of the institutions in this area which are such an oppression. Any society will require some institutionalized and social recognition of personal relationships. But there is absolutely no reason why there should be only one legitimized form – and a multitude of unlegitimized experience. What we should seek for is not the abolition of

the family, but the diversification of the socially acknowledged relationships which are today forcibly and rigidly compressed into it. This
would mean a plural range of institutions – where the family is only one
such institution, and its abolition implies none. Couples – of the same or
of different sexes – living together or not living together, long-term unions
with or without children, single parents – male or female – bringing up
children, children socialized by conventional rather than biological parents. extended kin groups, etc. – all these could be encompassed in a
range of institutions which match the free invention and variety of men
and women.

This is what we can fight for. Yet today women are confined within the
family which is a segmentary, monolithic unit, largely separated off from
production and hence from social human activity. The reason why this
confinement is made possible is the demand for women to fulfil these
three roles: they must provide sexual satisfaction for their partners and
give birth to children and rear them. But the family does more than
occupy the woman: it produces her. It is in the family that the psychology
of men and women is founded. Here is the source of their definition.
What is this definition and what is the role of the family in the ideology of
it as the basic unit of society today?

Radicals and Marxists
C. Crouch

Reprinted with permission from Colin Crouch, *Trade Unions: the Logic of Collective Action*, Fontana Paperbacks, 1982, pp. 24–32

Radicals

The institutional pluralist school takes existing institutions for granted,
and views employers and workers (or unions) as constituting two 'sides' in
a more or less balanced struggle. It is this which has been criticized by
those I have called here the 'radical' school. Goldthorpe, a major example
of this school, commenting on the Donovan report, asserted:

> Because the starting point is with industrial relations problems, which
> are taken as indicating some failure of regulative institutions, there is
> little concern to go, as it were, behind these problems and to enquire
> into the social relationships and modes of action *which throw strain on
> such institutions* in the first place; that is, which create, and express,
> social conflict. Nowhere in the Donovan report, or in the entire tradi-

tion of industrial relations writing on which it drew so heavily, is there to be found any systematic consideration of how the functioning of the economic system as a whole and of its constituent units of production is founded upon, and sustains, vast differences in social power and advantage; nor of how there are then generated – in undoubtedly complex ways – on the one hand, objective oppositions of interest, and, on the other, subjective responses of frustration, resentment and antagonism, and also in some degree aspirations and movements towards an alternative dispensation. [Original italics]

Alan Fox distinguished the pluralist and radical approaches in similar terms. His position is particularly interesting in that he was for several years one of the pluralist school, and had, only a few years previously (1966), set out that school's standpoint as contrasted with the 'unitary' school in a document prepared for the Donovan Commission. Indeed, in the wake of the Commission's report he had been co-author, with Alan Flanders, of a paper which remains the main example of industrial-relations specialists going directly to classical sociology. They turned to the work of Emile Durkheim to interpret British industrial-relations problems as essentially those of a failure of *normative* framework. However, by 1974 Fox was writing:

Unlike the pluralist, however, the radical does not see the collective organization of employees into trade unions as restoring a balance of power (or anything as yet approaching it) between the propertied and the propertyless. He may well agree that it mitigates the imbalance and thereby enables employees to challenge some kinds of management decision on issues of special and immediate importance for them. But a great imbalance remains, symptomized by the fact that there are many other types of management decision which employees might aspire to influence were they conscious of having the power to do so, but from which they are presently completely excluded.

In calling proponents of these criticisms 'radical' one is not referring to their political beliefs, but to their intellectual approach – though the latter does sometimes imply the former. What is radical is the determination of this school to dig deeper into the social structure for its explanatory variables; it does not remain at the level of the explicitly industrial-relations institutions, nor does it take for granted the character of industrial conflict. Attention is instead directed at the abiding inequalities of the employment relationship, which leads the radicals to stress the endemic nature of conflict and the fact that its sources lie beyond the reach of institutional tinkering.

Another important characteristic of this school is its concern with workers' attitudes, frameworks of action, ideologies. Examining the industrial world from such a perspective often provides an account which contrasts sharply with those of conventional wisdom. Thus, Goldthorpe, commenting on the perplexity often expressed as to why workers seem to prefer a combination of time-wasting during the day with long hours of overtime to a short but intensive working day, argues that not only does the latter require workers to raise the intensity of their effort, but it also underestimates 'the possibility that time-wasting at the employer's expense may in itself be gratifying to workers'. Taking Flanders to task for saying that to take such a view implies a cynical view of humanity, he continues that workers in modern industrial enterprises

. . . do often view their relationship with their employing organization in essentially calculative, 'money for effort' terms. Where this is so, it would then seem perfectly understandable that, under certain conditions, they might prefer to gain a certain level of earnings through a longer period of effort rather than through a shorter period of higher effort. . . . Furthermore, there is also extensive evidence of workers' concern to maintain their autonomy in the performance of their work tasks and roles and, to this end, to exert control of their own over basic features of the work situation – control over *time* being seen in various ways as highly important . . . it is not difficult to appreciate that being able to apply such control *against* management could be found inherently rewarding. In addition, in the particular instance of time-wasting, it needs also to be appreciated that 'time out' may sometimes serve a significant social function for the work group; that is, it may provide opportunity for various activities through which the solidarity of the group, and the shared beliefs and values of its members, are daily reinforced.

This kind of work is very much from the heartland of modern British sociology as it has developed over the past twenty years or more. Its theoretical base has been established by such writers as John Rex and David Lockwood. They have depicted society as an arena within which social actors (individuals as well as groups) pursue conflicting goals according to various beliefs about means and ends. These beliefs constitute their ideology or consciousness, though these writers, unlike phenomenologists and ethnomethodologists, never lose sight of the fact that a rational calculation of advantage in a context of real power relations is always at stake. Few prior assumptions are made about the identity of institutions, which are contingent on action, and virtually no assumptions are made about the contours of the overall system; indeed, a lot of energy has been devoted to demolishing the very concept of an elaborated social system, especially as it had been presented in the works of Talcott

Parsons. Certainly there are no assumptions that mechanisms exist in society to check and absorb conflict; rather, the society is seen as shot through with potential conflicts as different groups of actors pursue mutually incompatible goals. These authors have something in common with Marxist writers in their emphasis on the continuous possibilities for conflicts of interests, but do not agree that these conflicts always concern *class* interests.

This approach, stressing the subjective states of social actors and the effects these states have on structuring their pursuit of frequently conflicting goals, is not the only way of doing sociology; I have already noted that the industrial-relations institutional school tends, indirectly, to draw on the work of Parsons, whose structural functionalism is very different. But it is the approach which predominates among British sociologists, whether they are studying industrial relations or other social phenomena.

Another characteristic of this school is, in contrast with the institutionalists, its lack of involvement in practical consultancy or policy-making. While this is in no way related to the previous point about theory, the two characteristics combine to give the work of this school a very noncommittal character. It tends to correct or adjust popular conceptions (either by empirical refutation or by critical argument), and to point to the folly of superficial institutional tinkering, but then stands back, rarely asserting any positive positions about the nature of trade-union activity.

Marxists

Finally, there are the Marxists. There are many different strands of Marxism within and around sociology, partly because we are here dealing with a political movement as much as an academic school, with elements of theory being treated more as articles of faith than as items of imperfect and contingent knowledge; and partly because Marxism, as a 'rebel' movement, always outside the academic establishment, is particularly vulnerable to swings of transitory fashion. But behind all the differences certain major features unite most Marxists and distinguish them from many other scholars in the field.

If the radicals were differentiated from the institutional pluralists by their digging deeper into the social structure to find their explanatory variables, the Marxists take this process further. The cornerstone of Marxist analysis is the identification of the class relationship between capital and labour as the major determinant of social relations, the major explanation of why social actors behave the way they do or of why particular institutions exist. The endemic conflicts of capitalist society are, for Marxists, essentially class conflicts; and the motor of social change is the working out of the contradictions inherent in a class society. From that perspective any social explanation that does not reduce its variables to class terms, but spends time on intermediate factors without tracing them back to class, is inadequate. Something of the flavour of this standpoint is captured in the critique of Fox's radicalism offered by Wood and Elliott. They claim that, while Fox uses a Marxist framework in order to criticize Clegg and other pluralists, when he comes himself to propose changes he assumes the possibility of gradual social improvements which maintain the divide between managers and managed. Indeed, they consider that his approach to change assumes that employers (the dominant class) will be willing to carry out reforms; his stress on 'trust' relations between managers and employees is 'conservative . . . elitist and technocratic'. His approach is therefore not really much different from that of the pluralists, as he believes in the 'mutual survival' of antagonistic class interests.

Fox, replying to this criticism, claimed that Wood and Elliott had misrepresented his theory at certain points. In particular, the argument that he saw all change as coming from management was based on just one essay of his, which happened to have been directed specifically at a managerial audience; in his work as a whole he had by no means taken the view that reforms always proceeded from the top – very much the reverse. More important, he distinguished between a 'commitment to liberal pluralism' (i) which meant believing that countries like Britain, with deep social inequalities, *were* already adequately liberal and pluralist, and (ii) that which meant that one believed in the values of liberal pluralism as a means of action and a desirable goal. The fact that he held to (ii) did not imply that he believed (i). Indeed, he continued, it was the association of Marxism with blanket attacks on any kind of liberal pluralism that led many people to believe that Marxists were actually opposed to liberal and pluralist values in principle – a factor which then led them to reject even the valid insights of Marxist analysis.

Marxists differ among themselves, but several of them would respond to Fox's counterattack by saying that yes, they did reject liberal pluralism as a value and not just as a professed description of fact; that the pluralism that 'balances' a dominant management and a subservient work force can never be a genuine pluralism; and that there could be a true liberation of the workers only when that very difference between employer- and employee-interests that rests at the heart of pluralism was destroyed in revolutionary struggle. There are, then, various Marxist answers to the question of what will replace the division between managers and managed, and how pluralism among different interests within the work force will be expressed if the emphasis of the labour movement has hitherto been placed on a monolithic struggle between the massed forces of capital and labour. These answers have to find their own solution to the fact that, to date, all cases of successful revolutions carried out in the name of Marx have replaced the division between capitalist managers and workers with

one between state managers and workers, and have rejected all subsequent expressions of dissent and conflict among workers.

This is a subject to which we shall return, but it is not the end of the
problems of Marxist analysis. While trade unionism seems an obvious
subject for a Marxist approach, it does in fact present great difficulties for
Marxist theory – difficulties which date back to Marx's own relations with
trade unionists in nineteenth-century Britain. On the one hand, unions
are (or seem to be) an expression of class conflict, of workers' dissatisfaction with capitalist society. But trade unionism tries to resolve workers'
grievances *within* the employment relationship: it looks for concessions
and improvements from the capitalists and stops short of revolutionary
activity. Orthodox Marxist theory of early twentieth-century communist
parties solved the problem this way: the unions were useful for an initial
mobilization of the working class, but, after a point, workers with revolutionary potential had to move on to activity within the communist
party to become true revolutionaries. Thus, in the evocative phrase of
French communists, the union serves as a 'conveyor belt' for the party,
bringing workers out of the mass of the apathetic and delivering them to
the party. But in practice that kind of relationship always causes problems
for unions. The union becomes severely subordinate to the party, rarely
daring to take up issues without party guidance for fear that it might
overstep its prescribed role. Thus Lenin had very little use for trade
unions, either in his political writings or in his practical activity; free trade
unions did not long survive the Russian Revolution, but were absorbed
and refashioned by the Bolshevik Party, which was by then almost
synonymous with the state. Subsequently, no trade-union movement has
maintained its autonomy from the state following a communist takeover
of government. It is notable that the only significant autonomous union to
be founded within a communist society, the Polish union Solidarity, is not
Marxist and has very difficult relations with the Marxist Polish state. In
societies with large but unsuccessful communist parties, their associated
union movements have become notorious for their incapacity to respond
alertly to workers' demands without reference to the party. Such was for a
long time the position in Italy, and still is in France.

The historical background for the Marxist study of trade unions is
therefore not as encouraging as might be supposed. However, over the
past two decades or so, certain changes have taken place. First, disillusion
with the Soviet Union following repeated evidence of its internal
brutality, from the invasion of Hungary in 1956 onwards, led to the
desertion of the communist party in Britain and other European countries
by many political activists who still found themselves on the left of
established labour and social democratic parties, and who set about forming and joining small Trotskyist and other groups. The intellectuals of
these movements were now freed from doctrines of the central role of the

party. Second, from the 1960s on, and especially from around 1968, shop-floor militancy became increasingly important as an industrial phenomenon, and, given government involvement in incomes policies, as a political phenomenon too. Left-wing intellectuals were able to embrace this development without the constraints and ambiguities of orthodox communists, and saw in it the new social force from which a revolutionary transformation of society might spring. From this essentially political concern has come a stream of writing and research which has often considerably increased our knowledge of union activity and workers' militancy on the shop floor.

Social Inequality and Social Integration in Modern Britain
J. H. Goldthorpe

Reprinted with permission from D. Wedderburn (ed.), *Poverty, Inequality and Class Structure,* Cambridge University Press, 1974

The concern of this chapter is not to add to the detailed knowledge of the overall extent and pattern of social inequality in modern Britain, nor to produce any new synthesis of the information that exists. It is, rather, with the relatively neglected problem of the implications of inequality for social integration. Prior to broaching this problem, however, three points concerning the general nature of social inequality must be made.

First, social inequality, in societies such as ours, is manifested in a very wide variety of ways – wider than is generally recognized in public discussion of the matter. For example, in addition to great inequalities in the distribution of income and wealth, further marked inequalities are involved in the ways in which economic rewards are *actually gained* – most importantly, in the content of work tasks and roles. There is by now ample evidence to show that wide differences exist between occupations and jobs in the extent to which they offer possibilities of *intrinsic* satisfaction to the individuals engaged in them or, on the other hand, are a source of psychological or social deprivation. To take an obvious contrast, the inequalities in reward between professional employment and factory work are clearly not confined simply to the differences in their income levels.

Again, one aspect of inequality in work which it *has* of late been somewhat fashionable to point to, and to decry, is that of the status differences which operate among different categories of employee in most industrial organizations; for instance, in such matters as methods of payment, 'clocking-in' and lateness rules, toilet, canteen or car-parking arrangements, and so on. But discussion of these questions has usually been carried on without any reference to the far more basic inequality represented by the steep gradient of *authority* within such organizations – which, in fact, status distinctions serve largely to symbolize.

The tendency here illustrated to conceive of inequality in a piecemeal manner, rather than as a multiform and pervasive phenomenon, results from a failure to appreciate in what, fundamentally, social inequality consists. This leads to the second point.

Social inequality in all its manifestations can be thought of as involving differences in social power and advantage: power being defined as the capacity to mobilize resources (human and non-human) in order to bring about a desired state of affairs; and advantage as the possession of, or control over, whatever in society is valued and scarce. Power and advantage are thus closely related. Power can be used to secure advantage, while certain advantages constitute the resources that are used in the exercise of power. Moreover, different forms of power and advantage tend in their very nature to be convertible: economic resources can be used to gain status or to establish authority; status can help to reinforce authority or to create economic opportunities; positions of authority usually confer status and command high economic rewards, and so on.

In this perspective, then, the way in which inequality structures virtually the whole of social life can be readily understood. Differences in social power and advantage, simply because they imply differences across the whole range of life-chances, always tend, other things being equal, to become generalized differences. Furthermore, it is important to add that this effect operates not only from one area of social life to another but also through time. Inequalities of condition at any one point in time create inequalities of opportunity for future achievement. For example, the intergenerational aspects of this phenomenon could be said to constitute the central problem thus far for the sociology of education. The results of research in this field provide impressive evidence of how, notably through the agency of the family, the stability of social strata tends to be maintained – despite the growing importance of education to career chances and the development of policies aimed at reducing non-academic influences on educational attainment.

It has, therefore, to be recognized, thirdly, that structures of social inequality of both condition and opportunity – or, in other words, systems of social stratification – are inherently highly resistant to change. The members of higher strata have the motivation and, in general, the resources to hold on to their position and to transmit it to their children, while the members of lower strata are often caught up in vicious circles of deprivation. This is not, of course, to suggest that change in stratification systems cannot, or does not, occur; but rather that any significant reduction in the degree of inequality will require purposive, well-designed and politically forceful action to this end – that it is unlikely to come about *simply* as the unsought for consequence of technological advance, economic growth, or any such like secular trends. Such developments may well modify certain forms of inequality; but they appear just as likely to accentuate others.

Indeed, far from industrial societies having 'built-in' processes which steadily diminish inequality – as some writers have claimed – what is striking, at least in the British case, is the frequently very limited effect of even the deliberate pursuit of equality through governmental action. For example, as already implied, the egalitarian aspects of educational policy over the last half century or so have resulted in only a very slight lessening in class differentials in educational opportunity – even though over the same period an enormous expansion of educational facilities has occurred. In a similar way, major improvements in medical services and general standards of health have failed over a long period to produce any appreciable reduction in relative class differentials in infant mortality and in many kinds of morbidity. And finally in this respect the stability of inequality in income distribution over the last thirty years may be noted.

In sum, one may say that social inequality, as observed in present-day Britain, takes the general form of a substantially self-maintaining structure of social groupings differentiated multifariously and often extremely in terms of the power and advantages that their members enjoy. What, then, are the consequences of this inequality for the integration of British society, that is to say, for the extent to which the actions of individuals and groups tend regularly to comply with recognized norms, and to be thus consistent with, rather than in conflict with or unrelated to, the expectations and actions of other individuals and groups?

This question, in certain of its aspects, has in fact been examined by a number of recent writers who have adopted a similar initial approach. They have started from the observation that in Britain considerable and abiding inequality does not apparently give rise to deeply divisive conflicts in which the existing social structure, political institutions included, is frequently and fundamentally called into question. They have then gone on to infer from this, not unreasonably, that the resentment of inequality among the less favoured sections of the population is neither particularly widespread nor particularly militant – and especially if comparisons are made with the situation in certain other industrial societies. Thus, the somewhat more specific problem which emerges from this approach is the following: why is it that, given the prevailing degree of social inequality, there is no widely supported and radical opposition to the existing sociopolitical order, and that at all levels of the stratification hierarchy attitudes of acceptance, if not of approval, are those most commonly found? At this point, analyses tend to divide into two main types which one might conveniently label 'social psychological' and 'culturalist'. The first type is best displayed in the work of Runciman.

Briefly, Runciman's argument is that to account for the discrepancy between the objective degree of inequality in British society and the actual awareness and resentment of this inequality, we must consider the 'reference groups' in terms of which individuals in the lower social strata assess their position. That is to say, we must consider the other groups in society – real or imagined – with which members of less favoured groups habitually *compare* themselves in evaluating their rewards, opportunities and social deserts generally, and in relation to which their expectations and aspirations are formed. If, for instance, the reference groups adopted by a certain membership group are located fairly closely in the stratification hierarchy to the membership group's own position, then the degree of felt inequality is likely to be quite slight, no matter what the overall range of factual inequalities may be. A strong sense of grievance is only to be expected if reference groups are selected in a more 'ambitious' way so that considerable inequality is perceived and is then, on the basis of the comparison made, regarded as illegitimate and unjust. In other words, the degree of *relative* deprivation – deprivation which is subjectively experienced and which may thus influence political behaviour – is primarily determined *by the structure of reference groups* rather than by the structure of inequality itself as the sociologist might describe it.

Runciman's own research, using both historical and survey methods, indicates that among the British working class reference groups are, and generally have been, restricted in scope; and that while some variation in this respect can be traced over time and from one form of inequality to another, no consistent trend is evident towards wider-ranging comparisons. Consequently, the disruptive potential that social inequality might be thought to hold remains in fact suppressed: social integration is furthered through perceptual and conceptual limitations.

Turning secondly to the 'culturalist' type of analysis it should be said that this has been chiefly elaborated by American social scientists interested in the question of the social bases of stable and effective democracy. In treating Britain as one of the relatively few countries whose polity might be thus described, these investigators have been led to examine – with differing degrees of directness – such issues as the following. Why among lower social strata in Britain is there not far more alienation from a political system which is elitist in itself and under which many other forms of inequality persist? Why is there no longer in Britain, if indeed there ever was, a powerful class-based social movement seeking radical structural changes of an egalitarian kind, and prepared if necessary to challenge existing political institutions in pursuit of its objectives?

In the explanations that are offered for the absence of these possible threats to stable democracy, major emphasis is laid on the nature of

British 'political culture'; that is, on the pattern or 'mix' of attitudes which research has shown to exist in British society towards political institutions and political life in general. Like other countries in which democracy flourishes, the argument runs, Britain has, in the course of her historical development, built up a political culture of a distinctive type. It is one characterized primarily by the *balance* that holds, even across lines of class and party, between participant, activist attitudes on the one hand and acquiescent, passive attitudes on the other; between emotional commitment to political principle and cool pragmatism; between consensus on matters of procedure and conflict over particular issues.

Through their socialization into this culture from childhood onwards, it is held, the majority of citizens come to feel a sense of unfanatical, but generally unquestioning, allegiance to the established political order, and one that is unlikely to be seriously disturbed by any grievances they may have over the distribution of social power and advantage. Such grievances do not lead to alienation from the political system since there is wide acceptance of the 'democratic myth' – the myth that the individual can influence political decisions and outcomes – and the system itself is not therefore seen as exploitive. Moreover, attitudes towards the political elite tend to be ones of trust, if not of deference, and the exercise of governmental authority is generally accepted as legitimate. For example, in one study survey data are presented to show that manual workers who believe that there are inordinately powerful groups in British society (such as 'big business') are just as much prepared to allow Government a wide sphere of authority as are workers who do not share in this belief. In other words, grievances arising out of inequality do not tend to become so highly politicized that established political institutions and processes are themselves challenged. Political awareness is in any case at only a moderate level, and politics is only rarely a central life interest. Consequently, the availability of the ordinary citizen for involvement in 'unstabilizing' mass movements is low; the political culture effectively inhibits the radical political action which marked social inequality might otherwise be expected to generate.

Clearly, social psychological and culturalist points of view on the issue in question are not incompatible: they could, rather, be represented as complementary and mutually supportive on the following lines. Because the reference groups of lower strata have remained generally restricted, political issues stemming from social inequality have tended to be relatively 'mild' and capable of being resolved or accommodated by existing political arrangements. This has, therefore, helped a basically 'allegiant' political culture to form. Reciprocally, the development of such a culture has been inimical to the spread of ideological thinking – as, say, on the matter of social justice – which could lead both to a heightened awareness of inequality and deprivation and to greater recognition of their political dimensions. In short, social psychological processes of the kind examined by Runciman could be seen as a necessary condition of the political culture of British democracy, while this culture in turn, once established, favours the persistence of these processes.

Despite the various criticisms with which they have met, the analyses reviewed do, in my opinion, go some important part of the way to explaining why the consequences of inequality in Britain are not socially divisive in an extreme degree. But what has to be kept in mind, and what should be emphasized, is that for the most part these analyses treat the problem of inequality and integration only from one particular angle. As noted earlier the focus of interest is on the possible *political* implications of inequality; and what is in effect illuminated is chiefly the question of why among the British working class there is found no significant support for political ideas and movements of a revolutionary cast, nor even the widespread *incivisme* which characterizes sections of, say, the French or Italian working class. However, there are other major aspects of the problem which may be distinguished, and ones which have been curiously neglected. In particular, I would advance the view – as the central thesis of this chapter – that the most far-reaching implications of inequality for the integration of British society occur not in the political sphere but rather in that of economic life; and that they are manifested not in a situation of fundamental class struggle but rather in a situation of anomie; that is, in a situation in which to stay close to the original Durkheimian notion, there is a lack of *moral* regulation over the wants and goals that individuals hold. This contention can best be elaborated by reference to two closely related topics of current public concern: industrial relations and incomes policy.

In a paper – entitled 'The Reform of Collective Bargaining: from Donovan to Durkheim' – two leading authorities, Fox and Flanders, have in fact argued explicitly and at length that the British system of industrial relations is now in an anomic state. In the post-war period, these authors observe, the wants, expectations and aspirations of industrial workers have expanded notably, and not only in regard to wage levels but also in regard to such matters as security of employment, job rights and control over work organization. At the same time, generally high levels of employment have given many groups of workers the power to pursue their new goals with some effectiveness. A frequent outcome has then been that such groups have broken through the regulation of work relationships imposed by collective agreements at a national level and have secured agreements of a more favourable kind at company, plant or shop level. Thus, Fox and Flanders argue, industrial relations have become disordered in two main ways: first, as a result of the problems involved in developing new normative systems, capable of accommodating the new issues of industrial conflict which now arise; and second, and more seriously, because the solutions arrived at so far have tended to be *ad hoc* and piecemeal ones of only limited, local application. This tendency has therefore given rise to a proliferation of normative systems based on often unrelated or divergent principles; and such a situation is one rife with anomalies, frustrations and rivalries which constantly generate new tensions and conflicts both between employers and workers and between different sorts of workers: 'Disorder feeds upon disorder.' The consequences of this anomic state are then to be seen not simply in strikes and other dislocations of the productive process, but further 'in such things as chaotic pay differentials and uncontrolled movements of earnings and labour costs'. Thus, it is claimed, threats are posed to the long-term development of the economy (apart from the aggravation of short-term balance of payments problems) and there could, furthermore, be serious political implications: increasing disorder might generate popular demands for State intervention of an authoritarian kind which would mark the end of the present pluralistic and voluntary basis of industrial relations.

The analysis offered by Fox and Flanders is insightful and important. However, I would suggest that it is one that does not go far enough in revealing just how deeply rooted in the structure of British society is the 'disorderly' situation with which it is concerned; and, further, that this limitation results precisely from the fact that Fox and Flanders do not follow Durkheim in relating the problem of anomie to the problem of inequality. This argument can best be illustrated by reference to their recommendations for reform in industrial relations – that is, for the 'reconstruction of normative order'. Briefly, what they stress is the continuing need for an incomes policy, accompanied by the regularizing and rationalizing of collective bargaining from plant and company levels upwards. In this latter respect, they point to the availability and usefulness of such techniques as productivity bargaining and job evaluation and other means of measuring and rewarding different kinds of work. Through a programme of reform on the lines in question, they see the possibility of achieving a more logical wages structure, greater control over earnings and labour costs, and industrial relations institutions which, through being more adaptable to change themselves, will be better able to manage the conflicts that change inevitably produces.

Fox and Flanders recognize that there is no guarantee that such objectives will in fact be achieved, and they refer to the 'Promethean character' of the task of reform. None the less, I would argue that they still underestimate the difficulties that are involved: in particular, in creating an area of relatively rational and orderly inequality in place of the present 'wages jungle' *when this jungle is simply part of a wider structure of inequality which has no rationale whatsoever* – other, perhaps, than the principle of 'to them that have shall more be given'. For example, at one point in their paper, Fox and Flanders remark that 'The debate on incomes policy is often conducted within the trade union movement as if collective bargaining were simply a mechanism for pursuing social justice as between capital and labour, and its function of determining the relative fortunes of different groups of labour is ignored.' This may be fair comment, but it is still highly questionable if an incomes policy of the kind they favour can be effective in establishing a less chaotic and more equitable pattern of earning *within* the working class in the context of the *overall* degree of economic inequality which statistics on the distribution of income and wealth reveal. An industrial worker seeking a wage increase might be prepared to recognize that his claim was weak in comparison with that of, say, certain of his lower-paid workmates; but he would have no difficulty in finding other groups, possibly outside the working class, in relation to whom his claim could be much better justified – even assuming that his range of reference groups was not extensive. Moreover, it should be emphasized here that while restricted reference groups may inhibit feelings of grievance over inequalities, this is not to say they actually motivate individuals to *hold back* from attempting to improve their position, especially economically: limited social horizons are not, as Durkheim might have put it, a source of moral restraint.

Now it must be said that Fox and Flanders are well aware – indeed, they emphasize – that the normative regulation resulting from collective bargaining is unlikely ever to rest purely upon consensus; it will also be a product of the balance of power between the parties concerned and of their calculation of what, for the time being, is the most advantageous position they can achieve. What may further be involved, at least in initiating any reform, is some kind of third-party intervention – 'the forceful articulation of common norms by some authoritative source'. However, to follow Durkheim's argument closely here, one has to insist that in so far as the normative order in economic life is *not* based upon consensus, but is rather founded upon coercion or expediency, then the threat of anomie and of chronic malintegration remains – no matter what degree of internal logic or coherence normative systems may be given. For as Durkheim stresses, unless in modern society the regulation of economic life – and, crucially, the regulation of inequality – *does* have some accepted moral basis, then it is unlikely to be effective in any continuing way. To the extent that the normative order is imposed by superior power, fundamental discontent and unrest persist if only in latent form; to the extent that it results from the calculation of advantage under given (non-moral) constraints, it is likely to be called into question as soon as these constraints vary.

Thus, while proposals for reform of the kind that Fox and Flanders put forward might well endow collective bargaining institutions and procedures with a good deal more formal rationality than they at present possess, I find it difficult to believe that such measures could go very far towards ensuring *stable* normative systems, of either a substantive or a procedural kind, at any level of industrial relations. The absence of an accepted moral basis for economic life as a whole in our kind of society must always render precarious the norms which at any time prevail in any specific area – a plant, company, industry, etc. As but one illustration of this point, taken from Durkheim's own discussion of the problem, one may consider the implications of inequalities of opportunity for attitudes towards inequalities of condition. If the former are extreme and without effective legitimation, little consensus can be expected on the latter – even supposing that some hierarchy of social positions and role is generally acknowledged. For, as Durkheim argued, 'it would be of little avail for everyone to recognize the justice of the hierarchy of functions as established by public opinion, if they did not also consider just the way in which individuals are recruited to these functions'. While ever, then, British society is characterized by the present marked degree of inequality in educational and occupational opportunity, it is difficult to see that there is any basis for the achievement of what Fox and Flanders regard as the ultimate objective of industrial relations reform; namely, 'agreed normative codes regulating the production and distribution of wealth in modern industrial society' – or, at all events, agreement will for the majority remain highly qualified, reluctant or uncertain, and thus inherently *unstable*. One need not assume that rank-and-file industrial employees resent the inferior life-chances they have been accorded as keenly as the facts might warrant in order to claim that few will feel *morally* bound by the normative codes which govern their working lives. It is sufficient to ask from what source, given the nature of the British social order, such a sense of moral commitment might stem.

The conclusion must then be that the reconstruction of normative order in British industrial relations which Fox and Flanders pursue is something of an *ignis fatuus*. Within a society in which inequality exists as brute fact – largely without moral legitimation – 'disorderly' industrial relations cannot be understood as a particular pathological development which will yield to particular remedies: rather, to maintain a Durkheimian perspective, this disorder must be seen as 'normal' – as a generalized characteristic of societies of the type in question.

The structural features of British society which stand in the way of the reform of industrial relations are at the same time obstructive, as the foregoing discussion would imply, to the effective administration of an incomes policy. The aim of incomes policy, within a market economy such as our own, is usually stated to be that of controlling the growth of incomes so that inflationary tendencies may be kept in check while still preserving relatively high levels of employment and utilized capacity. However, it is essential to appreciate that an incomes policy is not, and cannot be, just another economic instrument – despite the attempt of certain technocratically minded economists to present it in this guise. Once a Government attempts to regulate incomes, in no matter how piecemeal or partial a fashion, it is forced into the position of arbiter on particular wage levels or wage changes, and issues of social justice thus inevitably arise and have in some way or other to be resolved. Indeed, Government spokesmen in Britain have been generally prepared to acknowledge this situation and even to claim that an incomes policy is, or could be, a means of enhancing social justice; for example, by ensuring a better deal for the lowest-paid workers. But it is basically on account of this normative aspect of incomes policy that its administration runs into serious problems which have not as yet been overcome, and which may, for reasons I shall shortly suggest, be self-aggravating ones.

At the root of the difficulty is again the fact that not only is the existing distribution of income and wealth in British society 'unprincipled' – but further that there appears to be little consensus on the principles which *ought* to apply when it is a question of maintaining or altering any specific income level or relativity. Survey data are of some relevance to this argument, but more significant is the great variety of frequently conflicting considerations which are actually invoked when pay issues are debated. Some criteria, for example, would entail at least the possibility of significant change in the existing pay structure – increased productivity, job evaluation ratings, 'absolutely' low wages or persisting manpower shortages: but other criteria, such as increases in the cost of living, the need to preserve a differential or maintain the social status of a particular group, are essentially conservative in their implications. Moreover, as Professor (now Lady) Wootton has pointed out, claims for more pay based on *any* of these often conflicting criteria can be, and usually are, couched in moral terms, or at any rate the economic arguments are related back to moral premises. Thus, one is again forced to the conclusion that little basis for moral *restraint* is currently to be found in British society – that, in other words, a condition of anomie prevails. Given the diversity of moral positions that are tenable in the existing state of public opinion, virtually any occupational group seeking a pay increase is likely to be able to find some kind of legitimation for pressing its case.

From this standpoint, then, it is to be expected that the amount of 'voluntary' support for an incomes policy will be insufficient to enable it to achieve its ends; and such an expectation seems to be generally in accord with British (and other) experience. Furthermore, even when control over incomes is in some way or other 'imposed', it still appears difficult, at least within the constraints on governmental authority that liberal democracy entails, for such control to be very effective for very long. A 'norm' for pay increases may hold up for a short-run period and even a complete 'freeze' may work under crisis conditions – as in Britain, 1966–7. But in the longer term control invariably seems to break down, most notably at the level at which coercive methods are least feasible – that is, at the grass-roots level of the individual enterprise. A tendency for the actual earnings of many groups of workers to rise above the intended norm, as a result of collective agreements or other less formal arrangements locally made, has to be reckoned as the besetting problem of incomes policy administration – and even, it seems, in 'centrally planned' economies such as that of the USSR.

Thus, as one economist, John Corina, has pointed out, 'the unpalatable facts of wage drift', once recognized, pose a hard dilemma so far at any rate as Britain is concerned. Either an attempt must be made to extend the range and increase the stringency of income control, to the point at which voluntary collective bargaining ceases to exist and at risk of building up a considerable pressure of opposition; or it must be accepted that, under existing conditions, incomes policy initiatives are inherently *unstable* in their effects, and that their progressive breakdown is to be anticipated as a matter of course. Unlike some of his colleagues, Corina is prepared to recognize that 'At bottom, the crucial tangles of incomes policy stem from the intangible concept of "social justice" in income distribution', and are inseparable from issues raised both by the existing structure of inequality and by the lack of accord on what form this structure should possess. As he pertinently asks: ' . . . how can incomes policy create consent where social valuations of incomes, within a given incomes distribution, are confused and often obscure?'

Moreover, one point which Corina does not consider is that attempts to implement incomes policy may have quite unforeseen consequences which in fact tend to build up the difficulties involved. It is not simply that a 'freeze' or period of tight control over incomes may be followed by heightened militancy in wage demands, threatening greater inflationary problems than before. There is a further, yet more awkward, possibility; namely, that through increasing information about, and interest in, differences between occupational rewards and conditions, the actual operation of an incomes policy will serve to broaden comparative reference groups among the mass of the population, and at the same time bring issues of equity and fairness into greater subjective salience. Thus, following Runciman's analysis, one would expect, in the case of the working class at least, a growing sense of resentment and grievance over the *status quo* and, in turn, a yet greater unwillingness to accept 'restraint' or to hold back in any way from the direct pursuit of their own maximum advantage. In other words, what are sometimes called the 'educative' functions of incomes policy may well have the effect of undermining the viability of such policy. To the extent that evaluations of income and other economic differences do become less confused and obscure, there is little reason to suppose that what will emerge will be greater consensus from one group or stratum to another: the far more likely outcome, given the prevailing degree of inequality, is that conflicts will become more clearly defined and more widely recognized – that the anomic state of economic life will be made increasingly manifest.

To recapitulate, then, the two central arguments have been the following: first, that social inequality in Britain appears to pose no direct threat to the stability of the political order – because this is, as it were, 'insulated' from the potentially disruptive consequences of inequality by a combination of social-psychological and cultural influences; but second, that the existence of inequality, of an extreme, unyielding and largely un-legitimated kind, does militate seriously against any stable normative regulation in the economic sphere – because it militates against the possibility of effective value consensus on the distribution of economic, and other, resources and rewards.

Social Justice
W. G. Runciman

Reprinted with permission from W. G. Runciman, 'Social Justice', the *Listener*, 29 July 1965

There are, broadly speaking, three different and mutually incompatible theories of social justice: the conservative, the liberal, and the socialist. In the conservative theory, social justice consists in a social hierarchy, but a hierarchy governed by a stable system of interconnected rights and duties. Those at the top are the holders not merely of privilege but of responsibility for the welfare of those below; and through the recognition that different strata in society have different functions to fulfil, the hierarchy is accepted without dissension or envy as long as the responsibilities imposed on each class are in fact properly exercised.

In the liberal theory, by contrast, there is also a hierarchy; but this hierarchy is only legitimate if it has been arrived at from a position of initial equality. The liberal is not against inequality, but against privilege. He demands equality not of condition but of opportunity. He places a value not on an elite of caste, or inherited culture, but of individual attainment. The socialist theory, finally, is the strictly egalitarian theory. It may or may not require as a corollary that the State should play a predominant part in economic affairs. This is really only a means to an end – the maximum of social equality in any and all its aspects.

All three of these theories are persuasive, and internally consistent. How, therefore, can one adjudicate between them? How, having looked at the social structure of twentieth-century England, are we to judge it by the standard of social justice except by appealing to whichever one theory happens to suit our own interests or temperament? By what possible criterion can one be shown to be any more or less arbitrary than the other two? There is no one just distribution of the national income, no one just constitution, no one just mode of social relations. But what it is worth looking for is a principle. We may be able to find not a set of rules for the one just society but a criterion by which a set of rules as such may be assessed. We want to be able to say, not 'Is this particular inequality unjust?' but, 'Does this inequality derive from a rule which could not be defended by appeal to the notion of justice?'

The notion of justice which best enables us to assess a system of inequalities is not the conservative, or liberal, or socialist notion as such, but one which goes behind all three. It is a notion of justice which has been recently put forward by Professor John Rawls of Harvard, and which may be summarized as follows: the essence of justice is fairness, and for an understanding of the concept of fairness the most appropriate model is that of a contract between equal persons. This does not mean in any sense a reversion to the theory of a social contract which actually happened in the state of nature. It means only that when assessing particular inequalities which we find we must ask one simple question: is this an inequality defensible by a principle which we could have agreed before we had any idea which of the unequal positions we should eventually occupy?

A just system, therefore, is a system to which people would have agreed if they had had to decide on the principles by which social systems were to be regulated before they knew either what their own system would be or what would be their own place in it. Suppose I had to decide on the principles by which education was to be run in my eventual society before I knew either where I would be placed in the social hierarchy or what the abilities or temperaments of myself or my children would be. Would I agree that the best education should go to the children of the richest parents? I think there is no doubt that I would not; and by this token any educational system of such a kind is demonstrably unjust.

Should no inequality be justified?

It might seem that this line of argument leads directly to the socialist view of social justice. You may feel that we would all, in the state of nature, have agreed that no inequality should be justified – that all jobs should be equally rewarded, that everyone should treat everyone else as a social equal, and that nobody should have more power than anybody else. But one of the virtues of Rawls's model is that it shows that what would have been agreed is not a total egalitarianism. In Rawls's state of nature, we should only have agreed that no inequality could be justified in our eventual society unless it followed from a principle agreed in advance of vested interest. The contract model is, therefore, fundamentally egalitarian, but only in this special sense. It requires all inequalities to be justified. But among those which it justifies there may well be some which would be justified also by the conservative or liberal theories of social justice.

The suggestion that everyone should receive an equal reward breaks down at once. If, as far as I know, I may turn out to be a man doing a difficult and responsible job with long hours, and to have in addition many dependants to support, I will surely want to be able to claim a higher reward than will be allotted to a man who has no dependants and an easy half-time job. I will, conversely, be prepared to concede this even if I in fact turn out to be the second man (having had, as far as I knew, an equal chance of being either). In fact, I shall be prepared to agree on three principles by which I shall be willing, if it so turns out, to be the loser. These principles, which in their various forms are familiar throughout the history of political theory, are need, merit, and contribution to the common good. By merit I do not, of course, mean moral virtue, but things like danger money; and the criterion of merit must also be linked with the third criterion: contribution to the common good – it would be absurd to suggest that, say, an outstanding solver of crosswords should be paid an extravagant income unless the solving of crosswords contributed in some widely accepted sense to the national welfare. But these three principles, however difficult their application in practice, would surely be agreed by people in the state of nature who did not yet know what their position in the social structure would turn out to be.

No acceptable formula

This argument obviously is not enough to show whether a coalminer contributes more to the national welfare than an architect, whether a laboratory technician should be paid more than a policeman, or whether the State should provide a family allowance for the first as well as subsequent children. But there is never going to be a formula which will answer such questions as these. The concept of social justice can only be brought to bear at a different level – the level at which we can establish the principles by appeal to which any divergence from strict equality can be justified.

If we picture ourselves in a state of nature, we can agree for a start that jobs requiring a long training and a high degree of skill and fulfilling an essential need should be accorded higher reward than where this is not so. We can also agree that any unemployed person willing to work should have a claim on the communal resources on the grounds of need; if I know that I have as good a chance of finding myself in this position as in any other, I shall surely want to stipulate in advance that I should have a claim on the communal resources even at the price of conceding this claim if I should turn out to be among the employed. This much might be agreed on any theory of justice; even the more extreme versions of the conservative or liberal theories do not nowadays require the unemployed to starve. But there are three consequences which follow from Rawls's theory of justice which are rather more important. The first is the importance of needs. The second is the irrelevance of conventional comparisons. The third is the requirement of redistribution.

The most obvious provisions that follow from this are hardly at issue in contemporary Britain. We have freedom of speech, restrictions on theft or assault, and universal suffrage. But there is still a case to be made for saying that there is less equality of power in our social structure than would be consonant with what would have been agreed from the state of nature. Whatever position I turned out to occupy in twentieth-century Britain, I would surely want a maximum of say in the decisions by which my life was governed; and any inequality of power would have to be justified in the light of this injunction. Would it not therefore be just that workers should have a greater say in management? The reasons why such demands have not been more strongly pressed is largely – perhaps even entirely – because they are impracticable. But because justice is impracticable it does not cease to be justice; and if the ordinary worker has less say in the decisions by which his working life is governed than we should all have wished to stipulate before knowing what our own location would be in the economy of industrialized Britain, then this is a social injustice.

But – and it is a big but – to show that a social structure is unjust is not to show either how it ought to be changed or even that it ought to. Would more people be happier in a just society? Even if they would, might not more unhappiness than happiness be caused in the transition to justice? Inequalities are always least resented when expectations are low; and, conversely, deprivations are most strongly felt when a previous expectation has been disappointed. This much, indeed, is a truism. But it has the important consequence that the reformer, in attempting to make society just, may risk causing as much unhappiness as he will cure. Whether a system is just or not has nothing to do with people's attitudes towards it; even if slaves preferred to be slaves, this would not make slavery just, and even if everyone was miserable under a just regime, this would not make it unjust. In the same way, the efficiency or even the workability of a system has no necessary connection with its justice. It never follows, from the fact that a system is unjust, that it must be undone, and it is only by recognizing this that a clear and useful appeal to the notion of social justice can be made.

The Class Bias

H. Spencer

Reprinted with permission from Herbert Spencer, *The Study of Sociology*, Appleton and Co., 1873, pp.241–6

Many years ago a solicitor, sitting by me at dinner, complained bitterly of the injury which the then lately established County Courts were doing his profession. He enlarged on the topic in a way implying that he expected me to agree with him in therefore condemning them. So incapable was he of going beyond the professional point of view, that what he regarded as a grievance he thought I also ought to regard as a grievance: oblivious of the fact that the more economical administration of justice of which his lamentation gave me proof, was to me, not being a lawyer, matter for rejoicing.

The bias thus exemplified is a bias by which nearly all have their opinions warped. Naval officers disclose their unhesitating belief that we are in imminent danger because the cry for more fighting ships and more sailors has not been met to their satisfaction. The debates on the purchase-system proved how strong was the conviction of military men that our national safety depended on the maintenance of an army-organization like that in which they were brought up, and had attained their respective ranks. Clerical opposition to the Corn-Laws showed how completely that view which Christian ministers might have been expected to take, was shut out by a view more congruous with their interests and alliances. In all classes and sub-classes it is the same. Hear the murmurs uttered when, because of the Queen's absence, there is less expenditure in entertainments and the so-called gaieties of the season, and you perceive that London traders think the nation suffers if the consumption of superfluities is checked. Study the pending controversy about co-operative stores *versus* retail shops, and you find the shop-keeping mind possessed by the idea that Society commits a wrong if it deserts shops and goes to stores – is quite unconscious that the present distributing system rightly exists only as a means of economically and conveniently supplying consumers, and must yield to another system if that should prove more economical and convenient. Similarly with other trading bodies, general and special – similarly with the merchants who opposed the repeal of the Navigation Laws; similarly with the Coventry-weavers, who like free-trade in all things save ribbons.

The class-bias, like the bias of patriotism, is a reflex egoism; and like it has its uses and abuses. As the strong attachments citizens feel for their nation cause that enthusiastic co-operation by which its integrity is maintained in presence of other nations, severally tending to spread and subjugate their neighbours; so the *esprit de corps* more or less manifest in each specialized part of the body politic, prompts measures to preserve the integrity of that part in opposition to other parts, all somewhat antagonistic. The egoism of individuals leads to an egoism of the class they form; and besides the separate efforts, generates a joint effort to get an undue share of the aggregate proceeds of social activity. The aggressive tendency of each class, thus produced, has to be balanced by like aggressive tendencies of other classes. The implied feelings do, in short, develop one another; and the respective organizations in which they embody themselves develop one another. Large classes of the community marked-off by rank, and sub-classes marked-off by special occupations, severally combine, and severally set up organs advocating their interests: the reason assigned being in all cases the same – the need for self-defence.

Along with the good which a society derives from this self-asserting and self-preserving action, by which each division and sub-division keeps itself strong enough for its functions, there goes, among other evils, this which we are considering – the aptness to contemplate all social arrangements in their bearings on class-interests, and the resulting inability to estimate rightly their effects on Society as a whole. The habit of thought produced perverts not merely the judgments on questions which directly touch class-welfare; but it perverts the judgments on questions which touch class-welfare very indirectly, if at all. It fosters an adapted theory of social relations of every kind, with sentiments to fit the theory; and a characteristic stamp is given to the beliefs on public matters in general. Take an instance.

Whatever its technical ownership may be, Hyde Park is open for the public benefit: no title to special benefit is producible by those who ride and drive. It happens, however, that those who ride and drive make large use of it daily; and extensive tracts of it have been laid out for their convenience: the tracts for equestrians having been from time to time increased. Of people without carriages and horses, a few, mostly of the kinds who lead easy lives, use Hyde Park frequently as a promenade. Meanwhile, by the great mass of Londoners, too busy to go so far, it is scarcely ever visited: their share of the general benefit is scarcely appreciable. And now what do the few who have a constant and almost exclusive use of it, think about the occasional use of it by the many? They are angry when, at long intervals, even a small portion of it, quite distant from their haunts, is occupied for a few hours in ways disagreeable to them – nay, even when such temporary occupation is on a day during which Rotten Row is nearly vacant and the drives not one-third filled. In this, anyone unconcerned may see the influence of the class-bias. But he will have an inadequate conception of its distorting power unless he turns to some letters from members of the ruling class published in the *Times* in November last, when the question of the Park-Rules was being agitated. One writer, signing himself 'A Liberal MP', expressing his disgust at certain addresses he heard, proposed, if others would join him, to give the offensive speakers punishment by force of fists; and then, on a subsequent day, another legislator, similarly moved, writes:–

'If "MP" is in earnest in his desire to get some honest men together to take the law into their own hands, I can promise him a pretty good backing from those who are not afraid to take all the consequences.
I am, Sir, your obedient servant,
"AN EX-MP"'

And thus we find class-feeling extinguishing rational political thinking so completely that, wonderful to relate, two law-makers propose to support the law by breaking the law!

In larger ways we have of late seen the class-bias doing the same thing – causing contempt for those principles of constitutional government slowly and laboriously established, and prompting a return to barbaric principles of government. Read the debate about the payment of Governor Eyre's expenses, and study the division-lists, and you see that acts which, according to the Lord Chief Justice, 'have brought reproach not only on those who were parties to them, but on the very name of England', can nevertheless find numerous defenders among men whose class-positions, military, naval, official, &c., make them love power and detest resistance. Nay more, by raising an Eyre-Testimonial Fund and in other ways, there was shown a deliberate approval of acts which needlessly suspended orderly government and substituted unrestrained despotism. There was shown a deliberate ignoring of the essential question raised, which was – whether an executive head might, at will, set aside all those forms of administration by which men's lives and liberties are guarded against tyranny.

More recently, this same class-bias has been shown by the protest made when Mr Cowan was dismissed for executing the Kooka rioters who had surrendered. The Indian Government, having inquired into the particulars, found that this killing of many men without form of law and contrary to orders, could not be defended on the plea of pressing danger; and finding this, it ceased to employ the officer who had committed so astounding a deed, and removed to another province the superior officer who had approved of the deed. Not excessive punishment, one would say. Some might contend that extreme mildness was shown in thus inflicting no greater evil than is inflicted on a labourer when he does not execute his work properly. But now mark what is thought by one who displays in words the bias of the governing classes, intensified by life in India. In a letter published in the *Times* of May 15, 1872, the late Sir Donald M'Leod writes concerning this dismissal and removal:–

'All the information that reaches me tends to prove that a severe blow has been given to all chance of vigorous or independent action in future, when emergencies may arise. The whole service appears to have been astonished and appalled by the mode in which the officers have been dealt with.'

That we may see clearly what amazing perversions of sentiment and idea are caused by contemplating actions from class points of view, let us turn from this feeling of sympathy with Mr Cowan, to the feeling of detestation shown by members of the same class in England towards a man who kills a fox that destroys his poultry. Here is a paragraph from a recent paper:–

'Five poisoned foxes have been found in the neighbourhood of Penzance, and there is consequently great indignation among the western sportsmen. A reward of 20/- has been offered for information that shall lead to the conviction of the poisoner.'

So that wholesale homicide, condemned alike by religion, by equity, by law, is approved, and the mildest punishment of it blamed; while vulpicide, committed in defence of property, and condemned neither by religion, nor by equity, nor by any law save that of sportsmen, excites an anger that cries aloud for positive penalties!

I need not further illustrate the more special distortions of sociological belief which result from the class-bias. They may be detected in the conversations over every table, and in the articles appearing in every party-journal or professional publication. The effects here most worthy of our attention are the general effects – the effects produced on the minds of the upper and lower classes. Let us observe how greatly the prejudices generated by their respective social positions, pervert the conceptions of employers and employed. We will deal with the employed first.

As before shown, mere associations of ideas, especially when joined with emotions, affect our beliefs, not simply without reason but in spite of reason – causing us, for instance, to think there is something intrinsically repugnant in a place where many painful experiences have been received, and something intrinsically charming in a scene connected with many past delights. The liability to such perversions of judgment is greatest where *persons* are the objects with which pleasures and pains are habitually associated. One who has often been, even unintentionally, a cause of gratification, is favourably judged; and an unfavourable judgment is formed of one who, even involuntarily, has often inflicted sufferings. Hence, when there are social antagonisms, arises the universal tendency to blame the *individuals*, and to hold them responsible for the *system*.

It is thus with the conceptions the working-classes frame of those by whom they are immediately employed, and of those who fill the higher social positions. Feeling keenly what they have to bear, and tracing sundry real grievances to men who buy their labour and men who are most influential in making the laws, artizans and rustics conclude that, considered individually and in combination, those above them are personally bad – selfish, or tyrannical, in special degrees. It never occurs to them that the evils they complain of result from the average human nature of our age. And yet were it not for the class-bias, they would see in their dealings with one another, plenty of proofs that the injustices they suffer are certainly not greater, and possibly less, than they would be were the higher social functions discharged by individuals taken from among themselves. The simple fact, notorious enough, that working-men who save money and become masters, are not more considerate than usual towards those they employ, but often the contrary, might alone convince them of this. On all sides there is ample evidence having kindred meaning. Let them inquire about the life in every kitchen where there are several servants, and they will find quarrels about supremacy, tyrannies over juniors who are made to do more than their proper work, throwings of blame from one to another, and the many forms of misconduct caused by want of right feeling; and very often the evils growing up in one of these small groups exceed in intensity the evils pervading society at large. The doings in workshops, too, illustrate in various ways the ill-treatment of artizans by one another. Hiding the tools and spoiling the work of those who do not conform to their unreasonable customs, prove how little individual freedom is respected among them. And still more conspicuously is this proved by the internal governments of their trade-combinations. Not to dwell on the occasional killing of men among them who assert their rights to sell their labour as they please, or on the frequent acts of violence and intimidation committed by those on strike against those who undertake the work they have refused, it suffices to cite the despotism exercised by trades-union officers. The daily acts of these make it manifest that the ruling powers set up by working-men, inflict on them grievances as great as, if not greater than, those inflicted by the ruling powers, political and social, which they decry. When the heads of an association he has joined forbid a collier to work more than three days in the week – when he is limited to a certain 'get' in that space of time – when he dares not accept from his employer an increasing bonus for every extra day he works – when, as a reason for declining, he says that he should be made miserable by his comrades, and that even his wife would not be spoken to; it becomes clear that he and the rest have made for themselves a tyranny worse than the tyrannies complained of. Did he look at the facts apart from class-bias, the skilful artizan, who in a given time can do more than his fellows, but who dares not do it because he would be 'sent to Coventry' by them, and who consequently cannot reap the benefit of his superior powers, would see that he is thus aggressed upon by his fellows more seriously than by Acts of Parliament or combinations of capitalists. And he would further see that the sentiment of justice in his own class is certainly not greater than in the classes he thinks so unjust.

/

The Welfare State
R. M. Titmuss

Reprinted with permission from Richard Titmuss, *Commitment to Welfare*, Allen and Unwin, 1968, pp. 195–8

The major positive achievement which has resulted from the creation of direct, universalist, social services in kind has been the erosion of formal discriminatory barriers. One publicly approved standard of service, irrespective of income, class or race, replaced the double standard which invariably meant second-class services for second-class citizens. This has been most clearly seen in the National Health Service. Despite strict controls over expenditure on the Service by Conservative Governments for many years it has maintained the principle of equality of access by all citizens to all branches of medical care. Viewed solely in terms of the welfare objective of non-discriminatory, non-judgemental service this is the signal achievement of the National Health Service. In part this is due to the fact that the middle classes, invited to enter the Service in 1948, did so and have since largely stayed with the Service. They have not contracted out of socialized medical care as they have done in other fields like secondary education and retirement pensions. Their continuing participation, and their more articulate demands for improvements, have been an important factor in a general rise in standards of service – particularly in hospital care.

But, as some students of social policy in Britain and the United States are beginning to learn, equality of access is not the same thing as equality of outcome. We have to ask statistical and sociological questions about the utilization of the high-cost quality sectors of social welfare and the low-cost sectors of social welfare. We have to ask similar questions about the ways in which professional people (doctors, teachers, social workers and many others) discharge their roles in diagnosing need and in selecting or rejecting patients, clients and students for this or that service. In the modern world, the professions are increasingly becoming the arbiters of our welfare fate; they are the keyholders to equality of outcome; they help to determine the pattern of redistribution in social policy.

These generalizations apply particularly when services in kind are organized on a universalist, free-on-demand basis. When this is so we substitute, in effect, the professional decision-maker for the crude decisions of the economic market-place. And we also make much more explicit – an important gain in itself – the fact that the poor have great difficulties in manipulating the wider society, in managing change, in choosing between alternatives, in finding their way around a complex world of welfare.

We have learnt from fifteen years' experience of the Health Service that the higher income groups know how to make better use of the Service; they tend to receive more specialist attention; occupy more of the beds in better equipped and staffed hospitals; receive more elective surgery; have better maternity care; and are more likely to get psychiatric help and psychotherapy than low-income groups – particularly the unskilled.

These are all factors which are essential to an understanding of the redistributive role played by one of the major direct welfare services in kind. They are not arguments against a comprehensive free-on-demand service. But they do serve to underline one conclusion. Universalism in social welfare, though a needed prerequisite towards reducing and removing formal barriers of social and economic discrimination, does not by itself solve the problem of how to reach the more-difficult-to-reach with better medical care, especially preventive medical care.

Much the same kind of general conclusion can be drawn from Britain's experience in the field of education. Despite reforms and expansion during the past fifteen years it is a fact that the proportion of male undergraduates who are the sons of manual workers is today about one per cent lower than it was between 1928 and 1947. Although we have doubled the number of University students the proportion coming from working-class homes has remained fairly constant at just over a quarter.

The major beneficiaries of the high-cost sectors of the educational system in 'The Welfare State' have been the higher income groups. They have been helped to so benefit by the continued existence of a prosperous private sector in secondary education (party subsidized by the State in a variety of ways including tax deductibles), and by developments since 1948 in provisions for child dependency in the category of fiscal welfare. Take, for example, the case of two fathers each with two children, one earning £60,000 a year, the other £1500 a year. In combining the effect of direct social welfare expenditures for children and indirect fiscal welfare expenditures for children the result is that the rich father now gets thirteen times more from the State than the poor father in recognition of the dependent needs of childhood.

Housing is another field of social policy which merits analysis from the point of view of redistribution. Here we have to take account of the complex interlocking effects of local rate payments, public housing subsidies, interest rates, tax deductibles for mortgage interest and other factors. When we have done so we find that the subsidy paid by the State to many middle-class families buying their own homes is greater than that received by poor tenants of public housing (local government) schemes.

These are no more than illustrations of the need to study the redistributive effects of social policy in a wider frame of reference. Hitherto, our techniques of social diagnosis and our conceptual frameworks have been too narrow. We have compartmentalized social welfare as we have compartmentalized the poor. The analytic model of social policy that has been fashioned on only the phenomena that are clearly visible, direct and immediately measurable is an inadequate one. It fails to tell us about the realities of redistribution which are being generated by the processes of technological and social change and by the combined effects of social welfare, fiscal welfare and occupational welfare.

How far and to what extent should redistribution take place through welfare channels on the principle of achieved status, inherited status or need? This is the kind of question which, fundamentally, is being asked in Britain today. And it is being directed, in particular, at two major areas of social policy – social security and housing. Both these instruments of change and redistribution have been neglected for a decade or more. We have gone in search of new gods or no gods at all. It is time we returned to consider their roles afresh and with new vision. Perhaps we might then entitle our journey 'Ways of Extending the Welfare State to the Poor'.

Social Selection in the Welfare State
T. H. Marshall

Reprinted with permission from T. H. Marshall, 'Social Selection in the Welfare State', *Eugenics Review*, vol. XLV, no. 2, 1953

It would be difficult to find any definition of the Welfare State acceptable to both its friends and to its enemies – or even to all its friends. Fortunately I needn't try to define it; I have only to explain what are the characteristics of the Welfare State which seem to me to provide a distinctive setting to the problem of social selection. I take the most relevant aspect of the Welfare State, in this context, to be the following.

First, its intense individualism. The claim of the individual to welfare is sacred and irrefutable and partakes of the character of a natural right. It would, no doubt, figure in the new Declaration of the Rights of Man if the supporters of the Welfare State were minded to issue anything so pithily dramatic. It would replace property in those early French and American testaments which speak of life, liberty and property; this trinity now becomes life, liberty and welfare. It is to be found among the Four Freedoms in the guise of 'Freedom from Want' – but that is too negative a version. The welfare of the Welfare State is more positive and has more substance. It was lurking in the Declaration of Independence, which listed the inalienable rights of man as 'Life, Liberty and the Pursuit of Happiness'. Happiness is a positive concept closely related to welfare, but the citizen of the Welfare State does not merely have the right to pursue welfare, he has the right to receive it, even if the pursuit has not been particularly hot. And so we promise to each child an education suited to its individual qualities, we try to make the punishment (or treatment) fit the individual criminal rather than the crime, we hold that in all but the simplest of the social services individual case study and family case work should precede and accompany the giving of advice or assistance, and we uphold the principle of equal opportunity, which is perhaps the most completely individualistic of all.

But if we put individualism first, we must put collectivism second. The Welfare State is the responsible promoter and guardian of the welfare of the whole community, which is something more complex than the sum total of the welfare of all its individual members arrived at by simple addition. The claims of the individual must always be defined and limited so as to fit into the complex and balanced pattern of the welfare of the community, and that is why the right to welfare can never have the full stature of a natural right. The harmonizing of individual rights with the common good is a problem which faces all human societies.

In trying to solve it, the Welfare State must choose means which are in harmony with its principles. It believes in planning – not of everything but over a wide area. It must therefore clearly formulate its objectives and carefully select its methods with a full sense of its power and its responsibility. It believes in equality, and its plans must therefore start from the assumption that every person is potentially a candidate for every position in society. This complicates matters; it is easier to cope with things if society is divided into a number of non-competing social classes. It believes in personal liberty because, as I choose to define it, it is a democratic form of society. So although, of course, like all States, it uses some compulsion, it must rely on individual choice and motivation for the fulfilment of its purposes in all their details.

How do these principles apply to selection through the educational system? The general social good, in this context, requires a balanced supply of persons with different skills and aptitudes who have been so trained as to maximize the contribution they can make to the common welfare. We have, in recent years, seen the Welfare State estimating the need for natural scientists, social scientists and technicians, for doctors, teachers and nurses, and then trying to stimulate the educational system to produce what is required. It must also be careful to see that the national resources are used economically and to the best advantage, that there is no waste of individual capacities, by denying them the chance of development and use, and no waste of money and effort, by giving education and training to those who cannot get enough out of them to justify the cost.

On the other side, the side of individualism, is the right of each child to receive an education suited to its character and abilities. It is peculiar, in that the child cannot exercise the right for itself, because it is not expected to know what its character and abilities are. Nor can its parents wholly represent its interests, because they cannot be certain of knowing either. But they have a rather ambiguous right at least to have their wishes considered, and in some circumstances to have them granted. The status of parental rights in the English educational system is somewhat obscure at the moment. There is no reason to assume that the independent operation of the two principles, of individual rights and general social needs, would lead to the same results. The State has the responsibility of harmonizing the one with the other.

So far I have merely been trying to explain the general meaning which I have discovered in the title of this lecture. As I have already said, I shall first limit this broad field by concentrating on selection through the educational system. I shall then limit it further to the two following aspects of the problem. I shall look first at the selection of children for secondary education and try to see what is involved in bringing it into harmony with the principles of the Welfare State. I choose this particular point in the selection process partly because of its intrinsic and often decisive importance, and partly because so much has recently been written about it. I shall look in the second place rather at the social structure and consider how far it is possible to achieve the aims of the Welfare State in this field – particularly the aim of equal opportunity – in a society in which there still exists considerable inequality of wealth and social status. In doing this I shall be able to draw on some of the still unpublished results of researches carried out at the London School of Economics over the past four years, chiefly with the aid of a generous grant from the Nuffield Foundation.

The Welfare State, as I see it, is in danger of tying itself in knots in an attempt to do things which are self-contradictory. One example, I submit, is the proposal to assign children to different schools, largely on the basis of general ability, and then to pretend that the schools are all of equal status. If this means that we shall take equal trouble to make all schools as good as possible, treat all the children with equal respect and try to make them all equally happy, I heartily endorse the idea. But the notion of parity of esteem does not always stop there; and I feel it really is necessary to assert that some children are more able than others, that some forms of education are higher than others, and that some occupations demand qualities that are rarer than others and need longer and more skilled training to come to full maturity, and they will therefore probably continue to enjoy higher social prestige.

I conclude that competitive selection through the educational system must remain with us to a considerable extent. The Welfare State is bound to pick the children of high ability for higher education and for higher jobs, and to do this with the interest of the community as well as the rights of the children in mind. But the more use it can at the same time make of allocation to courses suited to special tastes and abilities the better. It further seems to be that, for the purpose of selection on grounds of general ability, the objective tests are already accurate enough to do all that we should ever ask them to do, while, so far as 'allocation' is concerned, they will never be able to give a decisive verdict in more than a minority of cases, although they can be of great value in helping to decide what advice to give.

The problem which now faces us is more administrative than psychological. There is less to be gained by trying to perfect the tests and examinations than by thinking how to shape the structure of our educational and employment systems. It is better to minimize the effects of our decisions in doubtful cases than to imagine that, if we only try hard enough, we can ensure that all our decisions in such cases are correct. The word 'correct' has no meaning in this context; it is a bureaucratic fiction borrowed from the office where there is a correct file for every document.

By 'minimizing the effects of our decisions' I mean refrain from adding unnecessary and artificial consequences to acts whose real meaning and necessary consequences I have been urging that we should frankly recognize. A system of direction into distinct 'types of secondary school' rather than 'courses of secondary education'. . . must, I think, intensify rather than minimize the consequences. I am aware of the educational arguments on the other side, but do not intend to enter into a controversy for which I have no equipment. The other point at which artificial consequences may be added is the point of passage from education to employment. The snobbery of the educational label, certificate or degree when, as often, the prestige of the title bears little or no relation to the value of the content, is a pernicious thing against which I should like to wage a major war.

There is another matter on which the Welfare State can easily try to follow contradictory principles. It relates to occupational prestige, social class and the distribution of power in society.

Although the Welfare State must, I believe, recognize some measure of economic inequality as legitimate and acceptable, its principles are opposed to rigid class divisions, and to anything which favours the preservation or formation of sharply distinguished culture patterns at different social levels. The segregation when at school of those destined for different social levels is bound to have some effect of this kind and is acceptable only if there are irrefutable arguments on the other side. Further, a system which sorts children by general ability and then passes them through appropriate schools to appropriate grades of employment will intensify the homogeneity within each occupational status group and the differences between groups. And, in so far as intelligence is hereditary and as educational chances are influenced by family background (and I have produced evidence to show that they are), the correlation between social class and type of school will become closer among the children.

Finally, the Welfare State, more than most forms of democracy, cannot tolerate a governing class. Leadership and power are exercised from many stations in life, by politicians, judges, ecclesiastics, businessmen, trade unionists, intellectuals and others. If these were all selected in childhood and groomed in the same stable, we should have what Raymond Aron calls the characteristic feature of a totalitarian society – a unified elite. These leaders must really belong to and represent in a distinctive way the circles in and through which their power is exercised. We need politicians from all classes and occupational levels, and it is good that some captains of industry should have started life at the bench, and that trade unions should be led by genuine members, men of outstanding general ability who have climbed a ladder other than the educational one. It is important to preserve these other ladders, and it is fortunate that the selection net has some pretty big holes in it. It is fortunate too, perhaps, that human affairs cannot be handled with perfect mechanical precision, even in the Welfare State.

The Acquisitive Society
R. H. Tawney

Reprinted with permission from R. H. Tawney, *The Acquisitive Society*, Victor Gollancz, 1937, pp. 9–10

It is a commonplace that the characteristic virtue of Englishmen is their power of sustained practical activity, and their characteristic vice a reluctance to test the quality of that activity by reference to principles. They are incurious as to theory, take fundamentals for granted, and are more interested in the state of the roads than their place on the map. And it might fairly be argued that in ordinary times that combination of intellectual tameness with practical energy is sufficiently serviceable to explain, if not to justify, the equanimity with which its possessors bear the criticism of more mentally adventurous nations. It is the mood of those who have made their bargain with fate and are content to take what it offers without re-opening the deal. It leaves the mind free to concentrate undisturbed upon profitable activities, because it is not distracted by a taste for unprofitable speculations. Most generations, it might be said, walk in a path which they neither make nor discover, but accept; the main thing is that they should march. The blinkers worn by Englishmen enable them to trot all the more steadily along the beaten road, without being disturbed by curiosity as to their destination.

But if the medicine of the constitution ought not to be made its daily food, neither can its daily food be made medicine. There are times which are not ordinary, and in such times it is not enough to follow the road. It is necessary to know where it leads, and, if it leads nowhere, to follow another. The search for another involves reflection, which is uncongenial to the bustling people who describe themselves as practical, because they take things as they are and leave them as they are. But the practical thing for a traveller who is uncertain of his path is not to proceed with the utmost rapidity in the wrong direction: it is to consider how to find the right one. And the practical thing for a nation which has stumbled upon one of the turning points of history is not to behave as though nothing very important were involved, as if it did not matter whether it turned to the right or to the left, went up hill or down dale, provided that it continued doing with a little more energy what it has done hitherto; but to consider whether what it has done hitherto is wise, and, if it is not wise, to alter it.

When the broken ends of its industry, its politics, its social organization, have to be pieced together after a catastrophe, it must make a decision; for it makes a decision even if it refuses to decide. If it is to make a decision which will wear, it must travel beyond the philosophy momentarily in favour with the proprietors of its newspapers. Unless it is to move with the energetic futility of a squirrel in a revolving cage, it must have a clear apprehension both of the deficiency of what is, and of the character of what ought to be. And to obtain this apprehension it must appeal to some standard more stable than the momentary exigencies of its commerce or industry or social life, and judge them by it. It must, in short, have recourse to Principles.

Further Reading: **Values and Social Change**

R. ATKINSON, *Orthodox Consensus and Radical Alternative*, Heinemann, 1971.
R. BACON and W. ELTIS, *Britain's Economic Problem,* Macmillan, 1973.
C. BARNETT, *The Collapse of British Power*, Eyre Methuen, 1972.
D. BELL, *The Coming of Post Industrial Society*, Heinemann, 1974.
R. FORESTER, *The Microelectronics Revolution*, Blackwell, 1980.
I. GOUGH, *The Political Economy of the Welfare State*, Macmillan, 1979.
A. H. HALSEY, *Trends in British Society Since 1900*, Macmillan, 1972.
I. ILLICH, *Tools for Conviviality*, Fontana Paperbacks, 1975.
D. H. MEADOWES, *The Limits to Growth*, New American Library, 1974.

G. POGGI, *The Development of the Modern State*, Hutchinson, 1978.

K. R. POPPER, *The Open Society and its Enemies I* and *II*, Routledge and Kegan Paul, 1966.

A. R. PREST and D. T. COPPOCK, *The U.K. Economy*, Weidenfeld and Nicolson, 1982.

J. REX, *Discovering Sociology*, Routledge and Kegan Paul, 1973.

G. RODERICK and M. STEPHENS, *The British Malaise*, The Falmer Press, 1982.

A. SAMPSON, *Anatomy of Britain Today*, Hodder and Stoughton, 1965.

R. SCASE, *The State in Western Europe*, Croom Helm, 1980.

D. A. SCHON, *Beyond the Stable State*, Penguin, 1973.

J. SEABROOK, *What Went Wrong?*, Gollancz, 1978.

Textbook Reference

As we pointed out in the Introduction, this book of readings is not intended as a substitute for conventional textbooks, any more than it is hoped to supplant the reading of original materials.

The aims and intentions are that the easy availability of original material in the form of a reader will increase the value of courses organized round one or other of the major textbooks in the field, or a basic lecture course on modern Britain.

Accordingly we compiled a list of textbooks in most common use in teaching courses of this type, and in introductory sociology generally. We then traced out the major themes which seemed to be important within the institutional areas which form the framework of this book of readings, whether we had been able to select readings in these areas or not. Although there are doubtless many other texts which could be included and many more will be on the market within a short time, there seem to be advantages for the student in having a readily accessible summary of the comparative coverage of the major textbooks, and of the areas within which one is substitutable for another. In our experience, a good deal of disillusion and disappointment on the part of students can be associated with inappropriate advice about textbooks, and a lack of guidance about which texts are relevant for particular sections of a course.

The annotations are derived from a survey of the contents of each book. The roman numerals refer to chapters and the arabic numerals to pages in the relevant textbooks. Not all of these books, as will be noted, cover precisely similar ground, and some, for instance Halsey, are not strictly *textbooks* in the commonly accepted sense: all, however, provide introductory and reference material for courses on modern Britain. Some have been superseded but still remain on library shelves: in the present climate of economic stringency, some indication of comparative coverage may be useful to students.

Textbooks

V. AUBERT, *Elements of Sociology*, Heinemann, 1967.
T. BILTON *etal.*, *Introductory Sociology*, Macmillan, 1981.
T. B. BOTTOMORE, *Sociology: a Guide to Problems and Literature*, Allen and Unwin, 1962.
S. F. COTGROVE, *The Science of Society*, Allen and Unwin, 1967.
B. GREEN and E. A. JOHNS, *An Introduction to Sociology*, Pergamon, 1966.
A. H. HALSEY (ed.), *Trends in British Society Since 1900*, Macmillan, 1972.
M. HARALAMBOS, *Sociology*, University Tutorial Press, 1980.

H. M. JOHNSON, *Sociology: a Systematic Introduction*, Routledge and Kegan Paul, 1961.

G. D. MITCHELL, *Sociology: the Study of Social Systems*, University Tutorial Press, 1959.

T. NOBLE, *Structure and Change in Modern Britain*, Batsford, 1981.

J. RYDER and H. SILVER, *Modern English Society*, Methuen, 1970.   .

G. SERGEANT, *A Textbook of Sociology*, Macmillan, 1971.

H. J. SHERWIN and J. WOOD, *Sociology: Traditional and Radical Perspectives*, Harper and Row, 1982.

E. J. WILKINS, *An Introduction to Sociology*, MacDonald and Evans, 1970.

P. M. WORSLEY (ed.), *Introducing Sociology*, Penguin, 1970 (Worsley 1).

P. M. WORSLEY (ed.), *Modern Sociology: Introductory Readings*, Penguin, 1970 (Worsley 2).

The New Sociology of Modern Britain	1. Family	2. Community	3. Socialization	4. Work	5. Class	6. Power
Johnson	147–9, 155–60, 171–200	—	120–44	215–18, 235–45, 280–312	XVII, IX, 469–92, 516–35	XIII, XIV, 280–312, 587–624
Mitchell	53–76	40–50	140–50	115–16, 126–39	109–32	77–92, 126–34
Noble	IV	III	V	VI	VIII	IX
Ryder & Silver	IX, 107–16	II, 102–17	VI	VI	VII	III, X
Sergeant	III	—	IV	—	II	VI
Sherwin & Wood	IV, VII, X	69–70	VIII, XI	IV	II, III, XV	V
Wilkins	VII, XII	XIII	X	IX	VI	VIII
Worsley 1	III	VI	IV	V	VII	VII
Worsley 2	III	VII	IV	V, VI	VIII	IX, 265–74

Index